D0847991

Software Engineering Productivity Handbook

Jessica Keyes, Editor

Windcrest®/McGraw-Hill

New York San Francisco Washington, D.C. Auckland Bogotá
Caracas Lisbon London Madrid Mexico City Milan
Montreal New Delhi San Juan Singapore
Sydney Tokyo Toronto

Library of Congress Cataloging-in-Publication Data

Keyes, Jessica
    Software engineering productivity handbook / by Jessica Keyes.
        p.   cm.
    Includes index.
    ISBN 0-07-911366-4
    1. Software engineering—Handbook, manuals, etc.   I. Title.
    QA76.758.K49 1992
    005.1—dc20   92-23356
                                                                  CIP

1 2 3 4 5 6 7 8 9 0   DOH/DOH 9 9 8 7 6 5 4 3

ISBN 0-07-911366-4

*The editors for this book were Jeanne Glasser and Alan B. Danis, the designer was
Jacqueline J. Boone, the New York production supervisor was Suzanne Babeuf, and the
production supervisor was Katherine G. Brown. This book was set in ITC Century Light .*

Printed and bound by R. R. Donnelley & Sons Company.

For more information about other McGraw-Hill materials,
call 1-800-2-MCGRAW in the United States. In other
countries, call your nearest McGraw-Hill office.

Contents

Contributors

Jessica Keyes
TECHINSIDER
New York, NY

Sam Holcman
Computer & Engineering Consultants, Ltd.
Southfield, Michigan

Ken Horner
DRT Systems
New York, NY

Clive Finkelstein
Information Engineering Systems Corp.
Arlington, VA

Prof. Dr. Eberhard Rudolph
Fachbereich 2
Hochschule Bremerhaven
Germany

Ed Yourdon
American Programmer
New York City, New York

Roger S. Pressman, Ph.D.
R.S. Pressman & Associates, Inc.
Orange, CT

W.W. Everett
AT&T Bell Laboratories
Murray Hill, New Jersey

J. D. Musa
AT&T Bell Laboratories
Murray Hill, New Jersey

Barbara Zimmer
Hewlett-Packard Corporate
  Engineering
Palo Alto, CA

William G. Smillie
Coopers & Lybrand Management
  Consulting Services
Rosslyn, VA

Chris F. Kemerer
Sloan School of Management
Massachusetts Institute of
  Technology
Cambridge, MA

Michael W. Patrick
Sloan School of Management
Massachusetts Institute of
  Technology
Cambridge, MA

Pierre Deveaux
International Function Point User
  Group (IFPUG)
Westerville, Ohio

Scott A. Whitmire
Advanced Systems Research
Seattle, WA

Howard Rubin
Howard Rubin Associates
Pound Ridge, NY

Rajiv D. Banker
Carlson School of Business
University of Minnesota
Minneapolis, Minnesota

Robert J. Kauffman
Stern School of Business
New York University
New York, New York

Rachna Kumar
Doctoral Program in Information Systems
Stern School of Business
New York University
New York, New York

Philip Wallingford
Software Quality Automation
Lawrence, MA

Daryl Conner
ODR Inc.
Atlanta, GA

Vaughan Merlyn
Ernst & Young
Center for Information Technology
  and Strategy
Boston, MA

Elliot J. Chikofsky
Progress Software
Bedford, MA

Watts S. Humphrey
Software Engineering Institute
Carnegie Mellon
Pittsburgh, PA

Margaret H. Hamilton
Hamilton Technologies, Inc.
Cambridge, Mass

David Marca
Digtal Equipment Corp.
Nashua, NH

Craig D. Galler
SRA
Arlington, VA

J. Michael Corns
SRA
Arlington, VA

Barry Brown
BrownStone Solutions, Inc.
New York, NY

Lewis Stone
BrownStone Solutions, Inc.
New York, NY

David Friend
Pilot Software Inc.
Boston, Mass

Adam Kolowa
ParaSoft Corporation
Pasadena, California

Jon Flower
ParaSoft Corporation
Pasadena, California

H. Glen Weekley
Computer Task Group
Buffalo, NY

Marcel Markus
Computer Task Group
Buffalo, NY

Sudy Bharadwaj
Scientific Computing Associates
New Haven, CT

Timothy Mattson
Scientific Computing Associates
New Haven, CT

This book is most appreciatively dedicated to my clients and friends, old and new, my family, and editors.

Foreword

In *Soul of a New Machine,* Tracy Kidder details the riveting story of a project conducted at breakneck speed while under incredible pressure. Driven by pure adrenaline, the team members soon became obsessed with trying to achieve the impossible. For more than a year, they gave up their nights and weekends—in the end logging nearly 100 hours each per week. Somewhere buried in the midst of Kidder's prose we find that at the end of this project the entire staff quit. Not just one or two of them, but every single one!

The information technology field is ripe with stories such as this. Software development projects are usually complex and often mission critical. As a result the pressure on staff to produce is great. And sometimes, as in the Kidder example, even with success comes failure.

Successful software development projects (those that finish on time and don't lose staff members) all have something in common. Each of these projects, in some way, shape, or form, followed one or more principles of quality and productivity. Some of these principles are clearly intuitive; however, most are learned or culled from vast experience over a number of years and projects.

In today's competitive environment, information technology is a major partner with the business units. And because of this the push is on for enhanced software productivity and quality. Intuition, alone, is no longer adequate, nor can an organization wait until software developers learn their quality lessons over so many projects in as many years.

This book was written to push the information technology industry up that learning curve in one fell swoop. Included in this book are 69 chapters, 128 illustrations, and one diskette filled with techniques, policies, issues, checklists, and guidelines on quality, productivity, and reliability.

This book wouldn't have been possible without the help and encouragement of many people. First of all, I'd like to thank my husband and parents without whose unwavering support this book would not have been finished. I would also like to thank my editor at McGraw-Hill, Jeanne Glasser, who has been a great assistance as well as a good friend.

If there is one other person who was as involved in the publication of this book as I, it was my research assistant Kevin Chou. Kevin was a rare find. He already possessed two Masters degrees when I found him at my alma mater, New York University. He was pursuing yet a third degree while working simultaneously at IBM Poughkeepsie where he designs and implements the MVS operating system software. In spite of his IBM job and his schoolwork, Kevin still found time to assist me in uncovering the nuggets of gold that are found in Part 2 of this book.

But many other people were involved in this book as well—people like Clive Finkelstein, Roger Pressman, and John Musa. These people contributed their time and information willingly, and I offer them my grateful thanks.

JK, New York City, January 1993.

Preface

Much has been said and written about quality and productivity. Unfortunately, little of it is translatable to the everyday concerns that the software developer and his or her manager must face.

However, quality, productivity, and reliability are perhaps the most important concerns of both senior management—and the ultimate end-user. The three tenets of quality, productivity, and reliability should not be thought of as extra burdens on a job already burdensome. In fact, incorporating many of the techniques appearing in this handbook could very well reduce the software burden while making the job much more rewarding.

Software Engineering Productivity Handbook is positioned to be the definitive book on productivity and quality, reliability, measurements, policies, and procedures.

The information technology (IT) buzzword of the 1990s is productivity. With decreasing software budgets and increasingly demanding users and senior managements, technology directors need a complete guide to the subject of software productivity, which includes information about the very latest in metrics as well as information about how to make IT more productive. *Software Engineering Productivity Handbook* is that guide. It is a complete reference to the state-of-the-art in productivity and quality today. It accomplishes this by synthesizing the works of many academic and industry powerhouses into an easy-to-read reference manual for the thousands of IT staffers who need to know.

This handbook contains three parts. Part 1 is a series of contributions by the leaders in the IT industry. Part 1 contains 26 chapters offering a wide range of advice on inducing a quality environment in your organization. In chapter 4, the father of information engineering, Clive Finkelstein, offers us an inside look on how information engineering offers us a methodology to create strategic systems. Roger Pressman, in chapter 7, offers us some great advice on how to improve the software engineering practice, while Bell Labs' own John Musa and Bill Everett offer an advanced look at software reliability and productivity in chapter 8.

In chapter 14, the king of metrics, Howard Rubin, presents a detailed checklist for putting a measurement program in place in an organization. For those of you who have heard about function points, but wanted some more detailed information, Pierre Deveaux of the International Function Point User Group, offers a very specific methodology for counting function points in chapter 12.

Ed Yourdon contributes to the discussion in chapter 6 with a look at alternative development methodologies while Vaughan Merlyn and Daryl Conner discourse on management's role in orchestrating the change that comes with Computer-Aided Software Engineering (CASE).

Joining the contributors' list are New York University, MIT, Hewlett-Packard, Coopers & Lybrand, and the Software Engineering Institute at Carnegie Mellon. There is perhaps no other book today that offers such a wealth of expertise in one place.

In Part 2, we change gears from the "gems of wisdom" of industry leaders to a nitty-gritty, hands-on approach. Culled from the leading research from both academia and industry over the last few years, the remaining 42 chapters of this book offer you the techniques you need to install and implement a quality and productivity program in your organization.

In chapter 28 we find a technique for successfully converting prototypes to operational systems while in chapter 31 you will find a methodology for establishing a productivity-enabling software development environment.

The content of the handbook is extensive and inclusive. Everything from creativity improvement to the seven principles of quality leaders to guidelines for structured methodology to productivity through shared information technology.

And that's not all. I've included a description of John Zachman's framework, the guidelines for the Malcolm Baldridge Quality Award, and excerpts from the *IEEE Standard Dictionary of Measures to Produce Reliable Software*.

And all of this is in the language of the software developer.

In Part 3, I have provided you with a diskette which contains many of the checklists and guidelines that you have read about in this book. Since the goal of this book is to describe techniques that can be used to raise your organization's productivity in the area of information technology, I figured that I could raise yours quickly by providing you with some ready-made checklists.

Part

1

This section contains contributions by some of the most illustrious spokespeople in the information technology (IT) industry. Contributions range from philosophical discussions to "hands-on" instructions.

1

A Survey on IT Productivity/Quality

by Jessica Keyes

The Productivity Paradox

Businesses that expected a big productivity payoff from investing in technology are, in many cases, still waiting to collect. Let's step outside for a second and take a long, hard view of things—not on just measuring the productivity of the software engineering process, but on the concept of technology and productivity in general.

According to recent research by Prof. Paul Attewell of the City University of New York, "There is an absence or paucity of productivity payoffs from information technology [IT], despite massive investment in IT over the last 25 years."

In 1988 alone, U.S. companies invested some $51 billion in hardware, $20 billion in purchased software, and over $44 billion in computer services, representing 25% of a firm's capital stock. This huge commitment was made at the expense of other kinds of investments, while the U.S. bet that IT investment would raise economic productivity.

Instead of increasing productivity, though, computers often generate more work for the end user. Attewell points to a study by the Internal Revenue Service in which IRS auditors supplied with laptops experienced no productivity gain. In fact, the same work took longer to complete.

Companies are also adding layers of administrative overhead to manage their systems, according to Attewell. This need for systems expertise within the user department coincides with an upswing in the number of managers found within U.S. corporations. The computer systems create a demand for "hidden" data processing (DP) experts, whose official titles may be "claims examiner" or "financial analyst," but who really are gurus of the computerized system. Attewell said, "Managing IT systems is a natural for managers to claim they need more managers."

Systems are developed for the end user. However, unlike the pieceworker, whose productivity is easy to measure, the information worker's productivity is difficult to quantify. It is just as difficult to measure the quality of the software system being utilized as well as the effectiveness of the software developer.

By using measurements (commonly called *metrics*), it is possible to understand and manage the software development process. Perhaps more important, it is possible to measure the impact of change when a shift in methodologies (such as Computer-Aided Software Engineering, or CASE) or training procedures occurs.

The self-perception of software developer as "artist" has evolved to that of "engineer." The term *software engineering* is indicative of this change in perception from art to science.

Software artists insisted that measuring their work was as impossible as measuring Rembrandt's work. But with the emphasis on engineering comes the viewpoint that the software development cycle is process-oriented. Therefore, a method of measuring is not only possible, but required.

Why Bother to Measure?

The idea of measuring productivity is relatively new. Jerrold M. Grochow, a vice president of American Management Systems, Inc. (AMS), Arlington, Va., has questioned over 2500 people at up to 500 organizations over the last three years. He found that few IT organizations are quantitatively measuring productivity or quality.

Said Grochow, "As an industry, we have a dismal performance in this area. There is no other industry that knows so little about itself in a quantitative way."

The organizations measuring, or just beginning to measure, are primarily doing it for the same reasons. Software is becoming more complex while user demands and expectations are increasing. The need to develop better software in less time translates to a need to quantify the project's progress and the system's attributes.

A variety of productivity/quality metrics are available; choosing the most appropriate one can be as tricky as picking winning lottery numbers (see Fig. 1.1).

Measuring does have its detractors. Many "artists" still refuse to be measured. Ironically, measuring often produces the unusual effect of increasing productivity in just the areas that are measured.

In most situations, *metric* refers to the programming process only. But programming is the smallest part of the systems development life cycle. For an effective measurement program, each component of the cycle must include its own measures—or a measure must be used that encompasses the entire spectrum of development.

The software development process is one of the most complex processes a human can perform, according to T. Capers Jones, chairman of Software Productivity Research (SPR) in Burlington, Mass. Software development includes numerous formidable tasks. Although variations abound in the number of executable steps in a life cycle, most IT organizations perform the same functions.

Metrics must consider several esoteric items, such as *user involvement*, which correlates positively with productivity increases. Human factors must also be taken into account, such as the square footage allocated per programmer. (Jones' research has shown that a full 78 square feet of floor space increases programmer productivity more than any CASE tool.) Design, programming and quality factors must also be weighed.

Productivity/Quality Metrics

1) Lines of code
2) Pages of documentation
3) Number and size of tests
4) Function count
5) Variable count
7) Number of modules
8) Depth of nesting
9) Count of changes required
10) Count of discovered defects
11) Count of changed lines of code
12) Time to design, code, test
13) Defect discovery rate by phase of development
14) Cost to develop
15) Number of external interfaces
16) Number of tools used and why
17) Reusability percentage
18) Variance of schedule
19) Staff years experience with team
20) Staff years experience with language
21) Software years experience with software tools
22) MIPs per person
23) Support to development personnel ratio
24) Nonproject to project time ratio

source: TECHINSIDER

Fig. 1.1 Metric list.

Quality measurements are frequently overlooked in the race to implement on or before deadline. However, no matter what the time pressure, certain measures undertaken seriously can enhance the quality of output of any software investment (see Fig. 1.2).

Measurement of quality is often thought of as a manufacturing process. But this is changing, and the hardware manufacturers are leading the way. Geoffrey Roach, a marketing executive in the Marlboro, Mass., office of Digital Equipment Corporation (DEC), described the automated methodology used to run the 22,000 quality checks on the VAX Cobol compiler.

With 22,000 tests, it is impossible to test the compiler thoroughly; therefore, DEC wrote VaxScan, which looks at many micro-oriented measures such as rate of change and how much the program was tested. It also measures the introduction of new errors, and performs many other tests.

Quality Factors	1 = low to 5 = high
1) How easy is it to use?	1 2 3 4 5
2) How secure is it?	1 2 3 4 5
3) Level of confidence in it?	1 2 3 4 5
4) How well does it conform to requirements?	1 2 3 4 5
5) How easy is it to upgrade?	1 2 3 4 5
6) How easy is it to change?	1 2 3 4 5
7) How portable is it?	1 2 3 4 5
8) How easy is it to locate a problem and fix it?	1 2 3 4 5
9) Is the response time fast enough?	1 2 3 4 5
10) How easy is it to train staff?	1 2 3 4 5
11) Ease of testing?	1 2 3 4 5
12) Is the software efficient in terms of computing resources?	1 2 3 4 5
13) Ease of coupling this system to another?	1 2 3 4 5
14) Does the system utilize the minimum storage possible?	1 2 3 4 5
15) Is the system self-descriptive?	1 2 3 4 5
16) Does the system exhibit modularity?	1 2 3 4 5
17) Is there a program for on-going quality awareness for all employees?	1 2 3 4 5
18) Do you check supplier quality?	1 2 3 4 5
19) Is there a quality department?	1 2 3 4 5
20) Is this the "right" system to be developed?	1 2 3 4 5

Circle the number applicable to each measure. Add for total score.

Source: TECHINSIDER

Fig. 1.2 Quality factor matrix.

Roach tells the story of Deming, who fought unsuccessfully for quality measurements within the automobile industry. Deming was the American responsible for fostering quality as a buzzword in American industry even though he had to go to Japan to do it. The Japanese listened. The rest is history.

Deming's message is being taken seriously by the likes of Roach and others on the hardware side. That message is slowly getting through to mainstream corporate data centers.

The Original Metric

Those who measure most often use a simple source-lines-of-code (SLOC) metric. With this metric, however, there is room for variation. Conte, Dunsmore, and Shen

(1986) proposed this definition of SLOC: "A line of code is any line of program text that is not a comment or blank line, regardless of the number of statements or fragments of statements on that line. This specifically includes all lines containing program headers, declarations and executable and non-executable statements."

The SLOC metric is often further redefined into distinguishing the number of non-comment source lines of code (NCSLOC) from the lines of code containing comment statements (CSLOC).

Along with SLOC measurements, the weekly time sheet provides other gross statistics often used for productivity measurement. The total number of labor hours expended, divided by the total number of NCSLOC, provides an overall statistic that can be used to compare productivity from project to project.

One problem with the SLOC measurement is that it does not take into account the complexity of the code being developed or maintained. "Lines of code and man-months hide some very important things," said AMS' Grochow. For example, the SLOC measurement for a name and address file update program might be 600 lines of code per day.

On the other hand, the output for software that tracks satellites might be in the range of 40 to 50 lines of code per day. To look at this output on a purely gross statistical level, one would conclude that the name and address project was more productive and efficient than the satellite project. This conclusion would be wrong.

So, starting from this base, two researchers at the Massachusetts Institute of Technology's Center for Information Systems Research in Cambridge, Mass., examined this complexity issue. Chris F. Kemerer and Geoffrey K. Gill studied the software development projects undertaken by an aerospace defense contracting firm from 1984 to 1989.

The Kemerer and Gill team began their research by reviewing the original measure for complexity as developed by Thomas McCabe, now president of McCabe & Associates, a Columbia, Md., consulting group. In his article, McCabe (1976) proposed that a valid measurement of complexity would be the number of possible paths in a software module. W.J. Hansen (1978) interpreted McCabe's mathematical formula into four simple rules that would produce a numerical measure of complexity (i.e., the higher the number, the more complex):

- Add 1 for every IF, CASE or other alternate execution construct.
- Add 1 for every iterative DO, DOWHILE or other repetitive construct.
- Add 2 less than the number of logical alternatives in a CASE.
- Add 1 for each AND or OR in an IF statement.

The results of the Kemerer and Gill study showed that increased software complexity leads to reduced productivity. They recommended the use of more experienced staff and a reduction of the complexity of the individual software module. To reduce complexity, they suggested the establishment of a complexity measure that could be in use as the code was written, and adherence to this preset standard.

According to Kemerer, "The goal of these studies is to transfer the generally accepted processes of measurement from the manufacturing arena to the software arena. The problem with the software industry is that we think everything we're doing is new."

The Hewlett-Packard Way

Quality and productivity have been an explicit part of Cupertino, California-based Hewlett-Packard's (HP) corporate objectives. But only within the last two years has this objective filtered into the world of software development. To help develop and utilize metrics company-wide, HP created the Software Metrics Council. Today, 80 productivity and quality managers within HP perform a variety of functions, from training, to communicating the best software engineering practices and establishing productivity and quality metrics.

HP has adopted a methodology called Total Quality Control (TQC). A fundamental principle of TQC is that all company activities can be scrutinized in terms of the processes involved; metrics can then be assigned to each process to evaluate effectiveness. HP has developed numerous measurements (see Fig. 1.3).

The TQC approach places software quality/productivity assessment high on the list of software development tasks. When projects are first defined, the team, along with understanding and evaluating the process to be automated, defines the metrics that are to be used to measure the process.

When HP decided to revolve the future of the company around RISC-based architecture, software reliability was considered critical. The development of the systems software was the largest development effort in HP's history, and the first required

Hewlett-Packard Productivity/Quality Measurements	
Metric	**Goal**
Break-even time	Measures return on investment. Time until development costs are offset by profits.
Time to market	Measures responsiveness and competitiveness. Time from project go-ahead until release to market.
Progress rate	Measures accuracy of schedule. Ratio of planned to actual development time.
Post-release defect density	Measures effectiveness of test processes. Total number of defects reported during first 12 months after product release.
Turnover rate	Measures morale. Percentage of staff leaving.
Training	Measures investment in career development. Number of hours per staff per year.
Source: Hewlett-Packard	

Fig. 1.3 Hewlett-Packard's measurements.

multiple divisions to produce software that would be combined into a single software system.

Charles A. Krueger, a professor at the University of Wisconsin in Madison, points out the productivity paradox of budget versus getting to market—is it more important to stay within the targeted confines of money allocated, or to get the product out on time? He quotes a McKinsey & Co. study that indicates that going overbudget by 50% and getting a product out on time reduces profits by only 4%. But staying on budget and getting to market five months late reduces profits to a third. Said Krueger, "Productivity is really a measure of how successfully you are in achieving your results."

Hewlett-Packard came to the same conclusion as Krueger, and the company insisted on reliable software and on-time delivery. HP established the Systems Software Certification program to ensure measurable, consistent, high-quality software through defining metrics, setting goals, collecting and analyzing data, and certifying products for release. This program developed four metrics for the RISC project:

- Breadth—measures the testing coverage of user-accessible and internal functionality of the product.

- Depth—measures the proportion of instructions or blocks of instructions executed during testing.

- Reliability—measures the stability and robustness of a product and its ability to recover gracefully from error conditions.

- Defect density—measures the quantity and severity of reported defects and a product's readiness.

HP's results were impressive. Defects were caught and corrected early, when costs to find and fix them are lower. Less time was spent in the costly system-test and integration phases and maintenance. This reduced time resulted in lower overall support costs and higher productivity. It also increased quality for HP's customers.

HP's success demonstrates what a corporate-wide commitment to productivity and quality measures can achieve. The commitment to these gains was so strong that HP invested in full-time productivity and quality managers, which is indeed unique.

The Function Point Advantage

One of the bright spots on the measurement horizon is a concept called *Function Points*. Jones is an authority on the history and current usage of these newest measures.

A.J. Albrecht (1983), with IBM at the time, first proposed the Function Point concept. This metric is a combination of metrics that assesses the functionality of the development process. The Function Point metric achieves this by first counting the number of external inputs (transaction types), external outputs (report types), logical internal files (nonphysical), external interface files (files accessed by the application but not maintained/updated by it) and external inquiries.

Using a set of standards for assessing complexity, these components are then classified as relatively low, average, or high. Once the total number of function counts are computed according to a statistical formula, the second step assesses the impact of 14 general system characteristics:

- Data communications
- Distributed functions
- Performance
- Heavily used configuration
- Transaction rate
- On-line data entry
- End-user efficiency
- On-line update
- Complex processing
- Reusability
- Installation ease
- Operational ease
- Multiple sites
- Facilitates change

These values are then totaled to compute what is known as the Value Adjustment Factor (VAF). The VAF is then multiplied by the total function count to create the number of Function Points.

The one aspect of Function Point measurement programs that makes them so valuable is the presence of large databases of information that companies can use for comparison. SPR, for example, markets Checkpoint, a PC-based product that incorporates a database of over 4000 projects. Checkpoint is used to compare an organization with industry norms.

Dr. Howard Rubin, president of Howard Rubin Associates of Pound Ridge, N.Y., and a professor of computer science at Hunter College in New York, is the overseer of the Rubin Data Base, which has accumulated statistics on over 13,000 projects.

Aside from these external comparative databases, many in-house databases have been painstakingly accumulated. As Kemerer states in his thesis, "From a control perspective, organizations using a variant method would have difficulty in comparing their Function Point productivity rates to those of other organizations that switched methods, the new data might be sufficiently inconsistent as to render trend analysis meaningless."

Most people are using Function Points because it is the only metric that comes close to matching the economic definition of productivity, which is costs or services produced per unit of labor and expense. Using Jones' SPR research base of 400 studied companies, the national average was calculated to be five Function Points per person-month; IT groups averaged eight Function Points per person-month.

These numbers can dramatically increase with CASE tool usage to the degree that it is possible to achieve 65 Function Points per person-month with a full CASE environment and reusable code. As Jones points out, this metric will decrease when the development environment is new, but will regain momentum when familiarity with the toolset increases.

AMS' Grochow was an early believer in the Function Point concept. With over 2200 systems professionals and supporting 28 product lines, AMS needed a methodology that worked. The company has been measuring productivity for over ten years. The firm found that its traditional metrics of lines of code and work-months was hiding some very important information: Not all work-months are created equal.

According to Grochow, "There are experienced people and not-so-experienced people, expensive people and not-so-expensive people." If the company could find a way of optimizing this mix, then AMS would find increased productivity. To this end, AMS needed a measure that would foster economic productivity. Function Points filled the bill. But measurement cannot foster productivity alone.

Peeling Back Layers of Quality Equation

Companies in search of a silver bullet to the software development quality and productivity quandary will find themselves firing blanks, according to Ed Yourdon, father of Yourdon structured methodologies.

"One of the big problems in this country is that we tend to look for one silver-bullet solution to the production problem," said Yourdon, who sold his company several years ago and now is the publisher and editor of American Programmer, based in New York.

Quality and productivity are tightly linked; the approaches used to address these issues—metrics, methodology and CASE tools—must be interconnected. Yourdon suggests that simply throwing technology or methodology at the problem is not enough. IT departments, he said, must also use "peopleware" solutions (see Fig. 1.4).

For example, Yourdon said, one way to improve development is to hire better de-

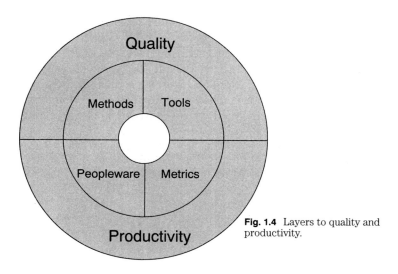

Fig. 1.4 Layers to quality and productivity.

velopers. This solution, he said, is the closest thing to a silver bullet.

"Rather than spend lots of money trying to bring in a new methodology, why not just bring in better people? Since we know that there is a 25 to 1 differential between the best and the worst people, and a 4 to 1 differential between the best and the worst teams, maybe the best way to improve productivity and quality is just to improve your hiring practices," Yourdon said.

"If you take a random group of 100 people and put them in a room with a complex programming exercise, one of them will finish 25 times faster than the others," Yourdon said. Another "peopleware" improvement to productivity, according to Yourdon, is to help managers improve their skills, as well as to foster a teamwork approach among developers. Yourdon believes "peopleware" solutions boost productivity and quality more than any tools or techniques.

Know Thy Business Model

The companies that will win the competitive battles of the '90s are those that will leverage their technology investments to create new possibilities. According to SPR's Jones, to make a productive contribution, IT needs "good management, good technical staff, including good estimators and testers, good measurements, good tools and a good methodology."

IT management can choose from many well-known and well-documented methodologies, the most popular being Martin, Gane/Sarson and Yourdon. According to Jones, "All of the methodologies are basically the same; the key is to use one."

Jones offers an analogy of painted houses versus those that are left bare. "These are the ones that get termites; the ones that are painted last a long time. It doesn't matter what color they are. The only thing that matters is the paint." But, according to Jones, only a small number of IT groups have even bought the paint.

The Software Engineering Institute, Pittsburgh, is the creator of a well-known, chart-software process maturity framework. The framework consists of five levels of maturity that an IT department goes through on its way to becoming completely optimized and productive (see Fig. 1.5).

An oft-quoted statistic is that 80% of us are sitting on top of level one (Basic Management Control). According to George van Schaick, Vice President of Information Management Software at Computer Associates (CA), this might be because the general computing public has not found exactly what it wants or needs from any one of these methodologies. Instead, "people are all back in their shops trying to put a little bit of what sounded good in one with what sounded good in another," said van Schaick. "They're asking 'is there a way for me to create my own version of these methodologies? And then have some tool that would enforce them for me?'" This, in fact, may be one of the largest inhibiting factors to the penetration of CASE into the IT market at large. Van Schaick continued: "CASE is nice, but useless if you don't follow any methodology. You might as well stick to a pencil and paper. You need to be able to tailor a CASE tool to individual environments. You would describe rules to it,

SOFTWARE PROCESS MATURITY FRAMEWORK

STAGE 1: INITIAL
-Ad hoc
-Little formalization
-Tools informally applied to the process
 KEY ACTIONS TO GET TO NEXT STEP:
-Initiate rigorous project management,
 management oversight, and quality assurance

STAGE 2: REPEATABLE
-Achieved a stable process with a repeatable level
 of statistical control
 KEY ACTIONS TO GET TO NEXT STEP:
-Establish a process group
-Establish a software-development process architecture
-Introduce software engineering methods and technologies

STAGE 3: DEFINED
-Achieved foundation for major and continuing progress
 KEY ACTIONS TO GET TO NEXT STEP:
-Establish a basic set of process managements to identify
 quality and cost parameters
-Establish a process database
-Gather and maintain process data
-Assess relative quality of each product and inform management

STAGE 4: MANAGED
-Substantial quality improvements
-Comprehensive process measurement
 KEY ACTIONS TO GET TO NEXT STEP:
-Support automatic gathering of process data
-Use data to analyze and modify the process

STAGE 5: OPTIMIZED
-Major quality and quantity improvements
 KEY ACTIONS TO GET TO NEXT STEP
-Continue improvement and optimization of the process
 Source: Software Engineering Institute

Fig. 1.5 Five steps to maturity.

rather than have it enforcing only the rules it came with."

Van Schaick clearly sees the relationship between methodology and measurement. "Until you master a methodology and have time to implement that methodology in a complete product, you can't measure it," he said. "It takes a good three or four months to get a mastery of the methodology, then it takes a good six months to implement it in an entire project life cycle. So you're a year down the road before you can find out if it even worked. Then you can begin measuring what differences you can get out of it."

Vaughan Merlyn, partner at Ernst & Young's Center for Information Technology and Strategy, Boston, is reported to have said, "The important part is learning to understand method." According to Merlyn, once an organization has established a methodology as a way of doing things, then the CASE tool is disposable.

In choosing a methodology, IT should understand the dynamics of the relationships between methodology, CASE, and measurement. Many interviewed for this chapter agreed that the proper sequence of implementation to foster the sought-after improvement in systems development productivity and quality is to develop a measurement program first, a methodology second and then choose a CASE product. Surrounding this trio are the issues of "peopleware," as Yourdon so succinctly labeled, perhaps the most important factor of all.

Soon, however, IT departments may not have to worry about the "right" order of implementation. There are some new techniques and tools that give new meaning to the term "integrated CASE" (ICASE). Where in most quarters ICASE means a toolset that sports both an upper-CASE (planning, systems analysis and design) with a lower-CASE (program generation) component, a newer definition of ICASE combines methodologies and techniques with automation.

Industry guru James Martin might have been the first to see this causal relationship between methodologies and automated tools. Rapid Application Development (RAD) is his latest contribution to the concept of information engineering.

The RAD technique produces higher productivity because of the way things are packaged. If you take the best person and give him a workstation with everything on it, that person can perform at an incredible level. James Martin calls this the "Swat team" approach.

Quality in an Era of Paradigm Shifts

Who among us doesn't remember the soulful tale of Alice? In her journey through Wonderland she comes upon the Queen of Hearts who, at one point in the fantasy, makes sport of the game of chess with live chess pieces, including our very own Alice. The Queen makes Alice run so fast, but Alice finds that she is merely running in place . . . running so very fast just to catch up.

Elliot Chikofsky, currently Development Director of 4GL Application Development Environments at the Bedford, Massachusetts-based Progress Software Corporation as well as associate editor-in-chief of IEEE Software magazine, uses this story as an analogy to describe where the information technology industry is vis-a-vis productivity and quality. According to Chikofsky, ". . . in essence, our productivity is masked by system complexity and continually rising demand for new systems . . . so like Alice, it seems like we're merely running in place."

Has productivity and quality risen? Or, like Alice, are more and more firms merely running in place, too tired from continual day-to-day operational battles or too shell-shocked from retrenching to support the new paradigms of client/server architectures and object-orientation to pay heed to what is now being referred to as Total Quality Management (TQM)?

Dr. Jerry Grochow is in the unique position of having been an industry observer for almost as long as there has been an information technology industry. Grochow has been tracking quality for at least as many years and, in his opinion, there's not really been much progress. "Overall, I'm relatively negative and cynical," is how Grochow reacts when the question of quality improvement is put to him. From his perspective, although there's certainly a lot of noise about quality programs, "it's a little hard to tell at this time how many of these quality programs are actually bearing fruit." In fact, quality improvements may have less to do with putting certain methodologies in place than in modifying human behaviors.

Grochow describes this phenomenon as the Hawthorne Effect: "This is an old business school phrase. Many years ago, sometime in the 1920s, some social scientists were studying the productivity of workers at a Western Electric plant in Hawthorne, Illinois. They discovered that when they turned up the lighting productivity went up. They also found that when they turned down the lighting productivity went up again." Grochow goes on to explain that what these social scientists found was that when the Hawthorne workers realized that people were paying attention to them they started to do better work.

TQM Meets the Black Hole

Even though the jury is still out on the effects of quality programs on the process of information technology, there's no doubt that the industry itself is extremely interested in its potential. According to Merlyn, "Less than 5% of IT organizations are doing this sort of thing." Even though TQM is strongly rooted in many industries as a whole, Merlyn quotes the statistic of 60–70% for the manufacturing industry: "IT tends to be a black hole."

But in spite of this rather bleak acceptance level, Merlyn's practice is burgeoning due to the increasing interest in the concept. Merlyn's methods are simple but dramatic. One starts off the process by understanding a single principle—that change is painful and lengthy. In fact, according to Merlyn, "To effectuate any kind of change you need something like a ten-year plan." But ten years is a long time and management's patience is short. So how can you motivate change over that time period?

The secret, according to Merlyn, is to make management extremely dissatisfied with the status quo. And to do that you need to look at the cost of the status quo. One way of accomplishing this is to examine the cost of poor quality.

By answering questions such as "what are we spending on detecting defects?" and "what are we spending on repairing defects?", the IT organization can begin to accumulate the statistics it needs to make the push for change. The data needn't be hard to track, in most cases it's already available through project management systems that track walkthroughs, reviews, defect rates, and the like. Merlyn cites the statistic that 40–50% of the IT budget is spent on fixing defects due to poor quality. With statistics like this it should be rather easy to, as Merlyn puts it, "motivate massive change."

Techniques to introduce TQM programs into what Merlyn refers to as "the black hole" of IT vary from company to company. Merlyn's Ernst & Young has a very specific methodology that they employ to accomplish this end (a quick look at it is presented in Fig. 1.6). But so does Coopers & Lybrand.

Based in Coopers' Washington, D.C., offices, Bill Smillie, a partner in the Technology and Finance Unit of the Federal practice, gets to do a lot of TQM consulting. It was here that Smillie got interested, as he puts it, "in what happens if you took appropriate elements of TQM and tried to apply them to software delivery organizations. We have developed a specific methodology for doing that. This methodology provides a framework for managing continuous improvement for software delivery."

As a systems integration veteran of over 15 years, Smillie has first-hand experience of the "endemic behaviors in most of us that got attracted to this business that are contrary to the quality tenets of TQM." One of these is the "code or die" syndrome. As Smillie describes it, "The greater the deadline pressures, the more we focus on 'I got to code right now.' This is a quality problem because it speaks to the fact that we are generally product oriented and when the pressure is on we fundamentally have no faith in the process and TQM says if you want to improve the quality of the product you focus on improving the process. So this is a behavior that gets us into trouble every time." In order to combat these behaviors that seem to sabotage the drive towards quality, Coopers & Lybrand modified their four-phase TQM

---

1. Create a massive discomfort with the status quo
   a. Look for numerical data
   b. Do a customer satisfaction survey
2. Use what was found in step 1 to get management sponsorship
3. Top management needs to make a visible and personal commitment to any quality program
4. Customers/suppliers must be involved in the TQM process
5. Define what the processes are
6. Have customers of the processes outputs determine what value measurements are
6. Form process (quality) imporvement teams that use these measures
7. Come up with ways to innovate or improve the process
8. Create an environment where the processes continually improve

Source: Vaughan Merlyn

Fig. 1.6 A quick approach to TQM.

methodology to suit the tenets of software engineering.

The centerpiece of the *assessment phase* of the Coopers & Lybrand methodology is a development of metrics by which the quality baseline is assessed and by which improvements over time can be measured. According to Smillie, "We do not have a list of a half dozen metrics. The choice of metrics depends upon the client. The reason is that quality is different things for different people. What you think are key quality issues should drive what you're trying to measure." In order to determine the appropriate metrics for any particular client Coopers consultants utilize a method that was first developed by NASA and then put into the public domain. Called goal-question-metric (GQM), it is a disciplined technique used to refine from key quality issues their individual components and ultimately the metrics that might be derived from them.

The second phase of the Coopers methodology, *planning*, is, according to Smillie, "based on what we see today, our vision or where we want to take ourselves. Here we look at the highest priority quality issues and think about what we want to do to build ourselves in that direction." The "plan" developed is actually a short list of things to do over the next six months. Referring to this list as "low-hanging fruit," Smillie stresses that the list must contain the greatest near term opportunities to increase quality.

The third phase, *process improvement*, is, according to Smillie, "actually a phase of experimentation." It is here that the low-hanging fruit can be picked, and if determined not to have any nutritive value to the process, quickly tossed aside. And finally, in the fourth phase of the Coopers TQM methodology, *integration*, the best things from these experiments are built into the organization.

What Smillie and Merlyn both stress is that TQM is actually a process by which one manages continuous improvement. As Smillie puts it, "You need to learn the lessons in as close to real time as possible and implement lessons learned across the organization. For quality programs to be successful you have to get scared enough to act. The manufacturing industry did this in the '80s. The '90s are the decade of fear in the IT world."

New Tools for More Complex Development

The decade of the '90s is most certainly the decade of fear in our industry. At the same time that quality has become a "hot ticket," so too has a cadre of new developmental and implementation paradigms dramatically shifted IT's perception of itself. Progress Software's Chikofsky knows this only too well: "When we move away from the glass-house (i.e., the mainframe) we upped the complexity of software management. Most organizations have not upped management practices to manage that." What Chikofsky is alluding to is the developmental shift that must take place when making the move from mainframe-based applications to the world of client/server. For Chikofsky the issue is really how to manage distribution. "When you go into a distributed system it is very important to have planned the data in different places . . . how it will be used . . . is it in the right place for efficiency."

Since efficiency and productivity are ever-present in the minds of today's IT managers, one might question whether or not the migration to today's more complicated technologies has served to increase productivity or decrease it.

Chikofsky's response: "We've introduced new tools that are more complex but demand for systems has gone up so greatly that it gives the appearance that our productivity has gone down . . . in essence, our productivity is masked by complexity and demand for new systems." Chikofsky goes on to say, "The key is the development environment. This is where CASE research is coming to fruition. Let CASE environments do a lot of the complex background work for the users."

Yourdon sees the effect of the extra layer of complexity added by the new developmental techniques of graphical user interface (GUI), Client/Server and the like, being mitigated by newer and more robust forms of CASE. "As soon as you say GUI you are saying Motif or something like that. You're almost taking for granted that developers will increase productivity because they will have a reasonably powerful workstation, etc., which they might not have had before."

Yourdon contends that while the methodology of building systems is independent of the tool, the tool itself makes implementing the methodology much easier, even for the traditional programmer. Today, along with newer and more robust forms of CASE tools, there are a plethora of language-oriented tools that make the job of programming in this brave new world a lot easier for the programmer to swallow. Yourdon gives us some examples: "A trivial example is Borland's C++, which is a combination of a text editor, debugger, link editor and more, which can all be open and visible to the programmer at the same time." For the programmer not too keen on making the move to C++ to develop GUI implementation systems, more familiar languages are making the change to add on the many features of C++ development. MicroFocus, one of the beacons of PC COBOL, will soon make available a version of COBOL which permits COBOL programmers to have multiple open windows—perhaps one for the text editor, one for compiling and one for debugging. According to Yourdon, "So even if a programmer keeps working in an old familiar kind of language and methodology and building familiar applications, he'll be doing it in an environment that is a lot more pleasant and productive to work in."

Measurement in the Brave New World

However, moving into these new paradigms of development presents the IT organization with a quandary. What type of metrics should be utilized that will effectively measure development in this brave new world? Is the old standard, lines of code, dead? Has the new kid on the block, Function Points, lost its utility?

According to Rubin, "The measurement field hasn't been changing very much at all to incorporate these new technologies (e.g., Client/Server, GUI)." Although still strongly behind the use of Function Points as a measure, Rubin admits that Function Points do have their limitations in dealing with today's more GUI-oriented systems. As Rubin puts it, "Function Points were created with a transaction notion of input and output. What do you do with the notion of color and motion? This is not reflected in the internal measure."

Today's systems, according to Rubin, "very much stress the envelope of measurement." Rubin goes on to stress that "there were really no good solid standards of measurement even for traditional environments looking back to the world of the 1970s and people are now trying to build on those very same things to deal with GUIs and object-oriented systems. There's a risk that a lot of technical size measures might start to fall apart." Recognizing the inadequacies of current measurement practices when used on today's more complex systems, Rubin's team has developed what he has termed a "consumer reports scorecard structure." Rubin's scorecard includes 13 categories of measures that can be further refined down to 156 business-oriented measures. This scorecard, or EKG, approach is so palatable to some developers that most recently a very large Northeastern bank managed a merger with another large bank using this approach.

Rubin is the first to admit that not all metrics are appropriate to all methodologies. As far as Function Points is concerned he is finding that "people are trying to stretch Function Points to work with the object-oriented world. I don't believe it's stretchable. We might as well use something new. We can't always use the past for the future."

Research is underway at MIT to do just that—find something new. Dr. Chris Kemerer, a professor at MIT's prestigious Sloan School of Management and Dr. Shyam Chidamber, also of the Sloan School, recently presented a paper on object-oriented design (Kemerer and Chidamber 1991). In this paper Kemerer asserts his position as perhaps the first person to talk about measurement for object-oriented systems. Since most client/server systems of the future and all GUI systems are object-based, the IT world is beginning to take notice of just this type of research.

Kemerer's paper proposes a series of six metrics that serve to measure the depth and breath of object-oriented design. While he is currently collecting statistics to verify his proposal, his list of six is worth mentioning even without validation. Figure 1.7 summarizes Kemerer's contribution. By perusing this figure it is easy to pinpoint how Kemerer's metrics differ from conventional measurements. Object-oriented metrics are specifically oriented to object-oriented methodologies that are quite different from conventional methodologies. Kemerer explains, "The notion is to try to go after those things that are different about the object-oriented approach. The one

Fig. 1.7 Metrics for object-oriented design.

Metric 1: WMC - Weighted Methods Per Class
Relates to the definition of complexity of an
object. The number of methods and the
complexity of methods involved is an indicator
of how much time and effort is required to develop
and maintain the object.

Metric 2: DIT - Depth of Inheritance Tree
DIT is a measure of how many ancestor classes
can potentially affect a class. It is useful to
have a measure of how deep a particular class
is in the hierachcy so that the class can
be designed with reuse of inherited methods.

Fig. 1.7 *Continued.*

Metric 3: NOC - Number of Children
        NOC is a measure of how many sub-classes
        are going to inherit the methods of a parent
        class. NOC gives an idea of the potential
        influence a class has on the design. If a class
        has a large number of children, it may require
        more testing of the methods in that class.

Metric 4: CBO - Coupling between Objects
        This is a count of the number of non-inheritance
        related couples with other classes. Excessive
        coupling between objects outside of the
        inheritance hierarchy is detrimental to modular
        design and prevents reuse. This measure is useful
        to determine how complex the testing of various
        parts of the design are likely to be.

Metric 5: RFC - Reponse for a Class
        The response set is a set of methods available
        to the object. Since it specifically includes
        methods called from outside the object, it is
        also a measure of communication between objects.
        If a large number of methods can be invoked, the
        testing and debugging of the object becomes more
        complicated.

Metric 6: LCOM - Lack of Cohesion in Methods
        LCOM uses the notion of degree of similarity of
        methods. Fewer disjoint sets implies greater
        similarity of methods. Cohesiveness of methods
        within a class is desirable, since it promotes
        encapsulation of objects.

source: Chidamber and Kemerer, MIT

that is the easiest to explain to most people is the notion of inheritance. Our metric is to measure depth of inheritance. In this way we can determine to what degree people are using inheritance." The goal here is to address the optimal mix of complexity and usability.

What Kemerer is referring to is actually the optimal use of the depth of inheritance. When a programmer uses no inheritance, he is not taking advantage of reusability and therefore negates productivity gains of the object-oriented technique. When the programmer "goes really deep" then, according to Kemerer, "This may also be bad since it will be hard to test it . . . indeed it may get to be too much for one person to keep in mind."

Even though Kemerer is well on his way to inventing the latest state-of-the-art in the form of measurement he, as is Rubin, is still keen on Function Points. As Kemerer puts it, "Measurements could coexist. Measurements might address two parts of the same problem, one is size the other is design complexity."

Given the trend toward complexity in software, coupled with a desire for increased quality, is there any wonder that IT managers all across the country are having a difficult time adjusting to the new status quo and are actively seeking out role models. In looking for role models to interview for this chapter, the author decided to look straight to hardware/software vendors. After all, they are developers too—and developers of software that is highly complex and has pushed into the new frontiers of client/server and GUI development. What better than to find out from the heads of development, then, just how they cut the mustard.

A View from the Top

Brian Magowan is Vice President and General Manager of Unisys' Software Products Group. In charge of all Unisys software, his responsibility crosses hardware boundaries, requiring his staff to master not only the mainframe but the DOS and UNIX worlds as well. In ensuring that quality reigns supreme, Unisys uses the SEI matrix to self-access their readiness for quality. According to Magowan, "A number of years ago we concluded that we didn't have a sufficient emphasis on software engineering quality issues. We made some decisions then that we are in the process of implementing now."

Under Magowan's stewardship, Unisys has implemented a TQM program in which quality and productivity is "everybody's job." Their first step was to train everyone, including programmers, in the basics of modern quality thinking. According to Magowan this course was not specifically geared to software engineering but rather emphasized the Deming approach to quality. The Unisys quality course includes everything from statistical process control to why quality is everyone's job and why quality leads to productivity.

What this translates to, as Magowan puts it, "is some general TQM thinking where different software engineering organizations get to apply that thinking to their own development life cycles." Where this approach has really paid off is in the lowering of the Unisys defect rate. Using an in-house automated system named PRIMUS, Unisys staff and customers can track defects both before and after release, enabling Unisys to, according to Magowan, "improve tests to make sure that we don't let software out that has bugs in it."

This emphasis on improved quality of their software product has broadened into more sophisticated issues that relate to completeness and marketability of their products. According to Magowan, "Our emphasis on quality forces us to concentrate on three key areas: defect rates, predictability of software performance, and product completeness."

This emphasis on quality is demonstrated by Unisys' commitment to bringing to the table products that can be used both internally and externally for automatic testing and in funding extensive R&D in the area of measurement.

In the first instance, Unisys markets the highly regarded LINC Interpretive test

Environment, which is CASE software that eliminates the need to regenerate systems during the test stage of application creation. Unisys LINC developers can change code and immediately verify proper operation to implement changes faster. This interpretive test environment comes complete with an on-line debugger for locating, analyzing, testing, and correcting logic errors as well as a statistics-gathering feature to ensure code efficiency.

At the other end of the spectrum, Unisys has played a pivotal role in the funding of Function Point measurement research by the esteemed Dr. Eberhard Rudolph, Professor of Information Systems at the Hochschule Bremerhaven in Germany. He is a well-known authority on productivity in application software development and in particular on Fourth Generation Languages, CASE tools and the Function Point technique. His most recent study, released in November 1991, surveyed the effectiveness of the Unisys LINC software development environment. According to the study, "The results indicate that LINC users can develop larger application systems than installations using conventional COBOL environments. Productivity gains of 5:1 to 10:1 were observed for application systems exceeding 2000 Function Points. Applications over 5000 Function Points can have gains of 20:1 and more." Though the Rudolph study measured solely the Unisys LINC environment, one can extrapolate that the newer software methods can play a large role in fostering productivity.

Digital Equipment Corporation knows this lesson only too well. DEC is another hardware/software vendor with a need for consistent quality and enhanced productivity across hardware platforms and software types. Tom Harris, Software Engineering Group Manager for the Commercial Languages and Tools Group based in Nashua, New Hampshire, is responsible for software developed across all platforms. In his long tenure at DEC he has managed the development of Motif, compilers, CASE tools, as well as project management systems.

Over the years Harris has refined some techniques that he successfully uses to develop quality software. The most important of these techniques is a clear definition, at the outset of the project, of its usability goals. As Harris explains: "If you are developing a spreadsheet, how will you know that someone can use it effectively, what other products will this be positioned against, what are some sample tasks and is the rate at which you do these tasks important?"

In essence, Harris arrives at these goals by working with his customers. According to Harris, "As it turns out this is a study in human factors." And in performing this human factors study Harris and staff have developed a number of techniques that run the gamut from knowledge acquisition to development of quantifiable measurement parameters, some of which are shown in the form of questions to be asked in Fig. 1.8. One of these is what Harris refers to as *contextual inquiry.* "In the context of someone doing their job, rather than put you in a lab and watching, why don't we work with you in the context of your job by running a small video camera off to the side." Harris sums up the DEC approach to fostering quality with a couple of phrases; a consistent process, good change control, and good testing tools.

The head of development of Oracle Corporation, maker of the Oracle relational database software, echoes DEC's Harris in his insistence on fostering quality. Alan Gater, Director of CASE Development, based in Chertsey, England, details the Oracle development strategy: "First we decide on what the users want to do, what is ac-

---

1. **How stable are the project's requirements?**
2. **Are you aware of and up to speed on your competitor's products?**
3. **What are you doing to build a quality product?**
4. **What do you need to do, or need to have, to improve quality?**
5. **At this stage of the project, what process are you using to help you understand where you are in repsect to quality?**
6. **What test coverage is planned?**

source: Tom Harris, Digital Equipment Corporation.

Fig. 1.8 DEC quality review questions.

tually intended, what are its major features. Then we do a full analysis of how that product should be developed." This analysis is based on discussions with both users and technologists. Not only does Oracle consider internal users but they have a wide base of cooperative business partners with whom they spend a lot of time. These are the Boeings and the Shells with whom Oracle spends much time in identifying what they require and how it should work.

Before Oracle is ready to delve into development on any one particular product they match the project to a set of guidelines (rules of thumb) that includes:

- No product will come out before it's ready.

- How many different development streams can we manage at one time?

- How much development can we actually afford?

- What is the list of features and functions that we must support?

This list serves to streamline the long list of possible projects that is presented to Oracle at any given time. As Gater puts it, "At some point we say we can do this much and not more. And then we prioritize the projects that do remain."

Oracle is so intent on quality that they are currently in the process of attaining ISO 9000 certification. From Gater's perspective, quality goes hand-in-hand with development: "Alongside every development plan we have a quality plan. And for each plan we have a list of deliverables or what we call acceptables."

Oracle's many development teams use the concept of acceptables to "prove" that they are delivering usable and quality-oriented software. According to Gater, "Our quality plan is something that each of the development managers has to produce to demonstrate that product quality is acceptable. It details how they are going to assure that what they deliver is adequate." Gater goes on to describe one of the formal processes that Oracle developers undergo in this vein: "We utilize something we call a formal structured hand-over. These sessions, which take about half a day, are attended by four people—one for each stage of development. We have the supplier—whoever it was that thought of the previous stage, the author—the coder of the current stage, the designer and the receiver, who is the person that is supposed to do something with the product. There is also a moderator. The idea behind the formal structured hand-over is that if you put the person who wrote the specification, the designer and the programmer together and they go through the design document in detail with the user a higher end-quality will result."

Perhaps the name that looms largest on the horizon in terms of heavy-duty software development is Computer Associates. Makers of a wide variety of software products that are available on an even wider array of hardware platforms, CA offers the reader an excellent role model. As Senior Vice President for Research and Development, Mark Combs, based on New York's Long Island, is ready to offer us a rare insight into the CA method of developing quality code. According to Combs: "We consider that developing a process is bigger than just a coding job. It's something that ties in the appropriateness of the product, performance, the way it integrates into the environment as well as just looking at a particular design for implementing a particular feature."

The centerpiece of the CA development strategy is their CA90 architecture. When developing new code, one of the things that they look for is how the new release is going to implement the CA90 architecture. According to Combs: "CA90 has a lot of business focus to it. It also has a lot of technical focus. It makes heavy use of common components and tools in creating software. This, almost by itself, contributes to a higher level of quality because we make very heavy use of common components and tools in creating our software."

Although the CA90 architecture was conceived at least ten years ago to deal with developing software that needed to integrate easily into the ever-changing IBM operating environment, the architecture provides CA real benefits in today's rapidly changing environment where multi-platform, GUI-oriented software is the norm. By insisting that all CA software adhere to a common set of rules all defined neatly within an architecture, CA assures itself that reusable and quality code are the yardstick by which it measures itself.

And in an era of rapidly changing technologies it is perhaps this yardstick that will matter the most.

Author Biography

Jessica Keyes is president of TECHINSIDER, a high-tech consulting research firm based in New York City. She is the publisher and editor of TECHINSIDER REPORTS and Computer Market Letter. As a columnist for PC AI and correspondent for many other trade publications such as COMPUTERWORLD and SOFTWARE MAGAZINE she has written well over 100 articles. She is the author of three other books: *The New Intelligence*, *The Handbook of Expert Systems in Manufacturing*, and *InfoTrends: The Competitive Use of Information*.

Ms. Keyes has over 15 years of practical experience in the technology field. Prior to founding TECHINSIDER, Ms. Keyes was Managing Director of Technology for the

New York Stock Exchange and has been an officer at both Banker's Trust and Swiss Bank Corp. Ms. Keyes received an M.B.A. from New York University.

Works Cited

Albrecht, A.J. 1983. Software function, source lines of code and development effort prediction: A software science validation. *IEEE transactions on software engineering*.

Conte, Dunsmore, and Shen. 1986. *Software engineering metrics and models*. Benjamin/Cummings Publishing Company.

Hansen, W.J. 1978. Measurement of program complexity by the pair (cyclomatic number, operator count). *ACM SIGPLAN notices*. March, 1978.

Kemerer, Chris and Shyam Chidamber. 1991. Towards a metrics suite for object oriented design. Presented at ACM Object Oriented Programming, Systems, Languages and Applications Conference. October 1991.

McCabe, Thomas. 1976. A complexity measure. *IEEE transactions on software engineering*.

2

A Systems Methodology
A Rating and Evaluation Guide

by Sam Holcman

Overview

About this chapter

This chapter provides an evaluation framework for selecting a systems methodology. It presents key questions along with rating scales to help you identify strengths and weaknesses in methodologies you might be reviewing for your organization.

The chapter begins with a perspective-setting discussion on methodologies. It then introduces five categories you should consider when selecting a methodology. Each category contains specific criteria stated in question form. Each question is followed by a brief discussion that helps you rate the methodology. The chapter concludes with charts you may use for making quantitative evaluations and for comparing methodologies.

How this chapter can help your organization

Every systems organization needs an effective methodology; however, selecting the best methodology remains a challenge. A methodology is not easily exchanged for another one if it does not meet expectations. Implementing a methodology represents a long-term commitment that requires investment in education and a certain change in culture.

Methodology selection is a serious step that should be taken based on quantitative evaluation rather than the influence of clever sales tactics. This chapter is designed to help you rate a methodology based on a specific set of criteria. Evaluating and comparing methodologies in this way can help your organization make a quality selection.

Introduction

Effective systems development

Systems play a critical role in today's business environment, directly affecting a corporation's ability to compete. As a result, systems organizations, responsible for the development and evolution of complex systems, experience pressure to improve both the quality and productivity of their work. However, effective systems development/evolution remains an elusive goal.

Today, organizations often rely on technologies such as Computer-Aided Software Engineering (CASE) to produce higher quality systems in less time. While CASE tools deliver necessary automation for systems organizations, they are just that— tools. CASE tools record, validate, and report on business and development decisions that have been made. But you cannot expect a CASE tool to tell you which systems to build, what the systems must do, how they should be designed, and similar items. Effective systems development requires a process that guides system decisions such as these. This process must evolve with the changing needs of the systems community and reflect improvements in methods, techniques, standards, and available technology. Such a process is the modern systems methodology.

What is a methodology?

Every mature engineering discipline embodies a methodology that expresses proven methods, techniques, and standards for developing its products. Complex products such as integrated circuits are not simply the result of advanced CAD/CAM technology. Rather, these circuits are made possible by the proven methods, techniques, and standards that electrical engineering employs to guide the engineering process.

A systems methodology guides the activities of developing and evolving systems, and it continually reflects improvements made in the development process. As such, a methodology is an evolving repository for systems development practices that have proved effective. But how can you determine whether or not a systems methodology will meet the specific needs of your organization? This question can be answered by evaluating the methodology.

How to use this chapter

This chapter is designed to help you evaluate a methodology on a quantitative basis. Twenty-six distinct criteria are divided into five categories: objectives, properties, components, functions, and services. Each criterion is presented in the form of a question followed by a discussion to guide you in evaluating the methodology under review. An eight-point rating scale, like the one shown here, is provided for each question.

"Sample" rating scale

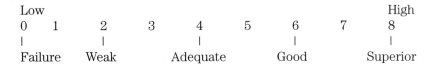

Low   High
0   1   2   3   4   5   6   7   8
| | | | |
Failure   Weak   Adequate   Good   Superior

To better interpret the low and high points, guide words specific to each question appear on each rating scale. All questions can be weighted according to the specific needs of your organization. After you finish rating all 26 criteria, your scores can be transferred to the charts at the end of the chapter. These charts allow you to add up methodology scores and to make overall evaluations and comparisons.

Objectives

Objectives reveal the intent of the methodology—what it claims to accomplish and what the user might expect of future releases. An effective systems methodology should meet the four objectives presented in this section.

Guide the systems development process

1. Does the methodology identify the steps necessary to produce each deliverable of systems development/evolution?

   The methodology user should be able to easily determine and execute the steps necessary to produce a selected deliverable. Low-rating methodologies might contain the necessary details within a narrative, but fail to present the details in a step-by-step manner. High-rating methodologies guide the systems process with explicit steps that define the following:

   —What must be done?   —How long will it take?
   —Why is the step done?   —How should it be done?
   —What is produced?   —Who will do it?
   —When should it be done?   —Which tools are to be used?

1. "Guide Process" rating scale

   Academic   Step-Based
   0   1   2   3   4   5   6   7   8
   | | | | |
   Failure   Weak   Adequate   Good   Superior

Serve as a central systems encyclopedia

2. Does the methodology house and deliver the details necessary for developing/evolving systems?

   The methodology is intended to be the single place where systems professionals house system policy, standards, methods, techniques, etc. A methodology that does not allow a systems organization to tie its naming conventions to deliverables, for example, will discourage its use.

   Low-rating methodologies force users to cross-reference and consult related documents to assemble the complete picture. High-rating methodologies link this information electronically for easy access.

2. "Centralize" rating scale

```
No Intent                                             Full Intent
 0      1      2      3      4      5      6      7      8
 |             |             |             |             |
Failure      Weak         Adequate       Good        Superior
```

Simplify the systems development process

3. Does the methodology simplify the systems development/evolution process?

    Some methodologies are developed with the notion that bigger is better, offering a vast quantity of detail but often containing unnecessary or weak content. In contrast, when the focus is on quality, detail is provided only to accomplish demonstrated utility.

    Low-rating methodologies contain overwhelming content. In many cases, the content is redundant or is based on a bulky design—one that contains an excessive ratio of audit and/or review steps for each productive step. High-rating methodologies employ an economy of expression by getting to the point, setting out essential steps, and progressively exposing detail.

3. "Simplify" rating scale

```
Pick & Choose                                           Essence
 0      1      2      3      4      5      6      7      8
 |             |             |             |             |
Failure      Weak         Adequate       Good        Superior
```

Standardize the systems development process

4. Does the methodology encourage and provide the means to implement a standard approach to systems development?

    A systems development methodology should drive standardization. It should establish and encourage a consistent vocabulary. It should provide the means to create a standard project approach for accomplishing each of a variety of projects, such as Accelerated Analysis, External System Design, Prototyping, Business Engineering, etc. Low-rating methodologies force the using organization to conform to its standards. High-rating methodologies supply a standards baseline (starting point) along with mechanisms to adapt the methodology to reflect the standards and practices of the using organization.

4. "Standardize" rating scale

```
Restrictive                                         Accommodating
 0      1      2      3      4      5      6      7      8
 |             |             |             |             |
Failure      Weak         Adequate       Good        Superior
```

Properties

Properties reveal the inherent qualities of a methodology and are useful in identifying potential strengths and weaknesses. Six distinct properties are considered in this section.

Customizability

5. Can any aspect of the methodology be customized to meet specific standards and practices of the using organization?

Studies indicate that most organizations either "shelve" or customize a methodology within 18 months after installation. A customizable methodology is one that can be modified, in place, and retain all of the features and functions of its original form.

The lowest-rating methodologies are simply not accessible in electronic form. Low-rating methodologies fail to incorporate necessary functions to support customization. A high-rating methodology treats customization as a key design requirement and can answer yes to the following questions without diluting its basic features and functions:

—Can the names of methodology components be changed to those the using organization is more familiar with?
—Can the descriptions of methodology components be changed?
—Can new components be added and related to existing components?
—Can component definitions (designs) be altered, extended, or deleted?
—Can new paths be defined to describe unique uses of the methodology?
—Can the underlying methods and deliverables be changed?

5. "Customizability" rating scale

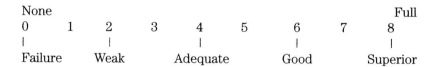

```
None                                              Full
0      1     2      3      4     5      6     7     8
|            |             |            |           |
Failure    Weak        Adequate      Good       Superior
```

Correctness

6. Can changes to the methodology be verified as correct?

A methodology with inconsistencies will be rejected quickly by the systems community. If the methodology is customizable, corrections can be made, but the question remains: are those changes correct? To allow for verifiable correctness, a methodology must be formally defined. This means that the methodology vocabulary is described via an underlying data model (or equivalent) to ensure terms are uniquely defined and consistently related. Likewise, methodology processes (its methods) are formally defined to ensure that each method produces a deliverable that contributes to the systems development/evolution process.

The lowest- rating methodologies are not expressed in a formal model and act as a barrier to verification. Low-rating methodologies have no automated means to assist in verifying correctness. High-rating methodologies are designed using formal models and reside in an automated environment that "understands" the models. This provides the opportunity to conduct computer-assisted verification of the methodology when it is first built and as it undergoes change.

6. "Correctness" rating scale

Unverifiable						Automatic Verification		
0	1	2	3	4	5	6	7	8
|		|		|		|		|
Failure		Weak		Adequate		Good		Superior

Compatibility

7. Does the methodology support current techniques and technology or is it based upon dated practices?

Systems development/evolution is continually improving. New techniques are introduced and methods change to better support new technologies, such as CASE, repositories, re-engineering, etc.

Low-rating methodologies are based on dated (pre-CASE, form-intensive) philosophies, which limit their effectiveness. High-rating methodologies assume the existence of such technologies/practices as:

—CASE
—Relational database management environments
—Client-server and cooperative processing
—Accelerated, user-centered development
—Business and technical engineering
—Integration (cross business area/system data and function sharing)
—Model-based development (use of modeling formalisms such as data models)

7. "Compatibility" rating scale

Outdated								Current
0	1	2	3	4	5	6	7	8
|		|		|		|		|
Failure		Weak		Adequate		Good		Superior

Completeness

8. Does the methodology cover all aspects of systems activities?

An effective systems methodology should address all the needs of a systems organization. Low-rating methodologies focus on a portion of the systems life-cycle, such as design and construction. High-rating methodologies incorporate the following phases:

—Planning—analysis and modeling of the business (organization) to determine which system projects to deploy, which business areas they affect, and when to deploy them.

—Analysis—discover, structure, detail, and verify business requirements for a particular business area.

—Design—engineer a system design from the business requirements.

—Construction—translate the system design into the solution system.

—Evolution—accept, consolidate, plan, and coordinate the release of changes to the deliverables of the above phases. Activities include change management, impact analysis, and change planning.

8. "Completeness" rating scale

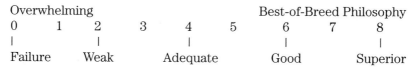

Incomplete   Complete
0   1   2   3   4   5   6   7   8
| | | | |
Failure   Weak   Adequate   Good   Superior

Conciseness

9. Can the methodology be realistically followed by the systems organization or does it present overwhelming details?

A methodology that simply houses all known knowledge of systems practices is ineffective as a coherent guide for systems professionals. Effective methodologies must be both complete and concise.

Low-rating methodologies offer an array of sometimes conflicting approaches from which the user may choose. High-rating methodologies provide the best-of-breed of past and current approaches. Higher-rating methodologies present one consistent philosophy that is succinctly expressed.

9. "Conciseness" rating scale

Overwhelming   Best-of-Breed Philosophy
0   1   2   3   4   5   6   7   8
| | | | |
Failure   Weak   Adequate   Good   Superior

Ability to subset

10. Can cohesive pieces of the methodology be extracted for use on focused projects?

An effective methodology supports paths that include methods and techniques designed to meet specific objectives, such as a path that guides the scoping of a business area. These paths should be easily extracted for use on focused projects.

Low-rating methodologies have limited or no support for this type of subsetting. High-rating methodologies allow the user to extract almost any coherent piece of the methodology. Once extracted, that piece may be operated on using the full features and functions of the methodology.

10. "Subsetting" rating scale

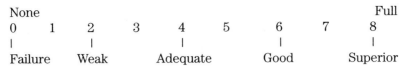

```
None                                              Full
 0      1      2      3      4      5      6      7      8
 |             |             |             |             |
Failure      Weak        Adequate       Good        Superior
```

Components

Components are the basic elements that represent the building blocks of the methodology. Components help reveal the capabilities of the methodology. This section looks at seven critical components.

Deliverables

11. Is the methodology driven by the production of deliverables?

The primary purpose of a methodology is to guide system development/evolution activities. These activities are measured by the quality and timeliness of deliverables. An effective methodology establishes deliverables as its goals and focuses on their production.

Low-rating methodologies are form- or process-based, while the primary architecture of a high-rating methodology is a deliverable chain. Other components (methods, techniques, roles, tools, objectives, etc.) of high-rating methodologies support the development and evolution of deliverables.

11. "Deliverables" rating scale

```
Implicit                                        Explicit
 0      1      2      3      4      5      6      7      8
 |             |             |             |             |
Failure      Weak        Adequate       Good        Superior
```

Methods

12. Is the methodology organized in terms of discrete methods that are linked by the deliverables they produce?

Methods are a key component of a methodology. Each method should have a purpose—to produce a deliverable. The methodology should incorporate precedence relationships among the methods to establish which serve as prerequisites for others.

A low-rating methodology has fuzzy boundaries for its methods. High-rating methodologies have crisply defined methods that are characterized by:

—Function—each method should perform one function. The function should be precise enough to be adequately profiled by its name in the form of a verb followed by a one- or two-word identifier. Examples: Discover Entity Types, Structure Data Model, Detail Entity Type.

—Deliverable(s)—ideally, each method produces one deliverable.

—Roles—the types of job functions (skills) required to perform the method.

—Tools—the CASE (or other) tools required to perform the method.

12. "Methods" rating scale

Fuzzy   Crisp

0	1	2	3	4	5	6	7	8
|		|		|		|		|
Failure		Weak		Adequate		Good		Superior

Techniques

13. Does the methodology provide techniques that describe how to conduct its methods?

A technique is a procedure that guides the execution of the method. A methodology's techniques incorporate empirically determined approaches that have proved effective in accomplishing the method.

Some low-rating methodologies have no techniques at all, while others have trivial or poorly expressed techniques. High-rating methodologies provide a dynamic collection of explicit techniques that are mapped to the method(s) they support.

13. "Techniques" rating scale

None   Throughout

0	1	2	3	4	5	6	7	8
|		|		|		|		|
Failure		Weak		Adequate		Good		Superior

Standards and practices

14. Can the methodology embody the standards and practices of the using organization?

Each organization has unique systems development guidelines, such as naming conventions. These guidelines should be integral to the organization's methodology.

Low-rating methodologies impose standards on the using organization. High-rating methodologies encourage the blending of organizational standards.

14. "Standards" rating scale

No Support   Full Support

0	1	2	3	4	5	6	7	8
|		|		|		|		|
Failure	Weak			Adequate		Good		Superior

Roles

15. Does the methodology identify the roles (types of job functions) that are involved in each method?

    Methods are performed by various practitioners, each with specific skills. An effective methodology links required skills with each method in order to identify appropriate roles. The roles reflect logical job functions such as Analyst, Database Designer, Project Manager, etc.

    Low-rating methodologies have general and/or inconsistent role identification. Treating the role as a key property of each method, high-rating methodologies provide a means to tie the using organization's roles directly to the methods.

15. "Roles" rating scale

```
None                                              Throughout
0       1    2      3      4     5     6     7     8
|            |             |           |           |
Failure     Weak         Adequate    Good        Superior
```

Tools

16. Does the methodology identify the support tools appropriate for the execution of each method?

    Effective methodologies should assume and allow for the use of CASE technologies to assist in the execution of its methods, and each method should identify the support tools required.

    Low-rating methodologies ignore implicitly suggested tools. High-rating methodologies clearly identify recommended tools for each method.

16. "Tools" rating scale

```
None                                              Throughout
0       1    2      3      4     5     6     7     8
|            |             |           |           |
Failure     Weak         Adequate    Good        Superior
```

Paths

17. Does the methodology allow for predefined paths that accomplish specific objectives?

    Since a methodology will rarely, if ever, be used in its entirety on a single project, it's critical that the user be able to establish predefined paths. These paths represent standard project structures that reflect sanctioned uses of the methodology within the organization.

    Low-rating methodologies offer one path. High-rating methodologies provide multiple paths and allow the user to select a path, customize a path, or build an entirely new path to meet specific objectives.

17. "Paths" rating scale

No Support   Full Support
0   1   2   3   4   5   6   7   8
| | | | |
Failure   Weak   Adequate   Good   Superior

Functions

Functions are the dynamic features of a methodology and help define such qualities as ease-of-use, flexibility, and extensibility. Four distinct functions are considered in this section.

Methodology management

18. Is the methodology expressed using formal models whose structural integrity can be automatically verified?

Informally expressed methodologies cannot be verified for correctness either manually or automatically. Methodology management refers to functionality that allows automatic verification of the formal models used to express a methodology. It also supplies a means to manage the changes that will occur to the methodology over time. The functionality required for effective methodology management is found in a CASE tool.

Low-rating methodologies are informally expressed using structured English or unverified models. High-rating methodologies are designed using formal models and are managed by a host CASE tool.

18. "Management" rating scale

Informal/Manual   Formalized/Automatic
0   1   2   3   4   5   6   7   8
| | | | |
Failure   Weak   Adequate   Good   Superior

Methodology navigation

19. Can the methodology be expediently searched to retrieve methodology information?

The value of a methodology's content is diminished if it cannot be located and retrieved efficiently. An effective methodology is accessible using a variety of approaches:

—Abstraction—allows review from several levels of abstraction so that the user can select any component at one level of abstraction and see its details (go to a lower level of abstraction).
—Context-Shifts—allows quick shifts in context so that the user can anchor on an object and quickly navigate to a set of related, but adjacent information.

—Perspective—allows the same information to be viewed from multiple perspectives so that, for example, the user can see methods hierarchically (showing parent-child relationships) or sequentially (showing dependencies).

In addition, the methodology should provide a contemporary window-based, mouse-oriented, graphical user interface (GUI). GUI inherently provides strong navigational capabilities and an intuitive interface for the user. Low-rating methodologies are paper-based, offer functionally weak navigational capabilities, or supply flashy navigational features that fail to address the needs of the user. High-rating methodologies provide navigational support linked to the way the methodology is used. Highest-rating methodologies deliver this support via a GUI-based interface.

19. "Navigation" rating scale

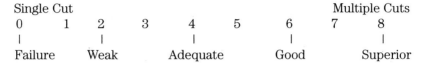

Handbook generation

20. Can select pieces of the methodology be published as project handbooks?

A project handbook is an electronic or paper-based subset of the methodology designed to support a specific project. The handbook complements the electronic form of the methodology by providing a convenient reference guide. The handbook is simply a generated report of methodology contents, with any changes to the methodology appearing in the paper version without human intervention.

Low-rating methodologies offer primitive printing capabilities or none at all. High-rating methodologies allow any portion of the content to be delivered in publishing-quality handbook form.

20. "Handbook" rating scale

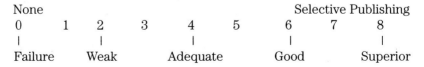

External interfaces

21. Can the methodology be ported to external software (tools)?

Interfaces with external software (project management software, desktop publishing packages, other CASE tools, etc.) enhance the power of an electronic-based methodology. For example, one portion of the methodology may be ported to a desktop publisher to produce educational materials for in-house courses. Another portion may be ported to a project manager to better drive systems projects.

Low-rating methodologies require manual intervention or offer little or no support to electronically interface with other products. High-rating methodologies provide an open interface for import and export of electronic information.

21. "Interfaces" rating scale

```
None                                      General Purpose
0       1    2    3    4    5    6    7    8
|            |         |         |         |
Failure     Weak      Adequate  Good      Superior
```

Services

Services identify the support provided by the methodology vendor. Several services are required to effectively implement a methodology within an organization. Five services are looked at in this section.

Education

22. Is the methodology supported by a complete line of educational services?

Effective education transfers information about the content and usage of a methodology into knowledge. Education should be conducted by a practitioner who can explain significant characteristics, clarify complex points, answer questions, and verify that learning is taking place.

Low-rating methodologies offer superficial education. High-rating methodologies support education on a level equal to the methodology itself.

22. "Education" rating scale

```
None                                            Full
0       1    2    3    4    5    6    7    8
|            |         |         |         |
Failure     Weak      Adequate  Good      Superior
```

Integration

23. Are services available to integrate the methodology with the standards, practices, and conventions of the using organization?

No commercially developed methodology will fit precisely with the using organization. As a result, an early implementation step is to integrate the methodology with the organization's existing standards, practices, and conventions. There are several key points of integration:

—Roles—some roles will require change to adjust their name or definition; some roles will be added or deleted; some will be split into several roles; some might be combined into one.
—Tools—each organization has a different mix of tools that will necessarily vary from those identified in the methodology and will require incorporation.

—Paths—a path describes a unique sequence of methods and steps designed to achieve certain objectives. Integration will adjust the methodology's default paths or introduce new paths to reflect the organization's sanctioned project approaches.

Low-rating methodologies offer no integration services. High-rating methodologies provide assistance in fitting the methodology to the organization.

23. "Integration" rating scale

```
None                                              Full
0      1    2    3    4    5    6    7    8
|           |         |         |         |
Failure    Weak     Adequate   Good      Superior
```

Demonstration

24. Is the vendor capable of demonstrating any aspect of the methodology on a real project?

Recognizing that there is no substitute for experience, an organization that is educated in a particular methodology can realize a significant head start in its implementation by observing the method in practice by professionals. This is best accomplished by putting the methodology to work on one of the organization's actual projects.

Low-rating methodologies are not able to demonstrate the methodology on real (versus pilot) projects. High-rating methodologies encourage demonstration on actual projects.

24. "Demonstration" rating scale

```
None                                              Full
0      1    2    3    4    5    6    7    8
|           |         |         |         |
Failure    Weak     Adequate   Good      Superior
```

Customization

25. Are services available to customize the methodology to incorporate the using organization's experiences?

Customizing is similar to adding new functionality to an existing, working system—it involves a careful weaving of new experiences without compromising the integrity of the methodology. Initially, the vendor has the strongest understanding of the design philosophy and content of the methodology. For this reason, the vendor should provide a service to help with the very first customization of the methodology. This service should lead to a process that allows the using organization to handle all future customizations on its own.

Lowest-rating methodologies claim that customization is unnecessary. Low-rating methodologies have no customization support. High-rating methodologies view customization as a necessary part of implementation and offer full services to meet this need.

25. "Customization" rating scale

None   Full
0   1   2   3   4   5   6   7   8
| | | | |
Failure   Weak   Adequate   Good   Superior

Implementation

26. Are services available to guide an effective roll-out of the methodology?

To effectively implement a methodology, the using organization will necessarily influence a change in culture. The organization can choose to manage the change or to allow the change to manage them. The management of cultural change involves proactive planning and execution. It treats change as a process with known characteristics—measures of risk, indicators of success or failure, defined roles, etc. An effective implementation service addresses these issues in the technical roll-out of the methodology.

Low-rating methodologies consider roll-out to be a simple distribution of the methodology. High-rating methodologies provide an implementation service to help manage cultural and organizational elements within the using organization.

26. "Implementation" rating scale

None   Full
0   1   2   3   4   5   6   7   8
| | | | |
Failure   Weak   Adequate   Good   Superior

Scoring the Methodologies

Itemized evaluation

The following chart provides a means to conduct a quantitative evaluation of several methodologies. Simply go back through the chapter and transfer the scores from each of the rating scales under the 26 evaluation criteria. Total these scores for each of the five categories and transfer them to the Overall Evaluation Chart.

Itemized Evaluation Chart
Methodology

Objectives
1.   Guide   ——
2.   Centralize   ——
3.   Simplify   ——
4.   Standardize   ——
Total   ——

Properties
5.   Customizability   ——
6.   Correctness   ——
7.   Compatibility   ——
8.   Completeness   ——
9.   Conciseness   ——
10. Subsetting   ——
Total   ——

Components
11. Deliverables   ——
12. Methods   ——
13. Techniques   ——
14. Standards   ——
15. Roles   ——
16. Tools   ——
17. Paths   ——
Total   ——

Functions
18. Management   ——
19. Navigation   ——
20. Handbook   ——
21. Interfaces   ——
Total   ——

Services
22. Education   ——
23. Integration   ——
24. Demonstration   ——
25. Customization   ——
26. Implementation   ——
Total   ——

Overall Evaluation Chart
Methodology

Category	Maximum
Objectives	32
Properties	48
Components	56
Functions	32
Services	40
Total score	208

Comparing methodologies

As you can see, the maximum possible methodology score is 208. While today's methodologies might strive to reach this level of precision, the criteria set forth in this chapter are demanding. Recognizing that the "perfect" methodology will likely never exist, the following ranges indicate a general rating of methodologies based on total scores:

- Low rating   0–103
- Average rating   104–155
- High rating   156–208

The chart and these ratings provide a means to compare methodologies quantitatively with an eye toward identifying strengths and weaknesses in specific categories. The objective of this comparative evaluation is to provide a useful base of information to assist you in making a difficult decision—the decision of selecting a systems methodology for your organization.

Summary

Qualities of an effective methodology

Today's systems organizations require an effective methodology that incorporates the best practices for systems development and evolution. What are the qualities that make for an effective methodology? The key features of such a methodology are summarized here.

The methodology serves as a central systems encyclopedia that guides, simplifies, and standardizes the systems development/evolution process. Recognizing that each organization is different, the methodology is customizable. It considers customization a key design requirement and provides functionality to accommodate diverse and ever-changing processes within an organization. It is expressed using sound formal models that can be automatically verified for correctness by technology such as CASE.

The methodology supports advanced systems development techniques and technologies. It covers all aspects of the systems lifecycle: the planning of systems projects, the analysis of business requirements, the design of solution systems, the construction of systems, and their ongoing evolution. The methodology is both complete and concise, serving as a coherent guide for systems professionals. It allows paths and pieces of content to be selected and extracted for application on specific projects.

The methodology establishes deliverables as its goals. It focuses crisply defined methods on the production of those deliverables. It is supported by explicit techniques that have proved effective in accomplishing the methods. Roles and support tools required to execute each method are clearly defined.

The methodology allows the using organization to integrate its standards and practices and to create predefined paths to meet its unique objectives. Content information can be searched and retrieved efficiently using several approaches, and portions of the methodology can be conveniently printed as project handbooks. The power of the methodology is enhanced through interfaces with external software.

The methodology vendor offers critical support services that include education, integration of the organization's existing standards and practices, demonstration on a real project, customization to embody the organization's experiences, and implementation assistance in the methodology's roll-out.

Author Biography

Samuel B. Holcman is founder and president of Computer and Engineering Consultants, Ltd. (CEC), Southfield, Michigan. His interests are in corporate business modeling, accelerated analysis techniques, and systems lifecycles. Holcman has developed a strategic planning methodology that is used by many Fortune 500 companies. He is co-developer of the widely used accelerated analysis (JAD-like) technique known as Rapid Analysis, which is explained in a multi-part tape series produced by Applied Learning (Deltak) Corporation.

Prior to forming CEC, Holcman spent 11 years at Ford Motor Company and was involved in data processing, finance, and engineering. He was also the vice president of a robotics and factory automation firm for two years.

Accomplishments include an invitation by the Chinese and United States governments to participate as the senior member of a technology delegation to the Peoples Republic of China. He also has been invited to be a member of a technology delegation to the Commonwealth of Independent States. In addition, Holcman has been contracted by McGraw-Hill Book Company to publish a book titled *A Guide to AD/Cycle*.

Holcman has a master's degree in electrical engineering from Wayne State University in Detroit and a master's in business administration from the University of Michigan—Ann Arbor. He is a member of numerous honor societies and professional organizations.

Computer & Engineering Consultants, Ltd. (CEC) is a practitioner firm that employs the principles of information engineering (IE) in business engineering, strategic planning, systems analysis, design, and development of information systems. Encompassing all phases of the systems lifecycle, CEC's services are tightly integrated, with each step in the development process building directly upon the work done in the preceding step. Housed in a CASE tool, ForeSight™ is a flexible, interactive methodology for developing and managing systems in the CASE environment, marketed by CEC.

3

Methodology as a Productivity Tool

by Ken Horner

Definitions

In trying to assess how methodologies and their use affect an organization's productivity, we first need to be sure that we agree on the definitions. *Methodology* is relatively simple—a collection of techniques or methods that one employs to perform a task. In my usage here, I also mean to include tools and the organizational policies and practices that support or surround the methods used to develop systems. Figure 3.1 presents one of the oldest concepts (Royce 1970), the step-wise progression of a developer from the initial definition to delivery.

The loops back to prior steps are meant to embody needed or unexpected rework, including the last, which implies that either something was missed that was important or that you are working in phases and can now go on to the next phase. When I first encountered this type of chart about 25 years ago, I was struck by the idea that the picture is saying that you will, in all likelihood, make a mistake; that it is allowable to reverse course and go back to start over. In the world I work in now, this may or may not be true; or if true, there may be considerable financial and/or reputational consequences. The proverb on my high school wood shop teacher's wall of "why is there never enough time to do a thing right the first time, but always plenty of time to do it over?" comes to mind. We could define productivity, or the lack thereof, in the example above by the number of rework attempts, the number of times we have had to double back—fewer would obviously be better.

However, defining systems development productivity more generally is somewhat harder. In a larger sense, we all know what we mean by it, but to understand how using a methodology could impact development productivity, we need to be a little more precise. Simply saying we are interested in the rate of code produced per day per programmer or in the number of Function Points produced per person month are not adequate definitions.

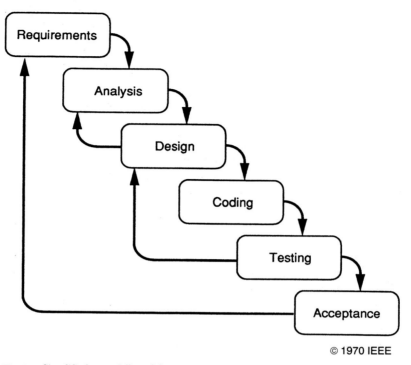

© 1970 IEEE

Fig. 3.1 Simplified waterfall model.

Differences in productivity among team members, whole teams, or organizations have been discernible empirically for some time even without a formal definition. Some "super" programmers really are quicker than others. Some teams produce finished products with few, if any, defects. Some organizations are known for their reputation in being able to deliver, on time, on budget. In attempting to identify how methodologies help an organization to be more productive, we can't look only at individual productivity (e.g., rates of code production), we must also examine other less obvious factors.

In the preface to his book, Watts Humphrey (1990) debunks several myths including the "myth of the super programmer." He states quite simply that even if an organization had the best people in the world, it would still need an "orderly process framework," and that one goal (my wording) of a good software development organization should be to "support them (the people) with an effectively managed software process." This is the essence of my hypothesis: we should see a large productivity impact if an appropriate methodology is implemented to support a well-managed team. The team will do better with it than they would do without it, all other things being equal.

A good working definition for our purpose here needs to encompass all the individual and organizational aspects of productivity, but still be compact. One useful definition has been offered by Charles Symons (1991). He describes three dimensions: (1)

the effectiveness of the work team, (2) their ability to deliver on target, and (3) the quality of what they do. In terms of measurable targets these are:

- Raw productivity = System size÷Work hours
- Delivery rate = System size÷Elapsed weeks
- Defect density = Number of defects÷System size

Trying to quantify "system size" above is hard, but use of Function Points methods can give repeatable results.

The last measure can be subdivided into functional (user viewpoint) and technical defects, which might include failure rate, maintainability, adequacy of documentation, or other measures. The quantifiability of the yardsticks is an important part of understanding and defining productivity. While more complex or detailed frameworks are possible, for our purposes here I believe this three-part definition works well and illustrates the tradeoffs between the different aspects of what is high productivity versus low productivity.

Background

In the 1960s, practitioners in the art of developing systems began to recognize that there was (or should be) a method to the madness. I'm not certain whether the concept came into being spontaneously or grew gradually (the literature is full of opinions of all sorts), but in several different areas, at roughly the same time, individuals, researchers, companies and governmental agencies began to think about developing systems in a more organized manner: the "waterfall chart" in Fig. 3.1 is one such example. In the mid-'60s, one of the predecessor firms to Deloitte & Touche (D&T), Touche Ross Bailey & Smart, was involved in a number of large and complex systems projects.

The senior practitioners working closely with each other on many of these assignments began to understand that having a structure was better than not having one. It provided support to a problem analysis team, and that, in some cases, just having a good checklist to consult really helped. Over a five-year period, they published a series of workbooks based on actual case examples, procedures and forms used in real projects, and "Hints from Heloise." The workbooks were aimed at documenting good practices in commercial systems development. Using today's terminology we would call this a "best demonstrated practices" approach, but at the time, because they were published with different color covers, these books were known internally as the "rainbow series." The series included focused efforts aimed at improving the state of our art as consultants in project management, system design, programming management, and systems management.

Looking at these four areas and thinking back on our earlier, three-part definition of productivity, these books comprised a set of methods, a methodology, and each workbook tackled an overlapping set of the three productivity characteristics. For example, the project management volume focused on the planning and task management aspects of delivering a system, the programming management volume on the delivery targets, and raw code production steps, and so forth.

This initial thinking that resulted in Touche's "rainbow series" methodology was undertaken for several reasons: (1) to codify what was thought to be good practices, (2) to allow experienced personnel to pass on to disparate project teams the benefits of their thinking, (3) to show customers that as consultants, Touche had a highly organized productive approach to helping them, (4) to help in managing the quality of the work, and (5) as materials that could be left behind at the client to help them after the fact as well. In essence, the technique books improved team productivity not only at the back end in delivering a system, but also at the beginning in helping to structure the customer's initial request.

About the same time, research was being done in many different places that began to lay the foundation of structured systems analysis and of improved development management processes. The early '70s saw these ideas expand and take root and methodology products were introduced by other "Big Eight" consulting firms, hardware vendors, and numerous systems consultants. By the time I joined Touche Ross in 1973, the workbooks had been redone at least once and had been shortened into two smaller volumes devoted to the management of systems development activity (Ditri, Shaw, and Atkins 1971) and the management of the MIS function itself (Shaw and Atkins 1972). Most of our clients had copies, as did every member of any project team with whom I was involved. While the books were more concise, they were less helpful to project teams and especially junior personnel because they weren't as instructional and weren't able to specify much in detail to the reader. Copies of the original "rainbow" versions, with their forms, worksheets, hints, and checklists, were guarded as prize possessions.

As an aside, I've often wondered that there might be a direct correlation between increasing complex methods approaches and a decreasing marginal utility or significant falloff in their effectiveness. I was never able to determine if it was just me or if there is some general "law of gravity" that organizations attempt to repeal when they put in place a large and imposing, rigid and complex rules structure. It seems appealing and intuitively correct to conclude that there must be, but I fear I'm not a good judge.

During the years 1965 through 1975, the major management concerns and the batch systems approach we took to meeting them were relatively unchanged. But in the mid-'70s as telecommunications, database file structures, and on-line systems became predominant issues, we launched another update effort and published a larger volume devoted solely to explaining our revised approach to systems development and the steps needed to successfully complete a major system with these new technologies. This revision also took a step backward and included full size versions of all the checklists and forms. The upgrading and revision effort continues today with Deloitte & Touche's current 4FRONT™ product (Deloitte & Touche 1991), which is not only a structured methods approach, but is also a robust and highly integrated set of books, computer-based tools, and training aides (Fig. 3-2).

Looking back it seems that about every five years D&T's consultants concentrated considerable effort in refining their thinking, and incorporated new elements of technical planning and execution. We did so, in general, because the systems landscape changed, or some part of the set of problems we faced with our clients

Project Management						
Strategic Planning	Tactical Planning	Appication- Software Package				
		Application- Custom Development				
		SDLC Management				
		Data				
		Technology				
Strategic Planning	Tactical Planning	Requirements Analysis	General Design	Detail Design And Specification	Construction And Testing	Conversion And Implementation

© Deloitte & Touche 1991

Fig. 3.2 Architecture and threads.

was not well addressed, or whole technical issue areas were left unresolved in the older approach. As a result, as each version took shape, it was larger, more complete and more structured than its predecessor. It also got better at focusing on what was really important—helping teams figure out what to do by seeing what has worked well in the past. We concluded that our methodology was, if nothing else, malleable because the more we continued to hammer on it, the better it conformed to our needs.

The other evident conclusion from this cycle of thinking and rethinking is that we continue to struggle to figure out what works. Growth and development of the methodology have encompassed changes in the following:

- The ideas themselves and process logic.

- The "coaching" provided and the form in which these good ideas are presented.

- The management process in which the methods are embedded.

- The commitment we make to conforming ourselves to our own standards, and in researching new approaches.

This same idea of a changing tool set must extend into the process-management thinking of organizations who use a methodology. What worked three to five years ago might or might not work today, depending on circumstance. I believe it is important to begin each new development effort by challenging our thinking, process choices, and standards. It is not safe to ignore the base issues and assume that this decision/evaluation/selection process isn't something that you have to worry about anymore—after all, you use a methodology don't you? It should take care of the risks. Well, unfortunately, it might not.

In thinking how to convey what I'm worried about here, the analogy to a craftsman planning to build a new piece of furniture is apt. The planning includes not only the drawings and selection of materials and finishes, but also the method of construction and the tools to be used to shape the components. Factored into this will be the budget the customer has in mind, the timetable, and the expertise of the craftsman. Has he done it before? If so, is the material familiar? Do his tools meet the demands of the tasks? Are *you* asking these kinds of questions when your teams begin a new development project? If not, how will your productivity be affected?

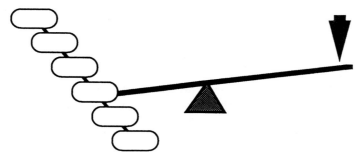

Fig. 3.3 Leverage on the life cycle.

Leverage on the Life Cycle

O.K. So we know that we agree on what productivity is and that a successful methodology must be dynamic and able to conform to new requirements, and that ultimately it must be usable by the practitioners if it is to have any effect.

Given that we agree on the above, this, then where is the methodology of greatest use or greatest value? In the most general sense, a methodology provides leverage in problem solving or problem avoidance as the systems problems we tackle grow more complex. The first builders of houses had common sense to help them in building walls to hold up the roof, and they didn't need much more. But it took hundreds of years of experimentation and failure to perfect an arch in a stone-walled cathedral. Rules of thumb and masonry-guild prescribed ratios then helped to ensure in new construction that the walls with these new holes were buttressed and thick enough to carry the roof load.

In building computer systems, we've seen much the same thing happen but in a more compressed time period. Science and engineering as analytical disciplines have supplanted much of the hand crafting aspects or art in developing software, especially as systems scale has increased. With this has come, in many organizations, the use of a methodology providing sequences of steps and checkpoints. But why do organizations need this type of device? Where is it of greatest use? From my experience, there are many signposts indicating need, including those where:

- Design scope spans the entire organization.
- Design scale or problem complexity is larger than a single person or small team can grasp.
- Large teams of users and technical people are involved.
- There is need to manage the activities over a time span of many months or years.
- You are building a baseline system as a foundation for future efforts.
- Risk of failure (no matter how you define it) is large.

A methodology is, at its root, a language and communications tool. It provides a common framework for discussion about the problems to be solved. It structures the development process and gives the project team a road map to follow. It provides "pre-flight" checklists to assure that all the needed elements are addressed. As part of our quality management program at DRT Systems, we perform a formal project risk assessment analysis when we prepare a bid on all systems jobs over 2000 hours of work. The risk assessment is geared toward understanding what "uncontrollables" are present and which parts of the methodology we employ will be most useful in managing the risk. We also revisit the risk assessment later on in the project to see if our assumptions have proven correct. We also try to double-team our estimating activities. It can really help to force a constructive argument at the outset of a bid process to see what two systems engineers come up with in their interpretations of "what's important."

Our methodology significantly helps in quickly creating a common vision of what we have to do. We spend very little time arguing about the process steps and focus instead on the work needed to produce the agreed-upon deliverables.

Does the leverage differ from stage to stage?

Most of the comprehensive methodologies in use today provide assistance at all stages of the systems life cycle. But the leverage might be different at each stage just as the tools used might be different. Leverage is inherently greater in the front end. Missing a major requirement or choosing the wrong platform technology are more damaging long term than recovering from an inadequate unit testing sequence for several modules of code.

A comprehensive methodology offers guidance to the developer at each stage and helps the team delineate what is to be done; what is to be included; and many times importantly, what is not to be done or included. Defining the scope or terms of reference is essential. In addition, given the emphasis on quality and engineered systems that is now in the forefront of development literature today, we need to define or specify what level of quality is needed and what exactly this means in terms of real and measurable targets. The user must also agree. As our earlier definition of productivity implies, simply saying that you want the system to be of high quality is not enough.

Without getting too elaborate, let's examine a simplified life cycle chain and identify the major leverage points.

Planning phase.   Here we find leverage in terms of estimation and planning tools, from a formal approach to defining enterprise-wide systems opportunities to the planning steps needed to undertake them. The methodology should guide the organization as it confronts the business issues in a logical manner and should help to identify the compromises and trade-offs explicitly.

By providing written guidance and examples, the methodology works to communicate to the users what they can expect to do as part of the project and what they can expect to see produced at different points. The methodology, in essence, removes uncertainty and reduces risk by surfacing questions as early as possible.

Joint applications-development techniques and good, experienced facilitators quickly get the whole team into the meat of the system issues and past the day-to-day, peripheral and background noise in the organization. Making progress quickly and obtaining high-quality results and well-thought-out compromises not only makes management happy, but also gives the team very solid, positive feedback that they are making change happen.

Design phase. In design, the tools and techniques get rolled out in force and the repository of good past ideas gets tapped. Creating new task lists from prior work-breakdown structures, and providing solid standards and end-product descriptions as examples, the team leaders are able to focus more time on offering coaching and advice and guidance to the staff. They avoid having to explain for the 50th time why it is important that all the data flow diagrams conform to the same diagram convention.

Working in an integrated development workbench environment using PC-based tools, the design team can benefit from the use of shared, jointly developed, work products much faster than in prior efforts. The whole design is more visible, and the efforts of the individual people more in synch. Even little things can be of great benefit—I contrast my own productivity now with a Macintosh versus what I used to get done with my trusty, green, IBM-flowcharting template.

Construction phase. Code-generating CASE tools do work, but even without them much of the hand work has been removed from writing code (using screen painters, debug aides, etc.). Today's raw code production rates are very high and syntax errors very low with these new techniques, so it is safe to say that we have seen a productivity benefit that probably affects all three of our definition points. But in addition, benefits accrue from the avoidance of work as well. Solid design planning, problem decomposition, and identification of key elements, such as common use services modules, early in design can really leverage a team. A good methodology will help the designers work toward these objectives as they move into the manufacturing stage.

The methodology should also help manage the assembly process as unit testing proceeds and libraries of working subsystems are integrated. The progress reporting, test management, and code review elements of the chosen methods package really pay off here. For example, research done on well-managed code inspections points to very large payoffs from simple, well done, process steps (75% of the mistakes caught are found in the preparation stage by the authors themselves; 10-fold improvements in the rates of defects produced in handwritten code, and so on) (Humphrey 1990).

Implementation phase. The comprehensive requirements and spec documentation called for in the methodology give the final stage real benchmarks against which to measure success. The methodology will have worked to curtail "requirements drift." Those new problems that have come into focus have been properly dealt with and integrated into the system. Since the team and the users already know and agree on what constitutes "acceptable," the integration testing and training moves quickly ahead.

Overall. Good methodologies also offer guidance in estimation and planning throughout a project. Having a decent project plan at the outset and then managing and measuring progress against that plan are essential for success. Today, the tool sets that come along with a particular methodology can also help by providing automated project management subsystems, estimation, productivity and risk-management data, libraries of detailed work-breakdown structure plans, prior design work repositories and sample end products for key deliverables. These go a long way toward helping the team get moving and fully committed to using the methodology because of the added value these components bring.

A good, or well-conceived methodology must also be flexible. For example, one internal developmental process model may not be the most appropriate for all occasions (e.g., sometimes prototyping is not the way to go). Factors such as the risk involved, the scale of the system, and the customer environment might all influence the decision of one process model or another. An essential element of a high-productivity methodology is that it be able to accommodate differing systems architectures and process-model approaches and still be useful.

Another flexibility issue comes from the omission of a step in the process or from a re-sequencing of steps. No methodology can be assumed to work right out-of-the-box in all situations. However, some have no built-in checks and balances that allow the developers to decide not to do something. By this I mean that the methods should provide the team with a way to determine that a specific step isn't appropriate or is unneeded. The methods should allow the team to be able to leave it out and work around the change in approach with no impact on the overall quality or risk. Forcing a team through a series of one or more useless steps which contribute little to the end result isn't just bad for morale—it wastes time and reduces the focus on the real issues.

Considerations

It would be overly simplistic to assume that there are no downsides to implementing or using a methodology. From my experience, and from an informal survey I recently ran with approximately 50 customers and experienced consultants with whom I have worked, all of whom have used one or more methodologies at some point in commercial systems development, there seem to be several common benefits and problems.

At least five, common denominator methodology "misuses" are identifiable:

1. Religious fanaticism—this is the situation where an organization holds to the theory that there can be nothing else but the methodology. A "methodology-centric" view of the world if you'll permit the use. Such rigidity is seldom useful or productive. It may also be a symptom of other poor management practices.

2. Bureaucracy—here the methodology gets wrapped up in a less-than-effective organization, which adds yet another layer of protection and excuse as to why no products are produced. Using a methodology in an organization which might already have top-down communications problems and seven or more management layers between the programmers and the management will not help. It will just cause people to push more paper.

3. The end in itself—very similar to bureaucracy is the failure resulting from the total focus on the process of developing systems and not on the end results. Personnel are indoctrinated into the process and become wedded to the idea that

step 16 must come after step 15 and before step 17, and that every last step must be completed and documented, even when it is obvious that performing the activities in a step will add no value to the result or that what they are doing has no real business benefit.

4. Using the wrong one—this is rare but is sometimes seen. The few cases I have seen personally seem to arise because a methodology in place has failed to keep up with the times. For example, having no methods that focus on JAD or on structured testing or, trivially, a customer's methodology which still requires the use of a paper screen layout form when screen painters and prototyping provide far faster and more effective user interaction. A methodology incorporating no guidance in data modeling would be of little help in implementing a system using a modern relational database system.

5. Lack of organizational penetration—the most common problem is still lack of consistent use, starting with lack of commitment by management. Project leaders who get trained and start off by trying to conform will tend to fall by the wayside if not encouraged and coached to do better. Martyn Ould (1990) identified "fourteen dilemmas of software engineering" that he concluded impeded the introduction of new techniques into organizations. Among the more notable examples of these "Catch 22's" are:

—We can't use a new method on a project until we shave seen it work on other projects.
—We could justify the use of a new method if we could quantify the costs of using it. But we use traditional methods even though we are unable to quantify the costs of using them, resulting in a continuation of the status quo and generally unreliable estimates.
—Tools that are generally applicable are generally weak. Strong tools are very specific and therefore generally inapplicable.
—An important feature of new methods is that they tend to be powerful in particular areas. This makes them generally inapplicable. The traditional methods are weak in all areas. This makes them generally inapplicable as well.

Many of these ring true in my own experience. I have heard people say things quite similar—as I'm sure you have. With impediments such as these, how much success can one hope for?

Positive Aspects

On the brighter side, we have in our work been able to see a growing number of specific examples where much more positive results have occurred. As one example, the impact on team productivity of introducing joint application development (JAD) ideas over the past ten years into our own methodology has been incredible. Providing the users with an environment in which they can effectively interact with a technical team who are charged with solving problems and not just creating elegant code, makes both groups happier in the end. The methodology provides a formal structure to the environment and the discussion. It eliminates the argument about "why we have to have the discussions" and reduces the politics in the meeting, and it allows team members to spend their energy on the real issues, what the market or the customer really want.

Recently published research about new twists on these concepts, such as advanced JAD and storyboarding development methods (Kirkpatrick 1992) and PC-based groupware products (Zahniser 1990) point to further gains in the future. Evidence from DRT Systems' recent work is less auspicious but nonetheless encouraging. LAN technology has allowed us to extend our tool set to include rudimentary "bulletin board" software accessed from the developer's workbench. This allows us to create developer conference sessions during which an argument can be thrashed out much more efficiently than in a group session around a chalkboard:

- The comments are more focused.
- Personal diatribes are reduced.
- The discussion is sequential and orderly even though everyone is typing at once.
- Everyone can listen to everyone else (no mumbling, no loud talkers).
- You can go back easily to a prior comment.
- Documentation is created at no cost for historical tracking.

Work on formal methods and small team quality management techniques using statistical methods also shows promise. Producing defect-free software efficiently using "clean room" techniques and structured specification methods is possible (Trammel, Binder, and Snyder 1992) and is becoming more commercially feasible. All these are important parts of implementing a modern methodology in an organization.

Communications

We have already discussed the importance of solid team communications and the role that a methodology can play to improve the process. Fred Brooks (1976) describes how poor estimating and the tendency to throw more bodies at the problem of slipping schedules could cause more problems than it solves. He concludes that communications interactions among team members grow with team size and contributes to a fall off in productivity (with resultant schedule slippage). A team leader simply cannot forecast or move end dates forward by dividing the man-months of work by ever larger numbers of people. One of the graphs Brooks uses illustrates a growth in the required time to complete as team size increases past a certain inflection point. The "marginal return" of adding another person actually becomes negative—things get worse not better.

While specific data from laboratory projects is hard to find, the intellectual argument is appealing. The hypothesis is that as team size grows, the amount of time spent on communications increases. In many cases the communications requirement (the need to talk to each other) grows much faster than team size. Consider one project being done by a three person team, A, B, and C for an external user, U. Assuming both pair and group discussions, the possible communication paths between all the parties are comprised by the 11 element set {AB, AC, BC, ABC, AU, BU,

CU, ABU, ACU, BCU, and ABCU}. If the team size expands to five members and two external users, 75% growth (four to seven) the possible communications set size grows from 11 to 56 (400% growth).

Large teams attack this problem using a methodology to provide structure and by decomposition, breaking the team and users into subteams and assigning parts of the project to each team. The communications flow is considerably reduced, but the risk due to isolation grows. Some aspect of one team's work may impact work being done by another. Without methodology and a structured framework to channel the analysis and discussion, the risk could be unmanageable. Applying a methodology that is used consistently in the groups helps bridge the communication gaps and also ensures that the work being done will be standardized and meet common objectives.

As a management tool

One of the obvious areas where a correctly implemented methodology will improve an organization's productivity is in the area of managing work done by external vendors. Having several different vendors work in a major MIS organization and having each of them produce good, but non-standard, work is a problem. Imagine having several different carpenters work on your house over a period of time installing doors, and having all the doors end up with no standard dimensions.

Judging from the evidence in terms of recent work that customers are asking us to do, many companies are becoming much more sophisticated in terms of what they are asking us, as systems integrators, to do for them than in past years. The requests (and the contracts behind the requests) have advanced from "build us a system" to "deliver this as a turnkey application, fully integrated." In addition, customers in many cases, are asking us to conform to their choices of development methodology, CASE tools, and design standards such as GUI interfaces. What we have found is that this type of request works well for both of us. Structure is good.

Just as our early evidence indicated that a well-trained analyst with a CASE tool can shift tools without great pain, a designer used to working in a controlled project environment using methodology x can shift as well. The retraining work at the outset can be focused on key differences and the near term tasks and not on the more general issues involved in convincing new developer staff that it is a good idea to use a methodology, or why they need to learn to structure their thinking. In addition, as the external vendor, it is much easier for us to assess the request for a new system if it is framed in terms defined by the methodology. With this information, we know the standard the customer expects, we know the deliverables they want to see, we know how they will be measuring progress, how they define their terms, how they want us to manage the project, and so forth. This kind of critical data goes a long way toward clarifying the request and getting the project off to a solid start by letting us begin with a better estimate and project plan and a well discussed agreement on how to proceed.

As organizations continue to downsize, we expect this trend to intensify. There will be greater reliance on external development resources, either custom or package, and it can be much easier to ask your external vendors to conform to a standard and measure their compliance than it may be to do it in-house with or without these standards. At a minimum, the external vendor doesn't have all the baggage to carry along of projects going on or past work that wasn't done to the new standard. Also, the vendor doesn't usually put up much in the way of a political argument. If you want all your doors to be 84 inches tall and 36 inches wide, then as your construction team we will see that you get them that way.

As a part of a quality management program

The focus on quality in services provided or products produced has become a topic of much interest in the past several years in numerous industries, not just systems. MIS organizations who in the past have struggled with gaining consensus on the guidelines for productivity are now faced with challenges in not only managing to produce a lot of code quickly, but to produce code that works. In our own computer systems development organization, we have spent a lot of time working on the quality management process.

In most things we do, DRT Systems' reputation, as well as the profits being generated by a project, depend heavily on the quality of the output. One of the things my high school shop teacher and many others have concluded is that "doing it right the first time" can be much cheaper in the long run. If we can produce systems or even sections of code that are on target in terms of meeting the customer's spec and which function properly, we are much more productive than otherwise—plus, our warranty expense is considerably reduced.

Quality management is another one of the areas where having a formal set of methods to manage the process and provide guidance and standards can be not only helpful but mandatory. A robust methodology will help to define the acceptable level of quality and communicate it to the team members. They will have gone through training together and learned what to expect from the steps in the process and from each other as they fill different roles on the team. The benefits obviously are leveraged toward large projects where risk is significant and where a formal quality process management approach might be layered on top of the normal project control structure, but it should not be ignored in small team efforts.

Future Directions

Today, researchers at the edge of development problems are creating and implementing concepts, tool sets, and computer architectures simply not thought possible five years ago. Ideas such as shared network parallel processing using languages like LINDA and the horsepower from the "under-utilized" MIPS of dozens of workstation computers on a network are radically changing the things that one can consider doing with computers in commercial settings. This unexpected payback from a decision to use a workstation approach is not fully understood, but the opportunity to use the equivalent of a distributed supercomputer is worth serious consideration.

Even more simply, the impact of a 20+ MIPS workstation, a fast network, and a fast disk array file server in a client server architecture is usable today and impacts both the types of systems which can be delivered and the developmental approach and the interaction with the users. In some cases, the tools will allow users to build whole sections of the application themselves without worrying about the technical issues (e.g., underlying database schemes, or managing relational integrity, or providing transaction rollback in case of failure).

In addition, we continue to have to cope with the billions of lines of code running on large mainframe or minicomputer systems that need maintenance support, process or design re-engineering, or replacement. Finding improvement techniques through better methodologies, technical tools, or training is worth millions of dollars to many organizations, both large and small.

Examples such as these illustrate the need for methodologies that are not stagnant. We already understand that the process-model techniques used to build a system may need to be different depending on the system architecture. In some larger sense, the methodologies of the future might have components similar to mathematical equations, developed over time through research, and each appropriate to a given class of problems to be solved. Serious and proficient developers might be masters of many techniques, tools, approaches, etc., and may need graduated training and retraining in more and more complex methodology constructs and concepts as they move ahead in their careers.

Summary and Conclusions

Implementing a methodology will, by itself, make no one more productive immediately. In fact, I think the implementation process will result in a net fall-off as development work done by certain key people is halted or slowed as they do the implementation work. Positive impacts over the next two to three years will come from the parts of the new methods that:

- Add structure, set standards
- Help build a base of repeatable methods, designs, and common knowledge
- Aid in communication
- Provide examples and guidance; establish a "coaching" or "mentor" environment
- Help quantify and measure results
- Support improved estimation
- Support improved task management
- Provide new tools
- Challenge team thinking and innovation

Our earlier definition of productivity incorporated physical measures to reflect how much improvement we get in unit production rates, timeliness, and quality through analysis of:

- Raw productivity
- Delivery
- Defect density

A methodology's tools, a formal structure, visualization aides, communications frameworks, standards, and other elements, make it almost impossible to conclude that you can have sustainable high productivity development without a well-implemented methodology. It is equally impossible to conclude that using a methodology properly will not result in at least some improved productivity.

In addition, as the organization moves forward and builds on its experience base, not only will it develop a better estimation database and see higher design reuse, but its reputation for success will advance. In large measure, credibility is what good management is all about. Your customers have to believe you when you give a target (or ask for a compromise to compensate for an error); the professional staff has to follow your lead and operate as a team without an overly large amount of short interval scheduling or unconstructive argument. The group needs to function as a well-coached team and be able to remember the playbook and occasionally run a no-huddle offense. As projects get large and technologies we use become more diverse, a methodology is even more essential in aiding an organization or a project manager in delivering on his or her objectives.

Author Biography

Ken Horner is a partner in the Management Consulting practice of Deloitte & Touche and is also Executive Vice President of a joint Japanese/American systems integration company, DRT Systems, owned by Deloitte & Touche and Tohmatsu & Co. Mr. Horner has been involved with systems development for over 25 years and has been with Deloitte & Touche since 1973. DRT Systems was formed 3 years ago with a mission to become a successful independent operation based on delivering high-quality systems to a growing global client base. Operations are now in place in both the far east and Europe as well as in five locations in the United States, and the company is continuing to grow rapidly to meet market demands.

Mr. Horner graduated from the Massachusetts Institute of Technology with bachelors and masters degrees in both engineering and management, and has worked in the aerospace and computer engineering fields as well as in consulting. This background has influenced his focus on complex systems integration as an engineering discipline and his interest in team building, methodologies, productivity and quality and technology management.

Works Cited

Brooks, F.P. 1975. *The mythical man-month*. Addison-Wesley.

Deloitte & Touche. 1991. *4FRONT™ methodology*. Release 2.0. Wilton, Ct.: Deloitte & Touche.

Ditri, A.E., J.C. Shaw, and W. Atkins. 1971. *Managing the EDP functions*. McGraw-Hill.

Humphrey, W.S. 1990. *Managing the software process*. Addison-Wesley.

Kirkpatrick, F. 1992. Here comes the payoff from PCs. *Fortune.* March 23, 1992: 93–102.

Ould, M.A. 1990. *Strategies for software engineering.* John Wiley.

Royce, W.W. 1970. Managing the development of large software systems. *Proceedings of the IEEE WESCON.* August 1970.

Shaw, J.C. and W. Atkins. 1972. *Managing computer systems projects.* McGraw-Hill.

Sommerville, I. 1989. *Software engineering.* 3rd ed. Addison-Wesley.

Symons, C.R. 1991. *Software sizing and estimating.* John Wiley.

Trammel, C., L. Binder, and C. Snyder. 1992. The automated production control documentation system: A case study in cleanroom software engineering. *ACM transactions on software engineering and methodology.* 1 (1): 81–94.

Zahniser, R.A. 1990. Building software in groups. *American Programmer.* 3 (7–8).

Information Engineering
Strategic Systems Development

by Clive Finkelstein

Introduction to Information Engineering

Information Engineering is an integrated set of tasks that guides an organization from strategic planning to the implementation of information systems. This chapter, based on Finkelstein (1992), discusses the emphasis that Information Engineering will take as we move into the 21st century. *Strategic Systems Development* integrates corporate strategic planning with systems development and database design, so that the resulting strategic information systems provide direct support to management for making decisions. Such integration draws on business and strategic planning expertise of managers and their staffs, and systems development and database-design expertise of data processing (DP) staff. Strategic systems development requires knowledge of Information Engineering as well as an understanding of strategic planning principles and practice.

Competitive pressures, business opportunities, and technological change constantly press in on both senior management and information technology staff. The computer industry provides some of the most fertile ground in the world for innovation and development. But unless this technology can be harnessed for competitive advantage, organizations can only react to change, rather than control their own destinies. This chapter discusses how Information Engineering may be used to integrate information technology with strategic planning. It provides a road map for navigation through what has often been a fog of too much information and jargon in the computer industry. The initial concepts of Information Engineering were first developed in 1972, and were refined over the period 1976–1981 (Martin and Finkelstein 1981). Since then, Information Engineering has been used to design and build information systems that reflect the business needs of organizations more effectively than do other systems-development techniques such as Software Engineering. My earlier book (Finkelstein 1989) provides an introduction to the evolution of Information Engineering and addresses its theory. My later book (Finkelstein 1992) is a how-to discussion of the application of Information Engineering.

Since 1981, Information Engineering has evolved into two main variants. The first uses the existing functions of an organization as the starting point; data needed by the functions are then defined. This approach is more DP-driven than the second variant. In this DP variant, business knowledge is incorporated from users often by interview; but significantly there is subjective interpretation of the users' input by DP personnel. This is sometimes referred to as "application Information Engineering," or DP-driven Information Engineering. It is supported by many of the Information Engineering software products on the market today.

The second variant is the subject of this chapter. It starts with the strategic plans set by management at all levels of an organization. From these plans are defined the data, and later the functions, needed to support those plans. This approach is more user-driven than the DP variant and is referred to as "enterprise Information Engineering," or "business-driven Information Engineering." It is defined (Finkelstein 1992) as follows: Information Engineering is an integrated set of techniques, based on corporate strategic planning, which results in the analysis, design, and development of systems that support those plans exactly. Information Engineering is applied by managers and users with no knowledge of computers, but instead with an expert knowledge of their business—in conjunction with expert systems that provide rapid feedback to management for refinement of the strategic plans.

With the business-driven variant, business managers and users are trained in the techniques of Information Engineering and apply these techniques directly rather than by interview; their defined knowledge is objectively interpreted by software to identify the functions and systems needed to achieve the strategic plans. This business-driven variant is supported by a number of Information Engineering expert systems software products available today. It starts with strategic planning.

Strategic Planning

There has been much research into and application of strategic planning in the last 30 years. Strategic planning has focused on three main disciplines (Fayey and Christensen 1986), (Huff and Reger 1987), and (Schendel and Hofer 1979):

- Strategy formulation, also called strategy content
- Strategy implementation, also called strategy process
- Strategic management, or the management of strategy

More and more, it is becoming evident that complexity of organizations precludes separation into these three categories. They are all interrelated: each provides feedback to, and receives feedback from, the other disciplines. They represent a life cycle for strategic planning (see Fig. 4.1). Recognizing this interdependence and complexity, Information Engineering uses a methodology called *strategic management planning*. This methodology permits the strategic management of planning and implementation with rapid feedback for the refinement of those plans. Strategic management planning uses an approach to focus on the development of organization structures and information systems (manual or automated) that directly support the strategic plans, both at the business unit level and at the corporate level. We will first discuss traditional strategic planning in more detail based on the above three disciplines. We will then consider some of the problems encountered before addressing strategic management planning.

Traditional strategic planning

Strategic planning, as we know it today, is generally accepted to have had its genesis in the 1960s with the works by Chandler (1962), Ansoff (1965), and Andrews (1971). These books resulted in an explosion of research into strategic planning. As new approaches were developed and applied to organizations, significant results were achieved. In this chapter we collectively refer to these approaches as the traditional strategic planning methods.

There were successes, as well as failures, as the body of experience grew. The failures were often due, in many respects, to problems associated with different requirements at separate stages in the strategic planning life cycle. These problems are illustrated in Fig. 4.1. They are summarized below.

Strategic Planning Life Cycle

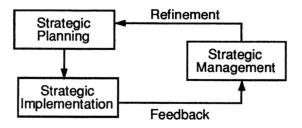

Problems with Traditional Strategic Planning

Strategic Planning	Limited strategic alternatives
Strategic Implementation	Ineffective communication
	Misinterpretation
Strategic Management	Long feedback cycle (3 – 5 years)
	Ineffective performance monitoring

Fig. 4.1 The problems with traditional strategic planning.

The evaluation of a strategic plan is difficult, often possible only by the pilot introduction of a new plan using part of the organization as a guinea pig. After assessing the results of the pilot plan, adjustments are made to the plan before it is introduced corporate-wide.

A greater problem is the time horizon before useful feedback is available for refinement of the plan. With pilot introduction, 6- to 12-months' operation under a new strategic plan might be required before an evaluation can be made. An assessment after the plan has been introduced corporate-wide might need 1- to 2-years' further operation before effective overall evaluation is possible.

The necessary changes to the plan then take more time: the result is a three- to five-year time horizon between strategic plans. But we live in a changing world. Tomorrow's competitive environment will not allow us the luxury of this start/stop approach to planning. Evolutionary, incremental adjustment to a plan over a short time period, through progressive refinement, is needed.

Integrating information systems with an organization's strategic plan; providing information needed by management for decision support, is another problem. Traditional systems development methods normally focus too low, mainly at the operational level, for decision support systems to be developed that are useful to management. Management and DP staff must work closely together to define decision-support needs: but they have difficulty communicating because of the jargon and different backgrounds of each group.

Discussing the consequences of all of these problems, Gray (1986) indicates that:

> Strategic planning as many text books describe it may not be around for much longer, but not for the reasons most critics give. If formal strategic planning vanishes in a few years, it will be because wherever it is undertaken it either gets better or it gets worse, depending on how well it's done: if you do it poorly, either you drop out or you rattle around in its mechanics; if you do it well, you evolve beyond strategic planning into strategic management.

Nolan (1987), in discussing the transformation of organizations to compete in the 21st century, comments:

> As the heartbeat of business quickens, we can no longer enter upon orderly phases of strategic planning every five years or so, followed by periods of implementation. Strategy must be monitored continuously, and implementation altered as strategies are adjusted. . . . Transformation entails changing everything about the business, while incorporating information technology at the same time.

Strategic management planning

Strategic management planning allows continual evaluation and refinement of the strategic plan at all stages of its development. It leads to precise implementation of the plan, with the development of information systems that support the plan exactly through the use of strategic systems development. The result is more effective decision support to management than is achieved by traditional strategic planning and systems-development methods. The methodology is based on much of the work by Drucker (1974) and Porter (1980; 1985). Figure 4.2 illustrates strategic management planning. Feedback is rapid, effective and precise, with clear communication and exact implementation. Wrong interpretation by lower-level managers during implementation, which presents problems in traditional strategic planning, can be identified and resolved early.

Managers at all levels are able to interpret the strategic directions from their perspective, using strategic data modeling in conjunction with an independent facilitator to aid strategic thinking. Feedback from more detailed data modeling at tactical and operational levels is available for strategic management review. All levels of the organization thus participate. There is clear identification of the benefits that address specific needs at each level. A corporate culture develops: planning becomes a normal part of each manager's job. There is also rapid feedback to senior management of new innovative opportunities. The result is integration at all levels of the organization: with its data, information and systems (both manual and automated) and new organization structures able to be integrated to achieve the strategic directions.

Because of its utility and the advantage of rapid feedback, strategic management planning is also used for continuing assessment and refinement of the plan in response to perceived competitive threats or opportunities. It allows an organization to respond rapidly to highly competitive situations if necessary. Where rapid response is not required, this method also allows management to introduce controlled, evolutionary changes that have already been evaluated and highly refined before introduction to the organization. Instead of using pilot introduction for evaluation of the defined strategic plan, strategic management planning uses the technique of goal analysis to provide rapid feedback that helps management to identify gaps or missed opportunities in the plan. This is achieved in days, rather than months as required by

Strategic Management Planning

Advantages of Strategic Management Planning

Strategic Planning	Strategic analysis of alternatives
Strategic Implementation	Effective communication through modeling with clear interpretation
Strategic Management	Rapid feedback cycle (weeks) Identifies performance criteria

Fig. 4.2 Advantages of strategic management planning.

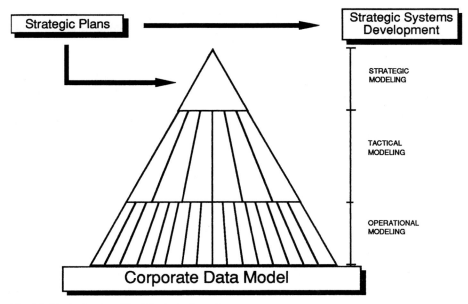

Fig. 4.3 Strategic plans identify strategic systems.

traditional strategic planning. Goal analysis can be applied not only at the highest corporate level, but also at lower management levels to ensure the correct implementation of the plan.

Strategic management planning is also integrated with systems development to develop strategic information systems that directly support the strategic plan. This is one of the responsibilities of the Chief Information Officer (CIO) (Canning Publications 1984). Direct strategic plan input is used to develop strategic, tactical, and operational models (see Fig. 4.3), designed by managers and staff charged with the responsibility for implementing the plan. Because these models are developed by business experts based on directions defined in the plan, they result in information systems that exhibit higher quality than systems traditionally developed by DP professionals.

Strategic Systems Development

Figure 4.3 shows the progressive development of these models using strategic, tactical, and operational modeling, with the strategic systems development method of Information Engineering. Strategic modeling from the strategic plans of a project area identifies a number of tactical areas. If the project area is the corporation, the strategic model is the foundation of a corporate data model—a major focus of the CIO. Tactical modeling of priority tactical areas identifies operational systems. Priority operational systems are then taken to full data detail through operational modeling. These all expand the corporate data model to tactical and operational detail in those areas. Process modeling derives procedures from data models, to implement manual or automated procedures as operational systems. But priority systems can be implemented long before the corporate data model is completed, as illustrated in Fig. 4.4.

This approach allows priority areas to be selected, and taken to full operational detail in individual implementation projects for business units as shown in Fig. 4.4. A high degree of concurrent development is the result. The corporate data model progressively expands based on this modeling feedback as discussed earlier; the concurrent business unit projects also apply the same methods to define and implement the operational databases and systems that they require. The result is the early delivery of priority systems and progressive evolution of the corporate data model as more projects move through to operational detail. Both of these are important objectives of the CIO. Systems development previously has worked on individual application systems. The later integration of these separate systems has been difficult. Bridges between systems have had to be built to enable them to work together; or instead, significant changes have had to be made in existing systems. This has often been compared to fitting together a complex jigsaw puzzle without an understanding of the overall picture.

The strategic model provides that overall picture—either corporate-wide or for specific business unit projects. The tactical models are sections of the jigsaw picture that should be put together first. Operational models are completed sections. The process models show how the pieces in these sections fit internally, and also how those sections are externally interfaced, or integrated, with other tactical and operational models and their process models. This is achieved by strategic systems development. Corporate and business unit strategic plans provide input to the analysis, design and generation methods used by Information Engineering, shown in Fig. 4.5.

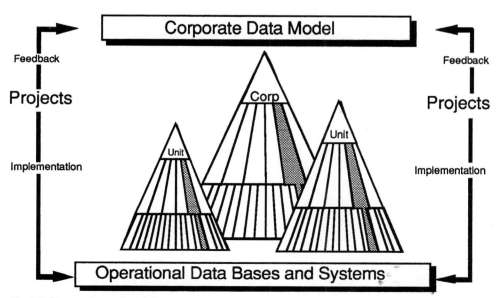

Fig. 4.4 Progressive project delivery.

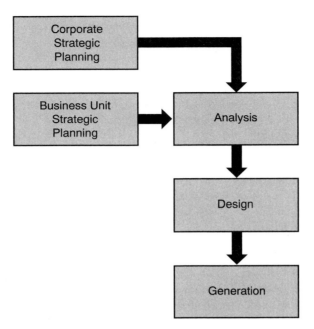

Fig. 4.5 Strategic plans provide input to development.

Strategic systems development is based on Information Engineering, which we will discuss shortly. Systems that have been developed with this approach can use the best hardware or software technologies available. They can be implemented using either traditional or relational Database Management Systems (DBMS or RDBMS). They use third, fourth or fifth generation languages, either conventional or object-oriented. The resulting systems can be implemented on mainframes, minis or micros—either centralized or distributed. These information systems can accommodate business and technological changes more readily than systems developed using traditional systems development methods based on Business Systems Planning (BSP) (IBM 1981) or Software Engineering (Yourdon and Constantine 1978; De Marco 1982). As summarized by Smith (1990): "The original BSP technique resulted in models (or architectures) too fuzzy or high-level to be implemented. Systems builders simply did not know how to transform the BSP study into actual data structures and working code."

Data-driven and Process-driven Methods

Information Engineering focuses on the information needs of an organization, rather than on its current procedures. It helps to identify the data that are fundamental to the operation of the organization, from which information needed by managers is derived. Data indicate which details the operational levels of an organization need, or what details are needed to measure achievement of specific goals or objectives set by management.

There may be many ways in which the data may be used or may be processed. These indicate how the data are used and are called "procedures." Similarly there may be many ways which indicate how defined goals or objectives may be reached; these are called "strategies." Strategies might comprise one or many procedures.

Many DP methods have been developed for the analysis and design of systems based on procedures. These include systems analysis and Business Systems Planning. They also include structured analysis and structured design. Because of their emphasis on procedures, these are all called "process-driven methods."

In contrast, Information Engineering focuses first on data rather than procedures, and is therefore called a "data-driven method." Other data-driven methods are based on the Warnier-Orr methodology (Orr 1977) and Jackson (1975) systems development methodologies. Each of these methods can be utilized by analysts for the analysis and design of both small and large systems. Information Engineering is, however, unique—as it can also be applied by users with no computer experience. They use it to analyze and design corporate-wide systems based on strategic plans set either for specific divisions or business units, or for the entire organization. They use it also to design the most effective organization structures based on those strategic plans.

It is now widely accepted that the data of an organization change slower than its procedures. Consequently, system designs based on data-driven methods have been found to be much more stable than systems designed using process-driven methods.

Information Engineering Overview

In this section we discuss the Information Engineering methodology in more detail. We then conclude the chapter with a discussion of current issues in systems development and strategic planning, describing their relationship with Information Engineering. We use the term *users* to refer collectively to managers and users. Those users with detailed expertise of the business we refer to as business experts. We will refer to systems analysts and business analysts collectively as analysts.

With business-driven data modeling methods, Information Engineering, business experts define high-level information models, as well as detailed data models. The analysts design systems from these data models, rather than by interviewing the users (the traditional way to design systems using process-driven methods). They design and develop systems and databases needed to satisfy the information defined by the data models.

Expert systems software generates the databases automatically for a variety of DBMS products. Analysts can then use systems development facilities and languages provided with these DBMS products to design and develop menus, screens, reports, and programs to process the data stored in the databases.

The quality of systems developed using business-driven Information Engineering has been found to be much higher than those developed using process-driven methods due to the rapid feedback that the users receive. Interestingly, systems are developed also much faster because of the greater business understanding of users. Users know the business. Analysts know computers. Each draws on expertise of their respective disciplines. The result is a design partnership: the users provide the business design; analysts provide the computer design.

The availability of managers and users with an expert knowledge of their business is an essential requirement. When these experts obtain rapid feedback from an evolving design, they are able to refine their strategic and business plans accordingly. This feedback is provided in small projects by analysts experienced in Information Engineering. In large projects, which may cover major parts of an organization, the availability of expert systems software to provide automated support to the Information Engineering methodology is essential.

Systems developed using Information Engineering are represented as blueprints of the data needed by users to carry out their jobs. This offers a visual representation of data, referred to as a data model. Strategic, tactical, and operational models are all examples of data models at different organizational or project levels. These data models can be defined by business experts without requiring any knowledge of computers. They illustrate the detailed business knowledge of those experts. They are an exact specification of business requirements for development of systems.

The Information Engineering Phases

Figure 4.6 summarizes the phases of Information Engineering, emphasizing two distinct stages: a technology-independent stage and a technology-dependent stage. The starting point is strategic business planning based on strategic management

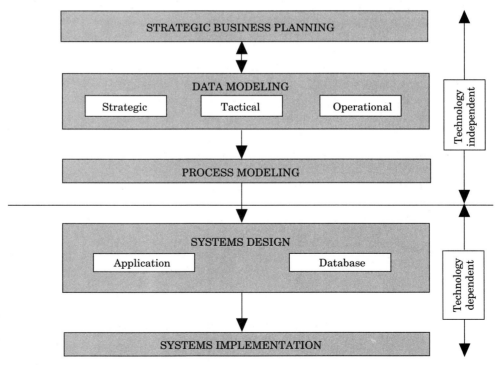

Fig. 4.6 Information Engineering phases.

planning as discussed earlier. Data modeling is then used to develop a corporate strategic model. Priority areas are taken to greater data definition detail through tactical and operational data modeling. Process modeling is used to define application systems. All of these phases address the technology-independent stage of Information Engineering, based on strategic management planning as discussed earlier.

Data modeling is then used to develop a corporate strategic model. Priority areas are taken to greater data definition detail through tactical and operational data modeling. Process modeling is used to define application systems. All of these phases address the technology-independent stage of Information Engineering.

The technology-dependent stage focuses on the systems design of applications and databases, for systems implemented in different hardware and software environments, either centralized or distributed. It is used to design object-oriented application systems and databases with relational or non-relational DBMS, and with either object-oriented languages or conventional third-, fourth-, or fifth-generation languages and development tools.

Figure 4.6 shows that strategic business plans are incorporated in technology-independent data and process models, so allowing a clear separation from technology-dependent application and database designs. Large productivity gains are achieved in strategic planning, systems development and maintenance, and result in high quality plans and systems. This is due to a four-level architecture, which allows us to place the business-driven variant of Information Engineering in context.

Four-level Information Engineering Architecture

Information Engineering addresses four architectural levels, shown in Fig. 4.7. This architecture separates data and process, and enables organizations to build databases and applications that can change rapidly to achieve competitive advantage. Level 1 is the business level, including the corporate vision and business plan. Level 2 is the logical level, which is technology-independent and develops the business model. Level 3 is the physical level, which is technology-dependent and develops system models. Level 4 is the platform level, which is site-dependent and represents implementations.

Level 1—the business level: This reflects the corporate vision as data, based on strategic planning statements defined at all management levels. Business plans then operate on those data, based on the planning statements and on business events which process the data.

Level 2—the logical level: Data models, developed from the planning statements based on the corporate vision, are technology-independent. Process models, developed from data models and also from business events based on the business plan, represent the business model.

Level 3—the physical level: Together, data and process models provide input to technology-dependent database designs. These database designs, and relevant process models, provide input to application design (which also feeds back to database design), so representing system models.

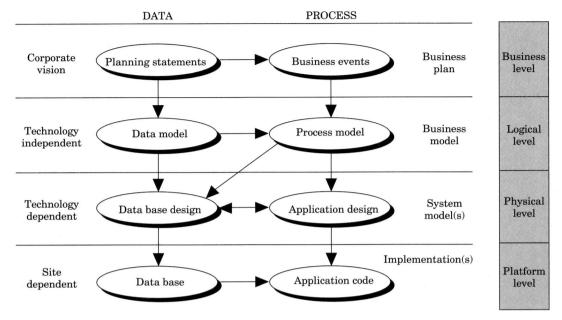

Fig. 4.7 Information Engineering four-level architecture.

Level 4—the platform level: The database design is physically implemented as site-dependent databases. These databases and the application design are implemented as application code that operates against the databases. Databases and applications can then be implemented on specific platforms that utilize the best available hardware, software and communications technologies.

This four-level architecture thus isolates changes at the business and logical levels from changes at the physical and platform levels. Because business rules are modeled as data (through process modeling) the business can change easily and rapidly. And new hardware, software, or communication technologies can also be introduced easily without requiring major redevelopment of systems. The massive systems development projects of the past, based on the traditional systems development methodologies, are replaced by incremental development and rapid delivery of priority systems and databases as an organization fine-tunes its data, information and knowledge resources for its competitive march into the future.

The components of a data model, linked to the management statements that drive that model, integrate redundant data versions in an organization. This data resource and its derived information resource can be managed for business advantage. Organizations now realize that they must gain control over the information needed to make critical business decisions about their financial, material and people resources to achieve any strategic advantage. Even more valuable is their knowledge resource: this is reflected in the business rules that are captured in the data model and implemented in process models. Information Engineering enables this knowledge resource to be used for competitive advantage. We will review how this is achieved in the following sections.

The Strategic Data Model

The strategic data model (see Fig. 4.8) not only defines the scope of systems development projects, it also represents a picture of the business. Strategic statements provide a textual definition of strategic plans. They provide input for development of the strategic data model comprising: the strategic data map; planning outline; planning statements; model views; data dictionary and associated reports. A strategic data model is used to design and build systems and databases based on the strategic plans. It is also used to design organization structures to implement those plans.

The strategic data model is thus the jig-saw picture that allows an organization to identify priority areas to be implemented first. This identification of priorities for implementation ensures that resources are optimally allocated. The strategic data model is the first view at the logical level, reflecting the business level as discussed earlier in Fig. 4.7. The tactical and operational data models, and the process models, that are also built at this logical level then represent the technology-independent business model.

The Business Model

The business model is based on the business plans, business rules, strategic and tactical statements, and business events of the project area (see Fig. 4.9). Through tac-

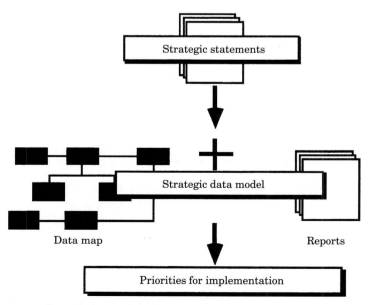

Fig. 4.8 Strategic data model allows optimization.

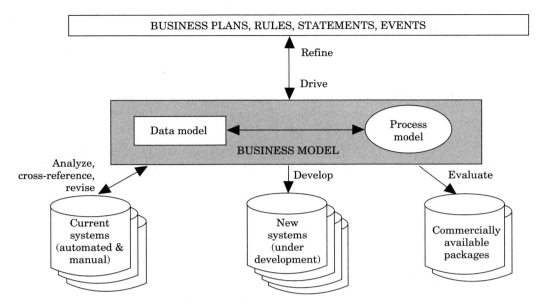

Fig. 4.9 Using the Business Model.

tical and operational modeling, the strategic model expands to greater data detail. Process modeling uses the data models, business rules and business events to derive processes: these data and process models thus represent the business model.

Because the business model exists at the logical level, it can be used to develop new systems or evaluate commercially available packages. An organization can thus analyze and plan migration from, or integration with, its current systems, both auto-mated and manual (see Fig. 4.9). It can also integrate new systems with packages for added functionality. Thus new systems, needed for tomorrow, can be fine-tuned to work also with the current systems and packages needed for today. Development re-sources can be concentrated on priority new systems, integrating them with current systems or packages where required.

Process Modeling

Process modeling derives process models from data models, based on business events. This is illustrated in Fig. 4.10. A business event will result in a business process that may use other processes. The business process may also respond to many other business events. A business process interfaces with many users, who must use many business processes.

Figure 4.10 shows that a business process may use many data access processes, which are generic procedures that can be reused as needed by many systems. A data access process will be used by many other business processes, and might use other data access processes. A data access process accesses data model components, which are data entities, associations, and attributes. These data model components will result in many data access processes; however this figure does not show the major benefits that accrue from process modeling—such as definition of business rules and conditional logic as data rather than program code, allowing an organization to change its systems and databases rapidly for competitive advantage. This and other systems development issues are discussed next.

Systems Development Issues

Information Engineering leads to gains in the productivity and quality of systems development: gains that are often dramatic. To conclude this chapter, we discuss some of the significant issues relating to systems development in the 1990s:

- Data administration and information resource management (IRM)
- Productivity and system quality
- Change management and evolution
- Migrating to alternative architectures
- Rule modeling to allow rapid business change
- Re-engineering and reverse engineering
- Object-oriented development

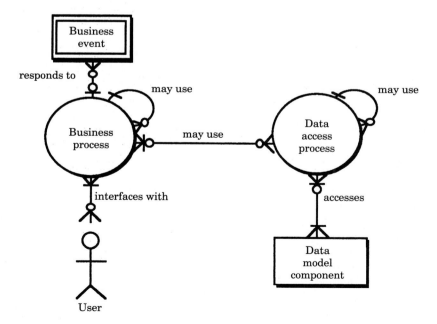

Fig. 4.10 Process modeling concepts.

Data administration and IRM

Information Engineering is a powerful vehicle to establish data administration and IRM functions. Data administration is a function that defines standards, stewardship, and control of the information in an organization. Information resource management has a similar purpose to data administration, but also includes the planning, organizing, and control of both technology-independent and technology-dependent data and process models and designs, defining configurations of hardware and software, and training of the people required to support the information systems of the organization. Establishing an information resource management function invariably leads to implementation of an information encyclopedia to manage the meta-data involved. This encyclopedia is the most important development issue affecting organizations today. Software will be available to manage this encyclopedia. Examples include IBM's Repository Manager and AD/Cycle, and DEC's Cohesion. The definition of the encyclopedia is achieved by Information Engineering.

Productivity and system quality

Much has been written in recent years regarding quality. Increased productivity with poor quality will not achieve the desired result—productivity and quality must both improve together. Because Information Engineering captures business requirements before creating solutions, quality is assured at every step of the process. The rigor in the techniques and phases of the methodology ensure that this initial quality is carried through to implementation. Use of the four-level Information Engineering architecture for change management (see Fig. 4.7) ensures that quality is maintained over time. Although it certainly costs an organization precious resources to establish and maintain the IRM function described earlier, the increase in productivity of systems development using Information Engineering more than compensates for this investment.

Change management and evolution

The four-level architecture used by Information Engineering provides a mechanism to manage change in an organization: both impact analysis and "what-if" planning can be carried out. Establishing and maintaining the architecture as part of the IRM function ensures that change can be managed in a controlled fashion. Traditional methodologies had maintenance as a separate phase. Now, however, we recognize that maintenance is a required response to some change in the business. Changes in technology or systems requirements require modifications to system designs and implemented systems. The addition, deletion or revision of a business rule requires evaluation from a broader perspective of the data and process models. This might lead to modifications in many systems. But we now see that by separating the technology-independent aspects of change management from technology-dependent implementations, maintenance is an evolutionary process that allows an organization to control its own destiny.

Migrating to alternative architectures

Once technology-independent data and process models have been developed for a functional area, they provide the basis for systems design and implementation. In some cases the target environment for implementation of a particular functional area may have already been specified. In many situations, however, the data and process models become the baseline to evaluate alternative technologies. This allows an organization to select the optimum configuration of hardware and software, based on the budget they have available, to meet their needs. It may be that more than one target environment will be required to satisfy the business needs depicted by the data and process models. Rather than merely interfacing these different environments, however, they can be fully integrated, so taking advantage of the key features of each environment.

Rule modeling to allow rapid business change

Business rules are modeled as rules data through process modeling. This enables business experts to capture details precisely as data, rather than in process logic, permitting rapid business change for strategic advantage. By modeling the rules that govern business logic controlling the capture of business facts, two clear advantages are realized. First of all, rule modeling refines the data model, ensuring that business data are precisely modeled. Secondly, a change in the business rules can be immediately accommodated when it occurs, with a fraction of the maintenance impact required by the traditional methods. By implementing the rules as data, business users quickly and easily implement business changes by changing rules data, avoiding the time delay and the expense of program modifications to systems.

Re-engineering and reverse engineering

The top-down approach to building data and process models, as discussed in this chapter, is sometimes referred to as re-engineering. It yields high-quality results in a short period of time, while also ensuring user understanding and buy-in of the end result. However it is not always an achievable starting point. For organizations with current systems that are not well-documented, a bottom-up approach, reverse engineering, might be necessary. Information Engineering uses business normalization and reverse engineering principles to extract database designs from data structures and program code. These become technology-independent data and process models, used to build databases and systems for different technology-dependent platforms. This process of reverse engineering is feasible for those organizations that are not subject to business change because of regulatory or other constraints. But it is not recommended where business plans or rules are changing, as it invariably takes more time than the top-down, re-engineering approach. Both approaches, however, lead to development of integrated databases and systems through object-oriented development.

Object-oriented development

The emergence of object-oriented analysis, design and programming has lead to a review of the traditional information systems development methodologies. The distinct sequencing of data, then process, inherent in business-driven Information Engineering ensures that objects important to the business are identified, defined well, and linked to the strategic management statements that govern their existence. The characteristics of object-oriented systems and databases (including abstraction, inheritance, identity, and encapsulation) are fundamental characteristics of Information Engineering. The object-oriented approach and Information Engineering have both conceptually arrived at the same point, but from different directions. Business-driven Information Engineering has evolved from a business perspective; object-oriented techniques have evolved from increasingly sophisticated attempts to structure systems development.

This means that object-oriented database management systems and programming languages are particularly well adapted to implementing the data and process models developed during the technology-dependent stage of Information Engineering. With Information Engineering, the ease of implementation, productivity, and quality gains that are achieved in a relational environment can also be realized in a non-relational environment. In an object-oriented environment using Information Engineering, design and implementation of systems can potentially be even easier than in these relational and non-relational environments.

Information Engineering thus enables an organization to maximize the advantages gained from emergent technologies. The benefits realized range from new insights into the strategic business vision of the organization, to detailed planning and optimization of new technologies. Both short- and long-term benefits are attained. Once established, the returns from implementing Information Engineering ensure competitive advantage and long-term success for the organization.

Strategic Planning Issues

We conclude by discussing a number of issues relating to strategic planning and organizational design:

- Strategic planning and refinement
- Information-based organizations
- Knowledge-based organizations
- Future organization structures

Strategic planning and refinement

Strategic business plans, at the corporate, business unit and functional area levels, are defined using strategic management planning. A strategic data model is developed based on those plans. Strategic, tactical, and operational data models, as well as process models, provide immediate feedback to management for refinement of the plans. They identify information-based and knowledge-based restructuring opportunities.

Information-based organizations

An organization's information resource is vital. The definition and management of this resource is essential for organizations to be able to compete in the turbulent years ahead, as emphasized by Drucker (1988): "We are entering a period of change: a shift from command-and-control organizations to information-based organizations of knowledge specialists." He commented that "businesses, especially large ones, will have little choice but to become information-based. . . . But as soon as a company takes the first tentative steps from data to information, its decision processes, management structure and work . . . begin to be transformed."

Applegate, Cash, and Mills (1988) indicate that top management will have centralized control with decentralized decision-making in such information-based organizations by using Information Technology to downsize and restructure the organization so that computer systems provide the communication, coordination, and control functions that were previously performed by middle managers. They emphasize that sophisticated expert systems and knowledge bases will help capture decision-making processes, moving the business eventually to a knowledge-based organization.

Knowledge-based organizations

Drucker continues this theme by saying, "To remain competitive—maybe even to survive—businesses will have to convert themselves into organizations of knowledge specialists." Information Engineering is used to capture an organization's knowledge resource in data models and process models, implemented as information systems and databases, or as expert systems and knowledge bases, thereby making this knowledge available to all who are authorized to access it. Drucker goes on to say, "The typical large business 20 years hence will have fewer than half the levels of management of its counterpart today, and no more than one-third the managers. It is more likely to resemble the hospital, the university, the symphony orchestra. For like them, the typical business will be knowledge-based."

Such organizations, to utilize their information and knowledge resources more effectively and operate with fewer management levels, will be structured differently to organizations today.

Future organization structures

The bureaucratic, divisional and coordinated organization structures that are used most commonly in business today are not very flexible or adaptable. Their databases, systems, and procedures, whether automated or manual, do not readily adjust to change. In contrast, a matrix organization structure is designed to adapt easily to rapid change. Its resources are closely managed, yet they can be allocated dynamically to projects or workgroups based on relative priorities. With an environment of rapid organizational change in the '90s and beyond, the existing systems of an organization—if developed using traditional methods—often have difficulty surviving change. They might need to be redeveloped. Databases and systems developed from data models using Information Engineering, however, enable organizations to navigate changes easier. But Drucker points to a future even beyond these structures, saying, "The organization will go beyond the matrix, and may indeed be quite different from it." We have no doubt that opportunities will emerge in the move to information-based and knowledge-based environments that suggest even more effective organization structures than we can imagine today.

Summary

In this chapter we discussed strategic planning and systems development. We saw that traditional strategic planning has suffered from many problems. Problems due to ineffective communication, or misinterpretation, of directions set by management are magnified by a long feedback cycle, typically 3–5 years, before information is available for refinement of the strategic plans.

We saw that strategic management planning emerged to address these problems. Continual evaluation and refinement of the plan at all stages of development, and also during implementation, is a characteristic of strategic management planning. Feedback is available to management within weeks, and sometimes even in days. This feedback is achieved through modeling at three levels of a project area—through strategic, tactical, and operational modeling. The project area can be a complete corporation, or a business unit, department, section, functional area, or an application area.

We also discussed systems development—the process-driven methods of Business Systems Planning, systems analysis, structured analysis and structured design, and the data-driven methodologies of Jackson, Warnier-Orr, and Information Engineering. We discussed that business changes bring about changes in procedures more often than changes in data on which the business is based. Systems developed using the process-driven methodologies might have to change greatly. But the systems developed using business-driven Information Engineering can accommodate business changes with less disruption, as they are based on a more stable foundation—data. We saw that strategic management planning, used with Information Engineering, results in strategic systems development.

Information Engineering has evolved dramatically since its original development in the 1970s, and its refinement during the '80s. It is now an integrated set of techniques that extend from strategic planning at the highest management levels to the analysis, design and implementation of information systems, decision support systems, and executive information systems. The databases and systems that are developed address the needs of managers and their staff more precisely than those built by traditional methodologies. With its use now by thousands of people in the management and user communities, and also by data processing staff, Information Engineering will continue to evolve in the '90s and into the 21st century.

Author Biography

Clive Finkelstein is the Managing Director of Information Engineering Services Pty, Ltd., in Melbourne, Australia, and is also the Founder and Chief Scientist of Information Engineering Systems Corporation in Alexandria, Virginia. These companies provide Information Engineering consulting and education support to MIS staff as well as business managers and their staffs. This consulting enables both users and MIS staff to design and implement systems based on the strategic plans set by management. He has over 30 years of experience in the computer industry. In 1972, based on his original work to bridge from strategic planning to information systems, he began developing the Information Engineering methodology. He is now widely recognized as the originator and main architect of Information Engineering, as used by corporations and governments around the world. He resides in Melbourne.

Mr. Finkelstein is the author of many articles on computing, including articles in two editions of the *Encyclopedia of computer science and engineering*, published by Van Nostrand Reinhold, with a second edition released in 1983. He has authored numerous papers on analysis and design, database design, and strategic planning throughout his career. This includes the first worldwide publication on Information Engineering; a series of six in-depth articles in Computerworld magazine in May and June, 1981, and in the Dec 16, 1991 issue.

He is the author of several books, including *Information Engineering*, co-authored with James Martin and published by the Savant Institute in 1981. He is the author of *An Introduction to Information Engineering*, published by Addison Wesley in 1989, and *Information Engineering: strategic systems development*, published by Addison Wesley in 1992.

Mr. Finkelstein presented papers at IBM Guide (1982 and 1986) and IBM Share (1982) in the United States, the 1982 State-of-the-Art Conference in Brazil, the Unilever Research Symposium in Great Britain in 1983, the Australian Computer Conference and Artificial Intelligence Conference in Australia in 1986, the CASExpo and the Expert Systems Conferences in Washington, DC in 1987, the 1988 Hong Kong Computer Conference, and the Australian Software Engineering Conference in Sydney, Australia, in 1991. In 1992 he is the invited keynote speaker at FIJICOM '92 in Fiji, the CASEWORLD '92 Conference in San Francisco, the Software Technology '92 Conference in Tokyo, the DAMA International Conference in Dallas, and is Conference Keynote Speaker at the Application Development World Conference in Philadelphia.

He conducted seminars on Information Engineering in 1989 in five cities across the United States. During 1991 he presented seminars on Strategic Systems Development in 24 cities in the United States and Canada, and 8 cities in Australia and New Zealand. He is scheduled to present 32 seminars in these countries again in 1992. He has conducted both public and in-house courses and provided consulting support for many US FORTUNE 1000 corporations, British companies, and Australian government and commercial organizations.

Prior to establishing Information Engineering Services Pty, Ltd., he worked for IBM for 15 years. In this period he held several technical, educational, and marketing positions with IBM in Australia. In the United States, in the early 1970s, he provided technical, educational, and marketing DB/DC support worldwide for IBM.

Mr. Finkelstein holds a Bachelor of Science degree from the University of NSW in Sydney, Australia, and was appointed a Fellow of the Australian Computer Society in 1972.

Works Cited

Andrews, K.R. 1971. *The concept of corporate strategy*. Homewood, Il.: Irwin.

Ansoff, H.I. 1965. *Corporate strategy*. New York, N.Y.: McGraw-Hill.

Applegate, L., J. Cash, and D. Mills. 1988. Information technology and tomorrow's manager. *Harvard business review*. Nov - Dec 1988.

Chandler, A.D. 1962. *Strategy and structure: Chapters in the history of the American industrial enterprise*. Cambridge, Ma.: MIT Press.

De Marco, T. 1982. *Software systems development*. New York, N.Y.: Yourdon Press.

Drucker, P. 1974. *Management: tasks, responsibilities, practices*. New York, N.Y.: Harper & Row.

Drucker, P. 1988. The coming of the new organization. *Harvard business review*. Jan–Feb 1988.

EDP Analyzer. 1984. *The chief information officer role*. 22 (11). Canning Publications.

Fahey, L. and H.K Christensen. 1986. Evaluating the research on strategy content. *Journal of management*. 12 (2).

Finkelstein, C.B. 1989. *An introduction to information engineering*. Reading, Ma.: Addison-Wesley.

Finkelstein, C.B. 1992. *Information engineering: Strategic systems development*. Reading, Ma.: Addison-Wesley .

Gray, D.H. 1986. Uses and misuses of strategic planning. *Harvard business review*. Jan - Feb 1986.

Huff, A.S. and R.K. Reger. 1987. A review of strategic process research. *Journal of management*. 13 (2).

IBM Corporation. 1981. *Business systems planning: Information systems planning guide*. IBM Reference No. GE20-0527. White Plains, N.Y.: IBM Corporation.

Jackson, M. 1975. *Principles of program design*. New York, N.Y.: Academic Press.

Martin, J. and C.B. Finkelstein. 1981. *Information engineering*. Carnforth, Lancs, U.K.: Savant Institute.

Nolan, R.L. 1987. What transformation is. In *Stage by stage*. 7 (5). Boston, Ma.: Nolan, Norton & Co.

Orr, K. 1977. *Structured systems development*. New York, N.Y.: Yourdon Press.

Porter, M.E. 1980. *Competitive strategy*. New York, N.Y.: Free Press, MacMillan Publishing.

Porter, M.E. 1985. *Competitive advantage*. New York, N.Y.: Free Press, MacMillan Publishing.

Schendel, D.E. and C.W. Hofer. 1979. *Strategic management: A new view of business policy and planning*. Little, Brown & Company.

Smith, W.G. 1990. The requirements for an IRM environment. In "Data base advisor." Column in *Data base newsletter*. May - June. Boston, Ma.

Yourdon, E. and L. Constantine. 1978. *Structured design: Fundamentals of a discipline of computer program systems design*. Englewood Cliffs, N.J.: Prentice-Hall.

Application Development Productivity in the '90s

by Prof. Dr. Eberhard Rudolph

Overview

This survey addresses the effectiveness of the Unisys LINC software development environment and evaluates the application software development performance of 11 organizations. The participating companies were drawn from the United States, Europe, Japan, Australia, and New Zealand. They operate in the financial, manufacturing, transport, and service sectors.

For each company, the size of a critical mission system was measured together with the overall development effort. The Function Point technique was used to evaluate the application size.

The results indicate that LINC users can develop larger application systems than installations using conventional COBOL environments. Performance gains of 5:1 to 10:1 were observed for application systems exceeding 2000 Function Points. Applications over 5000 Function Points can have gains in excess of 20:1.

This study identified as key indicators for efficient application development, the size of the development team, the use of prototyping methodology, and the inclusion of the system users into the development process. Organizations that ignore these factors will not fully exploit the potential of the LINC environment. Continuation of applying proven conventional COBOL development practices will result in lower performance.

Introduction

Productivity environments

During the past five years, Computer-Aided Software Engineering (CASE) environments evolved to automate and simplify application software development. Some of such CASE environments primarily address the planning and design steps of the development process; they are therefore referred to as "upper-CASE tools." Other environments focus on the implementation phase assisting in the actual construction of information systems. Such tools are known as "lower-CASE tools."

The computer press and specialized industry seminars, such as Schussel (1984), regularly address and praise the productivity tools. Jones (1991) and Martin (1991) postulate overall productivity gains of ten times and more compared with standard COBOL environments.

Despite such publicity, productivity environments gained only a modest acceptance, particularly in larger computer installations. Information system managers are cautious: they want to see facts instead of general perceptions.

The benefits of such tools in small applications is widely recognized. Typically lower-CASE tools, however, are seen as being limited to reporting or end-user query systems. There is some doubt voiced whether lower-CASE environments can address large and mission-critical applications.

As a consequence of perceived limitations of lower-CASE environments, IS managers often continue to use the conventional COBOL environments for most of their production work, which leads to mixed environments, often operating separately.

Continuing from an earlier study (Rudolph 1983), the lower-CASE environment chosen for this detailed and global survey is the Unisys LINC environment. Completed and operational LINC application systems were observed and measured. Comparisons with the earlier results can be found in appendix A.

Objectives

The purpose of this study is to provide quantitative field data for the use of lower-CASE environments. This survey reflects large application systems from a variety of organizations operating in different regions of the world. The objectives of this study are as follows:

- To analyze the use of LINC application development in well-known and successful organizations worldwide.

- To review the LINC productivity margin against conventional COBOL environments.

- To provide data on the size, quality, and productivity of large and heavily used application systems.

- To identify key success factors of efficient LINC application development.

Research Method

The data for this study were collected by conducting personal interviews at 13 installations. Each of these interviews lasted about one day. The performance of each project was measured by the application size to work-effort ratio of the systems developed.

In addition, information was gathered on the development methodology adopted, the team size and structure, the IS reward scheme, the transaction or activity rates of the developed software, the software and hardware environment, the IS experience of the staff, the involvement of end-users into the development process, the quality of the software, the perceived benefits of the application and the use of other additional programming environments.

Measure of effort

The effort of application development is derived from all activities associated with the development of the application. The work effort in this study includes the planning, design, implementation, and testing stages. It particularly contains the effort for the formal acceptance testing, quality assurance, and all other project-related overheads.

Porter (1988) suggested a helpful convention on time accounting in software development. His framework includes the time of the development team, support staff, consultants, and users.

End-users have a considerable involvement in specifying, developing, and acceptance testing in the LINC environment. Therefore, in this study the end-user time, whenever applicable, was included in the overall effort value as well.

The unit of effort was a person-hour. While some installations recorded very detailed information about the effort spent in application development, others had only very sketchy figures. In any case the total effort was reworked. Considered were the number of staff (plus users and contractors), the elapsed development time, and the actual hours worked (including overtime) per week. These times were checked with several independent staff members and with the applications users.

Not considered in the development effort were the costs of general support staff such as system programmers or database administrators. These tend to be only a few in LINC installations, but they can have a sizable impact in conventional environments.

Measure of size

Function Points were the measure of size in this study. This technique was first proposed by Albrecht (1979). Function Points quantitatively assess the size of information functions delivered to the user to support business functions. Since 1985, the Function Point technique has become the accepted standard for quantifying the size of software development projects. Over 1000 major organizations worldwide use this technique for software development management reporting. There is a North American-based, manufacturer-independent, International Function Point User Group (IFPUG) that provides standards and information exchange in Function Point measurements. Affiliated user groups exist in the Netherlands and Australia.

Details on how to count Function Points can be found in the IFPUG (1991) standards manual. Guidance in how to use the results of such Function Point counts is given by IFPUG (1991a). Indeed, some of the critical indicators suggested by IFPUG (1991a) were compiled and used in this survey.

The results of this study are based on release 3.1 of the Function Point counting practices as defined and published by the International Function Point User Group (IFPUG), which may be referred to for details.

Release 3.1 of Function Point counting rules differs from the original Albrecht counting rules (release 2) used in earlier studies. The release 3.1 changes generally do not substantially modify the results of earlier measurements. Based on ten application systems, Rumpf (1990) found that in his installation the change to release 3.1 rules reduced the old release 2 Function Point counts by 10%.

There is one area, however, where IFPUG release 3.1 considerably differs from the earlier standard. It credits special business function value to error and help messages for input functions. This can increase Function Point counts by up to 50% and makes comparisons with established figures difficult.

Since the other figures quoted in this survey did not yet use IFPUG release 3.0 or higher, the error messages and help functions were not counted separately as output functions as suggested by release 3.1. Instead, these error messages were considered as part of the input function to which they apply.

Several of the participating LINC users already record their Function Points and had a Function Point value for the application under observation. Irrespectively of existing Function Point counts, the Function Point values shown in this study were established during the site visits. The basis for the counts was the application implementation documentation (ISPEC listing). In all but two cases the installation count agreed with the revised count carried out during the visit.

Some installations used the automated Function Point counting facility of the LINC Design Assistant II (LDA II) upper-CASE tool. The results of that tool will depend on the quality of the source code (ISPEC) listing. Many of the ISPEC listings seen in this survey contained dead code, conversion aids, or internal technical functions. All of these would be counted by an automatic tool, but they do not represent any Function Points.

The majority of LINC users had large, integrated applications that have evolved over a number of years. All applications studied in this survey were completed and in production for more than six months. Two installations were surveyed, but their results had to be rejected since their applications were not in production at the time of the visit.

Most applications, however, have been used for over three years and have changed during those years. In the case of system modifications, the original development time was used to establish the work effort. Considering the subsequent enhancements, a distinction was made between the change of existing functionality and newly added features. Changed functions were considered since they existed in the original system. The Function Points of added functionality were not included in this study since the added functions did not exist originally (and did not require any work effort).

The application systems listed in this survey often represent only a small part of the total LINC applications available to the users of the participating companies. Limited time required that selections had to be made.

Contributing Organizations

Thirteen organizations from the United States (3), Europe (4), Australia (2), New Zealand (2), and Japan (2) provided the data for this survey. The individual site visits were made from April, 1990, through May 1991. Two of the reviewed applications could not be included in this survey because the systems were not yet used in production at the time of the interview. The 11 participants of the study were:

- Advance Bank—a rapidly growing Australian bank with assets of $A4.5 billion and 1.3 million customers holding 1.7 million accounts, which are served by 200 branches. From a DP staff of 100, 30 are trained in LINC, which is used for all new development. The system studied was the Visa card system supporting 60,000 cards and 6500 transactions per day.

- BASF Corporation—the US affiliate of the BASF Group with annual sales of $5.4 billion and 21,500 employees. The Plant Information System measured in this study runs on seven centers supporting 16 plants. The transaction rate per plant might reach 5000 per day.

- Ford Australia—Australia's largest car manufacturer uses the LINC environment for their material control system. The production costing system inspected is only a small part of that information system.

- Hertz New Zealand—the New Zealand Hertz rental car subsidiary has 120 employees and handles about 12,000 car rentals monthly. The car reservation system examined supports 60 terminals in 30 on-line locations and is also used by another 40 offices. The system processes 600,000 transactions per month and produces 6000 reports per month.

- Kawasaki Steel Corporation—a major Japanese integrated steel maker with net sales of over $7 billion and 18,000 employees. Kawasaki produces 10.9 million tons of steel annually. All software development is carried out by KSD, a 1160 staff subsidiary. The Iron Powder Production Control system investigated in this study was developed for the Chiba plant.

- Liberty Travel—the largest United States retail travel agency with $1 billion annual gross sales. With 2500 employees, this privately owned company operates 155 retail branches and 75 wholesale branches. The Space Allocation Reservation System measured handles 10,000 bookings and 2500 hotels weekly. The system processes over 50,000 activities daily.

- National Provincial—a major Great Britain building society with assets of £8.5 billion. 3300 employees serve 1.6 million investors and 334,000 mortgages through 321 branches. With a total staff of 253, the IS department uses LINC in two business systems while all other applications were developed in COBOL.

- NZ Steel—the main New Zealand steel mill with 2250 employees producing 600,000 tons of steel annually. Ninety-five percent of the commercial information systems are written in LINC. The Roll Production Control system studied supports 85 terminals and handles 16,000 transactions per day.

- Showa Line—the fifth-largest Japanese shipping line operating world-wide with a fleet of 121 ships. During the past four years the company halved its IS development staff to 12 and at the same time completed a Total Information system. The Trade Accounting system observed in this study is only a small part of that total information system.

- Skipton Building Society—a medium-sized Great Britain building society with assets of £1.66 billion, specializing in private residential mortgages. Fifty-six branches support 70,000 mortgage accounts and 250,000 savings accounts, using 400 terminals. The 13-person development staff writes all mainframe software in LINC. Some of their applications have become packages for the building society industry.

- Ziegler—one of Europe's largest transport companies with a turnover of $2 billion. With 5000 employees, the privately owned Belgian company has 140 branches in Europe. The freight forwarding system examined in this study handles 100,000 transports per month.

Results

Table 5.1 summarizes the productivity results found in this survey. The Function Point size listed next to the application name is given in adjusted Function Points. The Function Point Adjustment Factor (AF) reflects the complexity level of the application.

The elapsed time (in months) is taken from the planning stage to the completion of the functions included in the size count. This does not necessarily mean that the user had to wait that time before the first application was available. Typically information systems are delivered incrementally. A good example is application 2, the space reservation system. It took 57 months to grow to 6258 Function Points, yet the first functions were delivered after 5 months.

As pointed out earlier the overall effort includes overtime and end-user involvement. In addition, the effort reflects training, documentation, and acceptance testing. Acceptance testing alone often accounted for a substantial part of the overall development effort.

The activities per hour are an indicator for the relative use of the application. Typically, an activity would be a business transaction such as recording a sale, inquiring into an account, or producing a report. Some of the business activities could be sophisticated, such as costing a new car model.

Team size describes the average number of team members directly involved in the application development. Not included in the team size (but counted in the development effort) are staff involved in training and testing.

Productivity

The productivity results shown in Table 5.1 show a considerable variance between individual installations. The observed productivity ranges from 1.5 hours per Function Point to 26.6 hours per Function Point. The average productivity factor was 8.63 hours per Function Point. The size of the applications varied between 7266 Function Points to 634 Function Points.

Interestingly, the size had little influence on the productivity rates. The largest application had a productivity factor of 5.5 hours per Function Point while one of the smallest application had by far the highest factor of 26.6 hours per Function Point.

How do the LINC lower-CASE results compare with current COBOL environments? Table 5.1 shows, in its last three rows, average COBOL productivity rates for applications of 1000 to 3000 Function Points. Each of these three COBOL figures reflects the database and experience of leading industry consultants.

One of the largest commercial project databases (with over 2200 rigorously screened projects) is kept by Putnam. This database has been converted to Function

TABLE 5.1 Productivity results of the 1991 LINC survey.

application	size	AF	elapsed time [months]	effort [hours]	hours per FP	activities per hour	team size
1. forwarding system	7,266	1.21	72	40,000	5.5	20,000	2
2. space reservation	6,258	1.14	57	52,380	8.37	6,000	4
3. building society	4,128	1.04	21	35,380	8.5	1,000	11
4. car reservation	3,970	1.05	12	6,000	1.5	1,000	3
5. production control	2,511	1.05	41	20,340	8.1	300	3
6. visa card	2,364	1.11	15	16,590	7.0	750	4
7. plant information	2,205	1.04	16	25,920	11.75	600	9
8. production control	2,192	1.04	21	15,680	7.15	2,000	4
9. production costing	1,706	1.07	12	5,200	3.05	2	3
10. mortgage	1,620	1.12	13	43,128	26.6	5,000	27
11. trade accounting	634	1.0	27	4,740	7.47	250	5
COBOL (Putnam [1991])	3,000				32.0		
COBOL (Jones [1988])	2,500				40.0		
COBOL (Rubin [1991])	1,000				20.0		

Points. Looking at any recent project developments (completed after 1986), Putnam (1991) lists productivity rates of 16 hours per Function Point for projects of up to 1000 Function Points. For larger projects (with several thousand Function Points) the productivity rate drops to 32 hours per Function Point.

Interestingly, the two largest LINC projects of this investigation (applications 1 and 2) exceeded the largest projects of Putnam's database by almost 1000 Function Points.

Jones (1988) is more conservative and provides the following rule of thumb for rates: for small projects of a few hundred Function Points; 13 hours per Function Point. Medium projects of up to 1000 Function Points have a rate of 20 hours per Function Point. For large projects of several thousand Function Points, this rate grows to 40 hours per Function Point. Rubin (1991) also quoted 20 hours per Function Point for medium systems.

Figure 5.1 correlates the LINC results from Table 5.1 with the productivity rates of general development environments as discussed by Putnam (1991), Jones (1988), and Rubin (1991).

In the small systems area of up to 1000 Function Points, the difference between the LINC environment and conventional COBOL environment is not very visible. Well-managed conventional environments report development rates similar to those observed for LINC applications in this survey.

The differences to the COBOL environments become evident for larger applications of over 1000 Function Points. Here some LINC installations have expanded the application size to levels that are hardly matched by developments in COBOL environments. And they did so without a significant drop in productivity.

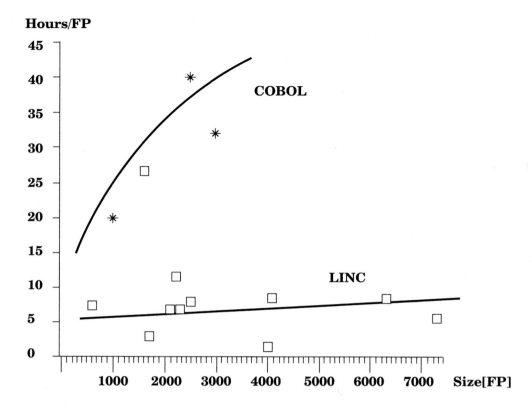

Fig. 5.1 LINC versus COBOL.

The capability to develop large systems without a significant drop in productivity was already noted in an earlier study (Rudolph 1983). The difference between the COBOL and LINC environments widens with increasing application size. Finally, Fig. 5.1 shows one LINC application that perfectly fits into the general COBOL performance rates. This is a reminder that the development environment has only a facilitating role.

Ultimately, productivity will depend on the management and the staff (both IS and user) of an organization. The development environment provides only an opportunity (but not a guarantee) for productivity. It is up to the installation to make full use of the capabilities of its environment. As pointed out by Martin (1991), productivity stands on four pillars: methodology, tools, people, and management.

Key success factors

To understand the differences in the observed results we must also look at the methodologies, people, and management of the participating organizations. Table 5.2 correlates some of their characteristics with the productivity results.

Productive LINC sites use LINC almost exclusively. This includes high-volume applications and batch jobs. Increasingly the sophisticated LINC users have direct communication with outside organizations. Hooks are provided by LINC software to interface to such external systems which are written in more appropriate system languages.

Most efficient users have adapted or replaced the formal and rigidly detailed standard development methodologies. Typically, they will refer to their approach as prototyping, which will generally mean that they have a clear procedure to set requirements and provide a conceptual design. Solutions then are incrementally developed and regularly verified with the user. The prototyping techniques used by the organizations surveyed are based on methodologies such as LSA, K-Pride, or Information Engineering. These methodologies, however, were not used for detailed design or program documentation.

It is interesting to note that those (few) organizations that provide a direct financial reward for achieving results have excellent productivity rates. In contrast all participating organizations that: did not fully involve the user in the development process; rigidly followed formal development methodologies; used team sizes greater than five staff members; and used several application environments experienced development rates of 10 hours per Function Point and more. These organizations contrast from the other LINC installations of this survey. Nevertheless they provided applications at rates which are only achieved by excellent COBOL environments. As one site put it, before using LINC they were never capable of developing applications of this size.

Table 5.3 provides an overview of the key success factors for application development. It should be noted that the average performance referred to in Table 5.3 will still be regarded as an excellent achievement in conventional COBOL environments.

TABLE 5.2 Development environment characteristics.

application	size [FP]	other language	user participation	hours per FP	methodology used	result reward	use LINC since
1. forwarding system	7266	none	full time	5.5	prototyping	yes	1984
2. space reservation	6258	none	full time	8.37	incremental	no	1985
3. building society	4128	none	close	8.5	semi-formal	no	1984
4. car reservation	3970	none	close	1.5	prototyping	yes	1987
5. production control	2511	COBOL	reviews	8.1	prototyping	no	1985
6. visa card	2364	COBOL	full time	7.0	prototyping	no	1983
7. plant information	2205	COBOL	reviews	11.75	prototyping	no	1984
8. production control	2192	none	full time	7.15	prototyping	no	1987
9. production costing	1706	COBOL	close	3.05	prototyping	yes	1983
10. mortgage	1620	COBOL	sometimes	26.6	formal	no	1986
11. trade accounting	634	COBOL	reviews	7.47	prototyping	no	1985

1) except for special interfaces to outside organizations

TABLE 5.3 Key success indicators.

Key factor	high performance	average performance
Tools	LINC only	mixed
Methodology	prototyping	formal
Team size	< 5	> 5
User Participation	full at all stages	restricted to planning

Quality

All organizations quoted quality rather than productivity as the prime reason for using LINC. They stated that without the LINC environment they would not be capable of providing the level of service to their users. Some installations have regular and independent user surveys addressing quality-of-service issues.

Each of the surveyed installations would express the quality of their LINC applications by the ease of change. Their users expect substantial changes within days and certainly not longer than weeks. Application backlogs of more than several months are not acceptable in those organizations.

One installation formally evaluated quality by recording the number of failures (for any reason) per system. It found the quality of the LINC systems to be three times better (less failures) compared with its COBOL applications.

Conclusions

The survey showed that a number of organizations world-wide develop and operate large and mission-critical information systems in the LINC CASE environment. Application development productivity varied depending on a number of key success factors. The competitive advantage of the LINC lower-CASE environment will depend on the size of the application and the culture of the LINC user.

The critical success factor is a flexible and responsive management style described by Martin (1991). Using such a style, a high level of productivity can be obtained even with conventional environments. Success with management techniques alone, however, is limited to small applications of several hundred Function Points. The lower-CASE environments enable the developer to extend high productivity to large applications of several thousand Function Points in size.

The LINC environment, however, offers a distinct advantage for large application system development. With applications of several thousand Function Points LINC productivity rates can still have a 5:1 advantage over conventional environments. More importantly large scale solutions can be implemented by small teams. The size of such solution is seldom reached in other environments.

LINC users who apply standard methodologies that were designed for conventional environments will yield conventional results. They will, however, exceed their capabilities and still compare favorably with other conventional installations.

Productivity and quality are management issues. Appropriate methodologies, team size, and user involvement are paramount to harness the potential of the LINC environment. Successful IS managers require the full support of their senior management. Executives have to care about software productivity and quality. Performance and quality need to be regularly measured. The results should be reported to senior management, and trends should be analyzed. Such regular reporting is vital to the management of the application development cycle. IS staff needs to be motivated and rewarded to be productive.

At present, the IS industry is dominated by mediocrity. One participating company received an auditor report that highlighted that their development costs were significantly less than the average industry figure. Their costs were, furthermore, not in line with their installed hardware value. This is not surprising since that company was one of the most efficient software developers in this study. The audit report, however, listed the low development cost as a concern for action, not as a credit.

Appendix

Comparison with the 1983 LINC productivity study

This first, detailed, Fourth Generation Language (4GL) productivity study was published by the University of Auckland, New Zealand in 1983 (Rudolph 1983). That work investigated 11 Unisys LINC 4GL application systems developed by six different organizations. In summary, that research found a 20-fold productivity advantage of LINC users against COBOL (or PL/1) environments. For the first time, quantitative evidence confirmed earlier, unsubstantiated claims of Martin (1982). The magnitude of these 1983 results was surprising. Further observations (Rudolph and Simpson 1984) confirmed the original figures.

Differences

Compared with the 1983 results, the productivity rates of LINC users have diversified. In 1983, only about one hour was required to produce a Function Point. In 1991, the average time to produce a Function Point is 8.6 hours, almost ten times higher. The average application system size, however, rose at the same time from 711 Function Points to 3168.

The differences between the 1983 and 1991 results stem largely from the characteristics of the organizations surveyed. All participating companies in the 1983 study were small organizations. Their management structure was not complicated, with entrepreneurial chief executives taking a direct interest in the development of their information systems. Decisions in such organizations were made without much delay. The companies surveyed in 1991 were large organizations that had to apply stringent development and implementation controls. Compared with 1983, the acceptance testing and quality assurance efforts were higher in 1991, therefore increasing the overall effort in application development.

Similarities

In the 1991 study a wider range of organizations could be observed. There are still organizations that come close to the 1983 results, but at the same time the average application size had a four-fold increase.

The conventional COBOL environment made up ground on the lower end of the application size scale. The original 20:1 advantage does not apply to information systems of less than 1000 Function Points. At the high end of application system size, however, the gap has even widened. The LINC environment can deliver application sizes of over 5000 Function Points in less than 10 hours per Function Point. At this magnitude, conventional COBOL environments have difficulties to deliver at all.

Author Biography

Dr. Rudolph is Professor of Information Systems at the Hochschule Bremerhaven in Germany. He is a well-known authority on productivity in application software development and, in particular, on fourth-generation languages, CASE tools, and the Function Point technique. He advises numerous corporations on evaluating and implementing software development environments. Professor Rudolph directs research on application development and software technology transfer.

He is co-author of the IBM GUIDE International workbook on *Estimating using Function Points*, the International Function Point User Group *Function Point counting practices manual*, and the Computerworld *Development World Product Briefings*.

His previous experience includes computer system management positions with mainframe manufacturers (IBM and XEROX), general management of a banking EDP organization (Northern Trustee Computerbank), government computer science research, and the introduction of an MIS undergraduate and graduate program at the University of Auckland.

Works Cited

Albrecht, A. 1979. Measuring application development productivity. *Proceedings of the joint SHARE/GUIDE/IBM application development symposium.* pp. 83–92. October 14–17, 1979. Monterey, Ca.

IFPUG 1991. *Function Point counting practices manual.* Release 3.1. The International Function Point User Group, 5008 Pine Creek Park, Westerville, OH 43081-4899.

IFPUG 1991a. *Function Points as an asset to management reporting.* Release 2. Feb. 1991. The International Function Point User Group. 5008 Pine Creek Park, Westerville, OH 43081-4899.

Jones, C. 1988. *A short history of Function Points and Feature Points.* Version 2. Burlington, Ma.: Software Productivity Research.

Jones, C. 1991. Using Function Points to evaluate CASE tools, methodologies, staff experiences, and languages. *Proceedings of the IFPUG spring conference.* pp. 2–38. April 2–5, 1991. Baltimore, Md.

Martin, J. 1991. *Rapid application development.* New York, N.Y.: MacMillan Publishing Company.

Porter, B. 1988. Measurement improvements through time accounting conventions. *Proceedings of the IFPUG spring conference.* pp. 16–19. May 16–19, 1988. Dallas, Tx.

Putnam, L. 1991. Using statistical process control for total quality management. *Proceedings of the IFPUG spring conference.* pp. 182–198. April 2–5. 1991.

Rubin, H. 1991. I/S measure and business value, bridging the gap, tracking key indicators. *Proceedings of the IFPUG spring conference.* pp. 298–329. April 2–5, 1991.

Rudolph, E. 1983. Productivity in computer application development. Working paper 9. Auckland, New Zealand: Dept. of Management Studies, Univ. of Auckland.

Rudolph, E. and G. Simpson. 1984. Evaluation of a fourth-generation language. *Proceedings of the joint international symposium on information systems.* pp 148–165. April 9–11. Sydney, Australia.

Rumpf, B. 1990. How to deal with changes to Function Point counting rules. *Proceedings of the IFPUG fall conference.* pp. 23–27. October 1–4. San Antonio, Tx.

Schussel, G. 1984. Fourth-generation productivity tools—a shopping guide for software customers. *Data management.* October, 1984. 42–46.

A Natural Productivity in Object-Orientation

by Ed Yourdon

Structured Techniques Remembered

By now the vast majority of software engineers around the world have a broad (though often remarkably shallow) understanding of the principles of structured programming, design, and analysis. I won't belabor the technical components of structured stuff here: instead, I'll offer some comments on the "paradigm shift" that the methodology represented when it was born in the 1970s.

Software methodologies, like all the other scientific disciplines throughout history, are developed by people—people with ambitions, emotions, likes and dislikes, occasional insights, and frequent blind spots. Software methodologies, political movements, and scientific breakthroughs are typically led by young people who, secure in their belief that everything in life can be categorized as black or white, become what Eric Hoffer calls "True Believers."

One of my memories of the early Yourdon inc. years is that we all passionately believed that our ideas had the power to change the world. We alone could save society from whatever ills threatened it: low productivity and software quality in the narrowest sense. But in our dreams of glory, we missionaries were convinced that data flow diagrams (DFDs) alone stood between Western civilization and the wicked Communists on the other side of the Berlin Wall.

I wish I could still believe that structured analysis—or, for that matter, information engineering, object-oriented techniques, or any methodology—had such power. One of the sad, sobering consequences of reaching middle age is the discovery that, by and large, it's all garbage: the best methodologies don't guarantee the technical success of most systems development projects, and technical success can't save a project from the larger issues of corporate politics in these whirligig days of mergers and downsizings. Meanwhile, time marches on: five years from now, few software engineers will even remember the Berlin Wall.

But long before I concluded that structured techniques would not, and could not, save the world, the methodology had already sown the seeds of its own destruction. Paradigm shifts are generally promoted by young revolutionaries who can afford to take radical positions because they have nothing to lose: when the revolution succeeds, movement leaders gradually come to depend more and more on the success of their paradigm to pay the rent, feed their followers, and maintain their ever-growing egos. Alternative paradigms come to be seen as competitors and are strenuously attacked by the True Believers as inferior, if not downright evil.

In 1975, Michael Jackson's JSP methodology was greeted with some curiosity and mild interest by the technical staff at Yourdon inc., but the marketing staff saw it as a distinct threat and attacked it with the fervor of white blood cells going after a virus. Fourth-generation languages (4GLs), prototyping, data modeling, and all manner of alternative approaches to systems development were also threats. When I remarked to one of our top salespeople that this was rather narrow-minded, he promptly calculated for me the amount of sales commissions he had lost in training and consulting competitions based on these "interesting" alternatives.

Meanwhile, the paradigm itself begins developing problems as it is applied to larger and more complex problems. Exceptions and special cases are discovered and grafted onto the side of a once-simple body of knowledge. Real-time systems, for example, were a terrible thorn in our side at Yourdon inc. in the '70s: the conventional DFDs were inadequate for modeling the critical issues in process control systems, air traffic control systems, and telephone switching systems. Finally, after being bloodied by clients like Dupont, Lockheed, and Foxboro, Ira Morrow, Paul Ward, and Steve Mellor grafted some real-time extensions onto the standard DFDs and appropriated state-transition diagrams (STDs) into the methodology.

Eventually, a methodology collapses under its own weight, attacked by a new generation of revolutionaries who are convinced that their paradigm will solve all the problems for which the older methodology is no longer adequate. Of course, in many scientific disciplines, such paradigm shifts take decades or even centuries: aside from the inertia associated with the True Believers, the fundamentals of the discipline itself typically don't change very rapidly.

But software development methodologies are ultimately driven by the possibilities afforded us by new generations of hardware. The structured techniques were developed in the days of batch computing and third-generation languages (3GLs). On-line systems with even the dumbest of terminals were a radical concept: graphical user interfaces were about as realistic as the technology in Star Trek. Times have changed—hardware is 100 to 1000 times more powerful than when Larry Constantine and I wrote *Structured Design* (Yourdon & Constantine 1979). It's obviously appropriate for the software development methodologies to change also. However, it's unrealistic to expect those who derive their income, stature, or self respect from the old methodologies to willingly accept such change.

So what? Well, if all this is true for structured techniques, it will come true for the OOPLers. If you're about to jump on the OO bandwagon, fine, but avoid the hysteria and the expectation that it will save Western civilization from . . . who? Saddam Hussein?

And watch out for a new aspect of the methodology religion game that didn't exist in the 1970s: the CASE vendors. At Yourdon inc., we had enough trouble changing our lecture notes when we modified our methodology, but the capital investment was essentially zero. If one of our pesky young instructors claimed that he had yet another new wrinkle on how DFDs really should be drawn, we would sit him in a corner for a month and tell him to write a book.

Today's CASE vendors, on the other hand, have invested millions in their products and have invited venture capitalists to participate with them in their efforts to grow rich. The conservative defense of whatever methodology their tool supports is a foregone conclusion; if you're interested in methodology evolution, you should take a close look at such meta-CASE vendors as Systematica and lpsys.

The Current Situation

Most of the structured techniques were developed in the 1970s, and many people assume that nothing much has happened since. What follows is a brief summary of the major developments that occurred in the 1980s and that are part of the "current" structured techniques.

The basic modeling tools were extended to deal with real-time systems. This required adding control flows and control processes on the DFD, as well as adding an entirely new modeling tool—the state-transition diagram. A variation is to show the control flows in one diagram and the data flows in a separate diagram.

Event partitioning was added to structured analysis, providing the analyst with a more effective method of developing a set of leveled DFDs than a strictly "top-down" approach offers. Surprisingly, many analysts and CASE vendors (including, it seems, IBM) are unaware of this approach, first documented by Steve McMenamin and John Palmer (1984).

A variety of data-modeling techniques gained popularity and credibility. Unfortunately, many designers and systems analysts feel they must make a binary choice between a process-modeling approach (that is, drawing only a DFD model of a system) and a data-modeling approach (using only entity-relationship diagrams (ERDS)). However, the best approach uses three models—DFDs, ERDS, and STDs—to model all three dimensions of a system.

CASE tools began to appear in the mid-'80s, initially as tools for automating the drawing of diagrams. Now, of course, CASE is an acronym for a much broader range of automated tools: most serious vendors intend to automate the entire life cycle of systems development, from business systems planning to maintenance and reverse engineering. (By the way, if structured analysis and structured design are so important, why is it that several CASE vendors don't use these techniques to build their products? Ask your friendly CASE vendor to show you the DFDs and structure charts that were used to build its product—you might be surprised by what the vendor shows you.)

Paradigm wars broke out between the fanatical followers of different methodologists. If you develop business data processing systems, your DP organization was compelled to choose from among the Gane-Sarson approach, the DeMarco-Yourdon approach, and the Warnier-Orr approach (or the LBMS approach in England, or the Merise approach in France, and so forth). If you developed real-time systems, you were given a choice between the Ward-Mellor approach and the Hatley-Pirbhai approach. The similarities among all these approaches are far greater than their differences, but you would never know this from listening to the people who market them.

The methodology of structured analysis changed. When first introduced in the 1970s, standard wisdom dictated that DFDs should first be used to develop a current physical model; that is, a model of the user's current implementation of his system. This was to be followed by a current logical model (a model of the "essence" of his current system), without regard to the manual or automated technology used to implement it. The third stage of structured analysis was a new logical model, followed by a new physical system.

During the 1980s we learned it could take so long to develop the two current models that the users might give up in disgust and cancel the project. Some consultants and textbook authors still haven't figured this out. But most practitioners who want to keep their jobs know they should ignore the user's current system as much as possible and begin almost immediately with a model of the proposed new system.

On the one hand, these changes were profound: it was virtually impossible, for example, to use vintage-1978 structured analysis to model real-time systems. On the other hand, the changes were incremental: if you had learned about structured techniques in the late 1970s, a one-day seminar in 1989 is all you would have needed to find out what had changed.

Scenarios for the Future

The structured techniques were responsible for much of the success I have enjoyed in the DP field. So why say adieu? Because the tools and concepts that served us well in the past won't necessarily serve us well in the future. This is true in all walks of life. People who grew up believing financial security could be achieved by putting money in a passbook savings account were badly disappointed by the raging inflation of the late 1970s. People who made their money by investing in the stock market during the bull market of the 1980s learned on October 19, 1987, that they could lose money as well as make money. Times change.

So what's changing in the field of systems development? What's going to be different about programming, design, and analysis in this decade? I believe there isn't just one future awaiting us, but a spectrum of futures. Arthur C. Clarke (1984) put this eloquently in the foreword to *Profiles of the Future*:

> All attempts to predict the future in any detail will appear ludicrous within a few years. This book . . . does not try to describe the future, but to define the boundaries within which possible futures must lie. If we regard the ages that stretch ahead of us as an unmapped and unexplored country, what I am trying to do is to survey its frontiers and get some idea of its extent.
>
> The detailed geography of the interior must remain unknown—until we reach it.

The future of systems development in company A may be quite different from that of company B, and the future within an individual organization will depend on a number of factors. Here are the likely scenarios for structured techniques:

- Ongoing evolution of the structured techniques

- Disappearance of the mystique of the structured techniques

- Complete automation of systems development, eliminating programmers

- Decreased development of new systems and the dominance of maintenance

- Replacement of idiosyncratic, one-of-a-kind systems with generic, vendor-supplied systems that can be tailored by the user

- Replacement of the structured techniques by 4GLs and powerful database management systems (DBMS)

Scenario 1: Ongoing evolution of the structured techniques

The structured techniques evolved gradually and might continue to evolve. I was more emphatic about this in 1988, arguing that "no doubt they will continue to evolve." But I now feel it's unlikely: none of us cares about structured techniques any more. Constantine and I are working with object-oriented methodologies, Tom DeMarco is working on peopleware and metrics, Chris Gane is involved with reengineering at Bachman, and Trish Sarson was last seen running an antique business. Wayne Stevens has probably suffered the cruelest fate of all, being stuck with the job of incorporating methodologies of all sorts into AD/Cycle.

In any case, so what? I don't foresee any fundamental, revolutionary changes—and if there are, they won't come from the current generation of fuddy-duddies. The next generation of software engineers, the kids in high school and college today, might come up with something revolutionary. Maybe they will invent a three-dimensional DFD, but why would they want to extend a paradigm from the 1960s?

Scenario 2: Disappearance of the mystique of the structured techniques

Structured programming, structured design, and structured analysis were never very difficult concepts. But because they represented such a radical departure from the accepted way of building systems, they had a certain mystique. Analysts attended five-day workshops to learn how to draw DFDs and still came away puzzled. Designers read the 600-page Constantine-Yourdon "orange monster" to learn about coupling and cohesion and were overwhelmed by the vocabulary. And while structured programming quickly permeated the curriculum of even high school programming courses, structured analysis and design were often reserved for computer science graduate students. Even today many CASE vendors strongly urge their customers to attend a three-day training course on the structured techniques in order to understand how to use their products.

But the mystique can't last forever; there are already signs that the structured techniques are being communicated to the masses. Universities are now teaching structured analysis and design at the freshman level; a few schools in New York and Chicago are teaching structured design in eleventh and twelfth grades. Remember, long division was a college subject in the Middle Ages.

Scenario 3: Complete automation of systems development, eliminating programmers

This, of course, is the dream of CASE vendors. In 1988 I wrote that we didn't have it then and that we probably wouldn't have full, automated code generation for another five years. In 1991 it is clear that a few vendors (notably Texas Instruments) can generate complete code from their CASE tools—as long as you are willing to live with COBOL and to limit yourself to a fairly narrow range of hardware and software platforms for your target system. But even where code generation is possible, most software engineers still want to see the code because they don't completely trust the quality of the generator, and they know that they'll have to do their debugging at the language level rather than at the diagram level. So it may well be another five years before we can consider the automation activity acceptably complete in the CASE industry.

Even when this happens, all that will be eliminated is the need to know something about structured design and structured programming. We will still need some form of systems analysis (be it structured or otherwise), because we will still have to provide the CASE tool with a description of the user's requirements.

Or will we? Another scenario that I predicted in 1988 (and for which due credit was given at the time to Rich Carpenter of Index Technology), was that CASE vendors would begin developing libraries of "templates" of generic systems. You want a payroll system? Rather than starting from scratch, why not use a set of DFDs, ERDS, and STDs for a generic payroll system that you could modify to meet the idiosyncrasies of your organization? When finished, you would have a complete "requirements model" of your own customized payroll system, which the CASE tool could turn into COBOL.

In 1991, this is still more a vision than a reality: Andersen Consulting was widely praised for introducing a CASE template called CUSTOMER/I for customer information systems, and other CASE vendors announced major efforts at creating reusable templates. But the practical results are far less impressive than, say, the use of class libraries in the OO world.

Scenario 4: Decreased development of new systems and the dominance of maintenance

Structured techniques have been applied primarily to the analysis, design, and development of new systems. But between 50 and 80% of the work done in most DP organizations is maintenance of old systems. General systems theory tells us that as an organism grows larger, more of its resources have to be devoted to maintenance: consider how much time dinosaurs had to spend each day just feeding themselves.

In 1988 I suggested that it would not be unreasonable to expect the Fortune 500 companies to spend 90% of their resources maintaining existing information systems by the early 1990s. If only 10% of the resources are devoted to building new systems, who cares about structured analysis? Indeed, structured analysis and design could disappear entirely if those few new systems are developed using 4GLs (see scenario 6).

This 1988 technology prediction appears to have been dead wrong: maintenance seems to have leveled off in most organizations. Capers Jones, software statistician par excellence, points out in his new book (Jones 1991) that the overall maintenance level in the software industry has not reached the dramatic levels of 80 to 90% that I feared.

Maybe that is due to another major technology trend that I observed in 1988, and that nobody on the planet could have overlooked—the continuing evolution of hardware technology. Hardware technology predictions for the next ten years still point to improvements of between a thousand to a million times beyond today's technology. We have historical evidence of this, of course, all through the 1960s, '70s, and '80s. Al Cutaia (1990), in his landmark book, provided detailed estimates of the ongoing advance of technology through the 1990s.

As hardware becomes dramatically more powerful, many large organizations will simply continue operating as they have and enjoy the advantages of being able to do things faster and cheaper. Thus, in the 1990s, there will still be a few IBM 1401 programs emulated and simulated on supercomputers. There will still be many second-generation sequential file-batch programs, and there will be countless online transaction-processing systems based on the concept of, as John Landry put it in a 1988 speech, presenting "dumb forms" to a dumb user at a dumb terminal.

Gradually, end users in large organizations—ranging from senior management to clerks and administrators—all begin to find profoundly new uses for these computers. They will discover new products, new businesses, new markets, and new ways of organizing and communicating. Just as the desktop PC revolutionized the business world of the 1980s, so the supercomputer of the 1990s, superpowerful, supercheap, and superminiaturized, will bring about radical changes.

Those radical changes, whatever they are, will inevitably create a need for new information systems—systems that cannot be patched together from odd bits and pieces of existing systems. Today's systems might continue to run or they might be scrapped, but new systems will be built in any case. To the extent that this is true, we will still need some form of software engineering—structured techniques, perhaps, or (more likely) object-oriented techniques—to build the new systems.

There is yet another possibility: not only will today's information systems be scrapped, but the organizations that built them might also be scrapped. Dinosaurs died because they couldn't adapt to changes in environment, and old Fortune 500 companies might suffer the same fate. It is quite possible that the systems developed to run on the new supercomputers will be built by new companies, and those new companies won't use classical structured techniques. They will follow scenarios 5 or 6.

Scenario 5: Replacement of idiosyncratic, one-of-a-kind systems with generic, vendor-supplied systems that can be tailored by the user

In 1988, I raised the following questions: If you were going to start a company tomorrow, from scratch, would you write your own payroll system? Would you design and code your own accounting system? Would you even consider hiring programmers to design and code a payroll or an accounting system for you? Obviously not! If you're going to start the Frummel Manufacturing Company, why on earth would you want to hire programmers or systems analysts? All they do is take up space and consume our precious supply of oxygen.

The paradigm for starting a new business today is fundamentally different from what it was over the last three decades. The reason for this is partly the appearance, around 1985, of sufficiently powerful (286-class and above) PCs with adequate, affordable hard disk storage. Along with the desktop PC, there appeared a potpourri of office automation technology, such as fax machines, Xerox machines, laser printers, smart phone systems, and local area networks (LANs), that makes it possible for a new business to run a fully automated office, and ultimately fully automated information systems, with little or no need for clerks, administrators, or secretaries.

By contrast, in the 1970s, office automation in a new business often consisted of nothing more sophisticated than an electric typewriter. When Toni and I started Yourdon inc. in 1974, we thought we were very advanced because, in addition to a 1966 IBM Selectric typewriter, we had a handheld calculator purchased from Hewlett-Packard for the outrageous sum of $600. The new-business paradigm of the 1970s inevitably required paper-based information systems: the profusion of paper required a small army of clerical and administrative people to type it, file it, stamp it, process it, send it out, log it in, and so forth.

And—this is the critical point—such a small army of people forms a tribal culture, and the tribal culture develops its own idiosyncrasies. (We also learned at Yourdon inc. that the tribal culture often has less to do with the fundamental business of the company than with the personalities of the people in the office.) The internal, day-to-day business policies and procedures of small company A are often totally different from the policies and procedures of small company B, even if both are in the same industry.

Sooner or later, the small business grows to the point where it needs a computer (or where it can afford the luxury of a computer). In our case, it occurred in 1976, two years after the formation of the business. But two years is long enough to develop a rich, complex culture and a mind-numbing array of peculiarities, special cases, and exceptions. If you're going to automate the business at that point, you generally end up automating the peculiarities and exceptions, too.

Thus the automated information system of medium-sized company A looks quite different from the automated information system of medium-sized company B. Each is a customized, one-of-a-kind system, built from scratch by a horde of programmers and systems analysts. If this is true of relatively small companies that have been in business for only a few years, imagine how much more difficult it is to automate the business policies of a century-old business, whose tribal folklore of idiosyncrasies is so rich and so subtle that much of it cannot even be articulated. And because it can't be articulated, structured techniques are required to provide abstract, graphical models of the business so everyone can communicate.

None of this is necessary for today's new business. At a modest cost, it can operate from day one with a full range of office automation technology. There's no need for a clerical army: with voice mail, fax machines, and word processors, the new business can sometimes escape hiring any clerical people. Thus no tribal culture, no idiosyncrasies.

Equally important, the new business can start up with vendor-supplied, generic application packages to handle the fundamental functions of payroll, order entry, invoicing, accounts receivable, accounts payable, general ledger, inventory control, and so on. These vendor-supplied packages have their own peculiarities and quirks, but more and more of them provide a facility for the user to tailor the package to his or her own needs. An example of this is SBT, a vendor that provides PC-based accounting software written in DBASE III. When you buy the software package, you get the DBASE III source code so you may tailor it to your heart's content.

Even if the application software packages couldn't be tailored, it wouldn't matter much: a small business in its formative stages can almost always adapt its policies and procedures to conform to the idiosyncrasies of the software package. And, during the past five years, there has been a definite trend for package vendors to release new versions of their software on an annual basis, with each version having more functionality, more flexibility, and better performance.

What does all this have to do with the structured techniques? Quite simply, it eliminates the need for them. If my business is conceptually simple, because it has few eccentricities and a nonexistent tribal culture, then I don't need abstract, graphical modeling tools to represent it. If I can buy a software package to carry out my information processing needs, I don't have to worry about structured design and structured programming.

None of this is relevant for most of the older Fortune 500 companies. On the other hand, remember that some Fortune 500 companies, such as Apple and Compaq, didn't even exist a decade ago. And these new companies have yet another reason for eliminating customized programming projects—they are growing too quickly to wait for an army of programmers to spend two years developing a system.

I'm not suggesting that General Motors and Exxon are going to disappear tomorrow or in the next decade. But it's important to remember that small, start-up companies have provided virtually all the new jobs in this country in the past ten years and that there has been a net loss of jobs in the larger companies. Small companies are going to play an increasingly important role in our society for the rest of this century. Some will grow to become Fortune 500 companies along the way, displacing dinosaur companies that will quietly disappear. And it's important to keep in mind that for many of those small companies, the structured techniques are an irrelevant anomaly of the idiosyncratic, elephantine systems.

Scenario 6: Replacement of the structured techniques by 4GL and powerful database management systems (DBMS)

If you do have to build a customized system from scratch, why not build it with a 4GL and a powerful (relational) database package? In 1988, I acknowledged that organizations like the New Jersey Department of Motor Vehicles had tried that with its on-line automobile registration system, and the inefficiencies of its 4GL had blown the system apart. But if it had hardware a million times more powerful than today's piggy machines, would the department have cared how many CPU cycles it was wasting?

In 1991 it is still questionable whether one can use a 4GL and a relational DBMS to build a high-volume transaction processing system. So for the next few years, the day-to-day operational systems at many banks, insurance companies, airline reservation operations, and the like, will continue to be built using COBOL and IMS and other archaic technologies. But it's a pretty safe bet that hardware technology will improve faster than the volume of transactions increases in these organizations.

The combination of fast PCs, better 4GLs, and more efficient LANs is making this a distinct possibility for an ever-increasing number of organizations. More and more systems will be built to run on desktop machines and to deal with modest numbers of transactions and processing requirements, and they will be built by end users who have neither the time nor the desire to draw DFDs.

Traditional Development Obsolete

For the systems developer, there are two worlds out there: the huge, old obsolete organizations, and the small, new start-up organizations.

In 1988 I suggested that if you were a programmer, systems analyst, or DP manager in an antiquated organization, and if your organization was still building large, complex, one-of-a-kind, transaction-processing systems with the Mongolian horde approach, maybe you could ignore everything I said. But I suggested that your days were numbered, and I still believe that. In the long run, these projects and the companies that build them are doomed, even though vast fortunes might be made and lost in the short term.

Competence in Autocoder, assembly language, and COBOL is no longer enough to guarantee that you'll have a job in this field in the 1990s. Unfortunately, the same is likely to be true of the structured techniques. The hot methodology for the '90s will be object-oriented. Actually, I believe the really hotshot skill for the next decade will be enterprise modeling—helping new, growing companies develop overall models of their businesses, from which information systems will be generated with no coding, no design, and no DFDs.

So, sayonara, once again, structured stuff. It was fun, but like our memories of the Berlin Wall, it's already beginning to fade.

Object-Oriented Design

Some call it revolution. Some prefer to think of it as evolution. Whatever you call it, something significant is going on in the object-oriented field. I believe that a discipline far more significant than just "object-oriented programming" is emerging, though the details aren't clear yet. In this section, I want to report on some research that Peter Coad and I have conducted and show you how we think a new object-oriented design paradigm will unfold.

Most of the object-oriented proponents are mucking about at the code level, communicating their ideas to one another in terms of Smalltalk, C++, or Eiffel: we refer to this group as the OOPLers because of their emphasis on Object-Oriented Programming Languages.

True, some of the OOPLers have begun to realize that if they want to work on large problems, it would be a good idea to carry out some kind of design before sitting down at their workstations and madly writing code. But what is object-oriented design (OOD)?

The entire object-oriented field (OOA, OOD, and OOP), is in the same state of turbulent evolution that the structured field underwent in the mid-'70s. A lot of good work has been going on in the OOP area for the last decade (though largely in ivory-tower research environments), just as a lot of good work was done by Dijkstra, Wirth, and Hoare in the structured programming field for years before the mainstream COBOL community heard about it. The transition from a code-level orientation to a design-level orientation and then to an analysis-level orientation, was marked by acerbic debates, conflicting terminology, and general confusion. The same seems to be true in the object-oriented field.

To get some additional insights and perspectives on OOD, Coad and I decided to gather together four of our more articulate and vociferous colleagues for a four-day brainstorming session in Coad's hometown of Austin. Other participants were Mike Rissman, a senior researcher at the Software Engineering Institute; Jeff McKenna, a Smalltalk consultant and editor of *Hotline on object-oriented technology*; Sam Adams, chief technology officer at Knowledge Systems, Inc., and a longtime Smalltalk programmer; and Hermann Schindler, a database designer and DB2 guru at Advanced Micro Devices. Each brought a different background and perspective to the meeting. We asked the participants to talk about the kinds of projects they work on and how they use the object-oriented paradigm to analyze, design, and implement their systems.

By the end of four days we were exhausted. We were also frustrated, for we had not answered all the questions we have about OOD. We did gain some valuable insights, and some "Aha's!" that helped us define a successful OOD methodology. The most important insights I got from the session concern:

- Teaching by example: the use of pattern languages
- The factors that affect the nature of design work
- Why OOPLers haven't seen the need for graphical models yet
- The nature of the analysis/design "twilight zone" for OOPLers
- The relationship of OOPLs and prototyping
- The importance of reusability
- The difference between SP/SD/SA and OOP/OOD/OOA
- The effect of small, fast OOPL projects on the learning curve

Teaching by Example: the Use of Pattern Languages

One of the most interesting ideas that came out of the brainstorming project was the notion of "pattern languages" for design. Rissman brought up the concept first, but everyone in the group referred to the same idea repeatedly using different terms: meta-models, domain models, and templates were three of the more common synonyms.

Rissman pointed out that his thoughts on pattern languages had been strongly influenced by the work of Christopher Alexander and his colleagues in a three-volume work (Alexander 1979), (Alexander, Ishikawa, and Silverstein 1977), (Alexander et al. 1975). Ironically, the work that Larry Constantine and I did in the 1970s in the structured design field was influenced by an earlier book by Alexander (1971).

Alexander and his colleagues are architects, and the thrust of their work is to help architects design villages and buildings. In *A pattern language* (Alexander et al. 1977), he suggests that buildings and towns are naturally designed from combinations of 253 "patterns."

All 253 patterns together form a language. They create a coherent picture of an entire region, with the power to generate such regions in a million forms, with infinite variety in all the details.

It is also true that any small sequence of patterns from this language is itself a language for a smaller part of the environment; and this small list of patterns is then capable of generating a million parks, paths, houses, workshops, or gardens.

For example, consider the following ten patterns:

- Private terrace on the street (140)
- Sunny place (161)
- Outdoor room (163)
- Six-foot balcony (167)
- Paths and goals (120)
- Ceiling height variety (190)
- Columns at the corners (212)
- Front door bench (242)
- Raised flowers (245)
- Different chairs (251)

This short list of patterns is itself a language: it is one of a thousand possible languages for a porch at the front of a house. One of us chose this small language to build a porch onto the front of his house.

Rissman's interpretation of this concept, with which McKenna and Adams enthusiastically agreed, was that we should not try to create designs "from scratch" for each new application. Instead, we should try to find a pattern that fits a broad class of problems. In Rissman's case, the class of problems was flight simulator systems for new-generation aircraft. Specific applications—for example, the flight simulator for the B-2 bomber—could be designed by looking at the required variations from the generic pattern.

This fits nicely into the concept of "application domain models" that Coad and I have been exploring. We believe that it should be possible to provide a handbook to system designers that says, "Look, if you're building a sales order entry system, you should expect to see these 20 basic classes of objects and the following class hierarchies. You might encounter some variations and extensions, but this is the general pattern."

In addition to a book that provides pictures of standard application patterns, why not have them built into a CASE product? The big question, of course, is, who invents these domain models? Alexander's theme is that patterns evolve naturally because the right patterns work, and the wrong patterns simply don't work. Indeed, I see this often in MIS organizations that build the same kind of application over and over again: a tribal folklore develops about the general pattern of the application. (Note, however, that if this were the full extent of the organization's software engineering sophistication, Watts Humphrey's process maturity model would characterize it as only a level 2 "repeatable" organization.)

Rissman warned that while an existing pattern can be stretched or modified to meet local circumstances, a major change in the scale or complexity of an application might cause serious problems. Inevitably, it will turn out that the old pattern cannot be successfully modified to fit the problem, and a new pattern must be found.

This situation brings me back to the same question—where does the new pattern, or *metamodel*, come from? After listening to our OOPL colleagues debate this question for several days, I think I might have stumbled upon a simple, but crucial, cultural difference between the OOPL community and the SA/SD/SP community: the OOPL community assumes that a pattern exists, and the job is merely to find it. The SA/SD/SP community, on the other hand, when faced with a problem that no longer fits into an old, familiar pattern, starts from scratch and tries to invent completely new solutions that might or might not fit a pattern. Why does this happen?

Why do OOPLers and SA/SD people work differently and approach problems differently? Why is their approach to patterns dissimilar? We tried to understand this by looking at some of the other issues affecting design.

The Factors that Affect the Nature of Design Work

It seems to me there are several key factors affecting the nature of design work.

The culture and politics of the organization

The Humphrey process model is one way of characterizing the difference between organizations. But OOPL development organizations, such as Adams's company, which builds all its applications in Smalltalk, have a very different culture from the typical SA/SD organization.

Because of the rich library of reusable components, there is a strong cultural tendency to approach new problems by saying, "How can we build this new system from things we already have?" This translates into the technical question, "What existing patterns (objects and class hierarchies) match, or almost match, the requirements of my system?" The SA/SD adherents know that reusability, like other Boy Scout virtues, is a good thing, but it's not a fundamental part of their culture.

The available implementation technology

Culture and technology go hand-in-hand. The library of reusable components used by the SA/SD community consists of individual, "atomic" modules. Sometimes, as in the case of the UNIX library, it is easy to see how modules can be connected and aggregated in useful ways. But this is a bottom-up process, which runs counter to the conventional wisdom of top-down decomposition.

The OOPL community, on the other hand, starts with a reusable library of high-level aggregates (class structures). This approach is typically neither top-down nor bottom-up but rather "design by exception." The question the OOPLers seem to ask themselves is: "What attributes and methods (services) do I need to extend, or override, or redefine in order to make this general class hierarchy of objects accomplish what I want it to do?"

The scale of the problem

There are several key differences between small-scale and large-scale systems. Small-scale systems typically have fewer hardware performance problems, so they can take advantage of 4GLs, OOPL technology, and the like. Equally important, they can be implemented by smaller teams, led by one person who can keep the entire "conceptual design" in his or her head. But perhaps most important, the large-scale systems are more likely to be perceived as one-of-a-kind systems by their designers. After all, who has ever built a Star Wars system before? What possible existing pattern could fit it? The small- and medium-scale systems are more likely to be the kind of systems that have been built before, so it's more likely that successful patterns exist for them.

The "distance" between the statement of requirements and the implementation of the requirements

One of the most difficult technical issues in the SA/SD world has always been the translation of a user-oriented SA model, involving an asynchronous network of DFD bubbles, into a technology-oriented SD model, involving a synchronous hierarchy of modules in a structure chart. This is because the "vocabulary" of a user requirements description is quite different from the vocabulary needed to describe the implementation of a system in a conventional 3GL.

For OOPLers, it appears that if you can describe the problem in a vocabulary that is natural to the users, you have also described the solution in a form that can be directly implemented in an OOPL. Coad and I have noticed, for example, that OOPLers have found the graphical notation we provided in our book, *Object-oriented analysis* useful for describing user requirements and the design of the system.

Why OOPLers Haven't Seen the Need for Graphical Models Yet

Because languages like Small talk and Eiffel are 10 to 100 times more powerful than are the conventional 3GLs, many of the programs and systems developed by OOPLers are only a few hundred or a few thousand lines of code. Hence, it appears that OOPLers communicate with one another about their design by actually looking at the code and reading it. Diagrams, or graphical models, do not have the mystical aura in the OOPL community that they have in the SA/SD community.

But I remember that on my first programming projects in the 1960s (the math library for a Fortran system and the assembler for the PDP-5 minicomputer), I didn't draw any diagrams either. I occasionally drew some cryptic pictures on the back of an envelope, but mostly I conceived of the solution to my problem in terms of my implementation technology (assembly language) and then started coding.

The key point today, I believe, is that the power of OOPLs allows a tiny group composed of two or three people to tackle projects that would have required 10 to 100 people and three to five years of effort in a 3GL environment. The tiny group doesn't need any pictures to communicate. What will happen when the experience of OOPLers on small projects (e.g., 1000 lines of Smalltalk) is scaled up to truly large systems requiring 10,000 to 100,000 lines of code? Sooner or later, noncoding issues will begin to dominate—the problem of precise, unambiguous communication between larger groups of developers and implementors, the problem of communicating with geographically separated users, and so forth. I believe that at this point, if not before, the need for graphical modeling tools will become increasingly apparent.

Christopher Alexander (1979) makes some interesting points about precision and diagrams:

> My experience has shown that many people find it hard to make their design ideas precise. They are willing to express their ideas in loose, general, terms, but are unwilling to express them with the precision needed to make them into patterns. Above all, they are unwilling to express them as abstract spatial relations among well-defined spatial parts. I have also found that people aren't always very good at it; it is hard to do. . . . If you can't draw a diagram of it, it isn't a pattern. If you think you have a pattern, you must be able to draw a diagram of it. This is a crude, but vital rule. A pattern defines a field of spatial relations, and it must therefore always be possible to draw a diagram for every pattern. In the diagram, each part will appear as a labeled or colored zone, and the layout of the parts expresses the relation which the pattern specifies. If you can't draw it, it isn't a pattern.

Sooner or later, the OOPL community will have to realize the same truth about large software designs: no matter how powerful Smalltalk may be, if you can't draw a precise picture of the pattern, it doesn't exist.

In an OOPL environment, the problem vocabulary and the implementation vocabulary are close enough that we might consider using the same graphical notation for OOA and OOD. This needs to be explored further, though. We might find that we require additional graphical notations to describe such things as the user-computer interface and the physical distribution of objects in a network.

The Nature of the Analysis/Design "Twilight Zone" for OOPLers

For people familiar with structured analysis and structured design, the transition from analysis to design may be difficult, but the distinction between the two is fairly clear. Indeed, the distinction might exist in their minds precisely because the transition is so difficult. Conversely, the OOPLers make much less distinction between the two. For them there is implementation, and then there is everything that precedes implementation.

Why the lack of distinction? Primarily because OOPLers combine the activities of analysis and design. As I listened to McKenna, Adams, and Rissman discuss how they had used an object-oriented approach on their typical projects, they bounced back and forth between issues that were clearly matters of user-specified requirements and issues that were clearly high-level implementation (design) issues. As I said, this is partly because OOPLers use a high-level implementation technology that allows them to think in terms of the user's vocabulary.

However, there are other reasons. In some cases, I fear that OOPLers are hackers of the worst kind, composing object-oriented code extemporaneously. Perhaps a more charitable way of saying this is that OOPLs come with such a powerful library and, at least in the case of Smalltalk, such a powerful development environment, that prototyping is remarkably easy. If you can build a real prototype just as quickly as you can draw a diagram that represents a formal design of your system, many people would choose the prototyping approach.

This has been further amplified by the small size (at least until now) of OOPL projects. A small project, combined with a very powerful implementation technology, means that one person is often sufficient to do the job. And in any situation where the same person does analysis, design, and coding, it has been difficult to separate the activities.

The Relationship between OOPLs and Prototyping

Why do OOPLers prototype? Because it's there. If you had powerful prototyping tools in your environment, wouldn't you use them? The more interesting question is: what use do OOPLers make of prototyping? The straightforward answer is: the same use that SA/SD developers do. They use it to build a working demonstration quickly in order to get feedback from the users. It gives them something to play with, something more real and tangible than a bunch of bubbles and boxes on a piece of paper.

I found that the veteran OOPLers go beyond this. They build prototypes to discover, early, where the hard parts of the system will be. As McKenna observed, "I try to find out what I don't know because I know that I can design and code what I do know." We need to explore this a little further because it suggests that object-oriented techniques might have been more successful than SA/SD on projects with ambiguous requirements, where it's very difficult to write a formal, precise statement of user requirements.

There is a more significant question: how does OOD help the developer discover more quickly what he really knows about the problem and what he doesn't? It may just be that OOPL environments provide faster and more powerful prototyping facilities than a 4GL does. Or it may be something more profound: by getting users and developers to think about the encapsulated combination of data and functions, it's possible that difficult, ambiguous aspects will come to the surface more quickly.

The Importance of Reusability

Reusability seems to be the golden word in the OOPL community, much as *cohesion* was the buzzword with structured design, and *essential (logical) model* was a buzzword with structured analysis. All OOPLers talk about the benefit of reusability, and, to their credit, they seem to take advantage of the concept with a vengeance. But reusability is a subtle and complex concept, and I believe we need more research to understand how OOPLers use reusability differently from SA/SD people.

For instance, I haven't discovered how the OOPL community justifies spending more time on a project to create new reusable components for a library. An automobile could be defined as an instance of class VEHICLE. Alternatively, one could define a new subclass *automobile* of class *vehicle*, with additional subclass attributes such as *operating-cost-per-mile*. Whether it is easier to do this in an OOPL environment than in an SA/SD environment is not the issue—the issue is whether the developer will spend the time thinking about the potential value of having a new subclass called *automobile*.

I also haven't figured out how the OOPL community solves the configuration management problem associated with a reusable library. For example, suppose my high-level *vehicle* class has an attribute of *weight*. The inheritance concept means that any subclass below *automobile* also has an attribute of *weight* unless it has been overridden or redefined. Now suppose I decide to change the definition of weight from pounds to kilograms. Is it any easier to gauge the impact of this change on all the subclasses of *vehicle* than it would be to gauge the impact of a similar change to a system developed with SA/SD techniques?

The Difference between SP/SD/SA and OOP/OOD/OOA

What, then, is the difference between the way "structured" people develop systems and the way "object" people develop systems? The differences are greater than some would suggest and less than others would believe. I don't know if it is useful to delineate the differences in detail, especially since there seem to be such emotional arguments from each camp about the stubbornness of the other camp.

During our brainstorming sessions, for example, McKenna and Adams complained that some prominent members of the SA/SD community (for example, Steve Mellor, Paul Ward, Meilir Page-Jones, Steve Weiss, and Dave Bulman) are trying to "objectify" their designs by first drawing data flow diagrams, and then gathering a bunch of bubbles around a common data store and calling each assembled bubble bunch an object.

"The problem is," they said, "that they first think about the problem in functional terms and then make a cosmetic effort to change the model to make it look like it's object-oriented! So they really look at the problem from a very different perspective than we do."

They were equally critical of data modelers, whose ERD models describe objects and relationships, but say nothing about the processing functions/methods/services that are to be carried out.

Yet when Coad and I asked the OOPLers to tell us how they develop a design of their various applications, the diagrams they drew to explain their work often turned out to be thinly disguised data flow diagrams! Adams also recommended the use of a "subsystem message flow diagram" that he had picked up from a General Electric software engineer, Frank Cubbage. This, too, turned out to be a data flow diagram. Attempts to convince McKenna and Adams of the true nature of the diagrams they were drawing were met with much skepticism.

Why bother arguing about design notation? Because notation (drawings) is one of the three major components of a design methodology: the other two are criteria for evaluating the goodness or badness of a design and "cookbook" strategies for creating designs.

The nature of a diagram has a strong influence on how one looks at a problem. Thus, the OOPLers argue that most SA/SD developers use data flow diagrams or structure charts as their major modeling tool and inevitably view the systems they build from a functional point of view.

But SA and SD are more than just diagramming techniques. A major component of SD, for example, is a collection of guidelines and criteria for evaluating different candidate designs for a system. This presupposes that there is more than one possible design to correctly implement some well-defined problem. I asked my OOPL colleagues if the same was true in their world. "Well, yes, of course," they replied. "There are many different ways to design a system in Smalltalk or C++ to solve a problem." So whether one works in an SA/SD world or an OOA/OOD world, one must eventually deal with the same question: How do you tell the good designs from the bad designs?

SA/SD practitioners are familiar with the concepts of coupling and cohesion as a way of evaluating intermodule and intramodule connections. They know that the guidelines of "span of control" and "scope-of-effect/scope-of-control" are useful ways of evaluating the morphology, or shape, or a hierarchy of modules.

Lo and behold! There are highly analogous criteria for evaluating an OOD design! Coupling and cohesion, span of control, and various other guidelines are just as meaningful, but there may be more "dimensions" to consider than in the SA/SD world—methods, classes, inheritance, messages, and collaboration among objects.

The Impact of Small, Fast OOPL Projects on the Learning Curve

A final insight from Adams was particularly fascinating for me. As he pointed out, the rapid prototyping and high productivity aspects of an OOPL like Smalltalk mean that a typical OOPLer works on 10 to 12 projects a year. This is in stark contrast to the experience of a typical SA/SD developer, who often works on the same project for two or three years.

"The result," Adams says, "is that an OOPLer's experiences are amplified. If he tries a design approach that works, he's likely to repeat that experience a dozen times in a year. If he tries something that basically doesn't work, he'll have that experience repeated several times within a matter of months. It's a lot easier to remember what you did on the last project." Adams went on to say that in his experience, it was only after the third time he built a particular kind of application that he felt he had really gotten the design "right."

Perhaps this is one reason OOPLers are more comfortable with the concept of looking for an existing pattern from which to generate new systems. If you build only three payroll systems in the course of a decade, each one at a different company, it's easy to treat each project as a unique experience. For OOPLers, the third project occurs within the first year, and by then you've got it right. After that, it's merely a matter of repetition.

Conclusion

What practical use can you make of this brainstorming effort in your shop? If you're already deeply entrenched in the object-oriented world, you may be tempted to discuss all this as the sniveling of an old bubble-drawer.

There are two fundamental messages you should be able to extract from this chapter:

1. A significant part of the OOPLers' success occurs because the OOPLs themselves are so powerful that a medium-sized system can be built by one or two people. But today's success can breed tomorrow's problems. What happens when OOPLs are used on huge projects that require Mongolian hordes of people? I have seen or heard of Smalltalk systems involving 5000 lines of code, or 15,000 lines of code, but nothing yet involving 500,000 lines of code.

   "But that would be equivalent to 5 million lines of COBOL!" you reply in dismay? My response is, "Right! And systems that large are beginning to be built!" So the OOPL community should try to learn whatever it can from the grizzled old SA/SD veterans (and from a generation or two earlier, as well) about the non-code-related problems of building truly huge systems.

2. The OOPL community and the SA/SD community actually do have some things in common. They may look at systems from a different perspective, and they may use different kinds of good systems. Some ideas about coupling and cohesion that were well articulated by the SA/SD camp can be borrowed by the OOPLers and re-expressed in their own vocabulary. This needs to be done, for most of the OOD work Coad and I have seen so far is highly informal.

And if your software engineer or data processing manager is from the "old school," wondering how to get ready for the brave new world of the object-oriented 1990s, I think there are some practical lessons to be learned:

■ It should be evident from this chapter that there are a number of deep intellectual issues surrounding the OOA/SA and OOD/SD schism. My impression is that the OOD methodology state-of-the-art is at the same level of maturity and stability as structured design was in the mid-1970s or structured analysis was in the mid-1980s.

   You don't get to be object-oriented just by switching your programming language. A COBOL shop is not likely to switch to Smalltalk overnight, though a number of scientific/engineering/systems shops are switching from older 3GLs to languages such as C++ and Ada. You can't just buy a book and send your designers through a course and get "objectified." If you're serious about making a switch from the structured camp to the object-oriented camp, consider having a brainstorming session with some of the more thoughtful and articulate people in your organization.

■ Just as the OOPLers need to worry about the problems they will face in the future when they work on large-scale projects, you should think about the qualitative benefits you can get from a technology that allows medium-size, real-world systems to be built by one or two people. Fred Brooks (1975) stressed the importance of maintaining the "conceptual integrity" of a design by ensuring that one or two "chief programmers" understood the entire design of even a large system. OOPLs combined with OOD and OOA may make it possible for the average software engineer to maintain the conceptual integrity of moderate-sized systems in his brain.

- While reusability is universally recognized as a great idea, the reality is that the SA/SD community has rarely, if ever, put the concept into practice. It's convenient to find a number of excuses for this or to blame it all on management, but perhaps it's time to admit that reusability will never be implemented in a practical way in an SA/SD world.

    I'm not ready to admit this personally because I believe that CASE tools offer the possibility of reusability at the design and requirements level. But I also believe that every DP manager has an obligation to look at his or her organization and ask whether reusability could be more easily accomplished in an OOD/OOPL environment.

- The OOPLers have shown us the power of using existing patterns, of looking at new systems as minor variations of existing systems. By watching how easily and naturally they construct systems, they suggest that the facility for recognizing patterns is within us all. Pattern languages for building software systems are just a small part of a larger phenomenon of patterns in our lives. As Christopher Alexander observes (1979):

    If I consider my lifestyle, I see that it is governed by a certain very small number of patterns of events which I take part in over and over again.

    Being in bed, having a shower, having breakfast in the kitchen, sitting in my study writing, walking in the garden, cooking and eating our common lunch at my office with my friends, going to the movies, taking my family to eat at a restaurant, having a drink at a friend's house, driving on the freeway, and going to bed again. There are a few more.

    There are surprisingly few of these patterns of events in any one person's way of life, perhaps no more than a dozen. Look at your own life and you will find the same situation. It is shocking, at first, to see that there are so few patterns of events open to me.

    Not that I want more of them. But when I see how very few of them there are, I begin to understand what huge effects these few patterns have on my life, on my capacity to live. If these few patterns are good for me, I can live well. If they are bad for me, I can't.

Note: This chapter was composed of excerpts from the November 1991 and March 1990 issues of *American Programmer*, of which Mr. Yourdon is Publisher and Editor-in-Chief.

Author Biography

Edward Yourdon is an independent management consultant, and is widely known as the developer of the "Yourdon method" of structured systems analysis and design. He is the publisher of *American Programmer*, a software journal that analyzes software technology trends in the United States and several other countries around the world.

Mr. Yourdon has worked in the computer industry for nearly 30 years, including positions with Digital Equipment Corporation and General Electric. He has worked on over 25 mainframe computers, and has been involved in a number of pioneering computer projects, and is currently deeply immersed in research in new developments in software engineering, such as object-oriented software development.

In 1974, Mr. Yourdon founded his own consulting firm, Yourdon inc., to provide educational, publishing, and consulting services in state-of-the-art software engineering technology. Over the next 12 years, the company grew to a staff of over 150 people, with offices throughout North America and Europe. As Chairman and CEO of the company, he oversaw an operation that trained over 250,000 people in major companies and government agencies around the world. The publishing division, Yourdon Press (now part of Prentice Hall), has produced over 100 technical computer books on object-oriented analysis, structured analysis, structured design and a wide range of other software engineering topics; many of these classics are used as standard university computer science textbooks. In 1986, Mr. Yourdon sold his company and returned to private consulting practice.

Ed Yourdon is the author of over 150 technical articles and has also written 18 computer books. His most recent books are Object-oriented analysis (1990), and Object-oriented design (1991). He is a regular keynote speaker at major computing conferences around the world. He holds a B.S. in Applied Mathematics from MIT.

Works Cited

Alexander, Christopher. 1971. *Notes on the synthesis of form.* 2d ed. Cambridge, Ma.: Harvard University Press.

Alexander, Christopher et al. 1975. *The Oregon experiment.* New York, N.Y.: Oxford Press.

Alexander, Christopher et al. 1977. *A pattern language.* New York, N.Y.: Oxford Press.

Alexander, Christopher. 1979. *The timeless way of building.* New York, N.Y.: Oxford Press.

Brown, Fred. 1975. *The mythical man-month.* Reading, Ma.: Addison-Wesley.

Clark, Arthur C. 1984. *Profiles of the future.* Holt, Rinehart, and Winston.

Cutaia, Al. 1990. *Technology projection modeling of future computer systems.* Prentice Hall.

Jones, Capers. 1991. *Applied software measurement.* McGraw-Hill.

McMenamin, Steve and J. Palmer. 1984. *Essential systems analysis.* Yourdon Press/Prentice Hall.

Yourdon, Edward and L. Constantine. 1979. *Structured design.* Yourdon Press/Prentice Hall.

7

Improving Software Engineering Practice
The Challenge of Technology Transition

by Roger S. Pressman, Ph.D.

Introduction

Cultures never appear and disappear overnight. They evolve over a long period of time—an entrenched culture slowly giving way to some new set of traditions, habits, and rules. Over the past 40 years, we have seen the growth, entrenchment, and slow decline of the first software-development culture. Today, a second software development culture, software engineering, is slowly displacing the first, but not without resistance and trauma. Cultural change is never easy.

In the 1950s and 1960s, a set of traditions, habits, and rules coalesced to form a culture for software development. Programming was an art form, performed by the anointed few who worked behind closed doors to produce "code." Few outsiders really understood software or the process through which it was created. Each programmer applied an ad hoc approach.

In fact, if a more disciplined approach to programming was discussed, the conversation often went something like this: "Specification? Why bother, we'll fill in the details as we go. Prototyping? Who has the time? Besides, we understand what the customer wants. Design? I do that while I'm coding. Testing? Sure, we'll whip up a few test cases and show that the program works. Documentation. What for? We'll be around to answer questions."

More than a few of us look at those early days with fondness. It was the "wild west" of computing, and in fairness, some excellent work was accomplished; but times change. Projects have gotten larger and more complex. Schedules have contracted. Teams, rather than individuals, build systems.

The first rumblings of a second culture for software development began in the late 1960s. An art form was to be displaced by an engineering discipline. Distinct methods, procedures, and tools were to replace coding as the operative mechanism for building applications and computer-based systems. Software engineering was born. But the entrenched culture—the programming culture—has not completely disappeared. Most software professionals and their managers recognize that change is in the wind. But many think the challenges of software engineering are only technological, and they are wrong. The challenges are also cultural.

Making the First Move: Common Questions

Technological and cultural change both begin with recognition. We must first recognize that problems serious enough to warrant change do exist. Next, we must recognize that practical solutions are available. Finally, we must recognize that technological solutions often result in cultural changes. When faced with a new technology and a new culture, it is natural to have a few questions. It might be worthwhile to examine some of the more common management questions.

We are very set in our ways, is change really possible? The modis operandi of every software development organization appears to be cast in concrete. The fact is that organizations change regularly: new tools, new people, new policies, new products and applications, and even new organizational structures are commonplace in the software-development community. Even if your organization is "set in its ways," a move toward a software engineering culture (and the changes it portends) is often essential for the continued production of high-quality systems. Change is certainly possible, but only if both managers and technical staff take a systematic approach to it.

We're going a million miles an hour, how can we make the time? This question is often asked by managers of young, high-technology companies that are growing at a precipitous rate, or in large, well-established companies that are experiencing a significant growth in software demand. It is true that rapid growth stretches resources to the limit. But it is also true that rapid growth exacerbates any underlying software development problems that do exist. The need for change becomes more important.

OK, we have to change, what do we do first? If this question is asked, the first thing has already been done—the speaker has recognized that change is required. Once the decision to change has been made, many managers and most technical people feel that immediate action is necessary. Although a "bias for action" is commendable, the road to a new software engineering culture must be viewed as a journey with many steps. Before beginning the journey, you must understand where you are now. Understanding your current location is the first thing that you should do.

We've worked hard to develop internal standards and procedures, isn't that enough? Although standards and procedures can help to guide technological change, they are not enough. Many software development organizations have fallen into an "S&P trap." That is, they have expended time and resources developing voluminous standards and procedures documents that few staff members understand or use. Just because an approach to software development has been codified, that does not guarantee it will be followed.

Should technological change be driven from the top down or from the bottom up? When successful technological change occurs, it usually occurs in a way that might best be called a "sandwich." Senior management establishes goals and provides resources, driving the process from the top down. At the same time, technical staff obtain education and apply methods and tools driving the process from the bottom up. Both meet in the middle.

Software engineering requires a new approach and a substantial learning curve, won't this cause upheaval? It is true that cultural change can cause upheaval if it is not managed properly. Therefore, our primary goal in implementing change is to do it in a manner that does not negatively impact the progress of ongoing projects. In a later section we discuss a strategy for implementing change that will minimize upheaval while at the same time having a reasonable likelihood of success.

What about project managers, won't they resist? If software engineering is viewed as a destabilizing influence, project managers will resist it. To gain the support of project managers, we must look at software engineering from their point of view and ask "what's in it for me?" The answer is simple—control. Software engineering procedures, methods, and tools will improve the manager's ability to control a project, something that every manager desires. Once the project manager recognizes this benefit, resistance will disappear.

Money is always tight, how do I get resource commitment from management? Too many requests for resources (to be allocated to software engineering transition) continue to use the "trust me" school of justification. That is, a request for resources attempts to sell middle and senior management on the overall qualitative benefits of new software engineering technology, without translating these benefits to the bottom line. Although this approach sometimes works, it is being viewed with increasing skepticism by many senior managers. For this reason, it is necessary to develop concrete measures of the software development process and establish an historical baseline that will enable quantitative justification to be made.

Why can't we just buy some good CASE tools and leave the rest alone? Any power tool can be a wonderful thing. Whether you are cutting wood, washing dishes or building computer software, a power tool can improve the quality of your work and the productivity with which you do it. But this is true only if you understand the methods and procedures that must be applied to use the tool properly. If a power tool is used without an understanding of the underlying procedures and methods, it can be both unproductive and even dangerous. Most of us wouldn't use a large chain-saw without first understanding the procedures and methods that guide its use. Few people would attempt to wash socks in a dishwasher. Yet, many software developers attempt to use sophisticated CASE tools with little more than a passing understanding of software engineering methods and procedures. Then, they wonder why "these tools" don't work for us.

Changing Technical Cultures

We have already noted that recognition is the first step toward cultural change. The next steps are a bit more complicated. Every software development organization has options when it comes to software engineering. These are sometimes so confusing that a paralysis sets in and no decision is made. But in other situations, management does make a decision. The following represent the most common responses:

Do nothing. After recognizing that change is required, management and technical staff may decide to do nothing, hoping that problems will fix themselves or that "we can continue like this for a few more years." In the software business, problems rarely cure themselves; in fact, problems (e.g., on-time delivery, questionable quality, poor maintainability) tend to become amplified as time passes.

Dictate change. Management has seen the light and then decides that the "techies will get on board or else." This dictatorial approach rarely works because technical staff must make the technology happen. Unless practitioners support software engineering, they will not apply it enthusiastically and can (in extreme circumstances) work to subvert it.

Push from the bottom. Practitioners often recognize the benefits of software engineering methods, procedures, and tools, and attempt to make the technology happen by trying to convince management that money should be spent. This is a reasonable approach if practitioner's efforts raise management consciousness, but it results in frustration if management provides no support or if dollars are spent with little planning.

Be systematic. The most successful adopters of software engineering have established a game plan for cultural and technological change and then executed it. They have recognized that the plan must be revisited frequently, that changes and iteration are likely, and that small failures will accompany successes. But through it all, a systematic approach is maintained.

Companies often begin the process of software engineering technology transfer by starting in the wrong place; they iterate endlessly, become frustrated, and stop, only to restart with a new team of people who repeat the mistakes of their predecessors. Sometimes, management will become frustrated and stop, never to restart, and thereby lose the benefits of software engineering technology. Most companies run into trouble because they take a relatively disorganized approach to the integration of software engineering. An organized, systematic approach is the only viable alternative.

An Implementation Life Cycle

A systematic approach to software engineering cultural transition begins not with a selection of new tools or methods, but rather with self-assessment. It proceeds through a series of steps that you can use to integrate software engineering and CASE effectively within your company. These steps form a software engineering implementation life cycle. The five steps that make up this life cycle are discussed in the paragraphs below.

Assessment

In many software development organizations, managers and technical staff are all too anxious to make technical decisions—to select technical methods and/or new CASE tools and then proceed at a rapid rate toward "modern" software development practice. The problem is that many of these same managers and technical people have a weak understanding of methods, tools, and procedures that are currently being applied within their organizations. Because of this they proceed without a good foundation, without understanding what needs to be changed and what can be left alone. To paraphrase Waterman and Peters in *In Search of Excellence*, these individuals take a "ready, fire, aim" approach!

The first thing that must be done as an organization moves toward the integration of software engineering technology is to "look in the mirror." That is, before you worry about technology transfer, take a hard look at your current software development practices.

The term assessment refers to both qualitative and quantitative information gathering. The methods that are currently being applied to develop software must be explicitly identified. In addition, the procedural context into which any methods are being applied, the tools that are being used, the modes of communication between customers and software developers, the amount of training that is provided to both technical practitioners and management staff, and many other issues must be considered. The understanding gained from a portion of an assessment establishes a qualitative foundation for decision making that must occur as culture transition takes place.

In addition to qualitative information, it is important to gather quantitative data—metrics that measure software productivity and quality on past projects. These data provide support for the justification of expenditures for software engineering and CASE and establish a baseline for comparison once change has been initiated.

I have found that an effective method for accomplishing information gathering is a software engineering process assessment that focuses on both qualitative and quantitative information. The process assessment makes use of a questionnaire that helps to organize the assessment step and allows you to gather specific information on the topics that I have mentioned above. There are three sources that can provide you with a list of appropriate questions. The first set of questions will help to you determine whether "the time is right" for change. The second set of questions will provide you with detailed technical insight into your organization and the technology that it applies. The third set will enable you to compare the current status of software engineering at your company against established norms.

A first set of questions. Barbara Bouldin (1989) suggests a set of ten initial questions that will help you to determine whether you should proceed with technological change:

1. Is your organization newly formed?
2. Are the functions your organization performs new to your organization?
3. Is your organization growing at a reasonably rapid rate?
4. Is your organization responsible for the development of new systems?
5. Is there a general attitude of optimism, and is morale high?
6. Is your technical staff utilizing tools or methods that improve productivity?
7. Does your management support the concept of productivity in any way?

8. Is your staff experiencing motivation problems?

9. Is your staff responsible for mature systems that are primarily in the maintenance mode?

10. Does your organization have a backlog of user (or customer) requests?

Bouldin argues that a positive response to the first five questions followed by a negative response to the last five should convince you to wait because your organization may need to mature a bit before the benefits can be properly recognized. A mixed response (yes/no) to all ten questions should lead to "soul-searching" with the decision to proceed based on other extenuating circumstances. A positive response to the last five questions is a key indicator that change should occur.

A second set of questions.   The second source of questions for a software engineering process assessment is contained in my book (Pressman 1988). The book contains a comprehensive questionnaire with more than 100 questions that focus on many aspects of software development practice within your organization. The categories queried include the following:

1. Company profile and business strategy

2. The role of software in the client's business

3. Software/hardware engineering organization

4. Interdepartmental issues

5. Staff characteristics

6. Software standards and procedures

7. Project case histories

8. Software problem areas (management view)

9. Software problem areas (technical view)

10. Software development strengths

11. Software documentation

12. Methodology issues

13. Reviews

14. Software products and pricing

15. Software acquisition

16. Software development tools

17. Supplementary data

18. Quantitative metrics

This list of questions is complemented by a "quasi-expert system" for evaluating the information gathered through the questionnaire. The quasi-expert system provides an explanation of the rationale for each question, an indication of likely responses, suggestion for next steps based on each response, and a set of second-level questions that can be used to uncover additional detail for targeted areas of concern.

A third set of questions.　The Software Engineering Institute (SEI), sponsored by the U.S. Department of Defense, and located at Carnegie Mellon University in Pittsburgh, Pennsylvania, has developed a comprehensive Software Process Maturity Questionnaire. The SEI questionnaire contains queries that expect "yes/no/don't know" responses. Topics covered include the following:

- Organization

  —Policies
  —Resources
  —Oversight
  —Communication
  —Training

- Project Management

  —Planning
  —Progress monitoring
  —Project control
  —Subcontract management

- Process Management

  —Process definition
  —Execution
  —Analysis
  —Process control
  —Process improvement

The responses to the SEI questionnaire can be "graded" to provide an organization with an indication of software process maturity and technology sophistication. Process maturity is graded on a scale of 1 to 5, where a grade of 1 implies an organization with a poorly defined software development process, and a grade of 5 suggests a high degree of control over the software development process that includes optimal management practices, good quality assurance procedures, and effective measurement.

No matter which questions are used, the bottom line is this: gather enough information so that you can gain an understanding of your organization, the application of technology within it, and the relative sophistication of the technology that is being applied. Without a detailed look in the mirror, your probability for success in the application of subsequent steps will drop dramatically.

The assessment step is only an entry point to the implementation life cycle. Once we have looked in the mirror, it is necessary to proceed towards the acquisition and installation of methods, procedures, and tools. However, before we can do this, it is important to establish a framework. Education is a key building block.

The education step

Most software developers know relatively little about software engineering. Although developers build software every day, they often use an ad hoc approach that has changed little since the 1960s. Detailed knowledge of modern methods, software engineering paradigms, and tools (including CASE) is inadequate.

Many managers view software engineering education as a perquisite. Rather than being viewed as a necessary activity that must be conducted to support the development staff, education is viewed as a reward to be offered only when work load is light, times are good, and projects are on schedule. The irony is that we often fall behind schedule on projects because people don't have an understanding of software engineering methods that might keep them on schedule. And because the project is behind schedule, staff members "don't have the time" to obtain training. In too many companies, software development staff receive fewer than three days of software engineering methods training per year. Although educational needs vary, a good rule of thumb is that software engineering staff should receive at least one, and as many as three weeks of methods education during the time required to achieve technology transition.

It is important to understand that education can take many forms. The most common is classroom instruction, conducted on-site or through public course offerings. However, other modes of education are also valuable. For example, video-based education in software engineering can prove especially useful when tight project schedules do not allow staff members to spend long periods of time away from the office or when new staff are being hired over a rather long period of time. Although video-based education does not contain the interactive element that is particularly beneficial in classroom work, it still provides a useful mode of information transfer.

In addition to formal modes of education delivery, a software engineering library should be established within the software development organization. For an expenditure of $5000 to $10,000, an organization can establish a reasonably comprehensive collection of textbooks and periodicals that serves to supplement formal education.

All education mechanisms send a set of important signals to practitioners. First, education tells them that software engineering is deemed important by management and that management is willing to commit resources to improve their technical capabilities. Second, it provides all staff members with a consistent source of information that can be translated into practical use. Third, it provides a foundation from which methods, procedures, and CASE can be selected and effectively applied. Last, it helps to "sell" the change of culture that comes as a result of greater knowledge.

So the next time you hear the complaint, "We don't have the time to educate," remember that a lack of education has likely caused the situation that doesn't allow you the time. If you think education is expensive (in time and dollars), consider the cost of ignorance!

The selection step

In the context of the software implementation life cycle, the selection step is three things: (1) an understanding of available methods, procedures, and tools for software engineering practice; (2) the definition of goals and criteria for selection of methods, procedures and tools; and (3) a rational mechanism for choosing, justifying and acquiring methods, procedures and tools.

The selection process is often confusing. A vast array of methods, procedures, and tools are available to the industry and the differences between them are often subtle. However, once the assessment and education steps have been conducted, the specific criteria required to make appropriate choices can be more easily targeted.

Technical criteria for selection of software engineering and CASE are important, but overall management goals are even more important. These goals are always the same—quality and productivity. Each technical criterion that is developed for the selection of a method, procedure, or tool should be traceable to one or both of these goals. If it is not, it should be rejected.

As the selection step proceeds, it will become necessary to present management with a detailed justification for the tools to be acquired, and the expenses to be associated with implementation of methods and procedures. To develop a believable justification, it is necessary to collect data from past projects to establish a baseline from which productivity and quality projections can be made. The following steps provide useful guidelines for effective justification:

1. Measure! Collect software metrics that enable you to assess past productivity and quality. Although a number of different metrics can be developed, the following (although controversial) are relatively easy to collect: dollars per line of code (many companies prefer the Function Point measure instead of the lines of code measure); dollars per defect; lines of code per person-month; defects per thousand lines of code; and dollars per page of documentation.

2. Using the approach described in the assessment step of the implementation cycle and the knowledge gained through education, select an appropriate tool set based on internal need.

3. Collect industry data that will serve to reinforce any projected improvements that are suggested during your justification.

4. Establish conservative projections of the percentage quality and productivity improvement to be expected when software engineering practice is applied. In general, improvements of between 10 and 25% per year can be obtained through the use of better methods and CASE tools.

5. Project demand for software over the next 12 to 24 months by estimating the total lines of code to be produced.

6. Compute the cost of new lines of code using the baseline average costs described in step 1 above.

7. Recompute the cost of new lines of code using the baseline averages reduced by the percent improvement projected in step 4.

8. Compute the cost savings. Cost savings are determined by computing the difference between cost of new development using past practice as an indicator (step 6) and the cost of new development determined in step 7.

9. Apply the steps above to software maintenance activities, but in this case, consider the cost of maintenance and the projected cost of re-engineering (rebuilding the application, rather than maintaining it).

Too many managers attempt to justify CASE tools and software engineering methods using only qualitative benefits. Few people argue that implementation of these new technologies results in improved product quality, better project control, improved product documentation, and overall improvements in specification, design, and testing. But senior managers want to understand justification in bottom line terms; that is, using return on investment as a motivation for CASE expenditures. The simple justification steps noted above can be used to provide this quantitative justification.

The installation step

Many organizations attempt to install software engineering technology by forcing a square peg into a round hole. Powerful tools are selected, but they address either the wrong aspects of software development or they are applied to the wrong problems by the wrong people. Frustration and confusion results and these tools often become "shelfware."

The first three steps of the implementation life cycle lay the foundation for installation—the strategy required to implement CASE tools and software engineering methods. Installation should be treated like a software project; that is, a work breakdown structure (WBS) of specific tasks for installation should be defined, responsibilities should be assigned to key individuals, milestones and deliverables should be identified, and a task network and overall project schedule should be developed.

In order to achieve successful installation, it is necessary to proceed incrementally. Some organizations attempt to install CASE and software engineering in one dramatic stroke, but such an approach is doomed to failure. A "big bang" approach introduces too much risk and overly complicates the introduction of new technology. It is better to install CASE tools, software engineering methods, and procedures in small steps, using each success as a stepping stone to the next installation activity.

Too many companies begin the installation step by developing a voluminous set of standards and procedures. Unless your company must use software engineering standards that are mandated by regulatory control (e.g., defense contractors), it is a mistake to write a 400-page standards document. Stated bluntly, it is unlikely that very many people will read the document. Would you?

At the early stages of installation it is better to write a "skinny" set of software engineering/CASE guidelines and have these guidelines evolve slowly into more formal standards and procedures. By developing guidelines first, practitioners can contribute to the evolution of a standards document and will ultimately have greater ownership in the end result.

When practitioners learn a new method, frustration is the most dangerous enemy. Lack of experience with a tool or method can often turn a trivial problem into a major source of frustration. Finding the answer (using vendor supplied manuals or an 800 customer-assistance number) is often a lengthy and confusing process that leaves the practitioner with a feeling that "all this isn't worth the effort."

In order to overcome this situation, one or more staff members should be given the role of a *systant*, which is a contraction for "system assistant" and was originally coined by Jerry Weinberg. The role of the systant is to act as a teacher/consultant/advisor in the use of new methods and tools during the installation step. A practitioner who becomes stuck while using a new method or tool, goes to the systant for assistance. By calling the systant on a local extension or walking to his or her office the practitioner gets an instantaneous solution to the problem. This rapid response tends to eliminate frustration and makes the installation of software engineering methods and tools much easier.

The evaluation step

There is sometimes a tendency to play ostrich when software engineering and CASE are installed. Some managers select and install the technology and then stick their heads in the sand, not spending nearly enough time evaluating whether or not the technology is working. The evaluation step performs an ongoing assessment of the CASE/software engineering installation process. We ask the same questions that were asked during the assessment step and perform both quantitative and qualitative data collection. In essence, we attempt to answer a single question—is the technology working?

During evaluation, both qualitative and quantitative data are collected. In fact, the guidelines suggested for the assessment step apply here as well. In addition to data collection, it is essential that you solicit feedback from practitioners to gain an understanding of the perceived effectiveness of software engineering methods, procedures, and tools. Regular debriefing sessions provide valuable insights and enable technical practitioners to contribute comments, criticisms, and concerns about their changing culture.

Summary

The five steps of the software engineering implementation life cycle are really nothing more than common sense. They suggest that you know where you are before you begin; that you understand the technology before you select; that you make choices based on bottom line issues (quality and productivity improvement); that you install the technology in a stepwise fashion; and that you continually evaluate what you've accomplished. So the next time you hear someone say, "This technology is interesting, but I don't know how to begin," just suggest common sense.

Note: This chapter was adapted from an article by the author that appeared in *Software Engineering*. New York, NY: Auerbach Publishers.© 1990 Warren, Gorham & Lamont. Used with permission.

Author Biography

Roger S. Pressman is an internationally recognized consultant and author in software engineering. He received a Ph.D. in engineering from the University of Connecticut, and has over two decades of industry experience, holding both technical and management positions with responsibility for the development of software for engineered products and systems.

Dr. Pressman is President of R.S. Pressman & Associates, Inc., a consulting firm located in Orange, Connecticut, that specializes in software engineering methods and training. He serves as principal consultant, specializing in helping companies establish effective software engineering practices.

Dr. Pressman is author of many technical papers, is a regular contributor to industry newsletters, and is author of six books. His book, *Software engineering: a practitioner's approach*, is the world's most widely used software engineering textbook. Another of his books, *Making software engineering happen* has been critically acclaimed as the first book to address the critical management problems associated with implementing software engineering technology. His latest book, *A manager's guide to software engineering* uses a unique question and answer format to present software engineering issues to managers.

Works Cited

Bouldin, Barbara. 1989. *Agents of change*. Yourdon Press.

Pressman, Roger. 1988. *Making software engineering happen*. Prentice Hall.

Pressman, Roger. 1993. *A manager's guide to software engineering*. McGraw-Hill.

Software Reliability and Productivity

by William W. Everett and John D. Musa

Introduction

Quality and productivity at times appear to be at odds with each other; that is, the feeling is that spending effort on quality attributes will reduce productivity. This is not necessarily true if you consider the following:

1. The role quality plays in product delivery.
2. The entire life cycle of the product and not just that part of the life cycle associated with building the product.

There are some key points to consider when considering quality and productivity. First, delivering a quality product requires striking the right balance among the level of quality desired by the customer, the price the customer is willing to pay, and the time frame in which the customer desires the product. (This suggests an extended definition of quality as achieving the balance between quality attribute levels, price, and delivery date that best satisfies the needs of the customer.) You do not best serve your customer if you deliver a high quality product but at a price the customer can ill afford to pay. Likewise, you are not serving your customer by delivering high quality at the expense of not being responsive to the needs of the market; that is, not delivering your product when your customer needs it. Understanding what this balance is helps you focus your development resources and hence be more productive than doing more or less than you need to.

Second, you must look across the entire life cycle of the product to assess productivity. Cutting corners early in the life cycle may make you appear to be more productive. But considering the possible rework that will occur later in the life cycle, these productivity gains are easily lost. These gains are also lost if you deliver a product that doesn't match your customer's needs.

The key to managing quality along with managing productivity is to have ways of measuring quality. These measures should be closely correlated to what the customer perceives as quality. There must also be a relationship between your quality measures and your productivity measures. This relationship allows you to know how changing one measure will affect the other. For example, when assessing whether changes to a development process will result in a productivity gain, you must consider the effect of the change on development cost and time and just as important on product quality. To assess the effect of process changes on product quality, you must be able to measure quality and you must be able to relate that measure to the changes being made.

This chapter focuses on reliability, an important quality attribute. To many, reliability is the most important quality attribute. For, after all, if the product doesn't work, what else matters. Reliability turns out to be a quality attribute that is directly measurable. It is also customer-oriented, as reliability is a quality directly experienced by the customer. This chapter also highlights how reliability of software products can be measured and modeled, and illustrates how reliability measures can be directly tied to productivity measures.

Specifically, this chapter singles out one part of a development process, namely reliability growth testing, and shows how the consumption of software test and repair resources are related to the improvement of reliability during testing. The next section summarizes some basic concepts in reliability. The final section discusses the relationship between testing resources and the improvement of reliability during testing.

Basic Concepts

Reliability and its importance

Reliability is the ability of a system or component to do its required functions for a specified period of time under stated operating conditions. This definition applies to both software and hardware products. With this definition, you are concerned with the failure-free operation of your product in your customer's environment.

Major surveys show that reliability ranks first on the list of customer satisfiers. With the increase in software that is embedded in products the proportion of failures attributable to software is increasing. Some projects report that the number of customer-reported software failures of their products exceeds the number of hardware failures.

Faults versus failures

You must make the distinction between faults and failures when considering software product reliability. A *fault* is a defect in the software code. The defect might be the result of an error made by a programmer in writing the software, or the result of errors in the design or requirements specifications referenced in writing the software. The fault might result from incorrect or missing instructions.

A *failure*, on the other hand, is the inability of a system to perform a required function. A failure can only occur during software operation. Faults are not synonymous with failures. Depending on the way the software is used, a fault might or might not cause a failure (or failures).

Fault-based measures are commonly used in the software development industry. They have helped in improving the quality of development processes in the past, and will continue to play an important role. However, users of software products experience failures, not faults. Customers are not so much concerned with how many faults there are in a software product. Instead, they are concerned with how often the product will fail and the effect that such failures will have on the job they have to do. Evaluating reliability of software from the customer's perspective requires failure-based measures.

Execution versus calendar time

Software failures occur only while software is operating. Operating time for software is referred to as *execution time* and is defined as the time during which a computer is processing instructions associated with the software. A direct measure of execution time is CPU time (e.g., CPU hour, CPU second). In cases where execution time cannot be measured directly, you can usually approximate it with other measures. These other measures should be related in some way to execution time. One other such measure might be the number of items processed by the software. The items could be calls processed by a telephone switch or commands executed by a transaction-processing system. To use this measure, the CPU time must be proportional to the number of items processed. There are other approximations to execution time. The occurrence of software failures is measured and modeled in terms of execution time.

Calendar time is the passage of time as people observe it. Measures of calendar time would be hours, days and months. Since people are concerned with failure occurrences relative to calendar time, there are ways of transforming reliability measures relative to execution time to corresponding measures relative to calendar time. For example, a tester would want to know how much elapsed time will occur in testing to reach a specified reliability level and not just the execution time.

Reliability and failure intensity

There are two ways of expressing software reliability. Reliability proper is the probability of no failure occurrences in a specified time period. The alternative, failure intensity, is the number of failures experienced per time period. The time period for both measures is expressed in terms of execution time. For example, you might determine the failure intensity of a software product in field operation (i.e., where no software fault removal is occurring) to be 8 failures per 1000 CPU hours. The corresponding reliability or probability of failure-free operation for, say, 10 CPU hours, would be 0.923.

Operational profile

Changes in operating conditions affect the observed reliability of software. Operating conditions determine which execution paths are followed and the state of internal data values as software instructions are being processed. This, in turn, determines when an execution path containing a fault will be followed, and when that fault is encountered under the right data conditions, that a failure will occur.

Operating conditions that affect software reliability are:

- The functions processed by the software
- The characteristics of the environment in which the software is operating
- The frequency that each of these are encountered while the software is being processed

For example, in an Automated Teller Machine (ATM) application, examples of functions might be "checking account balance inquiry," "savings account deposit," and "checking account withdrawal." Environment characteristics for a central ATM application program might be the types and numbers of ATM machines serviced by the program. A complete specification of the operating conditions for the ATM application would include the frequency that each function would occur on each type of ATM machine.

This characterization of operating conditions for software is referred to as an operational profile. Defining an operational profile is an important step in characterizing the reliability of your software product.

Reliability modeling

Models play an important role in characterizing the reliability of software products. Reliability models have two components: an execution time component and a calendar time component. The execution time component models failure occurrences are stated in terms of execution time. Various execution-time reliability measures can be derived using the execution time component model. The calendar time component translates these execution-time reliability measures into measures of calendar time.

There are two general classes of models: *reliability growth* models and *constant reliability* models. Reliability growth models are used when the underlying fault causing a failure is removed after the first failure occurrence. This occurs during system test or during field trials when active fault removal is underway. With active fault removal, the underlying faults causing failures are removed and the level of reliability improves over time. Constant reliability models are used when no fault removal is underway (for instance, during the post-release phase of a product between maintenance releases of the software). When the underlying faults causing failures are not removed, the level of reliability does not change. Both classes of models take into account random fluctuations of measures, so that quantities estimated by the models are usually expressed in terms of a "most likely value" and a confidence interval around that value. This chapter focuses on the use of reliability growth models during testing.

Applying reliability models

Figure 8.1 illustrates conceptually how reliability models are applied. During system test, cumulative failure occurrences up to the current time (vertical dotted line) are plotted versus execution time as in the left-hand plot. A reliability-growth model (the smooth solid-line curve in the left-hand plot) is then fitted to the failure data. The slope of the model curve at a particular time represents the failure intensity at

Cumulative failure counts

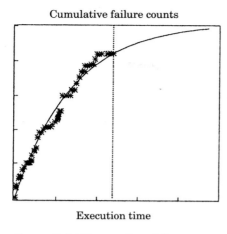

Execution time

Failure intensity

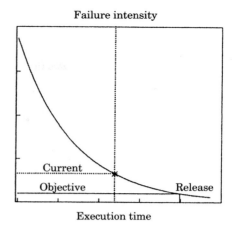

Execution time

Fig. 8.1 Reliability growth modeling.

that time. The slope (failure intensity) is plotted in the right-hand plot. The curve in the right-hand plot is then used to read off the current failure intensity and estimate the remaining execution time to reach a specified failure intensity objective (say, for product release).

Execution Time Component

Introduction

Reliability growth models express the cumulative number of failures as a function of execution time τ. In general, cumulative failures is a random variable. However, in the following, only the mean number of failures as a function of execution time, represented by $\mu(\tau)$ will be considered. The reliability models considered in this chapter are referred to as Non-homogeneous Poisson Process (NHPP) models. Such models are completely characterized by their mean value function $\mu(\tau)$, which is a monotonic increasing function of τ, that is, if $\tau_1 > \tau_2$, then $\mu(\tau)_1 > \mu(\tau)_2$. Another quantity of interest is the instantaneous rate at which failures occur. This is referred to as the failure intensity, $\lambda(\tau)$. With reliability growth models, failure intensity diminishes with time. It is defined as the derivative of mean failures; i.e.,

$$\lambda(\tau) = \frac{d\mu(\tau)}{d\tau} \quad (1)$$

Figure 8.1 illustrates the behavior of $\mu(\tau)$ and $\lambda(\tau)$ as a function of execution time τ.

Several different reliability growth models have been proposed in the literature. These models generally have two or more unknown parameters. Particular values of these parameters can be determined by fitting the models to failure occurrence data collected during test. The parameters of one model, however, can be related to characteristics of the software and the effectiveness of the fault removal process. This model, referred to as the Basic Execution Time (BET) model, will be used in the remainder of this chapter to illustrate the relationship between reliability and productivity. Readers interested in exploring reliability modeling further are referred to Musa, Iannino, and Okumoto (1987).

Basic execution time model

The functions $\mu(\tau)$ and $\lambda(\tau)$ for the BET model are represented by:

$$\mu(\tau) = v_0(1 - e^{-\phi\tau}), \quad (2)$$

$$\lambda(\tau) = v_0\phi e^{-\phi\tau} \quad (3)$$

This is a two-parameter model with parameters v_0 and ϕ. The parameter v_0 is the number of failures that would occur if testing were to continue indefinitely and the fault removal process were perfect. Since the underlying fault causing each failure is removed during reliability growth testing, v_0 also represents total faults that would be removed if testing continued indefinitely. Setting τ to 0 in equation (3) gives us the initial failure intensity $v_0\phi$. If each fault that is removed contributes the same to the initial failure intensity, then ϕ can be interpreted to be the failure intensity associated with each fault.

The BET model has other interesting properties that will be used later in this chapter. First, using equations (2) and (3), $\mu(\tau)$ can be expressed in terms of $\lambda(\tau)$ as

$$\mu(\tau) = v_0\left[1 - \frac{\lambda(\tau)}{v_0\phi}\right] \quad (4)$$

Likewise, equation (3) can be solved for τ to give an expression for τ in terms of λ.

$$\tau = -\frac{1}{\phi}\ln\left[\frac{\lambda}{v_0\phi}\right] \quad (5)$$

An example

The values estimated for the parameters of the Basic Execution Time model for a particular software product are:

$$v_0 = 156 \text{ failures}$$

$$\phi = 0.0078 \text{ per CPU hour}$$

(At first glance, it would seem that the units for ϕ would be "failures per unit time." However, remembering that ϕ is a "failure rate per failure," units of "failures" cancel out and one gets units of reciprocal time.) For this product, there will be 156 failures if the product were tested indefinitely. Using equation (3), the failure intensity at the start of testing (i.e., the initial failure intensity) is $156 \times 0.0078 = 1.2$ failures per CPU hour of operation. Product managers determined that customers would be satisfied if the failure intensity of the product were less than 2 failures per 1000 CPU hours, or 0.002 failures per CPU hour. Setting $l = 0.002$ in equation (3) and solving for τ, the amount of execution time that must transpire to attain that objective is

$$\tau = -\left(\frac{1}{0.0078}\right)\ln\left(\frac{0.002}{1.2}\right) \approx 820 \text{ CPU hours}$$

What would happen if the project decided to double the level of reliability delivered to the customer? This would equate to a failure intensity objective of 1 failure per 1000 CPU hours (0.001 failures per CPU hour). At first, you might expect the amount of execution time to double. However,

$$\tau = -\left(\frac{1}{0.0078}\right) \times \ln\left(\frac{0.001}{1.2}\right) \approx 909 \text{ CPU hours}$$

is required, an increase of only 11% in execution time.

Calendar Time Component—Modeling Costs

Introduction

This section will illustrate how the execution time component model can be used with the calendar time component to schedule and plan the costs associated with reliability growth testing. Costs are dependent on the amount of resources used during testing. This section starts by showing how resource consumption can be related to the occurrence of failures and passage of execution time during testing. The amount of testing, and hence the amount of resources consumed during testing, will depend on the failure intensity level that needs to be certified through testing. This section closes by illustrating how tradeoffs of cost versus failure intensity objective can be made. As costs equate into the price the customer must pay for the product, being able to do such tradeoff studies helps in determining the right balance between price and level of reliability.

The amount of resources used during testing depends on the number of failures detected and the passage of execution time. Consider the work done by testers in running tests and analyzing the output to determine whether a failure occurred. The number of staff hours of their work can be represented by X_T. First, the work needed to identify each failure and report it to software developers should be proportional to the number of failures that has occurred ($\mu(\tau)$). Second, the work needed to set up tests, monitor their progress, do the cleanup following each test run, and scan through all the output of the test to determine if a failure occurred should be proportional to the amount of processing that was done by the software. The processing done by the software is proportional to the amount of execution time expended (τ). Thus, as a first approximation, the amount of tester resource consumed in execution time τ can be represented by

$$X_T = \alpha_T \mu(\tau) + b_T \tau \qquad (6)$$

where α_T and b_T are proportionality constants. Note that equation (6) holds for all execution-time component models (i.e., any function $\mu(\tau)$ can appear in (6)). Constant α_T represents tester staff hours needed to handle each failure occurrence. Likewise, constant b_T represents tester staff hours to do τ units of execution time during testing.

However, testers are not the only resource that must be considered during testing. There are also the software developers who must locate and remove the underlying faults associated with a failure, and computing resources used by testers for running tests and by developers for isolating and removing the failures causing the failures. The consumption of developer resources (represented by subscript D) and computing resources (represented by subscript C) can also be represented by an equation similar to equation (6), namely:

$$X_D = \alpha_D \mu(\tau) + b_D \tau$$

$$X_C = \alpha_C \mu(\tau) + b_C \tau$$

In general, the consumption of all three resources can be related to $\mu(\tau)$ and τ by the following formula:

$$X_i = \alpha_i \mu(\tau) + b_i \tau \qquad (7)$$

where the subscript i = T, D, and C, and the parameters α_i and b_i represent the amount of each resource consumed for each failure and each unit of execution time.

Now, just a few words about equation (7). Tester resources (X_T) and software developer resources (X_D) are usually measured in terms of staff hours. Computing resources (X_C), on the other hand, are usually measured in terms of test lab hours. Interestingly enough, equation (7) has the same form no matter what the execution time component model is; that is, it depends only on the mean value function $\mu(\tau)$. For the BET model, equation (7) can be written as

$$X_i = \alpha_i v_0(1 - e^{-\phi\tau}) + b_i \tau \quad (8)$$

An example

The project described in the previous example found from experience that ¾ of a staff-hour of tester time is required for each failure that is detected during testing. This project has a semiautomatic test environment, allowing a tester to set up and run a series of tests without having to continuously monitor the tests. Hence, only 0.4 staff-hour is needed for each CPU hour of processing during testing. Thus, the tester resource consumption factors are:

$$\alpha_T = 0.75 \text{ staff-hour per failure}$$

$$b_T = 0.4 \text{ staff-hour per CPU-hour}$$

Building on the previous example, the product will be tested until the failure intensity objective of 2 failures per 1000 CPU hours is achieved. As previously computed, 820 CPU hours of processing was required. Using equation (8), the amount of testing resource consumed is

$$X_T = 0.75 \times 156 \times (1 - e^{-0.0078 \times 820}) + 0.4 \times 820$$

$$X_T = 116.8 + 328 = 444.8 \text{ staff-hours}$$

The project uses a loaded salary rate of $60 per staff-hour in figuring the costs of its testers. Thus, the cost of testing to a failure intensity objective of 2 failures per 1000 CPU hours is $444.8 \times \$60 = \$26,688$. As in the previous example, suppose the reliability level were doubled; i.e., the failure intensity objective were set to 1 failure per 1000 CPU hours. As previously computed, 909 CPU hours of processing would be required. Again, using a loaded salary rate of $60 per staff hour for testers and equation (8):

$$\$60 \times (0.75 \times 156 \times (1 - e^{-0.0078 \times 909}) + 0.4 \times 909) = \$28,830$$

which equates to only an 8% increase in testing cost.

Reliability and Development Cost

Having a model relating development costs to some measurable quality attribute allows project personnel to focus on development productivity to satisfy customers' desires for quality at a price they are willing to pay. As illustrated, development costs associated with reliability growth testing can be related to the level of reliability desired in the delivered product. There is a tradeoff in reliability growth testing. The longer testing continues, the lower the failure intensity will be when the product is released. However, the cost of testing and fault removal will go up. The increase in test costs with a decreasing failure intensity objective λ_{Obj} for the released product is illustrated by the dotted curve labeled "System Test Cost" in Fig. 8.2. On the other hand, stopping testing too early results in a higher failure intensity of the released product, which adds to the field failure costs after the product is released. If the execution life time of the product over all field sites is τ_F, then the number of field failures will be $\lambda_{Obj}\tau_F$, assuming the underlying faults causing the failures are not removed.

If a cost can be associated with each field failure, then the field failure costs will grow linearly with failure intensity objective at release λ_{Obj}. This is illustrated by the

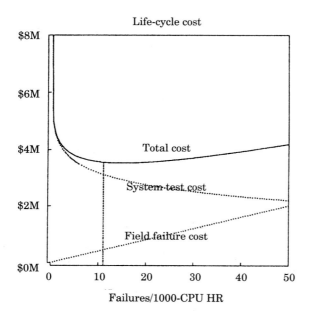

Fig. 8.2 Cost versus failure intensity objective.

dotted curve labeled "Field Failure Cost" in Fig. 8.2. The "TOTAL COST" curve in Fig. 8.2 is just the sum of the test and field failure costs. The solid curve in Fig. 8.2 shows that there is a failure intensity objective for which the "TOTAL COST" curve attains a minimum.

For the basic execution time model, the total cost can be easily expressed. Let C_i, where $i = T, C,$ or D, be the cost of each unit of tester, developer, and computer resource consumed during reliability growth testing. Let C_F be the cost of each field failure. Then using equations (7), (4), and (5) and the number of field failures, the total cost, C, can be expressed as:

$$C = \sum_{i = T, C, D} C_i X_i + C_F \lambda_{Obj} \tau_F = \sum_{i = T, C, D} C_i (\alpha_i \mu(\tau) + b_i \tau) + C_F \lambda_{Obj} \tau_F$$

$$C = \sum_{i = T, C, D} C_i \left[\alpha_i \left[v_0 - \frac{\lambda_{Obj}}{\phi} \right] - \frac{b_i}{\phi} \ln \left[\frac{\lambda_{Obj}}{v_0 \phi} \right] \right] + C_F \lambda_{Obj} \tau_F \quad (9)$$

The minimum value of equation (9) can be found by differentiating C with respect to λ_{Obj} and setting it equal to zero:

$$C = \sum_{i = T, C, D} C_i \left[-\frac{\alpha_i}{\phi} - \frac{b_i}{\phi \lambda_{Obj}} \right] + C_F \tau_F = 0 ,$$

$$\lambda_{Obj} = \frac{\sum\limits_{i = T, C, D} C_i b_i}{C_F \tau_F \phi - \sum\limits_{i = T, C, D} C_i \alpha_i} \quad (10)$$

Calendar Time Component—Modeling Schedule

Introduction

This section will illustrate how the execution time component model can be used with the calendar time component to estimate and plan the time associated with reliability growth testing. The amount of calendar time that elapses during testing depends on several factors:

1. The resource consumption during testing (the previous section showed how this is related to reliability growth and the execution time model)

2. The amount of resources available

3. What resource is the "limiting" resource during each testing period

Given the amount of calendar time that will elapse and information on how the calendar time will be scheduled (such as how many work hours there will be in a workday, the number of workdays in a work week, and the date that testing will begin), a completion date (i.e., the date when a particular failure intensity objective is achieved) can be projected.

The passage of calendar time is related to the consumption of resources. Let t_i represent the passage of calendar time associated with resource $i = T$, D, and C. Now t_i depends on two factors, the quantity of each resource available during testing N_i, and the utilization level ρ_i of each resource. The passage of calendar time for each resource can be represented by

$$t_i = \frac{X_i}{\rho_i N_i} = \frac{\alpha_i \mu(\tau) + b_i \tau}{\rho_i N_i} \quad (11)$$

Note that the passage of calendar time is a function of execution time τ. Using equation (11), the calendar time that would elapse if a particular resource were utilized at its capacity may be calculated. Interestingly enough, equation (11) has the same form no matter what the execution time component model is; that is, it depends only on the mean value function $\mu(\tau)$.

If the consumption of each resource is considered separately during test, calendar time t_i associated with each resource (i) could be translated into actual calendar dates using work schedule constraints. Such constraints are the number of hours in a workday, workdays in a week, and the occurrence weekends and holidays. However, the consumption of each resource cannot be considered independently because they are interrelated. Testers cannot test at their rated capacity if they do not have enough computing resources on which to run their tests. Likewise, developers will sit idle if testing has not detected enough failures for them to locate and remove underlying faults. Generally, one resource will be operating at full capacity. This resource is referred to as the "limiting resource." The passage of calendar time will be determined by this limiting resource during the period when it is limiting the full utilization of other resources. The consumption of the other two resources will be throttled by the limiting resource.

To determine the limiting resource, the rate at which calendar time changes with execution time must first be determined for each resource. Differentiating equation (11) with respect to τ provides this rate:

$$\left(\frac{dt_i}{d\tau} \right) = \frac{\alpha_i \left(\dfrac{d\mu(\tau)}{d\tau} \right) + b_i}{N_i \rho_i}$$

Using equation (1), the following can be obtained:

$$\left(\frac{dt_i}{d\tau} \right) = \frac{\alpha_i \lambda(\tau) + b_i}{N_i \rho_i} \quad (12)$$

The significance of equation (12) is that the rate of change of calendar time with respect to execution time can be represented as a function of failure intensity alone (i.e., the dependence on execution time is only through $\lambda(\tau)$). This property will be used later on.

The limiting resource (i) at any point of execution time τ is the resource for which its rate of change of calendar time

$$\frac{dt_i}{d\tau}$$

is maximum. To visualize this, consider a small period of execution time $\Delta\tau$. The amount of calendar time required by each resource (i) is about

$$\Delta\tau_i = \left(\frac{dt_i}{d\tau}\right)\Delta\tau$$

The calendar time that will transpire in $\Delta\tau$ will be the resource that requires the most calendar time during that time $\Delta\tau$, the other resources remaining idle for part of the time. Let

$$i(\tau) = \max\left(\frac{dt_i}{d\tau}\right), \text{ where } i = T, D, \text{ and } C$$

$$i(\tau) = \max\left(\frac{\alpha_i\lambda(\tau) + b_i}{N_i\rho_i}\right) \quad \text{where } i = T, D, C \quad (13)$$

Equation (13) says that the index (i) used to determine which resource is the limiting resource (and hence determines the passage of calendar time) is a function of time τ. Now $i(\tau)$ is a step function taking on particular values of T, D, and C during different periods of time as illustrated in Fig. 8.3.

The amount of calendar time that would elapse in τ of execution time can be expressed as

$$t = \int_0^\tau \frac{X_i(\tau)}{N_i(\tau)\rho_i(\tau)} \, d\tau = \int_0^\tau \frac{\alpha_i(\tau)\lambda(\tau) + b_i(\tau)}{N_i(\tau)\rho_i(\tau)} \, d\tau \quad (14)$$

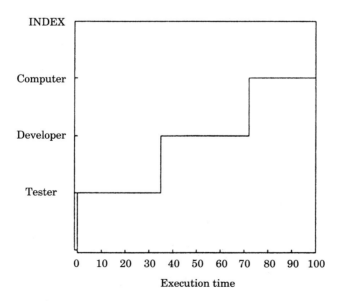

Fig. 8.3 Index function.

If there is only one limiting resource i during testing, equation (14) simplifies substantially as $i(\tau)$ is constant and becomes

$$t = \frac{X_i(\tau)}{N_i \rho_i} = \frac{\alpha_i \mu(\tau) + b_i(\tau)}{N_i \rho_i} \quad (15)$$

Note that equation (15) holds for any execution time component model. For the Basic Execution Time model, equation (15) becomes

$$t = \frac{\alpha_i v_0 (1 - e^{-\phi\tau}) + b_i \tau}{N_i \rho_i} \quad (16)$$

Although equations (13) and (14) appear at first to be difficult to solve, their solution is straightforward. First, note that the rate of change of calendar time (equation (12)) is a linear function of λ. This suggests expressing execution time τ as a function of λ; i.e., $\tau = f(\lambda)$. For example, for the basic execution time model, equation (3) yields

$$\tau = f(\lambda) = - \frac{\ln \dfrac{\lambda}{[v_0 \phi]}}{\phi} \quad (17)$$

The mean number of failures μ in equation (2) can be expressed in terms of λ as:

$$\mu(\lambda) = v_0 - \frac{\lambda}{\phi} \quad (18)$$

Now, equation (12) represents three linear functions of the dependent variable λ. Taking each of these three equations a pair at time, they intersect in three points. Denote these three points as λ_1, λ_2, and λ_3, where, without loss of generality, they can be ordered so $-\infty \le \lambda_1 \le \lambda_2 \le \lambda_3 \le \infty$. These three points divide the λ-domain into four intervals. In each of these intervals, one of the three linear functions represented by (12) is greater than or equal to the other two. This means that the corresponding resource is the limiting resource within that interval. Thus solving equation (13) reduces first to finding the solutions to the equations:

$$\frac{\alpha_T \lambda + b_T}{N_T \rho_T} = \frac{\alpha_D \lambda + b_D}{N_D \rho_D} \quad (19)$$

$$\frac{\alpha_T \lambda + b_T}{N_T \rho_T} = \frac{\alpha_c \lambda + b_c}{N_c \rho_c} \quad (20)$$

$$\frac{\alpha_D \lambda + b_D}{N_D \rho_D} = \frac{\alpha_c \lambda + b_c}{N_c \rho_c} \quad (21)$$

Note, that equations (19), (20), and (21) may have one, two, three, or no meaningful solutions, in which case there are respectively two, three, four, or only one interval. (Meaningful solutions for λ are those values of λ that are less than the initial failure intensity λ_0 and greater than 0 or a failure intensity objective, if one is specified.) Then, for each interval, the limiting resource can be determined by evaluating

$$\frac{\alpha_i \lambda + b_i}{N_i \rho_i} \qquad (22)$$

for each i = T, D, and C and taking that i for which equation (22) is a maximum. Substituting equations (17) and (18) into equation (15), the calendar time in each of the three intervals can be expressed as

$$t = \frac{\alpha_i \left[v_0 - \dfrac{\lambda}{\phi} \right] - \dfrac{b_i}{\phi} \ln \left[\dfrac{\lambda}{v_0 \phi} \right]}{N_i \rho_i} \qquad (23)$$

where i is the limiting resource in that interval. The amount of calendar time that elapses between two failure intensity values λ_1 and λ_2 in an interval where i is the limiting resource is

$$t_2 - t_1 = \frac{\alpha_i \left(\lambda_1 - \lambda_2 \right) + b_i \ln \left[\dfrac{\lambda_1}{\lambda_2} \right]}{\phi N_i \rho_i} \qquad (24)$$

An example

The project cited in the previous examples have two testers ($N_T = 2$) who will spend 100% of their time in testing the product ($\rho_T = 1.0$). Again, project experience is that a tester requires 0.75 staff-hour for each failure identified ($\alpha_T = 0.75$) and 0.4 staff-hours for each CPU hour of test processing that is done ($b_T = 0.4$). There are 10 developers in the project ($N_D = 10$) who will be spending 50% of their time ($\rho_D = 0.5$) locating and removing the faults that caused failures during testing. (Since only the first failure occurrence is counted during reliability growth testing, each failure corresponds to a fault that must be located and removed.) Project experience has been that 3.0 staff hours of developer's time is required to locate and remove a fault ($\alpha_D = 3.0$). Developer's time is not dependent on the amount of processing time that transpires during testing of the product, therefore $b_D = 0$. (This is generally the situation with many projects that have independent test teams. Developers are not involved in setting up test runs or monitoring their progress which the b factor takes into account.)

The project has two computers ($N_C = 2$) used by the two testers and these computers are dedicated to testing ($\rho_c = 1.0$). About a tenth of an hour of computer time is required for each failure that is identified ($\rho_c = 0.1$) and one hour of computer time is required for each CPU hour of test processing ($b_c = 1.0$). The project's re-sources and resource consumption factors are summarized in the following table.

Calendar Time Parameter	Tester	Developer	Computer
α_i - hours per failure	0.75	3.0	0.1
b_i - hours per CPU hour	0.25	0.0	1.0
N_i - quantity of resources	2	10	2
ρ_i - utilization	1.0	0.5	1.0

The project's failure intensity objective has been set to be 1 failure every 1000 CPU hour or 0.001 failure per CPU hour. The elapsed calendar time to reach this objective will first be computed assuming testers are the limiting resource. Although equation (5) could be used to compute the execution time τ to reach the failure intensity objective and then equation (15) to compute the elapsed calendar time, equation (24) will be used instead. This will illustrate how calendar times are computed for different failure intensity intervals. The value for λ_1 will be the initial failure intensity of 1.2 failures per CPU hour as computed in the previous examples. The value for λ_2 will be the failure intensity objective 0.001 failure per CPU hour. Using equation (24), the elapsed calendar time for this failure intensity interval is

$$\frac{0.75 \times (1.2 - 0.001) + 0.4 \times \ln\left[\dfrac{1.2}{0.001}\right]}{0.0078 \times 2.0 \times 1.0} = 239 \text{ staff hours}$$

However, testers may not be the limiting resource during the testing period. To check this out, equations (19), (20), and (21) are solved for values of λ that bound each of the intervals where one resource is limiting. These intervals are summarized in the first column of the following table. An interior point is selected in each interval as shown in column 2 of the table. The calendar time rate for the interior point is computed using equation (22) for each of the resources and recorded in the third through fifth columns. The limiting resource is that resource whose calendar rate in columns 3 through 5 is maximum (it is recorded in column 6).

Interval		Calendar Time Rate			Limiting
End-Point	Interior-Point	Tester	Developer	Computer	Resource
$-\infty$					
	0.1	0.237	0.060	0.502	Computer
1.08					
	1.09	0.609	0.654	0.555	Developer
1.10					
	1.12	0.620	0.672	0.556	Developer
1.125					
	10	3.950	6.000	1.500	Developer

From the table above, computers are the limiting resource in the failure intensity interval 0.001 to 1.08. Developers are the limiting resource in the interval 1.08 to 1.2. Using equation (24), the elapsed calendar time in each of these intervals can be computed:

$$\frac{0.1 \times (1.08 - 0.001 + 1.0 \times \ln\left[\dfrac{1.08}{0.001}\right]}{0.0078 \times 2} = 454.4 \text{ staff hours}$$

$$\frac{3.0 \times (1.2 - 1.08)}{0.0078 \times 10 \times 0.5} = 2.7 \text{ staff hours}$$

The total elapsed calendar time is 457.4 staff hours. Note, this is nearly twice the time needed if testers were the limiting resource. For this project, providing more computing resource will substantially improve productivity by reducing the elapsed time to do testing.

Reliability and Development Schedule

One important aspect of planning is to estimate when a specified level of reliability will be attained with a given set of resources. Having a model relating the consumption of resources to quality level allows a project to adequately plan resources so project schedule deadlines can be reached. This section illustrates how such planning can be done with reliability growth testing. Specifically, this section looks at how the scheduled completion date for reliability growth testing can be related to a failure intensity objective to be attained at that completion date. This is illustrated in Fig. 8.4.

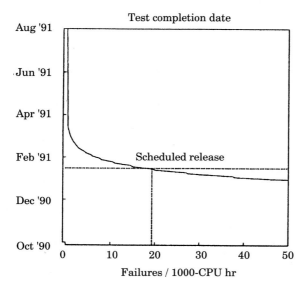

Fig. 8.4 Completion date versus failure intensity objective.

In Fig. 8.4, the test completion date is defined to be the date when a particular failure intensity objective λ_{Obj} is attained. The completion date depends on the test start date, the test resource consumption parameters, and the parameters for the execution time component model. The elapsed calendar time is computed using equations (8) and (9). Calendar dates can be computed from calendar time by knowing how many calendar hours there are in each workday, how many workdays in a work week, and which days of the week and month are workdays (i.e., people (ideally!) should not be scheduled to work on weekends and holidays). In the example illustrated in Fig. 8.4, testing began on December 1, 1990. As lower failure intensity objectives are considered, the curve shows that the completion date will move further and further into 1991.

Summary

One can view productivity as the use of project resources in a way that improves the delivery of products that meets the customer's quality needs at a price the customer is willing to pay and within a time frame the customer desires the product. In this context, measures of quality are needed along with measures of cost and schedule to effectively manage productivity. Not only are measures of quality needed, but these measures need to be related to cost and schedule. In this chapter, these ideas were illustrated with respect to one important quality attribute, namely reliability. This chapter highlighted how reliability growth could be measured and modeled during software product testing. It also showed how test resource usage and test period schedules could be modeled in terms of reliability growth. Finally, the chapter showed how these models allow projects to make the necessary tradeoffs to achieve a balance of cost, quality and schedule.

Author Biography

Bill Everett is a Distinguished Member of Technical Staff in the Quality Process Center at AT&T Bell Laboratories, Murray Hill, New Jersey. Bill has over 20 years of experience in software development and engineering, the last five in Software Reliability Engineering (SRE). Bill has not only been a practitioner in applying SRE on projects he has been associated with, but has also been instrumental in the technology transfer of SRE within AT&T. He has been involved in developing and delivering courses within AT&T on SRE. He has implemented an MS-DOS and UNIX version of SRE TOOLKIT, a set of software tools that support the application of SRE and are an integral part of the AT&T courses. He has worked as a consultant with a number of AT&T projects in implementing SRE in their development processes. Most recently, he has led a team that documented a "best current practice" for doing SRE within AT&T.

He has published a number of papers and given a number of talks and tutorials on Software Reliability and is a coauthor of AT&T's *Reliability by Design Handbook*.

Bill is a member of SIAM, IEEE Computer Society, and is an Associate Editor for IEEE Software magazine. He received a Ph.D. degree in Applied Mathematics from the California Institute of Technology and an Engineer's Degree from the Colorado School of Mines.

John D. Musa is Supervisor of Software Reliability Engineering at AT&T Bell Laboratories. He has varied and extensive experience as a software developer and software development manager. He has been involved in the field of software reliability engineering since 1973, developing two models (one with K. Okumoto) and making many theoretical contributions. These resulted in the publication of over 60 papers. He has been a leader in practical application of software reliability engineering to guiding engineering management decisions. Musa created two courses at AT&T to integrate this extensive experience in both theory and practice and impart it to software practitioners. In addition, he coauthored (1987) a widely acclaimed pioneering book *Software reliability: measurement, prediction, application*. He has extensive experience speaking and teaching on an international basis and has made a number of videos. He is currently actively involved in research and in organizing and leading the transfer of this technology into practice by software-based projects within AT&T. He is one of the founders of the IEEE Subcommittee on Software Reliability Engineering. As a result of his work, he was elected a Fellow of the IEEE for his "contributions to software engineering, particularly software reliability."

Musa is widely recognized as an international leader in software engineering and received an award for his outstanding innovative leadership. He is a founding editor of the Software Engineering Institute book series and an editor for the Software Engineering Encyclopedia. He is a member of the editorial board of Technique et Science Informatiques, was a founding editor and consulting editor of IEEE Software, and was an editor of IEEE Spectrum and Proceedings of the IEEE. Musa has been a chair and member of the Steering Committee for the International Conferences on Software Engineering. His wide participation and leadership in these and many other professional society, conference, and publication activities results in unusual breadth and depth of background and judgment continuing close contact with leaders and research in the field.

Musa has been an examiner for the AT&T Chairman's Quality Award. As such, he has training and experience similar to that of the examiners for the Malcolm Baldridge Award.

Works Cited

Musa, John, A. Iannino, and K. Okumoto. 1987. *Software reliability: Measurement, prediction, application*. McGraw-Hill.

Software Process Improvement at Hewlett-Packard
A Partnership Approach

by Barbara Zimmer

Abstract

With software now a vital component of virtually all Hewlett-Packard (HP) products, HP has dedicated significant resources to improving its software development processes. Software Quality and Productivity Analysis (SQPA) represents one of the early components of this effort. In its first four years, SQPA reviewed over 100 of HP's software development laboratories and provided a standard by which both individual labs and the company as a whole could evaluate their processes. Due in part to SQPA results showing a frustratingly slow rate of improvement, the company launched a major new initiative in 1990 designed to place HP among the leaders in software development practices. This paper discusses the history, methodology, impact, and results of SQPA at HP, and how they led to the Software Initiative.

HP's Quality and Productivity Commitment

Quality and productivity have been an explicit part of HP's corporate objectives throughout the company's history. The concepts might have seemed simpler in the less competitive years gone by, but HP has maintained its commitment in an increasingly complex business environment.

In the world of software development, HP's attention to productivity and quality has become more formalized in recent years in response to the demands of a dynamic and rapidly changing field. An early outgrowth of this response was a process assessment program called Software Quality and Productivity Analysis. A few words about the company's general organization and history will help put the discussion in context.

HP's corporate structure is built on many different divisions or operations that operate more-or-less autonomously. These separate entities are organized into various groups by product types. At the top levels of the hierarchy are product group sectors and finally, corporate management.

At the entity level, a division or operation will normally include manufacturing, marketing, and administrative functions as well as a research and development laboratory. The lab manager, who reports directly to the division manager, will have responsibility for several section managers, who in turn oversee project managers. The labs vary greatly in size, ranging from 50 to 150 people.

The roots of the current software quality and productivity effort are in the Corporate Software Quality Council, which grew out of a 1983 task force. The council set some software development guidelines involving the use of Total Quality Control methods and called on participation by Marketing, Manufacturing Support, and Field Sales Representatives. The most definitive result was the application of HP CEO John Young's 10X Quality Goals to software. These goals called for a tenfold improvement in the number of defects in the upcoming five years.

A new entity called Corporate Engineering was formed in 1984 to address these goals from a company-wide perspective. As part of Corporate Engineering, SQPA's original charter was based on the need to leverage HP's software development efforts in response to the evolution from a total technological approach to software development to one that includes consideration of culture, change agents, methodologies, and human factors. (It should be noted that throughout this paper, that "software" refers to both software and firmware development.)

Software Quality and Productivity Analysis

SQPA's major objective is to develop and implement a software-engineering review process and a software-management decision-support system. Its tactic is to assess the state of each HP lab and draw comparisons with other HP labs and the rest of the industry. It focuses on these eight key areas that affect software development:

- Methodologies
- Staff variables
- Project management and control
- Programming environment
- Tools
- Defect prevention and removal
- Physical environment
- Measurement

After measuring variables in each of these categories, the program identifies strengths and weaknesses, pinpoints areas for improvement, makes recommendations, and provides follow-up measures to show progress over time. In the process, a quantitative and qualitative baseline of key factors impacting software development is established.

The SQPA methodology is based on a set of standardized questions that have been checked for validity and reliability. The original questions were derived from a prototype developed by Capers Jones, an independent consultant who has done extensive research on software development productivity. This prototype was tested on 15 projects in typical HP environments to determine which questions should be used and to validate them for HP. The questionnaire has continued to evolve, reflecting HP cultural anomalies, changes in technology and HP management priorities, and incorporating what has been learned through SQPA team experience.

The current survey yields both verbal and numeric responses. It includes perception checks that help describe the state of the lab verbally and contribute to verifying consistency in the data, as well as some questions directed specifically to senior managers with both numeric and narrative responses possible. About 50% of the survey requires quantifiable responses that can serve as a basis for comparisons across different HP entities. This information is also compared to industry data compiled by Capers Jones.

In addition to being standardized and validated, the questions are tailored to HP's typical project-oriented environment. They address both strategic and tactical issues and enable quantification of the effects of tools and methodologies. It is important to note that there can be great ranges in the numeric answers, but the level of detail gathered is sufficient to identify differences and similarities across labs.

This detail can often reveal differences in lab environments that might be appropriate to the unique requirements of a given lab.

The SQPA Process

The SQPA process begins with a request from a lab, and a subsequent scheduling and information exchange. After the request, the lab will generally be asked for demographic data, organization charts, and product descriptions. The formal interviews with lab and section managers, a representative sample of project managers, productivity and quality managers (if appropriate), and a representative sample of engineers take place next, usually over two days, depending on the size of the lab. One engineer from the two-person SQPA team conducts each 1- to 2-hour interview using the questionnaires discussed previously. No written responses are requested. The SQPA interviewer records all numeric and qualitative responses.

Over half of the questions are multiple choice, asking for descriptions of tools, methods, and other elements of the development environment. Other questions, which also yield numerical results, ask for evaluations of activities or perceptions of the extent to which certain methods or tools are used. The interviewer also notes additional verbal descriptions of development processes as well as answers to open-ended questions, such as listing strengths and weaknesses. It is important to note that these comments are an integral part of the analysis, both in providing a context for the quantitative data and identifying additional areas of significance within the lab.

After the interviews, the SQPA team performs an analysis, including a statistical comparison with HP and industry data, and a narrative summary of key findings. The analysis is presented within a day or two to the R&D manager and anyone else he or she invites. The two-hour presentation consists of a description of strengths, constraints and weaknesses, graphs comparing the lab with HP and the industry in the eight key measurement areas, and recommendations for improvement. It is important that this immediate feedback session be interactive to clarify any misinformation or misperceptions and to prepare managers for the upcoming written report.

Over the next three to four weeks, the SQPA team confers on quantitative and verbal responses and consults with experts as appropriate to diagnose or prescribe specific activities. The final results are summarized in a formal written report containing graphs, text, and statistics, and sent to the R&D manager. The level of detail in the report can provide sufficient information on which to base specific improvement strategies. Finally, the database containing all the HP data collected to date is updated to allow for HP-wide trend analysis.

A sample overall profile using hypothetical data is illustrated in Fig. 9.1. The inverted scale makes this diagram a sort of "target," where the ideal profile converges upon the center with as much symmetry as possible. The different bands represent ranges of comparison with industry data based on a survey of over 3000 successful projects by Capers Jones. Criteria for success were finishing on time, within budget, and success in the marketplace. Activities in the 1–2.5 range are thus "Ahead of Norms" and are likely to contribute to the success of the project. Normal range is 2.6–3.5, and 3.6–5.0 is considered risky to the project's success.

Each small circle on the axes represents the composite average for all questions about a given category. The fictitious lab pictured in this profile is strong in staff vari-

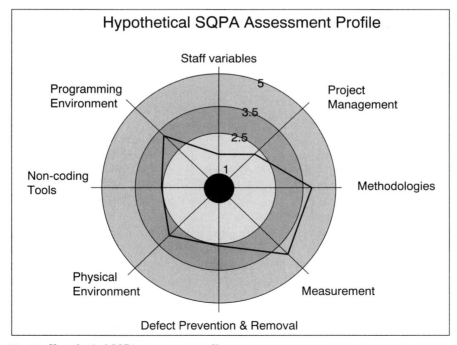

Fig. 9.1 Hypothetical SQPA assessment profile.

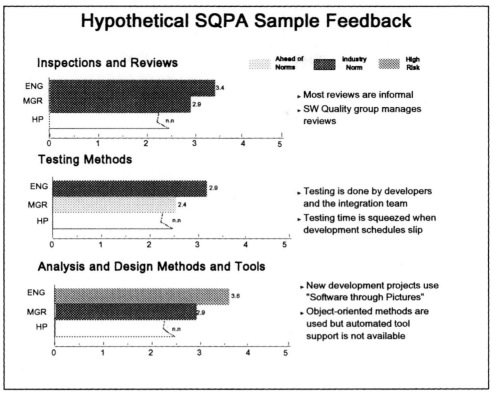

Fig. 9.2 Hypothetical SQPA sample feedback.

ables and project management, normal in defect prevention and removal, programming, and physical environment and non-coding tools, and weak in methodologies and measurement.

Figure 9.2 uses hypothetical data to illustrate some sample SQPA feedback. These graphs show composite averages to groups of questions about inspections, testing and analysis, and design. Engineer and manager responses are compared to each other and to company-wide results.

Other sections of the report include comparisons of engineers' and managers' evaluations of methods, tools, and overall aspects of the environment, and descriptions of the types of development undertaken and the tools used. A summary of strengths, constraints, and weaknesses is followed by specific recommendations. The recommendations are based on the SQPA observed best practices within HP, advice of consultants, as appropriate, and industry research.

The last step in the SQPA process is follow-up analysis to measure and report changes and improvements. This would normally take place 12 to 18 months later. Over 20 labs have now had follow-up analysis performed.

Benefits of SQPA

The SQPA program was initially announced at an annual conference for HP R&D laboratory managers. Interested managers who participated in the first reviews helped refine the original questions. The program's reputation has spread mostly by word-of-mouth and by periodic publications and presentations. The result has been a constant backlog of requests for analysis.

SQPA services have been offered free-of-charge and on a voluntary basis. No lab is required to have the analysis. The constant backlog of requests since the program's inception attests to its positive reception. Even when monetary charges were introduced for second-round reviews, requests have not diminished. Although individual participants have occasionally begrudged the initial two-hour commitment, post-analysis surveys have shown the respondents thought the time was well rewarded and could not and should not have been shortened.

Perhaps the principal reason why a lab would request SQPA is that there is no other measurement system or process for R&D labs that takes into account the major factors in the general development environment. Other existing methods measure only technical factors, while SQPA provides a broad cross-section of information covering all aspects of the environment, but at a detailed, project-specific level. And it does this with a minimal time investment from the lab. No individual should expect more than a two-hour time commitment.

A significant benefit of SQPA has been simply the opening of communication on some issues. In particular, for managers without software experience, the process can help them understand the issues and questions they should be asking their managers and engineers.

Among the most interesting revelations might be the differences in perceptions between project managers and section managers or managers and engineers. Engineers, for example, might complain of having to sacrifice features to meet deadlines, while managers in the same lab take pride in never giving up features in order to meet a schedule.

The success of SQPA rests largely on management's support and willingness to participate both in the review itself and in resulting activities. The methodology used to derive the results has proven very effective. Doing an interview rather than a paper survey assures greater consistency in the interpretation of both questions and answers, as well as flexibility in pursuing issues that might be unique to a particular lab or project. The initial interactive presentation of results gives the lab some immediate feedback and establishes realistic expectations of the overall formal written report.

However, while SQPA's flexibility is a desirable feature, standardization, in both the administration of the review and results drawn from the data, is a critical issue and is rigorously applied.

Confidentiality and ownership of the analysis results are also key issues. In order to create a maximum openness in the interview to elicit candid responses, the SQPA team assures that all individual lab data is strictly confidential and owned by the R&D manager. Although statistics and verbal comments are accumulated in the HP database, none of this information, when published, is associated with a particular lab or individual without prior permission.

Impact of the Analyses

Once the lab has received the formal report, it is the prerogative of the R&D manager to determine how to use the information and whether to ask for additional assistance from the SQPA team. The use of SQPA data, in practice, has been as varied as the labs themselves. In general, a prevalent short-term effect has been more attention being given to formal planning and measurement activities.

The results have also been used in different functional areas for things such as quality planning. One group used the analysis as a basis for a similar study of their documentation environment.

The educational value of the analysis to the labs has been seen in a number of forms. Some labs have presented the SQPA report along with their own improvement plan to the entire lab. Others have selected a few key areas from those that SQPA identified and delved deeper into the problems and possible solutions.

From a corporate perspective, the implications of SQPA are considerable. SQPA facilitates consistent use of common vocabulary metrics and common vocabulary. Much of this commonality is shared simply in the process of administering the survey and publishing the written report.

Establishment of a database containing quality and productivity data for labs throughout HP enables trend analysis. This data provides the basis for publications addressing specific quality and productivity issues and contributes to HP's continued focus on quality and productivity.

Shifting Resources from Pure Diagnosis to Prescription—the Software Initiative

SQPA data played a key role in persuading HP management to fund a major initiative aimed at software process improvement across HP. The SQPA results showed that while some divisions have used the SQPA results to instigate formal process improvement plans, others have not used them at all. Isolated cases of dramatic process improvement demonstrate what can be done, but remain anomalies as overall company trends have held steady.

Thus, while the benefits of SQPA have been many, it is clear that a standardized process assessment program alone will not impact HP's ability to bring higher quality products to market more efficiently. Consequently, HP has now launched the Software Initiative (SWI) to provide the necessary follow-up and support to effectively enhance HP's software development technology and process knowledge. SWI adds a full menu of prescriptive programs to complement SQPA's diagnostic services.

SQPA, itself, is now part of the SWI and has expanded its scope to include other assessment tools and methods, as well as a strategic planning support component. It has consequently been renamed the Software Process Assessment (SPA) program.

SQPA data, along with input from internal HP customers and other company process and product data, were instrumental in shaping the content and priorities of the SWI. The major areas of technical focus are Process Definition and Metrics, Reuse, Configuration Management, Maintenance, Rapid Prototyping, System Design, and Product Definition. Supporting these program areas are the SPA team and groups in Software Development Environments and Technology Transfer.

The SWI technical programs focus on software development processes with high payback potential, but which address varying HP entity needs. The Configuration Management and Maintenance programs are exploring solutions applicable to almost any development environment, while the Reuse program offers technologies appropriate to organizations with more mature processes. Systems Design, Product Definition, and Rapid Prototyping address activities occurring between idea and design, which translate customer views into designer views. Risk management is an essential part of this process.

SWI Partners with HP Divisions in Process Innovation and Process Improvement

While the SWI is being directed by Corporate Engineering, its success is predicated on joint efforts with entity productivity and quality groups, divisional and group management, and local project teams. Figure 9.3 illustrates this infrastructure and Fig. 9.4 shows how the program concept pairs corporate resources with divisional pilot projects to address specific software development process and environment issues. Over 40 proposals for pilot projects have been received and 15 are now underway in HP entities around the world.

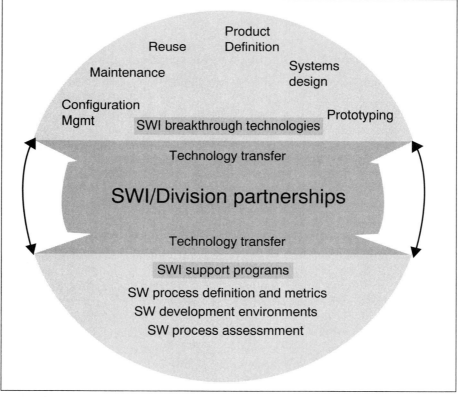

Fig. 9.3 SWI structure.

A Range of Products And Services

Information		Consulting
Publications	Conferences	Assessments
Handbooks	Classes	Pilot Projects
Reference Sheets	Videos	Collaborative Partnerships
	Tool Information	

Fig. 9.4   A range of products and services.

The pilot projects are the core of the SWI partnering approach to process improvement at HP. The proposals which are now underway were selected on the basis of many criteria, including business impact, management support, local commitment of resources, problem definition, consistency with SWI objectives, likelihood of success, and generalizability of the experience or solution.

One of the compelling lessons of the SQPA data is that for any given software development activity, there is probably at least one project team in HP which is doing it successfully. Clearly then, the challenge of the SWI is not only to discover new processes, but also to transfer those successful practices to other appropriate HP environments. Our approach to both developing and transferring knowledge and expertise centers on working directly with our customers—all HP people who develop software for HP products.

Different organizations, however, are at different levels of readiness for change. For example, a lab that is ready for a formal reuse program must have configuration management under control. Baselines, including technical environment, management and staff education, software technology, and an ability to measure and manage processes, need to be in place at the divisions to successfully utilize the technology being addressed by the SWI.

Thus a key deliverable of the SWI is not just recommendation and implementation support for specific technologies, but a model for when and how to adopt the appropriate technology for a specific environment and organization. The SWI works at raising the baseline environments and maturity levels that are the responsibility of individual HP organizations by building process improvement capability and transferring appropriate technologies. Elements essential to the improvement process include a maturity model defining appropriate sequencing of steps to incremental process improvement; guidelines for implementing change; and a transition cost model.

Past experience at Corporate Engineering has taught us that no single technology transfer activity is likely to bring sustained improvement in software development processes. Consequently, SWI programs are designed to deliver a spectrum of products and services that will support divisions in developing their own process improvement programs. Planned deliverables range from purely informational products to custom consulting services. Additionally, SWI programs support the entire cycle of process improvement activities from those with management focus to engineering technologies.

To date, SWI resources have been concentrated in process innovation activities in division pilot projects and in tapping resources from industry and academia. As candidate best practices are identified, SWI activities will shift more into product delivery.

HP is committed to making software development a core competency. SQPA and the Software Initiative embody significant efforts towards this end.

Author Biography

Barbara Zimmer has been with HP for ten years in positions in Finance, Information Systems, and Research and Development. As a member of the SQPA team, she participated in numerous lab reviews and was responsible for analyzing and communicating information about trends in software development processes at HP. This included initiating internal publications that summarized HP trends for upper management and explored specific software technologies and issues for HP's technical community. She also wrote HP's Software Quality and Productivity Guide, published in 1990, and available in an external version for distribution outside HP. She is currently working on technology transfer activities for the Software Initiative.

10

Managing the Quality of Software Development

by William G. Smillie

Introduction

With the maturation of the information age, custom systems and proprietary software have become some of the largest and most strategic assets of many corporations. Moreover, new systems and applications are called upon today to provide immediate and significant sources of competitive advantage to companies. These trends make the effective development of applications an ever-greater challenge as we find IS embedded in almost all corporate products and services.

Nevertheless, while software development productivity has improved over the past 20 years, perceived software quality has not. Problems with cost overruns, turn-around time, unmet requirements, and maintenance backlogs are all too familiar to both users and developers. Even the most venerable commercial application publishers have trouble delivering on introduction dates, features, and prices.

For example, according to Tom DeMarco (1984), 15% of all software projects with more than 100,000 lines of code failed to deliver anything useful. In 1989, according to Capers Jones, of all software projects over 64,000 lines of code, 25% failed to deliver anything, 60% were significantly over budget and behind schedule, and only 1% finished on time, on budget, and met user requirements.

In addition, a study of software engineering practice by the Software Engineering Institute (1991) shows the sorry state of the current software development process (see Fig. 10.1).

- At 86% of the companies assessed, the process is ad hoc or chaotic
- At 13% of the companies, the process is somewhat repeatable, but is driven by personal initiative and dependent on individuals
- At a mere 1% of companies, the process is defined and institutionalized

LEVEL	CHARACTERISTIC	% OF COMPANIES
1 Initial	Ad Hoc /Chaotic	86%
2 Repeatable	Initiative; Process dependent on individuals	13%
3 Defined	Qualitative; Process defined and institutionalized	1%
4 Managed	Quantitative; Process measured	0%
5 Optimizing	Improvement fed back into process	0%

Fig. 10.1 SEI levels.

The goal of software development organizations should be to go beyond these initial levels to the point where the process is closely managed and measured quantitatively, with improvements fed back into the process. In fact, some purchasers of systems will not do business with a software developer if the developer has not reached a certain minimum level on the SEI scale.

However, if information is to be managed efficiently and used effectively, the software development process must also be closely managed and guided by a comprehensive software quality-improvement program. The key is to establish a level of quality output that is defined by customer satisfaction—whether that customer is inside or outside the firm, a frustrated end user or a major client.

A New Concept of Quality

This new concept of quality means that the simple absence of defects is no longer a sufficient definition. Businesses are now requiring software developers to pursue excellence in the eyes of very broad constituencies. When one is faced with intense competition, customer satisfaction is the only definition of quality that matters.

Much of the recent literature on software quality has focused on error-free coding and the use of metrics to measure and improve upon the integrity of applications. While this is a good start, we must first realize that quality is not simply a tactical tool. Traditional metrics measure the software product, not the customer's satisfaction with it. Quality must be seen as the addition of value to applications throughout the development process.

Furthermore, users today are far more sophisticated in terms of software functionality and ease of use. This knowledge has been drawn from a broad base of experience with commercially produced, PC-based software. End users are also less tolerant of the time and cost to produce applications, in both absolute terms and with regard to predictability.

The Science Is Known

Ironically, good software engineering principles and methodologies are well known and well established—we have the ability to create quality software. The problem is that software development organizations collectively have not managed the process nearly as well as we would have hoped. At the very least, software development methodologies, techniques, and tools must be well defined and applied to the development process. In addition, the methodologies, techniques, and tools must also be applied consistently and institutionalized.

There are, nevertheless, examples of success stories at software development organizations that give us clues as to how to proceed. These examples include a software metrics program initiated at Hewlett-Packard (HP) (Grady and Caswell 1987) and a Total Quality Management program at Nippon Electric Company (NEC) (Murine 1988).

The essence of the HP example is a software quality metrics program that started in a small division of the company and was so successful that it expanded on its own to other parts of the firm. Managers in the division developed measurement systems to help manage the process of continuous software improvement. It resulted in benefits so evident that managers in other divisions sought to adopt the approach without direction from top-level management.

The benefits of the software improvement program were twofold. First, the simple act of measuring the software development process led to short-term productivity improvements. People naturally wanted to do better on the scale by which they were measured. Second, the program established a measurement foundation with which various competing methodologies, techniques, and tools could be evaluated.

In general, the metrics program helped managers understand the software development process better and measure its progress, making software management less subjective. It enabled engineers to estimate, schedule, and make critical decisions earlier in the development process. It enabled managers to evaluate the competitive position better, identify the best engineering practices, and, in many instances, it eliminated the fundamental causes of defects. Overall, the program encouraged the use of software engineering techniques as well as the definition of a long-term software development strategy based on a measurement of current practices and needs.

In our second example, NEC started to apply some of the concepts of a corporate Total Quality Management (TQM) program to its software development process. Over a seven-year period, the company collected data measuring the impact of TQM across all phases of the software development life cycle, including maintenance.

The overall result was an initial increase in costs in the early phases of the software development process of as much as 10%. However, the company rapidly found as much as a 36% decrease in costs after development was completed, and an additional decrease in maintenance costs of 51%. Over the course of the program, total cost savings in the software development life cycle approached 87%.

Total Quality Management

This brings us to the concept of software quality management, which is based on the principles of Total Quality Management. TQM is a philosophy of pursuing continuous improvement in a company or process through the integrated efforts of all the members of that organization. TQM is being successfully applied, in both business and government, as a way of meeting or exceeding customer expectations of quality every time a product or service is delivered.

The basic principles of TQM are as follows:

1. The focus of the process is on the "customers."
2. There must be total commitment from the top management of the company.
3. Performance is continuously measured quantitatively.
4. Employees must be empowered and given incentives to make changes.
5. The goal is continuous improvement of process and product, with no "acceptable" target level of quality.

The most important concept of TQM to remember is that it is a philosophy of doing business and not a development tool. TQM requires a corporate culture where all involved in a process are committed to the minimum goal of customer satisfaction and to the ultimate objective of customer delight—the discovery of value-added features that users never even expected to find.

In addition, TQM requires a high level of commitment from everyone involved in the software development process on up to the heads of the corporation. It also means beginning the difficult process of changing counter-productive behaviors within a software development organization and establishing a culture that supports a software quality management program.

Barriers to Developing Quality Software

As we have seen, the techniques and tools needed to develop quality software are generally available and can be used in a productive manner. However, at most companies, the software development process has not been managed well. The problem has been that the approach of the individuals involved in the development process has not been regulated and counter-productive behaviors have been allowed to become the norm.

In general, there are three typical behaviors prevalent in software organizations that have become barriers to the development of quality software. The first of these behaviors we have termed "Code or Die." Individuals who exhibit this behavior react to an application request with "you want it when? My gosh, I'd better start coding now." This knee-jerk reaction occurs because we've been brought up to focus on the end product, not the process. When the time frame is especially challenging, the methodology goes out the window and the immediate reaction is to start producing the product. With this behavior, quality will never be improved upon because the process is entirely ad hoc.

The second counter-productive behavior often seen in development organizations we have termed "The Artist in Me." The classic example is a development programmer who receives the design specifications for an application and says, "I can write a better program than this and provide more features." This excessive creativity often results in an application that is delivered late and over budget. These individuals believe that they are providing a better product when, in fact, the greatest quality concern among end users is the on-time delivery of requested applications. Software development organizations and individuals must refrain from defining quality on behalf of their end users.

The third behavioral barrier surfaces in the "Lots of Pain, Little Gain" scenario. This occurs when individuals do not take the time to apply the lessons they have learned. Yesterday's application development is viewed as a finite project performed in a vacuum rather than part of an ongoing software development process. Both programmers and engineers often feel that they are so busy that they do not have time to see their work as a continuous process, let alone to evaluate and improve upon it. When the opportunities for improvement have not been institutionalized, the successes that occur are, more often than not, based on chance.

Principles of Software Quality Management

The first issue that needs to be addressed in building the type of corporate culture needed to successfully implement software quality management (SQM) is the empowerment of employees. True empowerment can only be achieved by giving employees the responsibility, authority, and means to make improvements within their areas of expertise and the extent of their viewpoint. The process must also include special training, tools, and resources to identify and solve quality problems, plus the provision of rewards for successes.

The second general element needed for SQM to succeed is total commitment from top management, and the communication of that commitment down the line. The greatest obstacle to the success of SQM is resistance to change—resistance not only from programmers and engineers, but also from executives at the highest levels. Only with an across-the-board commitment to change can this resistance be overcome and counter-productive behaviors eliminated.

The third principle of TQM needed in the entire software development process is a focus on the customer and the notion that achieving customer delight is an ongoing process. The quest for quality is one of continuous improvement—there is no target level of quality.

This ongoing process begins with an initial assessment of the current level of software quality, a plan for improvement, the implementation of that plan, followed by a return to assessment for an ongoing cycle of continuous improvement. The most important tools used in this process are the metrics based on the components of an organization's major quality issues, which will be described in more detail later in this article. These measurements provide a benchmark as well as feedback from end users and direction for improvement for software development teams.

Finally, utilizing a software quality management program can provide the sources of competitive advantage that so many companies are searching for today. This conclusion is becoming more and more evident as information technology becomes an integral part of nearly all the products and services of a company. In addition, benefits of an SQM program for systems purchasers and developers include:

- Increased user satisfaction
- Systems that are easier to maintain
- A return on software investment
- Greater control over projects with improved risk management
- Fewer surprises

Therefore, establishing a quality software development process has a triple impact—it increases user satisfaction, enhances a company's competitive advantage, and improves the stature of the developers.

Achieving Quality Software Management

The first step into the future is for software developers to thoroughly know end users' requirements and their "wish lists." Much of the work currently devoted to enhancements and maintenance is the result of not really knowing user requirements either at the start or throughout the development process. This last part is the key: users must be involved during the entire development process to provide continuous feedback and fine-tuning. Without user involvement, the odds of missing the mark go up dramatically. The days of software development in a vacuum must end.

But how do software developers know if they are meeting user requirements or even understanding them? Obviously, IS professionals and end users will have to agree on requirements and explore the types of systems features that are most valuable to the end user. Not so obviously, an agreed-upon process to measure whether or not the requirements are being met must also be established.

Soon, systems developers will find that simply meeting requirements is not enough: they will want to fulfill users' wish lists. This is what is meant by providing value-added products and services. The ultimate objective is to delight end users by giving them features and benefits that they never expected to get, but on time and on budget.

The second step to the future is to think of software development as a continuous, flexible process rather than a series of discrete tasks. Then, by focusing on measuring and improving the process, the goal of continuous improvement will come naturally. Quality will become a dynamic element of the new software development process.

However, software development professionals are not always that accepting of a new way of doing business when it interferes with a process that is likened more to an art than a science. While it is true that software development requires genuine talent, the goal must be to apply that talent in a more effective and efficient manner.

Resources must be used to create more new solutions instead of fixing old ones. Programmers and engineers will have to become aware of their places in the process and how they affect the people before and after them in the process. The goal of "best-in-class" software developers must be to achieve excellence in the eyes of purchasers, users and other broadly defined customers.

Establishing the Dimensions of Quality

We believe that, among a myriad of choices, the specific dimensions of quality that contribute most to purchaser and user satisfaction include predictability, business impact, appropriateness, reliability, and adaptability. By predictability, we mean knowing and controlling the dimensions of the risk factors involved, such as delivery date, cost, and resources needed. Unfortunately, software development organizations have a terrible track record in predictability. Often, users would be willing to pay more and accept a later delivery date if they were just able to know about it in advance.

The business impact dimension of quality relates to whether or not an application provides a significant benefit to the organization, rather than just being technically elegant. Code that is full of bugs and relatively inefficient but does the job, can be thought of as terrific by users. On the other hand, an error-free application that is not particularly useful is not a winner.

Among the other quality dimensions, appropriateness means providing a solution that is suitable to the business and technical problems that end users want addressed. Reliability is whether or not the system will work for its users when it is needed. And adaptability means that the system and user support can be changed cost-effectively to meet the evolving needs of the end user.

By breaking each of these quality issues down into their key components and then formulating a measurement system based on those components, one can begin to get a quantitative handle on the software development process (see Fig. 10.2).

For example, predictability can be broken down into the three components of "on schedule," "amount of effort," and "cost." These components can then, in turn, be measured. "On schedule" could be quantified as the deviation from the estimated number of elapsed weeks for a project. "Amount of effort" could be quantified as the deviation from the estimated number of hours per phase and rework hours per phase. And "cost" could be quantified as the deviation from the estimated number of hours and rework hours multiplied by the cost per phase.

The key, then, to a software quality management program lies in whether or not the process can be measured. If a process cannot be measured, it cannot be understood, controlled or improved.

How Do We Get There?

In the next section we look in more detail at the measurement techniques, tools, and training needed for a software quality management program. The overall goal of SQM, however, will remain the same: a focus on customers and the development process, while continuously taking advantage of the lessons learned.

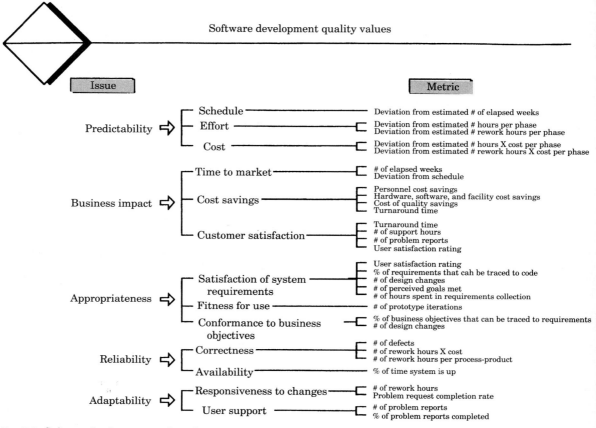

Fig. 10.2 Software development quality values.

Implementing SQM

Competition is the basic motivating factor for software development organizations that adopt an SQM strategy. The desire to be best-in-class, to keep up with improvements that others have made, or to improve customer satisfaction are foremost in their strategy. It may be a question of success, but it may also be a question of survival for these organizations—they must change fundamental ways of doing business.

Under SQM, software organizations have a structured development process that can be used by teams to build better solutions that everyone can own. However, the process must also be structured so the teams can act quickly. Speed is a critical success factor. The goal is to produce a more flexible and agile organization by empowering the work force and pushing accountability and responsibility down the line.

The key to improving the development process is to establish a measurement system, such as the one that was introduced in the preceding section. Success hinges on the fundamental act of measuring the process that is to be improved. Only by measuring the factors that affect software production is it possible to effectively manage those factors.

Unfortunately, many organizations spend too much time measuring the wrong things and not enough time measuring those items that make a positive impact. For a measurement system to be effective it needs to be tailored to the goals, objectives, and needs of the organization. It must also involve measuring process parameters as well as product and project parameters. Metrics are critical because they help answer the most important questions in an SQM program:

- Where are we now?
- Where do we want to be?
- Which direction must we move in?
- How far must we go?

In addition to identifying the correct metrics for an organization, a method must be put in place that enables the organization to use the metrics as the basis for an improvement program. As was mentioned before, this is a multi-phased process which begins with a benchmark assessment of the current level of software quality. The next step is to develop a plan for improvement, the implementation of that plan, followed by a return to assessment. The approach, described in detail below, provides for an ongoing cycle of continuous improvement.

Assessment

The purpose of the Assessment phase is to evaluate the organization's current environment and determine how well the organization meets or is likely to meet its customers' software quality requirements. In any Assessment phase, a measurement system must first be designed as a tool and to establish a quality baseline. The Goal/Question/Metric approach (Basili and Caldiera 1991) described below can be used to produce this measurement system.

During Assessment, it is important to understand the activities involved in the software development process as well as the organizational roles and responsibilities. The measurements currently being used by the organization must also be identified and assessed. Whenever possible, existing measures should be used as part of the quality assessment to promote familiarity and acceptance.

Nevertheless, the overall approach is to develop questions and metrics that have the greatest importance to the organization. This is achieved by focusing on the three dimensions of the goals of the Assessment: the phase under scrutiny, the relevant quality issue, and the role from which the phase and quality issue are viewed (see Fig. 10.3).

When conducting an Assessment, it may also be necessary to hold briefing sessions with respondents to clarify the meaning of some of the metrics. Moreover, respondents who feel that they are being imposed upon or are fearful of the measurement effort are likely to provide questionable data. It is especially important to make clear that the metrics are not being used as a mechanism for punitive ac-

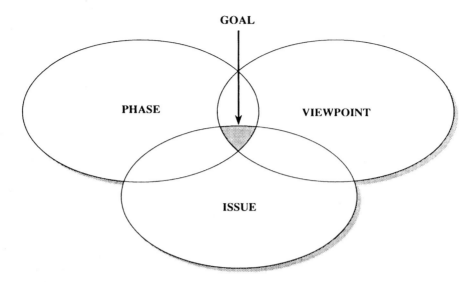

Fig. 10.3 Three dimensions of the assessment goal.

tions. Since many sensitive and perhaps embarrassing issues may arise during the Assessment, it is often easier for an outside third party to manage the process and gather data.

It is also desirable to collect the data during a fixed period of time with a specific deadline. During the Assessment period, the collection team should be available to answer questions and clarify procedures. After the data are collected, they are compiled, analyzed and translated into graphic depictions of the major findings. The key outcome of the Assessment is the identification of opportunities for improvement by studying the consolidated findings. This resulting list of opportunities is essential for the planning and implementation of pilot improvement projects.

Getting consensus from management as to the validity of the analysis and the opportunities for improvement is also essential. Specifically, the Assessment team must be sensitive to the possible misinterpretation of the findings and conclusions which may result in blame laying. Before moving on to Planning, the management sponsor must help the team identify potential trouble spots and devise methods for defusing them.

Planning

The analysis of the data collected during the Assessment provides the foundation for the quality improvement plan. The Assessment defines the organization's quality profile and identifies opportunities for improvement. The objectives of the Planning phase are to establish strategic and tactical direction, as well as consensus and commitment for improvements identified in the Assessment. A Process Improvement Plan is the final outcome of this strategic planning effort.

Typically, two types of problems surface as a result of the Assessment: ones with relatively simple, quick solutions and ones more deeply rooted in organizational practices, requiring a longer period to solve. To address the first type of problem, the organization must devise short-term, measurable projects with a consistent sequence encompassing the Plan/Do/Check/Act process (Demming 1986). The second type of problem requires an effort aimed at longer-term organizational and behavioral changes. The focus of the Planning effort will be on these long-term projects.

Nevertheless, a critical success factor for any SQM project is the perception that quality improvement is attainable. The quality improvement team's ability to achieve successes on the short-term projects will help to pave the way for the entire process. Furthermore, quick management decisions on short-term projects will show development staff that their improvement ideas have been taken seriously and that management is willing to take actions based on staff input.

Because participation and consensus of management is essential to the Planning effort, there is always considerable risk of delay. The Planning team must, therefore, conduct an intensive quality planning session with managers early in the process. Ideally, all of the planning work could be accomplished at such a session. At a minimum, the result of the meeting will be to define the "quality vision" and to establish the roles and responsibilities of the groups to be charged with the organization's quality program.

The organization's vision of what quality software means and where it expects to be must be agreed upon early in the Planning effort. Most organizations find that there are several areas where improvement efforts can be focused; however, trying to do too much at once is not a good idea. Priorities should be assigned to targets based on the following criteria:

- Criticality

- Cost

- Resources

- Timing

- Risks

- Opportunity for near-term success

The projects that are selected as top priorities will require further discussion and decisions regarding the manner in which the improvements are to be implemented. The result will be a prioritized statement of quality objectives, the process improvements to be achieved and the measurements that will demonstrate success. In addition, each quality improvement project should have:

- A mission statement that includes improvement goals

- Schedules and resource and cost estimates for each project

- An organization structure responsible for quality management

- Measurement procedures to validate the meeting of goals

In addition to establishing procedures, it is essential that top management realize the implications of committing to SQM. It must be understood that SQM is not a pilot program, but is an ongoing process to enhance the way the software organization conducts business. SQM requires changing procedures, cooperating with other departments, emphasizing the process, and changing management philosophies that are ineffective yet pervasive. If senior management is not willing to commit themselves, their organization, and their people to the process, an SQM program is probably not worth starting.

Planning for software quality improvement requires more than just top management commitment and sponsorship. It also calls for attention to cultural and behavioral issues. For example, the initial reaction of staff to a measurement program may be apprehension, fear and resistance. It must be shown that the program and data collected will be used for improvement purposes and not punishment. One or more short-term successes will demonstrate the real value of the measurement system. Also, a measurement system should indicate process and product strengths that need encouragement as well as weaknesses that need improvement.

The primary goals of the Planning phase of SQM are to define quality objectives and strategies for instituting improvement solutions. It is also important for the plan to establish the roles and responsibilities for the individuals and teams whose mission is to promote and oversee continuous quality improvements. The final product is a plan that prioritizes the quality objectives, details the means for achieving improvements in the short term, identifies and analyzes quality-related risks, and creates an agreed-upon framework to achieve long-term quality improvement objectives.

Implementation

Introducing measurement systems and the concept of continuous improvement will require far-reaching changes to an organization. During the Implementation phase, these changes begin to occur. Implementing the quality improvement plan means incorporating the measurement and improvement efforts into the organizational culture and discovering which behavioral changes need to occur. This effort, therefore, requires a corresponding change in the reward structure. A reward system should motivate the staff to change development procedures in a way that is consistent with the goals of the improvements efforts.

Once a new reward system is in place, Implementation should turn to those short-term projects that were identified in the Planning phase. These might include:

- Project-tracking techniques and tools
- Formalizing reviews and walkthroughs
- Implementing Joint Application Design (JAD) sessions
- Applying new approaches to testing

Most of the efforts at improvement will require training of staff and project management in the relevant techniques and tools. These training efforts must be undertaken with the same commitment and level of support given to the entire SQM effort.

If staff is not supported in its effort to change, all of the assessments and strategic planning sessions in the world will not effect change. For an SQM program to be successful, staff and management must be encouraged to experiment, take risks and take charge of improving the process.

Once the framework of rewards, training, and empowerment is established, the long-term process improvements can be attempted. These might include:

- Implementing risk management techniques
- Introducing a structured development methodology
- Instituting Rapid Prototyping techniques
- Evaluating and implementing new CASE tools

Institutionalization

Institutionalization requires that the lessons learned during Implementation be captured and transformed into organizational assets to form the basis of a continuous improvement culture. As a first step, the experiences gained in near-term improvement projects should be analyzed, packaged, and communicated to everyone in the organization. Successes must be validated and publicized. The experience is packaged into self-contained units including approach, results, techniques, tools, manuals, and training to transform the knowledge gained into the organization's culture.

The basic techniques for institutionalizing continuous quality improvement include:

- Analyzing the results of short-term projects and comparing the results with the targets defined in Planning.
- Synthesizing the experience into lessons learned, domain expertise, rules, and models.
- Packaging the experience as products that can be delivered to the organization.

Institutionalizing SQM requires comprehensive reuse of the experience from several projects or several phases of a project. Much of the work done at this stage of the program involves educating the individuals who develop and maintain software. This education involves not only formalized training on specific process improvements, but also formal and informal quality awareness education via the promotion of quality improvement successes.

SQM measurement systems

As was mentioned above, the first step in any software quality improvement program must be the design and development of a measurement system as a tool for accomplishing the Assessment phase and to establish a quality baseline. If something cannot be measured, it cannot be understood, managed or improved. The Goal/Question/Metric (GQM) approach described below can be used to produce this measurement system.

The GQM approach was originally developed for evaluating defects for a set of case study projects at the NASA Goddard Space Flight Center. The approach can be translated for use in software quality management because it allows control and improvement of a software project within the context of several other projects.

The GQM approach is used to define metrics over the course of the software project, process and product. GQM is structured in such a way that the

- resulting metrics are tailored to the organization and its goals;
- measurement data play an instructive role in the organization; and
- metrics and their interpretation reflect special quality values and different viewpoints (customers, developers, and maintainers).

The facets of the GQM approach are defined as follows:

- **goal** an objective of an organization with respect to quality, from a specific point of view, in a particular environment.
- **question** a set of questions used to characterize the way the Assessment of a specific goal is to be performed.
- **metric** a set of measurements associated with every question in order to answer it quantitatively.

The process used to develop a GQM model starts with a set of goals for quality issues in a specific organization. Based on these goals, operational definitions are developed in the form of questions or problems that characterize or evaluate quality within the limits established by the goal. Last, the measures needed to answer those questions or to check the process or product conformance to the goals must be specified.

Obviously, the reliability of the results of a measurement system and subsequent analysis depends on the accuracy and amount of data collected. It is very difficult to make good estimates with only a few pieces of data. It is for this reason that data collection over the long term provides more substantial benefits.

Conclusion

In general, a software quality management program based on a solid measurement system can point out the advantages and disadvantages of current development practices and encourage change. A measurement system can also help to justify the costs of user involvement in a quality program: the difference between the cost of rework plus extensive maintenance and the cost of up-front user input (see Fig. 10.4).

But managing software quality not only requires measurement, it also requires careful focus on the tailoring of organizational culture so that all members involved in the development process are provided incentives, empowered, supported by management, and committed to the goal of continuous improvement. With proper attention to the real issues that contribute to software quality and customer satisfaction, we can move forward and learn to improve behaviors and processes. This will not only benefit the customer but will contribute to the quality and success of the entire organization.

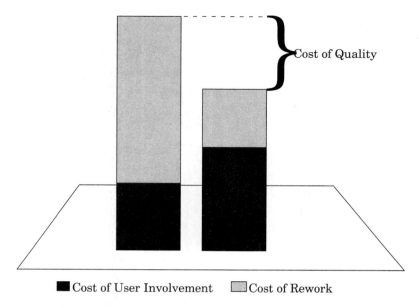

}Cost of Quality

■ Cost of User Involvement   ▢ Cost of Rework

Fig. 10.4 Cost of quality.

Author Biography

William G. Smillie is a partner in Coopers & Lybrand's Washington, D.C. Federal Systems Consulting practice and Partner-in-Charge of the Firm's Software Quality Management Practice. His practical approach to the issues of software quality have been gained through 17 years of experience in managing the design, development, and implementation of complex, on-line information systems. He is regularly asked to provide quality assurance reviews for a wide variety of Information Technology engagements and has led the development of the firm's methodology for managing continuous improvement in software quality. Mr. Smillie received a B.S. degree from McGill University and is a member of IEEE and the ASQC.

Works Cited

Basili, V.R. and G. Caldiera. 1991. Methodological and architectural issues in the experience factory. *Proceedings of the sixteenth annual software engineering workshop.* Greenbelt, Md.: NASA Goddard Spaceflight Center. December, 1991.

DeMarco, Tom. 1982. *Controlling software projects.* Englewood Cliffs, N.J.: Yourdon Press, Prentice-Hall.

Demming, W.E. 1986. *Out of the crisis.* MIT Center for Advanced Engineering Study. Cambridge, Ma.: MIT Press.

Grady, Robert B. and Deborah L. Caswell. 1987. *Software metrics: Establishing a company-wide program.* Englewood Cliffs, N.J.: Prentice Hall.

Jones, T.C. *Programmer productivity.* New York, N.Y.: McGraw-Hill.

Murine, Gerald. 1988. Integrating software metrics with software QA. *Quality progress.* November, 1988.

Software Engineering Institute. 1991. *Capability maturity model.* Pittsburgh, Pa.: Carnegie Mellon University.

Staffing Factors in Software Cost Estimation Models

by Chris F. Kemerer and Michael W. Patrick

Abstract

Many software cost estimation models have attempted to incorporate staffing variables such as personnel experience and capability. This chapter surveys such models and evaluates the extent to which accounting for staffing variables can improve their software project cost estimates. Current measures of ability, such as years of experience, appear to be poor indicators of individual capability differences and do little to improve model accuracy. Suggestions for improving these models through expanded effort in theoretical development are proposed.

Introduction

Software projects have a well-deserved anecdotal reputation for being late and over budget. This anecdotal evidence is supported with a number of research studies. Jenkins, Naumann, and Wetherbe (1984) report that of 72 medium-scale (average 10 month) software projects in 23 major US corporations, only 9% were completed within the scheduled manpower effort. The average effort overrun was 36%. Most projects (48%) completed with 75% extra effort, but some projects required three, four, and even five times the manpower effort of the original estimate.

A University of Arizona survey found an average, self-reported (191 of 827) over-run of 33%, and that only 16% of the respondents felt that software projects "rarely" or "never" experienced cost overruns (Phan, Vogel, and Nunamaker 1988). DeMarco and Lister (1987) report that in their survey of 500 software projects, 15% of all projects were so late they were canceled, and a full 25% of large (over 25 person-year) projects were canceled.

Heemstra and Kuster's (1991) survey of almost 600 European organizations revealed that over 80% of their software projects failed to meet their original time schedule. As expected, the larger the project, the more likely it was to slip. Whereas 71% of all projects completed within 10% of original budget, only 45% of the largest (>200 person-month) projects were within 10% of their original manpower estimate.

Most recently, van Genuchten (1991) presents the results of a number of studies that provide similar findings. When surveyed as to why software was late, van Genuchten found that the two most common answers were that personnel were not available (i.e., some other project was late) and "product related reasons" including "complexity of application underestimated."

Software cost estimation models attempt to more accurately estimate the effort required to develop a software project by using a mathematical formula of expected project inputs. The most frequently used input measure is the estimate of the size of the program in lines of code. The output of the model is usually an estimate of the effort in person-months.

However, use of these models in their current state of development is not a panacea for project management overruns. The Heemstra and Kuster (1991) study also demonstrated that software cost estimation models are not widely used or particularly effective when they are used. Only 14% of the projects surveyed used any kind of algorithmic cost estimation model at all. There was no significant difference in the magnitude of schedule slips between those projects that used a model and those that did not.

It is widely believed in practice that the single most critical factor to manage on a project is the staffing. Teams of the "the best" staff are widely believed to significantly outperform average teams. This belief is even sometimes raised to challenge claims for new tools or methodologies, arguing that the project was "stacked" with talented individuals, who were the primary reason for the success rather than the new tool. Given the belief in the importance of this factor, some cost estimation models attempt to improve their estimates by incorporating differences in the ability of the individual project team members.

This chapter surveys the published empirical literature that attempts to explicitly model the effect of alternative staffing policies. The main results of this survey are that, despite research spanning approximately two decades, little progress has been made in modeling the effect of these variables. Some suggestions are made for improving these models through greater incorporation of a stronger theoretical base.

Cost estimation models

The cost estimation modeling literature has been recently reviewed (Kemerer 1991) and will only be briefly summarized here. All software cost estimation models attempt to predict the effort as a function of various measured "factors":

Effort = <f>(factor1, factor2, ...)

Several researchers have measured a variety of factors and run a multiple regression to determine the most significant factors. For example, Walston and Felix

(1977) collected data on 68 factors, finding 29 to be of significance, and Chrysler (1978) collected data on 24 factors and found 14 to be statistically significant.

In all cases, the most significant variable was the actual "size" of the project, usually measured as lines of code. To improve accuracy, many models multiply the baseline effort by a modification factor $M(x_1, x_2, \ldots xn)$, which is a function of additional independent factors $x_1, x_2, \ldots xn$. The detailed COCOMO model, for example, uses 16 such modification factors (15 plus a "mode" overall variable). Many researchers feel that one of the most important modification factors is some measure of the differences between the individuals involved in the development team (Boehm 1981).

Table 11.1 summarizes the survey of software cost estimation model studies. Most of the columns are relatively self-explanatory, but the column marked "Productivity Output Measure" requires some further discussion. This column indicates how the study measured output, typically expressed in lines of code. This survey of software cost estimation models reveals a wide diversity in the method of counting lines of code. Most researchers did not count comments, but did count data (non-executable) statements. All studies counted new lines of code; Table 11.1 indicates whether reused (modified) code was counted as well. The columns indicate with a "Y" whether Executable, Data, Comment, and Overhead (developed but not ultimately used) lines of code were counted by the study.

The treatment of reused code varies significantly. Some studies, such as Walston and Felix (1977), ignore reused code completely. This was probably because it was not

TABLE 11.1 Surveyed studies.

Study	Num Proj	Min Size (KLOC)	Max Size (KLOC)	Avg Size (KLOC)	Type	Data Source	Language	Productivity Output Measure (Lines of Code)	Productivity Input Measure (Phases of Effort)
								N: New Lines R: Reused Lines E: Executable D: Data Lines C: Comments O: Overhead	R: Requirements Phase F: Functional Spec Phase D: Design, Code, Unit Test S: System Test Phase M: Management Effort P: Paperwork (Documentat'n) U: Units of Effort Measured
								N R E D C O	R F D T S M P U
[Sackman 68]	12	0.65 (Kobj)	6.14 (Kobj)		Experiment	SDC	Jovial, Assy	Successful Completion	Debug Hours
[Wolverton 74]	88	0.30	5.00		Military	TRW	Fortran, Assy	Object Code Words	Dollar Cost ($)
[Walston 77]	60	4.00	467.00	20.00	Scientific; DP	IBM	Several	Y n Y Y Y Y	Y Y Y Y Y Y Y Mo
[Chrysler 78]	31				DP	SW House	Cobol	15 FP-like measures	n n Y Y n n n Hr
[Lawrence 81]	278	0.01	6.00		Data Proc	Australia	Cobol, +	Y n Y n n n	n n Y Y n n n Hr
[Boehm 81]	63	1.98	966.0		Various	TRW	Several	Y Y Y Y n Y	n Y Y Y n Y Y Mo
[Bailey 81]	18	2.10	100.8	28.80	Scientific	NASA	Fortran	Y Y Y Y n n	n Y Y Y n Y ? Hr
[Behrens 83]	25	22 FP	435 FP		Data Proc	Equitable Life	Cobol, 4GL	New FPs only	n n Y Y n ? ? Hr
[Thadani 84]	1	210.00	210.00		Data Proc	IBM	PL/I	Y n Y Y n n	n n Y n n n n Hr
[Jeffery 85]	103	0.02	9.80		Data Proc	Australia	Cobol, PL/I	Y n Y n n n	n n Y Y n n n Hr
[Card 87]	22	32.80	159.00	62.00	Scientific	NASA/Goddard	Fortran	Y Y Y Y n n	n Y Y Y n Y ? Hr
[Gill 90]	65	0.22	128.00	15.60	Scientific	Aerospace	Fortran, Pascal	Y n Y n n n	Y Y Y Y Y n Y Hr
[Banker 91]	65	0.05 8 FP	31.00 616 FP	5.42 118 FP	Data Proc	Bank	Cobol	Y Y Y Y n n	Y Y Y Y Y Y Y Hr
[Kemayel 91]	200	n/a	n/a	n/a	Public Sector	Tunisia	Cobol	Y n Y Y n n	n n Y n n n n Mo

deemed a significant factor in the Federal Systems Division of IBM, which built large custom systems. The Software Engineering Laboratory of the University of Maryland has adopted the standard of a fixed 20% of reused code being counted as being "developed," and hence appearing in productivity measures (Bailey and Basili 1981) and (Card, McGarry, and Page 1987). Boehm (1981) offers a more complex, but relatively appealing approach in COCOMO. Given that the average project should spend 40% in design, 30% in coding, and 30% in testing, COCOMO calls for estimating the percentage of the original design, code, and testing effort that must be reproduced, and multiplying it by 0.4, 0.3, and 0.3, respectively, to get a weighted factor of the amount of work that must be reproduced. That factor is then multiplied with the old code size to get the "effective" number of lines developed by modifying the old code.

Note that one problem with using lines of code for the size estimate is that the final number of lines of code is not known at the start of the project, and so must be estimated. Albrecht and Gaffney (1983) proposed another size measure called *Function Points* (FPs), which counts the number of input files, output files, internal files, inquiries, and interface files. Function Points have been shown in some organizations to provide better predictors of effort than lines of code (Behrens 1983), and there is evidence that prediction equations based on FPs may be applicable between different organizations (Kemerer 1987). Some software productivity researchers have concluded that lines of code should be abandoned as a measure of software productivity output in favor of FPs (Jones 1991). Function Points are and will continue to be a fruitful area of software cost estimation model research.

Software managers generally divide software development projects into "phases" of requirements definition, functional design, detailed design, coding, unit test, and system integration/test. All of the software productivity studies surveyed measured the time that software engineers spend in the detailed design, code, and unit test phase. That still leaves several issues as to what other effort to measure:

1. How much of the "requirements definition" phase effort is measured, such as proposal preparation, user meetings, and background research?

2. How much of the "functional specification" phase is measured, e.g., the time spent by product planners or system engineers?

3. How much of "system testing" is measured? If the project is developed for an in-house customer, this effort is usually included. If the project is developed for an external customer, however, the customer may perform system testing that is not counted.

4. How much of the support staff effort is counted, including secretaries, building maintenance, personnel, and other general and administrative overhead?

5. How much of management effort is charged to the project, including reviews by senior managers, design-review time by non-project engineers, and similar items?

6. How much of the documentation effort is counted? In projects developed for the federal government, documentation is a significant portion of the effort.

7. How much of the engineers' "nonproductive" time is counted? Studies have shown that from 30% (Boehm 1981) to 50% (Brooks 1975) of software engineer time is not spent in activities that directly contribute to the final software product.

The "Productivity Input Measure" column of Table 11.1 indicates whether the study included the effort described in the preceding questions 1 through 6. As for measurements of nonproductive time, few studies indicate whether it was excluded. Table 11.1 indicates the granularity with which effort was measured. It is possible that studies that measured effort on the hour (Hr) level did not include non-productive hours. Studies that measured effort on the work-month level (Mo) are more likely to have included the nonproductive time.

Staffing Variables in Software Estimation Models

The distinguishing feature of the studies surveyed in this paper is that they included staffing variables as an explicit independent variable. In all cases, the models are attempting to account for differences in individual ability as a possible source of software productivity differences.

Individual differences: experimental results

In one of the earliest software productivity studies, Sackman, Erikson, and Grant (1968) measured the productivity of individual engineers solving the same problem with on-line terminals and off-line batch submissions. To their surprise, they noticed a 28:1 difference in the time between the fastest and slowest solution to the problem. This 28:1 ratio is widely and inaccurately cited as the range of individual programmer performance capability.

As clarified by Dickey (1981), the figure of 28:1 arose as follows: one subject programmed in assembly language in a batch mode and took 170 hours to solve an algebra problem. Another subject programmed in a high-level language on a time-shared system and took only six hours. The difference of 28:1 was caused partly by individual differences and partly by the deleterious effects of programming in a relatively time-inefficient language and in a time-inefficient manner. For individuals using the same language and the same system, the difference recorded by Sackman was only 5:1.

In response to Dickey, however, Curtis (1981) reaffirms individual differences by presenting another experiment in which three individuals took 39 minutes to find a planted bug and another individual took only three minutes, a 13:1 difference. (In fact, one individual never found the bug and quit after 69 minutes.) The Curtis study, however, is for a significantly smaller problem (minutes rather than hours).

The major unresolved issue for either of these studies is whether these ranges of performance in solving one small problem will be observed when the issue is scaled up to the full range of activities required of a practicing software engineer. Researchers cannot unequivocally generalize from the Sackman et al. data or the Curtis data that the long-term productivity of software engineers varies "on the order of a decimal order of magnitude." Furthermore, these small experiments do not strongly suggest that the same engineers will have similar productivity rates on different small problems.

In addition, it should be noted that controlled software experiments have also sometimes shown no significant correlation between performance and experience. Sheppard et al. (1979) found little correlation in small-scale experiments testing program comprehension and modification tasks. For debugging tasks, they found that programmers with less than 3 years experience showed correlation between debugging time and 1, 2, or 3 years of experience, but they admit this may be a statistical artifact of the wider variation in times reported for this low-experience group. The correlation was not present for programmers with more than 3 years experience.

Of more interest would be studies of much larger, typical problems. Unfortunately, the cost of such an experiment is prohibitive, so published studies of individual productivity differences on large projects are confounded by differences in the tasks themselves. Thadhani reports one small study with six subjects working on a large (210 KLOC) program, each doing separate tasks. The range of productivity was 4:1, from 1200 to 300 LOC/MM. DeMarco and Lister (1985) report, on page 45, a "composite of the findings of three different sources" that show an individual performance difference of 2.5:1 from the best to the median performer, and 10:1 from best to worst. These range differences are supported by their "coding war games" exercise performed by over 600 software engineers.

Individual differences: field studies

Current software cost estimation models attempt to account for individual differences indirectly—by assuming that other measurable factors, such as experience, may substitute for personal productivity. Usually, the staffing variables included in a model are measures of the experience of an individual, as measured in years experience with various facets of the project. Some models also add measures of the capability of the individual. Banker, Datar, and Kemerer (1991), for instance, used the performance ranking of the individuals as a measure of capability. Other models used subjective management classifications of capability. Table 11.2 classifies the staffing variables used by published software cost estimation models into eight categories, and shows which categories are used by which model. The human factor categories are:

- Total experience—the total professional experience of the engineer or team
- Language experience—the experience of the engineer/team with the programming language for the project
- System experience—the experience with the operating system or development environment
- Application experience—the experience with the software application domain
- Hardware experience—the experience with the hardware platform
- Programmer capability—a measure of the capability of the individual or team
- Management capability—a measure of the capability of the management or systems analysts of the team
- Education—the level of formal education of the individual or an average for the team

A major problem of all of the studies with more than one developer is how to assign a measure for a multi-person team. Although simple averages of years of experience could be applied, it does not appear that any study actually did this. In most cases a subjective determination is made to classify the team into one of a limited number of experience or ability categories. This is the approach, for instance, of both the COCOMO model (Boehm 1981) and the SPQR model of Jones (1986). Such arbitrary assignments, of course, diminish the repeatability of observed data and reduce the generalizability of the model.

Note that many popular cost estimation models, such as the SLIM model of Putnam (1978), do not require quantification of staffing variables per se. The SLIM model uses a "technology factor" constant to incorporate all factors other than project size and scheduled time. As such, it can be thought of as the correction factor "M." Putnam posits that this correction factor, or productivity index, stays within a narrow range for a given organization and changes relatively slowly over time. However, the SLIM database has observed productivity indexes for a single class of applications to vary by plus or minus 3 as a standard deviation. The difference between a productivity index of 12 and one of 6 is an effort estimation variation of as much as 4.23:1. Changing the index by even plus or minus one level changes the effort estimate by 60% (Mah and Putnam 1990). Therefore, the SLIM model allows for wide ranges in productivity.

Project team size

Programming-in-the-large is fundamentally a group activity. Weinberg (1971) was one of the first to recognize that improving psychological group dynamics would be likely to improve software productivity. He proposed "egoless programming" in order to improve group communication and effectiveness. Schneiderman (1980), in recognizing programming as a group process, advocates peer review and peer rating.

One of the easiest software metrics to measure is team size itself, and several researchers have investigated its impact on performance. The most famous anecdotal evidence is from Fred Brooks' experience on the OS/360 project documented in *The mythical man-month* (Brooks 1975). Brook's Law states that "Adding manpower to a late software project makes it later," due to increased communications and training efforts. Scott and Simmons (1975) documented the effect of increased communications due to different organizational styles, again showing how greater project communication requirements reduced productivity.

A thorough analysis of group size impact on productivity appears in the Conte, Dunsmore, and Shen (1986) textbook. They propose a Cooperative Programming Model (COPMO) developed by Thebaut and the authors at Purdue (1983). The generalized COPMO model is of the form

$$\text{Effort} = a + b \times \text{Size} + c \times (\text{Pbar})^d$$

where Pbar is the average team size, defined as $E \div T$, where E is effort in person-months and T is project duration in months. The Conte et al. textbook includes six databases of project size, effort, and time. They used these data to estimate a to be zero and d to be 1.5. They calculated a set of b and c parameters in b_i and c_i pairs for a set of "effort complexity classes." Using COCOMO's a priori modification factors, they defined four complexity classes and found the b_i and c_i for each class that minimize the Magnitude of Relative Error (MRE) measure for the COPMO model. With four such complexity class partitions, the COPMO model has an MRE of 25%, producing an effort estimate within 25% of the actual effort for 75% of the COCOMO database projects. This level of accuracy is consistent with best performance for current software cost estimation models.

Staffing Variables Impact on Software Cost Model Estimates

Human factors have had mixed success in improving software model accuracy. Studies that have successfully shown that more-experienced teams were more productive include those by Chrysler (1978), Walston and Felix (1977), Thadhani (1984), and Card, McGarry, and Page (1987).

Chrysler tested five programmer-related variables, including age and various types of experience, and found higher levels to all be associated with a reduction in the number of hours required to produce COBOL programs. Of the five, the single most useful predictor variable was "experience at this facility."

Walston and Felix collected data on a set of 60 projects by IBM's Federal system division in the 1972–1976 time frame. First of all, they calculated the productivity, in lines of code per work-month (LOC/WM) for each project. They collected data by a questionnaire on some 68 variables concerning the development environment, nature of the problem, and staffing variables. Of the 68 variables, 29 showed significant spread of productivity between the upper third and lower third of the variable ranges. Five of the 29 variables concerned staffing variables, and the results are shown in Table 11.2.

Thadhani measured the productivity of six programmers working on a large PL/I program. Although his primary interest was the effect of response time on productivity, he noted in his sample that the two experienced programmers produced at a higher rate than the four less-experienced programmers. The two experienced programmers produced 1200 and 900 LOC/MM, while the less-experienced programmers produced 600, 600, 400, and 300 LOC/MM. Such a study was too small to have a high degree of statistical significance, and as mentioned earlier, may have been confounded by the differences in the tasks performed by the engineers.

Card et al. measured a set of eight "technology use" variables (e.g., structured programming) and 12 "non-technology" variables (e.g., programmer effectiveness) along with LOC/MM productivity for 22 projects at NASA's Goddard Space Flight Center. The "programmer effectiveness" measure was "a weighted measure of the development team's general and application-specific years of experience." They found that this programmer effectiveness variable had the highest positive correlation with productivity. A variable called "computer use," which was computer time per line of code, had a slightly higher negative correlation, probably because projects in trouble had to spend more computer time. Together, these two variables accounted for 54% of the variation in productivity.

An ANCOVA analysis of the remaining variables showed that no other variable accounted for more than 5% additional explanation of variance. They also found that the programmer effectiveness variable had the highest correlation to software reliability. The range of staff application experience (2.9–5.0 years) and overall experience (7.0–11.0 years) appears to be low, and it is not clear to what extent the transformation to a "programmer effectiveness" measure affects the significance of the results.

TABLE 11.2 Human factors in surveyed studies.

Study	Staffing Variables: T: Total Experience, L: Language Experience, S: System (OS) Exp., A: Application Exp., H: Hardware Exp., P: Programmer ability, M: Manager Ability, E: Education								Results
	T	L	S	A	H	P	M	E	
[Sackman 68]	Y	Y		Y					High individual differences (28:1) in debug time, but confounded with different languages and on-line/off-line. Maximum 5:1 difference with same treatment.
[Wolverton 74]	Y								No correlation of programmer total experience with dollar cost of object code produced.
[Walston 77]	Y	Y	Y	Y					3:1 variation in productivity between extremes of five human factor variables.
[Chrysler 78]	Y	Y	Y	Y	Y				Reductions in programming time correlated with 5 different experience related variables. "Experience at this facility" most useful single predictor.
[Lawrence 81]	Y								No increase in productivity after the first year of experience.
[Boehm 81]		Y	Y	Y		Y	Y		Human factors are 5 of 15 factors which together reduce prediction mean relative error from 60% to 19%.
[Bailey 81]		Y	Y	Y		Y	Y		Human factors are 5 of 21 factors tested. Minimum model prediction error obtained without using any of them.
[Behrens 83]		Y							Experience factor did not improve model prediction error.
[Thadani 84]	Y			Y					Sample of 6 programmers on real-world application which showed 3:1 productivity differences between experienced an inexperienced engineers.
[Jeffery 85]		Y						Y	Follow-up to [Lawrence 81] with same results: no productivity increase after first year of experience.
[Card 87]	Y	Y							Experience had highest correlation to productivity (.53) of 12 non-technology and 8 technology factors.
[Gill 90]	Y							Y	Slight decrease of productivity with increased fraction of project time by highly experienced personnel. (Task complexity not controlled for.)
[Banker 91]				Y		Y			Ability and application experience not significant at usual levels after controlling for other factors such as project size.
[Kemayel 91]	Y	Y	Y	Y				Y	Two of five experience variables significantly correlated with productivity, but together explained only 7.5% of variance.

Other studies have failed to find significant effects of differences in experience level. An early study by Wolverton (1974) failed to find any correlation between experience and programming cost per object instruction. Lawrence (1981), and Jeffrey and Lawrence (1985) conducted two studies of over 350 programs prepared by 17

Australian organizations in 1976 and 1980. Their data showed very slight increases in productivity after the first year of COBOL programmer's experience, but no improvement in subsequent years. In general, they conclude (on page 55) by noting "a confusing relationship between education, experience, and productivity suggesting no clear trend of increasing productivity with education and experience." This confirms the experimental work by Sheppard et al. (1979), also showing early improvement with experience but no significant differences after the first few years.

Kemayel, Mili, and Ouederni (1991) studied the productivity of 200 individual Tunisian programmers, collecting data on 33 variables categorized as "personnel," "process," and "user-related" factors. Of the 33 variables, five were staffing factors—education, applications domain experience, programming language experience, virtual machine experience, and experience with the user community. Of these, only the last two were statistically significant, and these variables combined explained only 7.5% of the variation in productivity. They found very wide variation (15:1) in KDSI/MM productivity ratings, which they attribute to Tunisia's practice of tenured employment of even low-skill programmers.

One limitation of most of the studies cited above is that the researchers have done simple correlations of (typically) one experience variable and, for example, productivity. Such correlations might mask the effect of other variables that might be correlated with experience but are not controlled for in the model. Of the research surveyed here, Banker, Datar, and Kemerer (1991) reported the effect on the standard error when the human factor variable was removed.

They considered two variables: "No Experienced" (a dummy variable equal to 1 when no team member exceeded 2 years experience) and "Top Staff" (the percentage of project hours charged by individuals rated above average in the organization's performance review system). The "No Experienced" variable, and the "Top Staff" variable were not significant at usual levels (p = 0.41 and p = 0.11).

Another way to investigate the value added by the staffing variables in current cost estimation models is to examine the relative performance of these models and to determine factors common to the better-performing models. Interestingly, such an analysis suggests that the best software effort prediction models do not require the use of staffing variables as an independent variable. Of the models surveyed, the best results in terms of predicting the actual project values were obtained by Bailey and Basili (1981), using a baseline model and correction factors for the NASA Goddard data set.

Although they collected staffing variables data, they found that the correction factors for project complexity and development methodology alone were sufficient to build a model with a standard multiplicative error of only 16%. Conte, Dunsmore, & Shen (1986) also suggests a model (COPMO) that uses both estimated project size and team size, with modification factors only for project complexity, that achieves a mean absolute relative error of 21%.

From the above review it can be concluded that staffing variables, as currently operationalized, have not been shown to be a particularly useful addition in software cost estimation models. After accounting for measures of the project size, and modifying this estimate for project complexity differences and tool/methodology differences, additional correction for human performance differences appear to not significantly improve model accuracy. *Given that this result is at odds with what*

*practicing software managers believe about factors affecting project perfor-
mance, this suggests that more work is necessary to improve the modeling of
staffing factors.*

Future Research and Recommendations

The main difficulty with incorporating staffing variables in software cost models is
that it is not well understood why individual and team programming performance
varies. "We do not know if these differences are attributable to differences among
individuals' speed of information processing while programming, the nature of the
information processing themselves, or some combination of the two." (Laughery
and Laughery 1985). Weinberg (1971) suggests that differences in performance,
especially debugging speed, are probably due to the exact structure of the problem itself, and whether a similar exact problem has been seen before. If debugging
time is related to specific pattern matching, then studies of ranges of different
times to debug a small problem are not useful: the variation is only due to the variation of particular previously-solved problems. Supporting this difference is the
failure of almost all studies to show a correlation between tests of programming
skill and actual programming performance.

The most commonly accepted theories for accounting for individual differences
are the cognitive psychology theories of how programming knowledge is represented. These theories are surveyed in Laughery and Laughery (1985), and Curtis
(1990), and are only briefly described here.

Newell and Simon introduced a major theory of human problem solving via goal-
seeking production rules, today the basis of knowledge-based artificial intelligence
systems. Brooks (1977) applied the Newell and Simon theory to the programming
task by studying in detail a single expert programmer. He identified 23 protocols
used to produce code, themselves producing the 73 actions that generated the simple program under development.

He estimated that the total number of rules used by an expert programmer was in
the tens of thousands, consistent with the 31,000 rules estimated used by a chess expert. He argues that domain knowledge (the set of rules mastered), determines differences in programming skill. Schneiderman and Mayer (1979) propose that
syntactic and semantic knowledge is stored separately, so that, for instance, the algorithm for finding the largest integer in an array is stored independent of the form
of the FORTRAN program to implement it.

Program comprehension is a central skill for software maintenance and an important component of original software design. Robson et al. (1991) recently surveyed
the various psychological research on how programs are comprehended. They cite
48 papers studying the effectiveness of code artifacts on comprehension and various
other theories of program comprehension. As an example, Letovsky (1987) analyzed
the protocols employed by maintenance programmers in reading and understanding
programs, characterizing the process as an iteration of questions and conjectures.
He classifies these processes into a taxonomy of psychological constructs including:
slot filling, abductive reasoning, symbolic evaluation, discourse rules, generic plans,
and endorsement rules.

Brooks (1983) attributes individual differences in program comprehension performance to differences in programming knowledge, problem-domain knowledge, and hypothesis-confirmation search strategies. Soloway and Ehrlich (1984) identify two distinguishing components of expert programming skill to be programming "plans" or knowledge schemas and "rules of programming discourse," or useful coding conventions.

It seems apparent from the above that cognitive psychology offers a rich, complex, and growing set of theories to account for the observed differences in individual performance. Expert programmers may be those who have learned rules appropriate to the problem under examination. This includes semantic and syntactic knowledge of the computer language and computing environment, and often domain-specific knowledge as well. Vast individual differences in individuals may swamp any observed variation due to different treatments in programming experiments and software productivity studies. In an excellent critical review of programming psychology experiments, Sheil (1981) expresses the difficulty of measuring productivity differences as follows:

> However programmers' knowledge bases are actually organized, their existence and size seems clear. Hypotheses which posit differences in either individual aptitude or task difficulty are therefore, at best, extremely difficult to investigate, as the enormous size of the knowledge bases being drawn on imply that different individuals approach the same task with vastly different resources. Comparing their behavior is like contrasting the work of two tile layers, each of whom has covered an equivalent wall, working with radically difference sizes and colors of tiles. Similarity of pattern is unlikely.

Significant difficulties remain in measuring the richness of an individual's knowledge base and its conceptual fit to a problem's domain knowledge. Gibson and Senn (1989) for instance, found that programmers performing software maintenance tasks cannot reliably separate the syntactical complexity of a program's text from the semantic complexity of the modification task itself. Psychological constructs that cannot be distinguished cannot be measured.

Cognitive psychology offers a path for understanding why increases in, say, program size increase programming effort. It offers a diverse set of theories from which hypotheses can be drawn, measures defined, and experiments conducted. Vessey and Weber (1984) chide the computer science community for concentrating research on predicting dependent variable effects of structured programming, rather than understanding those effects. Their criticism applies to the entirety of software cost estimation model research.

Given the richness and complexity of the still-early understanding of software cognitive psychology, staffing variable measures like "years of application experience" are at best crude approximations of the differences among individuals. In addition, they do not at all address the issue of coordinating the mix of experiences and aptitudes of multiple agents in software development teams. It is, therefore, not surprising that such measures often fail to significantly improve the accuracy of software cost estimation models.

What are needed are more well-grounded variables that reflect these more complex notions of individual differences, most especially the staff/problem fit issue.

Author Biography

Chris F. Kemerer is the Douglas Drane Career Development Associate Professor of Information Technology and Management at the MIT Sloan School of Management. He received the B.S. degree, magna cum laude, in economics and decision sciences from the Wharton School of the University of Pennsylvania and the Ph.D. degree from the Graduate School of Industrial Administration at Carnegie Mellon University. Prior to his graduate studies he was a Principal at American Management Systems, Inc., the software services firm. His research interests are in the measurement and modeling of software development for improved performance, and he has previously published articles on these topics in leading academic journals, including *Communications of the ACM, IEEE Transactions on Software Engineering, Information and Software Technology*, and *Management Science*. Dr. Kemerer serves on the editorial boards of the *Communications of the ACM, Information Systems Research, The Journal of Organizational Computing, The Journal of Software Quality*, and *MIS Quarterly*, and is a member of the IEEE Computer Society, ACM and The Institute for Management Sciences.

Michael W. Patrick graduated from MIT with a BS and MS in Computer Science in 1980. He was the chief architect at Texas Instruments for the IBM Token Ring Chip Set, and has served on the IEEE 802.5 committee for local area networks. He has served as Research Associate at Ztel, Engineering Manager at General Computer Corporation, and Vice President of Engineering at Cryptall Communications Corp. He is currently a graduate student in the Management of Technology program in the Sloan School of Management at MIT.

Works Cited

Albrecht, A.J. and J. Gaffney. 1983. Software function, source lines of code, and development effort prediction: A software science validation. *IEEE transactions on software engineering*. SE-9 (6): 639–648.

Bailey, J.W. and V.R. Basili. 1981. A meta-model for software development resource expenditures. *Proceedings of the 5th international conference on software engineering*. 107–116.

Banker, R.D., S.M. Datar, and C.F. Kemerer. 1991. A model to evaluate variables impacting productivity on software maintenance projects. *Management science*. 37 (1): 1–18.

Behrens, C.A. 1983. Measuring the productivity of computer systems development activities with Function Points. *IEEE transactions on software engineering*. SE-9 (6): 648–652.

Boehm, B. 1981. *Software engineering economics*. Englewood Cliffs, N.J.: Prentice-Hall.

Brooks, F. 1975. *The mythical man-month*. Addison-Wesley.

Brooks, R. 1977. Towards a theory of cognitive processes in computer programming. *International journal of man-machine studies*. 9: 737–751.

Brooks, R. 1983. Towards a theory of the comprehension of computer programs. *International journal of man-machine studies*. 18: 543–554.

Card, D.N., F.E. McGarry, and G.T. Page. 1987. Evaluating software engineering technologies. *IEEE transactions on software engineering*. SE-13 (7): 845–851.

Chrysler, E. 1978. Some basic determinants of computer programming productivity. *Communications of the ACM*. 21 (6): 472–483.

Conte, S.D., H.E. Dunsmore, and V.Y. Shen. 1986. *Software engineering metrics and models*. Reading, Ma.: Benjamin-Cummings.

Curtis, B. 1981. Substantiating programmer variability. *Proceedings of the IEEE*. 69 (7): 846.

Curtis, B. 1990. Fifteen years of psychology in software engineering: Individual differences and cognitive science. In *Software state of the art: Selected papers*. ed. DeMarco T. and T. Lister. New York, N.Y.: Dorset House.

DeMarco, T. and T. Lister. 1987. *Peopleware*. New York, N.Y.: Dorset House.

Dickey, T.E. 1981. Programmer variability. *Proceedings of the IEEE*. 69 (7): 844–845.

Gibson, V.R. and J.A. Senn. 1989. System structure and software maintenance performance. *Communications of the ACM*. 32 (3): 347–358.

Heemstra, F.J. and R. Kuster. 1991. *Controlling software development costs: A field study*. University of Technology.

Jeffery, D.R. and M.J. Lawrence. 1985. Managing programming productivity. *Journal of systems and software*. 5: 49–58.

Jenkins, A.M., J.D. Naumann, and J.C. Wetherbe. 1984. Empirical investigation of systems development practices and results. *Information management*. 7: 73–82.

Jones, C. 1986. *Programming productivity*. New York, N.Y.: McGraw-Hill.

Jones, C. 1991. *Applied software measurement*. New York, N.Y.: McGraw-Hill.

Kemayel, L., A. Mili, and I. Ouederni. 1991. Controllable factors for programmer productivity: A statistical study. *Journal of systems and software*. 16: 151–163.

Kemerer, C.F. 1987. An empirical validation of software cost estimation models. *Communications of the ACM*. 30 (5): 416–429.

Kemerer, C.F. 1991. Software cost estimation models. In *Software engineers reference book*. ed. McDermid, J. Oxford, England, U.K.: Butterworth-Heinemann Ltd.

Laughery, K. and K. Laughery. 1985. Human factors in software engineering: A review of the literature. *Journal of systems and software*. 5: 3–14.

Lawrence, M.J. 1981. Programming methodology, organizational environment, and programming productivity. *Journal of systems and software.* 2: 257–269.

Letovsky, S. 1987. Cognitive processes in program comprehension. *Journal of systems and software.* 7 (4): 325–339.

Mah, M.C. and L.H. Putnam. 1990. Is there a real measure for software productivity? *Programmer's update.* 26–36.

Phan, D., D. Vogel, and J. Nunamaker. 1988. The search for perfect project manage ment. *Computerworld.* 95–100.

Putnam, L.H. 1978. A general empirical solution to the macro software sizing and estimating problem. *IEEE transactions on software engineering.* 345–361.

Robson, D.J., K.H. Bennett, B.J. Cornelius, and M. Munro. Approaches to program comprehension. *Journal of systems and software.* 14: 79–84.

Sackman, H., W.J. Erikson, and E.E. Grant. 1968. Exploratory experimental studies comparing online and offline programming performance. *Communications of the ACM.* 11 (1): 3–11.

Schneiderman, B. 1980. *Software psychology: Human factors in computer and information systems.* Cambridge, Ma.: Winthrop Press.

Schneiderman, B. and R.E. Mayer. 1979. Syntactic/semantic interactions in programmer behavior: A model and experimental results. *International journal of computer and information sciences.* 8: 219–238.

Scott, R.F. and D.B. Simmons. 1975. Predicting programming group productivity—a communications model. *IEEE transactions of software engineering.* SE-1 (4): 411–414.

Sheil, B.A. 1981. The psychological study of programming. *Computing surveys.* 13 (1).

Sheppard, S.B., B. Curtis, P. Milliman, M.A. Borst, and T. Love. 1979. First year results from a research program on human factors in software engineering. pp. 1021–1027. National Computer Conference. New York, N.Y.

Soloway, E. and K. Ehrlich. 1984. Empirical studies of programming knowledge. *IEEE transactions on software engineering.* SE-10 (5): 595–609.

Thebaut, S.M. 1983. *The saturation effect in large-scale software development: Its impact and control.* Ph.D. thesis. Purdue University Dept. of Computer Science.

van Genuchten, M. 1991. Why is software late? An empirical study of the reasons for delay in software development. *IEEE transactions on software engineering.* 17 (6): 582–590.

Vessey, I. and R. Weber. 1984. Research on structured programming: An empiricist's evaluation. *IEEE transactions on software engineering.* SE-10 (4): 394–407.

Walston, C.E. and C.P. Felix. 1977. A method of programming measurement and estimation. *IBM systems journal.* 16 (1): 54–73.

Weinberg, G.M. 1971. *The psychology of computer programming.* New York, N.Y.: Van Nostrand Reinhold.

Wolverton, R.W. 1974. The cost of developing large-scale software. *IEEE transactions on computers.* C-23 (6): 615–636.

12

Counting Function Points

by Pierre Deveaux

The International Function Point User Group

The International Function Point User Group (IFPUG) consists of over 500 companies. These companies include 29 of the Fortune 500, plus numerous large banks, utilities, insurance, transportation, retail, chemical, and other companies from virtually every industry. Aside from the 500 IFPUG members, another 200 companies are affiliated with IFPUG through the Netherlands Function Point Users Group (NEFPUG), and the Australian Software Metrics Association (ASMA). IFPUG is the most successful non-vendor sponsored organization of its kind.

The mission of IFPUG is to promote and encourage the use of Function Point Analysis and other software measurement techniques through the following value-added services:

- Member services
- Conference services
- Education services
- Function Point counting practices and professional certification
- National and international standards setting
- Industry publications
- Research studies

Members meet twice a year at conferences to discuss standards as well as the multi-million dollar impact that measurements can have on all aspects of business and government. IFPUG offers a seminar on software measurement in addition to workshops on how to count Function Points.

Information about measurement may be obtained from the group by writing to: IFPUG, Blendonview Office Park, 50008-28 Pine Creek Drive, Westerville, Ohio 43081-4899.

Function Point Analysis Overview

Objectives of Function Point Analysis

Function Points measure software by quantifying the functionality provided external to itself, based primarily on logical design. With this in mind, the objectives of Function Point Counting are to

- Measure what the user requested and received;
- Measure independently of technology used for implementation;
- Provide a sizing metric to support quality and productivity analysis;
- Provide a vehicle for software estimation;
- Provide a normalization factor for software comparison.

In addition to meeting the above objectives, the process of counting Function Points should be

- Simple enough to minimize the overhead of the measurement process;
- Simple yet concise, to allow for consistency over time, projects, and practitioners.

Summary of Function Point Counting

The Function Point metric measures an application based on two areas of evaluation. The first results in the Unadjusted Function Point Count and reflects the specific countable functionality provided to the user by the application. The second area of evaluation, which produces the Value Adjustment Factor (VAF), evaluates the general functionality provided to the user of the application.

Unadjusted Function Point Count. An application's specific user functionality is evaluated in terms of what is delivered by the application, not how it is delivered. Only user-requested and visible components are counted. These components are categorized into Function Types, and are categorized as either *Data* or *Transactional*.

Data Function Types include:

- Internal Logical Files (ILF)—internally maintained logical group of data
- External Interface Files (EIF)—externally maintained logical group of data

while *Transactional Function Types* include:

- External Inputs (EI)—maintains internally stored data
- External Outputs (EO)—data output
- External Inquiries (EQ)—combination of input (request) and output (retrieval)

Each Function Type is further categorized based on its relative functional complexity as Low, Average, or High.

Function Point values ranging from 3 to 15, depending on the Function Type and functional complexity rating, are assigned and totaled, producing the Unadjusted Function Point Count.

The Unadjusted Function Point Count is then weighted by the Value Adjustment Factor (VAF) to produce the final Function Point Count.

Value Adjustment Factor

The VAF is comprised of 14 General System Characteristic (GSC) questions that assess the general functionality of the application.

The General System Characteristics are:

1. Data communication

2. Distributed function

3. Performance

4. Heavily used configuration

5. Transaction rates

6. On-line data entry

7. Design for end-user efficiency

8. On-line update

9. Complex processing

10. Usable in other applications

11. Installation ease

12. Operational ease

13. Multiple sites

14. Facilitating change

The questions are answered using Degrees of Influence (DI) on a scale of 0 to 5.

0 Not present, or no influence

1 Incidental influence

2 Moderate influence

3 Average influence

4 Significant influence

5 Strong influence throughout

Types of Function Point Counts

Function Point Counts can be associated to either projects or applications. The three types of Function Point Counts are:

- Development (Project) Function Point Count—the Function Point Count associated with the initial installation of new software. This count measures the function provided to the end users by the project. It includes the functionality provided by data conversion and associated conversion reporting requirements. The Development Function Point Count, minus those Function Points associated with conversion activities, becomes the Application Function Point Count once the project is installed.

- Enhancement (Project) Function Point Count—the Function Point Count associated with the enhancement of existing software. This count measures the modifications to the existing application that add, change, or delete user function within the scope of a project. It includes the functionality provided by data conversion and associated conversion reporting requirements. When an Enhancement Project is installed, the Application Function Point Count must be updated to reflect changes in the application's functionality.

- Application Function Point Count—the Function Point Count associated to an installed application. It is also referred to as the Baseline or Installed Function Point Count. This count provides a measure of the current function the application provides the end-user. This number is initialized at the time the Development Function Point Count is completed. This count does not include the functionality provided by data conversion and associated conversion reporting requirements. It can therefore differ from the Development Function Point Count. It is altered every time an enhancement alters the application's function.

Boundaries

Boundaries identify the border between the application or project being measured and either external applications or the user domain.

Boundaries are used to establish the scope of the work product being measured. Additionally, they are used to establish data ownership and processing relationships that are required when conducting a Function Point Count. Associated measurement data (e.g., effort, cost, defects) should be collected at the same level as the application/project boundaries.

Application boundary

Look at the application from the user's point of view, what the user can understand and describe. The boundary between related applications should be based on separate business functions as seen by the user, not on technological concerns. Use the system external specifications or get a system flow chart and draw a boundary around it to highlight what is internal and what is external to the application. The boundary should be stable and correspond to how the application is maintained.

Development (Project) boundary

Again, look at the application from the user's point of view, what the user can understand and describe. Use the system external specifications or get a system flow chart and draw a boundary around it to highlight what is internal and what is external to the application.

Enhancement (Project) boundary

An Enhancement project's boundary must conform to the boundaries already established for the application(s) being modified. Separate or small phases, for the ease of development, should not be considered separate project boundaries.

Counting Rules

The Function Point metric measures the application based on two areas of evaluation. The first produces the Unadjusted Function Point Count, which is a measure of the specific, countable functionality provided to the user by the application. The second area of evaluation, which produces the Value Adjustment Factor (VAF), evaluates the general functionality of the application. This is done based on the 14 General System Characteristics discussed in detail in a later section.

The five function types discussed briefly below are discussed in detail in following sections.

Unadjusted Function Point Count

Unadjusted Function Points are calculated based on those components of an application that are requested and visible to the user. These components are categorized into Function Types. Function Types can be categorized as either Data or Transactional.

Data Function Types represent the functionality provided to the user to meet internal and external data requirements.

- Internal Logical Files (ILF) reside internal to an application's boundary and reflect data storage functionality provided to the user. Internal Logical Files must be maintained and utilized by the application.

- External Interface Files (EIF) reside external to an application's boundary and reflect the functionality provided by the application through the use of data maintained by other applications.

While both Internal Logical Files and External Interface Files contain the word "file" in their title, they are not files in the traditional data processing sense. In this case, file refers to a logically related group of data and not the physical implementation.

Transactional Function Types represent the functionality provided the user for the processing of data by an application.

- External Inputs (EI) reflect the functionality provided the user for the receipt and maintenance (add, change, and delete) of data on Internal Logical Files.
- External Outputs (EO) reflect the functionality provided the user for output generated by the application from Internal Logical Files or External Interface Files.
- External Inquiries (EQ) reflect the functionality provided the user for queries of Internal Logical Files or External Interface Files.

Internal Logical Files

Overview

Internal Logical Files represent an application's maintainable data storage requirements. Internal Logical Files are evaluated and contribute to the Function Point Count based on their number and relative functional complexity.

Definitions

An *Internal Logical File* (ILF) is a user-identifiable group of logically related data or control information maintained and utilized within the boundary of the application.

User-identifiable group of logically related data refers to data related at such a level that an experienced user would identify the data as fulfilling a specific user requirement of the application. The data analysis equivalent to such high-level logical groupings are singularly named *data stores* on a data flow diagram.

Control information is data used by the application to ensure compliance with business function requirements specified by the user.

Maintained is the ability to add, change, or delete data through a standardized process of application.

Methodology

Identification.   Identify all data that is

- Stored internal to the application's boundary;
- Maintained through a standardized process of the application;
- Identified as a requirement of the application by the users.

Group the data logically based on the user's view as follows:

- Group data at the level of detail at which the user can first categorize the data as satisfying unique requirements of the application.
- View the data logically. Although some storage technologies such as tables in a relational DBMS or a sequential flat file relate closely to Internal Logical Files, do not assume that one physical file equals one logical file.

Examples

To identify potential ILFs, look at the type of data stored and how a user would view or group the data, rather than the storage technology (such as tables, flat files, indexes, and paths).

Each type of data on the following list can relate to one or more ELFs, depending on the user's view.

- Application data (master files such as those for tax information and personnel information)
- Application security data
- Audit data
- Help messages
- Error messages
- Edit data

The following are ILFs:

- Backup data is counted only if specifically requested by the user due to legal or similar requirements.
- Internal Logical Files maintained by more than one application are credited to both applications at the time each is counted.

The following are not ILFs:

- Temporary files
- Work files
- Sort files
- Suspense files (files containing incomplete transactions from an External Input. Do not count unless data on the suspense file can be accessed or maintained by the user through unique External Inputs, External Outputs, and/or External Inquiries)

- Backup data required for corporate backup and recovery procedures
- Files introduced only because of technology used; for example, a file containing JCL required for job submission
- Alternate indices (an alternative physical access method)

Issues/resolutions

The following are not discussed in the Albrecht 1984 document and are decisions of the IFPUG Counting Practices Committee (CPC):

1. Backup files are counted only if specifically requested by the user to meet legal or similar requirements. Backup files required for normal backup and recovery procedures are not counted.
2. ILFs maintainable by more than one application are credited to both applications at the time each is counted.
3. Suspense/carry around files are counted as an Internal Logical File only if the suspense file can be accessed/maintained by the user through unique External Inputs, External Outputs, and/or External Inquiries.

External Interface Files

Overview

External Interface Files represent an application's externally maintained data storage requirements. External Interface Files are evaluated and contribute to the Function Point Count based on their number and relative functional complexity.

Definitions

An *External Interface File* (EIF) is a user-identifiable group of logically related data or control information utilized by the application, but maintained by another application.

User identifiable group of logically related data is defined as data related at such a level that an experienced user would identify the data as fulfilling a specific user requirement of the application.

Control information is data used by the application to assure compliance with business function requirements specified by the user.

Methodology

Identification.   Identify all data that is

- Stored external to the application's boundary;
- Not maintained by this application;
- Identified as a requirement of the application by the users.

Group the data logically based on the user's view as follows:

- View data at the level of detail at which the user can first categorize the data as satisfying unique requirements of the application.
- View the data logically. Although some storage technologies such as tables in a relational DBMS or a sequential flat file relate closely to External Interface Files, do not assume that one physical file equals one logical file.

Examples

When identifying potential EIFs, look at the type of data and how a user would view it, rather than storage technology (such as tables, flat files, indexes, and paths). Each type of data on the following list can relate to one or more EIFs, depending on the user's view:

- Reference data (external data utilized by the application, but not maintained on Internal Logical Files)
- Help messages
- Error messages
- Edit data (criteria)

The following are not EIFs:

- Data received from another application that adds, changes, or deletes data on an ILF (this is considered transaction data and, therefore, the process of maintaining the data is counted as External Input)
- Data maintained by the application being counted, but accessed and utilized by another application
- Data formatted and processed for use by another application is counted as an External Output

Issues/resolutions

The following decision of the IFPUG Counting Practices Committee (CPC) differs from the Albrecht 1984 document:

1. EIF is not credited to the "sending application": The Albrecht 1984 methodology credits External Interface Files to both the application maintaining the data and the application using the data by differentiating External Interface Files from External Inputs and External Outputs based on the directional flow and use of the data by the application.
2. Function type determination is based on how the application that receives the data utilizes them. If the data are used to update an Internal Logical File, it is either an External Input or External Output, depending on data flow. If the data are not maintained on an internal Logical File, it is an External Interface File regardless of the data flow.

Two issues have been raised with the Albrecht 1984 method of identifying External Interface Files:

1. Function Point counts must be updated if, subsequent to the count, access to an Internal Logical File is given to another application.
2. It cannot always be determined how the other application is using the data and various methods have evolved to handle this situation resulting in inconsistent counting rules.

To resolve these problems, only the application receiving the data can have External Interface Files. As a result, an application's Function Point count is dependent only on the application as it currently exists and not on future events or another application's use of data.

External Inputs

Overview

External Inputs represent an application's data maintenance and control processing requirements. External Inputs are evaluated and contribute to the Function Point Count based on their number and relative functional complexity.

Definitions

An *External Input* (EI) processes data or processes control information that enters the application's external boundary. The processed data, through a unique logical process, maintains an Internal Logical File. Control information is data used by a process within an application boundary to assure compliance with business function requirements specified by the user. Control information might or might not directly maintain an Internal Logical File. An External Input should be considered unique if it has a different format or if the logical design requires processing logic different from other External Inputs of the same format.

An External Input is considered unique if data is maintained on an internal Logical File, and the input format is unique, or the processing logic is unique.

Control information is data used by the application to assure compliance with business function requirements specified by the user. Do not include the input side of an External Inquiry.

Maintain is the ability to add, change, or delete data through a standardized process of the application.

Format is defined as unique data elements or a unique arrangement or order of data elements.

Processing Logic is defined as unique edits, calculations/algorithms, and/or sorts specifically requested by the user.

Methodology

Identification. Identify all processes that update an Internal Logical File. For each process identified:

- Consider each format a separate process if the data used by the process can be received in more than one format.
- Credit an External Input for each data maintenance activity (add, change, and delete) performed.

Examples

The following are External Inputs, assuming the above conditions are met:

- Transactional data: External data that is used to maintain Internal Logical Files
- Screen input: Count one External Input for each function that maintains ILFs. If add, change, and delete capabilities are present, the screen would count as three External Inputs.
- Batch input: For each unique process that maintains an ELF, count one External Input for each add, change, and delete.

Batch inputs should be identified based on the processing required to apply the data. One physical input file can, when viewed logically, correspond to a number of External Inputs. Conversely, two or more physical input files can correspond to one External Input if the processing logic and format are identical for each physical file.

One way to identify multiple External Inputs when processing one physical file is to look at the record types on the file. Exclude header and trailer records as well as those record types required due to physical space limitations. Look at the remaining record types for unique processing requirements and associate an External Input for each unique process. Do not assume a one-to-one correspondence between the remaining record types and External Inputs.

- Duplicate External Inputs: See Issues/resolution section.
- Suspense File Updates: See Issues/resolution section.

The following are not External Inputs:

- Reference Data: External data utilized by the application, but not maintained on Internal Logical Files.
- Input side of an External Inquiry: Data input used to drive selection for data retrieval.
- Menu Screens: See Issues/resolution Section.
- Logon Screens: See Issues/resolution Section.
- Multiple methods of invoking the same input logic, for example, entering "A" or "Add" on a Command line or using a PF key should be counted only once.

Issues/resolutions

The following are not discussed in the Albrecht 1984 document and are decisions of the IFPUG Counting Practices Committee (CPC):

1. Duplicate External Inputs: Input processes, which if specifically requested by the user, duplicate a previously counted External Input, are each counted. An example is a banking system that accepts identical deposit transactions, one through an Automated Teller Machine (ATM) transaction and a second through a manual teller deposit transaction.

2. Suspense file updates: Input processes that maintain either an Internal Logical File or a suspense/carry around file depending on edit evaluation, should be counted based on the following:

   —If the suspense/carry around file is accessed or maintained by the user, the suspense/carry around file is counted as an Internal Logical File. That being the case, count External Inputs for each data maintenance activity performed on both Internal Logical Files.
   —If the suspense/carry around file cannot be maintained or accessed by the user, count External Inputs for each data maintenance activity performed on the original Internal Logical File.

In either instance, the process of reapplying data from the suspense/carry around file to the Internal Logical File is not counted.

- Logon Screen: Screens that facilitate entry into an application and do not maintain an Internal Logical File are not External Inputs.

The following decision of the IFPUG Counting Practices Committee (CPC) is in agreement with the Albrecht 1984 document:

1. Menu Screens that provide only selection or navigational functionality and do not maintain an Internal Logical File are not counted.

External Output

Overview

External Outputs represent an application's output processing requirements. External Outputs are evaluated and contribute to the Function Point count based on their number and relative functional complexity.

Definitions

An External Output (EO) processes data or control information that exits the application's external boundary. An External Output should be considered unique if it has a different format, or if the logical design requires processing logic different from other External Outputs of the same format.

An external output is considered unique if: the output format is unique, or the processing logic is unique.

Control information is data used by the application to assure compliance with business function requirements specified by the user.

Format is defined as unique data elements or a unique arrangement or order of data elements.

Processing Logic is defined as unique edits, calculations/algorithms and/or sorts specifically requested by the user.

Methodology

Identification. Identify all processes that: send data external to the application's boundary, or send control data external to the application's boundary.

For each process identified:

- Consider each format a separate process if the data used by the process is sent in more than one format.
- Credit an External Output for each process.

Examples

The following are External Outputs, assuming the above conditions are met:

- Data transfer to other applications: Data residing on an ILF that is formatted and processed for use by an external application. Outputs are identified based on the processing required to manipulate the data. One physical output file can, when viewed logically, correspond to a number of External Outputs. Conversely, two or more physical output files can correspond to one External Output, if the processing logic and format are identical for each physical file.

  A method for identifying multiple External Outputs from the processing of one physical file is to look at the record types on the file. Exclude header and trailer records as well as those record types required due to physical space limitations. Review the remaining record types for unique processing requirements and associate an External Output for each unique process. Do not assume a one-to-one correspondence between the remaining record types and External Outputs.

- Reports: Each report produced by the application is counted as an External Output. Two identically formatted reports at the detail and summary levels are counted as two External Outputs. This is because each report requires unique processing logic and unique calculations.

- Duplicate reports: See Issues/resolutions section.

- On-line reports: On-line output of data that is not the output side of an External Inquiry.

- Error/confirmation messages: See Issues/resolutions section.

- Derived data: Derived data that does not necessarily update a File.

- Graphics: See Issues/resolutions section.

- Report Generators: See Issues/resolutions Section.

The following are not External Outputs:

- Help: See External Inquiry.
- Multiple methods of invoking the same output logic: For example, entering "R" or "Report" on a command line or using a PF key should be counted only once.
- Error/confirmation messages associated with function types other than External Inputs: For example, an External Output would not be counted for the error/confirmation messages associated to an External Inquiry.
- Multiple reports/unique data values: Identical reports that have the same format and processing logic, but exist due to unique data values, are not counted as separate External Outputs. For example, two reports that are identical in format and processing logic the first containing customer names beginning with "A" through "L" and the second having customer names beginning with "M" through "Z", are counted as only one External Output.
- Summary fields (column totals): Summary fields on a detail report do not constitute a unique External Output.
- Ad hoc Reporting: When the user directs and is responsible for the creation (through the use of a language such as FOCUS or SQL) of an undefined number of reports, no External outputs are counted.
- Query Language: A tool used in the ad hoc environment.

Issues/resolutions

The following decisions of the IFPUG Counting Practices Committee (CPC) are not discussed in the Albrecht 1984 document:

1. Duplicate reports: Identical reports, produced on different media due to specific user requirements, are counted as separate External Outputs. The processing required to produce different output media is considered to be unique processing logic. Identical reports, one on paper and one on microfiche, if specifically requested by the user, are counted as two External Outputs.
2. Graphical format: Graphical outputs should be counted as if they had been presented in textual format. Each different graphical display requested by the user should be counted as an External Output. Statistical data presented in a table, bar chart, pie chart, and exploded pie chart should be counted as four External Outputs.
3. Report Generator: Output developed for the user with a report generator should be counted as an External Output for each specified unique report. If a report generator facility is requested by the user as part of an application for do-it-yourself report generation: one External Input should be counted for each report definition parameter or unique command (e.g., select, compare, sort, merge, extract, calculate, summarize, format, etc.) requested by the user to control the report generation; one External Output should be counted for the total report program; and one Internal Logical File should be counted if a new file is created and saved.

The following decision of the IFPUG Counting Practices Committee (CPC) is in agreement with the Albrecht 1984 document:

1. Error/confirmation messages: An External Output should be credited for each External Input having error or confirmation messages.

External Inquiries

Overview

External Inquiries represent an application's inquiry processing requirements. External Inquiries are evaluated and contribute to the Function Point count based on their number and relative functional complexity.

Definitions

An External Inquiry (EQ) is a unique input/output combination that results in the retrieval of data required for immediate output, does not contain derived data, and does not update an Internal Logical File. An External Inquiry is considered unique if it has a format different from other External Inquiries in either its input or output parts or if the logical design requires edits and sorts different from other External Inquiries.

An *Input/output combination* is considered unique if: the input format is unique, or the edits and/or sorts are different, or the output format is unique.

Format is defined as unique data elements or a unique arrangement/order of data elements.

Derived data is defined as data that require processing other than direct retrieval, editing, and sorting of information from Internal Logical Files and/or External Interface Files.

Methodology

Identification. Identify all processes where an input triggers an immediate retrieval of data.

For each process identified:

- Verify that each input/output combination is unique and consider each unique input/output combination a separate process.
- Credit an External Inquiry for each process.

Examples

The following are External Inquiries, assuming the preceding conditions are met:

- Immediate retrieval of data: Selection of data retrieval is based on data input.
- Implied inquiries: Change/delete screen(s) that provide data retrieval capabilities prior to change/delete functionality are credited with an External Inquiry, provided the inquiry capability can and is used as a stand-alone function.

If the input and output sides of the External Inquiry are identical for both change and delete functions, count only one External Inquiry. If identical inquiry functions are available from the Change/delete screens and a separate Inquiry screen, count only one External Inquiry.

- Menus having implied inquiries: See Issues/resolutions section.
- Logon screens: See Issues/resolutions section.
- Help: See Issues/resolution section.

Two categories of Help are considered External Inquiries:

- Full Screen Help: A help facility that is dependent on the application screen displays help text relating to the calling screen. Credit one low-complexity External Inquiry per calling screen regardless of the number of Help panels/screens returned.
- Field Sensitive Help: A help facility, dependent on the location of the cursor or some other method of identification, displays help documentation specific to that field. Credit one External Inquiry per screen. Each field that is sensitive to Help should be considered as one DET on the input side.

The following are not External Inquiries:

- Error/Confirmation Messages: See External Outputs.
- Multiple methods of invoking the same inquiry logic: Multiple methods such as entering "I" or "Inq" on a command line, or using a PF key are counted only once.
- Help text: Help that can be accessed from multiple areas/screens of an application, or accessed and browsed independently of the associated application, is counted only once.
- Menu Screens: See Issues/resolutions section.
- Derived data: Derived data would be treated as an input/output versus retrieval of data.
- On-line Documentation: System documentation that is available on-line, in lieu of or in addition to that available in hard copy, is not counted. On-line documentation by itself should not be considered software function delivered.
- Test Systems: Test systems are included in system development and should not be counted.

Issues/resolutions

The following decisions of the IFPUG Counting Practices Committee (CPC) differ from the Albrecht 1984 document:

1. Menu screens: Screens that provide only selection functionality are not counted.

2. Menus having implied inquiries: Menu screens that provide screen selection and data retrieval selection input for the called screen are counted as External Inquiries, the menu being the input side of the EQ and the called screen being the output side of the EQ.

The following are not discussed in the Albrecht 1984 document and are decisions of the IFPUG Counting Practices Committee (CPC):

1. Logon screens: Logon screens that provide security functionality are counted as an External Inquiry.

2. Help: An inquiry pair where the input and the output (explanatory text) are both unique. Credit help text that can be accessed or displayed through different request techniques, or from different areas of an application, only once.

3. Duplicate output side: Identical queries, produced on different media due to specific user requirements, are counted as separate External Inquiries.

4. Graphical formats: Each different graphical display requested by the user should be counted as an additional External Inquiry.

5. User-Maintained Help Facility: A user-maintained help facility should be counted separately.

6. Independent Teaching (Tutorial) Systems: Computer Aided Instruction (CAI), Computer Based Training (CBT) Systems, or other independent software teaching systems that are different from the production system and maintained separately, should be counted as separate applications. Training systems that are identical to the production system should be considered as additional sites; do not count as separate functions, but consider the sites when calculating General System Characteristic 13 (Multiple Sites).

General System Characteristics

Each General System Characteristic (GSC) must be evaluated in terms of its Degree of Influence (DI) on a scale of 0 to 5. The descriptions listed under "Score as" are meant to be guides in determining the DI. If none of the guideline descriptions fit the application exactly, a judgment must be made about which DI most closely applies to the application.

The General System Characteristics are:

1. Data communication
2. Distributed function
3. Performance
4. Heavily used configuration
5. Transaction rates
6. On-line data entry
7. Design for end user efficiency
8. On-line update
9. Complex processing
10. Usable in other applications
11. Installation ease

12. Operational ease

13. Multiple sites

14. Facilitate change

The questions are answered using DI on a scale of 0 to 5.

0 Not present, or no influence

1 Incidental influence

2 Moderate influence

3 Average influence

4 Significant influence

5 Strong influence throughout

Data communications

The data and control information used in the application are sent or received over communication facilities. Terminals connected locally to the control unit are considered to use communication facilities. Protocol is a set of conventions that permit the transfer or exchange of information between two systems or devices. All data communication links require some type of protocol.
Score as:

0 = Application is pure batch processing or a stand alone PC.

1 = Application is batch, but has remote data entry or remote printing.

2 = Application is batch, but has remote data entry and remote printing.

3 = On-line data collection or teleprocessing (TP) front end to a batch process or query system.

4 = More than a front-end, but the application supports only one type of TP communications protocol.

5 = More than a front-end, but the application supports more than one type of TP communications protocol.

Distributed data processing

Distributed data or processing functions are a characteristic of the application within the application boundary.
Score as:

0 = Application does not aid the transfer of data or processing function between components of the system.

1 = Application prepares data for end-user processing on another component of the system, such as PC spreadsheets and PC DBMS.

2 = Data is prepared for transfer, transferred, and then processed on another component of the system (not for end-user processing).

3 = Distributed processing and data transfer are on-line and in one direction only.

4 = Distributed processing and data transfer are on-line and in both directions.

5 = Processing functions are dynamically performed on the most appropriate component of the system.

Performance

Application performance objectives, stated or approved by the user, in either response or throughput, influenced (or will influence) the design, development, installation, and support of the application.

Score as:

0 = No Special performance requirements were stated by the user.

1 = Performance and design requirements were stated and reviewed but no special actions required.

2 = Response time or throughput is critical during peak hours. No special design for CPU utilization was required. Processing deadline is for the next business day.

3 = Response time or throughput is critical during all business hours. No special design for CPU utilization was required. Processing deadline requirements with interfacing systems are constraining.

4 = Stated user performance requirements are stringent enough to require performance analysis tasks in the design phase.

5 = In addition, performance analysis tools were used in the design, development, and/or implementation phases to meet the stated user performance requirements.

Heavily used configuration

A heavily used operational configuration, requiring special design considerations, is a characteristic of the application (for example, the user wants to run the application on existing or committed equipment that will be heavily used).

Score as:

0 = No explicit or implicit operational restrictions.

1 = Operational restrictions do exist, but are less restrictive than a typical application. No special effort is needed to meet the restrictions.

2 = Some security or timing considerations.

3 = Specific processor requirements for a specific piece of the application.

4 = Stated operation restrictions require special constraints on the application in the central processor or a dedicated processor.

5 = In addition, there are special constraints on the application in the distributed components of the system.

Transaction rate

The transaction rate is high and it influenced the design, development, installation, and support of the application.

Score as:

0 = No peak transaction period anticipated.

1 = Peak transaction period (e.g., monthly, quarterly, seasonally, annually) anticipated.

2 = Weekly peak transaction period anticipated.

3 = Daily peak transaction period anticipated.

4 = High transaction rate(s) stated by the user in the application requirements or service level agreements are high enough to require performance analysis tasks in the design phase.

5 = High transaction rate(s) stated by the user in the application requirements or service level agreements are high enough to require performance analysis tasks and, in addition, require the use of performance analysis tools in the design, development, and/or installation phases.

On-line data entry

On-line data entry and control functions are provided in the application.

Score as:

0 = All transactions are processed in batch mode.

1 = 1% to 7% of transactions are interactive data entry.

2 = 8% to 15% of transactions are interactive data entry.

3 = 16% to 23% of transactions are interactive data entry.

4 = 24% to 30% of transactions are interactive data entry.

5 = Over 30% of transactions are interactive data entry.

End-user efficiency

The on-line functions provided emphasize a design for end-user efficiency, and include:

- Navigational Aids (e.g., function keys, jumps, dynamically generated menus)
- Menus
- On-line help/documents
- Automated cursor movement
- Scrolling
- Remote printing (via on-line transactions)
- Preassigned function keys

- Submission of batch jobs from on-line transactions
- Cursor selection of screen data
- Heavy use of reverse video, highlighting, colors underlining, and other indicators
- Hard-copy user documentation of on-line transactions
- Mouse interface
- Pop-up windows
- As few screens as possible to accomplish a business function
- Bilingual support (supports two languages; count as four items)
- Multi-lingual support (supports more than two languages; count as six items)

Score as:

0 = None of the above.

1 = One to three of the above.

2 = Four to five of the above.

3 = Six or more of the above but there are no specific user requirements related to efficiency.

4 = Six or more of the above and stated requirements for end-user efficiency are strong enough to require design tasks for human factors to be included (for example, minimize key strokes, maximize defaults, use of templates, etc.).

5 = Six or more of the above and stated requirements for end-user efficiency are strong enough to require use of special tools and processes in order to demonstrate that the objectives have been achieved.

On-line update

The application provides on-line update for the Internal Logical Files.
Score as:

0 = None.

1 = On-line update of one to three control files. Volume of updating is low and recovery is easy.

2 = On-line update of four or more control files. Volume of updating is low and recovery is easy.

3 = On-line update of major Internal Logical Files.

4 = In addition, protection against data lost is essential and has been specially designed and programmed in the system.

5 = In addition, high volumes bring cost considerations into the recovery process. Highly automated recovery procedures with minimum of operator intervention.

Complex processing

Complex processing is a characteristic of the application. Categories are:

- Sensitive control (for example, special audit processing) and/or application specific security processing.
- Extensive logical processing.
- Extensive mathematical processing.
- Much exception processing resulting in incomplete transactions that must be processed again; for example, incomplete ATM transactions caused by TP interruption, missing data values, or failed edits.
- Complex processing to handle multiple input/output possibilities; for example, multi-media, device independence.

Score as:

0 = None of the above.

1 = Any one of the above.

2 = Any two of the above.

3 = Any three of the above.

4 = Any four of the above.

5 = Any five of the above.

Reusability

The application and the code in the application have been specifically designed, developed, and supported to be usable in other applications.
Score as:

0 = No reusable code.

1 = Reusable code is used within the application.

2 = Less than 10% of the application considered more than one user's needs.

3 = 10% or more of the application considered more than one user's needs.

4 = The application was specifically packaged and/or documented to ease reuse, and application is customized by user at source code level.

5 = The application was specifically packaged and/or documented to ease reuse, and application is customized for use by means of user parameter maintenance.

Installation ease

Conversion and installation ease are characteristics of the application. A conversion and installation plan and/or conversion tools were provided and tested during the system test phase.
Score as:

0 = No special considerations were stated by user and no special set-up required for installation.

1 = No special considerations were stated by user, but special set-up required for installation.

2 = Conversion and installation requirements were stated by the user and conversion and installation guides were provided and tested. The impact of conversion on the project is not considered to be important.

3 = Conversion and installation requirements were stated by the user and conversion and installation guides were provided and tested. The impact of conversion on the project is considered to be important.

4 = In addition to (2) above, automated conversion and installation tools were provided and tested.

5 = In addition to (3) above, automated conversion and installation tools were provided and tested.

Operational ease

Operational ease is characteristic of the application. Effective start-up, back-up, and recovery procedures were provided and tested during the system test phase. The application minimizes the need for manual activities, such as tape mounts, paper handling, and direct on-location manual intervention.

Score as:

0 = No special operational considerations other than the normal back-up procedures were stated by the user.

1–4: Select the following items that apply to the application. Each item has a point value of one, except as otherwise noted.

—Effective start-up, back-up, and recovery processes were provided but operator intervention is required.

—Effective start-up, back-up, and recovery processes were provided but no operator intervention is required (count as two items).

—The application minimizes the need for tape mounts.

—The application minimizes the need for paper handling.

5 = Application is designed for unattended operation, which means no operator intervention is required to operate the system other than to start up or shut down the application. Automatic error recovery is a feature of the application.

Multiple sites

The application has been specifically designed, developed, and supported to be installed at multiple sites for multiple organizations.

Score as:

0 = No user requirement to consider the needs of more than one user installation site.

1 = Needs of multiple sites were considered in the design and the application is designed to operate only under identical hardware and software environments.

2 = Needs of multiple sites were considered in the design and the application is designed to operate only under similar hardware and/or software environments.

3 = Needs of multiple sites were considered in the design and the application is designed to operate under different hardware and/or software environments.

4 = Documentation and support plan are provided and tested to support the application at multiple sites and application is as described by (1) or (2) above.

5 = Documentation and support plan are provided and tested to support the application at multiple sites and application is as described by (3) above.

Facilitate change

The application has been specifically designed, developed, and supported to facilitate change. Examples are:

- Flexible query/report capability is provided.
- Business control data is grouped in tables maintainable by the user.

Score as:

0 = No special user requirement to design the application to minimize or facilitate change.

1–5: Select which of the following items apply to the application.
— Flexible query/report facility is provided that can handle simple requests; for example, and/or logic applied to only one Internal Logical File (count as one item).
— Flexible query/report facility is provided that can handle requests of average complexity; for example, and/or logic applied to more than one Internal Logical File (count as two items).
— Flexible query/report facility is provided that can handle complex requests; for example, and/or logic combinations on one or more Internal Logical Files (count as three items).
— Control data is kept in tables that are maintained by the user with on-line interactive processes but changes take effect only on the next business day.
— Control data is kept in tables that are maintained by the user with on-line interactive processes and the changes take effect immediately (count as two items.)

Function Point Calculation

The Function Point calculation is a three-step process. Step 1 produces the Unadjusted Function Point count. Step 2 produces the Value Adjustment Factor (VAF). Step 3 adjusts the Unadjusted Function Point Count by the VAF to produce the final Function Point Count.

The formula used by Step 3 varies depending on the type of count; Application (System Baseline), Development (Project), or Enhancement (Project).

Unadjusted function point calculation

The way you determine functional complexity depends on the Function Type. The two Function Types are as follows:

■ *Data Function Types* are Internal Logical Files and External Interface Files. The functional complexity of each identified Data Function Type is based on the number of Record Types (RET) and Data Element Types (DET).

■ *Transactional Function Types* are External Inputs, External Outputs, and External Inquiries. The functional complexity of each identified Transaction Function Type is based on the number of File Type Referenced (FTR) and Data Element Types (DET).

Once an application's components (specific data and processing requirement) have been categorized into the various function types, each component is assigned an Unadjusted Function Point value based on its functional complexity.

The Unadjusted Function Point Count value for each component is then summarized at the function type level and again at the application level. The resulting total at the application level is the application's Unadjusted Function Point Count and is used in the final calculation.

The following form may be used to facilitate the calculation of the Unadjusted Function Point Count:

Function Type	Functional Complexity				Complexity Totals	Function Type Totals
ILF	Low	×	7	=	_____	
	Average	×	10	=	_____	
	High	×	15	=	_____	_____
EIF	Low	×	5	=	_____	
	Average	×	7	=	_____	
	High	×	10	=	_____	_____
EI	Low	×	3	=	_____	
	Average	×	4	=	_____	
	High	×	6	=	_____	_____
EO	Low	×	4	=	_____	

Function Type	Functional Complexity			Complexity Totals	Function Type Totals
	Average	×	5	= _____	
	High	×	7	= _____	_____
EQ	Low	×	3	= _____	
	Average	×	4	= _____	
	High	×	6	= _____	_____

Unadjusted Function Point Count _____

Internal Logical Files. Each identified Internal Logical File is assigned a functional complexity based on the number of associated Record Element Types (RET) and Data Element Types (DET).

Record Element Type Identification: Record Element Types (RET) are subgroupings of Internal Logical Files based on the logical/user view of the data. The Data Analysis equivalent to such logical groupings are Data Entities. Internal Logical Files that cannot be subcategorized are considered to have one RET.

Data Element Type Identification: An Internal Logical File's Data Element Types (DET) are user recognizable, non-recursive fields residing on the Internal Logical File. Each field on the Internal Logical File is a DET with the following exceptions:

- Fields should be viewed at the user-recognizable level. For example, an account number or date physically stored in multiple fields is counted as one DET.

- Fields that appear more than once in an Internal Logical File because of technology or implementation techniques should be counted only once. For example, if an Internal Logical File is comprised of more than one table in a relational DBMS, the keys used to relate the tables are counted only once.

- Repeating fields that are identical in format and exist to allow for multiple occurrences of a data value are counted only once. For example, an Internal Logical File containing 12 monthly budget amount fields and an annual budget amount field would be credited with two DETs: a DET for the monthly budget amount fields, and a DET for the annual budget amount field.

- Each unique command/parameter is counted as a DET if an Internal Logical File is created and saved in a report generator facility requested by the user for do-it-yourself report generation.

Functional complexity assignment for Internal Logical Files is based on the following matrix:

Internal Logical File (ILF) Complexity Matrix

	1 to 19 DET	20 to 50 DET	51 or more DET
1 RET	L	L	A
2–5 RET	L	A	H
6 or more RET	A	H	H

Legend: RET = Record Element Type
DET = Data Element Type

Functional Complexity: L = Low
A = Average
H = High

Use the following matrix to translate an Internal Logical File's functional complexity to Unadjusted Function Points.

Internal Logical File (ILF) Unadjusted Function Point Table

Functional Complexity Rating	Unadjusted Function Points
L(ow)	7
A(verage)	10
H(igh)	15

External Interface File. Each identified External Interface File is assigned a functional complexity based on the number of associated Record Element Types (RET) and Data Element Types (DET).

Record Element Type Identification: Record Element Types (RET) are subgroupings of External Interface Files based on the logical/user view of the data. The Data Analysis equivalent to such logical groupings are Data Entities. External Interface Files that cannot be sub categorized are considered to have one RET.

One physical interface file can, when viewed logically, correspond to a number of External Interface Files. Additionally, multiple RETs can be associated to each External Interface File identified.

One way to identify different External Interface File RETs from one physical file is to look at the record types on the file. Exclude header and trailer records, unless specifically requested for audit purposes, as well as those record types required by physical space limitations. Each unique record type corresponds to a RET.

Data Element Type Identification: An External Interface File's Data Element Types (DET) are user recognizable, non-recursive fields residing on the External Interface File. Each field on the External Interface File is a DET with the following exceptions:

- Fields should be viewed at the user-recognizable level. For example, an account number or date physically stored in multiple fields should be counted as one DET.

- Fields that appear more than once in an External Interface File because of the technology or implementation techniques should be counted only once. For example, if an External Interface File is comprised of more than one record type in a file, the record ID field used to identify the records would be counted only once.

- Repeating fields that are identical in format and exist so that multiple occurrences of a data value can occur are counted only once. For example, an External Interface File containing 12 monthly budget amount fields and an annual budget amount field would be credited with two DETs; a DET for the monthly budget amount fields, and a DET for the annual budget amount field.

Functional complexity assignment for External Interface Files is based on the following matrix:

External Interface File (EIF) Complexity Matrix

	1 to 19 DET	20 to 50 DET	51 or more DET
1 RET	L	L	A
2–5 RET	L	A	H
6 or more RET	A	H	H

Legend: RET = Record Element Type
DET = Data Element Type

Functional Complexity: L = Low
A = Average
H = High

Use the following matrix to translate an External Interface File's functional complexity to Unadjusted Function Points:

External Interface File (EIF) Unadjusted Function Point Table

Functional Complexity Rating	Unadjusted Function Points
L(ow)	5
A(verage)	7
H(igh)	10

External Inputs. Each identified External Input is assigned a functional complexity based on the number of File Type Referenced (FIR) and Data Element Types (DET).

File Type Referenced Identification: A File Type Referenced (FTR) is counted for each Internal Logical File maintained or referenced and each External Interface File referenced during the processing of the External Input.

Data Element Type Identification: The Data Element Type (DET) count is the maximum number of user recognizable, non-recursive fields that are maintained on an Internal Logical File by the External Input.

Each field maintainable on an Internal Logical File by the External Input is a DET with the following exceptions:

- Fields should be viewed at the user-recognizable level. For example, an account number or date that is physically stored in multiple fields should be counted as one DET.

- Fields that appear more than once in an Internal Logical File because of technology or implementation techniques should be counted only once. For example, if an Internal Logical File is comprised of more than one table in a relational DBMS, the keys used to relate the tables would be counted only once.

Additional DETs are credited to the External Input for the following capabilities:

- Command line(s) or PF/Action key(s) that provide the capability to specify the action to be taken by the External Input are credited one additional DET per External Input, not per command PF/action key.

- Fields that are not entered by the user, but through an External Input are maintained on an Internal Logical File, should be counted. For example, a system-generated sequenced key, maintained on an Internal Logical File, but not entered by the user, would be counted as a DET.

Functional complexity assignment for External Inputs is based on the matrix shown in following matrix.

External Input (EI) Complexity Matrix

	1 to 4 DET	5 to 15 DET	16 or more DET
0–1 FTR	L	L	A
2 FTR	L	A	H
3 or more FTR	A	H	H

Legend: FTR = File Type Referenced
DET = Data Element Type

Functional Complexity: L = Low
A = Average
H = High

Use the following matrix to translate an External Input's functional complexity to Unadjusted Function Points.

External Input (EI) Unadjusted Function Point Table

Functional Complexity Rating Function	Unadjusted Points
L(ow)	3
A(verage)	4
H(igh)	6

External Outputs. Each identified External Output is assigned a functional complexity based on the number of File Type Referenced (FTR) and Data Element Types (DET).

File Type Referenced Identification: A File Type Referenced (FTR) should be counted for each Internal Logical File and External Interface File referenced during the processing of the External Output.

Data Element Type Identification: A Data Element Type (DET) should be counted for each user-recognizable, non-recursive field that appears on the External Output.

Each field on the External Output is a DET with the following exceptions:

- Fields are viewed at the user-recognizable level. For example, an account number or date physically stored in multiple fields is counted as one DET.

- Count a DET in the External Output for each unique command/parameter in a report generator facility requested by the user for do-it-yourself report generation.

- Count a DET for each type of label and each type of numerical equivalent in a graphical output. For example, a pie chart might have two DETs; one for designating the category, and one for the applicable percentage.

- Do not count literals as DETs.

- Do not count paging variables or system-generated time/date stamps.

Additional DETs are credited to the External Output for each summary or total field appearing on the External Output.

Error/confirmation messages: Count a DET for each distinct error or confirmation message available for display by the External Input. Implementation techniques, whether Batch Error Reports or an Error Message Area, Box, or Window, appearing on the External Input or a separate physical screen, such as a Message Frame, do not affect the functional complexity or number of External Outputs associated to a particular External Input.

Functional complexity assignment for External Outputs is based on the matrix shown below:

External Output (EO) Complexity Matrix

	1 to 5 DET	6 to 19 DET	20 or more DET
0–1 FTR	L	L	A
2–3 FTR	L	A	H
4 or more FTR	A	H	H

Legend: F3TR = File Type Referenced
DET = Data Element Type

Functional Complexity: L = Low
A = Average
H = High

Use the following matrix to translate an External Output's functional complexity to Unadjusted Function Points.

External Output (EO) Unadjusted Function Point Table

Functional Complexity Rating	Unadjusted Function Points
L(ow)	4
A(verage)	5
H(igh)	7

External Inquiries. Use the following steps to assign an Unadjusted Function Point value to each External Inquiry:

1. Calculate the functional complexity for the input side of the External Inquiry.

2. Calculate the functional complexity for the output side of the External Inquiry.

3. Select the higher of the two functional complexities. Using the EQ Unadjusted Function Point Table, transcribe the Complexity Rating to Unadjusted Function Points.

File Type Referenced Identification, Input and Output sides: A File Type Referenced (FTR) is counted for each Internal Logical File and External Interface File referenced during the processing of the External Inquiry.

Data Element Type Identification, Input side: A Data Element Type (DET) is counted for those fields entered that specify the External inquiry to be executed or specify data selection criteria.

Data Element Type Identification, Output side: A Data Element Type (DET) is counted for each user recognizable, non-recursive field that appears on the output side of the External Inquiry.

Each field appearing on the External Output is a DET with the following exceptions:

- Fields are viewed at the user-recognizable level. For example, an account number or date that is physically stored in multiple fields is counted as one DET.

- Fields that, because of technology or implementation techniques, appear more than once in an Internal Logical File should be counted only once. I do not count literals as DETs.

- Do not count paging variables or system generated time/date stamps.

Additional DETs are credited to the External Inquiry for each summary or total field appearing on the External Inquiry.

Help messages. The three categories of Help are Full Screen Help, Field Sensitive Help, and Help Subsystems. DET determination varies between each and is discussed below:

Full Screen Help: Credit a Low Complexity External Inquiry per calling screen regardless of the number of FTRs or DETs involved.

Field Sensitive Help: Credit an External Inquiry having a complexity, using the input side, based on the number of fields that are field sensitive and the number of FTRs. Each field sensitive field corresponds to a DET.

Help Subsystems: Specific counting rules are not available at this time.

Functional complexity assignments for External Inquiries are based on the matrices shown below:

External Inquiry (EO) Input Complexity Matrix

	1 to 4 DET	5 to 19 DET	16 or more DET
0–1 FTR	L	L	A
2 FTR	L	A	H
3 or more FTR	A	H	H

External Inquiry (EQ) Output Complexity Matrix

	1 to 5 DET	6 to 19 DET	20 or more DET
0–1 FTR	L	L	A
2–3 FTR	L	A	H
4 or more FTR	A	H	H

Use the following matrix to translate an External Inquiry's functional complexity to Unadjusted Function Points.

External Inquiry(EO) Output Complexity Matrix

Functional Complexity Rating	Unadjusted Function Points
L(ow)	3
A(verage)	4
H(igh)	6

Value Adjustment Factor Calculation

The Value Adjustment Factor is based on 14 General System Characteristics that rate the general functionality of the application. The 14 General System Characteristics are summarized into the Value Adjustment Factor. When applied, the Value Adjustment Factor adjusts the Unadjusted Function Point count ±35%, producing the final Function Point Count.

1. Evaluate the 14 General System Characteristics (GSC) on a scale of 0 to 5, producing a Degree of Influence (DI) for each of the General System Characteristic Questions.

2. Sum the 14 DIs to produce the Total Degree of Influence (TDI).

3. Insert the TDI into the following equation to produce the Value Adjustment Factor (VAF):

$$(TDI \times 0.01) + 0.65 = VAF$$

Where: TDI is the sum of the 14 Degrees of Influence
VAF is the Value Adjustment Factor

The following table facilitates the calculation of the VAF.

General System Characteristics (GSC)	Degree of Influence (DI) 0–5
1. Data Communication	_____
2. Distributed Processing	_____
3. Performance	_____
4. Heavily Used Configuration	_____
5. Transaction Rates	_____
6. On-Line Data Entry	_____

General System Characteristics (GSC)	Degree of Influence (DI) 0–5
7. Design for End User Efficiency	_____
8. On-line Update	_____
9. Complex Processing	_____
10. Usable in Other Applications	_____
11. Installation Ease	_____
12. Operational Ease	_____
13. Multiple Sites	_____
14. Facilitate Change	_____

Total Degree of Influence (TDI)

Value Adjustment Factor: VAF = (___ × 0.01) + 0.65
= (TDI × 0.01) + 0.65

Application Function Point Calculation

To produce the Application Function Point Count, complete the following formula:

(UFPB + ADD + CHGA − CHGB + DEL) × VAFA = AFP

where:

—FPB is the Application's Unadjusted Function Point Count before the enhancement project.

—ADD is the Unadjusted Function Point Count of those functions that were added by the enhancement project.

—CHGA is the Unadjusted Function Point Count of those functions that were modified by the enhancement project. This number reflects the functions after the modifications.

—CHGB is the Unadjusted Function Point Count of those functions that were modified by the enhancement before the modification.

—DEL is the Unadjusted Function Point Count of those functions that were deleted by the enhancement project.

—VAFA is the Value Adjustment Factor of the application after the enhancement project.

—AFP is the Application's Adjusted Function Point Count.

This formula can be used to either establish an application's initial Application Function Point Count or re-establish an Application Function Point Count after an Enhancement Project has modified the application's functionality.

(Do not include conversion requirements in an Application Function Point Count. If unavailable, the application's prior Unadjusted Function Point count can be calculated using the following formula:

$$AFPB \ VAFB = UFPB$$

where:

—AFPB is the Adjusted Application Function Point Count before the enhancement project.
—VAFB is the Value Adjustment Factor of the application before the enhancement project.
—UFPB is the Application's Unadjusted Function Point before the enhancement project.

When establishing an Application Function Point Count, functionality is only being added, and not changed or deleted, the formula in effect becomes:

$$ADD \times VAFA = AFP$$

where:

—ADD is the Unadjusted Function Point Count of those functions that were installed by the development project.
—VAFA is the Value Adjustment Factor of the application.
—AFP is the initial Application Function Point Count.

Development (Project) Function Point Calculation

To produce the Development (Project) Function Point Count, complete the following formula :

$$UFP \times VAF = DFP$$

where:

—UFP is the Unadjusted Function Point Count
—VAF is the Value Adjustment Factor
—DFP is the Development (Project) Function Point Count

Enhancement (Project) Function Point Calculation

To produce the Enhancement (Project) Function Point Count, complete the following formula:

$$((ADD + CHGA) \times VAFA) + (DEL \times VAFB) = EFP$$

where:

—ADD is the Unadjusted Function Point Count of those functions that were added by the enhancement project.

—CHGA is the Unadjusted Function Point Count of those functions that were modified by the enhancement project. This number reflects the functions after the modifications.

—DEL is the Unadjusted Function Point Count of those functions that were deleted by the enhancement project.

—VAFA is the Value Adjustment Factor of the Application after the enhancement project.

—VAFB is the Value Adjustment Factor of the application before the enhancement project.

—EFP is the Enhancement (Project) Function Point Count.

Author Biography

Pierre Deveaux is the Executive Director of the International Function Point User Group (IFPUG) in Westerville, Ohio

13

Applying Function Points to Object-Oriented Software Models

by Scott A. Whitmire

Introduction

Improving development productivity is an important issue facing our profession. As the problems we solve become more complex, the expectations of our customers also rises. At the same time, many organizations are facing cutbacks. The message is clear: we must learn to do more with less—if we don't, our competitors will.

In order to discuss productivity, we must first be able to measure it. *Productivity* is the ratio of input to output. The input is easy enough to measure: it is the sum of labor and non-labor costs for resources used on a development project. Measurement of output is much more difficult. Debate has raged long and fierce about how to measure our product. In fact, debate has raged long and fierce about just what our product is.

Many of us think of software products as systems; just look at the names we give them. A new view of software is emerging, and is correct, in my opinion. This view holds that a software product is but one component in a much larger system that includes people, machines, and other software applications, all working together toward the same goal. If we accept this view, we begin to judge the value of a software product not by its own characteristics, but by the utility it adds to the whole system. In this view, if an application does not contribute to the system at large, if it has no utility, it has no value.

As a result, we must measure as our output the functionality we deliver to the user, not the volume of the product. This means we need to be able to measure the size of the problem we are solving rather than the solution to that problem. Our output measure must be problem-based, not product-based.

Moreover, if we are to compare relative productivity differences between alternative development approaches, or technologies, our output measure must not be affected by our choice of technology. It must be technology-independent.

Traditional software size measures are both product-based and dependent on the choice of technology. They are product-based in that they measure characteristics of the existing product—the software. They are dependent on the technology in that their values can be deliberately influenced by the tools we use to solve the problem and the way we use those tools.

Function Points (Albrecht 1984) were originally developed to be both problem-based and technology-independent. I have used Function Points for over five years on projects with widely varying technologies with very good results. By good results, the estimates made using Function Points were more accurate than those made using other size measures, and the different values between applications were intuitively acceptable. Function Points were originally intended for use on traditionally developed business applications. I, and others, have been working on extending the use of Function Points to other types of software, such as scientific and real-time, and for software developed using new techniques, such as object-oriented development (Symons 1988), (Jones 1988), and (Whitmire 1991).

When I moved into object-oriented software development techniques, I was rather shocked at the state of measurement practice: for all intents and purposes, it did not exist. Those who push object-oriented software techniques are more concerned about methods and notation than measurement. Those who push measurement either assume the same old measures will still apply, or brush off object-orientation as just another fad. Object-orientation, at least for me, is not just another fad. It maps very well to the way I have always thought about and designed software. Furthermore, I have found traditional software measures to be lacking when applied to object-oriented software.

They either measure properties that are no longer appropriate, or they produce meaningless or even misleading results, particularly at the engineering level. At the organization level, object-oriented development represents such a change in thought processes, and even organization structures, that traditional methods of productivity measurement and estimating are hopelessly inaccurate.

This chapter focuses on applying Function Points to object-oriented software models. When I first tried this, I made an interesting discovery. When applied to object-oriented software using the application boundary, Function Points still measure delivered functionality; they work as they always have. When the boundary is moved to surround individual classes, Function Points become a measure of class complexity.

Even though this appears to violate not only the intent but accepted practice of Function Points, the idea was useful enough that I pursued it. When I presented this material to a meeting of the International Function Point Users Group (IFPUG), the organization that maintains the counting rules and promotes the use of Function Points, the results were interesting. Those people who had done some object-oriented software were invariably interested and could see value in the approach. Of the others, some were only skeptical, but could see where I was going. No one opposed the idea outright.

The use of models for our purposes is important and worth a brief discussion. Most of the time and effort required to calculate the Function Point value of an application is used to convert the physical implementation back into the logical models from which it was built. By starting with the models, as we would during a development project, we will find that counting Function Points is both easy and fast. It is far easier, in fact, than estimating other characteristics such as lines of code. If you don't believe me now, you will.

By the end of this chapter, we will have counted the equivalent of four applications. When I present this material to a conference, this takes about an hour. My brief experience with object-oriented software indicates that it is nearly impossible to build an application of any consequence without first building system models. So, it is not unreasonable to expect them to exist.

We will start with a brief introduction to Function Points, including their history and definitions. We introduce a case study to which we apply Function Points at two levels. First, we apply them at the conventional, application level. We map the counting rules to elements of an object-oriented model. We discuss some of the uses for the Function Point value at this level. Then, we move the boundaries, and apply Function Points at the class level. We then discuss the uses to which we can put this value. Finally, we explore the relationship between application level Function Points and class level Function Points.

Introduction to Function Points

Function Points were developed by Allan J. Albrecht in 1979 as part of an effort to measure the productivity across an organization using many different software development technologies. He sought a measure of output that was independent of the effects of the technology to facilitate organization-wide or cross-organization measurement.

The original definition of Function Points counted External Inputs, External Outputs, External Inquiries, Internal Files, and External Interface Files. The number of instances of each element type was multiplied by a weighting factor. These weighted values were summed to produce an Unadjusted Function Point Total. This total was then adjusted up or down for overall problem complexity by as much as 25%. The amount of the adjustment was based on expert judgment. This first version of Function Points suffered from a lack of guidance for identifying and counting the element types, and the method used to adjust the Function Point value was very subjective and somewhat limited.

In 1984, Albrecht (1984) refined Function Points, adding three complexity levels for each element type, providing more help with identifying instances of each element type, and providing a more objective way to adjust the value for overall problem complexity. The unadjusted total can be raised or lowered by up to 35%. Since 1984, Function Points have gained wide and increasing usage. The definition and counting rules are now maintained by IFPUG.

Like the 1979 version, the revision counted five element types: External Inputs, External Outputs, External Inquiries, Internal Logical Files, and External Interface Files. Inputs, outputs, and inquiries are concerned with data that cross the boundary to another entity, whether a human user or another application. Internal files describe the data the application must retain over time, and represent the application's data model. External Interface Files have come to mean data maintained by another application that is accessed directly for reference (IFPUG 1990).

An important concern is the placement of the boundary that separates the application from its environment. This boundary is important since it determines what can be considered an instance of an element type. This chapter discusses two distinct placements for this boundary.

The first step in counting Function Points is to identify instances of each element type. With logical system models, this is fairly easy (Putnam and Myers 1992). The second step is to determine the level of complexity as low, average, or high, for each instance using a matrix of values. Figures 13.1(a) through 13.1(d) show the complexity matrices for inputs, outputs, internal files, and external files, respectively. Inquiries are rated using the input matrix for the input part of the transaction, the output matrix for the output part of the transaction, and using the highest rating which is normally the output side.

The File Types Referenced (FTR) in the figures is a count of the Logical Internal Files accessed or updated by an input, output, or inquiry transaction. The acronym DET is for Data Element Types, and is simply the number of data elements or fields involved in the transaction. Record Types (RET) refers to the number of logical groups of data within a Logical Internal or External Interface File. For example, a customer order is often a complex structure consisting of a header group, one or more line item groups, followed by a trailer group. This structure would be counted

	1 to 4 DET	5 to 15 DET	16 or more DET
0 or 1 FTR	L	L	A
2 FTR	L	A	H
3 or more FTR	A	H	H

(a) External Input

	1 to 5 DET	6 to 19 DET	20 or more DET
0 or 1 FTR	L	L	A
2 or 3 FTR	L	A	H
4 or more FTR	A	H	H

(b) External Output

	1 to 19 DET	20 to 50 DET	51 or more DET
1 RET	L	L	A
2 to 5 RET	L	A	H
6 or more RET	A	H	H

(c) Internal Logical File

	1 to 19 DET	20 to 50 DET	51 or more DET
1 RET	L	L	A
2 to 5 RET	L	A	H
6 or more RET	A	H	H

(d) External Interface File

Fig. 13.1 Complexity matrices.

Description	Level of Complexity			Total
	Low	Average	High	
Inputs	__ x 3 = __	__ x 4 = __	__ x 6 = __	
Outputs	__ x 4 = __	__ x 5 = __	__ x 7 = __	
Inquiries	__ x 3 = __	__ x 4 = __	__ x 6 = __	
Internal Files	__ x 7 = __	__ x10 = __	__ x15 = __	
External Files	__ x 5 = __	__ x 7 = __	__ x10 = __	
Total Unadjusted Function Points				

Fig. 13.2 Calculating unadjusted function point total.

as one Logical File—it is a single structure—with two record types: one for the header and trailer information, and one for the item information.

In most cases, each table or data set in a normalized database will be a Logical Internal File. If a table is part of a larger logical structure, as is the case with the customer, the whole structure is treated as a single file, and each table is a record type.

After all instances of each element type have been assigned a level of complexity, a table similar to the one in Fig. 13.2 is completed. For each row in the table, the number of instances of that element type for a given level of complexity is multiplied by the indicated weighting factor. The weighted values are summed across the row and entered into the Total column on the far right of the figure. When all of the rows are completed, the total column is summed down to give the Unadjusted Function Point Total.

At this point, the General Systems Characteristics are applied to determine the adjustment factor. These 14 characteristics are valued from 0 (no influence) through 5 (significant influence) throughout the application. The 14 values are added, multiplied by 0.01 to create a percentage, then added to 0.65 to determine the adjustment factor, which can range from 0.65 to 1.35, ±35%. The Unadjusted Function Point value is multiplied by this adjustment factor to arrive at the Function Point Index. The 14 characteristics are: data communication, distributed processing, performance requirements, heavy usage, transaction rates, on-line data entry, design for end-user efficiency, on-line update, complex processing, usable in other applications (designed for reuse), ease of installation, ease of operation, multiple sites, and designed to facilitate change.

For our purposes, we do not need to apply the General Systems Characteristics, since they do not change the relationships between the application and class levels, and require substantial knowledge of both the domain and the implementation. We will be using the Unadjusted Function Point value throughout the rest of this chapter.

I should point out now that I will be straying from accepted Function Point practice when we consider class level Function Points. The application level Function Points we discuss later do follow accepted practice. Although current counting rules do not provide for counting classes, the rules presented for counting aggregate structures follow the spirit of current practice and lead to comparable results. The class level Function Points are almost a complete departure from accepted practice.

Although the counting rules are the same, moving the boundaries begins to focus on the implementation, rather than the problem, and decreases the purity of Function Points. For this reason, it is necessary to use the application level Function Points to measure productivity, quality, or to compare results between projects or organizations. Class level Function Points should only be used at the engineering level within a project, and for estimating development or maintenance effort. These uses will be discussed in greater detail later.

The Case Study

Before we begin to use Function Points, it will help to introduce the application models. We will be using the object structure models for two applications: order entry and inventory, and accounts receivable. The applications share a significant portion of the capabilities of several classes. The degree to which applications share classes is important—it is a measure of the reuse, both actual and potential, in an application inventory.

Figure 13.3 shows the model for the order entry application. The notation is from Embley, Kurtz, and Woodfield (1992) and is summarized in Fig. 13.4. I use this notation for several reasons: it is easy to draw using pencil and paper, it allows for leveling, it produces clean diagrams, and it provides different notations for different types of relationships. I will stop short of recommending it over the other available notations (see Bibliography for references on object-oriented modeling notation),

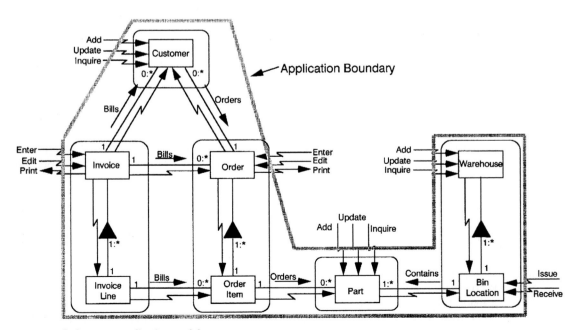

Fig. 13.3 Order entry application model.

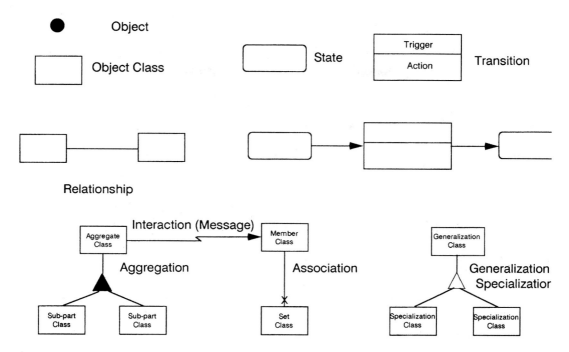

Fig. 13.4 Notation symbols.

because notation choice should be governed by personal tastes and the communication needs in any given circumstance.

The shaded line in Fig. 13.3 is not part of the notation, but shows the application boundary. Likewise, the rounded boxes surrounding the classes are not part of the notation, but show the class boundaries. The external inputs, outputs, and inquiries are shown as one-headed arrows, or interaction links, that cross the application boundary. The internal files are the classes themselves. There is not a one-to-one correspondence between classes and Internal Logical Files, which we will explore later.

Before we proceed, permit me a small digression to discuss one issue. The concept of an External Interface File is becoming obsolete. Under current counting rules, an external file is a file that is maintained as internal data by some other application and is accessed directly as reference data by our application. Transfer files created for the express purpose of passing data between applications are counted as an input or output, depending on the direction of the transfer. Under modern programming practices, and certainly under object-oriented techniques, externally maintained data are never accessed directly.

For our application to get data from another application, a message is passed requesting the pertinent data, which is then returned. In most cases, these will be counted as external inquiries. Sometimes, they will be inputs, and in others, outputs. We will not concern ourselves with External Interface Files, since we will almost certainly never encounter one.

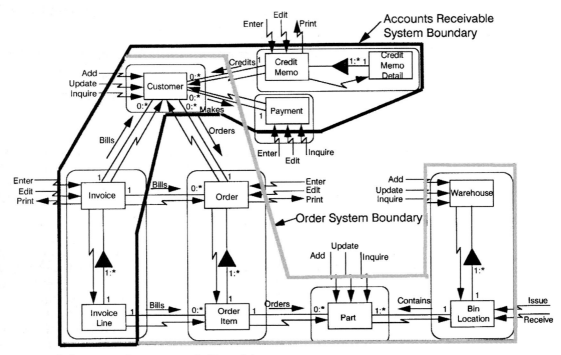

Fig. 13.5 Order entry and accounts receivable models.

Figure 13.5 shows the addition of the second application, accounts receivable. Note how the application boundaries overlap. We will first count Function Points at the application level, then at the class level. Since IFPUG Function Points include elements only related to data structure, we will only show the object structure models with the interaction links. Several people have proposed extensions to Function Points, including Charles Symons (Mark II Function Points) (Symons 1988), Capers Jones (Feature Points) (Jones 1988), and myself (3D Function Points) (Whitmire 1991). Many of these extensions measure elements from other dimensions of the problem, and would require more models.

Application Level Function Counts

Our first use of Function Points will stick to accepted practice and measure at the application level. This means an interaction link must cross the application boundary in order to be counted as an input, output, or inquiry. After we identify all instances of each element type, we apply the Function Point calculation algorithm to arrive at the Unadjusted Function Point count.

Our first task is to place the application boundary. Some models include the entire larger system. Others will include only the software portion of the system. With a model that includes the entire system, we must determine where the boundary lies between the software and the rest of the system. To do this, draw the boundary around the classes that are internal to the software. This becomes the application boundary. Our case study models only the software portion of the system, so the application boundary is the model boundary.

Inputs, outputs, and inquiries are interaction links that cross the boundary. Do not rely on the arrowheads to determine which is an input or an output. The arrow will always point from the initiator of the link to the receiver of the link. In object-oriented terms, the arrow points from the sender of the message to the receiver. Whether a link is an input, output, or inquiry depends on the direction of the flow of data. In an input, data will flow from outside to inside. In an output, from inside to outside. In an inquiry, the data will flow in both directions for each transaction. Determining the direction of data flow requires some knowledge of the application domain. Good labels on the interaction links also help.

Each input, output, and inquiry is assigned a level of complexity using the matrices in Fig. 13.1(a) and Fig. 13.1(b). Each class accessed by a transaction is counted as a file type referenced. For the order entry application in Fig. 13.3, all of the inputs are low complexity, and the outputs are all average complexity. The inquiries are all dominated by the output side, and are low complexity. These counts are entered in the table in Fig. 13.6(a).

Application Level

Description	Level of Complexity			Total
	Low	Average	High	
Inputs	12 x 3 = 36	x 4 = ___	x 6 = ___	36
Outputs	x 4 = ___	2 x 5 = 10	x 7 = ___	10
Inquiries	2 x 3 = 6	x 4 = ___	x 6 = ___	6
Internal Files	5 x 7 = 35	x10 = ___	x15 = ___	35
External Files	x 5 = ___	x 7 = ___	x10 = ___	
Total Unadjusted Function Points				87

(a)

Object Level

Description	Level of Complexity			Total
	Low	Average	High	
Inputs	12 x 3 = 36	x 4 = ___	x 6 = ___	36
Outputs	x 4 = ___	2 x 5 = 10	x 7 = ___	10
Inquiries	10 x 3 = 30	x 4 = ___	x 6 = ___	30
Internal Files	8 x 7 = 56	x10 = ___	x15 = ___	56
External Files	x 5 = ___	x 7 = ___	x10 = ___	
Total Unadjusted Function Points				132

(b)

Fig. 13.6 Function points for order entry.

Except for classes that participate in an aggregation relationship and some generalization classes, every class within the application boundary will be an Internal Logical File. For aggregations, the entire structure is a Single Logical File. Each class becomes a RET for purposes of assigning a complexity level. Logical files are entities in the user's view. The order is a single conceptual entity with two parts. Each part is a record type, but the whole structure is one logical file. This is true of the warehouse and invoice structures, as well.

Generalizations and specializations present another opportunity for an exception from the one class, one file principle. If the generalization is truly part of the application domain, it is counted as a separate logical file. Often, however, the generalization is added for the convenience of the model builder, and is not important to the application domain expert. When this is the case, it is not counted as a logical file, or as a record type—the data elements are added to each specialization. Specialization classes are always counted as separate logical files.

Once all of the logical internal files are identified, they are assigned a complexity level using the matrix in Fig. 13.1(c). For our order entry application, the results are added to the table in Fig. 13.6(a).

We now have all of the information we need to calculate the Function Point value. Figure 13.6(a) shows this value in the lower right-hand corner to be 87 Unadjusted Function Points for the order entry application.

We count the accounts receivable application in a similar manner. The result is shown in Fig. 13.7(a). The figure contains the Function Points contributed by the full inventory, consisting at this point of two applications. For reference, the accounts receivable application contributes 80 application level Function Points. Note that the value of the combined inventory is less than the sum of the two applications. Application level Function Points are not additive. This is due to counting transactions that cross shared boundaries only once. The inventory boundary is the union of all of the component application boundaries.

When we use application boundaries, we count instances of element types in each application that uses them. Thus, we seem to double count some instances, especially Internal Logical Files. This is appropriate for productivity measurement. An application consists of functionality regardless of its source. This is reuse in action.

One of the ways we can increase our development productivity is to increase the degree with which we share software components between applications. To measure this degree of sharing, we need to count the components in every application that uses them. We see the benefits of reuse when our delivery rate, Function Points per work month, starts to increase, or when the inverse, hours per Function Point, begins to decrease.

Application level Function Points can also be compared with Function Point counts from applications developed using other techniques. We have effectively normalized the effects of using object-oriented techniques. With this information, we can measure the relative cost or benefit of moving to object-oriented development.

The cost per Function Point can be determined on an average basis by multiplying the productivity rate (hours per Function Point) by the average hourly cost of a di-

Application Level

Description	Level of Complexity			Total
	Low	Average	High	
Inputs	20 x 3 = 60	__ x 4 = __	__ x 6 = __	60
Outputs	__ x 4 = __	4 x 5 = 20	__ x 7 = __	20
Inquiries	4 x 3 = 12	__ x 4 = __	__ x 6 = __	12
Internal Files	9 x 7 = 63	__ x10 = __	__ x15 = __	63
External Files	__ x 5 = __	__ x 7 = __	__ x10 = __	
Total Unadjusted Function Points				155

(a)

Object Level

Description	Level of Complexity			Total
	Low	Average	High	
Inputs	14 x 3 = 42	__ x 4 = __	__ x 6 = __	42
Outputs	__ x 4 = __	3 x 5 = 15	__ x 7 = __	15
Inquiries	14 x 3 = 42	__ x 4 = __	__ x 6 = __	42
Internal Files	11 x 7 = 77	__ x10 = __	__ x15 = __	77
External Files	__ x 5 = __	__ x 7 = __	__ x10 = __	
Total Unadjusted Function Points				179

(b)

Fig. 13.7 Function points for both applications.

rect labor hour. This cost can be calculated using either direct labor costs or fully burdened labor. Both numbers are valuable. The accuracy and purity of the cost value is determined by the accuracy and purity of the hours used in the productivity rate. The cost per Function Point can be used to bid on projects, to place a dollar value on the application inventory (a very large number for most organizations), or to benchmark the organization against its competitors.

Class Level Function Points

The big difference between application level Function Points and class level Function Points is the placement of the boundaries. For the class level, we draw a boundary around each class. To identify the classes for boundary purposes, we use the same rules we used to identify application level Logical Internal Files. Aggregations are viewed as a single class. Each participating class becomes an internal file for the aggregation. All generalizations are counted as classes because they participate in their own relationships and might be subject to different constraints than their specializations. The rounded boxes in Fig. 13.3 and Fig. 13.5 show the class boundaries for our two applications.

Inputs, outputs, and inquiries are interaction links that cross a class boundary. Note that some previously invisible interaction links, those that linked two internal logical files, are now counted. Again, you cannot depend on the arrows to distinguish an input from an output. You must know the direction that data is actually flowing through the link. The Function Point count for the class level view of the order entry application is given in Fig. 13.6(b). The value is higher because of the previously invisible inputs, outputs, and inquiries.

In many object-oriented methods, a class is assumed to have one input and one output per attribute, in addition to the interactions required for the problem domain (see Coad and Yourdon (1990) and (1991), for example). Do not count these implicit transactions. Count only those inputs and outputs that are required by the problem. The attributes contribute to class complexity by entering into the complexity of both internal logical files and transactions.

When we add applications, as we do in Fig. 13.5, we count only the classes and interactions that are added. For class level Function Points, we count a given instance of an input, output, inquiry, or internal file only once. The combined results for the order entry and accounts receivable applications are given in Fig. 13.7(b). The accounts receivable application contributes 47 class level Function Points. Note that because we count only the new classes and transactions, class level Function Points are additive.

One use of class level Function Points is for estimating new applications and changes to existing applications. You can use application level Function Points, but they do not map to the actual changes as cleanly as do class level Function Points. For existing software, class level Function Points are better for estimating the maintenance effort because they directly measure the software to be added or changed. While application Function Points measure the delivered functionality, class level Function Points measure the volume of product required to deliver that functionality. In this sense, class level Function Points are more product-based than problem-based.

Class level Function Points have at least one other use that will be of direct benefit to software engineers. A class or object is a data structure wrapped in a layer of function. Access to the data is provided by the functions. Together, a class's data and functions exhibit dynamic behavior. In other words, a class has all of the characteristics of an application, but on a smaller scale. It is accepted that application level Function Points measure the complexity of an application. Likewise, class level Function Points measure the complexity of the class. Given two classes, the class with the higher class level Function Point count is the bigger and more complex of the two.

More traditional measures of complexity do not apply well to classes. Experience has shown that the line count for object services is, on average, much smaller than for traditional functions (Software Development 1991). Likewise, Cyclomatic Complexity (McCabe 1976) measures the logic structure of blocks of code. Cyclomatic Complexity cannot be used to measure the logic structures represented by inheritance or aggregation relationships. In addition, object-oriented software does not exhibit the flow of control found in traditional software. Let's face it: the paradigm has changed, and our old measures just don't work beyond the individual service level. Since classes exhibit characteristics more like applications than functions, it makes sense to use an application measure to assess class complexity. Class level Function Points perform this function very well.

The Function Points used in this chapter, at both levels, are the standard Function Points used throughout the business software community. Like applications, classes have dimensions of data, function, and control (Whitmire 1991). To more completely measure class complexity, consider using one of the Function Point extensions mentioned earlier (Feature Points or 3D Function Points).

The Relationship between Levels

Figure 13.8 shows the relationship between the Function Point values taken at the application and class levels. With the first application, the class level value is higher. As applications are added, the two values, summed over the entire inventory, begin to converge. At some point around three applications, the class level value becomes the lower of the two. As more applications are added, the difference becomes greater. This difference is due to the sharing of class data and services between applications. The shared functionality is counted at the application level in each application that uses it, but only once for the class level value.

The class level value represents the actual volume of software in the inventory. The application level value represents the leveraged benefit from the inventory. The larger the difference between the two values, the more leverage. The actual relationship between these values depends to a large degree on the amount of sharing between applications. This degree may change over time in unstable and unpredictable ways. In some cases, the growth in the value of one or both levels may not be linear.

The degree of inventory leverage is measured by taking the ratio of application level Function Points to class level Function Points. The higher the value, the higher the leverage. This ratio is very similar in concept to the interest rate earned on an in-

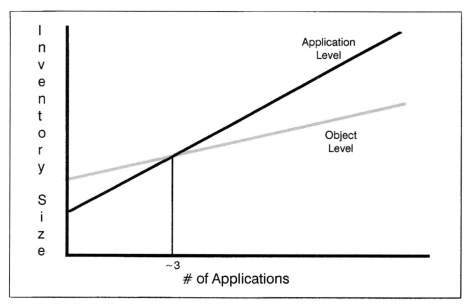

Fig. 13.8 Relationship between application/function points.

vestment. The class level Function Points represent the investment, and the application level Function Points represent the payback. The ratio between them is the rate of return, or interest rate.

On a development project, the Function Point values at both levels can be calculated as soon as the models are nearing completion and potential reusable software is identified, such as interface and database managers. The application level value should include the entire application, in keeping with current Function Point practice. The class level value should include only the classes to be added or modified. Then, the ratio between them measures development efficiency for this development project. It can also be viewed as the rate of return received on the invested labor and non-labor costs.

Summary

In order to be improved, software engineering productivity must be measured. To measure productivity, we must measure the size of the output. To compare the productivity effects of different development approaches, we must have an output measure that is not affected by the approach. Function Points are known to have this property. Taken at the application level, Function Points show the relative cost or benefit of object-oriented software development.

Taken at the class level, Function Points measure the complexity of a class. By their very nature, Function Points indirectly measure the internal complexity by directly measuring externally observable characteristics. By design, this is how the class appears to the rest of the world. Classes behave like whole applications, and it makes sense to measure them as such.

The ratio of application level Function Points to class level Function points can be calculated for both the entire application inventory and for individual projects. For the inventory, it is a measure of functionality received for functionality built. The higher the ratio, the more you are leveraging your resources. On a project, the ratio is the return on investment in terms of functionality, and a measure of the level to which you are reusing your existing inventory.

As a practicing software engineer, I use class level Function Point value extensively in object-oriented design evaluation and estimating. It is a practical and useful value. I have not found a measure of object complexity that is as satisfactory. Of course, class level Function Points alone are insufficient to assess design complexity or quality. They must be used as part of a set of metrics in accordance with a defined process and established project goals. But that is a matter for another work.

Author Biography

Scott A. Whitmire has been developing software applications for over ten years. He holds a Master of Software Engineering from Seattle University, and has developed applications in accounting, manufacturing, production control, executive information, project management, and development and systems tools.

Throughout his entire career, Mr. Whitmire has searched for methods, tools, and techniques that would allow him to tackle bigger problems with better quality and in less time. Technical by nature, he appreciates the value of measurement to the engineering process. He has been using object-oriented techniques, particularly modeling and design techniques, for over two years.

Mr. Whitmire is active in the software engineering profession. He is a member of the IEEE and participates in the development of software engineering standards. He is also an active participant in the International Function Point Users Group, where he advocates the extension of Function Points into new areas. He is currently an independent consultant in systems and software engineering, and is employed as a software engineer at Boeing Computer Services in Seattle, Washington.

Works Cited

Albrecht, A.J. 1984. *IBM CSI&A guideline 313, AD/M productivity measurement and estimate validation*. New York, N.Y.: International Business Machines Corp.

Coad, P. and E. Yourdon. 1990. *Object-oriented design*. Englewood Cliffs, N.J.: Yourdon Press.

Coad, P. and E. Yourdon. 1991. *Object-oriented analysis*. Englewood Cliffs, N.J.: Yourdon Press.

Embley, D.W., B.D. Kurtz, and S. N. Woodfield. 1992. *Object-oriented systems analysis—a model driven approach*. Englewood Cliffs, N.J.: Yourdon Press.

IFPUG. 1990. *Function Point counting practices, release 3.0*. Westerville, Oh.: International Function Point Users Group.

Jones, T.C. 1988. A short history of Function Points and Feature Points. Draft article. Cambridge, Ma.: Software Productivity Research, Inc.

Putnam, L.H. and W. Myers. 1992. *Measures for excellence*. pp. 67–73. Englewood Cliffs, N.J.: Yourdon Press.

Software Development. 1991. Private conversations. The developers of two interface libraries, one in C and one in C++, noted that the average function length in C++ was five to ten lines of code. The C++ library was just over half the size of the C library, but contained far more functionality. Similar informal results have been heard from people who have rebuilt a traditionally developed application in other object-oriented languages.

Symons, C.R. 1988. Function Point analysis: Difficulties and improvements. *IEEE transactions on software engineering*. SE-14 (1): 2–11.

Whitmire, S.A. 1991. 3D Function Points: Scientific and real-time extensions to Function Points. Unpublished white paper. Seattle, Wa.: The Boeing Company.

McCabe, T.J. 1976. A complexity measure. *IEEE transaction on software engineering* SE-2 (4): 308–320.

Additional Reading

Page-Jones, M. and S. Wiess. 1991. *Object-oriented analysis and design: the synthesis model*. Tutorial presented at Software Development '92. Wayland Systems, Inc. Bellevue, Wa.

Wirfs-Brock, R., B. Wilkerson, and L. Wiener. 1990. *Designing Object-oriented software*. Englewood Cliffs, N.J.: Prentice Hall.

Putting a Measurement Program in Place

by Howard Rubin

The Importance of Baselining and Benchmarking

Perhaps the biggest challenge facing information technology (IT) organizations in the 1990s is to establish the linkage between their work efforts and business value. The starting point for establishing this linkage is to obtain a total picture of the IT organization and relate it to the production of value for the business. The key element in making the connection is the creation of an IT baseline—a quantitative view of where you are today—that focuses on the six basic factors that are the drivers of IT business value: the applications and project inventory; the IT organizational structure and human resources profile; the management practices portfolio; the delivery process methodology; the technology infrastructure; and the business–IT interface. Once complete, the baseline provides a framework for comparing your organization against competitive benchmarks and a context for improvement and innovation.

In answer to the question, "Why should anyone read this?" there are two proverbs that truly characterize the state of software-systems development and maintenance today: "If you don't know where you are going, any road will do," and, "If you don't know where you are, a map won't help!"

Less than 10% of software-producing organizations worldwide have any kind of ongoing measurements program. Only one out of every six organizations that start measurement programs are successful. These findings are in agreement with some recent analyses undertaken by the Software Engineering Institute (SEI) of Carnegie Mellon University. The SEI developed a methodology for classifying an organization's "software process maturity" into one of five levels (see Fig. 14.1), which range from Level 1, the Initial level (where there is no formalization of the software process), to Level 5, the Optimizing level (where methods, procedures, and metrics are in place

Fig. 14.1 Levels of software process maturity.

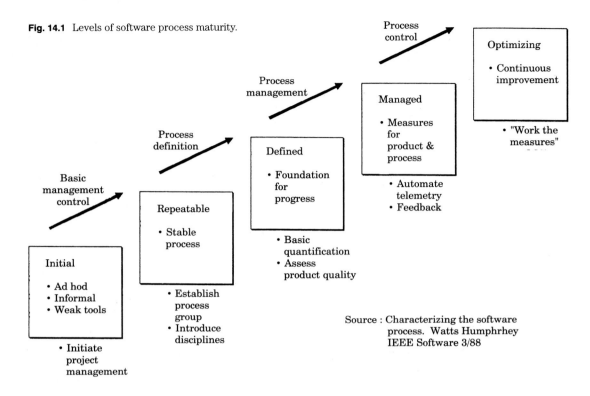

Source : Characterizing the software process. Watts Humphrhey IEEE Software 3/88

with a focus toward continuous improvement). The result of their study showed that about 85% of organizations surveyed in the United States were at Level 1.

How to Get Started: Assess Your Measurement Readiness

The first step to take is to carefully assess your "measurement readiness." Answer the following questions as a basis for setting the direction for your measurement strategy. Each answer is scaled from 0 to 5. Mark your answers on the chart provided in Fig. 14.2.

1. How intense is the organization's desire to improve its performance?
   0 = No desire, 5 = Intense.

2. Is the enterprise willing to invest time and money to improve systems performance with measurement?
   0 = No, 5 = Funds and people are allocated.

3. What is the current level of the systems skill inventory in regard to being able to use metrics?
   0 = None, 5 = Already in wide effective use.

4. To what extent are measurement concepts known and understood by the systems staff?
   0 = No staff have been exposed, 5 = Staff is 100% trained.

5. Is the systems culture adverse to using measurements at the organizational and individual level?
   0 = 100% against, 5 = Anxious to implement.

6. To what extent is a support structure in place to foster measurement practices and perform metrics technology transfer?
   0 = No infrastructure, 5 = Team in place.

7. Are tools and repositories for acquiring and analyzing metrics data in place?
   0 = No, 5 = Full suite and warehouse available.

8. Does the systems organization understand its role in the businesses processes?
   0 = No, 5 = Yes, the business processes are documented and tracked through metrics.

If the answers to all of these questions is at the low end of the scale, your organization's measurement readiness is quite low. Radical change will be needed to get things going. A good starting point for getting started is to contact professional societies so that experiences in measurement can be shared and exchanged. Good contacts can be made through the International Function Point User Group (IFPUG), the IEEE Computer Society, the Quality Assurance Institute, the Gartner Group, and at seminars offered by Digital Consulting, Software Quality Engineering, and Extended Intelligence.

If your readiness is somewhat higher at the "enabled ring," you are ready to "bite the measurement bullet" and build your baseline. Two actions should be taken in parallel: reinforce your measurement infrastructure by acquiring automated tools to ease the pain of data collection and analysis; mobilize measurement by building a rapid baseline using the structure that is outlined here and producing a measurement program design. Embark on a 30-day mission to collect and analyze information using the 80/20 rule as a guide. Then, consolidate your metrics findings for your baseline into a single-page picture covering each of the six driver areas. Next, relate the baseline to published benchmarks. However, don't stop there. Translate the opportunities found to business terms as a basis for providing value from your efforts.

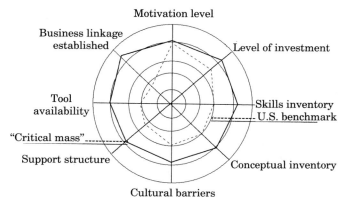

Fig. 14.2 Measurement readiness.

This is the step that will bring focus to all the work and will provide a platform for transformation and ongoing use of measurement.

Building Your Baseline (If you don't know where you are, a map won't help, but longitude and latitude aren't enough)

Productivity and quality (read the latter as "freedom from defects") seem to be the watchwords (or perhaps buzzwords?) today for assessing IT performance in the worlds of software development and support. A lot of energy is focused on how to measure these, but the truth of the matter is that no matter how you measure them, only measuring productivity and quality does not provide a complete picture. Establishing a baseline goes beyond just productivity and quality. A complete baseline involves assessing an IT organization's current portfolio of projects and applications, its human resources and organizational structure, its management practices and processes, the technology infrastructure, and most importantly, business factors that drive the computing function. Figure 14.3 shows the six areas that should be "baselined" as a platform for benchmarking and target setting.

Although completing the baseline picture appears to be time-consuming and exhaustive, it need not be. The typical time it should take for this activity is less than 30 days, using a dedicated team of no more than three persons (consultants allowed, of course). Remember, the goal is to create a workable and useful organization profile rather than 100% complete data collection: the 80/20 rule applies here.

How to Do It

The approach for assessing the baseline performance of an organization involves a "divide and conquer" approach by viewing the baseline as containing the aforementioned six segments that can be combined in a single comprehensive picture. The baseline segments follow.

Applications and project portfolio baseline

The "software side" of a typical IT organization creates new software applications or modifies existing applications. This baseline segment is targeted at creating an inventory of the applications and current projects as they exist today—as-is. This includes key descriptive information and metrics relating to:

- Demographics (age, language, implementation date, technology platform, tools and techniques used, etc.)
- Financial history (cost to build, cost to maintain, cost to use, cost to operate)
- Size (lines of code, Function Point counts)
- Support information (number of staff, number of requests, average request size)
- Quality attributes
  - —Rating of functional quality by the user (ability to support user requirements in terms of functionality, accuracy, reliability, data quality etc.)

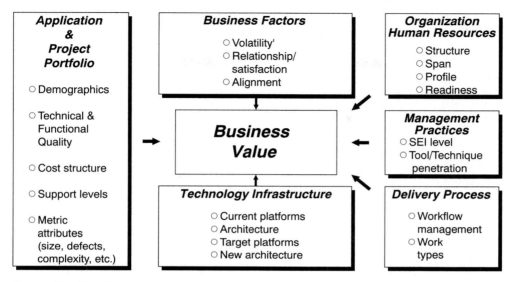

Fig. 14.3 The 6 baseline components.

—Rating of technical quality by systems staff (design strength, complexity, architecture, maintainability, portability, inter-operability, etc.)
—Problem history
—Defects found per line of code or Function Point

- Productivity attributes

—Support ratios (lines of code or Function Points per support staff member)
—Original delivery rate (lines of code or Function Points per team member per month)

Systems organization and human resources baseline

This baseline segment provides a profile of the "people side" of the IT equation. Included are:

- Organizational chart (functional)

- Average managerial span of control

- Human resource profile

—Skills inventory
—Educational inventory
—Training history
—Team and individual profiles, such as Meyers-Briggs

- Work distribution (percent of people and dollars expended on development versus support

Ultimately, the question that this segment answers is, "Do we have the right resources to support our business today and in the future?"

The production of an organizational "readiness footprint," in the context of the ability to assimilate new technology, is a major baseline output. This parallels the measurement readiness footprint used earlier in this chapter, but concentrates on software technology instead of on measurement. Assessment questions include:

1. How intense is the organization's desire to improve its performance?
   0 = No desire, 5 = Intense.

2. How much is the organization willing to invest to improve its performance?
   0 = Nothing, 5 = Up to $100,000 per professional.

3. What is the current level of the systems skills inventory in regard to software engineering?
   0 = Abstractions and models are not used at all, 5 = Formalization and models used by all.

4. To what extent are basic software engineering concepts known and understood by the systems staff?
   0 = No staff have been exposed, 5 = Staff is 100% trained.

5. Is the systems culture adverse to using new tools, techniques, or innovations?
   0 = Yes, 100% against, 5 = Anxious to implement.

6. To what extent is a support structure in place to foster measurement-software engineering-technology transfer?
   0 = None, 5 = In-place team of critical mass exists.

7. What is the current software engineering platform?
   0 = Dumb terminals, 5 = Client-server workstations.

8. What is the development to support ratio?
   0 = 0/100%, 5 = 100%/0%.

Plot your results on a circular scale, as you did with the measurement assessment. However, this time plot a profile of where your organization should be in each dimension—either in regard to a particular technology (such as CASE), or to the overall software process (such as SEI Level 3). The gaps that become apparent are those that need to be filled in order to transform your organization to where it should be.

Management practices baseline

The focus of this baseline segment is on how the existing resources work. This segment involves narrative information gathering and summarizing. It deals with answering basic questions about management practices, such as:

- How are planning and prioritizing done?
- How does the organization translate requests into systems?
- How defined is the systems development life cycle?
- What is in the organization's tool inventory and what is actually used in practice?

- What is organization's current software process maturity level? (Perform a formal or informal SEI assessment.)

This information is typically gathered through interviews and workshops, which are conducted to assess the rigor, actual end-use, and effectiveness of these practices.

Delivery process baseline

This is the baseline segment in which representative development and maintenance projects are examined in detail to measure schedule and effort productivity and quality. It is also necessary to go beyond these and assess other factors likely to affect productivity and quality. By determining delivery and support rates at the project level and comparing them to external benchmarks, an organization can create a framework to measure the impact of potential changes and identify opportunities. Furthermore, the framework will provide a clear basis for understanding the potential effect that tools, such as CASE, can have on the overall delivery rate and product/process quality.

Typical metrics collected at the project level include:

- Lines of code or Function Points per professional, by project size
- Lines of code or Function Points per work month by project size
- Defects per line of code or function discovered before and after implementation
- Percent of defects originating from each life cycle phase
- Point in life cycle where defects were found
- Percent of defects removed by phase

Technology infrastructure baseline

This segment of the baseline identifies the current and proposed delivery and production environments. Many companies are wrestling with the possibility of shifting from mainframe to workstation-based development in an effort to reduce costs while increasing productivity. Here is where the steps that can be taken to accomplish this goal most effectively are evaluated. Again, in reference to CASE, typical benefits can be found in reducing mainframe data-center charges and increased developer productivity.

Business factors baseline

Perhaps the most important component of any baseline is the mapping of the linkage between the software engineering function and the business' performance. The way to get at this is through executive interviews with major systems customers to develop an understanding of the combination of internal and external factors that might be changing the business fundamentally. Understanding the volatility of your customers' environments sets the stage for examining how the systems organization is aligned to support the business. This is supplemented by interviews with key end-users to identify those projects that are not currently being worked on that could provide a measurable difference in the way the business is run. The essence of this

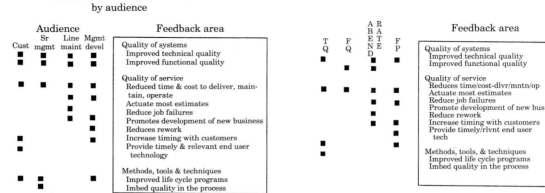

Fig. 14.4 Audience analysis sample charts.

baseline segment is to determine how business-value is created by the systems area from the vantage point of the business. This also sets the stage for defining business value level metrics.

The results of this baseline segment should be visualized as a table (see Fig. 14.4) that separates those interviewed into peer group audiences. For each audience, the cross-reference table should show which performance assessment areas are key to them. Another table should then be constructed to link each performance area to the measurements that support it. This set of tables is essentially your measurement program design document.

Making the Connection to Business Value

The baseline process described here illustrates how organizations can get a total picture of their systems function and link it to the production of value for their business. Each baseline segment represents one of the six drivers of business value. This provides a clear focus for implementing software measurement, both within the context of the as-is baseline and the benefits of the "to-be" business-based analysis.

To demonstrate contribution to the business, however, it is absolutely critical that a systems organization install a metrics "dashboard." With proper instrumentation, it can be used to monitor and manage organizational performance as well as to clearly identify the systems contribution to business value.

The exact business measures can be derived by extending the Business Factors Baseline segment. If shareholder, external business customers, and internal business customers are included in addition to the IT audiences, a complete dashboard framework will result. The resultant two tables will show what performance improvement looks like to each constituency and will also show what the suitable indicators (metrics) are. Using this as a framework, two types of dashboards should be constructed; one containing the navigating gauges, and the other containing the destination gauges used to declare success.

Using External Benchmarks with Your Baseline

If you have constructed your IT baseline in accordance with the guidelines given, you are in the enviable position of being able to assess your IT performance against "best-in-class" benchmarks. A few key charts have been provided with this chapter to provide you with a baseline/benchmark snapshot. Follow the steps below to construct your snapshot:

Applications portfolio

- On Worksheet Chart 14.1 (lines of code) or Worksheet Chart 14.2 (Function Points) mark a point for each application for which you have computed the support ratio (either lines of code or Function Points per support professional).

- On Worksheet Chart 14.2, fill in the percentage of your total portfolio that is in each of the following categories: low functional quality (FQ) and low technical quality (TQ); high FQ and low TQ; low FQ and high TQ; high FQ and high TQ.

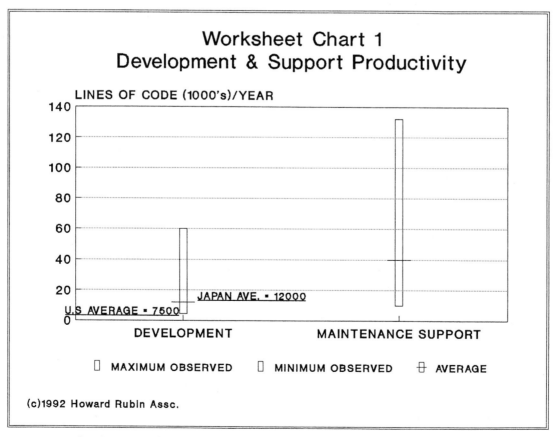

Worksheet 14.1 Development and support productivity.

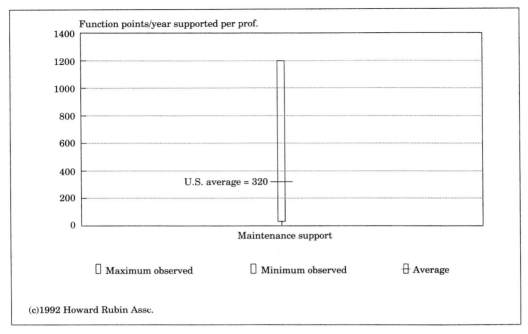

Worksheet 14.1A   Support productivity ranges.

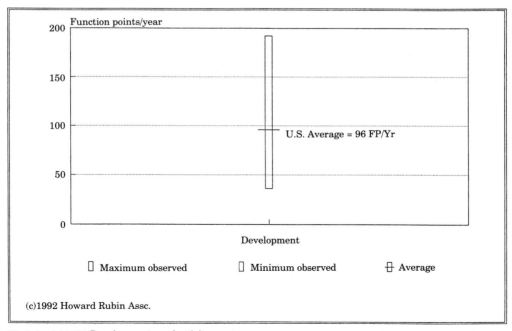

Worksheet 14.1B   Development productivity ranges.

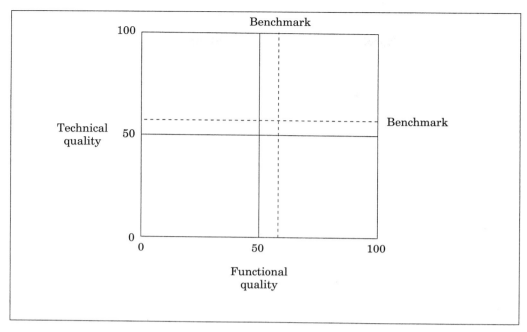

Worksheet 14.2 Application portfolio characteristics.

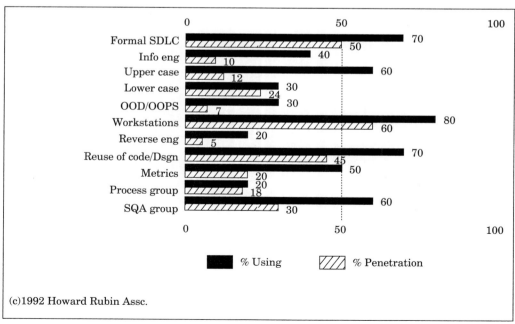

Worksheet 14.3 Tool/technique inventory—US data.

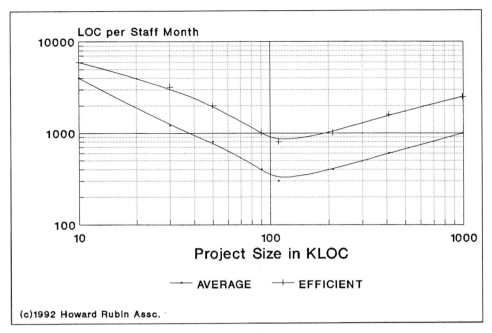

Worksheet 14.4 Effort productivity in KLOC/staff month.

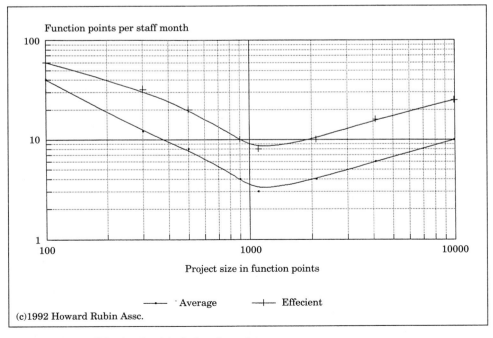

Worksheet 14.4A Effort productivity in function points.

Technology infrastructure

- For tool and technique listed in Worksheet Chart 14.3, indicate what percent of its target audience are using it in the intended manner at least 80% of the time.

Delivery process

- Mark a point on Worksheet Chart 14.4 (lines of code) or Worksheet Chart 14.5 (Function Points) for each project that you have assessed in terms of delivered lines of code or Function Points per person month.

- Mark a point on Worksheet 14.6 that represents either the average number of post-implementation defects detected per Function Point or lines of code.

Management practices

- Using Worksheet Chart 14.7 place an X in the segment that most clearly relates to your SEI process maturity rating.

Organization and human resources

- Using Worksheet Chart 14.8, mark the point that indicates your IT average span of control.

- Answer the organizational readiness assessment questions and plot your results on Worksheet Chart 14.9.

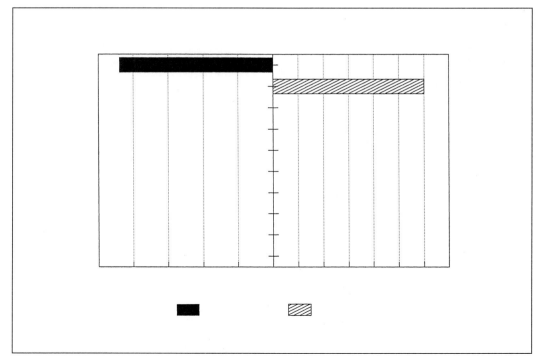

Worksheet 14.5 Defect density.

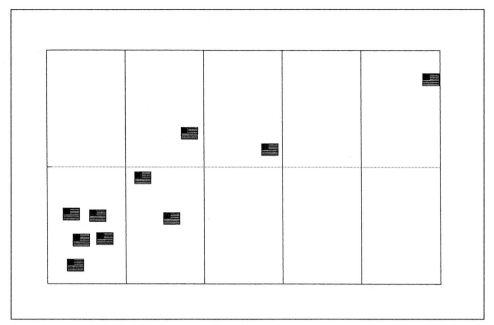

Worksheet 14.6 U.S. software process maturity.

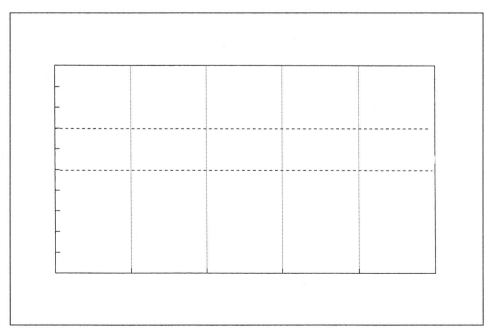

Worksheet 14.7 Span of control.

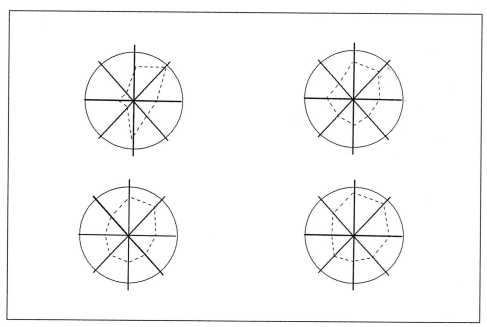

Worksheet 14.8 Organizational readiness.

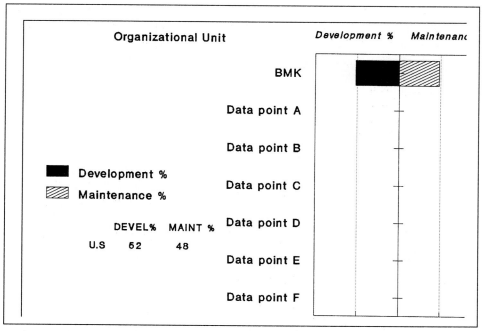

Worksheet 14.9 Development: maintenance distribution.

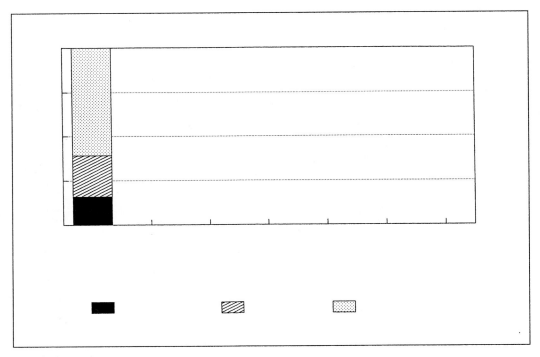

Worksheet 14.10 Maintenance distribution.

- Using Worksheet Chart 14.10, indicate the percent of resources allocated to maintenance and development. At a more detailed level, categorize your distribution into corrective, adaptive, and perfective maintenance.

Although these charts provide only a snapshot in a nonindustry-specific manner, they will allow you to get value from your baseline through comparisons with the provided benchmarks.

The Bottom Metrics Line

The benchmark data provided on these charts are real. The bottom line for many of the organizations at the top end of the performance spectrum has also been measured in business terms—a true "bottom line." In terms of the business value, these top-performing organizations were typically viewed by their companies as a critical part of a competitive strategy. In some instances, the results were that the IT organization contributed significantly to the company's ability to produce its products at half the cycle time and cost of its competitors, with 80% less rework, while deliveries were more than 90% on-time. In these same instances, competitors were plagued by long product-development times and late deliveries—the primary cause given by the business community: the software was either late or faulty. Enough said!

How Do You Improve Your Bottom Line?

The issue for the 1990s is not "to measure or not to measure." The real issue is one of transforming performance and producing business value through computing. Metrics play a pivotal role for benchmarking, baselining, and target setting.

The road to transformation is a difficult one. It still involves the basics—knowing where you are, where you are going, and how you are going to get there. By combining the notions of baselining, dashboard construction, target setting, and parallel approaches to change through readiness assessment, transformation is possible for any organization committed to go on the trip (see Fig. 14.5).

The good news is that "making transformation happen" and "making measurement happen" have a lot in common. The bad news is that the latter is a shallow goal and that there isn't any single metric (nor will there ever be) that will magically get you there by itself.

After completing the baseline, your organization should know where it is, be able to determine where it is going, and be ready to determine "which road will do." How-

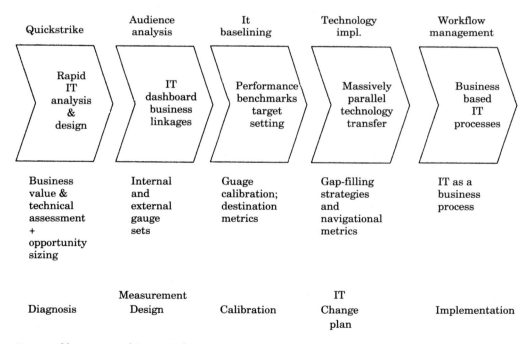

Fig. 14.5 Measurement driven transformation process.

ever, the role of measurement, baselines, and benchmarks does not stop at this point. It really only begins.

Author Biography

Dr. Howard A. Rubin is a Full Professor and former Chair of the Department of Computer Science at Hunter College of the City University of New York, and CEO of Howard Rubin Associates, Inc. Dr. Rubin is the originator of the project-navigation concept and author of the world's leading commercial tools for software estimation and planning—CA-ESTIMACS and CA-PLANMACS. Most recently he has developed the CA-ADVISOR expert software strategy and tactics analysis system, the RA-METRICS measurement repository, the FPXpert expert system for Function Point counting and analysis, and the Software Quality Management System for defect tracking and analysis. Dr. Rubin is also a former Nolan Norton Research Fellow.

Through his product experience and research, Dr. Rubin has collected data on more than 13,000 software projects as a basis for analyzing software productivity and quality trends. As a result he is an internationally recognized consultant and speaker in the areas of measurement, productivity, and software process dynamics.

In the area of software measurement, Dr. Rubin is the creator of the I/S measurement dashboard and is a pioneer in linking I/S investment to business value. His Audience Analysis methodology for measurement program design and his QUICK-STRIKE methodology for I/S process redesign have been adopted by industry leaders desiring to increase the value of computing to their enterprise. In the area of CASE, Dr. Rubin is the developer of the CASE/IM Implementation Methodology for ensuring effective technology transfer of tools and methods.

In 1987 Dr. Rubin formed Howard Rubin Associates, Inc., an outcome-oriented product and services organization focusing on applying his techniques to improve software engineering processes. Today, HRA is the leading organization specializing in software metrics, organizational transformation through measurement of business value, and value-driven process redesign.

Tracking the Life Cycle Trajectory
Metrics and Measures for Controlling Productivity of Computer-Aided Software Engineering (CASE) Development

by Rajiv D. Banker, Robert J. Kauffman,

and Rachna Kumar

Abstract

This paper proposes a new vision for the measurement and management of development productivity related to Computer-Aided Software Engineering (CASE) technology. We propose that productivity be monitored and controlled in each phase of software development life cycle, a measurement approach we have termed *life cycle trajectory measurement*. Recent advances in CASE technology that make low cost automated measurement possible have made it feasible to collect life cycle trajectory measures. We suggest that current approaches for productivity management involve the use of static metrics that are available only at the beginning and end of the project. Yet, the depth of the insights needed to make proactive adjustments in the software development process requires monitoring the range of activities across the entire software development life cycle.

This can be accomplished only with metrics that can measure performance parameters in each phase of the life cycle. We develop metrics that have the ability to measure and estimate software outputs from each intermediate phase of the development life cycle. These metrics are based on a count of the objects and modules that are used as building blocks for application development in repository object-based CASE environments. The viability of such object-based metrics for life cycle trajectory measurement has been empirically tested for the software construction phase using project data generated in Integrated CASE development environments.

Software Productivity and the CASE Opportunity

CASE tools are believed to represent an industrial revolution in the market for software development. They have changed the dynamics of software development from essentially a manual, craft-work-like process to a more automated, rigorous and standardized engineering discipline. In this paper, we examine new approaches and opportunities presented by this changed development environment for managing software development performance. We argue that CASE has the potential to improve control of software development productivity by allowing measurement of software outputs across the entire development life cycle.

The quest for improving software productivity

The sheer size of corporate investments in software indicates the extent of the hopes that senior managers place in wresting business value from it (Davis 1988; Benson and Parker 1986). For example, industry specialists estimated that by 1990 the total investment in existing, developed and purchased software was in the neighborhood of 13% of the United States' Gross National Product, a staggering $527 billion (Ramamoorthy et al. 1984). Other projections reveal an annual increase in software development budgets at the rate of 9% to 12%, exceeding $150 billion per year by 1990 (Boem and Papaccio 1988; Gurbaxani and Mendelson 1987). However, software development is regarded as a major bottleneck in exploiting the potential of IT (Grammas and Klein 1985). Substantial backlogs of software development exist in organizations of all sizes and in many different industries, and they are reported to be increasing at a rapid rate (Sprague and McNurlin 1986; Yourdon 1986).

One study even reported the existence of "hidden backlogs," consisting of user needs that were not formally requested or commissioned; these hidden backlogs were estimated at 535% of known backlogs (Alloway and Quillard 1983). Reports of software projects months behind schedule and far over budget are also quite common. As a result, senior management perceives that it is critical to find ways to better control the production of corporate software assets.

A common intermediate goal for senior software development managers is to improve the productivity of applications development and the quality of applications execution. The low productivity of software development operations is attributable to a number of factors (Alavi 1985; Boem and Papaccio 1988; Kang and Levy 1989; Senn and Wyenkoop 1990). Table 15.1 lists the major ones among these.

Improvement of productivity can be achieved by streamlining the life cycle of software creation through the introduction of new development techniques. As a result, in recent years we have witnessed the introduction and adoption of many new software development tools and techniques. These include: structured programming; rapid prototyping and protocycling; fourth generation languages (4GLs); object-oriented and graphical analysis; design and development techniques; and data-oriented methodologies.

The most recent addition to this list is CASE tools. Input Inc., a California-based research firm, has indicated that about 6% of annual software expenditures by American firms in 1989 were attributable to application development tools in gen-

TABLE 15.1 Factors responsible for inefficient development.

```
•  Customized application development practices which redevelop from
scratch the fundamental procedures and processes that are common across
applications or business units in an organization.

•  Outdated and error-prone development methodologies that postpone effort
to the back end of software development life cycle when the software is
coded and implemented; this results in significant additional hidden costs
of maintenance.

•  Increased complexity, size and scope of the functionality to be
incorporated into software for meeting user needs in the competitive
environment of a firm's business.

•  The labor-intensive nature of software development, which renders
software quality and productivity very vulnerable to the skills of the
personnel used for development.

•  A growth rate in user needs for IT applications that exceeds the growth
rate of the supply of experienced and well-trained development staff.
```

eral. In terms of dollars, this puts the total expenditure in the range of $6 billion or more, and spending on such off-the-shelf application development tools is conservatively estimated to be growing at a 19% annual rate (Moad 1990).

The promise of CASE productivity

CASE is often touted as the most promising of all the new tools, and certainly it is the fastest-growing segment. Two different surveys have indicated that between 55% and 75% of organizations have adopted CASE tools for various development projects including pilot projects, departmental projects, and corporate-wide applications (Burkhard and Jenster 1989; Sentry Market Research 1990). Analysts also predict that the CASE market will grow at 35% to 45% per year, to something on the order of $1 billion in the early 1990s (McClure 1989).

CASE technologies and the methodologies that they promote aim to transform the process of software development. Paralleling the structure of production in other industries, such as automobile manufacturing, home construction, and computer hardware manufacturing, CASE is enabling a move of the software enterprise from an assembly industry to a process industry. This means that each product is no longer custom built. Instead, production occurs through the use of prefabricated components and reusable templates, plans, and procedures (Pollack 1990). CASE supporters and firms investing heavily in CASE argue that software automation and the "modular software" approach is the key to increasing productivity, controlling quality, and introducing predictability into the software development process.

An analysis of the structural and functional dimensions of CASE technology helps to identify the major characteristics of this methodology that contribute towards potential improvements in development productivity. These have very broadly been classified by various authors as the standardization of the software development process, and the automation of software development activities (Burkhard and Jenster 1989; McClure 1989; Senn and Wyankoop 1990).

Standardization of software development is at the heart of the "modular approach" to software creation. It enables the reuse of existing software components, which saves the effort in writing, testing, and implementing portions of the software currently being developed (Hall 1987; Jones 1984). Standardization can lead to reduced development time as well as an improved software quality. Automation addresses tedious or routine manual tasks such as verification, validation, and consistency checking, in early development phases, or error checking in code. This not only reduces the labor required for performing these tasks manually, it also ensures that these tasks are performed satisfactorily and uniformly. It also supports an increase in the quality of delivered software.

Thus, standardization and automation can contribute significantly towards development productivity by impacting the efficiency and effectiveness of software creation. Efficiency increases productivity directly by increasing software output per unit input by software developers when a CASE methodology is used to develop software. Effectiveness impacts productivity indirectly by ensuring that CASE-developed software accomplishes the business goals of the organization and, therefore, the software output is relevant and has maximal value. The efficiency and effectiveness dimensions of CASE development are described in Table 15.2.

A natural question would be the verification of the promised productivity benefits of CASE. Although reports on CASE claim a myriad of benefits, ranging from 300% productivity increases to "zero-maintenance" program code, only a few studies report rigorously substantiated productivity benefits (Kemerer 1987; Norman and Nunamaker 1989; Vipond 1990). Most studies report on successful (or confessional) implementations of CASE methods or on surveys compiling usage proportions and profiles of CASE tools (Burkhard and Jenster 1989; McClure 1989; McNurlin 1989). Banker and Kauffman (1991) have presented some of the first empirical results to substantiate large productivity gains from using CASE development techniques, especially the leverage created when a firm implements a software reusability strategy.

This paper examines how management reporting needs to be recast to support the goal of controlling software productivity as much as possible with the tools available in the new environment of CASE. It develops a new vision for the management of the software development life cycle in the presence of integrated CASE technologies via automated software metrics and measures. We make the case that tracking the life cycle trajectory of software projects, made possible by automated analysis of the software development process, helps management to control productivity in a way that was not possible before CASE.

Controlling CASE Development Productivity

A new vocabulary for tracking software development performance

We propose a framework to measure, control, and influence software development performance that builds upon the distinguishing characteristics of CASE environments. We find that existing approaches to the estimation of software development

TABLE 15.2   CASE: Cost impacts of improved efficiency.

MAJOR SOURCES OF CASE BENEFITS	COST IMPACTS	
	EFFICIENCY DIMENSION	EFFECTIVENESS DIMENSION
Productivity Gains	Reuse supports creation of larger amount of software for given level of labor	Products of CASE development create a reusable software infrastructure for the firm, further lowering costs.
Speed of Development	Has potential to help reduce existing backlog of software projects	Allows for flexible, timely response to rapid changes in business goals
Accuracy of Development	Reduces debugging and maintenance costs by lowering error rates	Supports optimizing the functionality of software to meet business/user needs
Methodological Consistency of Development	Provides management with new leverage to manage development labor efficiency across projects	Permits management to make "optimizing" decisions about software labor deployment: software projects need labor with similar toolsets
Traceability of development operations	Enables efficient tracking and coordination of project activities documented on the computer	Enables continuous checking and feedback of project correspondence with initial business specifications
Higher Functionality of Software Product	Brings creation of very complex software within the bounds of routine project development practices	Supports development of visionary projects w/ "blue sky" functionality, and also encourages innovative IT uses
Less onerous technical personnel training requirements	Has potential to combat labor shortages, by reducing the knowledge-intensiveness of software development	Ensures that delivered software is not a function of new programming team's preferences, but dependent on a more fundamental business analysis
Makes the maintenance phase manageable	Maintenance costs are lowered by ensuring that code is highly modularized and well-documented with facilities of the CASE development environment	More careful monitoring of maintenance phase costs can help management to identify the optimal time to stop maintaining and rebuild from scratch to lower overall cost

productivity and the measurement of subsequent development performance only provide single point measures—when a project begins or when it has reached completion. Such stat-ic measures for estimation and efficiency analysis do not provide sufficiently detailed or relevant information for proactively managing the software development process.

By contrast, dynamic measures for software development performance can help management monitor and control performance through the entire software development life cycle. We refer to this concept of dynamically measuring and estimating performance in each phase of the development life cycle as "tracking the life cycle trajectory" of a software project. The life cycle trajectory approach monitors performance parameters of interest in each life cycle phase and visually depicts the progress of the project along the measured performance dimensions.

Static, single-point software development metrics are snapshots of the results of software development production performance. Dynamic metrics capture the development process on video tape, enabling management to play the action back at will as it occurs, to better understand it, and then to control and improve overall project performance.

Boehm (1981) has equated the problem of accurately estimating development costs for a software project with the problem an author has in estimating the number of pages a book will have when the plot has just been sketched out. Static metrics would only support the comparison of the initial estimate of the length with what the author subsequently writes. But dynamic metrics are meant to describe the process of producing the book, as the author adjusts the plot, resolves problems in the relationships among the characters, or deals with a crucial mental block that hampers the writing. Figure 15.1 contrasts the richness of the information provided from dynamic versus static measures.

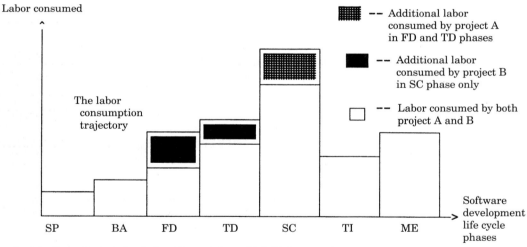

Assumptions: Project size in function points and total labor equal
    for A and B.

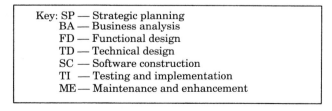

Fig. 15.1 Labor consumption trajectories.

The figure depicts the trajectories of labor consumed by two software projects, A and B. Initially, both are estimated to consume approximately the same level of resources during the life cycle. Suppose, however, that management's estimates are inaccurate to an equal extent for both projects. In this situation, we would observe two similar cost estimates and also two similar variances between the estimated and actual costs. Such static metrics might suggest that management take the same kind of action to improve "similar" projects in the future. But note that the labor consumption trajectory suggests that the software development processes occurring in each project were quite different.

Let us assume that the area under the phased labor consumption curves and the size of the resulting software are the same for both projects. Project B required relatively more effort during technical analysis and functional design, while Project A consumed more labor during the construction phase.

Similar sketches for the life cycle trajectory could be made for other performance measures such as productivity, defects, the development team's expertise profile, and so on. In CASE environments, tracking the life cycle trajectory of "software reuse" is another dimension that offers a diagnostic performance sketch. The point is that utilizing such full-trajectory information makes it more likely that managers will ask the right questions. For example: Were the functional design problems experienced due to the qualities of the resulting application or the analysis and design staff? Was the skill mix or experience level of the staff of Project B unsuited to the development requirements of the project?

Managers can ask more general questions as well. For example: How much reuse occurs in software development, and what is the extent of its leverage on productivity? Does the skill mix or the experience level of the staff assigned to a project influence the trajectory of its labor consumption or productivity?

However, such life cycle trajectory metrics only become feasible in the CASE environment because the phase activities and phase boundaries are better defined and more rigidly enforced than in the pre-CASE era. In keeping with the automated character of CASE development, measurement mechanisms can also be built into the CASE toolset enabling management to carry out continuous, low cost monitoring.

Automating life cycle trajectory measurement

In effect, we are advocating the collection of finer and more perfect information in the context of software development cost control, but only to the extent that it is relevant. The collection of more information in a decision setting can be justified only after a careful consideration of the costs and benefits of that information. Traditional software development environments were unable to support the delivery of such information as the life cycle progressed without forcing a project manager to incur unacceptably high costs. But CASE changes this cost/benefit relationship.

The benefits of measurement. The value of software development life cycle information to the project manager is a function of the actions that can be taken based on the information, and the consequences that the actions might produce (Demsky

1985). First, measures that are collected should be able to resolve decision options. Dynamic life cycle metrics enable actions that influence subsequent software development activities in a manner illustrated in the previous section.

Second, there is not much value in collecting measures with accurate up-to-the-minute detail if the software operations cannot (or need not) be controlled to that level of fineness. This is likely to be the case in the early phases of development, when order of magnitude estimates of labor may suffice. Figure 15.2 depicts the high variability and unpredictability of project costs when estimations are made in the earlier phases.

Efficient control measures in these phases could be rough first approximations because they cannot resolve very finely the management actions by cost control. In the later phases, more accurate, refined measures of the costs and cost drivers will better support decision making for cost control.

The costs of measurement. The other issue in committing to trajectory measures is an acceptable cost to implement them. Considerations regarding the decision value of the information affect the nature and design of suitable metrics. Clearly, the cost of measuring should not exceed its decision value, or else it will reduce management's motivation to measure. Johnson and Kaplan (1987) suggest that the reduction in information collection and processing costs no longer justifies highly aggregated, low-detail process information. They comment on page 144 ". . . that managers [were] not inclined to compile [disaggregated and] accurate data reflects

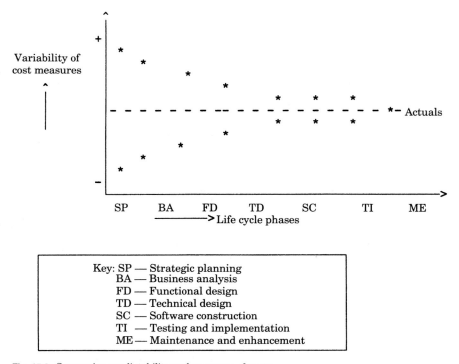

Fig. 15.2 Successive predictability and accuracy of costs.

their judgment on the costs and benefits and feasibility of such information, not a lost sense of what information is relevant to [operational] management decisions."

This suggests that managers might have been convinced of the value of measuring across the life cycle, but the cost of such measurement would have deterred them. The cost of collecting data and providing prompt reports for each life cycle phase of software development was too high in the manual programming era to permit the real time trajectory tracking we are now advocating.

But, today's CASE development environments make it possible to automate the measurement and collection of software life cycle trajectory metrics. The reduced cost of automated measures no longer requires managers to contend with irrelevant, aggregate measures on complex and critical software development processes. The challenge, therefore, is to develop dynamic life cycle performance measures for software development that will be amenable to automation and repeated collection at a minimal cost. Only automated measures and metrics for tracking the life cycle trajectories of CASE projects provide ongoing control information such that their decision value outweighs the costs.

In fact, product development in this area is underway for a number of CASE development environments, including Texas Instrument's IEF (Mazzucco 1990), Andersen Consulting's Foundation (Hidding 1990), and Seer Technologies' High Productivity Systems CASE tools (Banker et al. 1991). These firms are undertaking the construction of automated metrics facilities at a one-time cost, to defray the cost of repetitive measurements to be made in the future.

Control framework for life cycle trajectory measures

Software development productivity is defined as the ratio of the size of software output to the costs required to produce it.

$$\text{PRODUCTIVITY} = \frac{\text{SOFTWARE SIZE OUTPUT}}{\text{DEVELOPMENT EFFORT INPUT}}$$

Since the size of software output from the development process is an external specification as defined by the project description, it is not regarded as controllable. Thus most approaches to controlling productivity focus on ways and methods to control the cost of inputs into the development process, that is, development effort in the software context.

Effective cost control systems should deliver three basic capabilities to software development management (Shah 1981):

1. Measurement—the ability to unambiguously and consistently measure costs associated with identifiable units of work.
2. Estimation—the ability to accurately estimate and forecast cost measures.
3. Variance analysis—the ability to isolate variances between estimated and actual cost measures, enabling corrective measures to be taken to reduce the discovered variances.

We next examine these components more closely, as each relates to our proposal for life cycle trajectory metrics.

Measuring the costs associated with software development should take into account all inputs into the software production process. Costs arise from a number of sources, such as development labor, hardware resources, business transactions, and so on. However, development labor is by far the largest, most significant, and most variable cost component (Horowitz and Munson 1984). Therefore, the measure for the cost of development usually considers only labor inputs and is in terms of the number of person-days or person-months logged on the software project by the development team over the entire life span of the project.

The second requirement, the ability to accurately estimate costs, is required because managers gauge how well an activity is being performed by comparing actual and estimated performance. Whatever its sophistication, a specific software development performance measurement system cannot be effective in controlling the process unless it incorporates a set of standards that managers can agree upon and use as anchors on which to base their performance expectations. The limited ability of software managers to estimate the time required and costs of development has long been a major shortcoming, and was first brought to the attention of the systems development community by Brooks in his essay, *The Mythical Man-Month* (Brooks 1975). Even experts tend to underestimate software project development times, and in spite of this awareness projects continue to be behind schedule and budget.

Sometimes, irrational political perspectives influence the cost estimation process, and meaningful managerial actions for improving estimation can be implied (Lederer et al. 1990). Advances in more formal approaches to measuring software size have centered on empirical models that predict development time based on historical relationships between software size and development labor. Models, such as COCOMO, ESTIMACS and SLIM, exemplify these formal approaches (Kemerer 1987).

The third requirement, the ability to isolate variances between estimated and actual cost measures, is a diagnostic capability that answers an important question: "What is the cause for the difference between estimates and actuals?" Providing a satisfactory answer requires an understanding of cost drivers—those development attributes that impact and mediate the conversion of development labor into software product. In software development, as in most production processes, the size of the software output is the most important cost driver. But attributes of the development process have also been found to impact development labor (Scacci 1987; Boehm 1981). These attributes can be classified into program attributes (e.g., reliability requirements), environment attributes (e.g., main memory constraints), personnel attributes (e.g., average experience of project team), and project attributes (e.g., type of development tool used).

DEVELOPMENT-EFFORT-INPUT= f(SOFTWARE-SIZE-OUTPUT,
OTHER-COST-DRIVERS)

In software development, the impact of project development attributes on the labor effort required for delivering the system is not a simple relationship. The impact depends on both the life cycle phase of the software project as well as the value of other attributes (Boehm 1981; Vicinanza et al. 1990). Once managers are able to diagnose the causes for the deviation in performance, they should be able to understand what actions are appropriate or necessary to influence the factors causing the deviation. This ability to influence cost drivers, like isolating the causes of variances, is again dependent on an understanding of the nature and effect of the cost drivers.

For example, applications with the project attribute high reliability have been found to be adversely affected in terms of development time in the functional design phase, but to a lesser extent than in the coding phase. Similarly, if the personnel attribute for a project is high experience for the development team, reliability considerations would not impact development time as much as if the attribute were low experience.

So, we see that the cost drivers are phase-dependent and also may exhibit joint effects. This is summarized in the expression below.

$$\text{DEVELOPMENT-EFFORT-INPUT}_p = f_p(\text{SOFTWARE-SIZE-OUTPUT}_p, \\ \text{OTHER-COST-DRIVERS}_p)$$

This considerably complicates the isolation and correction of variances, and meanwhile places a premium on obtaining better and more detailed diagnostic information similar to that advocated in our life cycle trajectory measurement proposal.

Life Cycle Trajectory Approaches for CASE Productivity

In order to implement a dynamic productivity control system incorporating trajectory measures, we need to identify sound bases for designing metrics that measure DEVELOPMENT-LABOR-INPUT, SOFTWARE-SIZE-OUTPUT and OTHER-CASE-COST-DRIVERS in each development phase.

Identifying measures

- DEVELOPMENT-EFFORT-INPUT: These measures for each life cycle phase can be obtained from existing measurement approaches. Existing labor-tracking systems generally account for labor hours over the entire life cycle. These labor hours can be totaled at the end of each phase. Linking labor-tracking systems to automated software development performance analysis facilities with the proposed trajectory metrics would also help to motivate measurement.

- CASE-COST-DRIVERS: Phase measures for the CASE-COST-DRIVERS require a more substantive change in existing approaches. The prerequisite for establishing measures for cost drivers is the identification of relevant cost drivers: those attributes that significantly affect labor input costs in the different phases. In a CASE development environment, only some factors will impact the software development process enough to make a significant difference in the input labor hours. Thus, the set of relevant software cost drivers identified in prior research needs to be revised, based on what can be learned from new research on CASE development performance.

  Although more exhaustive, empirical verification is still needed, some preliminary evidence exists to suggest that in CASE environments DEVELOPMENT-TEAM-EXPERIENCE and NEW-OBJECT-PERCENT impact development labor significantly (Banker and Kauffman 1991). DEVELOPMENT-TEAM-EXPERIENCE can generally be measured with subjective rating methods for each phase.

  A bigger challenge is to develop life cycle trajectory metrics for NEW-OBJECT-

PERCENT and SOFTWARE-SIZE-OUTPUT from each phase. NEW-OBJECT-PER-CENT refers to the use of existing software in order to build an application. Reused software adds to the size and functionality of the delivered software product without requiring a proportionate amount of development labor. This justifies its inclusion as an important cost driver for DEVELOPMENT-EFFORT-INPUT. NEW-OBJECT-PER-CENT is measured in terms of the proportion of reused code in the total SOFT-WARE-SIZE-OUTPUT.

$$\text{NEW-OBJECT-PERCENT} = \frac{\text{TOTAL SOFTWARE-SIZE-OUTPUT}}{\text{UNIQUE SOFTWARE-SIZE-OUTPUT}}$$

Since NEW-OBJECT-PERCENT is expressed in terms of a proportion of SOFT-WARE-SIZE-OUTPUT, both drivers can be measured by the same units of work output. Thus, measures for both SOFTWARE-SIZE-OUTPUT and NEW-OBJECT-PERCENT are dependent on identifying work output measures from the development process. This requires identification of measurable units of work at the end of each of the life cycle phases.

Identifying measurable units of work from phases was not easy until the advent of CASE development tools. In traditional development environments each life cycle phase did not have a unit of delivered work that could be measured with any degree of accuracy. For example, the work done in the business analysis phase was partly represented by diagrams on paper and partly in the analyst's mind. Similarly, a considerable portion of the work completed in the functional design phase went undocumented because of verbal communications between the analyst and the programmer, unwritten contracts, and so on (Dhar, Ramesh, and Jarke 1989; Sasso and VcVay 1990; Turner 1986).

An illustration of trajectory metrics: CASE repository objects

CASE technologies make it possible to capture outputs from each life cycle phase. The discipline of CASE development produces well specified, rigorously defined outputs from each life cycle phase. These outputs can form the basis for unambiguous work unit measures.

In keeping with the standardization and reusability aspects of CASE environments, measures for monitoring phase outputs should utilize relevant parameters of the prefabricated components that form the basis of the "modular approach." In related work, we explored the possibility of monitoring the use and nature of these prefabricated components themselves, which have been called "objects" (Moad 1990). The results indicated that because objects act as building blocks to construct the functionality of the software in repository-based CASE environments, they can be used to represent the outputs of development in efficiency metrics.

Objects represent specific, well-defined functions in handy, ready-to-use chunks of code. An object need only be written once, and all subsequent applications that need to deliver the same functionality could merely reuse existing objects. In addition, the definitions and code content of objects in CASE environments are frequently stored in a centralized repository. Examples of objects that are often utilized in repository-based CASE environments are: RULES, SCREEN DEFINITIONS, USER REPORTS, and so on. The complexity of the objects written afresh by a programmer, the level of reuse of existing objects by a programming team, and the total number of objects of all types used to build an application provide a natural avenue along which the design of trajectory metrics can proceed.

In integrated CASE environments (ICASE) (i.e., those that automate development in all the life cycle phases), application development is a process of successive refinement of objects as development progresses from the earlier life cycle phases of business analysis and design to the later phases of testing and implementation. For additional details on an integrated CASE environment (ICE) that has some of these features, see Banker et al. (1991). The objects created at the business analysis phase are abstract, higher level representations of functionalities required by the application. Each subsequent lower level object of the later phases goes one step further in instantiating the functionality of the previous phase's object, until finally the code is written in the construction phase.

Objects created in earlier phases lay out a road map for subsequent refinement that may occur, or the development of additional objects in later phases. Thus, a study of the deliverables at the end of each life cycle phase of CASE development would enable the specification of outputs at each stage. Table 15.3 illustrates this perspective by identifying objects that would be useful to gauge output phase-by-phase. The examples draw on experience we gained in a field study of CASE at the First Boston Corporation and Seer Technologies. The object names are used as illustrations of generic outputs that can be identified from the different life cycle phases.

The Business Analysis phase defines the scope and functions of the system in terms of user requirements. The output of business analysis in CASE environments is a model of the processes and the data involved in the business system. The approach is based on the concepts of the Entity-Relationship (E/R) model developed by Chen. This phase often uses tools such as an E/R diagrammer or a process hierarchy diagrammer, and typically outputs objects such as ENTITIES, PROCESSES, and RELATIONSHIPS (between ENTITIES and PROCESSES). These are objects defined according to the E/R model, and their total number and complexity as they exist in the repository at the end of this phase can be used to measure the work output from the business analysis phase.

Similarly, the Functional Design phase translates business requirements to the specific needs of the application's users, including features, functions, interfaces, and so on. It uses tools such as a report painter or a window generator, and typically outputs objects such as RULES, WINDOWS, VIEWS, and RELATIONSHIPS (between RULES, WINDOWS, VIEWS, and so on). The Technical Design phase further refines the functional specification of objects by including: the data structures; data flows; and files referenced, input or output. Examples of objects produced in this phase are FIELDS, FILES, RULES details, and so on.

Software Construction involves adding details to the software for compiling at the source level. Actual code is generated only during the application's run-time. Reusable objects need merely retrieve software construction details from the repository while objects that have to be written from scratch will require much more labor. Thus, the NEW-OBJECT-PERCENT will affect DEVELOPMENT-EFFORT-INPUT very significantly in this phase. (We are currently studying what the relevant object outputs will be for the Testing/Implementation and Maintenance/Enhancement phases.)

TABLE 15.3 Possible Object metrics for CASE life cycle.

LIFE CYCLE PHASE	POSSIBLE OBJECT METRICS	ILLUSTRATIVE OBJECT HIERARCHY AND COMMENTS
Business Analysis	Entities, Processes, Relationships	**APPLICATION** Business Entity #1 Business Process #1 Relationship
Functional	Rules, Windows, Views Relationships	Rule Set A Rule Set B Rule Set C Windows Relationship
Technical Design	Fields, Files, Rules (details)	Files Referenced — Fields Rule Content
Software Construction	Objects built, Objects reused	Above hierarchy must be "navigated" while querying for objects instantiated with code and comprising full functionality. Also must query within and across project hierarchies to identify occurrence of reused objects.
Testing/ Implementation	Number of platforms, Number of objects	Currently under investigation.
Maintenance/ Enhancement	Number of revisions made to objects	Currently under investigation.

To sum up our argument, repository-based objects can act as distinct and identifiable units of work from each life cycle phase of CASE development. The total number, complexity or size, and origin (reused versus written-from-scratch) of objects can be used to measure SOFTWARE-SIZE-OUTPUT from each phase. As explained earlier, the NEW-OBJECT-PERCENT cost driver, dependent on the same unit of work as SOFTWARE-SIZE-OUTPUT, can also be distinctly measured USING object-based metrics for each phase. This equips us with productivity metrics to track the life cycle trajectory of CASE developed projects.

Implementing object-based trajectory metrics

In an exploratory study conducted earlier (Banker et al. 1992), we empirically tested the proposal for object-based trajectory metrics for the construction phase of the

CASE life cycle. Data were obtained on software projects developed and produced with a multi-million dollar ICASE tool built by a large investment bank in New York city. The objective of the study was to evaluate the performance of an object-based metric for the "Software Construction" phase. Performance of the metric was judged on the basis of its ability to, 1) measure the cost driver SOFTWARE-SIZE-OUTPUT, and 2) estimate the DEVELOPMENT-LABOR-INPUT for project delivery.

Each project was manually counted for the number of construction phase objects in the final delivered software. The sum of the instances of all object types used for application development in the construction phase was defined as the first object-based metric for this phase. We called this metric OBJECT-COUNTS. A second metric was defined as the effort-weighted sum of the instances of all object types used in the construction phase. The weighting with effort accounts for different amounts of labor required to develop each object type for inclusion in the code for the software project. This metric was called OBJECT-POINTS.

$$\text{OBJECT-COUNTS}_{\text{Construction Phase}} = \sum_{t} \text{OBJECT-INSTANCES}_t$$

$$\text{OBJECT-POINTS}_{\text{Construction Phase}} = \sum_{t} \text{OBJECT-EFFORT-WEIGHT}_t * \text{OBJECT-INSTANCES}_t$$

where

$t =$ object types used to create application in the Software Construction phase;

$\text{OBJECT-INSTANCES}_t =$ total number of instances of object type t in an application;

$\text{OBJECT-EFFORT-WEIGHT}_t =$ average development effort associated with the construction of object type t;

Table 15.4 presents correlations between the two object-based metrics defined above and Function Points, a metric for the size or functionality of the output delivered by a software project to the end user (Albrecht and Gaffney 1983). We utilize it as a metric for SOFTWARE-SIZE-OUTPUT. Its ability to estimate DEVELOPMENT-EFFORT-INPUT has also been investigated and implemented. The Function Point procedure requires counting the occurrence of five function types (Inputs, Outputs, Logical Files, External Interfaces and Queries; for details of the Function Points procedure, see Dhar et al. (1989). These units of software work output refer to the aggregate product delivered; they are not geared towards identifying the output in each phase. Thus, as currently defined, Function Points cannot be used to implement the life cycle trajectory measurement approach to controlling productivity.

In the exploratory study, we viewed obtaining high correlations between Function Points metric and the object-based metrics being tested as indicators of the validity of the new metrics. Such convergent validity with the well-established and well-validated Function Points metric provides preliminary evidence that the object-based metrics are measures of the same construct that Function Points purports to measure, i.e., the size and functionality of delivered software as given by SOFTWARE-

TABLE 15.4 Performance of Object-based construction phase metrics.

METRIC	CORRELATION WITH FUNCTION-POINTS	VALUE OF R-SQUARED
OBJECT-COUNTS	0.89	0.70
OBJECT-POINTS	0.86	0.73
FUNCTION-POINTS	–	0.75

SIZE-OUTPUT$_{\text{Construction Phase}}$. As Table 15.4 indicates, the OBJECT-COUNT and OB-JECT-POINT metrics were highly correlated with Function Points. OBJECT-COUNTS had a correlation of 0.89, and OBJECT-POINTS had a correlation of 0.86 with Function Points.

The estimation capability of the object-based metrics was assessed by evaluating their performance in an estimation model to accurately predict the DEVELOPMENT-EFFORT-INPUT that will be consumed for developing a project in the construction phase. Two separate regression models were estimated to predict development effort (the dependent variable) in terms of the output metrics, Function Points, OBJECT-COUNTS, and OBJECT-POINTS (one of these occurred as the independent variable in each model). Results of the regression indicate the extent to which the object-based metric is able to explain the variance in DEVELOPMENT-EFFORT-INPUT. The results shown in Table 15.4 reveal an R2 comparable to the Function Points metric (0.70 and 0.73 for OBJECT-COUNTS and OBJECT-POINTS respectively, compared to 0.75 for Function Points).

The above research results suggest the viability of the object-based metrics. The two metrics tested, OBJECT-COUNTS and OBJECT-POINTS, performed well as measures for SOFTWARE-SIZE-OUTPUT from the Software Construction phase. They also successfully predicted the total DEVELOPMENT-EFFORT-IN-PUT required for delivering the completed projects. It remains to test their predictive capability for DEVELOPMENT-EFFORT-INPUT in the Software Construction phase alone. Research is also underway to further define and test object-based metrics for the remaining phases of the CASE life cycle. This is required before the life cycle trajectory measurement approach can be more fully implemented.

Conclusion

In view of the large costs of software, systems for controlling software development should be designed to more closely support the operations and the strategy of the organization. The technology necessary to implement the approach to software development monitoring and control that we advocate is different from what exists in manual software development shops currently. But today, CASE makes implementing our vision of software development tracking increasingly possible.

Research contribution

The paper has described a conceptual framework for the development of managerially relevant procedures to enhance software control with life cycle trajectory metrics. We also suggested that automating software control is appropriate and feasible in CASE environments, and that this changes the basic cost-benefit relationship that exists for software project performance tracking. The low cost of measurement made possible through automated analysis and the availability of repository-based objects as distinct, identifiable units of development work from each life cycle phase combine to make integrated CASE environments an ideal test-bed for research.

Our approach to implementing dynamic control measures forms the first step in a broader attack on CASE project planning and project management methods. Control of software development activities in each phase will support project management activities from the earliest phases of the software life cycle. Tasks such as scheduling, identifying staff requirements, and performing resource planning can be performed on a phase-by-phase basis rather than a project-by-project basis. Moreover, these plans can be revised dynamically as the actual development performance of a phase becomes known. Such an approach will allow more powerful project planning which can more readily adapt to unanticipated changes in performance or parameters.

Research agenda

Our proposals for dynamic trajectory measures open up several new lines of research inquiry for the future.

1. Empirical evidence to identify relevant cost drivers for CASE development environments would provide valuable insights into the nature of the cost drivers and the metrics required to track them.

2. Research to validate and specify object outputs as measures of work from each of the different phases is needed to provide a rigorous, empirical basis for justifying the implementation of our cost control framework for CASE development.

3. Another important extension within our productivity control framework would be to study and compare the estimation accuracy and ease of existing and proposed measurement approaches. Our work on OBJECT-POINTS represented an initial step in this direction.

We are now involved in investigating the estimation performance of object-based trajectory metrics for phases other than Software Construction. This should result in an integrated cost accounting system for CASE performance tracking which makes use of the features of this development environment. This opens up the opportunity for software production to be integrated with strategy formulation to enable a firm to minimize its strategic software costs.

Note: We wish to acknowledge Mark Baric, Gene Bedell, Tom Lewis and Vivek Wadhwa for the access they provided us to data on software development projects and managers' time throughout our field study of CASE development at the First Boston Corporation and SEER Technologies. Another version of this paper was presented at a conference entitled Integrating Information Technology and Analysis: How to Deliver Systems Your Clients Will Love, sponsored by the College on the Practice of Management Science of The Institute of Management Science (TIMS/CPMS), and the Operations Research Society of America (ORSA). All errors in this paper are the responsibility of the authors.

Author Biography

Rajiv D. Banker holds the Arthur Andersen Chair in Accounting and Information Systems at the Carlson School of Management, University of Minnesota. He received a doctorate from Harvard Business School, specializing in planning and control systems. He currently serves on the editorial boards of six journals and as co-editor of the Journal of Productivity Analysis. He has published over 40 refereed articles. His research interests include strategic cost management, measuring the business value of information technology, assessing software development and maintenance productivity and the economics of information.

Robert J. Kauffman is an Assistant Professor at the Stern School of Business at New York University, where he has taught since 1988. He completed his masters degree in international affairs at Cornell University, and was later employed as an international lending and strategic planning officer at a large money center bank in New York City. He received a doctorate in Information Systems from the Graduate School of Industrial Administration, Carnegie Mellon University in 1988.

His current program of research involves developing new methodologies for measuring the business value of a broad spectrum of information technologies, using techniques from management science and economics. He has published refereed articles in MIS Quarterly, Journal of Management Information Systems, Information and Software Technologies, and elsewhere.

Rachna Kumar is currently in the Doctoral Program in Information Systems at the Stern School of Business, New York University. She received the Master of Business Administration degree from the Indian Institute of Management, Ahmedabad, in 1983. Her current research interests focus on productivity measurement and cost estimation for CASE environments. Her dissertation work involves a field study of the performance of object-based productivity metrics in the various CASE life cycle phases.

Works Cited

Alavi, M. 1985. High-productivity alternatives for software development. *Journal of information systems management*. 2 (4): 19–24.

Alloway, R.M. and J.A. Quillard. 1983. User managers' systems needs. *MIS quarterly*. 7 (2): 27–41.

Albrecht, A.J. and J.E. Gaffney. Software function, source lines of code, and development effort prediction: A software science validation. *IEEE transactions on software engineering*. 9 (6): 639–647.

Banker, R.D., R.J. Kauffman, C. Wright, and D. Zweig. 1991. Automating output size and reusability metrics in an object-based Computer-Aided Software Engineering (CASE) environment. Center for Research in Information Systems Working Paper Series. May 1991. Stern School of Business, New York University.

Banker, R.D., R.J. Kauffman. 1991. Reuse and functionality: An empirical study of Integrated Computer-Aided Software Engineering (ICASE) technology at the First Boston Corporation. Forthcoming in *MIS quarterly*. Fall 1991.

Banker, R.D., R.J. Kauffman, and R. Kumar. 1992. An empirical test of object-based output measurement metrics in a Computer-Aided Software Engineering (CASE) environment. Forthcoming in the *Journal of management information systems*. Winter 1992.

Benson, R.J. and M.M. Parker. 1986. Enterprise wide information management: Strategic planning for information technology - an introduction for the business executive. IBM Publication G320-2775. IBM Los Angeles Scientific Center.

Boehm, B.. 1981. *Software engineering economics*. Englewood Cliffs, N.J.: Prentice Hall.

Boehm, B.W. and P. Papaccio. 1988. Understanding and controlling software costs. *IEEE transactions on software engineering*. 14 (10): 1462–1477.

Brooks, F.P., Jr. 1975. *The mythical man-month*. New York, N.Y.: Addison Wesley.

Burkhard, D.L. and P.V. Jenster. 1989. Applications of Computer-Aided Software Engineering tools: Survey of current and prospective users. *Database*. Fall 1989: 28–37.

Davis, G.B. 1988. Commentary on information systems: Productivity gains from Computer-Aided Software Engineering. *Accounting horizons*. 2 (2): 90–93.

Demski, J.S. 1985. *Information analysis*. Reading, Ma.: Addison-Wesley Publishing.

Dhar, V., B. Ramesh, and M. Jarke. REMAP project: An environment for supporting requirements analysis and maintenance. In *Proceedings of artificial intelligence and software engineering symposium, AAAI-89*. Spring Symposium Series. March, 1989. Stanford, Ca.

Dreger, J.B. 1989. *Function Point analysis*. Englewood Cliffs, N.J.: Prentice Hall.

Grammas, G.W., and J.R. Klein. 1985. Software productivity as a strategic variable. *Interfaces*. 15 (3): 116–126.

Gurbaxani, V. and H. Mendelson. 1987. Software and hardware in data processing budgets. *IEEE transactions on software engineering*. SE-13 (9): 1010–1017.

Hall, P.A.V. 1987. Software components and reuse—getting more out of your code. *Information and software technology*. 29 (1): 38–43.

Hidding, Gezinus. 1990. Personal communication. Andersen Consulting.

Horowitz, E. and J.B. Munson. An expansive view of reusable software. *IEEE transactions on software engineering*. SE-10 (5): 477–487.

Johnson, H.T. and R.S. Kaplan. 1987. *Relevance lost: The rise and fall of management accounting*. Boston, Ma.: Harvard Business School Press.

Jones, T.C. 1984. Reusability in programming: A survey of the state of the art. *IEEE transactions on software engineering*. SE-10 (5): 484–494.

Jones, T.C. 1986. *Programming productivity*. New York, N.Y.: McGraw-Hill.

Kang, K.C. and L.S. Levy. 1989. Software methodology in the harsh light of economics. *Information and software technology*. 31 (5): 239–249.

Kemerer, C.F. 1987. An empirical validation of software cost estimation models. *Communications of the ACM*. 30 (5): 416–429.

Kemerer, C.F. 1989. An agenda for research in the managerial evaluation of Computer-Aided Software Engineering (CASE) tool impacts. *Proceedings of the 22nd Hawaii international conference on systems sciences*. pp 219–227. January 1989. Hawaii.

Lederer, A.L., R. Mirani. B.S. Neo, C. Pollard, J. Prasad., and K. Ramamurthy. 1990. Information system cost estimating: A management perspective. *MIS quarterly* 14 (2): 159–178.

Mazzucco, F. 1990. *Automation of function counting techniques*. Texas Instruments.

McClure, C. 1989. The CASE experience. *Byte*. April 1989: 235–244.

McNurlin, B. 1989. Building more flexible systems. *I/S analyzer*. October 1989.

Moad, J. 1990. The software revolution. *Datamation*. February 15, 1990: 22–30.

Norman, R.J. and J.F. Nunamaker, Jr. 1989. CASE productivity perceptions of software engineering professionals. *Communications of the ACM*. 32 (9): 1102–1108.

Nunamaker, J.F., Jr., and M. Chen. 1989. Software productivity: A framework of study and an approach to reusable components. In *Proceedings of the 22nd Hawaii international conference system sciences*. pp. 959–968. January 1989. Hawaii.

Pollack, A. 1990. The move to modular software. *New York Times*. April 23, 1990: D1–2.

Ramamoorthy, C.V., A. Prakash., W. Tsai, and Y. Usnda. 1984. Software engineering: Problems and perspectives. *IEEE computer*. 17 (10): 191–209.

Sasso, W.C. and M. McVay. 1990. The constraints and assumptions of systems design: A descriptive process model. Center for Research in Information Systems Working Paper #137. September, 1990. Stern School of Business, New York University.

Scacchi, W. and C.M.K. Kintala. 1987. Understanding software productivity. Technical report CRI-87-67. Los Angeles, Ca: Computer Science Department, University of Southern California.

Senn, J.A. and J.L. Wynekoop. 1990. Computer-Aided Software Engineering (CASE) in perspective. Working paper for the Information Technology Management Center, College of Business Administration, Georgia State University.

Sentry Market Research. 1990. CASE research report. Westborough, Ma.

Shah, P. 1981. *Cost control and information systems*. New York, N.Y.: McGraw Hill.

Sprague, R.H. and B.C. McNurlin. B. C., Eds. 1986. *Information systems management in practice*. Englewood Cliffs, N.J.: Prentice-Hall.

Turner, J.A. 1986. Understanding elements of systems design. In *Critical issues in information systems research*. ed. R. Boland and R. Hirscheim. New York, N.Y.: John Wiley.

Vicinanza, S., M.J. Prietula, and T. Mukhopadhyay. 1990. CASE-based reasoning in software effort estimation: A theory, a model, and a test. In *Proceedings of the eleventh international conference on information systems*. December, 1990. Copenhagen, Denmark.

Vipond, S.A. 1990. Achieving the transition to Computer-Aided Software Engineering: A longitudinal study of change and adaption in two software development groups. Working paper. April 1990. MIS Research Center, Carlson School of Management, University of Minnesota.

Yourdon, E. 1986. Whatever happened to structured analysis? *Datamation*. 32 (11): 133–138.

Automating Software Testing

by Philip Wallingford

Introduction

The need for *effective* software testing and quality assurance has reached emergency status. The costs of not testing software and the costs of testing software have both exploded.

Unfortunately, there are many examples of disasters caused by buggy software that was released into production. Examples include large communication networks being shut down, lost ticket reservations, and the loss or damage of other enterprise-critical information. For companies producing software products, the economic damage of these mistakes resulted in financial crisis. The competitive environment of the software industry in the early '90s is making *quality* a product differentiator.

Many software development organizations now need a larger staff (and budget) to test the software than the staff needed to develop it. In many cases, the staffing requirements are uneven, resulting in the hiring of expensive contracting to do the testing. The situation is becoming worse with the release of increasingly complex software products that must operate reliably in a distributed multi-user environment. For example, how will a company validate its software's operation on a local area network (LAN) with 50 or 200 concurrent users?

What created this crisis? You can find the answer by comparing the growth of software complexity with the growth of testing technology. Software has experienced fantastic increases in complexity, along with the need for distributed systems, graphical user interfaces, and highly interactive applications. On the other hand, software test technology—as practiced—has not advanced much since the beginning of the computing era. Software is still tested, largely, by people performing manual tests. The common myth that "software can't be tested" needs to be stated more accurately as, "Software can't be tested with the traditional testing approach." With today's software there can never be enough people spending enough time at enough keyboards to measure software quality.

The only solution to this problem is through the application of improved testing methods and, in particular, automated methods. Automation must be applied beginning at the test design phase, through test development and execution. The techniques are well known—the technology is becoming available and serious implementation can begin.

A New Perspective

A simple way to introduce software test automation is to review questions commonly asked of those responsible for software test and quality assurance (QA):

- How many problems have you found?
- How much time have you taken to find them?

The inquirers know that these questions aren't really the right ones, but they have come to accept that these questions are the only ones for which there are, typically, answers. The questions they would like to ask are:

- How complete is the testing?
- If the testing is not complete, when will it be?
- What is the reliability of the software today; that is, if I release the software to the marketplace, what will the failure rate be?

Although these two sets of questions have some similarities, there is an immense gap in the level of knowledge needed to answer each set. The knowledge is accessible and, ironically, can ultimately be attained with less technological acumen than that found in today's testing and QA organizations.

We find the explanation of this contradiction by realizing that the knowledge gap can be closed by the application of systematic engineering discipline and, especially, by applying automated test tools.

Unfortunately, this inspiration does not lead to an easy reconstruction of testing methods. Although straightforward, the path to the new technology is long and will demand great dedication. The gratification, however, will be manifest in a test method that is more predictable, of lower cost, and is faster than today's test methods.

A Strategy for Test Automation

Many software organizations have experimented with test automation. The common scenario is to start with a capture/playback tool because it automates what they are already doing. A *capture/playback tool* captures a user's operations and mimics them during playback to retest the software.

This approach is understandable and has value, but it is not a serious implementation of test automation if it is the only test. In the absence of test generation and test design tools, the human tester remains the bottleneck in producing the tests. The tester can never record enough operations to provide adequate testing. Without sufficient foresight and design time, the recorded scripts are not maintainable—

making their proposed reuse of suspect value. Perhaps most important, like most manual testing, there is not enough thought given to what measures are being used to monitor the success of the test. Without a measurement system and the test management tools to maintain it, automated tests reveal no more about the test process than their manual counterparts.

Test automation has to be approached by defining the objective criteria used to judge the progress of the test; what data will be collected and what analysis will be used to determine when the testing is complete?

There are two fundamental approaches to data collection in software testing. The first approach collects failure data, primarily based on "black-box" or functional tests, and fits the data to a Software Reliability Growth model to determine the software's readiness for operation. Several models have been proposed, based on different data-collection techniques and statistical methods applied.

The second approach establishes measures of testing completeness based on some criterion, and collects the associated data to measure progress. Common among these are various coverage measures that show how much the software has been tested. Of particular interest are structural, or white-box, coverage measures, such as control branch or data-flow, but functional coverage measures are also common.

Of course both of the approaches can be used. Once an approach has been selected, a Test Repository must be established as a place to save test items and measurement data in a structured, retrievable way. The volume of data required to support automated testing is enormous. It is not uncommon in a modest testing program, to require tens of thousands of test cases and to generate thousands of test incidents. A program of this scale will also require a team, whose members need accurate and timely access to this data. A Test Repository is intended to provide this access.

Test design tools are needed to automate the test generation using control or data-flow graphing, domain analysis, syntax testing, state graphing, or other structured design processes. The combined complexity of software programs and design tasks associated with these design techniques makes automation a must.

Other tools must automate test execution (including capture/playback), collect the data quickly, and reliably and save them in the Test Repository. Lastly, management tools assist in maintaining the Test Repository, generating various reports and analyzing the data to answer the questions previously cited. The following sections describe these building blocks in more detail.

The Testing Process

Software testing automation has to be based on a well-defined process that is to be automated. Many common test practices today are ad hoc and directed by the wrong influences, such as, automation, other than configuration control, but they define where automation can be applied in the design, development, execution and analysis (or QA) stages of the process.

These later stages are the target for an automated process. A view of an automated test system, in Fig. 16.1, shows how these activities relate to each other.

The most familiar activity is test execution, the "driving" of software with various test cases and recording results. The results that are monitored during test execu-

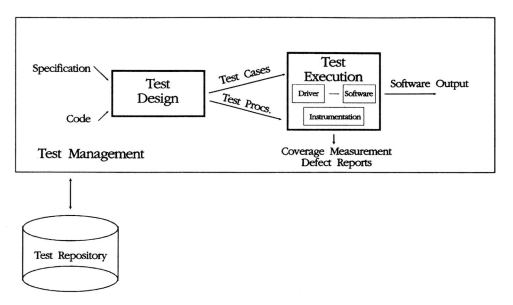

Fig. 16.1 Testing activities.

tion might include the software output or some internal (less observable) measures, such as code statement coverage. Some form of "instrumentation" is commonly employed to capture the results.

Test design/development is the process of creating the test cases from structural (e.g., code) or functional (e.g,. specification) sources. Test design is based on a chosen strategy for defining test completion; examples include code execution coverage, function point coverage, data flow coverage and software reliability or failure intensity.

Test management includes the tracking of test data, including test cases, procedures and defects. Test planning, including scheduling, is included in this activity.

QA applies broadly to all of the activities. Its function is to interpret test results to determine product reliability and process improvements.

The activities are integrated through a common data model. The model describes a Test Repository that all tools access to store and retrieve data.

Implementation

A full implementation of test automation must address all of the major test activities mentioned above. There are, however, reasonable approaches for adopting the technology in phases.

The first consideration in implementing test automation is to define the testing goals with measurable and objective criteria. Examples of these criteria are requirement coverage, path coverage, and reliability.

The next step is to establish the measurement and management system that will provide organization of the test design and development process and the interpretation of test results in terms of the test criteria. If software reliability is a test criterion, for example, then the measurement system must support, at least, the data collection needs (e.g,. failure times in terms of execution time). Further, the measurement system must have the reliability modeling capability for producing the desired metrics.

Initial testing methods will probably be functional, that is, testing against specified requirements. Although the test design is still a manual effort, their execution can be automated with test drivers, such as capture-playback systems. (Ultimately test design tools can generate test cases for these same drivers.)

Test coverage tools are beneficial even during functional testing. Management tools to organize and measure requirements coverage are a necessity for any serious functional tests. Code coverage tools can be applied to functional tests in a limited way. Statement coverage or profilers can operate with limited information about code structure. Function "call trees" can also be built for monitoring program execution and analyzing the results, using the program's "load map". The call trees describe which program functions were called.

As test automation advances, structural, testing techniques will be introduced. Early experience will likely be with branch testing, followed by more sophisticated and more effective methods, such as data-flow and domain testing. Structural testing demands automation, from design through execution and coverage monitoring.

The following sections present some of the system architectural issues around implementing test automation.

Test Repository

At the core of the test system architecture is the Test Repository. The Test Repository is a central facility used to store, organize, and validate all information necessary to support a robust departmental, and ultimately corporate-wide, testing and QA program. Examples of information maintained by the Test Repository include:

- Reference information

  —IEEE, DOD, and ISO standards documents
  —Corporate standards

- Test Documentation

  —Test plans
  —Test design specifications
  —Test procedure specifications
  —Test case specifications

- Test procedures

- Test cases

- Test logs

- Failure data

  —Incidents
  —Problems

The Test Repository also provides access to existing source code libraries to enable, for example, automated static analysis, code metrics, or structural test case generation.

The central technology in the Test Repository is a robust database management system. All test data are cross-referenced through this facility to maintain configuration control in an evolving product release cycle. For example, queries can be made to determine that test cases might have to be reviewed if a particular software module changes.

The Test Repository also supports group testing efforts with security and record-level locking features.

A general schematic of the Test Repository and associated data facilities is shown in Fig. 16.2.

The Bulletin Board System (BBS)/E-Mail is a facility for sharing information prior to its submittal to the Test Repository. It is used during the test development process as an informal mechanism to facilitate communication.

The Library is the storage facility for the test assets themselves, test procedures and test cases, and other variable length test data, e.g., core dumps, test images, etc. Entries in the Library are indexed and cross-referenced by the database, but the data itself is saved in the Library. Librarian functions provide "check-in" and "check-out" facilities for released test items for version control, and protection against developers making "asynchronous" modifications to the released items.

The Archive is a facility for securing periodic copies of the Test Repository. It has recorded in it historical information that facilitates keeping a journal of changes so that, if necessary, they can be "unwound" from newer copies.

All of the test automation tools use the Test Repository as their information "back plane." The data model for the Test Repository must be fully disclosed and access to it facilitated with published access methods.

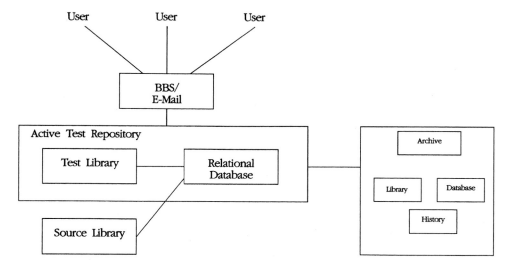

Fig. 16.2 Repository schematic.

Test Execution

Test execution tools are the most ubiquitous of all test automation tools. Execution tools automate the application of test cases to the software under test and provide data about the software's performance, be it functional or otherwise. Execution tools of the capture/playback are most common. With these tools a user's (keyboard and mouse) operations are captured into a script that is subsequently played back on a later software release to verify consistent operation. This test approach is called *regression testing*; the software is checked to ensure that it has not regressed to an earlier state. Capture/playback tests are usually black box tests performed during system test.

Traditionally, test scripts are saved in some proprietary format, often uneditable. However, because test scripts need to be adapted to changes in the software being tested, the need to modify the scripts exists. In tools that allow editing of the scripts, the scripting language is also proprietary. Furthermore, the scripting language is usually low level, dealing, for example, with mouse movements that are difficult to interpret, let alone modify.

The scripting language should be integrated with a standard programming environment, such as Basic or C. Building the scripting capability on such a standard brings all the power of a full programming tool to test scripting, reduces training requirements, and enables integration of many third-party software packages.

The scripting language also becomes the vehicle for delivering other automated tests, generated not by recording a user's actions, but by automated test generation techniques.

Test execution tools provide many ways to monitor the software's performance. Built-in test cases allow screen images to be compared, output data to be examined, file or window existence verified, interprocess communication to be monitored, and correct file contents to be checked. User-defined test cases can also be integrated into the scripts. Also significant is the existence of "wait states" that allow the software under test to stay synchronized with other system resource, such as network traffic.

Other software or system performance can be monitored with test execution tools. System resource, i.e., memory, stack usage, and disk space, can be monitored. Performance of the software under varying system configurations can be measured. Coupled with test design tools that analyze the structure of the software, test execution tools can also capture information about test coverage, such as statement, branch, path and data flow.

Test Design

Test design automation tools are, currently, the least-used tools of automation. Their absence is only a sign of the immaturity of testing methods. (In fact test design, itself, appears to be absent in many instances: "Build the test first; design it later!")

Test design tools will become the most important elements of the tool set because they will remove the last large labor component in building test suites. They are also the (only) instruments for generating the large numbers of tests that will be required to achieve "adequate" testing.

The definition of *adequate* is critical in determining when enough testing has been done. The common definition is based on available testing resources with little regard to fundamental measures of software quality; that is, keep testing until the promised delivery date. More scientific measures are based on criteria such as branch and path coverage, data-flow coverage, or reliability. It is the function of good test design to define the test cases that provide these measures.

Test design can be addressed to functional or structural (typically unit) tests. Design automation tools for functional tests are hampered by the lack of formal software requirements or functional specification languages. As a result, the test coverage has to be defined by interpreting these natural language descriptions. Automation tools can be applied to this activity to catalog and organize the test coverage points and associated test cases. When organized this way, this data can be used to easily generate reports of coverage completion.

Design automation can also be applied to recorded test scripts (with a capture/playback tool, for example), especially when the scripts exist in the form of a high-level language. For example, if a script is recorded to populate cells in a spreadsheet and to verify the results of calculation, then an automation tool can generate hundreds of variations of input/output data sets (test cases) that can be read by the script during playback. This is best accomplished by describing the inputs and outputs in a formal syntax (Backus-Naur Form, for example) and applying a general-purpose Test Data Generator.

Structural testing lends itself better to automated test design because the software code exists as a formal description of how the software operates. (Note that "how it operates" is not necessarily the same as how it is meant to operate, but that's another subject.) From this formal description, structural test design can be highly automated. The schematic of a system to do this is shown in Fig. 16.3.

The Code Analyzer is specific to the source language and parses it into a canonical form. From this, form-control flow or data-flow graphs can be developed. From the data-flow graphs, the particular coverage elements can be generated. Coverage elements are paths, branches, all-uses data paths, domains, etc., depending on the coverage criterion. These elements are then used by the Code Instrumentor so that coverage can be monitored during program execution. The Predicate Interpreter retraces the code predicates (conditional statements) to the software inputs. These

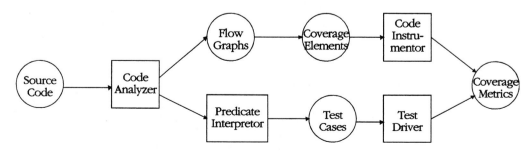

Fig. 16.3 Automatic testing system schematic.

inputs become test cases that are applied to the software with a Test Driver. As the Driver executes the software, the instrumented code logs information that becomes the measure of coverage completion.

Variants of this test design system, based on different testing strategies, can be developed. The important point is that most effective testing strategies are too difficult to undertake without an associated set of Design tools.

Static analysis

The above section describes test design to support Dynamic Analysis, that is observing the software while it is executing.

Static Analysis is another design approach based on inspecting the characteristics of a program without executing it. This is a more limited analysis, but has value in achieving early indicators in the development process of the software's "quality," or at least its testability.

Static Analysis is a common component of certain software development tools. Compilers and "lint" programs, for example, check syntax, type checking, unused data, etc. Considerably more analysis can be performed than is common with these tools. Examples of this extended analysis include finding unexecutable paths and unreachable data states. As with Dynamic Analysis tools, automation is required to perform Static Analysis.

Metrics

Metrics, in the context of software testing, are a specific result of Static Analysis. Metrics are quantifiable indices of a program's complexity. They range from simple statement counts to measures based on structural analysis.

Metrics are used like other Static Analysis to get visibility, early in development, of the difficulty of testing. As such they are useful predictors for testing schedules. Better yet, they can be used to gate the passage of software from the development groups to the testing organizations.

Test Management

The management of a software test and QA program requires a system to monitor progress and measure results. If taken seriously, this system demands a sophisticated tool to free the management activity from tedious and clerical tasks. Meeting the demand with homegrown tools is no more rational, in the presence of viable commercial tools, than an accounting manager building his own general ledger system. Tools must also be integrated with design and execution tools so all are accessing a common set of data.

The functions of test management tools are to maintain the Test Repository and to analyze and report on the data stored in it. These tools empower the QA, test, development, product management and customer service staffs to see a unified view on the status of a testing program.

Framework

Recently an industry effort has been initiated to define standards for test and QA tools that enable them to cooperate. This initiative is described as a *Framework for Software Test* and is modeled after similar framework initiatives in the CASE and CAD industries.

The framework is a standard environment modeled on the test process, which facilitates management of the testing process and automation of individual testing activities where possible. Through open specification of a supporting data model and interfaces between cooperating test activities, it enables integration of test tools from different sources. It serves to communicate and enforce a structured workflow through the testing process, thereby improving staff productivity. Finally, it enables consistent measurement points that allow the process to be monitored with the goal of accurately evaluating the effectiveness and cost of the testing activities and reporting quality metrics that reveal the completeness and correctness of the software under test.

The primary goal of the framework is to facilitate the delivery of a productive testing and quality assurance environment to its end-users. To achieve this goal it must also serve the needs of toolmakers and system designers and integrators.

For the end-user, the framework provides a flexible, configurable user interface to accommodate the needs of different kinds of end-users, for example, test managers and test technicians. In addition to a consistent and intuitive user interface, the framework also supports configurable work flows. Access to different data, from source code to defect statistics, is available from a shared repository of project information.

For the toolmakers and system integrators, the framework provides well-documented interfaces to the shared data and the user interface services.

Sources of Tools

Software test tools are available from two main sources. One source is commercial tool vendors who produce testing tools. A few companies have emerged whose entire product line is focused on testing—a clear indication of the importance being placed on testing tools by the vendor community. These products are reviewed in the trade press and, in some cases, may be purchased for evaluation.

The second source is public institutions, such as colleges and government agencies. Tools from these organizations represent leading-edge technology, and often can be obtained for the media cost. These tools should be considered, however, only after the source of support for them is identified.

Several good tool surveys are available. The consulting firm, Software Quality Engineering, publishes an annual review of commercial tools, sorted in many different ways, such as target system or tool classification, to facilitate their selection. Another source is *Software testing and evaluation* by DeMillo, McCracken, Martin and Passafiume. This survey references many of the tools available from public institutions as well as from commercial sources.

For Further Reading

Many excellent texts have been published on the subjects of software testing and quality assurance. While none are dedicated to the issues of test automation, most provide good discussions of the methods and technology that are the basis of test automation. A few of these works are cited at the end of this chapter; all of them have valuable bibliographies.

Summary

Software testing can be automated. In fact it must be to become an effective means of quality assessment and, ultimately, quality assurance. If there is any doubt of the verity of this, the progress of computer hardware testing should be considered. With many of the same methods described above, hardware testing is being performed with highly sophisticated testing systems. The testing has become critical to the success of manufacturers in that business. What is striking is the logical complexity of the hardware devices being tested. These devices are nothing less than software programs frozen in hardware. The software development community should be prepared to adopt the same engineering discipline.

Author Biography

Philip Wallingford is founder and president of Software Quality Automation (SQA), Inc. of Lawrence, Mass. The company is focused on providing automation tools for software testing and quality assurance and has released several best-selling products.

Mr. Wallingford received a B.S. degree in Engineering Physics from the University of Maine in 1974. He has spent his career in various engineering organizations, developing new technology ranging from 3-D CAD/CAM systems to multi-media applications. SQA was founded from an accumulated set of observations of how unproductive most software testing environments were, and how automation tools could provide dramatic benefits.

The author is a member of the IEEE Computer Society and the ACM. He can be reached at SQA; 1 Parker St., Lawrence, MA, (508) 689-0182.

Additional Reading

Beizer, B. 1990. *Software testing techniques*. 2d ed. New York, N.Y.: Van Nostrand Reinhold.

DeMillo, R., McCracken, Martin, and Passifiume. 1987. *Software testing and evaluation*. Menlo Park, Ca.: The Benjamin/Cummings Publishing Company, Inc.

Hetzel, W. 1988. *The complete guide to software testing*. Wellesley, Ma.: QED Information Sciences.

Myers, G. 1979. *The art of software testing*. New York, N.Y.: John Wiley & Sons.

17

Winners and Losers
Management's Role in Orchestrating the Change that Comes with CASE

by Daryl Conner and Vaughan Merlyn

Introduction

Automating software development is almost invariably a more arduous process than initially expected. To add value, automation inherently causes changes in organizational structures, work practices, roles, relationships, and responsibilities. Dealing with the far-reaching consequences of these changes often stretches management's capacity to the limit.

Recognizing the characteristics of successful change projects can help management better understand its role in implementing comprehensive Computer-Aided Software Engineering (CASE) environments. In nearly 20 years of international research and consulting work, ODR Inc. has identified the decisions and actions that separate the winners from the losers in implementing change. Winners are those organizations that achieve their change objectives on time and within budget. Losers are those that never achieve their change objectives, or do so only after investing a great deal more time and money than they anticipated. The companies studied represent nearly every segment of the global business market, including Fortune 500 corporations, governmental agencies and non-profit institutions throughout the United States, Canada, Europe, South America, Asia, Australia, South Africa, and the Soviet Union.

In its study of software development automation, the Ernst & Young Center for Information Technology and Strategy found that ODR's "winners and losers" analysis is particularly applicable to CASE implementation projects. This chapter applies ODR's research to the challenges of CASE implementation, examining 11 of the major characteristics that separate winners from losers. In this context, CASE refers to all contemporary forms of software development automation object-oriented approaches, methodologies, repositories, and so on.

Note that the subject of ODR's study is major change, such as installing a comprehensive CASE environment or implementing integrated CASE tools and new methodologies. If the change is minor (such as the employment of small "point" tools or a limited implementation with a single project team), the principles of organizational change management will still apply, though not as critically.

The following discussion uses examples from real situations. However, to highlight the principles at work, the examples are unidentified. In real-life situations, there is rarely a one-to-one correspondence of principle and example. Usually, many principles are operating simultaneously, and that is the case here as well. For the sake of brevity, we will isolate aspects of the situation to illustrate the principle even though it may appear artificial without the full context.

Management's Attention to Disruption Prior to Implementation

- Winners required that special attention be applied to any change that significantly disrupted those affected by the decision, regardless of whether there were positive or negative implications.

- Losers were only concerned when negative reactions were obvious or inevitable.

A major insurance company was frustrated by a lack of progress with its CASE implementation, even though the potential of CASE was obvious and everyone was positive about the methodology. Those charged with implementing CASE at the firm took time to explain the implementation plan to the software developers and provided substantial opportunities for the developers to attend tool and method classes. But few of the developers attended the classes, and they stubbornly continued old development practices. The need to manage change is often ignored or underestimated because of positive perceptions of the initiative. These positive feelings often mask the difficulty of the implementation and the natural resistance to change. Thus the implementation typically falters.

It is important to understand that major change is disruptive whether it is regarded as positive or negative. When people face a situation that is significantly different from what they anticipated, their expectations are disrupted and ambiguity is increased. Humans avoid ambiguous situations; we strive for as much control of our environment as possible. This is why resistance inevitably accompanies major change.

"We don't have to worry about change here as everyone is in favor of the CASE initiative." That is a dangerous assertion. Everyone might indeed feel positive about CASE, but the implications of the new methods must still be addressed. This means that new skills must be teamed, new relationships formed, and new expectations established. Even if CASE is welcomed, its implementation means leaving the known and comfortable, and moving toward the unknown and threatening.

While the disruption associated with software development automation cannot be eliminated, its effects can be managed. Recognizing the patterns of the human response to change, and factoring these responses into the implementation plan allows the inevitable resistance to be more easily understood and thus easier to influence.

Management's Decisions Prior to Implementation

- Winners accurately determined when implementation planning warranted concern.
- Losers could not determine when special implementation planning was required.

Implementation means putting a new tool, technology, or work practice into effective use. Yet, there are often situations in which CASE is thought of as simply a technical, developmental tool. As such, it is approached tactically. Management assumes that if the right tools are selected, the promised benefits of CASE can be reaped immediately.

Evaluation committees/teams, who spend months evaluating dozens of CASE products and attending seminars, are not the be-all-to-end-all. An evaluation team might lavish great care and attention on the evaluation-and-selection process, but it generally ignores or grossly underestimates the need for implementation planning and resources.

Usually, the implementation of a comprehensive CASE environment is extremely disruptive and might involve major change at many levels. The shift from a manual to a computerized process is one of the most obvious differences. Conversion to automation first requires an explicit definition of the process, and then requires decisions on how to simplify, standardize, and automate the process. This is far more complex than simply installing tools into an existing manual process and harvesting the benefits of automation.

A second level of change that comes with CASE is the shift from valuing productivity (do the development work as quickly as possible) to valuing quality (do the right things right the first time). While "back-end" CASE (code generators, fourth generation languages) addresses development speed and efficiency, "front-end" CASE (planning, analysis and design) deals with effectiveness. It's important to keep in mind that speed is not the goal. The subtleties of moving quickly versus moving rigorously and carefully take time and experience to appreciate and properly manage.

CASE changes the relationship between Information Services (IS) and the end user. IS no longer acts as a job shop for the user but forms a technology partnership with the user. These role changes and shifts in responsibility can have deep ramifications for most people.

At the most personal level, CASE shifts the software developer's skills from an art form to an engineering discipline and from an individual activity to a group effort. Skills change from technical skills and creative coding, to analysis, design, teamwork, communication and business skills, and creative problem solving.

We have found that those who are most successful with CASE have approached it as a strategic initiative. Those who succeed understand that the introduction of CASE is not an isolated, tactical step. It has a pervasive, strategic impact on the software development process and organizational structure. Winners also recognize the need to exercise special care when introducing CASE. There is a high risk that human factors—such as resistance—will inhibit successful implementation. But, most importantly, those who succeed with CASE realize that the high, long-term costs of not implementing CASE far outweigh the initial costs of implementation.

Management's Approach to Initiating Change

- Winners knew that change would not occur unless the pain of staying with the status quo became obvious.

- Losers assumed the change would occur of its own accord.

A major telecommunications company had a vision of what CASE could do for them and believed that implementing CASE was a priority. It had established a task force that drafted a comprehensive implementation plan. Unfortunately, the plan assumed that everyone in the organization shared the task force's conclusion. The plan failed to win the support of senior user management, which was more interested in addressing the application backlog than in sanctioning a major capital expenditure by MIS. The plan was shelved.

The problem at the telecommunications company was that no connection had been established between the pain as experienced by the users—the application backlog—and the remedy as envisaged by MIS-the CASE implementation.

A model developed by Kurt Lewin, an MIT researcher and author, helps explain how change is motivated and throws light on the telecommunications company's situation. In Lewin's model, organizations remain in the static state because the forces of change are counterbalanced by the forces maintaining the status quo. Change will occur only if this state of equilibrium is disturbed by either increasing the forces of change, reducing the restraining forces of the status quo or both.

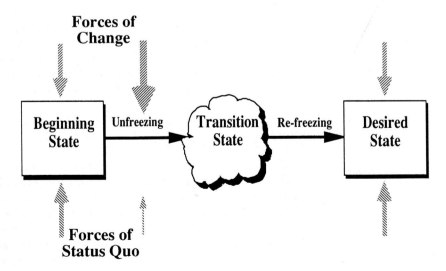

Forces of Change

Beginning State — Unfreezing → Transition State — Re-freezing → Desired State

Forces of Status Quo

ERNST & YOUNG
Center for Information Technology and Strategy

Fig. 17.1 The stages of organizational change.

Most CASE implementations begin without a clear understanding of the forces maintaining the status quo, and only a vague notion of the forces of change. Management says that it wants to see improvement, but it does not really know the costs of the current state. Although the status quo seems undesirable, it is not unacceptable. As the costs and disruptions of change surface, the status quo begins to look more desirable than the chaos of change. Eventually, the commitment to the change evaporates and the project is aborted. The CASE tools become "shelfware," and yet another opportunity to improve software development has been missed.

To begin the change process and affect what Lewin called the "unfreezing" of the status quo, management must reduce the forces maintaining current organizational behavior. This is usually achieved by revealing discrepancies between the current behavior and the desired behavior. For example, organizations typically begin a quality-improvement program by assessing the current costs of poor quality, such as the cost of nonconformance. Once these numbers are known, management is much more likely to seek quality improvement, even if this change is painful. In these cases, the status quo has become unacceptable.

To reveal the pain of the current state, one might ask such questions such as: What is the cost of not using information engineering and software engineering approaches? What has been the cost of building islands of automation that now require a multitude of interfaces and cannot respond to business changes or to management's need for information? What is the cost of maintaining a program at the level of code rather than at the level of design specifications? Where is the benefit of years of analysis with no accurate, up-to-date documentation to reflect its results?

While it is important to diminish the forces that restrain change—such as group performance norms, fear of change, employee complacency, and high investment in existing skills—it is also critical to increase the forces that facilitate change. Management can emphasize these facilitating forces, such as outside competition, new reward structures, new career opportunities, and new skills, by building a "case for CASE," either by identifying potential benefits or by completing successful pilots. Again, the benefits must be relevant to the level of sponsorship sought.

Executives are not impressed by increasing Function Point delivery rates by 80% with CASE. Similarly, development managers are not motivated by delivering software six months sooner to gain an extra 20% market share for the new product or service the software supports. Sometimes, we can transform restraining forces into facilitating forces. For example, a rightsizing project might be an excellent catalyst to motivate change to a CASE environment.

Management's Approach to Implementation

- Winners approached change as a process and demonstrated a high tolerance for ambiguity.

- Losers approached change as an event and demonstrated low tolerance for ambiguity.

Lewin's model describes a "transition state" between the existing state and the desired state. The transition state is an ambiguous situation. Existing beliefs, behavior, values and attitudes are no longer valid, and new ones have not yet been institutionalized.

Facing ambiguity can lead to strange behaviors. CASE implementations can stall over conflicts between old and new standards. (This can even happen in situations where standards were ignored before the CASE tools were brought in.) CASE implementation might also lead to major conflicts between programmers and data administrators and between information center and development center personnel.

Full CASE proficiency can take from 18 to 24 months to achieve. Unfortunately, data-processing professionals tend to have a particularly low tolerance for ambiguity. They become impatient in the transition state, and the CASE implementation easily gets derailed.

Management's Orchestration of Key Roles during Implementation

- Winners viewed the orchestration of certain roles in the change process as essential to successful implementation.

- Losers assume that issuing directives was synonymous with successful implementation.

Ignoring the roles of personnel essential to the implementation process frequently impedes the progress of CASE implementations. Most of these sort of implementation failures stem from a lack of sponsorship.

The *change sponsor* is the individual or group that legitimizes the change with official support and resources. As such, the sponsor should have the appropriate political power and authority as well as an understanding of the scope and depth of the change. With this understanding and authority, the sponsor should become visibly and personally involved in the change project.

Insufficient sponsorship can hinder otherwise smooth-running projects. A bank's development manager was implementing CASE quite well until he hit a brick wall trying to enlist user support for the Joint Application Design (JAD) sessions suggested by the CASE methodology. To the development manager and his people, user participation made all the sense in the world. It mystified him that the users did not share this vision. How could their reluctance to provide critical JAD resources be overcome? A higher level of sponsorship was necessary. In this case, the IS steering committee, which included senior user management, had power over the recalcitrant users.

Another key role in the change process is that of *change target*, the individual or group who must actually change their knowledge, skills, attitude, or behavior. In CASE implementations, those who fill the change target role encompass a broader and more diverse selection of people than is usually anticipated. Organizations often perceive CASE as an issue for developers only. In reality, CASE may affect data administration, database management, the information center, the development center, and the end user in some way, often dramatically. Managers must thoroughly assess the target's perspective, and they must meaningfully involve the targets in the change process.

A third role is that of change agent, the individual or group responsible for implementing the change. Change agents must have a number of different skills, human as well as technical. They must understand the dynamics of change, be effective communicators and excel at interpersonal relationships, team building, and conflict resolution. They must also, of course, believe in the change.

A public utility in the midst of a CASE implementation was suffering severe negative reactions among the development group. The CASE implementation team (the agents of change) had skilled technicians who believed strongly in CASE—almost to the point of obsession. This had become a problem, particularly because many of them lacked the requisite people skills. Their obsessive beliefs in CASE came across as pedantic, and their attitudes toward anyone who was not as devoted to CASE were at best impatient, at worst confrontational. Changing the mix of implementation team members, sensitizing them to the human issues and training them to empathize with developers gradually overcame the resistance. The CASE implementation is now proceeding smoothly.

A final key role is that of *change advocates*, those who want to achieve a change but are not in a position to legitimize the change. Many frustrated CASE advocates try to fulfill the role of change agent, even though they have not yet secured sponsorship. Their implementation efforts are almost always doomed to failure.

Advocates must recognize that implementation will not succeed without the proper sponsorship and careful management of change. They must not confuse their roles with that of sponsor or change agent. As advocates, they must work to secure sponsorship rather than try to implement CASE. (Of course, they can be working on pilot projects and other activities to help convince the sponsors, but they should not confuse securing sponsorship with executing fully sanctioned, broad CASE implementation.)

Management's Avoidance of Black Holes during Implementation

- Winners recognized the danger of the black hole phenomenon and succeeded in minimizing its occurrence.

- Losers fell victim to the corporate black hole.

A *black hole* is a region in space where gravity is so great that nothing, not even light, can escape from it. In the corporate universe, a black hole is a gap between senior managers who want the change to happen (initiating sponsors) and targets with whom change must occur. The symptoms of a corporate black hole are the failure to demonstrate sufficient sponsorship at all levels and the subsequent gap that occurs between strategic rhetoric and tactical reality.

There are usually several sponsors at many different levels in an organization. The initiating sponsor is typically, though not necessarily, a senior manager. Again, his or her key requirement is the political power to legitimize the change. Initiating sponsors start the ball rolling and build the commitment of sustaining sponsors within middle management, who directly influence the change targets.

The change message must be effectively carried throughout the organization; this means that the sponsorship role must cascade from top management (initiating sponsors) to middle management (sustaining sponsors). Initiating sponsors have middle management as change targets. These middle managers will, in time, become sustaining sponsors, with change targets at the next organizational level. How effectively this cascading effect is achieved and how well the power to legitimize change is delegated—these are the critical aspects to avoiding corporate black holes.

Management's Commitment during Implementation

- Winners demonstrated strong commitment by playing an active part in "sponsoring" change.

- Losers assumed that no further involvement was necessary once the decision for implementation was made.

In many CASE initiatives, senior management supports the idea of software development automation and demonstrates this by approving a budget and implementation plan. But it is common that management neglects making its commitment visible to the rest of the organization. Having "bought into" the CASE initiative and approved the expenditure, the sponsors believe that they have displayed sufficient commitment; now they can move on to other, "more important" things. Others, however, read the apparent disinterest as lack of commitment, especially if these major decisions have effects that conflict with the implications of previous major decisions.

Another telecommunications company experienced significant resistance to a software development automation project. The firm's developers did not believe that management was serious about software development automation and thought that this latest project was simply installing the "tool of the month." Senior management was flabbergasted when they heard that their employees did not believe that they were committed to CASE. They said, "How could that be the case when we had approved the budget and signed a memo about the project kickoff?" Surely that was evidence of commitment, they thought. Unfortunately, but typically, it was not enough. The "memo method" is especially insufficient if the organization has a litany of failed projects and hollow rhetoric.

Sponsors must make their commitment visible and tangible. They must thoroughly understand the depth and scope of the change and its impact on the organization. They must appreciate the resources required for the change to be successful and be committed to making these resources available. Sponsors must also appreciate the human impact of the change, empathizing with the targets. They must demonstrate strong public and private support for the change, promptly rewarding those who facilitate the implementation process or expressing displeasure with those who inhibit acceptance of the change. They also must ensure that the change process is monitored to track progress or problems.

Management's Synergistic Behavior during Implementation

- Winners convinced their organization that synergistic teamwork was a necessity for successful change.

- Losers encouraged teamwork but were incapable of achieving it.

When individuals or groups work together to generate more benefits to the organization than they consume, synergy is present. A synergistic work team produces a result that is greater than the sum of its individual parts. Synergy can flourish when the members of a team have both a common goal and a genuine interdependence. Not only are they working to achieve the same objective, they also need each other to achieve it.

The ability for sponsors, change agents, and targets to recognize mutual goals and needs and work together synergistically is indispensable to successful change. With CASE, teamwork among members of the development group and synergy between developers, users, and data administrators is crucial. Because CASE requires a complex web of common goals and interdependent actions, managers must ensure the creation and maintenance of synergistic working relationships.

A major textiles manufacturer, noted for its exceptional achievement in total quality management, has established a culture that not only values but relies on teamwork for problem solving and quality improvement. Management strongly supports the quality culture, and teams form across organizational boundaries. Participation is balanced, ground rules clearly established and decision processes clearly communicated. Most importantly, there is little fear and high trust, so teams are confident about putting forward ideas about improvement.

Management's Approach to Resistance during Implementation

- Winners viewed resistance as a natural and understandable human reaction to disruption.

- Losers thought of resistance as an inexplicable force that mysteriously affects people.

Individuals do not resist change so much as they resist the implications of change. Sources of resistance are categorized into three groups: barriers to understanding, barriers to acceptance, and barriers to acting.

Barriers to understanding might include a lack of appreciation of the need for CASE, doubt about the benefits of CASE, or poor communication about the nature of the CASE implementation. These barriers could exist simply because information has not been communicated, or they could result from inconsistent behavior from management or the change agents. The CASE initiative often comes from an elite group, chartered to explore CASE tools and other software development automation possibilities. But many times, this elite group does not do an adequate job of involving the rest of the organization or communicating the rationale for CASE, the strategy for future development and the implications of the initiative.

Barriers to acceptance tend to be more emotional. People may understand the need for CASE, but just not accept that CASE is the right solution. Emotional factors that might cause barriers to acceptance include a lack of security, a threat to self-confidence, or a perceived loss of organizational power. Programmers may feel that CASE will eventually eliminate their jobs. They may feel threatened, thinking that they will not be able to learn and apply the new techniques associated with CASE or that end users and junior individuals may adopt the new techniques more readily.

Barriers to action can develop from organizational problems, such as a lack of supporting resources. A firm might not have enough workstations or consulting resources to support a CASE implementation, or these barriers might result from a simple lack of skills. For example, analysts might not have the interpersonal or communication skills typically required for joint sessions with end users (such as JAD).

Resistance is inevitable, and its causes must be brought to the surface and addressed if the change is to go smoothly. The change agent's skills are critical to understanding the nature of resistance and dealing with it effectively.

Management's Response to Resistance during Implementation

- Winners responded to resistance as an inevitable part of the change process that must be expected and managed.

- Losers viewed resistance as avoidable, and if it occurred, it represented someone's failure.

All major changes—even positive ones—produce resistance. During a change that is originally perceived to have positive implications, there is a predictable pattern of increasing and then decreasing pessimism over time. For example, a major bank selected a sophisticated CASE product that relied on the information engineering methodology. At first, there was high enthusiasm for CASE. This stage could be described as "uninformed optimism."

After several weeks of JAD sessions, a couple of false project starts, shifts in end-user priorities, and some technical problems with the CASE tool, pessimism increased and the mood changed to "informed pessimism." Doubts about the CASE initiative came to the surface and several team members began to question the wisdom of committing a critical project to CASE approaches. As pessimism increased, some project participants became quite antagonistic toward CASE, spending more energy attempting to demonstrate what they saw as the looming problems of CASE than trying to achieve the goals of the project.

Management was committed, however, and the CASE project had strong leadership. The antagonistic team members were replaced, and the covert resistance and negative feelings were carefully brought to the surface and addressed. The informed pessimism turned to "hopeful realism" as the project turned the corner, and the benefits of extensive planning and analysis were realized. The mood then turned to "informed optimism," and the project was implemented successfully.

Increasing pessimism is a result of resistance, a certain response to the implications of change. There are many potential reasons for resistance, some blatant, others quite subtle. Sometimes resistance is expressed overtly; other times it is covert. Whatever its causes and however it is expressed, resistance must be anticipated, brought to the surface and managed.

Resistance does not represent someone's failure. It is a price of change that must be paid in order for the change to succeed. The price can be either paid up front in the form of prevention payments, or it can be paid later as excessive change costs or failure. There is no avoiding the price for change.

Management's Structure and Discipline During Implementation

- Winners demanded that structure and discipline be applied to the planning and execution of all major or changes.

- Losers allowed "spray-and-pray" approaches during implementation.

CASE evaluation and selection are usually managed conscientiously. Oftentimes, pilot projects are also carefully planned and managed, with hand-picked team members and meticulous project monitoring. When moving from the pilot to full roll-out, however, management often resorts to a spray-and-pray approach: they throw resources at the project and hope that everything works out. Management buys tools and workstations, provides basic training and issues edicts. With this done, management views the CASE implementation as a "done deal."

Meanwhile, cracks begin to show in the CASE initiative. Concepts of a shared data resource crumble under the weight of multiple modeling teams, whose work will just not consolidate. Some projects become bogged down in "analysis paralysis." Others experience massive escalation in scope and are canceled. There are problems getting the right level of user involvement. Some project teams contend that the chosen tools and methodologies are not suited to their projects, so they revert to traditional methods. Other projects are on too short a fuse to accommodate the teaming curve and are given special dispensation to bypass CASE for the time being.

The same sort of time and care devoted to the selection of tools and workstations must also be invested in the project's actual implementation. As a precursor, this investment must take the corporate culture into full consideration. An organization's pattern of shared beliefs, behaviors and assumptions is so strong that any time a change conflicts with the culture, the culture always wins. Therefore, it is advisable that the plan be designed and modified to conform to the culture or the culture converted to fit the plan (but changing in organization's culture is extremely difficult and requires massive commitment, substantial investment of resources and highly skilled change management).

New tools, basic instructions, and declamatory memos are obviously not the full range of a CASE implementation project. Sustained training must be provided not only in the technical realm but in the human arena as well. This is especially necessary to ensure that change agents have the necessary skills in communications, team building, and change management. In addition, implementation managers must not only address questions of data sharing, project scope, and user involvement in the project's initial stages but constantly revise their approaches based on employee feedback and departmental status reports.

Conclusion

The past few years are rich with lessons from hundreds of organizations that have either succeeded or failed in managing the sort of change that comes with implementing CASE. These examples offer instruction to current managers of CASE implementations. CASE enthusiasts can espouse at length the technical benefits of structured analysis and design. But it is apparent that the technical benefits of software development automation can come to fruition only if equal emphasis is placed on using a structured process for orchestrating the human aspects of implementation.

Note: This article was excerpted from *Chief Information Officer Journal*. Copyright © 1992 by Faulkner & Gray, Inc. Reprinted with permission from *Chief Information Officer Journal*, Spring 1992, published by Faulkner & Gray, New York.

Author Biography

Daryl Conner, president and CEO of ODR Inc., is an internationally recognized leader in the change management field, educating and advising executives around the globe. Mr. Conner developed ODR's Managing Organizational Change™ (MOC™) methodology based on his nearly 20 years of research and practice in organizational settings.

ODR is an international consulting firm that specializes in helping organizations manage change. Based in Atlanta, Georgia. ODR is dedicated to transferring MOC methodology to organizations across the nation and around the world. Thousands of business leaders in the United States, Canada, Europe, South Africa, South America, Asia, Australia, and the former Soviet Union use the methodology to ensure the successful planning and implementation of major change projects.

ODR serves a wide range of clients, including Fortune 500 corporations, government agencies, non-profit institutions, and multinational firms.

A prolific author, Mr. Conner has written more than 60 publications, including journal and magazine articles, monographs and chapters of books on the subject of change management. His first book on change management will be published by Random House in 1992. Mr. Conner has a master's degree in psychology.

Vaughan Merlyn is a Partner in Ernst & Young's Center for Information Technology and Strategy in Boston. He is an authority on the subject of software development automation and continuous quality improvement in Information Systems. Vaughan pioneered the application of Total Quality Management and Organizational Development methodologies to the implementation of software development tools.

He is a very popular speaker in the industry, and has lectured throughout North America, Europe, Australia, Japan, and the Far East for a decade. His insights and opinions have been regarded as among the most influential for the leading vendors and users of CASE technology.

Prior to joining Ernst & Young, Vaughan was chairman and co-founder of CASE Research Corporation, internationally recognized as a leading expert on Computer-Aided Software Engineering (CASE). CASE Research merged with Ernst & Young early in 1991. CASE Research's depth of work in this field included hundreds of public speaking appearances, respected research publications, frequent quotes in the trade press, as well as founders of the International CASE Users Group and sponsors of the Annual CASE Users Conference.

Vaughan designed and chaired the CASE benchmarks seminars, which were held worldwide, and served as conference Chairman for the Annual Meeting of the International CASE Users Group.

Prior to forming CASE Research, Inc., Vaughan was Executive Vice President for Altergo Software Inc., a leading developer and vendor of software productivity tools.

Vaughan serves on several advisory boards, including the Center of Project Management at Boston University, the Center for the Innovative Application of Technology, at Washington University, and the Information Engineering area of concentration of the Masters in Information Management Degree Program through the School of Technology and Information Management at Washington University in St. Louis. Vaughan has published widely on the subjects of application development automation, organizational change management, and total quality management applied to the Information Services function.

Vaughan was born in London, England, holds a B.Sc in Electrical Engineering from the University of Salford, and is a member of ASQC, ACM and SIM.

18

Why Do Many Good Tools Fail in Practice?

by Elliot J. Chikofsky

Introduction

For good software tools and systems development methods to succeed as productivity tools in industry, two critical factors are required. The tools need to be based upon a solid design that scales up to large project use. Then the use of the tools must be based upon sound management practices in the support of tools. While sound tool design has been the subject of many papers and conferences, the area of sound management practices for tool use continues to have too little attention. Yet without proper management, the best tools can easily fail.

Over the last 20 years, the development of software engineering tools has grown and matured. This progress has resulted in the field called CASE, which is primarily the industrialization of reasonably well-understood software technologies. The period of time it has taken to reach this stage is not unreasonable for such a transition to the widespread practical application of software tools. Studies of technology transfer in a number of different industries have generally supported the notion that it takes 15 to 20 years for a new technology to reach sufficient maturity for general use.

But in the meanwhile, many otherwise excellent software tools have not been transferred successfully from the laboratory to industry. They have not made it beyond the pilot project stage into real, productive use in organizations.

Clearly, one reason for this is that many of these tools were inherently unable to scale up to the reality of large projects. But that is not sufficient to explain the wide range of tool failures. In re-examining the last 20 years of software tool introduction, and reviewing my own experience as a tool developer and technology advocate, I contend that many tools fail because organizations do not recognize the symptoms of their own mismanagement of tool acquisition, tool introduction, and continuing tool use.

We must recognize that the management of tools does not end with their introduction. Too many organizations face the initial issues of bringing the tool in and then forget to manage the technology in regular practice. While tools and CASE environments are introduced to improve the organization's productivity, these tools require more effective management approaches to achieve this objective. Without reviewing management's approach to tools in use, organizations unknowingly lose the very productivity benefits they strove to achieve.

Problems Begin in Tool Acquisition

Many of the problems of tool use are direct results of an organization's approach to tool introduction. There are seven key symptoms that signal mismanagement in productivity tools acquisition and introduction. The first three symptoms relate to acquisition goals, real project involvement, and pilot projects.

Symptom 1: Window shopping. Organizations often shop for tools without well-defined goals. If you walk around the tools fair of one of the many CASE marketing shows and pick up a list of clients from each vendor of a brand new tool, what do you see when you compare the lists? The same major company names appear over and over again on the long lists of well-known corporate clients. These companies buy at least one or five of everything. Many such organizations have Tool Finder as an implicit or explicit job role—someone who is charged with locating and bringing in technology to try. But the organizations fail to assign responsibility for successful transition of the tools found into user projects.

Symptom 2: Transom transfer. Acquired tools are frequently thrown over the wall or through the transom to development projects. Many organizations isolate the real users from the acquisition of tools. The user project teams are not consulted regarding the real needs to be satisfied for real projects. Instead, they receive new tools that looked good to the Tool Finder and to upper management but may have little direct value to solving the problems at hand. Tools thrown over the transom often become shelfware on the other side.

Symptom 3: Pilotless projects. Too many organizations conduct pilot projects without support. For a pilot project of a software tool to be most useful, there should be some up-front agreement on the criteria for success. The parties to this agreement should include management, prospective user from other projects, and the pilot team. However, organizations go into pilot projects hoping that what they do will magically achieve the support and respect they failed to arrange before starting the project. They also go on with the project without determining how their work will be judged. This is frequently a recipe for disaster.

In contrast with these first three symptoms, the transition-successful Tool Finder relies on a well-defined set of objectives, often the result of corporate strategic or project management tactical planning efforts involving multiple projects or departments. Pilot projects are most successful when planned with the informed and interested participation of users and management.

Through the use of well-arranged pilot projects, organizations can identify the correct scope in which new methods and tools can succeed, and where they need to be engineered to the appropriate scale. The involvement of prospective users allows for interested observers of the pilot, and for the cultivation of relationships that could allow for the later success of the tools involved.

The next three symptoms relate to the perceived degree of change the tools will require or foster and its effect on the acceptance of the tools.

Symptom 4: Edict. Some organizations try to introduce new technology solely by executive fiat or management edict. Without grassroots support among project teams, mandated tools may be followed without fervor or embraced in name only. Resistance to edicts can be subtle, but still result in major problems for the acceptance of tools.

Symptom 5: Revolution. Implementing revolution without evolution can inhibit success. Organizations and people do not like drastic change, making it hard to succeed by introducing revolution. Tools and methods that require analysts or project groups to work in a manner that departs significantly from their experience and understanding have been harder to introduce and get accepted. This implies that it can be quite difficult to change to better tools and methods that are more demanding, recognizing the uphill effort needed to gain acceptance.

It is easier to garner support with an evolutionary approach to tool introduction. It is often best to encourage use by introducing tools or features that are supportive of the way the organization works now.

Building on such a foundation, it can be easier for the organization to accept improvements and advanced features in the future. By customizing new tools to better capitalize on familiar aspects and procedures of the potential audience, it should be possible to improve the implementation process and aid their acceptance.

Symptom 6: Off-the-shelf adoption. We think of organizations adopting tools as they come from the tool vendor. But, for a tool or method to be accepted in an organization, it must adapt to the corporate culture. This adaptation occurs in several ways. The project management procedures of the organization provide a framework into which the products of the tool must be fit. The contractual obligations of the organization constrain, and often mandate, the deliverables of the development process which the tool must meet.

Many organizations looking to acquire methods have not been satisfied with implementing the methods in off-the-shelf form. Instead, they have selected what they consider to be the best and most applicable aspects of several methods, often covering different life cycle phases or different modeling perspectives, and have welded them together into a new corporate method. For an example of a corporate integration of methods, see Kathleen Mendes' article (1980).

The adaptation of methods means that tools to support methods must be able to adapt to be successful. The best tools are able to be customized and evolve with the organization's needs without extensive intervention by the tool developer.

The last symptom relates to the impact of marketplace diversity on acquisition decisions.

Symptom 7: Deadlock. With so many alternative approaches in the marketplace regarding software engineering tools and methods, some managers are at a loss to find reasonable criteria to make informed decisions. This is further compounded by the organization's lack of identified goals. The drive to examine each and every tool on the market for the "best" solution has caused many organizations to go into a form of "acquisition deadlock." Another new tool entering the marketplace causes a new round of deliberation.

Organizations that have broken the cycle early and have chosen some initial tool set, knowing that it is probably not a perfect choice, have better handled the technology introduction hurdle. These organizations are now better prepared to receive and utilize second- and later-generation tools.

Forgetting to Manage Tool Use

Organizations introduce tools with a lot of attention to detail because of the up-front investment of resources. So, one would expect to find a healthy management interest continue into monitoring—or at least occasionally reviewing—the tools in regular use. However, most organizations never revisit their tool use. Once a tool gets beyond initial introduction, many organizations seem to forget that the technology still needs to be managed. They allow implicit management decisions and inattention to become the norm.

By not watching what is happening, management encourages the rise of many pitfalls and misconceptions that impede the effectiveness of tools and methods in practice. Without periodic re-examination, many user practices become the accepted or "proper" way to use the tool, without regard for their overall impact on productivity. Together, these pitfalls form a very successful strategy for losing the productivity gains that the organization thinks it has achieved.

Pitfall 1: Underestimating the effort required. Tools tend to take a lot more time and effort than we initially think they do. There are many examples of organizations failing to comprehend and allocate the resources required for successfully extending the introduction of tools into new project teams and helping them to scale the learning curve. This is compounded by allowing people to take short cuts that, in many cases, are not savings in the long run.

New users undergo a progression through stages of tool familiarity: introduction, first education, initial experience, re-education, then finally productive expertise. By presuming expertise too early, and by failing to account for re-education as part of the process, we artificially shorten our estimates of the required effort.

Pitfall 2: The first student syndrome. Training of users is often treated as overhead or holiday boondoggles. We give it insufficient support. In many organizations, the first person to attend a training class is expected to come back to the office and teach everyone else. This shortchanges everyone in the process. You don't learn a tool in the classroom. You learn a tool by using it. The classroom exposes you to the capabilities of the tool, application possibilities, and what features are where. By actually using the tool on a project of your own, you really learn the tool and find out its strengths and weaknesses. When the first student tries to train the rest, that student doesn't get the opportunity to really learn the tool, and the rest of the students have a teacher who doesn't really know the subject.

Pitfall 3: Introducing a savior. Tools have often been brought in as the salvation of projects in crisis—the worst possible scenario for tool introduction. Projects that are already projected to be overdue, over budget, understaffed, and under-supported are not suitable candidates for new technology. This fact is all-too-often ignored.

We tend to forget that saviors usually come with their own rule sets to be followed. To get the benefit, you have to be willing to adhere to the rules. Yet many organizations try to use tools as magic wands to get them out of trouble without being willing to adopt and follow the rules the tools require.

Pitfall 4: Assuming organizational stasis. Having chosen the right tool for the job, an organization may have failed to notice that the job has changed. Because of how long it can take to gain acceptance for a tool as a regular part of the development process, we may not notice differences in the environment.

In fact, the very introduction of the tool may have changed the organization's balance of power between project leaders or managers. One department has gotten upper management support for new technology, while another has not. By not recognizing changes to the organization and its culture, we can miss opportunities or fail to recognize impediments to success.

Pitfall 5: Presuming one size fits all. We often try to apply the same tool in the same way to all projects. Tools in place are often overused—without examining whether they are really appropriate solutions. The adage "if you have a hammer in hand, every problem begins to look like a nail" is particularly true of the recent history of software tools.

There is also a tendency to ignore the tool's real purpose. The reality of the intended job in the organization might match the apparent purpose of the tool, but might not match the tool developer's intended purpose for the tool. Many copies of early analysis and design tools have been put to use as over-qualified word processors, with little regard to their analytic facilities and true potential.

We also fail to customize the tool to the need. Tools are often introduced without adequately tailoring them to the organizational environment. The existing facilities of the tool may never have been examined to choose appropriate defaults for the project at hand, and to select project management options. Further, the tool may not have been constructed for adaptation. There may, in fact, be another model or variation which would be more appropriate.

Pitfall 6: Blaming the tool. No matter what happens, it's the tool's fault. Tools are easy scapegoats and get blamed for a lot of management mistakes and inattention.

Pitfall 7: Failing to recognize economics. It is important to keep in mind the economic incentive for tool use: the profit motive. A productivity tool's purpose is to allow the user to do more with the same or less resources. More might be measured in volume, quality, or shortened time.

Costs

Benefits

Fig. 18.1 Benefits versus costs.

In deciding to introduce the tool, someone concluded that the benefits outweighed the costs. The costs for introducing tools are most often very visible: software, training, and computer facilities. Benefits are less visible and less tangible. They may be in terms of savings, improvement in quality of products, improvement in productivity, and the ability to tackle otherwise unmanageable problems. Benefits are usually harder to measure than costs and clearly take much more time to accumulate.

Organizations often have only vague notions of the benefits to be achieved. In examining the use of existing tools, it is useful to ask some key questions: Is management still waiting for the benefits to be realized? Who is expecting the benefits—specific users, first-level management, or top-level management? Are those benefits still applicable to the continued use of the tool?

Pitfall 8: Failing to define productivity. Most tools are promoted and acquired based upon objectives dealing with productivity, yet most organizations have not considered what they mean by productivity. In 1981 IEEE articles, Tony Wasserman pointed out that for many organizations "teaching all developers the skills of touch typing . . . might have a greater impact upon productivity than would the introduction of new software tools or design techniques."

We often relate productivity to efficiency—building it faster—when what our real goal should be is effectiveness—building the right thing better. This leads us to mistakenly follow form instead of content in our use of tools and methods.

Without a viable definition of the organization's productivity objective, effective measures of progress are not possible. As the Cheshire Cat pointed out to Alice, if you don't know where you want to go, which direction you go doesn't matter.

Pitfall 9: Using methods half way. Organizations claim to follow structured methods, but many follow the form and not the content. They implement the visual attributes of a method—the diagram types and symbols or the notation of data dictionary—but not the rules of the method or the analytic tests for good quality designs. Larry Constantine, a founder of structured design who recently returned to the software engineering after a ten year hiatus, observed that "it's almost as if no one read past chapter three in any of the texts."

When users of automated data-flow diagrams don't push the analysis button for DFD Balancing, and when users of structured design don't recognize and understand the key terms such as "cohesion" and "coupling," how can their organizations hope to reach the potential of their investment in software tool technology?

Failing the Learning Curve

Most people view the learning curve as something the organization goes through once to achieve productive efficiency. This is not true for many organizations—they keep repeating the learning curve. By not having mechanisms in place to preserve and exchange expertise between project teams or departments, they implicitly encourage projects to cover the same ground again. In such cases, the organization never quite attains the productivity benefits it should expect from the effort put in.

The learning curve is not a rise to a plateau. Organizations can lose the productivity they've gained by allowing what they've learned to decay over time.

The Learning Curve

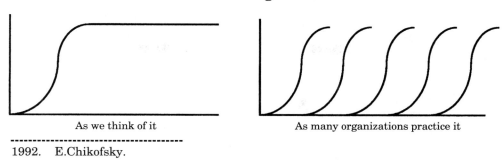

As we think of it   As many organizations practice it

1992.   E.Chikofsky.

Fig. 18.2 The learning curve.

Winning Back Productivity

There are, however, various techniques that organizations have used effectively to better manage the learning curve and stop reinventing the wheel regarding tool use.

Strategy 1: Create a review plan. Management should establish a plan and mechanisms for regularly reviewing and assessing the use of tools in the organization. How are they being used? What are the existing barriers to use? Are the features of the tool being used effectively? Are some features not being used at all? Are all aspects of the users' work being satisfied by the tools in use? Periodically examining such questions can lead to a better understanding of tool use in the organization and can allow management to detect problems which impede productivity.

Strategy 2: Elude political boundaries. It is important to provide meaningful support to new projects and users, regardless of political boundaries in the organization. When the staff under one manager can't talk to the staff under other managers doing similar work, the productivity potential of the entire organization suffers. By transcending such political barriers of the organization, there can be greater savings and benefit from tool use.

Some organizations have found it useful to establish internal user groups for specific tools. These groups meet regularly to encourage the sharing of knowledge and expertise among users from diverse parts of the organization. They provide new users with a ready source of answers, and can help to establish organization-wide conventions for use of the tool. Internal user groups also provide a ready source of interested users to participate in the periodic tool review process.

Strategy 3: Sanction training. Make training a valuable and respected part of the tool process, both in introduction and continuing use. Start by avoiding the presumption that someone who has been to one class can train the rest of the new users. Then also recognize that providing review and advanced training to existing tool users can recharge their batteries and provide new insights into more effective ways to use the technology. This can help rejuvenate projects and organizations which have come to suffer from anemic tool productivity.

Strategy 4: Tailor the training to the audience. Too many organizations accept off-the-shelf courses from tool vendors and training providers. Courses set up for an unknown audience of mixed backgrounds and interests can be made more effective by having them tailored to your specific user audience. Instead of using generic examples, have the instructor include meaningful problems and illustrations which capitalize on your users' prior experience and knowledge.

It's also useful to apply the tool in levels with new users by matching features of the tool to their needs and levels of expertise. Teaching new users in depth all of the detailed features of a complex tool in one training class is of marginal value. It is better to have a beginner's course, covering an overview of the tool with detail on essential start-up activities, followed by a period of regular on-the-job use. Then bring the users back for a review and more advanced training. This approach strengthens the confidence of the users and provides a sound basis for productive tool use.

Strategy 5: Explain conventions and standards. It is also important to provide "how to" documentation tailored to the organization and your type of projects. Don't just rely on manuals from the tool vendor. Have experienced users from successful projects describe what approaches work best and explain the conventions and standards they used.

Strategy 6: Mobilize materials from prior projects. To leverage the potential for reusability, make prior projects accessible. Do you know where the materials are for the last project you were part of? How about the one before that? All too often, finished projects have become shelf-fillers that are lost to all but the most ardent investigator.

Strategy 7: Update conventions and standards. It is also critical to review and revise conventions and standards to reflect real project experience. Assign responsibility in each project team for the documentation of the problems and pitfalls encountered in tool use and how the project got around them. Sharing this knowledge with other project teams will help the whole organization avoid needlessly repeating the learning curve.

Conclusion

Productivity tools are only part of the solution to achieving productivity in system development. Management practices of the user organization regarding the use of tools have to be as effective at fostering productivity as the tools themselves.

There are many ways in which an organization can unknowingly fail to realize the benefits expected from productivity tools. The tool acquisition process, operational issues, and the treatment of the learning curve each contribute to a potential loss of productivity. By periodically re-examining our explicit and implicit management decisions regarding tools, we can be sure that we are getting the value we need out of tool technology.

Making software tools more successful requires that we make our approach to managing them more successful. The best tool is no substitute for poor management.

Author Biography

Elliot J. Chikofsky chairs the Technical Committee on Software Engineering of the IEEE Computer Society and is a member of the society's board of governors. He is a consultant and author on information systems development, reverse engineering, and reengineering, and is a lecturer in Industrial Engineering and Information Systems at Northeastern University in Boston. He serves as secretary of the International Workshop on CASE and president of the Reverse Engineering Forum. Mr. Chikofsky was a development director for Progress Software (4GL/RD BMS) and was director of research at Index Technology (Excelerator/CASE), where he was a principal member of IBM's AD/Cycle Information Model Working Group.

Works Cited

Mendes, Kathleen. 1980. Structured systems analysis: A technique to define business requirements. *Sloan Management Review*. Summer, 1980.

19

Software and the Factory Paradigm

by Watts S. Humphrey

Abstract

The software factory concept was originally proposed to improve software development productivity through standardized tools, methods and component reuse (Bemer 1969; McIlroy 1959). This paper discusses the factory paradigm, relevant lessons from early manufacturing experience, and the problems with the traditional factory system in the United States and much of the western world. The implications of this experience for working professionals in general, and for software professionals in particular, are discussed, and a continuous process improvement paradigm is outlined that relates factory-like disciplines to the software environment. Some successful experiences with disciplined software methods are also noted and suggestions given for expanding their use.

Introduction

The perceived lack of structured and predictable software practices has led many managers to search for ways to impose rigor and discipline on their software operations. In many organizations, software has grown more rapidly than the overall business, while at the same time the software has become progressively more critical to business success. Mounting software costs, coupled with chronic unpredictability, have thus led to increasing management frustration. By comparison, the more traditional engineering and manufacturing operations (which have generally produced the bulk of corporate revenue), have seemed far more manageable. Consequently, there has been a growing management interest in introducing factory-like methods to control software development. Clearly, the hope is that by imitating the factory, the quality and productivity of software development will approach that of other business elements.

Although this approach is entirely sensible, it does have some risks. As historically practiced in the western world, the basic factory approach has been to reduce each task to a routine procedure, mechanize it, and therefore reduce both labor content and human error. There are, however, two issues that are important, and one is the principal subject of this paper; these traditional factory methods are no longer effective for the production processes that they were designed to handle. Japanese industrial successes amply demonstrate that this historical approach is a poor model for software process improvement.

The second problem is an all-too-common management propensity to search for quick and easy answers. In the case of software, this often takes the form of automation; some fancy new tool or environment will somehow magically straighten out an otherwise chaotic software operation. Unfortunately, when a sophisticated process is automated, its strengths are magnified and its weaknesses accentuated. Automation might make an effective software process more effective, but a chaotic one even worse—often at considerable expense. Many managers who are not familiar with software issues thus emphasize tools and ignore the critical need for better management and technical methods. Tools are important—unquestionably so—but they should not distract us from the greater need for appropriate process management methods.

We discuss here the pros and cons of the factory paradigm and why software must follow a similar but slightly different path. Whereas it is true that many of the disciplines that have been useful in factories can also be applied to software, it is also true that the same problems that have caused the factory paradigm to break down will be serious problems for software.

Some Lessons Learned from the Industrial Revolution

Factories were originally introduced in the textile industry in England nearly 200 years ago. Centralized production solved the serious transportation bottlenecks of the home-centered production systems used in the 1700s. As these small mills were merged into centralized factories, economies of scale became apparent. Space was more efficiently utilized, central supervision was possible, and raw materials supplies could be more readily financed. Centralization also led to better tooling and centralized power sources. In parallel with these advantages, however, there were many management abuses. Early factories made extensive use of child labor, and the factories often dominated entire communities or towns. This early period of employee exploitation by management led to aggressive unionization and to the western tradition of labor/management confrontation.

Taylor (1911) established the theoretical foundation for these early factories. He proposed structuring repetitive work into small, well defined elements that could be assigned to each worker. The work was studied and defined, and each worker was told precisely how each task should be handled. This mechanistic approach assumed that the workers had no feelings, capabilities, or motivations, and that they should be used much like machines or beasts of burden. Direct outgrowths of Taylor's theories were piecework and production norms. These same basic concepts are often used today when dealing with productivity issues, both in factories and with software.

Taylor's approach was probably appropriate for the early factories. Previously, workers had lived a largely serf-like existence with little formal education and no structured work habits. The factory system effectively turned undisciplined workers into effective production units. Unfortunately, over time, this same approach led to many counter-productive management methods, some of which have persisted to this day, such as piecework quotas, quantitative tracking of individual workers, and performance-related pay. These methods may seem natural to many managers, but they are all based on the principle that management knows the most effective process and that poor performance is the worker's fault. The process is thus a management creation that is imposed on the workers, and the workers are obliged to perform or be penalized.

The Breakdown of the Factory System

In 1924, Mayo, from Harvard University, undertook a study of Western Electric's plant at Hawthorne, Illinois (Mayo 1933). The original purpose of this study was to find the proper mix of lighting and other environmental conditions that yielded the highest worker productivity. Mayo started by adjusting the lighting level in the Western Electric factory. As expected, a test group's productivity continually increased as the lighting level was improved. Unexpectedly, however, a control group's productivity increased at the same time. After some time, Mayo decided to reset all the conditions to their original values. They reduced the lighting progressively and eliminated newly introduced benefits, such as flexible rest breaks and longer lunch periods. However, instead of a drop in productivity, both the test and control groups' productivity reached an all-time high.

These results were so unexpected that Mayo launched a series of interviews to learn precisely what was happening. He found that the mere existence of the study demonstrated management interest and made the workers feel better about their environment and their work. By asking the employees what they felt, the employees were made to feel important. In fact, many workers said that this study was the best thing the company had ever done. As a consequence of their better feelings, not surprisingly, they did better work. These initial results from the Hawthorne studies were the first conclusive demonstrations that workers' attitudes are a critical factor in determining their performance.

These concepts were further extended by McGregor, who characterized a new approach of worker involvement as Theory Y, as opposed to the earlier approach that he called Theory X (McGregor 1960). For example, Theory X assumed that the workers were not motivated and needed to be either punished for their failings or rewarded for better performance. On the other hand, Theory Y assumed that the workers were both motivated and willing to work if the management encouraged them and showed interest in their work. Not surprisingly, neither of these extremes has turned out to be entirely effective. On one hand, it is true that various forms of motivation and reward can be useful in achieving superior performance. Conversely, workers do not make good machines, and any system that treats them in a mechanized and inhuman way is not likely to achieve consistently effective results.

During the Second World War, significant steps were taken to couple these concepts to statistical management techniques and apply them to war production. These efforts increased United States factory output during the war years and, over time, they led to significant advances in statistical management methods. Shortly after the Second World War, Deming (1982) attempted to introduce these same methods to United States manufacturing. Unfortunately, he found little interest. But these methods were widely accepted in Japan. As is now well known, the Japanese embraced Deming's theories and demonstrated, beyond question, that higher quality and productivity can be achieved by following a different approach to that of the traditional Taylor-based factory.

Deming's points are given in Fig. 19.1 (Deming 1982); as can be seen, these are almost the antithesis of Theory X. Deming recommends encouraging employees to own their own working process and convincing management that production problems are not typically caused by workers, but by an ineffective process. He also insists that management owns the process and that it is management's responsibility to initiate and sustain process improvement.

The effectiveness of Deming's methods was best demonstrated by experiences at General Motors and Toyota (Business Week 1981). Over a period of years, General Motors averaged less than one employee suggestion per year, of which only 31% were adopted. Toyota employees averaged 17.8 suggestions per year, of which 90% were adopted. This difference clearly shows the distinction between these two approaches. In the case of General Motors, the process is viewed by the workers as immutable and static; a regime to which they must adapt. On the other hand, the Toyota workers see the process as serving them; when they see ways to improve it, they make suggestions, almost all of which Toyota management supports and adopts. As Cusumano (1987) points out, "The most important contributions to production improvements of Toyota appeared to lie in the management policy area—process analysis, standardization, and worker discipline and cooperation."

The Implications of the Factory System for Working Professionals

To shed light on people's behavior, Maslow (1954) established a five-level hierarchy of human needs. In his view, the most fundamental needs for food and shelter are closely followed by the need for personal safety. These needs are rarely denied to working professionals, but most people need the third level of support, membership in a social group. After gaining this security, needs then escalate to the fourth level—the desire for recognition and status. Finally, at the apex of Maslow's hierarchy is self-actualization. This is where the individual seeks the personal satisfaction of accomplishing a difficult task. This highest need is satisfied when professionals overcome all obstacles to achieve a creative or demanding success. As Maslow has shown, a clear prerequisite to effective self-actualizing performance is the professional's need to be recognized as an important part of the organization, not merely as an inanimate cog in some larger impersonal system.

Professionals also need some control over their working environment. They do not like to be given orders or detailed direction. They like some choice in their working

1.	**Create constancy of purpose toward improvement of product and service, with the aim to become competitive and to stay in business, and to provide jobs.**
2.	Adopt a new philosophy. We are in a new economic age. Western management must awaken to the challenge, must learn its responsibilities and take on leadership for change.
3.	**Cease dependence on inspection to achieve quality. Eliminate the need for inspection on a mass basis by building quality into the product in the first place.**
4.	End the practice of awarding business on the basis of price tag. Instead, minimize total cost. Move toward a single supplier for any one item, on a long-term relationship of loyalty and trust.
5.	**Improve constantly and forever the system of production and service, to improve quality and productivity, and thus constantly decrease costs.**
6.	Institute training on the job.
7.	**Institute leadership (see point 12). The aim of leadership should be to help people and machines and gadgets to do a better job. Leadership of management is in need of overhaul, as well as leadership of production workers.**
8.	Drive out fear, so that everyone may work effectively for the company.
9.	**Break down barriers between departments. People in research, design, sales, and production must work as a team, to foresee problems of production and use that may be encountered with the product or service.**
10.	Eliminate slogans, exhortations and targets for the work force asking for zero defects and new levels of productivity.
11.	a. **Eliminate work standard (quotas) on the factory floor. Substitute leadership.**
	b. **Eliminate management by objective. Eliminate management by numbers, numerical goals. Substitute leadership.**
12.	a. Remove barriers that rob the hourly worker of his or her right to pride of workmanship. The responsibility of supervisors must be changed from sheer numbers to quality.
	b. Remove barriers that rob people in management and in engineering of their right to pride of workmanship.
13.	**Institute a vigorous program of education and self-improvement.**
14.	Put everybody in the company to work to accomplish the transformation. The transformation is everybody's job.

source: W.E. Deming (6)

Fig. 19.1 Deming's 14 points.

assignments, and they want their concerns recognized by management. In fact, the reason many technical professionals seek management positions is to protect themselves from being managed by someone else. As an MIT scientist said (Kaplan 1981), "If you don't take responsibility for supervising others or for going after the money, doing all the things you could care less about . . . then somebody else will do it, and you will be directed by that person."

The Principles of a Better Paradigm

In establishing a more effective software development paradigm, it is appropriate to focus on the means to include professionals in the development and continuous improvement of their working process. There are several reasons for this focus. First, the historical concentration on product management in most software organizations has not been very effective. Second, the traditional factory systems in use in the western world do not provide a very encouraging role model; many traditional United States industrial organizations are not competitive with the more dynamic process-oriented industries of Japan and the Far Fast.

A process approach is also most appropriate when the workers perform tasks that require both technical competence and judgment. Here, management is generally unable to provide detailed direction on all aspects of the work and must rely on the worker's creativity and imagination. In software, for example, management is often unable to determine even the project status without consulting the professionals. Here, the traditional view of an all-seeing management imposing a precise process on the working population is totally impractical.

The process paradigm also requires that management recognize its obligation to provide a motivating climate for its employees. Management must define objectives, establish resources, assign responsibilities, and furnish capital facilities. The employees then participate in developing their process, executing it, and continually improving it. Management can then reasonably expect its workers to produce good quality results.

Compare this with the traditional top-down factory philosophy, where the management defines the work, establishes the precise methods, pays the workers when they operate according to plan, and penalizes them when they do not. Improvement suggestions are not expected or welcomed, and there is latent management/employee antagonism.

Continuous Process Improvement

The basic principles of the software process paradigm are given in Fig. 19.2 (Humphrey 1989). Four key actions are required to make this paradigm work.

- Each major process activity is assigned an owner, who is responsible for maintaining and improving it in concert with, and in response to, the suggestions made by the professionals involved.

- A mechanism is established to ensure that these process improvements are actually used in each phase of the work. Such a mechanism for the design phase, for

---

People management

- The professionals are the key to the programming process, and they must be intimately involved in its development and improvement.
- Management must focus on programming defects not as personal issues but as opportunities for process improvement.

Process support

- Special process groups are established.
- Necessary management and professional education is provided.
- The best tools and methods are obtained and used.

Process methodology

- The process is formally defined.
- Goals and measurements are established.
- Statistical data are gathered and analyzed to identify problems and to determine causes.

Process control

- Management practices are established to control change.
- Periodic process assessments are conducted to monitor effectiveness and identify necessary improvements.
- Procedures are established to certify process quality and implement corrective actions.

source: W.S. Humphrey

Fig. 19.2 The principles of software process management.

example, would be an initial meeting where the entire design team would review the tasks to be performed, agree on the basic requirements for the work, and set their goals for the design phase (Jones 1985).

- Process improvement is incorporated as a part of every task. A standard form, such as the process improvement proposal (PIP) shown in Fig. 19.3, is provided so anyone who encounters a problem or has an improvement idea has a ready means for submitting it to the process owner.

- Each PIP is tracked in much the same way as bug reports are in traditional software development. Feedback is provided to the PIP originator, both when priority is established and when the process improvement is implemented or rejected.

One way to view software process improvement is to consider the analogy with software maintenance. Software enhancements and repairs traditionally involve some or all of the phases of requirements, prototyping, high-level design, detailed design, implementation, and test. During this cycle, both the product design and its implementation are maintained under configuration control, and every change and bug report is recorded and tracked. The software process paradigm can be viewed in an analogous way; the process goes through similar requirements, design, implementation, and test phases, and any PIP and process change is recorded and tracked.

```
Process:_____Date:_____PIP Number:_____:

Originator:_____Job Name:_____Job#:_____:

PROBLEM:
Type of Problem:_____:
_____:

How Found: _____:
_____:
When Found (task #)                    Who Found:   _____

IMPACT:
Product Impact:_____:
_____:
_____:
_____:

When Encountered:         Process Task:_____:
Comments:_____:
_____:
_____:
_____:
_____:

Who Determined:          When:_____:

SUGGESTED/IMPROVEMENT (Specific changes, forms, etc.):
_____:
_____:
_____:
_____:

RESOLUTION REPORT (COPY TO ORIGINATOR):

Who Resolved:                    Date:_____:

What Done:_____:
_____:

source: W.E. Humphrey
```

Fig. 19.3 Process improvement proposal form (PIP).

The Effectiveness of the Software Process Paradigm

To date, this software process paradigm has been used only to a limited degree in the United States (Humphrey, Kitson, and Kasse 1989). Cusumano, however, has described the effectiveness of these same methods for several leading Japanese software firms (Cusumano 1989): Hitachi doubled productivity in one year, reduced late projects from 72% to 12% and reduced bugs per machine in the field by eight times; Toshiba more than doubled productivity and reduced bugs by up to seven times; NEC improved productivity from 26% to 91% and reduced bugs by one-third; and Fujitsu reduced bugs by 19 times in eight years and improved productivity by two-thirds. Although this information is uniquely Japanese, Cusumano points out that these same methods are also being used successfully in the United States but to a limited degree only.

The reasons why this software process paradigm is effective are as follows:

- Since the professionals participate in process definition, they own the process and feel responsible for making it work.

- This not only provides the individuals with a feeling of participation, but it also gives them a high degree of control over their working environment. When something does not work as they feel it should, they are willing and able to initiate the needed changes.

- The professionals are also in partnership with management. When they make suggestions and when management responds with capital and resources, they see the results. This partnership creates a far more effective working environment than the traditional management/professional mistrust that exists in many software organizations.

- The continual emphasis on process improvement throughout the project life cycle constantly challenges the professionals to perform superior work.

One consequence of such an environment is that the professionals are more likely to resist arbitrarily imposed changes. One example would be a management drive to install some new tool or environment. If this directive did not spring from a worker suggestion or a clearly recognized need, serious resistance should properly be expected.

Launching a Continuous Software Process Improvement Program

The key steps in initiating such an improvement program are (Humphrey 1989a):

- Assess the organization. Conduct an orderly study, determine the key problems and initiate appropriate improvement actions.

- Establish a software engineering process group (SEPG) to focus on and lead process improvement. If no one is working on process development, improvement is unlikely, as the process will rarely improve without conscious effort.

- Establish an automation planning and support group (APSG). This responsibility should be assigned to someone who is part of, or closely associated with, the SEPG and is capable of leading the CASE planning and implementation work.

- Plan, manage, and track process improvements with the same discipline used to plan, manage, and track the projects.

In this work, it is important to recognize the nature of process problems; they are defined issues that inhibit the professionals' performance of their work. If a problem does not meet this definition, it is not a process problem. Although there may be many management problems, they should be recognized as quite distinct from process issues. Management needs are typically addressed by adjusting the process requirements. It is clear, for example, that progress tracking, quality indicators, and capacity measures are valid management needs that should be accommodated by the process design.

This overall framework for process improvement must also include a focus on improved tools and methods. Every standard, measurement, and form is a kind of tool that should also be used to address identified process needs, rather than merely being introduced because someone thinks it is a good idea. It is important, however, to recognize that tools are rarely useful unless they are applied to defined problems.

Obviously, automation is an important part of all software process activities. After first establishing a full-time SEPG, an associated APSG should be given responsibility for planning and supporting CASE implementation. These two groups then form the core resource for continued software process development and automation.

Since people's abilities, the available technology, process methods, the business environment, and project needs all change with time, the automation support for the software process must also change and evolve. It is thus essential to maintain continuing resources to plan, support, and control CASE installation and evolution. This also requires a system for reporting and tracking CASE problems, mechanisms to periodically assess the users' needs, and the capability to test and prototype changes before putting them into general use.

Training is the area that is most frequently overlooked in software organizations. Professional programmers often will not accept and may not even be able effectively to use advanced tools, processes and methods unless they are adequately trained. The lack of adequate training often causes time-consuming and expensive mistakes, and it is always frustrating and demotivating. Training is, however, also generally expensive. In just one organization, the tool-training needs for a 30-person programming shop costs $162,000, not including the required instructional hardware and software (Humphrey 1989a). Although training is expensive, it is rarely as expensive as not training.

Economics

Today, software processes are essentially unique to particular projects, and it is not yet clear how much can be transferred from one organization to another. On the other hand, process development is expensive, and if every organization needs to build its entire process from scratch, our field is likely to remain a handcrafted specialty. When, for example, it is more costly to develop the process than to implement the project, process development makes little economic sense. As process development and customization costs decrease, and as the benefits of an orderly process framework become more apparent, it will be more reasonable for each project to define or adapt its process before launching a new product development.

Therefore, the need is to establish standard process definition formats and support mechanisms, to establish process frameworks, and to evolve a growing library of available process definitions. It is also important to identify those process elements that are most amenable for general use. There is ample opportunity for continued research and development in this area.

Managing Continuous Change

There is a growing literature about the process of causing organizational change (Humphrey 1987). It typically starts with an unfreezing phase, where people are made aware of current problems and the available opportunities for improvement. An assessment and the subsequent action planning process can often cause unfreezing.

The second phase, implementing the change, is far more difficult and time-consuming. Here, significant resources are often required, as are extensive training, support and various prototyping or test activities. During this phase, the organization undergoes a complete transformation. At the outset, at best only a few people are performing the desired process. At phase conclusion, however, all or most of the people are doing their jobs as intended.

The third change phase, refreezing, is where the change is established as a permanent part of the organization. It is incorporated in the operating procedures, standards might be established or functional groups might be charged with ensuring that the desired process steps are consistently performed.

Throughout the change process, various key roles are performed:

- The champion identifies the need for change and convinces an executive to sponsor or support it.
- The sponsor legitimizes the effort, provides the needed resources, and assists in overcoming obstacles.
- The change agents lead the change activity. Their job is to overcome resistance by including increasing numbers of the organization's staff in the change process.

An effective change process typically requires extensive training and the dedicated support of one or more change agents. A committed executive sponsor, however, is always required.

Conclusion

Whereas traditional United States factory methods are not appropriate to software development, the more dynamic and successful methods espoused by Deming (1982), and widely practiced in Japan, are a useful model. They not only provide a framework for addressing many traditional United States management problems, but they also are eminently suited to the creative aspects of software development.

The application of these methods to software, however, requires considerable care. An assessment should be made to define the organization's status, and an orderly improvement program should be launched. This requires resources and continuing management focus. The result, however, is not just a better process but a sound foundation for continuing process improvement.

Acknowledgments

The author would like to thank Ed Averill, Dave Kitson and Jim Over for their helpful review comments; Jim Morris for the extensive references and materials he provided on Japanese software and practices; and Dorothy Josephson for her great help with manuscript preparation. This work was sponsored by the U.S. Department of Defense. This article was reprinted from "The Software Engineering Journal," September 1991, with permission from IEE Publishing Department, Stevenage, Herts, England.

Author Biography

Watts S. Humphrey founded the Software Process Program of the Software Engineering Institute (SEI) and is a research scientist on the institute staff. The role of the Software Process Program is to provide leadership in establishing advanced software engineering processes, metrics, methods, and quality programs for the United States Government and its contractors.

From 1959 to 1986 Humphrey was associated with IBM Corporation. Among his assignments, he was responsible for IBM's commercial software development, including the first 19 releases of OS/360. He also managed IBM's Endicott, New York, development laboratory and was IBM Director of Policy Development. Most recently he was Director of Programming Quality and process, IS&TG. In that position he was responsible for establishing plans and implementation programs to improve the quality and productivity of IBM's 370 programming systems development.

Humphrey is an IEEE fellow and a member of the Association of Computing Machinery. He serves on the Board of Examiners for the Malcolm Baldridge National Quality Award. He is the author of three books: *Managing the software process*, Addison Wesley, 1989; *Managing for innovation - leading technical people*, Prentice Hall, 1987; and *Switching circuits with computer applications*, published in 1958. He has been issued five United States patents.

Humphrey holds a bachelor's degree in physics from the University of Chicago, a master's degree in physics from the Illinois Institute of Chicago, and a master's degree in business administration from the University of Chicago. He has taught graduate electrical engineering at Northeastern University.

The SEI, located in Pittsburgh, Pennsylvania is a federally funded research and development center operated by Carnegie Mellon University under contract to the U.S. Department of Defense. The objective of SEI is to provide leadership in software engineering and in the transition of new software engineering technology into practice.

Works Cited

Bemer, R.W. 1969. Position paper for panel discussion: The economics of program production. In *Information processing 68*. pp. 1676–1677. Amsterdam: North Holland.

Business Week. 1981. Putting workers into workmanship. pp. 1320–1321. 23 February 1981.

Cusumano, M.A. 1987. The "software factory" reconsidered: An approach to the strategic management of engineering. MIT industrial liaison program report 9-22–87. May 1987.

Cusumano, M.A. 1989. The "software factory" - a historical interpretation. *IEEE software*. March 1989: pp. 23–30.

Deming, W.E. 1982. *Out of the crisis*. Cambridge, Ma.: MIT Center for Advanced Engineering Study.

Humphrey, W.S. 1987. *Managing for innovation, leading technical people.* Englewood Cliffs, N.J.: Prentice Hall.

Humphrey, W.S. 1989. *Managing the software process*. Reading, Ma.: Addison-Wesley.

Humphrey, W.S. 1989. CASE planning and the software process. *Technical report CM-U-SEI-89-TR-26*. Pittsburgh, Pa.: Software Engineering Institute, Carnegie Mellon University. May 1989.

Humphrey, W.S., D.H. Kitson, and T.C. Kasse. 1989. The state of software engineering practice: A preliminary report. In *Technical report CMU/SEI-89-TR-1*. Pittsburgh, Pa.: Software Engineering Institute, Carnegie Mellon University. February 1989.

Jones, C.L. 1985. A process-integrated approach to defect prevention. *IBM System Journal*. 24 (2): 150–167.

Kaplan, G. 1981. We look at ourselves: The reacher. *IEEE spectrum*. 18 (8): 46.

Maslow, A. 1954. *Motivation and personality*. New York, N.Y.: Harper and Row.

Mayo, E. 1933. *The human problems of an industrial civilization.* New York, N.Y.: Macmillan.

McGregor, D. 1960. *The human side of enterprise*. New York, N.Y.: McGraw-Hill.

McIlroy, M.D. Mass produced software components. In *Software engineering: Reports on a conference sponsored by the NATO Science Committee.* ed. Naur, P. and B. Randell. pp. 155–158. Brussels, Belgium: Scientific Affairs Division, NATO.

Taylor, F.W. 1911. *The principles of scientific management*. Harper and Row.

Increasing Quality and Productivity with a "Development before the Fact" Paradigm

by Margaret H. Hamilton

Introduction

If system design and software development were true engineering disciplines, a system, no matter what kind or how complex, could be assembled without errors. It could be developed and safely changed for new requirements and ported to new target architectures in minimum time with minimum resources. With traditional methods, these goals will not be realized. New products, such as those which fall in the category of CASE, are intended to "engineer" development. Most of them are based on an attempt to automate parts of the traditional life cycle when the real problem could be the life cycle model, itself.

The desired focus is to approach a means for designing and developing systems that maximizes quality and productivity. There are two ways to accomplish this: one is curative, and one is preventative. For example, a curative means to obtain quality is to continue testing the system until the errors are eliminated; a preventative means is to keep errors out in the first place.

Productivity has its counterparts. One could use a curative approach and speed up a particular design and development process by adding resources, such as people or processors; in this case, productivity might be gained with respect to meeting a schedule, but lost with respect to resources needed to accomplish that process. Or, one could use a preventative approach and find a more efficient way to perform a process or eliminate it altogether and reach the desired results.

Some believe reuse is a major step towards realizing both the goals of quality and productivity. (One rationale is: if something with no errors is reused to obtain a desired functionality, time and money will not be wasted in developing that new system because it will not have the errors of a newly developed system. In this sense, reuse may be viewed as a preventative approach.) Of those approaches, many suggest various object-oriented techniques, whereas others, including functional programming proponents, find such techniques lacking.

For successful reuse, a system has to be good enough to reuse, and must be reused for each development requiring equivalent functionality. This means starting from the beginning of a life cycle, not at the end of the life cycle, which is typically the case with traditional methods; then a system is reused for each new phase of development. No matter what kind, every ten reuses saves ten unnecessary developments.

Some suggest maximizing automation, which is a formal reuse of a mechanized process, as a major step. Again, a process must be worth reusing if it is to be automated. (Sometimes, in fact, the use of automation might even result in a system that is less effective than before and decreases productivity in its production.) Techniques are also suggested that reuse knowledge, such as in the application of expert systems.

Many suggest an increase in user friendliness. For example, a front-end definition of a requirements environment could look friendly at first glance but be very unfriendly when applied to serious design and development. Time is wasted because the concepts used or learned lack derivability or continuity. For example, requirements might be defined with a friendly method that causes development to become a more difficult task than before. Or, requirements might be defined with more than one friendly method, but the definitions cannot be integrated in a straightforward manner. Derivability and continuity are related to reuse because they inherently save time in not having to perform unnecessary and ad hoc processes.

However they are solved, the critical issues of the traditional development process are dealt with too late and after the fact. Often, they relate to reusability. Take integration. It happens too late. For example, in defining requirements, data flow is defined using one method, state transitions another, dynamics a third method, and data structure using still another method. Once these aspects of requirements are defined, there is no way to integrate them. Designers are forced to think and design this way because of the limitations of the methodologies available to them. Integration is left to the devices of a myriad of developers well into the development. The resulting system is hard to understand, objects cannot be traced, and there is no correspondence to the real world. If requirements cannot be understood, how can they be reused and why would we want to reuse something that does not lend itself to integration?

Errors are eliminated too late. Why are they allowed in, in the first place? Believe it or not, it is the accepted practice with traditional methods that a system is defined by actually putting errors into it and propagating them throughout development. Interfaces are incompatible. The system and its development are out of control. Once again the developers inherit the problem. Why would anyone want to reuse something if it were full of errors? Similarly, flexibility for change and handling the unpredictable are provided for too late. Requirements are defined to concentrate on application needs of the user, but they do not consider that the user usually changes his mind. As a result, porting is a new development for each new architecture, operating system, database, graphics environment, and language or language configuration; critical functionality is avoided for fear of the unknown, and maintenance is the most expensive part of the life cycle.

Why reuse something in today's changing market if it is not portable or adaptable? Preparing for parallelism and distributed environments happens too late. Often, when it is known that a system is targeted for a distributed environment, it is first defined and developed for a single processor environment and then redeveloped for a distributed environment. Another unnecessary development.

The ability to create reusable definitions happens too late. Requirements definitions lack properties to help find, create and use commonality. Modelers use informal and manual methods to find ways to divide a system into its functional natural components, or blocks of components, for not only reuse but for first-time use. The result is redundancy instead of reuse. Again, errors propagate accordingly. Automation, an inherently reusable process, happens too late. Systems are defined with insufficient intelligence for automated tools to use them as input. Instead, a definition is given to developers to manually convert to code. A process that could have been mechanized once for reuse is performed over and over again, creating new errors each time.

When automation is possible, it is often incomplete across application domains, or even within a domain, resulting in a need to complete the documentation or code manually. It is often inefficient and/or hard wired to a particular architecture, language or even a particular version of a language.

Run-time performance analysis (decisions between algorithms or architectures) happens too late. Insufficient information is provided to define system performance. A system is defined without considering how to separate it from its target environment. This results in design decisions that depend on analysis of outputs from exercising ad hoc implementations and associated testing scenarios. Why not, instead, analyze reusable intelligent definitions, statistically?

Design integrity is considered too late. It is not known if a design is a good one until its implementation has failed or succeeded. Usually, a system design is based on short-term considerations; knowledge is not reused from lessons learned. Development is then driven towards failure.

When critical issues are dealt with after the fact, a system's quality and productivity in producing it are unacceptable. True reuse is ignored. System integrity is reduced at best. Functionality is compromised. Responding to today's rapidly changing market is not practical. Deadlines are missed. Time and dollars are wasted. The competitive edge is lost. Opportunities are gone.

The Solution

The solution is *Development before the Fact*. Each system is defined with properties that control its own design and development. With this new paradigm a life cycle inherently produces reusable systems, realized in terms of automation. Unlike before, an emphasis is placed on defining things right the first time. Problems are prevented before they happen.

Each system definition not only models its application but it also models its own life cycle. A system inherently integrates all aspects of its own objects and the combinations of functionality using these objects; maximizes its own reliability and flexibility to change; capitalizes on its own parallelism; maximizes the potential for reusing its own definitions, and the potential for its own automation; and supports its own run-time performance analysis and the ability to understand the integrity of its own design. Systems are inherently positioned for maximizing their own reuse. They are developed with built-in quality and built-in productivity assurance.

Once understood, the characteristics of good design may be reused by incorporating them into a systems language for defining systems. The answer lies not in the techniques, but in the language properties used. This language has the capability to define any aspect of any system and integrate it with any other aspect. These aspects are directly related to the real world.

This same language may be used to define system requirements, specifications, design, and detailed design, for functional, resource, and resource allocation architectures throughout all levels and layers of "seamless" definition. This would include hardware, software and peopleware. (The functional architecture defines what it is the user of a target system wants to do. Associated resource architectures define the potential execution environments for the functional architecture. The resource allocation architecture is the system that maps the functional architecture to one of a possible set of resource architectures.)

This language is used to define and integrate implementation-independent, function-oriented decompositions with implementation-independent, object-oriented decompositions. It defines and integrates these decompositions (control hierarchies), with networks of functions and objects. It can be used to define systems with diverse degrees of fidelity and completeness. Such a language can always be considered a design language, since design is relative. One person's design phase is another person's implementation phase.

This language has mechanisms to define mechanisms for defining systems. Although the core language is generic, the user language, a by-product of a development, can be application-specific, since the language is semantics-dependent but syntax-independent.

The first step in building a Development before the Fact system is to define a model using the systems language. (This model is a tentative representation of a system or theory that accounts for all of its known properties.) The model is automatically analyzed to ensure a proper definition. A fully production-ready software implementation, consistent with the model, is then automatically generated for a selected target environment (e.g., C or Ada). If the selected environment has already been configured, it's automatically selected; if not, the generator is configured (e.g., for VHDL, EDIF, C++) for that environment before it is selected. The resulting system can then be executed. If the desired system is software, it can now be tested for user-intent errors and operational after testing. Application requirements changes are made to the requirements definition, not to the code. Target architecture changes are made to the configuration of the generator environment, not to the code. If the real system is hardware or peopleware, the software system serves as a simulation upon which the real system can be based.

Development before the Fact Approach

With the Development before the Fact approach, every system is defined as an integrated, hierarchical, functional, and object-oriented network based upon a unique concept of control (Hamilton and Hackler 1990). This approach is used throughout a life cycle, starting with requirements and continuing with functional analysis, simulation, specification, algorithm development, analysis, system architecture, configuration management, software implementation, testing, maintenance, and reverse engineering. It is used by system engineers, software engineers, test engineers, managers, and end users; and it provides a framework of automation to aid the organization in focusing on defining and implementing process improvement, such as SEI Levels 1 through 5 (Humphrey and Sweet 1987).

The Development before the Fact approach had its beginnings in 1968 with the Apollo space missions when research was performed for developing software for man-rated missions. This led to the finding that interface errors accounted for approximately 75% of all errors found in the flight software during final testing. They include data flow, priority and timing errors at both the highest and lowest levels of a system to the finest grain detail. Each error was placed into a category according to the means that were taken to prevent it by the very way a system was defined. A theory and methodology was derived for defining a system such that this entire class of interface errors would be eliminated.

The first technology derived from this theory concentrated on defining and building reliable systems in terms of functional hierarchies (Hamilton 1986). Since that time, this technology was further developed to design and build systems with Development before the Fact properties in terms of an integration of both functional and type hierarchies.

Integrated modeling environment

The philosophy behind this approach is one of reusable building blocks, where reliable systems are defined in terms of reliable systems. Only reliable systems are used as building blocks and only reliable systems are used as mechanisms to integrate these building blocks to form a new system. The new system becomes a reusable for building other systems.

Every model is defined in terms of functional hierarchies (FMaps) and type hierarchies (TMaps). FMaps and TMaps guide the designer in thinking through his concepts at all levels of system definition and design. With these hierarchies, everything you need to know (no more, no less) is available. All model viewpoints can be obtained from FMaps and TMaps including data flow, control flow, state transitions, data structure, and dynamics.

On an FMap there is a function at each node that is defined in terms of and controls its children functions. For example, the function "build the table" could be decomposed into and control its children functions "make parts and assemble." On a TMap there is a type at each node that is defined in terms of and controls its children types. For example, type "table" could be decomposed into and control its children types "legs" and "top". Every type on a TMap comes with a set of inherited primitive operations. FMaps are inherently integrated with TMaps by using these primitive operations. Each function on an FMap has one or more objects as its input and one or more objects as its output.

FMaps are used to define, integrate, and control the transformations of objects from one state to another state (e.g., a table with a broken leg to a table with a fixed leg). Each object resides in an object hierarchy (OMap) and is a member of a type from a TMap. Primitive operations on types defined in the TMap reside at the bottom nodes of an FMap. Primitive types reside at the bottom nodes of a TMap. When a system has all of its object values plugged in for a particular performance pass it exists in the form of an execution hierarchy (EMap). A system is defined from the very beginning to inherently integrate its own real world definitions.

Typically, a team of designers will begin to design a system at any level (this system could be hardware, software, peopleware or some combination) by sketching a TMap of their application. This is where they decide on the types of objects (and the relationships between these objects) that they will have in their system. Often a Road Map (RMap), which is an index of FMaps, will be sketched in parallel with the TMap. Once an agreement has been reached on the TMap, the FMaps begin to fall almost into place for the designers because of the natural partitioning of functionality (or groups of functionality) provided to the designers by the TMap system. The TMap provides the structural criteria from which to evaluate the functional partitioning of the system (e.g., the shape of the structural partitioning of the FMaps is balanced against the structural organization of the shape of the objects as defined by the TMap). With FMap and TMap hierarchies, all system viewpoints are integrated. They inherently divide a system into functionally natural components and groups of functional components that naturally work together.

Primitive control structures

All FMaps and TMaps are ultimately defined in terms of three primitive control structures: a parent controls its children to have a dependent relationship, an independent relationship, or a decision-making relationship. A formal set of rules is associated with each primitive structure. If these rules are followed, interface errors are "removed" before the fact by preventing them from happening. As a result, all interface errors (75% to 90% normally found during testing in a traditional development) are eliminated at the requirements phase. The use of the primitive structures supports a system to be defined from the very beginning to inherently maximize its own reliability.

A use of the primitive structures is shown in the definition of the FMap for the system MakeATable (see Fig. 20.1). The top node function takes in "finish, flatWood, roundWood" as its inputs, and produces Table as its output. MakeATable, as a parent, is decomposed with a Join into its children functions MakeParts and Assemble. MakeParts takes in as input "finish, flatWood, roundWood" from its parent and produces Top and Legs as its output. Top and Legs are given to Assemble as input. Assemble is controlled by its parent to depend on MakeParts for its input. Assemble produces Table as output and sends that output to its parent.

MakeParts, as a parent is decomposed into its children, MakeLegs and MakeTop, which are controlled to be independent of each other with the Include primitive control structure. MakeLegs takes in part of its parent's input and MakeTop takes in the other part. MakeLegs provides the Legs to its parent and MakeTop provides the Top. MakeTop, as a parent is decomposed into its children, FinishSoftWood and FinishHardWood, where the children are controlled with an Or

Operation: MakeATable.
FMap:

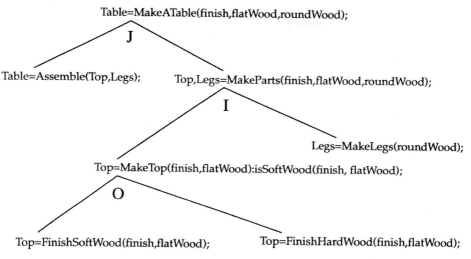

Table=MakeATable(finish,flatWood,roundWood);

J

Table=Assemble(Top,Legs);   Top,Legs=MakeParts(finish,flatWood,roundWood);

I

Legs=MakeLegs(roundWood);

Top=MakeTop(finish,flatWood):isSoftWood(finish, flatWood);

O

Top=FinishSoftWood(finish,flatWood);   Top=FinishHardWood(finish,flatWood);

Fig. 20.1 Operation: MakeATable.

such that either one or the other will be performed. Here, both children take in the same input and provide the same output since only one of them will be performed for a given performance pass. Notice that input (e.g., finish), is traceable down the system from parent to children and output (e.g., Table), is traceable up the system from children to parent. All objects in a Development Before the Fact system are traceable.

With experience using these structures, it was discovered that a system defined with them results in properties that support real-time distributed environments. Each system is event-interrupt driven. Each object is traceable and reconfigurable, and each has a unique priority. Independencies and dependencies can readily be detected and used to determine where parallel processing is most beneficial. With these properties, a system is defined, from the very beginning, to inherently maximize its own flexibility to change for the unpredictable and to capitalize on its own parallelism.

Defined structures and parameterized types

Any system can be completely defined using only the primitive structures, but less-primitive structures can be derived from the primitive ones and used to accelerate the process of defining and understanding a system. For example, user-defined structures and parameterized types can be created for asynchronous, synchronous, and interrupt scenarios used in real-time, distributed systems. Similarly, retrieval and query structures can be defined for client-server database management systems. Non-primitive structures can be defined for both FMaps and TMaps. Rules for the non-primitive structures are inherited from the rules of the primitive structures.

With the use of mechanisms such as defined structures, a system is defined from the very beginning to inherently maximize the potential for its own reuse. CoInclude is an example of a system hierarchy pattern that happens often when using primitive structures (see Fig. 20.2a). Its FMap was defined with primitive structures, Include and Join. Within the CoInclude pattern, A and B are the only leaf node functions that change. The CoInclude pattern may be defined as a non-primitive structure in terms of more-primitive structures using the defined structures concept. This concept was created for defining reusable patterns.

Included with each structure definition is the definition of the syntax for its use (see Fig. 20.2b). Its use (see Fig. 20.2c) provides a "hidden repeat" of the entire system as defined, but explicitly shows only the elements that are subject to change (i.e., functions A and B). The CoInclude structure is used in a similar way to an Include structure except that with the CoInclude, the user has more flexibility with respect to repeated use of an object state, ordering of objects, and selection of objects. Each defined structure has rules associated with it for its use just as with the primitive control structures. Rules for the non-primitives are derived from the rules of the primitives.

Async, shown in Fig. 20.3, is a real-time, communicating, concurrent, asynchronous structure. The Async system was defined with the primitive Or, Include and Join structures and the CoInclude non-primitive structure. It cannot be further decomposed, since each of its lowest level functions is either a primitive function or a previously defined type (under End, see Identify2:Any, and Clone1:Any, each of which is a primitive operation on any type), recursive (see Async under DoMore), or a variable function for a defined structure (see A and B under Process). If a leaf node function does not fall into any of these categories, it can be further decomposed or it

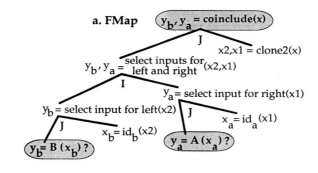

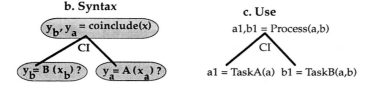

Fig. 20.2 FMaps, syntax and use.

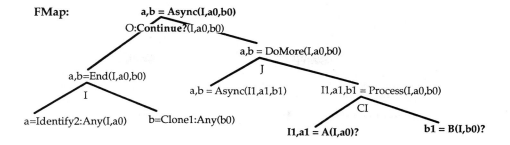

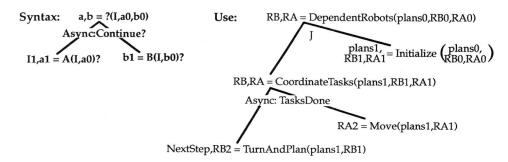

Fig. 20.3 Async.

can refer to an existing operation in a library, or an external operation from an outside environment. A use of Async is also shown here. TurnAndPlan and Move are dependent, communicating, concurrent, and asynchronous functions in the system DependentRobots. The two robots in this system could work together to perform a more complex task, such as building a table. Here one phase of the planning robot, RB, is coordinated with the next phase of the slave robot, RA. With the use of mechanisms such as defined structures, a system is defined from the very beginning to inherently maximize the potential for its own reuse.

A system: the integration of FMaps and TMaps

So far we have discussed properties in terms of FMap examples. Let us now look at Fig. 20.4 for a complete system definition for a manufacturing company that has been defined in terms of an integrated set of TMap(s) and FMap(s). This company could be set up to build tables, employing robots to perform tasks using structures such as those previously defined. Since this system is completely defined, it is ready to be developed automatically to full production, ready-to-run code. In this system's FMap, FullTime_Employee has been decomposed to primitive operations on types in TMap, MfgCompany. MfgCompany has been decomposed until its leaf nodes are primitive types or are defined as types that lead to primitive types.

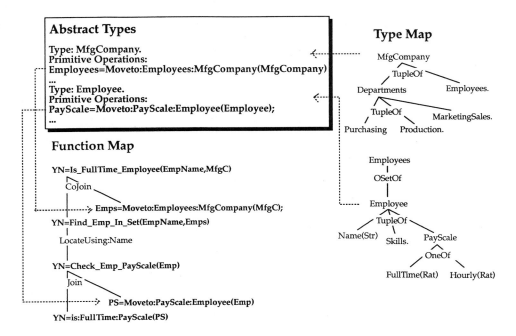

Fig. 20.4 Function maps and Type maps.

Reusability can be used within a TMap model by using parameterized types. A *parameterized type* is a defined structure that provides the mechanism to define a TMap without its particular relations being explicitly defined. Each parameterized type assumes its own set of possible relations for its parent and children types.

System, Is_FullTime_Employee, uses objects defined by TMap, MfgCompany, to determine if an employee is full time or part time. In this example, TMap, MfgCompany is decomposed into Departments and Employees in terms of a parameterized type, TupleOf. A TupleOf is a collection of a fixed number of possibly different types of objects. Departments is also decomposed in terms of TupleOf into Purchasing, Production, and MarketingSales. Employees is decomposed in terms of OSetOf. An OSetOf is a collection of a variable number of the same type of objects (in a linear order). One of the children of Employee is decomposed in terms of the parameterized type, OneOf. A OneOf is a classification of object types of different types from which one type is selected. Each parameterized type has a set of primitive operations associated with it for its use.

Abstract types that are decomposed with the same parameterized type on a TMap, inherit the same primitive operations. So, for example, MfgCompany, Departments, and Employee inherit the same primitive operations from parameterized type, TupleOf. An example of this can be seen in FMap Is_FullTime_Employee where both types, MfgCompany and Employee, use the primitive operation MoveTo that was inherited from TupleOf. Here each use of the MoveTo is an instantiation of the Child = MoveTo:Child:Parent (Parent) operation of the TupleOf parameterized type.

For example, Employees=MoveTo:Employees:MfgCompany(MfgCompany) allows one to navigate to an employees object from a MfgCompany object. A type may be non-primitive (e.g., Employees), primitive (e.g., FullTime as a rational number), or a definition that is defined in another type subtree. When a leaf node type has the name of another type subtree, either the child object will be contained in the place holder controlled by the parent object (such as with Skills), or a child reference object (a reference to an external object) will be contained in the child place holder controlled by the parent object.

The TMap provides universal primitive operations that are inherited by all types (for example, Copy). The universal primitive operations are used for controlling objects and object states. They create, destroy, copy, reference, move, access a value, detect, and recover from errors, and access the type of an object. They provide an easy way to manipulate and think about different types of objects. With the universal primitive operations, building systems can be accomplished in a more uniform manner. TMap and OMap are also available as types in order to facilitate the ability of a system to understand itself better and manipulate all objects the same way when it is beneficial to do so.

TMap properties ensure the proper use of objects in an FMap. A TMap has a corresponding set of control properties for controlling spatial relationships between objects. One cannot, for example, put an object into an object structure where an object already exists (one cannot put a wheel on a truck where a wheel already exists); conversely, one cannot remove an object from a structure where there is no object to remove; a reference to the state of an object cannot be modified if there are other references to that state in the future; reject values exist in all types, allowing the FMap user to recover from failures if they are encountered.

Run-time performance analysis considerations

When designing a system environment, it is important to understand the performance constraints of the functional architecture. Another important consideration is to have the ability to change configurations rapidly and at will. A system is flexible to changing resource requirements if the functional architecture definition is separated from its resource definitions. The same language is used to define functional architectures, resource architectures, and the allocation of functional architectures to resource architectures. The allocation definition defines how the elements of the resource architecture are applied to the functional architecture.

Constraints. The meta-language properties of the language can be used to define global and local constraints for both FMaps and TMaps. Constraints can be defined for both FMaps and TMaps. If we place a constraint on the definition of a function (e.g., Where RobotA takes between 2 and 5 seconds), then this constraint will influence all other functions that use this definition. Such a constraint is global with respect to the uses of the original function. Global constraints of a definition may be further constrained by local constraints placed in the context of the definition that uses the original function definition (for example, where function RobotB uses F Where F takes 3 seconds). Function F could have a default constraint that holds for all uses such as Where Default:3 seconds. If however, RobotB is defined to take 2 seconds, then RobotB overrides F. The validity of constraints and their interaction with other constraints can be analyzed by either static or dynamic means. The property of being able to trace an object throughout a definition supports this type of analysis. This property provides the ability to collect information on an object as it transitions from function to function. As a result, one can determine both the direct and indirect effects of functional interactions of constraints.

The separation of resources.   There are many ways to define a system. Figure 20.5 shows three different definitions for system Transfer2Blocks. The first two definitions are architecture dependent. The third one is not. The first system, Transfer2Blocks, implicitly assumes 1 Robot as its resource. If more robots become available, the functional architecture with its implicit resource architecture and resource allocation architectures would have to be changed to take advantage of its new resources. Such is the case with the second model that was defined to imple-

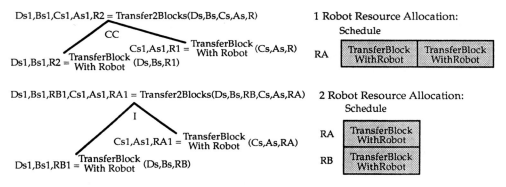

Resource Architecture Dependent Definitions

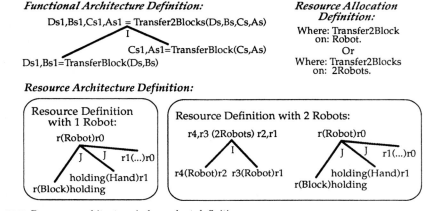

Fig. 20.5 Resource architecture independent definitions.

ment the system with 2 Robots. It will not work with one robot or any set of more than two robots. In both the first and second models, a change from one architecture version of the system to another affects the input and output list of every function. There is also a structural difference in the FMaps for the two implicit resource allocations of the first two models. One has a CC control structure and the other has a I control structure.

The third system model provides a solution that is more flexible to changing requirements than the first and second models, since changes made to the third model based on changing user needs do not affect other architecture models. The functional architecture definition can remain the same for any resource architecture. The alternate resource architecture models can also remain unchanged to perform the user's requirements. A resource allocation architecture definition defines the way in which the resources of the resource architecture are applied to the functional architecture. Two different resource allocation architectures are shown here which have been defined based on the alternative resource architectures. The only system that would change to switch from one robot to two robots or more would be the resource allocation specification. In this example only the Where statement would change. This is an example of a technique that can be used to define a system to inherently support its own run-time performance analysis.

Using the above separation method, the functional architecture model can remain the same, and therefore be reused for any resource architecture. The resource architecture models can also remain unchanged and become a reusable. The only system that would change when going from one resource architecture to another would be the allocation architecture. The use of constraints along with the method of defining a functional architecture to be independent of its resource architectures provides for a system to inherently support its own run-time performance analysis.

Design integrity

The "goodness" of a system design can be evaluated based upon attributes of the particular FMaps and TMaps used to define it. For example, the number of layers in a TMap, the degree of strong typing used in that TMap, the number of inputs and outputs associated with each function in the FMaps, the size of the FMaps and TMaps, and the degree of movement around a TMap to accomplish each functional task in an FMap all come into consideration. It becomes increasingly clear with each new development experience that a system can be defined from the very beginning by reusing knowledge of what makes a good design to inherently support its own analysis for design integrity.

Object-oriented properties

Development before the Fact systems are, by their nature, object-oriented from the beginning. The definition space is a set of real-world objects, defined in terms of FMaps and TMaps (see Fig. 20.6). Objects, instantiations of TMaps, are realized in terms of OMaps. An execution of a system, an instantiation of an FMap, is realized in

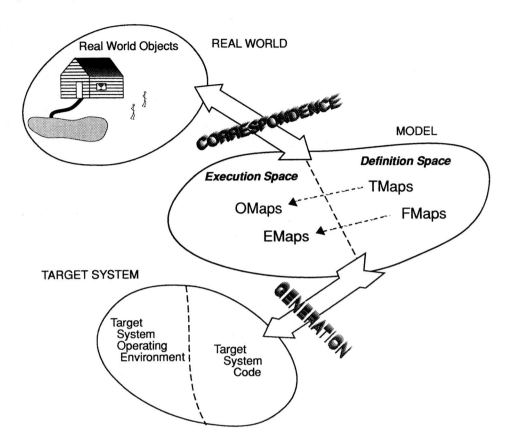

Fig. 20.6 Real world modeling.

terms of an EMap. From FMaps and TMaps, completely production-ready target system code or documentation is automatically generated and is ready to execute. Systems are constructed in a tinker toy-like fashion. Such a technology changes the way software is developed just as word processing changed the way in which offices were managed. The building blocks are definitions, independent of particular object-oriented implementations. Properties of classical object-oriented systems, such as inheritance, encapsulation, polymorphism, and persistence are supported with the use of generalized functions on OMaps and TMaps.

The Tool Suite: An Automation of the Technology

One automation of the Development before the Fact paradigm is the 001 tool suite. The tool suite, an automation of the technology, itself is a Development before the Fact system because it was used to define and generate itself. It encompasses "above upper", upper, middle, lower and "below lower" phases of development (see Fig. 20.7). Although the tool suite is a complete design and development environment, it can coexist with other tools. The tool suite, defined and generated with itself, ensures that the Development before the Fact approach is used correctly. It is layered onto primitives that are implemented in a language for a given native computer environment. A developer can use the tool suite either to prototype a system or to fully develop that system resulting in fully production-ready, quality code.

The tool suite provides an interface and an editor for defining FMaps and TMaps in either graphical or in textual form. The capability exists for a user to define a Road Map (RMap) hierarchy that provides an index to his system of FMaps, TMaps, and defined structures. At any point during the definition of a model, it may be submitted to the Analyzer, which ensures that the rules for using the mechanisms are followed correctly.

When a model has been decomposed to the level of objects designated as primitive and has been successfully analyzed, it can be handed to the Resource Allocation Tools (RATs) that automatically generate source code from that model for any type of application. These RATs are generic in that they interface with diverse language, data base, graphics, operating system, and machine environments. The Type RAT generates object-type templates for a particular application domain from a TMap(s). The Functional RAT generates source code from the FMaps. The code generated by the Functional RAT is automatically connected to the code generated from the TMap and code for the primitive types in the core library, as well as, if desired, libraries de-

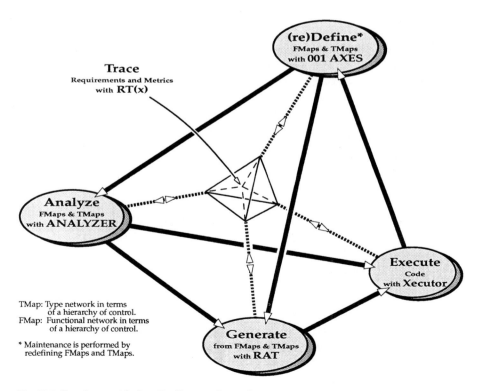

Fig. 20.7 Development before the Fact product suite.

veloped from other environments (the tool suite has an open architecture and can therefore be configured by the user to generate code to interface with outside environments).

The generated code can be compiled and executed on the machine where the tool suite resides (the tool suite currently resides in the VAX/VMS and UNIX X Window, Motif, C, and Ada environments); or, it can be ported to other machines for subsequent compilation and execution. User-tailored documents and metrics, with selectable portions of a system definition, implementation, description, and projections (e.g., parallel patterns, decision trees, and priority maps) can also be automatically generated by the RAT. Once a system has been RATted, it can be executed and debugged using the OMap Editor, a tool that provides a means to view and instantiate objects. Functions can be concurrently developed by other users, using FMaps and TMaps, and then be dynamically bound to a currently active user OMap Editor session.

At this time the tool suite provides automatic debugging and finds an additional set of errors dynamically (e.g., it would not allow one to put an engine into a truck if the truck already had one. The tool also will notify the developer about the impact in his system of any changes, and demotes those areas that are no longer valid). At the beginning of the performance testing phase, the remaining set of errors to be found is approximately 15% to 20% of what it would have been in a traditional design and development environment.

The Xecutor , an alternative to the RAT, allows the user to execute or simulate a system before implementation in order to observe characteristics such as timing, cost, and risk. The Requirements Traceability RT(x) tool generates metrics and allows the user to enter a requirements document into the system and trace between these requirements and corresponding FMaps and TMaps throughout system specification, detailed design, implementation, and final documentation.

With the use of the tool suite, a development process is automated within each phase and between phases beginning when the user first inputs his thoughts and ending when testing his ideas. The same language and the same tools are used throughout all phases, levels and layers of design and development. There are no other languages or tools to learn. Each development phase is implementation-independent. A system can be automatically "RATted" to various alternative implementations without changing its original definition. The tool suite takes advantage of the fact that a system is defined from the very beginning to inherently maximize the potential for its own automation.

Productivity Results

Many systems have been designed and developed with the Development before the Fact paradigm, including those that reside within manufacturing, aerospace, software tool development, database management, domain analysis, transaction processing, process control, and simulation environments. The definition of these systems began either with the definition of the original requirements or with requirements provided from others in various forms. The process varied from one extreme of interviewing the user to obtain the requirements to the other of receiving written requirements that were far too detailed. Written requirements were also provided to us in English, 2167A format, or in terms of other requirements/specification languages. We have analyzed our results on an ongoing basis in order to understand more fully the impact that properties of a system's definition have on the productivity in its development.

Productivity was analyzed with several of these systems, as shown in Fig. 20.8. Earlier systems were defined and developed for Los Alamos National Laboratory and SDIO (Hamilton and Hackler 1990). The first was Defensive Technology Evaluation Code (DETEC). It was performed in two parts and took six calendar months. For the first effort, 22,000 lines of fully production-ready C code were automatically generated by the tool suite described above. Some 26,300 lines were generated for the second effort. The first effort took 7 man-months and the second effort took 2.75 man-months. Productivity was higher in the second effort since knowledge gained and mechanisms developed in the first effort were reused in the second effort.

Productivity gains with the Development before the Fact paradigm varied from 14:1 to 48:1 when compared to conventional C-system developments. The conventional life cycle was based on 10 lines of code per day (Boehm 1981), starting with a basic compiler, linker, and standard run-time libraries to work with; we determined

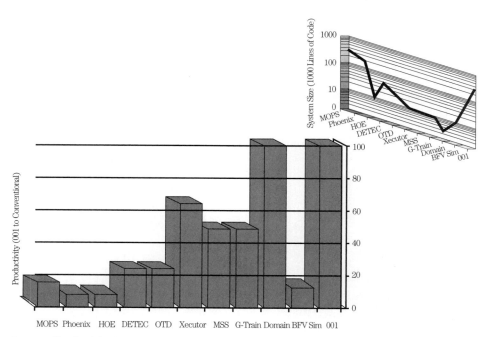

Fig. 20.8 Productivity increases exponentially.

that if all C experts with access to a specialized reusable library (equivalent to the core library of the tool suite) were to develop this same system, then the productivity gains would have been more like 2:1 to 8:1.

Productivity was even higher with later first-time efforts since the tool suite was more mature and had more reusable capabilities available. Eighteen months after DETEC, Object Tracking and Designation (OTD) was developed at a 26:1 productivity gain. This compares to a 25,500 statement system in C source lines developed in a highly structured and modular conventional development environment, or a 15,000 statement system in C source lines being produced by very experienced C experts with a generic reusable library equivalent to that of the tool suite. The Executor was developed and tested with four man-weeks of effort, a 65:1 productivity gain, with 13,000 lines of C being generated. The Executor interfaces with many complex modules; therefore, it is a more complex system than its size would suggest. Its productivity was higher because the developer understood his requirements before he began development.

Other systems analyzed for productivity include the simulation of vehicles within an aerospace environment, process control within a manufacturing environment, and transaction processing for banking. The tool suite design and development effort has the highest productivity at 100:1. It is a real-time client server application with almost 500,000 automatically generated lines of code. Its productivity is significantly higher because it has been under development using itself for several years and reusability has been capitalized on to a great extent.

Several developments with the traditional waterfall model (see Fig. 20.9) have been enhanced with traditional CASE tools that are used for the different phases (or

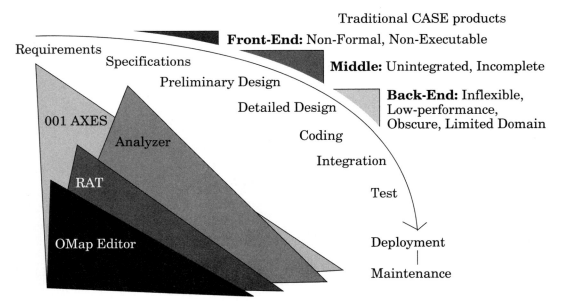

Fig. 20.9 Development before the Fact compared to CASE.

different aspects within a phase) of development. There are many issues raised with this approach of using point tools, as opposed to a system tool. There is the difficulty of integrating from one phase to another, and within a phase when combining different methods. When one tool or platform is changed, other tools are required to change. More often than not, there is the need to use manual methods to bridge these gaps and finish the development of a system. With the Development Before the Fact approach, however, the same methods, language and tools can be used for all aspects and all phases of development.

Figure 20.10 shows the Development before the Fact systems engineering and software development environment. This figure focuses on the open architecture aspects of this approach. The RAT, for example, can be configured to generate systems in languages of choice, such as C, Ada and, English; the core primitives can be configured for architectures, data bases, graphics, math libraries, operating systems, network protocols, and users libraries of choice. The next components to be added to this environment are the architecture-independent operating system (AIOS) and the Anti-RAT.

The AIOS has the intelligence to understand the semantics of functional, resource, and allocation architectures defined with Development before the Fact properties. It can use this information to automatically determine sets of possible effective matches between functional and resource architectures. The Anti-RAT performs the reverse function of the RAT. With the Anti-RAT, systems in existing languages such as FORTRAN, or an informal specification language, can be reversed engineered to a Development before the Fact system and then regenerated or generated to the language of choice such as C or Ada.

The Development before the Fact approach provides a new set of alternatives to the program manager for reverse engineering. There are several alternatives. A system could more realistically be completely redone, since the process, with this approach, results in a system that is more reliable and is developed with much higher productivity than before. Another alternative is to hook into existing libraries at the core primitive level and reuse portions of existing code considered worth reusing. Or, existing code can be anti-RATed to a Development before the Fact system definition that can then proceed through the RAT process to generate the desired output. There are advantages to each of these approaches depending on the requirements of the user.

Summary

Our experience strongly confirms that both quality and productivity increase with the increased use of Development before the Fact properties. For the most part, this has to do with the inherent reuse capabilities of Development before the Fact systems. Taken together, many of these properties can be mapped to a combined integration and abstraction of the best parts of some the newer, yet more traditional, methods. Yet, systems developed with before the fact properties do not exhibit many of the known shortfalls of these methods; each of these methods presented a partial solution, and it was not possible to find a perfect mate to integrate that partial solution with to form a total system solution. Further, implementation inefficiencies often resulted from taking an indirect path to a solution forced by attempting to

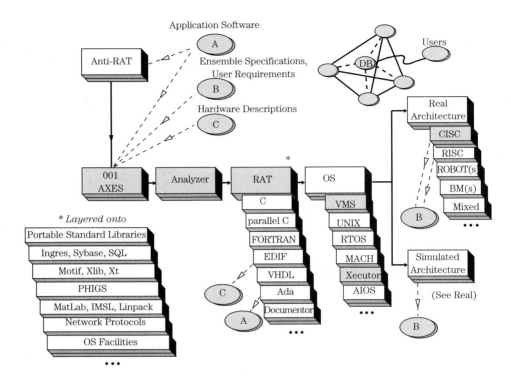

Fig. 20.10 Development before the Fact environment.

integrate methods that are not a functionally natural fit. These approaches still suffered from "after the fact" development. "After the fact" development is often redundant where reuse is abandoned for most of the life cycle. Productivity gains over traditional approaches can be significant with a before the fact paradigm since reuse is inherent.

The paradigm shift occurs once a designer realizes that many of the things that he used before are no longer needed to design and develop a system. For example, with one formal semantic language to define and integrate all aspects of a system, diverse modeling languages (and methodologies for using them), each of which defines only part of a system, are no longer a necessary part of the process. There is no longer a need to go to great lengths to reconcile multiple techniques with semantics that interfere with each other and then not be able to automatically produce complete production-ready systems.

Techniques for bridging the gap from one phase of the life cycle to another are no longer needed since this approach is seamless. Techniques for maintaining source code as a separate process are no longer needed, since the source is automatically generated from the requirements specification. Verification (i.e., the process of verifying that the implementation matches the requirements) becomes an obsolete process as well. Techniques for managing paper documents can be replaced by entering requirements and their changes directly into the requirements specification database that supports the requirements, such as generating documentation from them. Testing procedures and tools for finding the majority of errors are no longer needed because those errors no longer exist. Programming can become an art relegated once more to a select few.

With Development before the Fact, all aspects of system design and development are integrated with one systems language and its associated automation. Reuse naturally takes place throughout the life cycle. Functions and types, no matter how complex, can be reused in terms of FMaps and TMaps and their integration. Likewise, objects, instantiations of types, can be reused as OMaps. Scenarios, instantiations of functions, can be reused as EMaps. Environment configurations to diverse languages, operating systems, and database systems can be reused as RAT environments. Because of these properties, a system can be automatically and rapidly developed with high quality and high reliability without a compromise in efficiency, completeness, or production readiness. It can be safely reused to increase even further the productivity of the systems developed with it.

Often, the only way to solve major issues or to survive tough times is through innovation. This can be accomplished by creating new methods or by creating new environments for using new methods. Here, leadership is a key. Generally, innovation leading to preventative methods is superior to innovation leading to curative methods. Methods can be derived from mistakes by turning them into successes. One process is to first recognize problems and then categorize them in terms of how to prevent them in the future. This is followed by the derivation of practical solutions. The process is then repeated by looking for new problem areas and repeating the same scenario.

The Development before the Fact approach was derived from the combination of steps taken to solve the problems of the traditional after the fact approach. The next step is to find the most effective means to introduce this new paradigm to management, systems engineers and software developers. The solution is in the results.

Author Biography

Margaret H. Hamilton is the founder and CEO of Hamilton Technologies, Inc., which markets the 001 CASE tool based on the tenets of the Development before the Fact productivity-enhancing architecture discussed in this paper.

From 1965 to 1976, Hamilton was director of the APOLLO on-board flight software program and director of the software engineering division of The Charles Stark Draper Laboratory at MIT. There she created a theory for defining and developing reliable systems. She then founded and was CEO of Higher Order Software from 1976 to 1984, where the first CASE product in the industry was developed. Its emphasis was to support the development of reliable-software-based systems. She founded HTI in 1986 to create methods and tools for developing cost-effective quality software.

Hamilton has authored numerous articles in the field. She is the 1986 recipient of the Augusta Ada Lovelace Award for Excellence from American Women in Computing.

Works Cited

Boehm, B.W. 1981. *Software engineering economics*. Englewood Cliffs, N.J.: Prentice-Hall.

Hamilton, M. 1986. Zero-defect software: the elusive goal. *IEEE spectrum*. 23 (3): 48-53.

Hamilton, M. and R.Hackler. 1990. 001: A rapid development approach for rapid prototyping based on a system that supports its own life cycle. *IEEE proceedings, first international workshop on rapid system prototyping*. June 4, 1990. Research Triangle Park, North Carolina.

Humphrey, W.S. and W. L. Sweet. 1987. A method for assessing the software engineering capability of contractors. CMU/SEI-87-TR-23, ESD/TR-87-185. Pittsburgh, Pa.: SEI, Carnegie Mellon. September 1987.

Requirements Elicitation and Specification for Computer-Supported Cooperative Work

by David Marca

Introduction

Quality software engineering starts with correct requirements. Over several decades, people have proposed many system requirements elicitation methods and specification languages. Most are designed to help obtain correct requirements and to express them without error. Yet, software engineers still struggle to develop correct system specifications. This point is especially germane to specifications of very large systems (e.g., telephonics), systems that exhibit complex behavior (e.g., concurrent engineering), and systems that rapidly evolve (e.g., collaborative group work).

Part of the difficulty stems from software engineering tradition, where systems analysis methodologies have been used to describe systems from an information flow perspective. This tradition is founded on the often unquestioned assumption that a correct specification based on information and its flow will yield a correct system. While this assumption served the computing industry for many years, people have recently noticed that this assumption is rapidly losing its utility.

Some researchers suggest that an alternate framework is required for augmenting existing requirements-engineering practices to enable more correct specifications of large, complicated, and dynamic systems. The language-action perspective of Winograd and Flores is such an alternate framework. This perspective suggests that correct specifications are developed by analyzing information according to the context within which that information is created, used, archived, and destroyed (as opposed to analyzing just its flow). Recent experience indicates that this perspective is particularly useful during the specification of systems that support groups engaged in cooperative work.

The goal of this chapter is to put forth two ideas. First, at least one alternate framework exists for improving requirements elicitation methods and specification languages. Second, traditional methods and languages can be improved using this alternate framework for the domain of cooperative work. To accomplish this goal, the language-action perspective is used to create a general framework for systems analysis. This framework is then used to improve a system requirements elicitation method and specification language.

As a running example, Structured Analysis And Design Technique (SADT), a well-known systems analysis methodology, is augmented using the language-action perspective. Some of the augmentations are well-known (e.g., rapid prototyping) and some are new (e.g., analyzing commitments and their context). Regardless of the degree to which they are known and practiced, the improvements are presented to demonstrate how requirements elicitation methods and specifications languages can be consistently augmented from a fundamental conceptual framework. This writing is, therefore, a sharing of ideas, insights, and experiences about improving systems analysis.

This research was originally undertaken during the development of the COmmitment Negotiation and TRACking Tool (CONTRACT) system. The chapter includes actual events during that project, and the ideas and insights those events generated for both the users and the systems analysts. These experiences are given to suggest that correct specifications can be developed with users in a timely way, and that those specifications can represent the richness and complexity of the social interactions occurring in a workplace. Portions of the resulting software specification are also presented, with discussion of how the specification aided the work of the people who actually helped develop it.

Traditional Systems Analysis in the Context of Group Work

Systems analysis is a tradition made up of practices and languages for developing system descriptions. Typically, systems analysis practices are the methods for eliciting requirements, and systems analysis languages are the means by which those requirements are expressed. For example, SADT was created for accurately describing systems and their operations (Marca and McGowan 1988; Ross 1977; Ross and Schoman 1977; Stockenberg 1989). Thus, SADT embodies both elicitation methods and a language for systems analysis. SADT elicitation methods include face-to-face interviews and an iterative process for developing and reviewing specifications. The SADT language is made up of simple graphic symbols that have explicit, associated meanings. Together, the SADT graphic language and iterative modeling process form a comprehensive methodology for eliciting and describing system requirements.

Group work is an aspect of human endeavor typified by people who have explicit intentions to collectively create something. For example, several executives could draft a business charter, an engineering team could design a new product, a group of geographically dispersed researchers could coauthor a paper. Software that supports this kind of work is being termed *groupware* (Johansen 1988; Tazelaar 1988), and the general field of study is being called *computer-supported cooperative work* (Greif 1988). The domain of cooperative work is gaining increased attention by both software engineering researchers and practitioners. As a result, there is a growing awareness that group work is very complex and dynamic. Let us now see how systems analysis methodologies such as SADT are traditionally used to elicit the requirements of group work situations and to specify requirements for cooperative workplaces.

To date, some groupware projects have employed traditional systems analysis practices for developing their systems. For example, one project prototyped a software system for maintaining individualized "pots" of information created by people during weekly meetings (Begeman et al. 1986). This system, which was not able to sufficiently reestablish people's work context from meeting to meeting, was developed by studying people from behind one-way mirrors. From this and other similar experiences (Grudin 1988; Zuboff 1984), one might say that the computing industry as a whole may be unaware that traditional systems analysis practices might be inadequate for developing effective software for groups. To explain why this might be so, let us first look at current requirements elicitation practices to see how they strongly influence what appears in the software specification.

Traditional requirements elicitation in the context of group work

Software requirements are specified in part from the assumptions made about how people intend to use that software to accomplish their work. That is, assumptions influence the content of a requirements specification. For example, during the practice of systems analysis, software engineers rely on their assumptions about the way they expect people to use the future system. They call upon these assumptions while they elicit and interpret requirements and while they write the specification. These assumptions also carry over directly into the software design. How people create these assumptions for themselves is the pivotal issue with regard to eliciting correct requirements.

Some insight into this issue can be gained by reviewing the everyday practice of systems analysis. Traditionally, systems analysts study people working at their individual desks, offices, or places of work. The assumptions made from this detached kind of systems analysis are effective for designing software for the desktop, that is, for the individual (Tang 1991). Historically, this software has been very effective for addressing problems of a computational nature (e.g., spreadsheets). Unfortunately, those same assumptions do not necessarily transfer to groups because group work is about human interaction, and ordinary assumptions about the work of individuals fail to map to the complex social situations that arise when groups of people work in a cooperative manner (Grudin 1988).

To see why this happens, let us investigate a group who attempted to develop an electronic meeting-scheduling system. In one organization, managers keep their work schedules in on-line calendars because they have direct secretarial support. However, potential meeting participants rarely keep their work schedules in on-line calendars because their secretarial support is minimal. Automatic meeting scheduling, seen as beneficial by the managers, is seen as a burden by potential meeting participants because they have to do extra work to maintain their calendars while receiving no perceived benefit from that work. This system was actually built but never used! The specification for the tool was correct with regard to information management, but this had little value because everyone in the organization did not consider the final system to be usable (Grudin 1988). That is, the specification did not consider the way the system had to be used by all concerned parties.

This experience suggests that present-day systems analysis practices might be inadequate for gaining an appropriate understanding of group interaction. For example, traditional systems analysis practices such as interviewing give the systems analyst a certain kind of knowledge about the system—knowledge based on individual perspectives. On the one hand, such knowledge is valid, and the perspective of each person in a group is an important part of a full understanding of a system (Marca and McGowan 1988; Ross and Schoman 1977). On the other hand, individual perspectives alone are insufficient for completely describing what is required to support the group's interaction (Bullen and Bennett 1990; Winograd and Flores 1986). The research to date has identified three basic inadequacies in traditional requirements elicitation practices.

First, traditional systems analysis emphasizes studying users from afar. For example, the SADT process helps a systems analyst elicit requirements from users through face-to-face interviews, typically conducted away from the actual place of work. The SADT process also advocates iterative review of documented requirements by users (Ross and Schoman 1977). One could say that these practices tend to distance systems analysts from the actual system. For example, the closest one typically gets to the actual work being done by people is to observe the system in operation by walking through the work site. In addition, one-on-one interviews encourage people to talk about their work, as opposed to actually doing the work in front of, or with, the systems analyst (Bodker et al. 1988; Ehn 1988). Such practices lead to a detached analysis of the system.

Second, traditional interviewing techniques emphasize questioning individuals on how they do their particular job or work tasks. For example, systems analysts often remove a person from their work site and then ask them to explain the way they work. The nature of this questioning style makes it difficult to discover how the work of one person actually affects the work of others, and vice versa (i.e., the human interaction aspects of the work). This is because the person being interviewed has an individual perspective of his or her work. In addition, interviews conducted apart from the moment-by-moment activities of work allow for the possibility of people literally forgetting what they actually do—hence the facts given to the interviewer could be incomplete or wrong.

Third, traditional systems analysis places an emphasis on defining software requirements in documents often containing graphical diagrams with associated written text. To obtain "correctness," these documents are typically developed in an iterative fashion (i.e., authoring, then reviewing and then revising). Such specifications and their traditional iterative review process are useful in the very early part of system development because they create a baseline from which to build an initial version of the system (Ross and Schoman 1977). Unfortunately, common practice usually sees these specifications as the only requirements for the system. Traditionally little, if any, software requirements elicitation and validation happens at the actual work site—the place where group interaction, nuances, and "special cases" are directly experienced (Bodker et al. 1988; Ehn 1988; Kyng 1991).

Traditional specification languages in the context of group work

Traditional systems analysis languages are typically made up of graphic symbols and interconnections, each of which represents a system characteristic. Most systems analysis methodologies associate one specific system characteristic to one graphic symbol, thereby requiring the drawing of many different symbols to create a specification. In the case of SADT, a systems analyst describes the activities, information, and physical components of a system using just boxes and arrows. This simplicity is achieved because SADT associates special meaning to the way arrows touch boxes (Ross and Schoman 1977).

To explain, as the upper left quadrant of Fig. 21.1 summarizes, traditional SADT interprets: a box as an activity, an arrow touching the left side of the box as an input, an arrow touching the right side of the box as an output, an arrow touching the top of the box as a control, and an arrow touching the bottom of the box as a mechanism. This notation is an artifact of SADT being a methodology rooted in general systems theory (Marca and McGowan 1988). This fact distinguishes SADT from all other widely-used systems analysis languages (DeMarco 1978; Gane and Sarson 1979; Jackson 1983) that have their origins in software design. As Fig. 21.1 shows, the origin of software design gave other languages fewer fundamental concepts for representing systems.

SADT interprets a single box with the arrows that touch it to be a system transformation, the basic building block of a specification. In addition, SADT not only applies special meaning to the way arrows touch boxes, but it also applies special

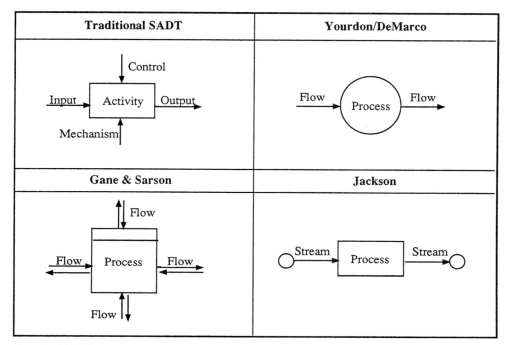

Fig. 21.1 SADT language.

meaning to the way boxes are interconnected by arrows. This gives the SADT graphic language the ability to represent system characteristics such as coordination and feedback (Ross and Schoman 1977). Specifically, traditional SADT represents feedback with two boxes connected by input and output arrows, and coordination with two boxes connected by control arrows.

Figure 21.2 gives three interrelated examples of these SADT representations. Transformation is depicted as a single box representing a manufacturing assembly activity, with arrows representing parts, tools, the blueprint, and the final assembly. Feedback is shown as the assembly activity feeding faulty assemblies into a reclaim activity, which feeds reusable parts back to the assembly activity. Coordination is presented as the assembly activity telling how many parts it needs to an ordering activity, which in turn tells the assembly activity the availability of those parts.

The fact that the SADT language can easily represent transformation, feedback, and coordination allows SADT practitioners to describe a wide variety of systems: computer-aided manufacturing (Bailey and Thornhill 1990; Ramirez 1989), real-time systems (Stockenberg 1989), banking (McDermott and Cottrell 1989), decision support (Ellis 1989), process improvement (Preston 1989), technology planning (Thornhill 1989), software engineering (Freeman 1987; Snodgrass 1989), and enterprise integration (Pyryemybida 1989; Royce and Nolan 1989).

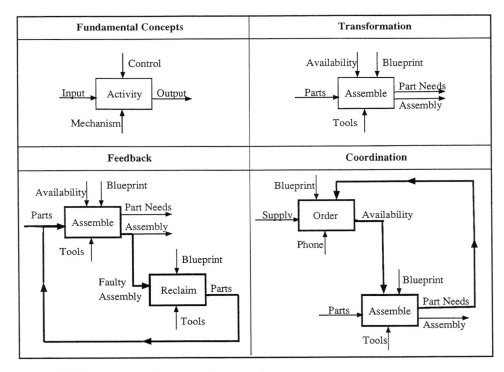

Fig. 21.2 SADT represents major system characteristics.

Coordination and feedback are important to represent with a specification language. These characteristics are often exhibited by automated systems, such as those just mentioned. Furthermore, coordination and feedback are critical aspects of systems dominated by human interaction (Malone 1985). A variety of these interactions can always be observed in the way people cooperate in the workplace. For example, people negotiate their work tasks, they often renegotiate those tasks before the work is complete, and they often give feedback if the results do not meet initial expectations. Thus, a systems analysis language needs to have graphic representations for coordination and feedback before it can be used to describe the ongoing cooperation embodied in a group work situation.

The focus on cooperation is of growing importance to the CSCW field. For example, CSCW researchers have noted that human interaction plays a dominant role in the design of software (Bullen and Bennett 1990). This observation is in contrast to the traditional view that technology is the sole design center for automated systems. It suggests that specification languages have to be able to describe interaction in its fullest sense. Thus, a systems analysis language must be able to describe much more than just coordination and feedback. Additional system characteristics such as goals (Dardenne et al. 1991), intentions (Marca 1991), and roles (Vamos 1991) must also be easy to represent.

These facts suggest that traditional systems analysis languages can only be used to correctly describe a cooperative workplace only after appropriate augmentation. In other words, additional meta-concepts must be added to traditional systems analysis languages before they can have sufficient descriptive power for the domain of cooperative work. For example, imagine augmenting the SADT box-and-arrow language so it can describe people coauthoring documents, coordinating related tasks, providing feedback to each other, or any other collaborative situation in a typical workplace. Descriptions of the work goals, the roles people play, and the intentions behind people's actions would all have to be part of such specifications.

The augmentation just described seems plausible, at least for some systems analysis languages. For example, extensive experience using the SADT methodology indicates that it has suitable descriptive mechanisms in its graphic language and because there is precedent for augmenting SADT to handle other specific application domains (Brackett and McGowan 1977; Schoman 1979; Stockenberg 1989). However, the augmentation cannot be done on the language without considering how the language will be used in practice. As it turns out, the entire practice of systems analysis needs to be reexamined before a systems analysis methodology is augmented so it can describe a cooperative workplace. The next section explains why this has to occur.

A Language-action Framework for Systems Analysis

As stated earlier, systems analysts have traditionally sought to model the information flow of systems. This tradition has been profoundly shaped by software engineering practice, which fundamentally considers "information" as a "thing" that needs to be managed by computers. In line with this tradition is how we currently consider the computer to be a machine for facilitating the exchange of information. This assumption leads us, for example, into seeing mail systems as exchangers of messages across a computer network. Similarly, we often consider the computer to be a machine that manages information and makes computations. This assumption leads us, for example, into seeing database management systems as organizers and providers of information.

As systems analysts, we have all experienced workplaces and have, by tradition, modeled their processes in terms of tasks and information flow. For example, system analysts are currently trained to be able to study a department of people, understand the paper forms they use, document how those forms are passed from person to person, extract the people's information needs by the way those forms are used, and specify appropriate automated support. This kind of systems analysis works well, for example, when an anticipated computer system is being designed to merely replace all or part of the paper flow in an organization. This tradition has led to the development of "well-defined" processes, where the specifications of the process describe paper flow, information processing, and how to use automated systems.

However, as systems analysts, most of us have also experienced the workplace as something more than just paper flow or tasks or procedures. Often, the workplace appears to be very dynamic, where even the most well-defined process has a plastic quality to it. This plasticity refers to the way the process evolves due to the changing circumstances around it (Ehn 1988). This quality is most often attributed to the ability of people to constantly redesign their work. This design comes about because people constantly notice and evaluate the changing conditions that surround their work. Based on these observations and evaluations, the work is redesigned, despite the existence of rules or procedures.

For example, consider a manufacturing process for assembling computers. This cooperative activity is a process that people consider to be quite "fixed." Upon close examination, however, one notices people continually adjust their tasks to suit their personal, ever-changing work context (Marca 1989a). Take, for instance, the situation where a person assembling a computer changes the order of the steps based on his or her knowledge of part availability on the floor for that day. In this case, that person is not strictly following "the process." They are, instead, accomplishing their work goals in the most expedient and efficient way, based on their observations and evaluations of their work setting. So if people are not following a fixed process, what is going on in the workplace?

Conversations in the workplace

In the case of computer manufacturing, people spend a considerable amount of time talking to each other. On closer study, it was discovered that people spend time conversing, mostly to align their organizations and teams in order to accomplish the coordination needed to build a computer (Marca 1989a; Marca et al. 1987; Mudge 1971). For example, computer companies often create "new product groups" to expedite and coordinate the hand-over of hardware prototypes from engineering to manufacturing organizations. Thus, one could say that the role of this group is primarily an orchestrator of conversations between engineering and manufacturing personnel. Therefore, one could describe this group in terms of the conversations it creates and manages. Furthermore, the description has specific meaning within the overall setting of transferring the design of a computer from one major organization to another.

Systems analysts practicing traditional requirements elicitation methods can experience extreme difficulty creating specifications of this kind of work from the perspective that the information is the thing to be studied. This perspective does yield a specification that accurately describes the information artifacts and their flow through organizations. However, the result is not a complete description of group work. A vital part of a group's work is their conversations (Winograd 1987): who they speak with, what they agree upon, and the business reasons surrounding those discussions. Thus, systems analysis practices must also consider the situations within which the information is created, used, and destroyed. In other words, specifications must contain descriptions of the context for the information.

For example, consider how the electronic meeting scheduling system previously described was developed. The people who designed the system focused primarily on the information kept by the on-line calendar tool. They focused on the tool's database, exploited its existence, and created a system that correctly manipulated its information elements. By tradition, this is a perfectly acceptable software engineering practice. This was, however, a primary reason for the system being rejected. To explain, had these people elicited how the information was actually acquired—by secretaries negotiating meeting times with engineers who consulted their appointment books—they might have noticed the user disparity that ultimately caused the system to fail. In other words, their traditional practices blinded them from the vital aspect of the system—the conversations that resulted in scheduled meetings.

In conjunction with traditional requirements elicitation methods, the traditional languages used during requirements specification often lack the representational power to express the situations in which information is created, used, and destroyed. For example, the Entity-Relation-Attribute language (Batra et al. 1990) can be used to describe the information objects of the electronic meeting scheduling system, but it cannot represent how those objects change over time. Similarly, object-oriented design (Booch 1983), with its ability to describe "access methods" for objects, would also have been ineffective because this approach has no meta-concept of "conversation," nor one of its special forms called "negotiation," the absence of which prevents the design of access methods critical to implementing a usable system.

Information in context

These examples illustrate the difficulty typically experienced when using traditional requirements elicitation methods and specification languages for group work situations. The key to solving this dilemma lies in a change in fundamental perspective—to consider the information's context. To explain, systems analysis for the domain of group work can be improved by first considering an alternate framework for understanding how people cooperate. The paradigm put forth by Winograd and Flores (1986) implies focusing first on the conversations people have during their work, and secondly on the information content of those conversations. Let us briefly explore this paradigm to see how it provides a design center from which an alternate framework for systems analysis can be created.

Using the Winograd and Flores paradigm, a systems analyst would have to learn how to identify and analyze conversations. To start acquiring this skill, one can approach the practice of system analysis with the following general question: "How do I fundamentally shift my focus away from 'people just sharing information' and consider instead 'people having conversations'?" By continually asking this question during systems analysis, one can see the results of a group's work being artifacts created from what people said they would do. For example, here are real examples of conversations for redesigning computers that one can imagine happening in a large computer company:

Declaration: The president of a company declares, "We build workstations." This declaration creates a context within which engineers can start designing workstation-class computers.

Assertion: A marketing expert claims "We estimate that people will buy 1000 workstations per week over the next year." This assertion defines the economic viability of workstation redesign projects.

Assertion: A project manager claims "If, in four months, we can implement a redesign that saves $100 per computer, we can spend up to $100,000 to make that change and recover the cost over the product's life." This assertion determines the business value of the redesign effort.

Promise: An engineer says "I will be able to finish estimating the cost of the workstation redesign only by the end of next week." This promise impacts the work of those people relying on that estimate.

Notice how these statements interrelate and build upon each other. In fact, each statement creates a context within which the next statement can be made. In this sense, "context" can be thought of as a business situation and a corresponding rationale within which specific, future work takes place. In other words, each of the statements creates a situation in which other statements can be made. The cascading effect continues from general to specific, thereby setting the context for future action and the creation of artifacts in line with the original declaration. One could therefore say that speaking these statements in some sense creates the action. Hence, Winograd and Flores (1986) give the name "language-action" to this perspective because of the role language plays in group work.

Looking at the workplace from a language-action perspective, one sees "conversation," and not just "information," being fundamental to people's work. The emphasis on conversations brings a systems analyst face-to-face with the human aspects of the work. Group work is thus seen as fundamentally social in nature, where the work is understood by the social interactions (i.e., the conversations) that take place (Ehn 1988; Whiteside and Wixon 1988; Winograd 1987). And so the language-action perspective suggests focusing first on the social interactions in the workplace, and focusing second on information within the context of these interactions. In short, the framework opts for "information in context" instead of "information flow."

"Information in context" can be thought of as an additional, major concept for systems analysis. Upon this concept, improvements to existing requirements elicitation methods and specification languages can be made so that people can distinguish more system characteristics. Armed with the "information in context" concept, an analyst can first study the human aspects of a system as a precursor to studying the technical aspects of that system. The concept is therefore a major augmentation to the practice of systems analysis. The augmentation potentially gives specifications more completeness and richness.

With these insights, formerly missing from the general practice of systems analysis, requirements elicitation methods and specification languages can be augmented for describing workplaces where people carry on a variety of complicated and interconnected conversations. Shifting one's fundamental perspective is a serious step—it requires changing the foundation upon which existing systems analysis practices are based. The potential reward is just as serious: more complete and correct specifications, which can lead to the development of computer systems that support cooperative work in an efficient and effective manner. The next two sections describe what impact a fundamental perspective shift could have on current systems analysis methods and languages.

A New Interpretation for Requirements Elicitation

Given the language-action framework as a foundation, what new requirements elicitation methods are necessary and useful? The language-action framework suggests a focus on the conversations occurring in the workplace. Conversations happen at such a rapid pace, and change so frequently and unpredictably, that traditional elicitation methods, such as interviewing, are not practical. To date, a more useful general practice is to understand the conversations in the workplace by directly experiencing the ongoing work (Bodker et al. 1988; Bullen and Bennett 1990; Ehn 1988; Whiteside and Wixon 1988; Wixon et al. 1990). The intention is to immerse the systems analyst into the ongoing work (Spradley 1980).

Incorporating people's actual work experiences into the elicitation process is a general augmentation approach. The goal is to create elicitation methods that enable systems analysts to correctly understand the totality of human activity that makes up the work. A rich body of anthropological field work (Spradley 1980) can be used to augment elicitation methods. If properly augmented, these methods can enable systems analysts to focus on the immediate, ongoing work. By their practice, they would also provide the opportunity to continually discover detailed social aspects of the work. Experience has shown that such practices can elicit both functional and non-functional requirements, such as usability goals (Marca 1991).

For example, in contrast to the use of "detached" systems analysis methods, some groupware projects choose participatory practices as their standard way of working. Take, for instance, the case where system analysts worked side-by-side with typesetters of a newspaper (Ehn 1988). They did so to first understand how newspapers are typeset, and second, to improve typesetting practices in conjunction with designing the automated system. The result was satisfactory to the typesetting union because the redefinition was done by both the systems analysts and the typesetters. This project invented the practice of "participatory design," opting for learning about typesetting by actually composing newspapers with typesetters.

Let us now explore how traditional requirements elicitation practices might be augmented to acquire an understanding of the social interactions occurring in a specific group. Our sample group is "an expediting team" who oversees computer redesign projects. The computer redesign work is a concurrent engineering activity, whose goal is to reduce the manufacturing costs of that computer (Mudge 1971). To achieve this cost avoidance goal, redesign is done to particular computer parts, and those design changes are introduced somewhere in the computer's lifetime of production. The savings incurred over the remaining life of the computer is the realized return on the investment. An expediting team was "the user" of a software system called CONTRACT (Marca, McKenna, and White 1987). This system was developed to support the expediting team in its management of several ongoing redesign projects.

Understanding the user's work by doing it

The development of the CONTRACT system centered around the expediting team. In order to understand the nuances of, and surrounding, the interaction among people in the computer redesign setting, systems analysts actually worked with the users (see Fig. 21.3, box 1). They learned how to manage a redesign effort and contributed to many project decisions. Being engaged in the actual work gave systems analysts first-hand, direct understanding of that work. Through these experiences they began to understand, for example, how different people may perceive various aspects of a given redesign project differently.

Over time, these experiences enabled systems analysts to form accurate definitions for, and conceptual models of, the human activities critical to computer redesign. In other words, they learned both the social and technical details of the work.

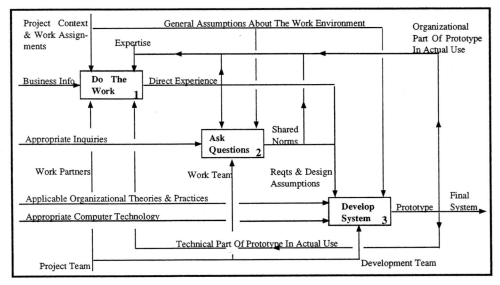

Fig. 21.3 Overview of a requirements elicitation method.

For example, during the CONTRACT project, system analysts worked as part of the expediting team. Each system analyst had a partner who taught them how to oversee cost-effective efforts for redesigning computers. That experience gave the systems analysts a first-hand understanding of the people, the skills, and the conversations required to make a redesign effort successful. This involved understanding how a variety of design experts cooperated with each other. Take, for instance, the need for a redesign to be evaluated from multiple viewpoints: cost, technical feasibility, material availability, and manufacturing process complexity. To perform this evaluation, many different people from all over the company have to concurrently review the redesign and immediately share their findings.

Due to the concurrent engineering nature of computer redesign, people sometimes must resolve conflicting recommendations. It is common, for instance, to discover that the dramatic cost reduction gained by using a lightweight material is offset by the dramatic complexity handling this material adds to the manufacturing process. Such situations call for all parties to be present during the redesign, so that a true cost reduction can be obtained. From a systems analysis perspective, the only way to obtain such facts about a group work event is to experience the event first-hand. As part of the redesign team, analysts became immersed in the work. This immersion gave them access to the work narrative, that is, the moment-by-moment conversations about the work.

Eliciting the requirements for a group cooperating at work becomes easy when analysts participate in the work. Access to the work narrative is achieved during "active" or "complete" participation (Darroch and Silvers 1982; Kockelmans 1967; Spradley 1980). Active participation is when the analyst seeks to do the work, with a goal of learning. Complete participation is when the analyst does the work as an ordinary member of the team. Such participation brings systems analysts close to their users, even though they may initially participate as novices. This closeness tends to have a significant, positive impact on the specification and the process by which the specification is developed. In particular, participation in the work has been found to be superior to intuitions about the work developed from detached observations (Bodker et al. 1988; Ehn 1988).

For example, as the systems analysts actively participated on computer redesign projects, they learned the complexities of the process. Some of this learning was gained during on-the-job discussions with users on how encountered redesign situations could be correctly supported with software. These discussions led to a specification of a concurrent engineering process that correctly handled those specific situations. As the participation level of the systems analysts grew, they were able to hold more sophisticated discussions. During one of these discussions, users explained the profitability criteria for redesign projects—the key management metric. This learning was then used to learn how the business value for a redesign is computed. The result was a simple, general algorithm for computing the monetary payback of any given redesign.

Uncovering group norms and shared work practices

Through active or complete participation, systems analysts create opportunities for people to share their work practices; that is, how they accomplish their tasks. One very informative and detailed look at the work happens when obtaining the group's interpretation of their ongoing work (see Fig. 21.3, box 2). Eliciting this interpretation requires asking questions to the entire team at the same time, during a close-knit endeavor, to uncover their norms and their shared work practices. Such an activity is called "group interviewing" (Ehn 1988; Mumford 1983). A group interviewing session provides both systems analysts and users with an opportunity to better understand the work being done as it actually progresses right before their eyes.

One way to support group interviewing is with a specially designed room. For example, during the CONTRACT project, systems analysts noticed that users often met as a team to do group problem solving of difficult cases. So, group interviewing sessions were held with the entire user team in their meeting room, modified slightly to resemble the one given in Fig. 21.4. This modified room allowed the team to solve redesign problems as a group, and it also allowed people to share with each other how they actually solve those problems. For example, one time the team discussed an alternate type of screw. Its new shape and material composition had to be verified to be superior. The team leader outlined the verification process, and specific people contributed their knowledge about specific parts of the process. In the end, the team had described the work from both individual and team perspectives.

During meetings like the above, SADT diagrams of the process were periodically sketched in front of the group. Sometimes, documents were referred to, or phone calls were made to other people, to clarify or verify detailed facts. During these sessions, senior team members explained a variety of criteria for successful redesign projects (e.g., manufacturing process redesign costs, material cost, part availability, product hardware usability, part rework costs). These explanations heightened each person's work because everyone learned the business issues surrounding redesign projects as well as the managerial techniques for expediting such projects. As it turned out, these issues and techniques were not even commonly known nor understood among all the members of the expediting team—a common occurrence (Ehn 1988; Mumford 1983).

Once the modified meeting room received regular use, the systems analysts on the CONTRACT project realized a significant improvement in their productivity. Specifically, the collaborative authoring sessions substantially compressed the SADT Author/Reader Cycle. Before the room, it took about one day to draw four diagrams, get them reviewed, and revise them based on everyone's comments. This approach typically took one week to develop four or five correct diagrams. The group interview-

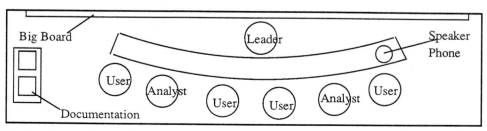

Fig. 21.4 A group interviewing room.

ing room enabled diagrams of the redesign process to be drawn right in front of those actually engaged in the process. Upon seeing the diagram, users immediately commented on the diagram's validity by demonstrating why it was inaccurate or deficient. This led to few misunderstandings. This approach typically took one day to develop four correct diagrams.

This elicitation method is advantageous for three reasons. First, no time is wasted distributing documents that might not be reviewed in a timely manner, which is a very serious problem for many systems analysis efforts (Brackett and McGowan 1977). Second, one avoids the recurring problem during follow-up interviews of users, forgetting what they actually said or wrote during the original review (Weinberg 1982). This reduces the chance of people giving systems analysts incomplete or wrong information. Third, feedback is often given in the form of demonstrations, which greatly reduces the chance for misinterpretation (Ehn 1988). In summary, eliciting the group's interpretation of their work—by asking questions while users are engaged in their work—can shorten the time it takes to develop a correct specification.

Rapid prototyping for validating requirements

The complex and dynamic nature of human interaction puts an extreme demand on the usability of software systems designed to support group work (Zuboff 1984; Whiteside and Wixon 1988; Kyng 1991). This calls for rapid prototyping at the actual work site (see Fig. 21.3, box 3). In this context, "prototyping" is taken to mean that the system, regardless of its current level of capability, be used in actual work situations (Stefik et al. 1987; Whiteside et al. 1988; Tatar et al. 1991). Similarly, "rapid" is taken to mean that the speed at which meaningful system changes are seen by the users is fast by comparison to their work rhythm (Ehn 1988; Kyng 1991). Thus, the art of rapid prototyping hinges on determining what constitutes a "meaningful" change.

For example, an initial specification of the CONTRACT system led to a prototype that was used to manage a few, very simple redesign projects. From the use of this first prototype, many of the initial software requirements for supporting the expediting team were verified by seeing the people actually use the system on a day-by-day basis (Marca, Schwartz, and Casaday 1987). One such use was the recomputation of monetary payback based on renegotiated commitments. After just one day of use, the expediting team noticed the formulas did not work as expected. After a software change during that evening and subsequent use the next day, the formulas operated correctly. Thus, a rapid prototype can make simple the discovery and correction of invalid system requirements by comparing actual versus expected system behavior (Liqui 1989).

Rapid prototypes are also very useful for discovering missing requirements (Purtilo, Larson, and Clark 1991). For example, an early version of the CONTRACT system, which supported very few redesign projects, was implemented with a limited number of information objects and their interrelationships. As each new redesign project was supported by the tool, the number of missing information objects quickly dropped to zero. So by taking the approach of supporting redesign projects of ever-increasing complexity, the value of the CONTRACT system grew incrementally as each new project was supported. This led to adding only small amounts of new functionality to support each new redesign project—a technique commonly known as step-wise system development (Freeman 1987; Jones 1986; Liqui 1989; Mills 1983).

A New Interpretation for Specification Languages

Given the language-action framework, what specification language syntax is necessary and useful? Examine any traditional specification language from the language-action perspective, and you may notice the lack of meta-concepts crucial for representing cooperative work situations. For example, the CONTRACT project used traditional SADT to create models of computer redesign endeavors. From the very first use of the language, it was evident that traditional SADT could not easily represent language-action concepts such as conversation and context. There is no simple way using the meta-concepts of input, output, control and mechanism to directly represent the concept "information in context."

Therefore, to have utility in the domain of cooperative work, the fundamental concepts of the language-action perspective must be used to augment the fundamental syntax of a specification language. Augmentation is needed because the meta-concepts of traditional specification languages easily represent work flow or information flow—resulting in models that reveal a perspective where being precise about the information flow has value. Unfortunately, this kind of precision has limited utility for representing group dynamics as conversations. From the language-action perspective, which sees work as group interaction, specification languages and their resulting models have to describe work as interrelated conversations that occur within a given context.

To see why this may be so, consider the situation where a person is trying to follow a set of work rules, but is unable to do so because the context for that work is inappropriate. Imagine we are following a plan to redesign a specific computer, and halfway through the redesign we discover the computer is not selling as expected. This drop in sales causes the planned savings to fall below acceptable business limits. The original plan can no longer be followed and must be revised! The drop in sales is actually a context that negatively impacts the plan. A specification for supporting this work that fails to accommodate a changing sales context would lead to a system that could not handle the full range of cooperation typical in redesign projects.

Now consider a description of the conversations people have with the contexts in which those conversations take place. Such a description allows a systems analyst to identify a particular work situation and to then see what conversations, actions, and people are required to produce the most effective results. In the example just given, a description of this kind would first identify falling sales as a context. The specification would then tie this context to the conversations for replanning the redesign project. This approach represents (and ties together) the business situations and the corresponding work tasks in a way that creates a description of cooperative work from the language-action perspective.

Augmenting the syntax of a specification language

The first step in augmenting the syntax of a specification language starts by examining its graphic primitives. For example, the syntax of the traditional SADT language is defined to be:

1. Boxes represent activities
2. Arrows that touch the left sides of boxes represent inputs
3. Arrows that touch the right sides of boxes represent outputs
4. Arrows that touch the tops of boxes represent controls
5. Arrows that touch the bottoms of boxes represent mechanisms (Ross 1977).

Thus, as Fig. 21.2 shows, traditional SADT interrelates four arrows, each having a distinct meaning, with a single box. Most unique to this syntax are the way top arrows govern the actions performed by boxes and the way bottom arrows suggest possible implementations of those actions.

The second augmentation step involves changing the meaning of some or all of the graphic symbols of the language. In other words, the goal is to leave the graphic symbols untouched, and to simply change their meaning! It is rare in the computer industry today to find software engineers willing to retain an existing graphic language and simply reinterpret its meaning. (It is far more common to see entirely new graphic languages or symbols be created for new concepts.) Yet this is the true potential for the language-action framework—to reinterpret, as opposed to replace, existing technology. In the case of SADT, this reinterpretation is very plausible, since SADT graphics have been reinterpreted to address other problem domains, such as information systems (Marca and McGowan 1982) and real-time systems (Stockenberg 1989).

For the domain of cooperative work, the reinterpretation takes the fundamental meta-concepts directly from the language-action framework (i.e., action, conversations, contexts, people) and associates them with the SADT graphic symbols. As Fig. 21.5 shows, care was taken to ensure the new meaning given to each specific graphic symbol was done in a manner as consistent as possible with traditional SADT. Thus: boxes represent action; arrows that touch the left and right sides of boxes represent conversations; arrows that touch the tops of boxes represent contexts; and arrows that touch the bottoms of boxes represent people. This syntax results in a simple way to depict the context for conversations and to suggest which groups hold those conversations.

With this syntax, the conversations of a cooperative work situation can be represented. More importantly, higher-level constructs can be formed to represent commonly occurring patterns of conversation. For example, Fig. 21.5 gives two such patterns: "action dialogues" and "establishing context." Action dialogues occur when an existing conversation, created in one context, is reinterpreted in a second context, and thereby generates another conversation. Contexts are established when conversations, created by a particular person or group, become the context within which other conversations are generated. As is demonstrated later in this chapter,

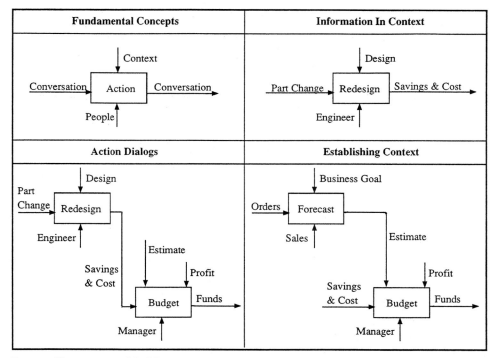

Fig. 21.5 How augmented SADT represents group interaction.

having this kind of representational power is absolutely essential to correctly specifying cooperative work.

Reinterpreting specification models

Since the use of specification languages results in models, how is a model interpreted within the language-action framework? The SADT language is used to draw
diagrams of boxes interconnected by arrows. These diagrams are drawn in such a
way as to describe the cooperative work situation in ever-increasing detail. This is
done through a process where all the details of a particular box are represented by
an entirely different diagram. This method is called hierarchical decomposition or
step-wise refinement (DeMarco 1978; Jackson 1983; Ross 1977). The result is a collection of diagrams that fit together into a hierarchical description that exposes details in a controlled and reliable manner. Such a collection of diagrams is referred to
as a model.

Unlike other systems analysis methodologies, SADT places importance on explicitly defining the characteristics of a model before it is drawn in its entirety. For example, a systems analyst typically defines the following SADT model characteristics:
purpose, viewpoint, boundary, and precision. The purpose defines what questions
will be answered by the model. The viewpoint names the person or group through
which the system is described. The boundary defines the overall system and its en-

vironment. The precision specifies how detailed the model has to be to meet the purpose (Ross and Schoman 1977). Therefore, just like for its language, traditional SADT gives specific meaning to its model characteristics based on the information flow perspective.

Thus, the meaning of each SADT model characteristic also has to be examined and possibly reinterpreted to reflect the shift away from representing work as tasks and information, and towards representing work as conversations and contexts. Interestingly, other problem domains to date have not required a reinterpretation of SADT model characteristics (Marca and McGowan 1982; Stockenberg 1989). This is due to the information flow perspective being fundamental to their analysis. The language-action framework does require reinterpretation of the characteristics of SADT models because the meanings associated with a model's components are dramatically different from the traditional interpretation:

- A Model is developed to describe one or more people working collaboratively, detailing what they say (conversations), what they do (actions), and the situations (contexts) within which work conversations occur. For example, the CONTRACT project created a model of computer redesign as a concurrent engineering endeavor.

- The Purpose is a set of questions about conversations, actions and their contexts. A question has the general form, "Given a particular context, what now will people say and do?" Answers to these questions provide the understanding needed to design the system. For example, the CONTRACT computer redesign model can answer the question, "Given a drop in sales for a particular computer, what conversations are re-examined or initiated?"

- The Precision defines the level of granularity for conversations, below which no additional value is gained. For example, the precision of the CONTRACT computer redesign model is "all conversations and contexts necessary to redesign a computer and to determine the cost-effectiveness of that redesign."

- The Viewpoint defines the person, group, role, etc., from which all conversations are interpreted. Describing the workplace from a single viewpoint keeps the interpretation consistent, and thus consistent answers to the question set are obtained. For example, the viewpoint of the CONTRACT computer redesign model is the expediting team that oversees redesign projects.

- The Boundary defines the range over which the conversations and the actions take place. Since conversations take place between people, the Boundary marks the "organizational interface" (Malone 1985) between groups. The boundary is thus useful for specifying how the resulting system will fit into the workplace. For example, the boundary of the CONTRACT computer redesign model is the team that expedites redesign efforts.

Figure 21.6 contrasts the new interpretative framework for SADT models against its traditional interpretation. Notice how the meanings for both language and model characteristics are consistently taken from the fundamental concepts of the language-action framework. Notice too how these meanings are carefully chosen, so as

SADT Model Characteristics	Semantics From An Interpretive Framework Of:	
	Information Flow	**Information In Context**
Content	Tasks and information.	People's work context, conversations and actions.
Purpose	Find out how the system generates outputs given certain inputs.	Find out what people say and do in a particular work context.
Precision	How detailed tasks and information have to be.	How detailed conversations have to be.
Boundary	System Interface.	Organizational Interface.

Fig. 21.6 Two interpretations of SADT model characteristics.

to create a complete and coherent framework. This augmentation is possible for three reasons: first, SADT is a methodology designed to represent complex subjects with very simple syntax; second, SADT applies carefully chosen meanings to the syntax of its language and to the characteristics of its models; and, third, those meanings are open to reinterpretation. If a specification language can claim all three of these properties, it too can be augmented to represent cooperative work from the language-action perspective.

A Specification Architecture for Describing Coordination

The framework for systems analysis, the requirements elicitation methods, and the reinterpretation of a specification language and its models, together form a methodology for specifying cooperative work. In the case of our running example, the earlier sections augment traditional SADT into a systems analysis methodology appropriate for describing cooperation and coordination. Based on just the theory, it seems plausible that augmented SADT can be used on actual systems analysis project whose goal is to develop specifications of group work. For example, imagine using augmented SADT to specify the iterative authoring and reviewing of a single computer redesign drawing.

In practice, however, the complexities of cooperative work situations scale up quickly and change rapidly, especially when the work involves many people and artifacts. In contrast to the previous example, imagine using augmented SADT to specify how dozens of people concurrently author and review numerous interrelated computer redesign drawings. Doing systems analysis under these circumstances requires the specification of cooperative work to be developed in small, easy-to-maintain sections. When confronted with similar circumstances, other engineering disciplines create architectures that define the sections of the specification, how to independently develop each section, and how to connect sections together in meaningful ways (Rubenstein 1975).

Interestingly, current CSCW theory lacks a specification architecture appropriate for describing large-scale cooperative work situations. To better understand why, and what kind of, specification architectures are appropriate for computer supported cooperative work, let us investigate one aspect of cooperative work, commitment negotiation, as well as some systems developed specifically to support this human activity. These systems are commonly called "coordination programs" because they coordinate the actions of people by managing the commitments behind those actions. Fundamental to these systems is the view that "coordination" is a language-based endeavor, centered around how people negotiate their work tasks. As background, a brief history of some past research and prototype systems is also given.

Coordination programs

A coordination program is the generic name currently given to one kind of software tool for supporting cooperative group activity (Winograd and Flores 1986). From a software engineering perspective, coordination programs are distinguished from traditional software applications in that they contain embedded protocols that describe how a group cooperates (Winograd and Flores 1986; Marca 1989). One can think of these protocols as performing two basic functions. First, they contain logic for manipulating the informational content of conversations. Second, they contain logic for guiding people through the steps that control how that information is manipulated. Many have studied the role and utility of embedded protocols of cooperation (Cohen 1980; Smith 1980).

The coordination programs built to date differ dramatically in the way they choose to implement embedded protocols. For example, early coordination programs like Monster (Holt and Cashman 1981) and XCP (Sluzier and Cashman 1984) took the approach of specifying group work as a set of procedural rules. These rules defined the sequential work tasks and the information that interrelates those tasks. The coupling-cohesion rules of structured design (Meyers 1978) tell us that sequentially-based designs are often hard to modify. Not surprisingly, many rule-based specifications were found to be somewhat limited in the kinds of group work situations they can describe (Marca, Schwartz, and Casaday 1987).

To explain, people using this approach found it difficult to specify rules without also considering their execution sequence. Take, for instance, a specification of a process for reviewing computer redesigns that describes a materials expert annotating the design with comments before a manufacturing expert reviews the design. Describing the review task of the manufacturing expert would have to include reading, evaluating, and sometimes ignoring the comments of the materials expert. Sequencing the two tasks in this way adds complexity to the specification. Now consider the case where the manufacturing expert reviews the design before the materials expert. The original sequencing does not allow for this situation, and unnecessarily limits how people work.

Experience to date indicates sequential specifications of cooperative work are difficult to quickly and reliably modify when the work process changes (von Martial 1990). This is especially true when process changes are frequent and unpredictable (Kraut, Dumais, and Koch 1989). Therefore, other researchers attempt to specify coordination by writing rules that define work tasks that are independent of time (Bowers 1988; Lai and Malone 1988). The advantage of this approach is that task sequencing is decided by the group as they are using the system to do their work. This allows the group to always be in a position to readjust the sequencing of their work tasks to suit the current situation.

For example, consider a computer redesign being reviewed concurrently by both material and manufacturing experts. The task of evaluating a computer redesign from the viewpoint of handling materials can now be specified independently from the tasks of reviewing the design from a manufacturing process viewpoint. Coordination programs like COSMOS (Bowers 1988) adopt this approach, and use a declarative specification language to define "timeless" work tasks. The advantage of such coordination programs is their flexibility to adjust to changing work situations (i.e., context changes) and their ability to support those situations on a team-wide or personal level.

Another approach is based on the concept that considers conversation being common to all work (Winograd 1986). This approach utilizes the language-action perspective previously described. Coordination programs developed from this perspective concentrate first on defining the commitments people make to each other, and second on defining how those commitments are negotiated. These systems consider commitments to be a general class of information, with negotiation being a method that operates on that information class. Two well-known coordination programs have been designed using this approach: CHAOS (DeCindio, DeMichelis, and Simone 1986), which emphasizes elaborate negotiation protocols, and The Coordinator (Flores and Ludlow 1981), which processes mail messages according to a fixed negotiation protocol.

Two shortcomings exist in all of the aforementioned theories and systems for supporting large-scale cooperative work endeavors. The first shortcoming is the lack of a scalable requirements specification methodology augmented using the language-action perspective. A scalable methodology is one that has proven its effectiveness for specifying systems of any size and complexity (Brackett and McGowan 1977).

Augmentation using the language-action perspective (Winograd and Flores 1986) means embedding its fundamental concepts directly into the specification language, thereby increasing the likelihood that any cooperative work situation can be described. The CONTRACT project addressed this first shortcoming by augmenting the traditional elicitation methods and specification language of SADT.

A specification architecture

The second shortcoming is the lack of an architecture that would increase the likelihood of developing a flexible and maintainable specification. Such an architecture would have to identify, separate, and encapsulate the major elements of a cooperative work endeavor, as well as the coordination support provided by the program (Marca, Schwartz, and Casaday 1987). From the language-action perspective, these elements would be the conversations and their associated contexts, the information embodied in the conversations, and how conversational information is maintained. The architecture would, therefore, not only separate the concepts of context, conversation, and negotiation, but it would relate these concepts to each other in a meaningful way, thus providing requirements traceability.

Such an architecture can be created using the established software engineering approach of developing multiple, interconnected models (Booch 1983; Marca 1989a;

Ross and Schoman 1977; Stockenburg 1989). The "multiple models" approach first recommends developing a set of small models, where each model focuses on just one aspect of the system. The approach then recommends connecting each model in some meaningful way to the other models, thereby forming a network that can be traversed in a variety of ways. Applying this approach results in the architecture summarized by Fig. 21.7, which encapsulates the major elements of coordination into three corresponding and interlinked models: the Cooperation Model, the Conversation Model, and the Negotiation Model.

In this architecture, the Cooperation Model describes the conversations of a team and the contexts in which those conversations occur. This model links the surrounding business enterprise to the team's conversations and actions. The Conversation Model defines the informational content of the conversations. This model links the team's work to appropriate database objects for supporting the details of that work. The Negotiation Model describes the process by which the informational content of the work conversations are maintained through the process of negotiation. This model links database objects with methods appropriate for maintaining their accuracy and integrity.

The utility of a specification architecture depends a great deal on three factors central to issue of producing quality systems analysis artifacts (Weinberg 1982; Freeman 1987). First, the characteristics and content of the models must clearly and unambiguously distinguish the meta-concepts of the problem domain. Second, the story told by each model must be easy to create and understand, and yet at the same time be substantive. Third, each model must be easily insertable and removable, without altering any other model in the network. To achieve these goals, the architecture given in Fig. 21.7 creates a level for each kind of model. Creating distinct levels provides two major benefits to the systems analyst.

First, the levels separate the meta-concepts, thereby constraining what aspect of coordination can be described by a particular model. This keeps each model simple, yet substantive. For example, the Conversation Model describes the informational content for particular commitments without it needing to know the details of how that information is maintained. Those details are completely defined in the Negotiation Model. Similarly, the Cooperation Model specifies the situational context for any particular conversation detailed in the Conversation Model. The Conversation Model

Augmented SADT Model Architecture			
Level	Model	Content	Architectural Intent
1	Cooperation	Contexts And Resulting Conversations	Isolate the conversations and explain why they take place.
2	Conversation	Informational Content Of Conversations	Isolate the informational content of conversations.
3	Negotiation	Negotiation Process	Isolate how conversational information is maintained.

Fig. 21.7 A specification architecture of interconnected models.

is thus separated from the details of the circumstances within which conversations originate and are interpreted.

Second, the levels define a hierarchical connection scheme for linking models together in a way that ensures traceability. This scheme is a predictable interlinking mechanism because it requires a model lower in the architecture to link only to a model immediately higher in the architecture. For example, the negotiation protocol described in the Negotiation Model pertains only to particular objects in the Conversation Model. Therefore, links are made only between the Negotiation Model and the Conversation Model. Similarly, the conversations identified in the Cooperation Model are detailed in the Conversation Model, which means that links are made only between the Cooperation Model and the Conversation Model. This results in a hierarchical model network, where links from Cooperation Models to Negotiation Models never occur.

Specifying Software that Coordinates Human Activity

We have described a process for creating a complete systems analysis methodology for cooperative work using: a language-action framework for systems analysis; methods that elicit requirements contextually; "information in context" concepts embedded within a specification language; and an architecture of specialized, interconnected models. The claim is now made that if a traditional systems analysis methodology is scalable and has language constructs for representing coordination and feedback, it can be augmented to have sufficient elicitation practices and representational power for specifying computer-supported cooperative work.

As evidence for this claim, let us now study how the complete augmented SADT methodology can be used to specify a cooperative workplace and software requirements for supporting that workplace. The particular system we will study is called CONTRACT, which stands for COmmitment Negotiation and TRACking Tool (Marca 1989a). This system helps an expediting team manage the commitments for computer redesign projects. The specification describes the work of the team, the informational content of their work commitments, and a process for negotiating those commitments. Following the augmented SADT methodology, a Cooperation Model, a Conversation Model, and a Negotiation Model are developed. Here are some details about each of these models.

The Cooperation Model

The Cooperation Model is created using the augmented SADT specification language. It occupies Level 1 in the architecture, and describes the business situations for the expediting team and the conversations the team has when a particular business situation arises. To create this model, an analyst works alongside users in order to understand and define the work contexts and their resulting conversations (Marca 1989a). For example, industry standards sets a context within which conversations arise about how a redesign will be implemented. Each context and conversation is worked into the model, thereby evolving it into a generalized description of cooperation for the team.

The resulting model is a network of boxes and arrows, which associates business situations and conversations. An important aspect of the Cooperation Model is its ability to show how particular conversations can, at a later time, become the context for future conversations. For example, read Fig. 21.8 and find where "Problems," one result of "Implementing" a "Part Change," becomes a second context within which future Part Change proposals are made. Here is an example demonstrating the model's ability to describe how particular conversations can become the context for future conversations—a common occurrence in concurrent engineering endeavors such as redesigning computers.

The Cooperation Model for a workplace is a springboard to specifying the software support for that workplace. To start specifying the design, SADT arrows in the Cooperation Model are used to create the information objects in the Conversation Model. These objects are, in turn, linked to the method that defines how they are negotiated. This approach results in a set of integrated models that provide traceability and enable software to be written in a direct manner with little additional translation. To date, while traceability is a concern of large traditional software systems development (Ross 1977; Brackett and McGowan 1977; Freeman 1987; Stockenberg 1989), little has been written about the need to trace a groupware system back to its workplace requirements.

The Cooperation Model's ability to describe a workplace so it can be linked to a software design is seen as a distinct benefit to groupware developers. For example, the specification of the expediting team's view of computer redesign contained contexts such as "Product Volumes," the estimates of how many computers will be sold over a particular period of time. This context became an information object in the CONTRACT database, and it was used to compute the total cost savings for a redesign project. For one project in particular, this computational capability enabled the expediting team to provide facts to their senior management on why that project should not be canceled. This enabled the project to return a cost savings so significant, it more than paid for the entire development of the CONTRACT system.

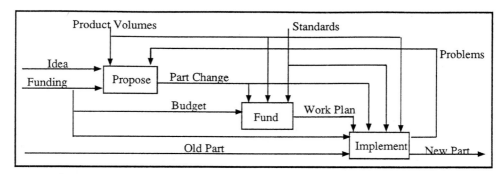

Fig. 21.8 Some contexts and conversations for redesign.

The Conversation Model

The Conversation Model is an Entity-Relation-Attribute model (Batra, Hoffer, and Bostrom 1990), appearing at Level 2 in the architecture. This model defines the informational content of each relevant conversation people have while they work. The model is created by first evaluating each SADT arrow found in the Cooperation Model, and secondly creating conversation types, one type for each relevant conversation. Using standard database design techniques (Booch 1983), these conversation types are then turned into database object definitions. A conversation type can be created from a single SADT arrow, or several SADT arrows can be aggregated to form a single conversation type.

To see how this is done, look at the Conversation Model given in Fig. 21.9, and notice how "Product" and "Part" are two separate conversation types. Two reasons can be found in the Cooperation Model to explain why they are considered distinct. First, Product Volumes are the context within which a Part Change is proposed. Second, Product Volumes are also the context within which Part Changes are implemented. By distinguishing the Product conversation type from the Part conversation type, the Conversation Model allows for those conversations to be managed separately. This ability is crucial, because it enables computations that determine the business value for commitments—a capability missing from every other coordination program to date.

The quality of the Conversation Model is directly correlated to how well the systems analyst employs the SADT concept of "viewpoint" (Sampio and Freeman 1991). The use of viewpoint is a means to obtain clear, consistent requirements. For the Conversation Model, skillful use of viewpoint is essential for producing a useful specification of conversation types. To explain, the model becomes useful only when its conversation types are defined from a single viewpoint. Utility is obtained because the single viewpoint consistently interprets every particular act of speech as a commissive or an assertion. This allows anyone reading the model to consistently interpret one person's promise as another person's assertion.

For example, Product Volumes are promises when seen from the viewpoint of salespeople. These same statements, however, are seen by the expediting team as assertions. The expediting team considers them assertions because they are the context for determining the business value of a Part Change. To explain, Product Volumes are the expected sales for a computer over its lifetime. Thus, they represent the money that can pay back the investment of a redesign project. Therefore, a Part Change is interpreted as a promise (i.e., a commissive) for redesigning a part so it costs less to manufacture. Similarly, Product Volumes are the facts (i.e., the assertions) about the future sales of a particular computer that uses that part.

The concept that some people interpret some conversations as negotiable while they interpret other conversations as facts is a new CSCW concept. The concept of viewpoint is widely used by traditional SADT practitioners (Ross 1977; Ross and Schoman 1977; Marca and McGowan 1988). However, its widespread use by those specifying both traditional and groupware systems lags the SADT community. The utility of this concept, to distinguish the different interpretations people place on conversations, suggests that software engineers as well as CSCW researchers and practitioners might consider using viewpoint when specifying their systems.

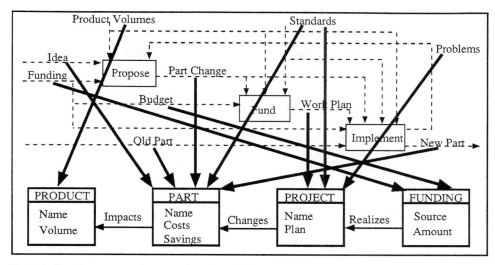

Fig. 21.9 Creating conversation types from description.

The Negotiation Model

The Negotiation Model is created by drawing State-Transition Diagrams (Winograd and Flores 1986). Each diagram defines a protocol (Cohen 1980: Smith 1980) for maintaining the information elements of one conversation type. At Level 3 in the architecture, the Negotiation Model defines methods for object types in the Conversation Model. In general, separate protocols for each conversation type often provide additional system flexibility. For the domain of cooperative work, however, a single protocol might be sufficient—one that implements a "conversation for action" (Searle 1969). This conversation, occurring between a specific "Asker" and a specific "Doer" can be thought of as the way two people talk to each other to accomplish a particular work task.

For example, Fig. 21.10 gives a portion of the CONTRACT protocol that defines a conversation for action. Notice how the specification architecture allows the protocol to be linked to only those conversation types requiring negotiation. For instance, Part conversations are promises, and so they have an attached protocol. In contrast, Product conversations are assertions, and so they have no attached protocol. Here is where the specification architecture provides flexibility. As stated above, a quality Conversation Model, drawn from just one viewpoint, distinguishes promises from assertions. To implement a shift in viewpoint, one need only change the links between diagrams in the Negotiation Model and objects in the Conversation model!

This capability provides several benefits. First, changes to any diagram in the Negotiation Model simultaneously affect all conversation types to which that diagram is linked. This improves the maintainability of the specification. Second, the resulting coordination program can be used by every person engaged in the same cooperative work endeavor—all each person needs to do is state their viewpoint. This makes the software tailorable. Third, a person playing a role cannot inadvertently engage in a conversation to which they are not authorized. This ensures information security. These benefits result from exploiting the principles found in object-oriented programming and applying them to groupware systems (Kyng 1991).

There is an additional advantage to having protocols provide all the logic for maintaining the informational content of conversation types, independent of the rest of the specification. This engineering can be exploited during system implementation—the user interface of the coordination program can be driven from these state-transition diagrams! For example, the CONTRACT system has a spreadsheet interface to its commitment database. Each row of the spreadsheet includes the commitment, the proposed due date, the committed due date, and the actual date of completion. By typing a date in the corresponding column, the user is either requesting, committing, counter-offering, renegotiating, or completing the commitment. Since the protocol knows the commitment's state, it restricts where the user can enter a date by graying and locking out columns.

This capability avoids users from having to understand the actual protocols. Instead, users are provided with a more abstract user interface, which presents protocols by generating automatic displays of state changes and restricting user input. This capability is critical for groupware in general. For example, early coordination programs were not accepted by their users, primarily because people felt that formal speech acts did not match their work terminology (Carasik and Grantham 1988). Users of the CONTRACT system had the same complaint. So the software interface just described was designed to eliminate the need for users to select a speech act before entering data. The CSCW literature to date has no such engineering solution for the problem of mismatches between speech act protocols and people's work terminology.

Interventions in the Work of Users and Systems Analysts

The goal of this chapter was to put forth two ideas; first, at least one alternate framework exists for improving requirements elicitation methods and specification

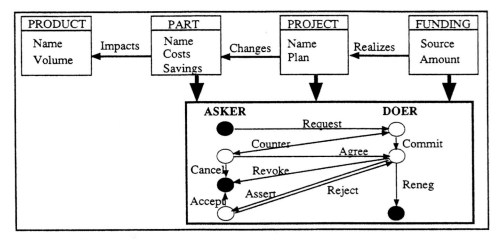

Fig. 21.10 Linking protocol to negotiated conversation types.

languages; second, demonstrating this framework can be used to improve traditional methods and languages for the domain of cooperative work. The chapter introduced the language-action framework, augmented the traditional SADT methodology according to that framework, and specified a coordination program using the augmented methodology. Along the way, some insights into systems analysis were declared, some ways of augmenting elicitation methods and specification languages were put forth, and some actual project experiences were recounted.

As this story unfolded, the examples gave glimpses into how the work of the systems analysts and the work of the expediting team changed in major ways. The systems analysts saw the workplace as a network of conversations, and shifted their focus towards information as it occurred in changing contexts. In addition, they acquired assumptions about the workplace by experiencing it as the users did, and verified those assumptions as the work took place. The expediting team improved their skills as they shared their norms and group practices. In addition, as they began to see their work as conversations, they started focusing on how to better manage those conversations and how to challenge the assumptions behind their work.

From these experiences, one could say that adopting the language-action framework created an alternate perspective from which the practices of both the systems analysts and the expediting team were significantly changed. Adopting this alternate perspective was not only an intervention into the practice of systems analysis, it was an intervention into the workplace as well. Some have said that whenever people practice systems analysis, they intervene in the ongoing work (Zuboff 1984). The effect happens before the first diagram is drawn. It happens when the system analysts and users first meet. From then on, the workplace changes. To close this chapter, let us explore the effect some interventions had on the people involved in the CONTRACT project.

Some effects on workplace practices

One effect on workplace practices was improved learning and teamwork. Users said the joint work on major project problems during the group interviewing sessions gave junior team members more opportunity to learn. The junior people not only contributed to redesign projects, they saw how to identify and resolve the major problems that commonly occurred on projects. By the end of the systems analysis effort, those people who had no prior expediting experience were managing their own projects. The sessions also brought different experts in the company together for group problem solving. Users said having the group interviewing room gave them a consistent place to convene collaborative work.

While the expediting team enjoyed improved learning, the team's leader experienced faster business decisions. Once redesigns became conversations that occurred in changing contexts, users created an ability to compute the business value of a redesign. First, they modeled redesigns as Part Change promises and Product Volume assertions. Then, they multiplied the negotiated savings for Part Changes by the asserted Product Volumes. The resulting profit was then compared against the negotiated cost for the Part Change. The CONTRACT system allowed this computation to occur at any time, thus providing vital decision making data to users within seconds.

The CSCW research cites the need for such capability (Flores and Ludlow 1981; Halasz 1988; Lai and Malone 1988; Winograd 1987). Yet, to date, no other coordination program has demonstrated an ability to compute business value for commitments.

Team leaders also acknowledged that planning remained consistent with business goals. Users defined the business goal for computer redesign as follows: "The savings promised for a Part Change must pay back its redesign costs four-fold." Once users saw Part Changes as promises, the systems analysts helped users distinguish "originally promised" from "newly proposed" dates. Both dates were then added to each promise in the CONTRACT database, and the protocol was modified to properly maintain their values during a negotiation. Once this was done, users queried the database to see which renegotiated Part Changes no longer met the business goal. This capability enabled the expediting team to consistently pass company audits—something users never accomplished before.

Planning also became simpler. Users and systems analysts discovered a point of diminishing returns with regard to the granularity of recorded commitments. Users explained the discovery in this way: "It is not necessary to record that two people will meet to review the funding status of a redesign project. It is critical, however, to record the decisions made in that meeting." Thus, all commitments made during redesign projects were not recorded—only those that affected the redesign itself or its business value. These are: expected product sales, part redesigns, needed funding, and return on investment goal. Despite a strong interest in commitment management, no CSCW research to date has put forth the concept of diminishing returns for recorded commitments.

Another effect was higher quality redesigns. Users defined quality as follows: "Part Changes must work as designed." Once Part Changes were being managed as commitments, the analysts helped users distinguish "when the engineer asserts the redesign is done" from "when the project leader accepts the redesign." Once these states were added to the negotiation protocol, Part Changes could be properly closed. Users said once they saw these states as distinct, they saw the need to define clear acceptance criteria for each redesign. The criteria specified such things as availability, strength, cost, manufacturability, and so on. Clear criteria ultimately resulted in fewer problems when Part Changes were implemented—a trouble spot on prior redesign projects.

Some effects on systems analysis practices

One effect on the practices of systems analysts was a better way of eliciting the group's work requirements. Analysts saw an immediate benefit of doing the work, as it created a social rapport with users. Once this rapport was created, questions about the ongoing work could be asked in a way that did not demean the users' traditions. In addition, group interviewing sessions created shared interpretations of the work. This interviewing style improved team skills even before the first version of the system was coded. As the system was developed, the rapid prototyping approach at the work site enabled immediate validation of system capability. Prototyping scenarios that addressed ever-increasing project complexity was a way to systematically grow system capability.

These practices resulted in better design assumptions. Systems analysts said that directly experiencing the users' work brought them close to their users (Marca 1989). This closeness gave the systems analysts experiences from which to build their assumptions about how computer redesign is achieved. These assumptions were superior to their previous intuitions about designing software to support concurrent engineering endeavors. For example, before the project, systems analysts had an intuition that a commitment had only one date—the due date. As they worked on redesign projects, they saw the value users saw in keeping recording, maintaining, and displaying three dates for the same commitment—the proposed date, the committed date, and the actual date.

Compressed review cycles was another positive effect. The group interviewing sessions held in the special meeting room shortened the traditional SADT Author/Reader Cycle (Ross and Schoman 1977) by a factor of five. This cycle, which advocates draft passing (Tang and Minneman 1991), places users and systems analysts outside the work, thereby permitting inaccurate and lengthy dialogues. Interviewing in the midst of the work permits more accuracy and brevity, because the users' words are always matching the action. With this approach:

1. No time is wasted distributing documents that might not be reviewed in a timely manner

2. The problem of users forgetting their work practices or their comments during follow-up interviews is avoided

3. Inaccurate descriptions about the work are minimized

System analysts also experienced better ways of specifying the requirements of group work. They invented how to augment graphic specification languages for describing the root concepts of information in context. The augmentation then allowed a workplace to be represented as interrelated conversations, where some conversations become the context for others. In addition, systems analysts discovered how conversations act as either assertions or promises, depending on the viewpoint taken by the person. They also saw how a single viewpoint gives a consistent interpretation of the conversations. When promises were distinct from assertions, systems analysts could identify those conversations needing a negotiation protocol. And by separating the protocol from the conversations, protocol changes could be automatically applied across all promises.

During the CONTRACT project, systems analysts gained new insights about coordination programs. They noticed how recording completion criteria for commitments improves people's productivity. They discovered how recording only the essential commitments can simplify project plans. Through the user's eyes, systems analysts saw how a coordination program can compute the business value of a commitment. They also generated ideas and designs for displaying multiple dates that succinctly explain the history of a commitment, converting embedded protocols into methods for information objects, and activating or deactivating those methods depending on the user's viewpoint. Lastly, they discovered how a user interface can abstract away the need for users to understand speech acts.

Closing Remark

The reported effects experienced by both users and systems analysts suggest the language-action framework, and the systems analysis methodologies augmented according to that framework, have merit in the domain of computer-supported cooperative work. In fact, the framework and the augmented methodologies could be considered tools for looking at the social aspects of people's work. One might therefore say the above interventions were positive because people took into account the social aspects of their work before designing the computer support for that work. Whether or not the reported effects came directly from applying the language-action framework is not as significant as the framework's potential for shifting people into noticing the social aspects of their work.

As system analysts, we choose to be either responsible or not responsible for the social aspects of peoples' work and for the interventions our systems analysis practices make in the workplace. Research indicates that computer professionals do not realize that they always make these choices when they build a system, regardless of whether they make the choices consciously or not (Zuboff 1984). When systems are developed without this awareness, the quality of people's work can degrade dramatically. For example, some have experienced a decrease in those social interactions that made their work enjoyable and fulfilling after automation occurred (Zuboff 1984). So, what might be at stake for us as systems analysts is finding ways to combine a responsibility for the social quality of the workplace with our technical expertise.

Acknowledgments

The CONTRACT coordination program was developed within Digital Equipment Corporation by the Intelligent Systems Technology Group, and was usability engineered by the Software Usability Engineering Group. The project was sponsored in part by the Engineering & Technology Group of Computer Systems Manufacturing. The author would like to thank John Bennett, Terry Winograd, and John Whiteside for their extremely valuable review, guidance, and support during earlier writings that led to this paper. Thanks also go to Clement McGowan for his recent technical coaching that added clarity to this work.

The views expressed in this work are those of the author, and do not represent the views of Digital Equipment Corporation.

Author Biography

David Marca is a Principal Software Engineer at Digital Equipment Corporation in Nashua, New Hampshire. Currently, Mr. Marca consults for and trains engineers and managers in the area of Socio-Technical Systems Design. He also designs groupware systems to support the software engineering practices at Digital.

Mr. Marca's career goal is to see software industry practices include: direct experience during systems analysis, user participation during design, and social responsibility during system development and deployment.

Mr. Marca is a member of the Institute of Electrical and Electronic Engineers (IEEE), the Association for Computing Machinery (ACM), and the Computer Professionals for Social Responsibility (CPSR). He is the holder of a United States patent in coordination technology and is the coauthor of a book on Groupware, published by the IEEE in 1991.

Works Cited

Bailey, J. and D. Thornhill. 1990. Product change process: meeting digital's future needs. *Proceedings of the IDEF users group*. April 1990.

Batra, D., J. Hoffer, and R. Bostrom. 1990. Comparing representations with relational and EER models. *Communications of the ACM*. 33 (2).

Begeman, M., P. Cook, C. Ellis, M. Graf, G. Rein, and T. Smith. 1986. Project NICK: Meetings augmentation and analysis. *Proceedings of the 1st conference on computer-supported cooperative work*. December 1986.

Bodker, S., P. Ehn, J. Knudsen, K. Morten, and K. Madsen. 1988. Computer support for cooperative design. *Proceedings of the 2nd conference on computer- supported cooperative work*. September 1988.

Booch, G. 1983. *Software engineering with Ada*. The Benjamin/Cummings Publishing Company.

Bowers, J. 1988. Local and global structuring of computer-mediated communication: developing linguistic perspectives on CSCW in COSMOS. *Proceedings of the 2nd conference on computer-supported cooperative work*. September 1988.

Brackett, J. and C. McGowan. 1977. SADT to large systems problems. SofTech Technical Paper Number TP059. January 1977.

Bullen, C. and J. Bennett. 1990. *Groupware in practice: An interpretation of work experiences*. MIT Center for Information Systems Research.

Carasik, A. and C. Grantham. A case study of computer-supported cooperative work in a dispersed organization. *Proceedings of the conference on human factors in computing*. May 1988.

Cohen, P. 1980. Elements of a plan-based theory of speech acts. *Cognitive science* 3 (3).

Dardenne, A., S. Fickas, and A. Van Lameswerde. 1991. Goal-directed concept acquisition in requirements elicitation. *Proceedings of the 6th international workshop on software specification and design*. October 1991.

Darroch, V. and J. Silvers, ed. 1982. *Interpretive human studies: An introduction to phenomenological research*. University Press of America.

DeCindio, F.,G. DeMichelis, and C. Simone. 1986. CHAOS as a coordination technology. *Proceedings of the 1st conference on computer-supported cooperative work*. December 1986.

DeMarco, T. 1978. *Structured analysis and system specification*. Yourdon Press.

Ehn, P. 1988. *Work-oriented design of computer artifacts*. Almqvist & Wiksell International Publishers.

Ellis, R. 1989. IDEF as a decision support system in a CIM enterprise. *Proceedings of the IDEF users group*. May 1989.

Flores, C.F. and J. Ludlow. 1981. Doing and speaking in the office. In *DSS: Issues and challenges* ed. Fink and Sprague. London: Pergamon Press.

Fisher, G., A. Lemke, T. Mastaglio, and A. Morch. 1991. The role of critiquing in cooperative problem solving. *ACM transactions on information systems*. 9 (3).

Freeman, P. 1987. *Software perspectives: The system is the message*. Addison-Wesley Publishing Company.

Gane, C. and T. Sarson. 1979. *Structured systems analysis*. Prentice Hall.

Greif, I. 1988. *Computer-supported cooperative work: A book of readings*. Morgan Kaufmann Publishers.

Grudin, J. 1988. Why CSCW applications fail: Problems in the design and evaluation of organizational interfaces. *Proceedings of the 2nd conference on computer-supported cooperative work*. September 1988.

Halasz, F. 1988. Reflections on notecards: Seven issues for the next generation of hypermedia systems. *Communications of the ACM*. 31 (7).

Holt, A. and Cashman, P. 1981. Designing systems to support cooperative work. *Proceedings of the 5th international conference on computer software and applications*. November 1981.

Jackson, M. 1983. *Systems development*. Prentice Hall International.

Johansen, R. 1987. User approaches to computer-supported teams. Symposium on technological support for work group collaboration. Paper number P-143. July 1987.

Johansen, R. 1988. *Groupware: Computer support for business teams*. The Free Press.

Jones, C. 1986. *Programming productivity*. McGraw-Hill Book Company.

Joyce, R. and M. Nolan. 1989. Interactive knowledge acquisition for tomorrow's enterprise. *Proceedings of the IDEF users group*. May 1989.

Kockelmans, J., ed. 1967. *Phenomenology: The philosophy of Edmund Husserl and its interpretation*. Anchor Books, Doubleday Press.

Kraut, R., S. Dumais, and S. Koch. 1989. Computerization, productivity, and quality of work life. *Communications of the ACM*. 32 (2).

Kyng, M. 1991. Designing for cooperation: Cooperating in design. *Communications of the ACM*. 34 (12).

Lai, K. and T. Malone. 1988. Object lens: A spreadsheet for cooperative work. *ACM transactions on information systems*. October 1988.

Liang, L., S. Chanson, and G. Neufeld. 1990. Process groups and group communication. *IEEE computer*. 23 (2).

Luqui. 1989. Software evolution through rapid prototyping. *IEEE computer*. 22 (5).

Malone, T. 1985. Designing organizational interfaces. *Proceedings of the conference on computers and human interaction*. April 1985.

Marca, D. 1989. Experiences in building usable meeting support software. *Proceedings 1st groupware technology workshop*. August 1989.

Marca, D. 1989a. Coordinators: Guidelines for groupware developers. *Proceedings of the 5th international workshop on software specification and design*. May 1989.

Marca, D. 1991. Specifying groupware requirements using direct experience. *Proceedings of the 6th international workshop on software specification and design*. October 1991.

Marca, D. and P. Cashman. 1985. Towards specifying procedural aspects of cooperative work. *Proceedings of the 3rd international workshop on software specification and design*. August 1985.

Marca, D. and C. McGowan. 1982. Static and dynamic data modeling for information design. *Proceedings of the 6th international conference on software engineering*. September 1982.

Marca, D. and C. McGowan. 1988. *SADT: Structured analysis and design technique*. McGraw-Hill Book Company.

Marca, D., N. McKenna, and S. White. 1987. Computer-aided support for coordination technology. *Proceedings of the 1st workshop on computer-aided software engineering*. May 1987.

Marca, D., S. Schwartz, and G. Casaday. A specification method for coordinated work. *Proceedings of the 4th international workshop on software specification and design*. April 1987.

McDermott, J. and R. Cottrell. Application of IDEF to banking. *Proceedings of the IDEF users group*. October 1989.

Meyers, G. 1978. *Structured design*. Addison-Wesley Publishing Company.

Mills, H. 1983. *Software productivity*. Scott, Foresman and Company.

Mudge, A. 1971. *Value engineering: A systematic approach*. Library of Congress Number 70-145618.

Mumford, E. 1983. *Designing human systems*. Manchester Business School.

Packer, M. 1985. Hermeneutic inquiry in the study of human conduct. *American Psychologist*. October 1985.

Preston, R. 1989. Process improvement through IDEF methodology. *Proceedings of the IDEF users group*. May 1989.

Purtilo, J., A. Larson, and J. Clark. 1991. A methodology for prototyping-in-the-large. *Proceedings of the 13th international conference on software engineering.* May 1991.

Pyryemybida, S. 1989. An enterprise description—a case study. *Proceedings of the IDEF users group.* October 1989.

Ramirez, M. 1989. IDEF applications to production systems definition. *Proceedings of the IDEF users group.* May 1989.

Ross, D. 1977. Structured analysis: A language for communicating ideas. *IEEE transactions software engineering.* 3 (1).

Ross, D. and K. Schoman. 1977. Structured analysis for requirements definition. *IEEE transactions on software engineering.* 3 (1).

Rubinstein, M. 1975. *Patterns of problem solving.* Prentice-Hall Incorporated.

Sampio, J. and P. Freeman. 1991. Requirements validation through viewpoint resolution. *IEEE transactions on software engineering,* 17 (12).

Schoman, K. 1979. *SADT and simulation.* SofTech Technical Paper number TP072. May 1979.

Searle, J.R. 1969. *Speech acts.* Cambridge, Ma.: Cambridge University Press.

Sluzier, S. and P. Cashman. 1984. XCP: An experimental tool for managing cooperative activity. Conference on Office Automation. August 1984.

Smith, R. 1980. The contract net protocol: High level communication and control in a distributed problem solver. *IEEE transactions on computers.* C-29 (12).

Snodgrass, B. 1989. Information asset management using IDEF. *Proceedings of the IDEF users group.* May 1989.

Spradley, J. 1980. *Participant observation.* Holt, Rinehart and Winston.

Stefik, M., G. Foster, D. Bobrow, K. Kahn, S. Lanning, and L. Suchman. 1987. Beyond the chalkboard: Computer support for collaboration and problem solving in meetings. *Communications of the ACM.* 30 (1).

Stockenberg, J. 1989. Extending IDEF for modeling and specifying real-time systems. *Proceedings of the IDEF users group.* May 1989.

Tang, J. 1991. Findings from observational studies of collaborative work. *International journal on man-machine studies.* 34 (2).

Tang, J. and S. Minneman. 1991. VideoDraw: A video interface for collaborative drawing. *ACM transactions on information systems.* 9 (3).

Tatar, D., G. Foster, and D. Bobrow. 1991. Design for conversation: Lessons learned from cognoter. *International journal of man-machine studies.* 34 (2).

Tazelaar, J. 1988. In depth: Groupware. *BYTE magazine.* December 1988.

Thornhill, D. 1989. IDEF: A management perspective. *Proceedings of the IDEF users group*. May 1989.

Vamos, T. 1991. Cooperative communication: Computerware and humanware. *Journal of organizational computing*. 1 (1).

von Martial, F. 1990. A conversation model for resolving conflicts among distributed office activities. *Proceedings of the conference on office information systems*. April 1990.

Weinberg, G. 1982. *Rethinking systems analysis and design*. Scott, Foresman and Company.

Whiteside, J., J. Bennett, and K. Holtzblatt. 1988. Usability engineering: Our experience and evolution. In *Handbook of human-computer interaction*. ed. Martin Helander. North Holland.

Whiteside, J. and D. Wixon. 1988. Contextualism as a world view for the reformation of meetings. *Proceedings of the 2nd conference on computer-supported cooperative work*. September 1988.

Winograd, T. 1986. A language/action perspective on the design of cooperative work. *Proceedings of the 1st conference on computer-supported cooperative work*.

Winograd, T. 1987. A language/action perspective on the design of cooperative work. *Journal of human-computer interaction*. Volume 3.

Winograd, T. 1988. Where the action is. *BYTE magazine*. December 1988.

Winograd, T. and F. Flores. 1986. *Computers and cognition*. Norwood, N.J.: Ablex Publishing Company.

Wixon, D., K. Holtzblatt, and S. Knox. 1990. Contextual design: An emergent view of system design. *Proceedings of the conference on human computer interaction*. April 1990.

Zuboff, S. 1984. *In the age of the smart machine*. Basic Books.

22

The Reengineering Life Cycle

by Craig D. Galler and J. Michael Corns

Introduction

Reengineering is rapidly replacing original development as the primary vehicle for keeping up with ever-evolving business requirements. New compiler technologies allow us to salvage both the source code and the existing-system design, making the already prohibitive costs of new development even less attractive.

Reengineering, simply defined, is the renovation or reclamation of existing (legacy) computer systems. The first part of the reengineering process is *reverse engineering*, the recovery of the legacy system design. The next step, logically enough, is *forward engineering*, which applies modern development methodologies to the system using CASE tools. A complete reengineering process applies these techniques to the technical components of the legacy system as well as the business model and the environment the system is meant to support. Typically we use RE to indicate reengineering, which is increasingly appropriate as reengineering embraces other disciplines such as redesign, remodeling, reimplementing, rewriting, etc.

Although new products and methodologies are rapidly being developed to support reengineering, the field is not without its share of problems, the worst of which is exaggerated and unrealistic expectations. Since the idea of reengineering is to save as much of the original investment as possible, management and users are disappointed that the cost of reengineering can be significantly greater than the original investment in the system. This increase over original development costs is still less, however, than the cost of developing the same system today, even with the latest in CASE technology.

Reengineering is not a magical process that gets an existing application system from one environment to another. It has a life cycle that requires planning, design, platform deployment, development, configuration management, and testing, like any new development effort. However, the reengineering life cycle is significantly different from the system development life cycle, in spite of those who believe that because of similarities between the two activities, simply adapting original development methodologies is sufficient to meet the requirements of reengineering. This is not true. Reengineering is the art of taking applications that have been developed in unrestrained surroundings and transferring their functionality into a highly regulated environment.

Another expectation problem is with the reengineering products themselves. Today's products facilitate, but do not automate, reengineering. They can automate structure-flow and data-flow analysis, convert code syntax, restructure source code, provide configuration management, extract data, migrate databases and unit test; but individually they address only small portions of the reengineering challenge.

It is unlikely that there will ever be a single global reengineering product, even within higher level language boundaries. COBOL, as an example, is a programming language with a highly standardized set of rules and constraints. Over the years, however, it has been polluted with platform dependencies introduced by a maze of productivity tools and system software interfaces. To completely and accurately address each of these COBOL varieties with a single off-the-shelf product would be impossible. Therefore, most reengineering products limit their scope in order to better address individual source and target development environments.

In spite of all these difficulties, several successful reengineering projects have been completed using automated tools and methodologies. The common factors in these success stories are a thorough understanding of the reengineering objectives, careful selection of the tools available to help meet these objectives, and assembling a staff capable of properly supporting the effort.

The Plan

Emerging methodologies assist in the identification of what, where, why, and how to go about reengineering a system. They provide guidelines to address the broader ramifications of reengineering large, diverse systems. They also establish a framework for evaluating, clarifying, and implementing the reengineering objectives for existing systems. The methodology is critical to the success or failure of the reengineering effort, so each one proposed should be carefully examined. Is the methodology a complete reengineering guideline, from assessment to production? Is it easily understood and adaptable to your specific objectives? Does it provide adequate intermediate checkpoints for determining the current status of the reengineering project? Finally, does it provide procedures for quick alterations to the approach?

Reengineering methodologies should also provide techniques for assessing the current state of the legacy system, factors for prioritizing the reengineering process, guidelines for identifying and selecting the reengineering and target products sets, and procedures for implementation and testing of the new system. Most importantly, the methodology should fit the reengineering category.

The Objective

To define the reengineering objective, you must first recognize the level of reengineering needed. Do you need to restructure source code, recapture design, migrate hardware platforms, elevate maintenance cultures to those of new development, integrate workstation processing, address new business requirements, or all of the above? One objective of reengineering is clear: *do it only once*. To accomplish this, platform dependencies in existing applications must be isolated to allow for easier adaptation to future technologies.

Reengineering projects fit into four distinct categories:

- Analysis and restructuring
- Maintenance conversions
- Technology rehabilitations
- Process reclamations

Analysis and restructuring efforts provide information about legacy systems that can be used for clean-up, restructuring, and documentation. These efforts are not intended to migrate a legacy system from one environment to another; rather they address specific shortcomings in existing systems. Generally, a full reengineering methodology is not needed for analysis and restructuring, since these efforts are usually part of normal system maintenance.

Maintenance conversions move legacy systems, with very little functional change, into a standard technical environment for maintenance and continued development. Typically they involve the integration of the existing applications into some type of increased programmer-productivity environment, such as CASE, 4GL, or PC development platforms. This type of facelift is an attractive option for aging systems, since the associated costs and risks are relatively low. On the other hand, the benefits are also limited.

Maintenance conversions reduce maintenance and development costs and tend to ease hardware requirements, but because the systems are functionally unchanged, they have very little impact on day-to-day system usage costs. In many cases, maintenance conversions are used as the first phase in a more complete reengineering effort in order to minimize the risk associated with more ambitious reengineering projects.

Technology rehabilitations, like maintenance conversions, elevate the legacy system to a consistent technology. In addition, they change one or more of the technical aspects of the system. The most common technical rehabilitation is updating data access methods. For example, the reengineering process might move the old system from a sequential, indexed, or hierarchical database to a relational database structure. Other common technical upgrades include changes in VDT forms processing, transaction processing, and operational environments. Technology rehabilitations tend to decrease user access by improving information availability. This type of project has a relatively high risk because major upgrades in technology may force changes in the functional behavior of the system.

Process reclamation begins with the independent development of a new business model and environment. In other words, you reengineer the business. The new model is compared to the legacy system to identify segments of the existing system that can be reengineered and reused, replaced with an existing package, merged with other information systems, or completely redeveloped. Process reclamation naturally results in the greatest benefits, since it can significantly improve the systems contribution to the business unit it supports. Process reclamations also provide the greatest economic rewards since they concentrate on improving the efficiency of the business model rather than simply improving the supporting technology.

The Investigation

The first step in the reengineering process is to assess the legacy systems, focusing on business value and technical quality. Business value is measured by how well the system meets business needs, the costs of operating and maintaining the systems, and overall ease-of-use. Technical quality is assessed on the size of the system, technical characteristics, staff knowledge, code quality, and maintenance environments.

Assessments provide a baseline to rate legacy systems relative to their readiness or suitability to reengineering. The best type of assessment is one in which individual users and technical support staff are interviewed by an impartial interviewer. Conducting personal interviews, instead of distributing printed surveys, allows the interviewer to focus answers on the primary issues and place boundaries on interpretations caused by differences in terminology, procedures, or personal biases.

Assessment surveys will not expose any major revelations about existing systems. On the contrary, they tend to validate what is instinctively known about the system. The value of the assessment comes from its forced objectivity, which supports subsequent decisions concerning the disposition of the legacy system. The assessment should be a short process. Its primary purpose is to help decide which systems are suitable for reengineering, and to justify discarding systems that are not. Once the decision to reengineer is made, more in-depth subsystem assessments and technical profiles can take place. Even for a large inventory of systems, there are assessment procedures that can provide this level of analysis in four to eight weeks.

The assessment survey should also provide a common vocabulary to use across the entire inventory of systems. In many cases, different groups supporting or using the system will define their status in terms of their local problems, requirements, or operating processes. Without the global perspective of the system assessment it can be very difficult to reconcile these conflicting views.

Once the systems have been selected for reengineering, based upon the initial survey, the assessment continues with the technical profile. The technical profile should address the program population, ownership, technical characteristics, architectural dependencies, code quality, regression test facilities, configuration management capabilities, data characteristics, productivity tool penetration, and documentation quality. A variety of tools are currently available to assess the quality of the system's existing code, its technical characteristics, and the level of complexity. These tools should be used whenever appropriate since the equivalent manual efforts are subjective and time consuming.

Once the assessments are finished, they can be used to prioritize candidate systems, select reengineering products, assemble the reengineering workbench, and identify the pilot project. The assessment is the foundation of the implementation plan and details reengineering specifications.

The Tools

Many reengineering tools are available to facilitate the various aspects of reengineering, including analysis tools, smart code browsers, and language remodelers. Analysis tools provide information about the application's code quality, process flow, and data flow. These products produce process flow and invocation diagrams and extensive cross-reference reports. The effectiveness of these tools corresponds directly to the amount of analysis that is needed for the reengineering project.

Smart code browsers provide "hypertext" cross-referencing of source code and diagrams, system level views, execution-based flow analysis, and the application documentation. They are most effective in process reclamation and technical rehabilitation projects, where there is greater need for human interfaces to specific technical information.

Language remodelers directly alter application source code and are used for syntax, platform, and even language conversions. They usually provide little analysis information outside of the directly manipulated areas. Consequently, language remodelers are very important in maintenance conversions and technical rehabilitations, both of which attempt to use as much existing code as possible, but are not as important for process reclamations.

Another important product consideration is the targeted maintenance and development environment. If the target environment is a CASE product, it must be able to accept the reengineered applications without jeopardizing the integrity of the CASE environment. Product stability is also important, since the reengineering effort will stress the CASE product to its extremes.

Reengineered applications, originating from outside the regulated development environments, tend to present the CASE tool with unlikely scenarios that expose obscure weaknesses in the CASE tool's capabilities. For this reason, CASE products that can be customized through an open architecture and allow specialized routines or macros to be built into the system are the best choice for reengineering targets.

Other products available to assist the reengineering effort are: automated test-script generators and recording tools for regression testing; configuration management and version-control tools for organizing the files of both the old and new systems; and source code comparison utilities for analyzing programs, data, and test results.

Since there is no single, complete reengineering tool, the reengineering effort will normally collect a variety of tools based on the methods and objectives of the job at hand. These tools must be carefully selected, customized and integrated into a seamless *Reengineering Workbench*.

The Workbench

An automated reengineering project requires a suite of tools to provide assistance in all phases of the effort. The ideal reengineering workbench consists of off-the-shelf reengineering products augmented by custom syntax parsers and a relational repository. Sometimes classified as language remodeler, *syntax parsers* play an important role in the reengineering process by providing a bridge between the original system and existing tools in the workbench. If, for example, variations in COBOL dialects are causing a high failure rate in the off-the-shelf products, a syntax parsing utility can be used as a preprocessor to smooth out syntax variations and reduce the failure rate to a more acceptable level.

The focal point of the reengineering workbench is a relational repository, which helps to integrate the various product sets and recycle data between phases of the project. A central relational repository is useful in every phase of a reengineering project, from assessments through testing, turnover, and documentation. As an example, the relational repository can be used to augment process-flow diagrams produced by a reverse engineering tool. The diagrams demonstrate application processes using naming conventions from program division, section, and paragraph tags. These diagrams might not provide enough information to easily identify a program's functionality.

To provide the level of information needed, several tools can be combined to isolate data-element manipulation from the system level down to the individual program paragraphs and populate the repository with the extracted information. The relational views of data-element information can then be combined with the process-flow diagrams to help define and/or isolate function segments throughout the system. This type of close interaction among the tools in the reengineering workbench is very common, so it is important to select the tools wisely.

The Prototype

During the construction of the reengineering workbench, a portion of the old system should be selected as a pilot project to performance test the workbench and the assumptions around which it was designed. The pilot should be as small as possible, but must be representative of the system and the challenges it represents. A good pilot should consist of not more than 5% of the legacy system, and should be reasonably self-contained to provide easy testing and validation of the process.

Pilot testing helps isolate and remove unanticipated roadblocks from every phase of the reengineering cycle before the entire reengineering staff is committed to the effort. It also provides accurate timing information that can be used in adjusting implementation schedules, manpower loading and costs. Finally, and most importantly, it provides an opportunity to compare the project's final results with the original objectives to ensure compliance.

Unanticipated problems with the reengineering workbench will inevitably surface when it is applied to the actual legacy applications. In fact, the primary function of the pilot project is to identify and correct problems. To correct the problems, management will need to carefully weigh the costs of additional product tuning against increased manual intervention. If, for example, a problem appears in translating some of the source programs, further investigation might reveal that correctly tuning the workbench would require more work than applying the changes to the reengineered programs manually. The decision is simple: you want the most cost-effective solution. It is not important to ensure that the reengineering workbench resolves every syntactical nuance. After all, from the manager's perspective the reengineering workbench is the vehicle, not the objective.

It is not unreasonable to expect to achieve a 90% to 95% level of automation in the reengineering process if the reengineering workbench is properly selected and tuned, the pilot system is an accurate representation of the complete system, and the appropriate technical staff is in place.

The Final Design

The next step in the reengineering life cycle is the development of the reengineering specification. This is done after the reengineering workbench has been deployed and tested, the objectives, methodologies, assessments, tools, and the pilot test is complete. This specification serves two purposes. First, it establishes a vehicle for management approval of the design and approach. Second, it serves as a checkpoint for reengineering technicians to document the modifications to each of the legacy programs in each stage of the project. The reengineering specification should include detailed information on the tools and operational aspects of the reengineering workbench, and documentation on the actual alterations made to the legacy applications.

Source and target files structures should be documented and fully correlated to the data element level. System operational and maintenance environments should be described along with the reengineering considerations made to optimize these environments. Finally, the specification should include step-by-step instructions for all procedures along with checklists and test-scripts setup for the reengineering factory.

The Factory

The results of the reengineering project are measured by the reengineering factory, in which reengineered applications are processed using manual or automated test-script scenarios for unit testing and sign-off. All the effort put into assessments, tool selection, workbench design, pilot tests, and detailed specifications, is focused on making this last step as efficient and seamless as possible. If there are serious problems in this phase, the productivity of the entire project might rapidly deteriorate. The previous steps are all conducted by a small core of key staff members and technicians, but the reengineering factory normally has the additional overhead of much larger staffs including project management, Q/A, testing, version control, and technical standards similar to a new development effort.

The People

It is critical to a successful reengineering effort to have experts in each technical discipline needed by the reengineering effort. Experts are needed for information about the legacy environment, the reengineering process, the reengineering tools, and the target environment. They must be conversant with the various programming styles and products sets in each environment in order to help translate usage patterns, limitations, and alternatives into useful reengineering criteria. The project also requires engineers to construct custom parsing utilities, provide integration expertise for the off-the-shelf products in the reengineering workbench, and support for configuration control and the deployment of the workbench.

Expertise in the various components of the reengineering life cycle is very important in establishing the reengineering criteria. For example, the experts in the original environment need to recognize patterns and identify potential problems in the source programs, and understand their implications. Next, the reengineering experts need to predict how the various reengineering products are going to react to the techniques and patterns used in the source. If the products reject a significant number of source programs, the parsing expert needs to develop methods for broadening the acceptance boundaries. Finally, the target expert needs to analyze the proposed output and determine whether or not it will fulfill the objectives of the project.

The Bottom Line

Although the costs are significantly less than original development, reengineering is by no means easier. Schedules are tighter, program throughput is greater, and minor difficulties can escalate into major crises. Just as in original development, however, the care and effort expended in planning is more than made up by a smooth and efficient production phase.

Before the commitment is even made to the project, the existing system should be analyzed for its reengineering feasibility and the level of reengineering to be achieved should be clearly understood. Next, the reengineering team must organize the tools and staff necessary to implement a sound methodology and carry out the reengineering effort. Most importantly, to avoid reengineering again, the entire development environment and associated cultural values need to be elevated to modern CASE environments.

Qualified consultants, good products and sound methodologies make up only part of a successful effort. The rest comes from a solid commitment from management, the technical staff and the end users to reengineer to the best advantage of the business.

Author Biography

Craig D. Galler is a Reengineering Specialist for Systems Research and Applications Corporation (SRA) in Arlington, Virginia. For the past 17 years, Mr. Galler focused on system engineering products and developed various product sets for both the mainframe and workstation computer environments. For SRA, Mr. Galler is responsible for reengineering project feasibility analysis and product design. His most recent efforts involve the design and adaptation of SRA's Parser for Host Exploration (PHX) product set to reverse engineer several legacy applications and provide automated Function Point analysis using a specialized relational repository. In addition, Mr. Galler participated in the design of two metric-based survey methods for assessing the feasibility of reengineering and downsizing legacy systems to workstation-based environments.

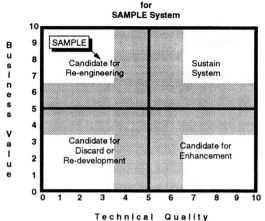

System Qualifier Matrix
for
SAMPLE System

Summary

Business Value 7.6
Technical Quality........2.3

The System Qualifier Matrix graphically illustrates the results of the business value and technical quality assessment of an existing system in this case system SAMPLE. It is completed by taking the average response to the questions in the business value portion of the Reengineering System Qualification Survey (RESQU) and plotting the Y axis. Then, using the average response to the questions in the technical quality/ characteristics portion of the survey we can arrive at the value for the X axis.

As you can see, each quadrant can be interpreted to signify a possible approach with the system surveyed. For example, if the system scores high on business value and low on technical quality, it is a likely candidate for a technical re-habilitation re-engineering approach. Conversely, if the system scores low on business value and high on technical quality, the system should be used as a baseline for major functional enhancements. It is important to realize that this survey is to be used as a rapid assessment vehicle for analyzing the state of an existing application system and to facilitate presenting the results of the analysis in such a way that all levels of individuals associated with the system can easily understand.

You will also notice a shaded area of the System Qualifier Matrix. These shaded areas represents border zones between the quadrants. If the results of the survey on an application system, or any subordinate portion of an application system, positions in any unshaded portion of the System Qualifier Matrix, then the directive for the approach should be clear. If the results position in the shaded areas of the matrix, you may find a combination of approaches may be necessary.

This summary area is used to briefly describe the application system or portion of the application system surveyed.

Fig. 22.1 System qualifier matrix.

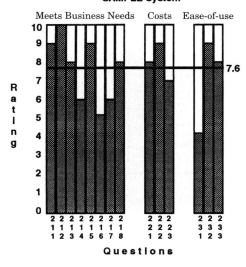

Summary

The Business Value Graphical Summary illustrates the results of the interview for assessing the business value of a system. It is completed by plotting the response to the business value related questions of the Reengineering System Qualification Survey (RESQU). These values are averaged for placement on the Y axis of the System Qualifier Matrix.

Presenting the data in this fashion allows you to quickly focus on areas for further analysis. For example, in answering the questions, the user has indicated a high response to the questions that are oriented towards 'Meets Business Needs' and "Costs' but low responses to questions oriented towards 'Ease-of-Use'. This could indicate that with some system modifications that included additional menus, help screens, or automated documentation, the business value could be raised significantly.

This summary area should be used to describe any patterns and/or any drastic dips or rises in the graphics illustrated above.

Fig. 22.2 Business value graphical summary.

Business Value Survey Results

Meets Business Requirements

2.1.1	Criticality Measure	9.0
2.1.2	Intended Requirements Coverage	10.0
2.1.3	Ratio of System/Job Completeness	8.0
2.1.4	Ability to Meet Future Requirements	6.0
2.1.5	Stability of Business Requirements/Market	9.0
2.1.6	Complexity Factor	5.0 *
2.1.7	Perception of Maintainability	6.0
2.1.8	Auditability/ Accuracy of the System	8.0

Costs

2.2.1	Enhancement Costs	8.0
2.2.2	Operational Maintenance Costs	9.0
2.2.3	Hardware Consumption Costs	7.0

Ease-of Use

2.3.1	Documentation	4.0
2.3.2	System Performance	9.0
2.3.3	Training Requirements	8.0

Summary

The Business Value Survey Results records the actual numeric values given in response to the business value questions of the Reengineering System Qualificationr Survey(RESQU). All responses which are below 5.0 are shaded for highlight.

This summary area should be used to publish any notes relative to the interviewee's comments regarding the rating for any particular question.

Fig. 22.3 Business value survey results.

Technical Quality Graphical Summary
for
SAMPLE System

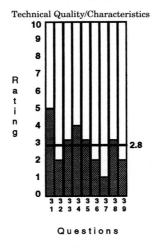

Questions

Summary

The Technical Quality Graphical Summary illustrates the results of the interview for assessing the technical quality of a system. It is completed by plotting the response to each technical quality and characteristics question of Reengineering System Qualification Survey (RESQU). These values are averaged for placement on the X axis the System Qualifier Matrix. Presenting the data in this fashion allows you to quickly focus on areas for further analysis.

This summary area should be used to describe any patterns and/or any drastic dips or rises in the graphics illustrated above.

Fig. 22.4 Technical quality graphical summary.

Technical Quality Survey Results

Technical Quality/ Characteristics

3.1	System Size	5.0
3.2	Technical Characteristics	2.0
3.3	Technical Staff Knowledge	3.0
3.4	Program Code Quality	4.0
3.5	Complexity Factor	3.0
3.6	Configuration Management	2.0
3.7	Regression Test Quality	1.0
3.8	System Testing Potential	3.0
3.9	Transferability of Technical Support	2.0

Summary

The Technical Quality Survey Results records the actual numeric values given in response to the questions in technical quality/characteristics questions of the Reengineering System Qualification Survey (RESQU). All responses which are below 5.0 are shaded for highlight.

This summary area should be used to publish any notes taken relative to the interviewee's comments regarding the rating for any particular question.

Fig. 22.5 Technical quality survey results.

23

Selecting and Integrating a Repository Workbench

by Barry Brown and Lewis Stone

Overview

This chapter provides a set of tools for understanding the value of a repository workbench. A framework is provided that the organization can use to quantitatively assess competitive repository products. A set of guidelines is provided to assist the organization in preparing for a repository implementation and metrics are provided to assist the organization in the important task of measuring the effectiveness of the repository solution.

How This Chapter Can Help Your Organization

As a whole, this chapter provides extremely important information about the value of the repository approach to the organization. Repository selection is a serious step that should be taken based on quantitative evaluation rather than the influence of clever sales tactics. This chapter is designed to help you rate a repository workbench based on a specific set of criteria. Evaluating and comparing repository workbenches in this way can help your organization make a quality selection.

Introduction

According to J. Martin (1989):

> The corporation of the future will be run with a vast mesh of interacting computers and data-based systems. It will be impossible to manage and build the procedures to take advantage of this technology without some form of information engineering, appropriately automated. The encyclopedia, which is the heart of information engineering, will be a vital corporate resource.

Effective Information Resource Management

There are many roads to productivity. The one least traveled, but perhaps most profitable, is the one where software tools are integrated in a manner producing accessible and timely information.

The three keywords here are information, tools, and integration. Information, a buzzword of late, really is the most important asset a company owns. With the proper utilization of it, information becomes a potent competitive force. And in today's very global—and very competitive economy—information might, in fact, be the deciding factor in determining the color of the organization's bottom line.

Understanding that information is a resource to be valued, organizations made a heavy investment in information technology. This investment, to the tune of billions of dollars, included development of new systems as well as the purchase of a variety of software tools.

Software tools are decidedly two-flavored. On the one hand there are the end-user oriented tools that include report writers and 4GLs, and on the other hand, there are the tools that specifically target the development function. These tools run the gamut from compilers to data administration tools. What was common among all of these tools is the decided lack of interconnectiveness—or integration.

Lack of integration is a subtle defect with a powerfully negative impact on the productivity (and competitiveness) of an organization. It translates to the inability of information to be managed in a consistent and non-redundant fashion. Because software tools have seams, information can't flow easily from one tool to another, forcing organizations to either manually move the information between tools—or worse, to create redundant and conflicting information stores.

The industry, recognizing the ramifications of these problems, began to move in the directional of what is often referred to as "development frameworks." IBM's AD/Cycle, DEC's Cohesion, and Unisys' ASD framework are three prime examples. The goal of these frameworks is a pointed orientation towards communications. That is, AD/Cycle or ASD's goal is to provide a boundary-less environment to spur the free flow of information through the use of standards and guidelines for the development of software tools. While development frameworks are most certainly a laudable goal, the major drawback is that, for the most part, these frameworks are only philosophies.

Software vendors began to stake claims to components of the development framework almost immediately. But for the most part, the integration problems persist. The missing component, that which enables a seamless environment, is a repository workbench.

A repository workbench has three functions. It is a repository. It provides tools. And it forms the "connecting glue" of the development framework: in other words, integration.

A short and standard definition of a *repository* is an organized reference to the data content of something. That something could be a system, a database, or a collection of all the files, program's databases, and manual records maintained by a large organization. While the definition of tools should be self-evident, in this context it is not.

Tools in a repository workbench environment encompass a broad spectrum of functionality that goes beyond what is commonly available. The last component of the repository workbench equation is integration. It is this component that meshes the repository and the repository-based tools into an organization's environment. The net sum of the repository equation is the ability to better leverage the skillset of a wide range of the organization's staff—from data administrators to programmers to analysts and to the end-users themselves. And it is this leveraging of skillsets that leads to a dramatic increase in productivity.

The remainder of this chapter assists the reader in three areas: evaluating the benefits of a repository workbench solution, planning for its implementation, and measuring it.

How to Use This Chapter

In upcoming Section I—Evaluating the Repository Workbench, a quantitative approach is taken to assist the reader in understanding the features of a repository workbench and compare these features across competitive products. Twenty-three distinct criteria are divided into three categories—repository, integration, and tools. Each criteria is presented in the form of a set of features. To quantify the assessment, each criteria should be rated in terms of its importance to the organization. A rating, or weight, of 1 to 3 should be used, where

1 = Not important to the organization
2 = Required by the organization
3 = Very important to the organization

Next, each of the features describing the criteria should be rated according to how well the vendor fulfills the requirement. A scale of 1 through 5 should be used, where

1 = Fails
2 = Weak
3 = Adequate
4 = Good
5 = Excellent

After you finish rating all 23 criteria, your scores can be transferred to the charts at the end of this chapter. These charts allow you to add up repository scores and to make overall evaluations and comparisons.

In Section II—Preparing for the Repository Workbench, a series of checklists is provided to assist the reader in deciding whether or not a repository workbench solution is desirable and in developing a plan for repository workbench implementation.

In Section III—Repository Metrics, a series of measurements are provided to assist the reader in determining how well the repository is being utilized.

Section I. Evaluating the Repository Workbench

Selecting a repository workbench is not a simple process. Repository workbench software is quite complex, and the selection process mirrors this complexity. Since a repository workbench offers a composite of functionality, the evaluation team needs to review three discrete levels of functionality: the repository component, the workbench component, and the integrative component. What follows is a set of categories to assist in this process. Each category represents a different level of functionality that a product of this type should have.

Repository. The *repository* is the heart of the repository workbench. It is much more than a data dictionary. It stores information about objects—whether those objects be file definitions or process rules. The following sections itemize the major attributes of a repository. An effective, and robust, repository should meet the objects presented in this section.

Initial data capture

For the most part, objects required to be entered into the repository are objects that already reside in catalogs, files, databases, CASE encyclopedias, or as part of a program (i.e., working storage as well as the procedure division). Scanning enables an organization to quickly populate the repository through the importation of objects from a pre-existing source. Among the facilities that a robust repository product provides are:

Weighting: 1 2 3	Rating
Scan program source - file sections	1 2 3 4 5
Scan program source - working storage sections	1 2 3 4 5
Scan program source - procedure divisions	1 2 3 4 5
Scan copybooks	1 2 3 4 5
Scan multiple copybooks	1 2 3 4 5
Scan database catalogs	1 2 3 4 5
Scan CASE encyclopedias	1 2 3 4 5
Scan databases	1 2 3 4 5
Provide the ability to repopulate the repository as many times as necessary through versioning	1 2 3 4 5
Provide collision resolution	1 2 3 4 5
Multi-level impact analysis	1 2 3 4 5

Tracking

A repository should have the ability to keep detailed information about objects. The repository defines an object as more than the traditional data definition. An object may be a field, a file, a procedure, or a system. Because the repository maintains detailed information about objects, the organization has an excellent opportunity to track the status of many of the formal processes that form the underpinnings of IT. A robust repository should be able to:

Weighting: 1 2 3	Rating
Keep track of jobs	1 2 3 4 5
Keep track of programs	1 2 3 4 5
Document data content of files and databases	1 2 3 4 5
Document data processed by programs, jobs, systems	1 2 3 4 5
Document reports and screens	1 2 3 4 5
Document schedules	1 2 3 4 5

Document backup and retention	1 2 3 4 5
Document maintenance responsibilities	1 2 3 4 5

Source and use

All organizations are different in the policies, methods, and procedures of their IT process. The repository workbench must integrate itself as well as acting as an integrator of these policies, methods, and procedures. The repository workbench must be flexible enough to:

Weighting: 1 2 3	Rating
Support data model	1 2 3 4 5
Support information center usage	1 2 3 4 5
Support application generator	1 2 3 4 5
Support life cycle methodology	1 2 3 4 5
Support distributed processing	1 2 3 4 5
Document communications network	1 2 3 4 5
Maintain hardware inventory	1 2 3 4 5
Support data security planning	1 2 3 4 5
Support forms control	1 2 3 4 5
Support change and problem control	1 2 3 4 5
Support procedures and standards for repository update and maintenance	1 2 3 4 5

User access

In studies on productivity, it has been shown that it's the user interface that has the greatest impact on the usability of the system. For the function of data administration, a flexible user interface is mandatory if the organization is to leverage the resources of skilled professionals. The repository workbench product should offer the following features:

Weighting: 1 2 3	Rating
Mainframe-based:	
Easy to use	1 2 3 4 5
Contextual help facility	1 2 3 4 5
SAA/CUA compliant	1 2 3 4 5
Customizable	1 2 3 4 5
Pull-down menus	1 2 3 4 5
Pop-up windows	1 2 3 4 5
Fast-path commands	1 2 3 4 5
Client/Server based:	
GUI	1 2 3 4 5
Graphical representation of E-R model	1 2 3 4 5
Point and click	1 2 3 4 5
Multiple platforms	1 2 3 4 5
CPI-C	1 2 3 4 5

On-line	1 2 3 4 5
Batch	1 2 3 4 5

Dialog

A robust repository dialog should provide a simple, intuitive means for maintaining and querying information assets as well as accessing tools. Features should include:

Weighting: 1 2 3   Rating

Contextual menus	1 2 3 4 5
Menus rebuilt automatically as tools added	1 2 3 4 5
Self-maintaining	1 2 3 4 5
E-R rule-based data-entry screens	1 2 3 4 5
Project-based menus	1 2 3 4 5
Context-sensitive feedback	1 2 3 4 5
Reusable panels	1 2 3 4 5
Scrollable panels	1 2 3 4 5
Spreadsheet-like displays	1 2 3 4 5
Customize forms	1 2 3 4 5
End-user SQL queries	1 2 3 4 5
Project-defined SQL queries	1 2 3 4 5
Multi-level impact analysis	1 2 3 4 5
Attribute anchoring	1 2 3 4 5
Meaningful labels for DB names	1 2 3 4 5
Multiple text types	1 2 3 4 5

Extensibility

A robust repository workbench is not rigid. It should support growth. This growth should not be limited to merely data definitions. In an object-based environment a repository workbench should have the flexibility to add new sources of information as well as new tools, reports, and procedures. Each of these is defined as an object. Extensibility features should include:

Weighting: 1 2 3   Rating

Dialog assistance	1 2 3 4 5
Automatic rebinding	1 2 3 4 5
Automatic creation of repository table spaces	1 2 3 4 5
(Re)creation of repository indices	1 2 3 4 5
Reorg	1 2 3 4 5
Error handling and correction	1 2 3 4 5
(Re)granting of table privileges	1 2 3 4 5
Integration with repository tools	1 2 3 4 5
Ability to "add-on" in-house tools	1 2 3 4 5
Ability to "add-on" 3rd party tools	1 2 3 4 5
Ease in defining migration rules	1 2 3 4 5

Ease in defining security	1 2 3 4 5
Ease in defining validation rules	1 2 3 4 5
Ease in defining integrity rules	1 2 3 4 5
Ease in defining derivation rules	1 2 3 4 5
Ease in defining domain constraints	1 2 3 4 5

Project control

A repository workbench must provide facilities to automate the enforcement of corporate and project standards and procedures, and control distribution of repository resources. Capabilities should include:

Weighting: 1 2 3   Rating

Project-oriented security requirements	1 2 3 4 5
Clone function for rapid project definition	1 2 3 4 5
Access/update/migrate privileges	1 2 3 4 5
Ability to subset E-R types	1 2 3 4 5
Life cycle phase authorization	1 2 3 4 5
Project parameterization	1 2 3 4 5

Versioning

The repository workbench must provide a comprehensive set of facilities for supporting, monitoring, and auditing the evolution of repository definitions. This feature makes it possible to plan and implement the maintenance procedures that become necessary as systems mature and require modifications. A robust repository workbench provides the following capabilities:

Weighting: 1 2 3   Rating

Use of variation name attribute	1 2 3 4 5
Unlimited number of variations	1 2 3 4 5
Support of revision number attribute	1 2 3 4 5
Ability to perform set-level operations:	
Set-rename	1 2 3 4 5
Set-delete	1 2 3 4 5
Set-copy	1 2 3 4 5
ANSI IRDS support	1 2 3 4 5
Alias support	1 2 3 4 5

Life cycle phase management

Supporting an organization's methodology(s) is an essential role of a repository. A robust repository workbench provides an organization-extensible means for defining the various stages of object evolution. These stages are referred to as *life cycle phases*. Transition rules define the movement of an object from one phase to another. Relationships between entities based upon their respective life cycle phases should be verified to ensure proper migration results. Managing life cycle phases and object migration is a vital function within a repository if it is to control and participate in an organization's development and maintenance methodology. Features should include:

Weighting: 1 2 3	Rating
Customizable controls	1 2 3 4 5
Ability to add or remove life cycle definitions	1 2 3 4 5
Transition rules	1 2 3 4 5
Migration paths	1 2 3 4 5
Relationship-state rules	1 2 3 4 5
Project-controlled life cycle phases	1 2 3 4 5
Versioning within life cycle phase	1 2 3 4 5

Integration. Developmental frameworks like AD/Cycle are philosophies. For the most part, software engineering tools, such as CASE, maintain key positions within this framework but do little to integrate themselves effectively to other tools in other quadrants of the framework—or even other tools within the same quadrant. The objectives in this section, if met by the tool being evaluated, will assure the organization that the repository will be seamlessly *integrated* with repository tools as well as in-house developed and third-party tools.

Architecture

A repository workbench is a unique hybrid of repository, tools and an integrative vehicle. In order to support this three-fold functionality, the underlying architecture of a repository workbench product must provide both openness—and an extensible framework. The organization must be able to easily integrate into—and expand upon framework. The architectural features of a robust architectural framework include:

Weighting: 1 2 3	Rating
Object-based approach	1 2 3 4 5
Extensible	1 2 3 4 5
Easily configurable	1 2 3 4 5
Easily modifiable	1 2 3 4 5
Easy integration	1 2 3 4 5
Underlying meta-meta model	1 2 3 4 5
Vendor supplied meta-model	1 2 3 4 5
Security, backup, and recovery	1 2 3 4 5
Referential integrity	1 2 3 4 5

Standards

The basis of any open framework is the standards upon which it rests. For this framework to integrate fully with an organization's environment, the framework must conform to and support the standards and guidelines that the industry has embraced. Additionally, the repository workbench must provide the organization with the ability to support the standards that it has developed as a part of its policy and procedures. This includes:

Weighting:	1 2 3		Rating
AD/Cycle			1 2 3 4 5
DB2			1 2 3 4 5
IRDS			1 2 3 4 5
QMF			1 2 3 4 5
SAA/CUA			1 2 3 4 5
LU6.2			1 2 3 4 5
DRDA			1 2 3 4 5
CPI-C			1 2 3 4 5
Organizational naming conventions			1 2 3 4 5
Organizational keywords and abbreviations			1 2 3 4 5
Organizational custom rules			1 2 3 4 5

Gateways

The basis of a repository product is information, which is not, however, confined to a single source. A repository product must provide the organization with a series of gateways that allow the organization to export and import information between these information sources (e.g., CASE tools, various databases, and files). Since it is expected that the organization will have multiple requirements for gateways, the most robust of repository workbenches will generically define a gateway bridge that provides a commonalty of approach across diverse products. Features should include:

Weighting:	1 2 3		Rating
Generic bridge architecture			1 2 3 4 5
Bidirectional bridge			1 2 3 4 5
Upload/download facilities			1 2 3 4 5
Check-in/check-out			1 2 3 4 5
Collision resolution			1 2 3 4 5
Impact analysis			1 2 3 4 5
Import/export capabilities			1 2 3 4 5
Bulk population ability			1 2 3 4 5
Repopulate through versioning			1 2 3 4 5
Default rules			1 2 3 4 5
Variable name mapping			1 2 3 4 5
Catalog import			1 2 3 4 5
Source import from multiple catalogs			1 2 3 4 5
Flat file import			1 2 3 4 5
VSAM import			1 2 3 4 5
IMS bridge:			
Store and manage IMS objects			1 2 3 4 5
Generate copybooks, PSBs, DBDs			1 2 3 4 5
Impact analysis across objects			1 2 3 4 5
IMS SQL reporting writing			1 2 3 4 5

CASE bridge

A very specific gateway is the one required by CASE tools. The gateway allows CASE objects to be integrated into the repository with the goal of permitting CASE users to have a more efficient way of controlling, securing, reporting, and distributing specifications captured in their workstations. A robust repository can be thought of as a clearinghouse between workstations and CASE products. The repository workbench should provide management tools that enable the organization to share data resources. This includes:

Weighting: 1 2 3	Rating
Shared model between different tools	1 2 3 4 5
Support change control	1 2 3 4 5
Report on design and analysis	1 2 3 4 5
Upload CASE product encyclopedia:	
Reporting	1 2 3 4 5
Rehearsal	1 2 3 4 5
Extend the definition of CASE objects	1 2 3 4 5
Reusability	1 2 3 4 5

Services

A product is only as good as the service provided by the product vendor. Towards this end the following features should be evaluated:

Weighting: 1 2 3	Rating
Continuous support	1 2 3 4 5
Toll-free hotline	1 2 3 4 5
Timely assistance	1 2 3 4 5
Trial period provided	1 2 3 4 5
Customer references provided	1 2 3 4 5
Support during trial	1 2 3 4 5
Quality of staff	1 2 3 4 5
Maintenance program	1 2 3 4 5
Product improvement schedule	1 2 3 4 5
Responsiveness	1 2 3 4 5
Track record	1 2 3 4 5
Tailored training program	1 2 3 4 5
On-line documentation	1 2 3 4 5
Manuals	1 2 3 4 5
Newsletter	1 2 3 4 5
User groups	1 2 3 4 5

Workbench integration

The repository workbench creates a productive environment where repository information is integrated with an extensible toolset. This approach offers you the flexibility to incorporate both your existing tools and those which you may consider in the future. Tool integration capabilities include:

Weighting: 1 2 3	Rating
Ability to integrate user-defined tools	1 2 3 4 5
Ability to integrate third-party packages	1 2 3 4 5
All tools accessible through on-line dialogue	1 2 3 4 5
Extensible end-user interface	1 2 3 4 5
Well-documented API	1 2 3 4 5
Easy incorporation into menu system	1 2 3 4 5
User security	1 2 3 4 5
Customizable help dialogs and messages	1 2 3 4 5

Tools. A robust repository workbench needs to supply a series of tools that takes advantage both of the repository and its integrative prowess. The features described in this section are those of a robust environment.

Tool development environment

Being able to integrate tools to the workbench is only one side of the coin. The other side is in being provided with the facilities to develop in-house tools. A tool development environment should possess the following capabilities:

Weighting: 1 2 3	Rating
Vendor-supplied shell programs	1 2 3 4 5
Vendor-supplied subroutine libraries	1 2 3 4 5
Comprehensive assistance	1 2 3 4 5
Encapsulation	1 2 3 4 5
In-house tools developed invoked through dialog	1 2 3 4 5
Vendor-supplied tools reusable	1 2 3 4 5

Groupware

Productivity is greatly enhanced when a facility is provided for project teams and users to communicate with each other. This is often referred to as *groupware*. Within a repository environment this can be accomplished through the use of electronic mail. Features available should include:

Weighting: 1 2 3	Rating
Electronic mail available	1 2 3 4 5
Messaging to project members	1 2 3 4 5
Messaging to users	1 2 3 4 5
Batch output messaging	1 2 3 4 5
Edit output and resend	1 2 3 4 5
Reusable method	1 2 3 4 5

Reporting

Various levels of the organization require access to the repository for reporting. On one level, the end users require access to the repository to retrieve information about the type of information available within the organization. On the other hand, data administration staff has a real need to control the transition of information within the repository. Both levels of user access must be supported. Reporting features include:

Weighting: 1 2 3		Rating
QMF reporting interface		1 2 3 4 5
FOCUS reporting interface		1 2 3 4 5
Canned reports should include:		
Repository detail		1 2 3 4 5
Catalog detail		1 2 3 4 5
Repository/catalog comparison		1 2 3 4 5
Table column cross-reference		1 2 3 4 5
Table structure/element cross-reference		1 2 3 4 5
Logical/physical element reference		1 2 3 4 5
Logical entity cross-reference		1 2 3 4 5
Structure circular references		1 2 3 4 5
Catalog statistical and action summary		1 2 3 4 5
Repository/catalog comparison		1 2 3 4 5
Repository content detail		1 2 3 4 5
Catalog content detail		1 2 3 4 5

Impact analysis

In non-repository systems, a large percentage of nonproductive time is spent in determining the impact of change. Analysts and programmers must manually review documentation and program source listings to evaluate the extent of change necessary as well as the length of time it will require to make those changes. This can be a lengthy process. A repository-based system automates this process through the function of impact analysis. Automatic impact analysis deconstructs the repository to determine the level of change required. The impact analysis function should include the following capabilities:

Weighting: 1 2 3		Rating
Multiple level		1 2 3 4 5
Nested impact analysis		1 2 3 4 5
Interactive as well as batch		1 2 3 4 5
Immediate maintenance capabilities		1 2 3 4 5
"Uses" and "where-used" displayed concurrently		1 2 3 4 5

Scripting

Database administrative procedures are extraordinarily complex. The complexity of many of these tasks implies that the staff member involved must have the highest degree of skill and exercise the utmost level of care. In organizations that wish to leverage the skill set of the average user, increase the speed at which a task may be completed, or wish to deploy vast functionality across differing layers of the organization, what is required is the means to decrease the complexity level of the activity and thereby reduce the risk of error. A repository-based scripting facility provides this functionality. Capabilities should include:

Weighting: 1 2 3	Rating
Recursive script development	1 2 3 4 5
Ability to invoke any vendor-supplied tool	1 2 3 4 5
Ability to invoke any vendor-supplied report	1 2 3 4 5
Ability to invoke any vendor-supplied script	1 2 3 4 5
Ability to invoke any in-house tool	1 2 3 4 5
Ability to invoke any in-house report	1 2 3 4 5
Ability to invoke any in-house script	1 2 3 4 5
Batch mode	1 2 3 4 5
Commit points and breakpoints	1 2 3 4 5
Script status feedback	1 2 3 4 5
Parameterized	1 2 3 4 5
Vendor-supplied base start-up scripts	1 2 3 4 5
Cut-and-paste facility	1 2 3 4 5
Invoked by electronic mail	1 2 3 4 5

Forms

Forms provide the ability to establish external layout definitions that serve to present a modified view of the objects within the repository without altering the objects. Though the definition of objects in the repository is not altered, the user view may be modified to afford the greatest expediency in utilization of the repository without having to write code. Features should include:

Weighting: 1 2 3	Rating
Project level modification	1 2 3 4 5
Order of presentation	1 2 3 4 5
Alteration of the prompt label	1 2 3 4 5
Alteration of the annotation	1 2 3 4 5
Modification of display rules	1 2 3 4 5
Modification of item length	1 2 3 4 5
Customization of the default values	1 2 3 4 5
Object-orientation of form	1 2 3 4 5
Maintainable via a method	1 2 3 4 5
Accessible through dialogue menus	1 2 3 4 5
Accessible via scripting	1 2 3 4 5

Generation

Since the repository acts as the central clearinghouse for corporate information resource management, the repository must have the ability to act in concert with definitions used by application-development and end-user tools. To enhance productivity, consistency and security the repository workbench must have the ability to generate syntax. This includes the ability to:

Weighting: 1 2 3	Rating
DDL, DML syntax including:	
Create	1 2 3 4 5
Drop	1 2 3 4 5
Grant	1 2 3 4 5
Revoke	1 2 3 4 5
Bind	1 2 3 4 5
Rebind	1 2 3 4 5
Free	1 2 3 4 5
Generate and execute mode	1 2 3 4 5
Generate and save mode	1 2 3 4 5
Copybook generation	1 2 3 4 5
DBD, PSB for IMS	1 2 3 4 5
DCLGENs	1 2 3 4 5

Managing relational tables

A repository workbench needs to be more than just a repository. Facilities to manage the underlying database should be fully integrated into the toolset. These tools should provide the ability to:

Weighting: 1 2 3	Rating
Unload/reload databases	1 2 3 4 5
Create and drop objects	1 2 3 4 5
Referential integrity support	1 2 3 4 5
Grant and revoke commands	1 2 3 4 5
Bind, rebind and free commands	1 2 3 4 5
Reorg, runstats and copy commands	1 2 3 4 5

Section II. Preparing for the Repository Workbench

Preparing for any software implementation requires careful planning and control. In the case of a repository workbench, where information, systems, and integration factors must be considered, even more care is urged for a successful implementation. A series of checklists is provided for this purpose.

Pre-planning action items

1. Standardize the names, definitions and physical descriptions of data elements used in all programs.

2. Document which data is kept in which files, databases, or schemas.

3. Document which reports and screens are produced by which programs jobs and systems.

4. Document which programs, jobs, and systems access and update which data elements in which files, databases or schemas.

5. Document which modules and subprograms are included in which programs.

6. Document processing schedules, file back-up and retention and responsibilities for program and jobstream maintenance.

Questions to ask for sizing of data collection effort

1. How many systems are there?

2. What is the quality of system documentation?

3. If documentation is inadequate, can the required data be obtained from the original developers or users?

4. How many programs are in each system?

5. How good are the run books and program documentation?

6. Have these been kept up-to-date as changes have been made?

7. Are job control statements kept in a single file or library?

8. Are program source statements kept in a single file or library?

9. Is some sort of source library maintenance system in use?

10. Is library content really kept up-to-date?

11. How many FILEs, DATABASEs, and SCHEMAs are there in each system?

12. How many different record types are there?

13. How many different relational tables are there?

14. Are standard record descriptions used?

15. Are they kept in a central library?

16. Are data element names standardized?

17. Are the names meaningful?

18. Are good definitions available?

19. Is there documentation of coding structures?

20. How well are reports, display screens and input transactions documented?

21. Can the data content be obtained from user manuals?

22. If the information above is not readily available, how will it be obtained? Who will compile it?

23. Who will do the actual work of preparing repository input?

24. How will it be done?

25. Can part of the data be obtained by scanning source programs or copy libraries?

26. Who will review edit lists and resolve naming discrepancies and other problems?

Questions to ask concerning technical and operational issues

1. Will the repository always be running? System initialization must be amended to include this.

2. Will reports be produced automatically on some predetermined schedule? Will they be triggered by specific events, such as the implementation of a new system? Will they be on a run on request basis? Who will initiate the jobs to produce the reports? How will they be distributed? How will special requests be handled?

3. How will repository problems be reported and resolved?

4. Will computer operations think of the repository as a production system?

5. Will procedures for the turnover of new systems or system changes incorporate steps that will ensure that the repository has been correctly updated?

Questions to ask about security

1. Who should be allowed to access what? Can project teams alter data that they think of as their own?

2. Will passwords be controlled and changed from time to time? Will they be changed when employees leave or are discharged?

3. Does repository software provide mechanism to prevent access to repository via means other than the repository software?

Questions to ask concerning redundant and inconsistent data

1. Can you identify all occurrences of the same information?

2. Can you determine which elements are calculated, or derived and how?

3. Will you know the original sources of all elements?

4. Will you know the uses of the elements?

5. Can the repository implementation help to determine whether there are procedures or programs to ensure consistency?

6. Will the repository implementation provide for validation rules and criteria?

7. Does it provide for data consistency and integrity rules?

8. What about procedures to ensure that such rules are actually entered in the repository?

Questions to ask about complexity and interdependence

1. Does the repository help us determine who actually uses the reports or screens?

2. Does it help identify screens and reports that really contain the same information?

3. Does it help identify the tasks and procedures that require use of the information contained in the reports and screens?

4. Will it help improve documentation?

5. Will it decrease complexity by providing reusability?

Section III. Repository Metrics

These criteria measure how well a repository/repository collects, maintains, and retrieves information about data. The objectives of these measures are to offer users cost-effective means of retrieving relevant information and reducing information overload. Five criteria are proposed to evaluate data dictionaries/repositories: relevance, consistency, common use among information systems, degree of automation, and degree of security.

DBA objective metrics

The following criteria measure how well each commercial repository/repository product fulfills the DBA's objectives.

Relevance: this criteria measures the effectiveness of retrieving correct information in response to a request. It is measured by two factors—recall and precision.

$$\text{Recall} = \frac{\text{Number of matching data elements retrieved by a product}}{\text{Maximum number of matches possible}}$$

$$\text{Precision} = \frac{\text{Number of matching data elements retrieved by a product}}{\text{Number of data elements retrieved by a product}}$$

Consistency: this criteria measures the performance of the product in removing redundancies and storing the minimum number of elements from which all other elements can be derived. The result will be what James Martin refers to as a canonical data repository—a minimal and non-redundant representation of data elements in an enterprise.

$$\text{Consistency} = 1 - \frac{\text{Number of elements in the final repository}}{\text{Number of elements in the original data dictionaries}}$$

Common use among different IS: this criteria measures whether the product can be consistently applied to standardize IS in different departments and operations within an IS organization. Current trends toward integrating networks and information systems to build integrated repository-network management environments make it important that repositories handle multiple environments. Deciding which repository to use as the central repository may depend on a repository's flexibility in handling a variety of software and hardware. The common use criteria measures this flexibility:

$$\text{Common Use} = \frac{\text{Number of elements standardized using particular product}}{\text{Number of elements standardized in the organization}}$$

Degree of Automation: an active repository uses substantially less manpower than a passive repository. In response to an inquiry, an active repository can locate the elements and find out who has access to them. The repository then directs the database management system to obtain those data elements. On the other hand, passive data dictionaries have no tie-ins to the operating system and require the user to write programs to gain access to the elements. This criteria measures the extent to which a product makes it easy for a DBA to standardize and store elements.

$$\text{Degree of Automation} = 1 - \frac{\text{Time spent in training and using product}}{\text{Total time available}}$$

Degree of Security: Overall security depends on managing the access controls to the various data elements. Access control limits have to be defined for each user and violations acted upon.

$$\text{Degree of Security} = 1 - \frac{\text{Number of security failures}}{\text{Number of attempts to breach}}$$

Repository workbench metrics

The following metrics measure additional attributes of the repository workbench.

Redundancy: one of the objects of a repository solution is to act as the single source for all information flows. To measure how successful the repository implementation is requires knowledge concerning the number of objects stored in the repository versus the number of objects stored, simultaneously, in different sources.

$$\text{Redundancy} = \frac{\text{Number of redundant objects}}{\text{Total number of objects}}$$

Intuitive Access: one of the most important, but underrated, features of a repository workbench is its user interface. The more intuitive the dialogue, the more the repository workbench will be used. Frequency of use translates into higher productivity. A low rating implies need for tuning, and/or, training.

$$\text{Intuitiveness} = 1 - \frac{\text{Number of users requiring manual}}{\text{Total number of users}}$$

Level of impact analysis: this metric measures both how well the impact analysis function is being utilized.

$$\text{Level of impact analysis} = \frac{\text{Number of levels being accessed}}{\text{Total number of levels in the E-R model}}$$

Integration: this metric determines the progress of the tool integration effort. Since a repository workbench enables complete tool integration, the level of integration implies progress—or lack of it.

$$\text{Integration} = \frac{\text{Number of tools integrated}}{\text{Total number of tools in use}}$$

Scoring the Repository Workbench

The following chart provides a means to conduct a quantitative evaluation of several repository products. To use this chart, simply transfer the scores from each of the rating scales under the 23 criteria. To transfer the score, multiply the rating (1 through 5) by the weighting (1 through 3).

	Product A	Product B
1. Initial data capture		
2. Tracking		
3. Source and use		
4. User access		
5. Dialogue		
6. Extensibility		
7. Project control		
8. Versioning		
9. Life cycle		
10. Architecture		
11. Standards		
12. Gateways		
13. CASE bridges		
14. Services		
15. Workbench integration		
16. Tool development		
17. Groupware		
18. Reporting		
19. Impact analysis		
20. Scripting		
21. Forms		
22. Generation		
23. Table management		

Author Biography

Barry Brown and Lewis Stone are co-founders of BrownStone Solutions, Inc., which has been a leader in relational dictionary products since early 1987. Their emergence onto the scene was, at the time, heralded as a pioneering effort in bringing IBM-repository-compatible, dictionary workbench capabilities to the DB2 administration and development environment.

The derivation of the BrownStone suite of products stems from the diverse Arthur Andersen consulting careers of its two founders. During Stone and Brown's tenure, where both were heavily involved in major DB2 projects, it was noted that time and time again they were required to spend hours in building a framework for the efficient administration of DB2 systems across their diverse client base. Over the years, across industries and applications, Stone and Brown noted that this framework was indeed generic and, if developed into a software workbench, could provide enormous benefits to utilizing the tool. The goal was to develop a highly efficient, high-performance object-oriented, and therefore truly extensible, DB2 workbench or Data Dictionary Solution.

Upon departure from Arthur Andersen, Stone and Brown were able to implement their theories, and their initial product, as consultants for The First Boston Corporation. Calling themselves BrownStone Solutions, Inc., Stone and Brown were able to rigorously test the technical and theoretical underpinnings of their prototypical data dictionary toolset.

Within a six-month time period, Stone and Brown were able to develop the first release of the DataDictionary/Solution (DD/S). It was during this time period that Stone and Brown combined their expert technical knowledge with their practical consulting experience to develop the basis, or philosophy, that is still maintained within the company today.

Lewis Stone obtained his degree from Rensselaer Polytechnic Institute. Barry Brown obtained his degree from Albany State.

Works Cited

Martin, J. 1989. *Information engineering, book I: Introduction.* Englewood Cliffs, N.J.: Prentice Hall.

Martin, J. 1990. *Information engineering, book II: Planning and analysis.* Englewood Cliffs, N.J.: Prentice Hall.

Sankar, C.S. 1991. Evaluation criteria for data dictionaries. *Journal of database administration.* 2 (1).

24

How to Build a Successful Visual Information Access System

by David Friend

Introduction

There are many recent innovations in information technology that significantly affected the way we do business or conduct our lives. At my local grocery store, for example, UPC bar-coded products are laser scanned and the total is electronically charged to my bank account. Colleagues drive to work through a toll booth that senses their car passing through and automatically debits the toll from their account. Automatic teller machines (ATMs) can dispense cash any time of day or night. I can call my travel agent 24 hours a day, 365 days a year and book a flight nearly anywhere in the world.

Most such examples are process or transaction-related applications. They facilitate the efficient expediting of a service or function. In the process, data is collected—data on what I bought, data on how much money I spent, data on how and where I drive, data on my use of cash, how often I fly, how much gas I buy, how quickly I pay my bills, and on and on. Behind the scenes in marketing, manufacturing, and finance departments, all this new data is starting to create a revolution of another sort—the reporting systems of the future are starting to take shape.

The kinds of reports traditionally used in business do not directly reflect what is happening at the point of the ultimate transaction between vendor and customer. Typically they reflect some financial results that are the secondary or tertiary effect of the primary transaction. For example, if I drive up to my local Exxon filling station and decide to splurge on a tank of high-test, my purchase just becomes a small component of the filling station's next order from the distributor, which in turn becomes a very small component of the distributor's next order from the refiner. My buying habits are unknown to the refiner, and therefore he can't tune his marketing to get me to repeat my purchase decision more frequently.

All this new data is a gold mine waiting to be exploited. The old reporting methods won't do it, so a new breed of reporting system is emerging. It's what Microsoft's Bill Gates refers to as "information at your fingertips." It's a new way of thinking about information access and the technologies that are implied.

What Is Visual Information Access?

Figure 24.1 illustrates a Visual Information Access system.

At a very general level, most computer software programs fall into three categories; those used to get data into a database, those used to get data out of a database, and database programs themselves. For the most part, data are collected through automated processes (such as cash registers, production line bar code readers, ATMs, etc.) or through manual data entry programs (transcribed from, say, insurance claims forms, sales orders, purchase orders, etc.). The databases themselves have changed over the years from being largely customized file systems that are part of the application to generalized (mostly relational) databases that are purchased separately from the applications. We'll be focusing on getting data out of the database, and to some extent the database technology itself.

The business of getting data out of a database falls into two general categories; service-related queries (such as accessing your credit card balance), and management reporting.

In recent years, most service-related queries are performed on-line using specialized software which is highly tuned to the specific service. An example would be computerized telephone directory assistance. Management reporting, on the other hand, has basically been done with paper. In fact a class of software called "report

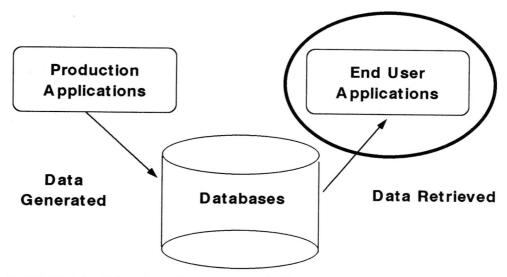

Fig. 24.1 What visual information systems are concerned with.

writers" has evolved to help developers more efficiently produce paper reports. Visual Information Access (VIA) systems are evolving as the on-screen successors to paper-based reporting systems.

The Problem with Paper

The problem with paper-based reporting stems from the automated data collection techniques, which, coupled with the dramatically lower cost of processing such data, has turned paper output into a severe bottleneck. Higher speed printers and more paper will not solve the problem. Over the past five years, the amount of computer-generated paper has increased 14% per year, to a total in 1991 of nearly 600,000,000,000 pages. Meanwhile, recent surveys show that the usefulness of such printout is declining—approximately 98% of the printouts are never looked at and essentially go from printer to trash can without ever seeing the light of day. There is so much data to look at and so many possible ways to aggregate and view the data that no amount of printout can ever anticipate even a fraction of the users' needs.

Another problem is speed. Most business processes run on a day-to-day basis. While paper-based reports were fine for most monthly financial statements, the logistics of printing and distributing a large number of reports on a daily basis are daunting. In a world of accelerating processes, faster deliveries, lower inventories, and highly competitive service, data distribution which relies on paper is too slow.

The only solution to this problem is to give the users themselves the power to link directly to data using electronic means. As the infrastructure of PCs, networks, and servers becomes as ubiquitous as the in-box, mail truck, and trash can, information workers at all levels of the organization will be turning to their PCs rather than traditional paper reports for the information they need to do their jobs. Rather than using report writers to churn out paper-based reports, they will be using VIA tools to design specialized human interfaces to the live databases.

There are fundamental differences between report writers and visual information access systems. For one thing, paper-based reports are canned "images" of data, as opposed to live numbers. VIA is not simply a matter of transferring paper-style reports to the computer screen. Rather, such on-screen reporting deals with live interactions with the underlying data and the ability of the user to immediately alter their view of the data in a nearly infinite number of ways. Visual information access is a combination of database access technology, data transformation, visual data representation, and data navigation techniques.

The Three Pillars of VIA

The "Three Pillars" of Visual Information Access systems are based on an open-architecture that allows software modules to be snapped together to form complete systems as shown in Fig. 24.2.

There are three essential components to a Visual Information Access system. First, and the one with which most people immediately identify VIA, is the GUI front end. This component is the "visual" in VIA. It is also the component that ultimately defines what kind of applications can and cannot be built from a human interface standpoint.

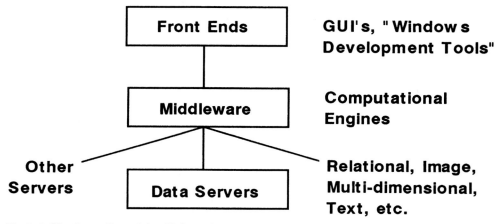

Fig. 24.2 The three pillars of visual information access.

It is also the part of the system that typically requires the most programming and development effort.

The second most obvious component of any VIA system is the back end data server. In most cases today, this back end server is an SQL relational database, such as Oracle, DB2, SQL Server, Ingres, etc. While relational databases are good general purpose data stores that can accomplish nearly anything in batch mode, for many types of live reporting applications they do not provide adequate speed. Hence VIA brings about a need for different, more specialized data servers that are more tailored to particular types of data and queries.

Finally, there is frequently a need for some sort of computational engine that sits between the database server and the GUI. The Gartner Group refers to this class of software as "middleware" for reasons which are obvious from the above diagram. The need for middleware is not appreciated by many people attempting to build VIA systems today.

The Need for Middleware

Some reporting systems can be built by simply putting a GUI front end onto a relational data server. However, the GUI still needs to be "data driven" and use dynamic menus to maintain independence of application and database.

Since the need for middleware is probably the most poorly understood aspect of VIA, let's examine this first. To begin with, some applications can be built without middleware. Such applications are typically those that require little or no transformation of the raw data and which use the underlying database in a way that offers adequate response time. For example, the speed of an SQL relational database can usually be expressed in terms of an approximate number of records accessed per second. For example, Oracle running on one of our VAXs was recently clocked at about 120 records per second.

An application that needs to retrieve only one or two records per screen will work quite nicely. An application that requires that 10,000 records be retrieved and aggregated for each screen will be too slow to be usable. An example of an application which might work fine would be a human resources application in which the user is locating and retrieving individual records on individual employees. Where such an application might get into trouble would be if the application were able to allow users to ask questions such as "let me see the total salaries and FICA taxes for all employees except executives." If there are 10,000 employees, this kind of query might be unacceptably slow.

Speed is not the only reason that one needs middleware. Consider a simple and highly plausible situation where sales data are stored on a daily basis and the user wishes to see the data displayed on his or her screen in weekly form. If your only tools are an SQL database and a GUI front end, how will you convert the days to weeks? Periodicity conversions are not as trivial as you might think because they need extensive knowledge of the calendar; they need to know about holidays, fiscal years, calendar years, 4-4-5 accounting periods, leap years, and so forth. Furthermore, all data do not convert the same way. To get weekly sales, you add up the days. To get weekly inventory, you don't add up the days, you take inventory at the end of the period, or perhaps an average over the period in question. It turns out that there are over a dozen different common rules for time series data aggregation. The periodicity conversion program in one of Pilot's products cost over $2 million to develop, so I have a good appreciation for the complexities of what appears to be a simple problem.

Another example of an application where middleware would probably be required might be anything requiring forecasting. For example, suppose a company has a database with daily sales data and the user wishes to see the actual daily numbers and a statistical forecast showing where he will be at the end of the month versus the forecast. Statistical forecasting is not something that is easily done with either SQL or most front-end products. Again what is required is a computational engine (middleware) that extracts data from the database, computes the statistical forecasts, and then passes all the data along to the front end for display.

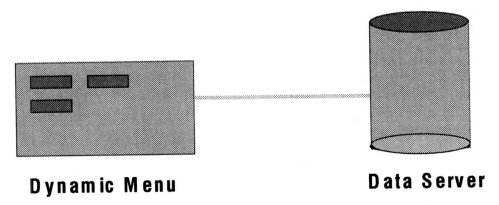

Dynamic Menu   **Data Server**

Fig. 24.3 GUI needs to be data driven.

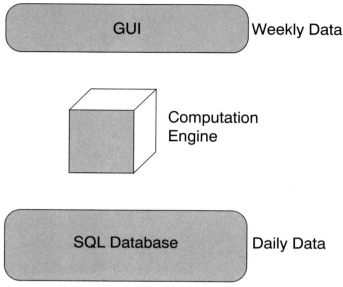

Fig. 24.4 A "middleware" computation engine.

Front-end GUIs

Front-end GUIs generally fall into three categories:

1. General purpose "Windows Application Tools"

2. Friendly SQL interfaces

3. Visual Information Access tools

Visual Information Access tools, such as Pilot's LightShip, are specifically designed to create end-user applications that access information in a semi-structured way. For example, I use a VIA application that allows me to look at current sales activity by product and sales region and compare these numbers against forecast and pipeline. While the data in this application are stored in an SQL database, my "view" of this data has nothing to do with SQL or relational data structures. I am simply presented with a screen that allows me to navigate from one view of data to another by pointing and clicking with my mouse. I never see the words "field," "record," or "select" or any other database terminology—just terms that are of specific meaning to my company's sales organization. My VIA tools have been used to create a unique application that insulates me from the structure of the underlying database.

More general purpose Windows development tools, such as Microsoft's Visual Basic, Borland's Object Vision, Asymmetrix's Toolbook, and so forth, can usually be made to deliver VIA-like functionality. However, all of these tools require learning a programming language and require significantly more development effort. In some cases, because of the general purpose nature of the product, certain functions will run unacceptably slowly and maintenance will be too costly.

All of these tools are "object oriented." The difference between a VIA tool whose purpose is limited to reporting applications, and general purpose Windows development tools is in the kinds of objects utilized to build an application. For example, one of the most basic capabilities of any reporting tool is the ability to display a properly formatted table of numbers, e.g.:

	Actual	Budget	Variance
Sales	$13,420.01	$13,200.00	$220.01
Expenses	$10,204.00	$10,000.00	$204.00
Net Profit	$3,224.01	$3,200.00	$24.01

A properly formatted table of numbers is a basic part of any reporting system. A VIA tool ought to include a "document object" that can produce such tables with minimum development effort.

In a "programming" product like Visual Basic, the developer has no "table object" that automatically knows how to deal with arrays of numbers, so all of this must be created by writing many lines of computer code. A VIA tool, on the other hand, ought to include a table object that can be simply connected to a source of data using "point and click" methodology. Maintenance is also effected by the different kinds of tools. Changing the dollar signs to Deutchmark signs, for instance, should be as simple as clicking on the table and changing the chart object characteristics. With a programming language development tool, the table is programmed using string manipulation, and the programmer would have to find all the instances of dollar signs and replace them. He would also have to change all the uses of commas and periods which are used differently when expressing values in Deutchmarks.

Another example of native VIA capabilities should be the ability to read the contents of a cell on the screen. For example, a logical way to allow a user to see the details of "Sales," "Expenses," or "Net Profits" in the above table would be to allow the user to simply point to the word on the screen and click the mouse. A VIA tool should be able to read the word you are pointing at and allow that word to be used in the next query to the database. Most general purpose Windows development tools will only feed back the X-Y coordinates of the mouse. It requires you to write the code to figure out what word the user is pointing at.

A third example is basic business graphs, such as bar charts or line charts. If graphical objects exist at all in general purpose Windows tools, they will be primitives such as rectangles, lines, circles, and so forth. Again, a great deal of effort is required to turn these primitives into an attractively designed bar chart with properly spaced scaling and so forth. A VIA tool, on the other hand, ought to support a "chart object" which can be visually linked to a table of numbers. Creating a bar chart in a VIA tool is considered basic reporting functionality and ought to take no more than a few minutes to set up.

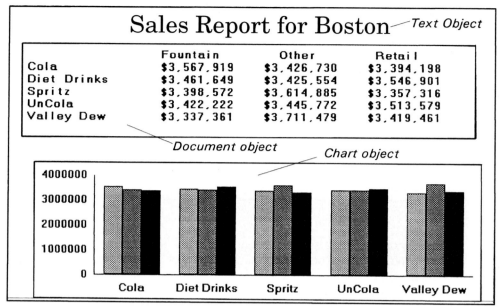

Fig. 24.5 Example of report screen.

"Friendly query tools," such as Cognos' Power Play or Pioneer Software's Q+E represent the third major category of GUI front-ends. These tools are specifically oriented toward allowing nontechnical users formulate SQL queries without having to know the SQL syntax. These SQL query generators can make a useful adjunct to other GUI front ends that have more application-building capabilities.

Back-end Database Servers

Relational databases are good general purpose tools for storing and retrieving simple numerical data and short text strings. They are particularly useful where the inherent structure of the data maps nicely to the row and column format of a relational table. The classic example of a good use of a relational table is a human resources database with one record per employee. A good relational database can locate and retrieve an employee record in a few hundredths of a second.

Some data, however, are inherently structured in a way that maps awkwardly to a relational database. Sales and marketing data are the most obvious multidimensional data. For example, a major retailer uses an SQL database to collect daily sales data from 1200 retail stores. They carry 30,000 different products and wish to store three years worth of daily sales data in order to facilitate year-to-year comparisons. In third normal form, the SQL table looks like this:

PRODUCT	STORE	DAY	SALES	PRICE
Prod A	A	1	2310	15
Prod A	A	2	130	15
Prod A	A	3	0	15
Prod B	A	1	4312	6
Prod B	A	2	0	6
Prod B	A	3	0	6
Prod A	B	1	145	15
Prod A	B	2	1340	15
Prod A	B	3	0	15
etc...				

A typical relational database containing 3rd Normal Form Data, 1200 stores, 30,000 products, and 3 years of daily data results in a database with 36 billion records. If a database user wanted to total the sales for any one store for a week, the query would require that $30,000 \times 7 = 210,000$ records be retrieved and aggregated. Using DB2 on a typical IBM mainframe, this query would take approximately 1000 seconds, or roughly 16 minutes.

Another problem with this particular database is that not every product is sold in every store on every day—there are a lot of zeros (this is known as "sparse data"). Also,

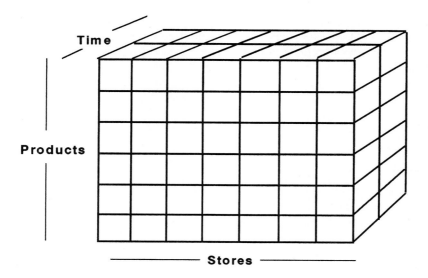

Fig. 24.6 Spreadsheet productivity.

the price of each product tends to repeat day after day. Rather than repeat a price in the database day after day, it would be more efficient if the database stored price changes only. A database that dealt efficiently with all the zeros and redundant price data could store the same information in a fraction of the disk space.

The right way to store this kind of data is in a multidimensional data server. A multidimensional database is an n-dimensional cube of data, which is designed to perform row and column arithmetic at spreadsheet speeds.

A multidimensional data server is a much better "fit" for this data. Now the user can perform row and column arithmetic at spreadsheet speeds and it would be reasonable to expect that our 16-minute query could be speeded up by at least one order of magnitude. This could mean the difference between a usable VIA application and one that is too slow to be usable.

There are other kinds of data structures that lend themselves to other specialized data servers. For example, many applications require access to text information, rather than numerical data. For such applications, a data server that can do a high-speed full text search might be essential. Other applications need to store and retrieve images, maps, or diagrams, while still others need to be able to access voice or full motion video. The point is that data warehousing is one thing, but live data access is another. A database to support production transactional processing might be entirely different from the server in which the data is staged for live access and analysis.

Conclusion

The world is quickly getting used to the idea of turning to a computer screen rather than a stack of paper for their day to day information needs. Live data reporting presents a new set of technological challenges and is promoting the creation of many new products. VIA tools will soon be an integral part of nearly every significant database application. As you migrate to this new way of providing reporting, the most important fact to keep in mind is that most reporting systems in the past have been based on batch processing. To make the leap to VIA, you have to think about more than a friendly front end to your SQL databases.

Author Biography

David Friend founded Pilot Software in 1983. Pilot introduced the first commercial Executive Information System (EIS) in 1984, and Mr. Friend has often been cited as the father of the EIS industry. He has written dozens of articles on EIS and is a regular speaker at trade shows and industry conferences. In 1991 he was featured on the cover of Datamation magazine.

In 1991, Mr. Friend engineered Pilot's acquisition of the software arm of Thorn EMI, TECS, which gave Pilot a strong presence in the DSS market and direct operations in most European countries. Today Pilot's worldwide operations employ approximately 300 people.

Prior to Pilot, Mr. Friend founded Computer Pictures Corp, one of the first companies in the business graphics software market. He authored the company's flagship product called "Trend Spotter." Mr. Friend served as Chairman of Computer Pictures until its acquisition by Cullinet Software, Inc., in 1982.

Before joining Computer Pictures, Mr. Friend was President of ARP Instruments, Inc., which was one of the first manufacturers of music synthesizers. ARP was the synthesizer of choice for many of the world's most famous rock bands and jazz musicians and Mr. Friend became well known as a pioneer in the electronic musical instrument industry.

Mr. Friend holds bachelor's degrees in music and engineering from Yale University where he was a Scholar of the House. He was a David Sarnoff Fellow at Princeton University's Graduate School of Engineering. He is currently a trustee of Berklee College of Music and the Boston Chamber Music Society and is a former trustee of the New England Conservatory of Music.

25

The Productivity Impact of Parallel Processing

by Adam Kolowa, and Jon Flower

Introduction

The demand for computer performance is still the dominating force pushing back the boundaries of high technology. Although there is significant demand for "better" in the computing arena, "faster" is still the most often-heard cry, and "faster at any expense" is really the underlying thought.

The last decade saw explosive growth in microprocessor power, and it might be expected that this will continue for at least the next few years. Despite this, however, nobody appears to seriously question that computers with multiple processors will become prevalent in the next decade. It is not unreasonable to expect, for example, that all machines will have more than a single processor by the turn of the century. From the most powerful supercomputers to the desktop workstation or personal computer, all new machines are moving in this direction. An important question, therefore, is what does this mean to software users and developers?

In the ideal case it wouldn't really mean anything. The multiprocessor systems would be designed so that their use was a transparent extension of current computing methods. All of the old (and new) tools would integrate seamlessly into the new environment. With our current understanding of the breed, however, this appears to be a pipe dream. The reality is that we can only expect to reuse all of the old technology if we pay the price of having the multiprocessor system run in a multiuser mode in which each individual user sees only the performance of a single processor, but more users can do useful work simultaneously. While this is clearly of some benefit, it is not really the reason why most systems turn to parallel processing.

In this chapter we explore some of the concepts involved in the "parallel" use of multiprocessor systems and their impact on software engineering practices and the tools required to support them.

What Is a Parallel Computer?

Surprisingly, after ten years of work in the field it is even hard to reach consensus on this question. A simple definition involving a simple "head count" of the number of CPUs means that most automobiles must be classed as parallel computers. Similarly a graphics workstation with an accelerator or even an IBM PC with a math co-processor would qualify.

In fact, these are multiprocessor systems—it just so happens that they have been integrated so well that most programmers don't see the difference. The compiler, for example, normally takes care of whether or not a program should take advantage of a floating-point processor and a library takes care of graphical accelerations which depend on underlying hardware.

As such, these are multiprocessor systems that have successfully avoided becoming "parallel computers." The latter are really the newly emerging machines in which there are typically many processors, each able to do the same type of operation. This last is really the key to "parallel processing" because it opens up the possibility to the user of achieving better performance by somehow using more than one of a similar component on the same task.

Consider, for example, a personal computer working on a database update. In most systems a single CPU is responsible for computing relationships between entries and also managing the disk accesses needed to bring the required data into memory and store the computed results. One can also imagine using two processors: one to do the numerical work and another to manage the disk. Fortunately this type of "parallel processing" is one that we understand fairly well. I/O is, after all, "different" from numerical work and we can easily see the difference between the two activities and write code to deal with it. We might even expect some operating system to be able to do this automatically for us.

The problems come to the fore when we consider adding a third processor to share the burden of the numerical work. Suddenly the picture changes because while the two-processor scenario is quite simple to understand, the three-processor variant has two CPUs working on the same type of task. Whereas the two-processor scenario can be implemented by dividing up the functionality of the original program, the three-processor picture requires that we divide up the work within a single function.

Of course, an easy solution is to merely use the third processor to update someone else's database. Until we have as many processors as databases to update this is a feasible alternative. No single database update runs any faster, but more people get work done in a fixed time interval. Unfortunately this is not enough. As the demand for information expands in the next decade we will need to perform ever more complex operations on ever more data, in the same amount of time, or even faster than we do now. The only way this can realistically be achieved is by having more than one processor share the work in a complex task.

What Is Parallel Software?

Once we have decided that we must make use of multiple processors within a given task, the question arises of how this is going to be achieved. We could hope that some sort of magical CASE tool or operating system will be available for our old codes on the new multiprocessor systems. Of course this isn't going to happen. One thing that we've definitely agreed on over the last ten years is that programs that work on multiple processors are different from those that work on single processors. Of course, the types of differences are not agreed on. There are many camps that each have their own ideas of how to go about this and their own set of hardware that best supports their style.

An important topic, however, is "what needs to run on what?" We basically have two types of hardware: single processor and multiple processor, and two types of applications: those that run on single processors and those that run on multiple processors. We can combine these to form four possible combinations as shown in Fig. 25.1. The trick is to figure out which matches with which and how.

The easy one is that we expect single processor codes to run on single-processor machines. That is what most people are doing today and what is supported by all the power of the software engineering process.

We are also agreed that multiprocessor codes will be running on multiprocessor systems. Of course there are many different types of multiprocessor system and many different types of multiprocessor codes, so it is not obvious how these match up in detail.

If single-processor codes could somehow be made to run on multiprocessor machines there really would be no problem and this chapter would already be over. Many people are desperately working on exactly this problem, including us.

	Single processor code	Multi-processor code
Single processor hardware	✔	?
Multi-processor hardware	?	?

Fig. 25.1 Single and multiprocessor hardware and software.

Strangely, it is often the remaining category that ends up being the most important—"can a multiprocessor code execute on a single processor machine?"

If the answer to this question is "no," we can expect to be in for a tough time in the next decade because commercial software developers will be forced to make the transition to parallel architectures "cold turkey." Probably they will spin off either small development teams or even new companies to pursue the multiprocessor versions of their applications while simultaneously developing their old codes to keep their existing customers happy. Eventually the parallel processing group will have a product but if it doesn't run on single-processor machines, it must forever live on a different development track from the single-processor code. Pretty soon the single and multiprocessor versions will each have different features and will probably end up as separate products. Of course the company may realize this before actually starting up the parallel effort and abandon it as hopeless. In the last few years we have actually seen this scenario played out with monotonous regularity by the major proponents of parallel processing.

The key for the next few years, we believe, is to make sure that parallel programs run on single-processor machines so that the development of one doesn't necessarily destroy the other. Note that an extremely important effect of this decision is the fact that we must concentrate on parallelizing codes that use existing languages like C and FORTRAN rather than inventing new ones solely for simplifying our task. Then we actually have some chance of developing turn-key applications in which the customer can decide how much performance to pay for but be guaranteed of the same functionality regardless of the cost. In the meantime we will continue to pursue the goal of making single processor codes work on multiprocessor systems.

The Problems of Parallel Software

If the previous discussion left one with the feeling that parallel processing is horrendously difficult we will work through an example that will, hopefully, show that "different" is really a more appropriate word than "difficult.'

An example—adding a column of numbers. Consider the somewhat trivial exercise of adding up a column of numbers in a table. Although this is clearly a simple problem it is still the basis for an enormous amount of the world's computing.

This problem is normally solved by writing a program with the logic shown below:
Set total = 0
Loop over items in list adding current item to total
Print the total

Obviously this is expressed in different ways in different computer languages, but the logic is the same. Pictorially this can be represented as above. We present the input data, compute the sum and print the result as shown in Fig. 25.2.

Now assume that two processors are available to perform this task as discussed previously. How can we take advantage of these to perform the job faster?

To a human being the answer is quite simple. If our list consists of 2 million entries, we should add up the first million in one of the processors and the other million in

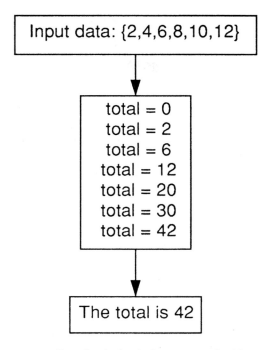

Fig. 25.2 Data flow in the single processor algorithm.

the other. We might, then, imagine a parallel program that looked like the following variant of the previous example:

Set total = 0
Loop over items in "our half" of the list adding current item to total
Print the total

Carrying out this process on the example data shown above gives something analogous to that shown in Fig. 25.3.

Clearly something is wrong with the logic in the above program: we forgot to add up the sums computed in the two processors. The correct logic is more like:

Set subtotal = 0
Loop over items in "our half" of the list adding current item to subtotal
Combine subtotals to make total
Print the total

Pictorially we now have the situation shown in Fig. 25.4 and the answer is finally correct.

Although the logic of our program is now correct, the problem is not really solved in the engineering sense because we have to worry about the implementation of the algorithm on whatever hardware we have at hand. This, unfortunately, opens up another set of issues.

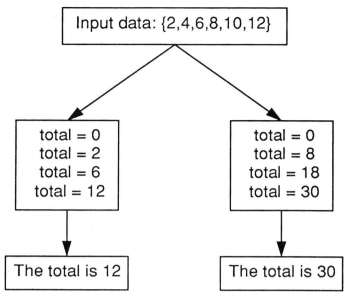

Fig. 25.3 Data flow in the incorrect multiprocessor algorithm.

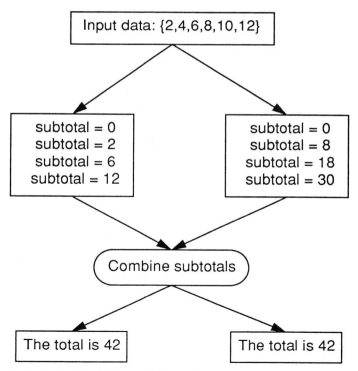

Fig. 25.4 Data flow in the parallel algorithm.

Converting Ideas into Algorithms

Up to now we have built a conceptual model of the program that computes the total of a set of numbers, but we haven't actually turned it into working code. If we were designing for a single-processor architecture, we would have many choices at this point.

Choices in implementation methods

For an application this simple we would probably proceed straight to writing code in a particular high-level language: C, Fortran, Ada, C++, Smalltalk, LISP, etc. Alternatively, we might use a higher-level tool to build the code by presenting a formal specification of what it is to do or by drawing pictures.

When the target is a parallel machine the options are much more restricted since few high level programming methods exist for such architectures. On the other hand there is enormous variety in the types of multiprocessor architecture for which the code may be targeted, and within each class there are numerous ways of actually expressing the parallel processing nature of the algorithm.

The message passing model

For the sake of argument we will discuss a machine architecture in which the processors communicate by sending messages to each other.

Conceptually, therefore, we would create two copies of the code that computes the subtotals and load one into each of two processors. Each program would then compute its subtotal and then combine it with the other processor's contribution to get the final result. One way in which we could conceive of performing this last operation is to have the second processor send its subtotal to the first, where it is added to the subtotal in that node. Finally the first processor sends back the total to the second. This process is shown in Fig. 25.5.

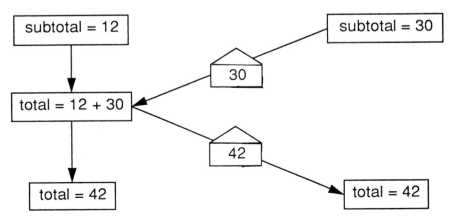

Fig. 25.5 Combining subtotals in a single processor.

While there is nothing wrong with this scheme, it shows another area in which multiprocessor algorithms can be tricky. Let us assume that we are adding a large enough list of numbers that we need to use several hundred processors instead of two. Dividing the list of numbers to be added is simple enough as is computing the subtotals. But now consider what happens if we pursue the original line of thought and simply have each processor send its subtotal to the first to be added and then receive the computed total. If we run this method on 500 processors 499 nodes will send out messages and then receive responses, for a total of 998 messages. Bearing in mind that interprocessor communication is normally much slower than computation, we may easily end up in a situation in which the advantage gained by computing subtotals separately in each node is lost when computing the total. This situation is shown in Fig. 25.6.

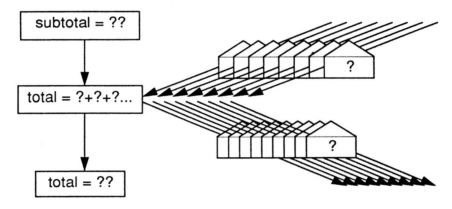

Fig. 25.6 Combining many subtotals in a single processor.

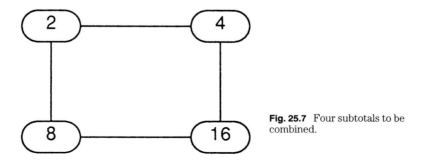

Fig. 25.7 Four subtotals to be combined.

A better way of combining values

Of course, this problem also has a solution. Consider the situation where only four nodes are involved, each with a subtotal as shown in Fig. 25.7. Note that the figure shows the subtotals arranged at the corners of a square, which helps to explain the smarter way of combining the values.

Consider the algorithm shown pictorially in Fig. 25.8. In the first step, the two processors on the left of the square exchange their subtotals with the corresponding processor to the right and combine their results to make a new subtotal. In the second step, each processor on the top of the square exchanges its new subtotal with the processor below it and similarly updates its value.

At the end of these two steps each processor has computed the correct total, and only four messages have been sent instead of the six in the original method. Even better, the two messages sent in the first step can both travel at once as can the two in the second step. The net result is that the "clever" algorithm requires only two time units while the "stupid" one needs six. (The messages in the slower method can all travel to the first processor at once, but this node must read them one after another. Similarly it must send responses to each node in turn.) In general, it is easy to show that the faster algorithm requires a number of messages proportional to the logarithm to base 2 of the number of processors, so in the case where we need to use 500 processors for our task the smart algorithm is almost 100 times faster than the original!

Other parallel processing architectures

Of course, we have addressed here only the type of parallel computer in which processors communicate by sending messages. Other architectures are possible, of which the most common are the "shared memory" machines in which multiple processors share data directly. At first glance, this type of architecture looks easier to program, but it actually has its own problems. In the current scenario, someone would need to coordinate access to the running totals so that one processor doesn't accidentally update a value that is being read by another processor.

What Have We Learned?

We have constructed a very simple program and examined some of the pitfalls involved in creating a parallel version of the code. Should one conclude that parallel processing is too difficult for practical use?

We believe that the answer is "no" as long as developers use the correct tools. Just as development for a single processor architecture can be significantly enhanced by using the right tools and methods, parallel processing can be made simpler with the correct tools. In fact we believe that for many of the most useful algorithms and applications, parallel processing is no harder today than writing single-processor codes—it's just different.

Basically the problem concerns not the parallel nature of the underlying system, but the tools that we have to implement our ideas. In practice it is straightforward to

Step 1. Horizontal Exchange

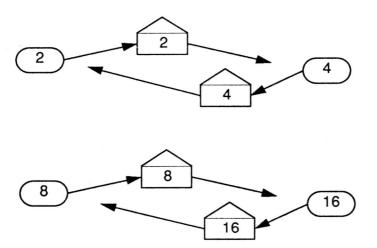

Step 2. Vertical Exchange

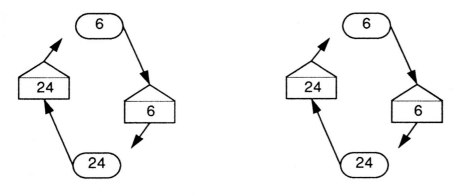

Step 3. Done

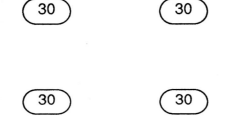

Fig. 25.8 A faster method for combining subtotals.

"see" parallel versions of single-processor applications just as it was easy to understand what the parallel version of our "table total" program should do. The problems come when these ideas are turned into operational code.

Having realized that parallel computers create most of their problems by merely being different from their single-processor counterparts, an extremely important issue comes up—the proliferation of parallel processing architectures. We originally broke down the computing world into four categories based on single and multiprocessor hardware and single and multiprocessor codes. If we now have to break down the multiprocessor categories into tens or even hundreds of subcategories based on the hardware and software architectures of the parallel computers, all will be lost and chaos will result.

The first requirement, therefore, for dealing with these machines is that there must be a uniform model of the entire breed of parallel computers for the developer to use.

A Productivity-Enabling Parallel Software Architecture

The following issues must be addressed:

- Presentation of a "virtual" parallel architecture that spans all physical architectures and allows programmers to proceed without detailed knowledge of the underlying components.

- Sophisticated and optimized libraries to perform all of the commonly occurring operations, such as the "combine" task described in the previous sections.

- Compatibility with existing "conventional" behavior in areas such as I/O and graphics, but with extensions to provide for parallel programs.

- Development and debugging tools.

CASE

As yet, CASE methodology has had little impact in the parallel processing arena, probably because the other issues appear to be more urgent: without a decent debugger for parallel codes, you can't really expect to make much progress in any direction. In the future, however, we expect that CASE tools and their derivatives will play an increasingly important role, possibly more so than in the single processor world.

The basic issue is that we have a long way to go before multiprocessor applications can be created automatically. In the interim we will have to use semiautomatic methods in which users can guide programming tools. Already in construction, for example, are tools that diagram both the logical structure of an application and the relative CPU times spent in its various parts, with the goal of allowing a human being to guide the construction of a parallel version of the code. Clearly, these have a lot in common with existing CASE tools. It is even to be hoped that by making such tools compatible with existing CASE technology a specification-driven parallel program generator can be created.

Conclusions

The most important conclusions that must be drawn from the last few years work are that:

- Multiprocessor hardware architectures are inevitable and will be more common that single-processor systems by the end of this decade.

- Multiprocessor systems will have to be used as parallel computers rather than just multiuser machines because performance demands are increasing so rapidly.

- Multiprocessor algorithms are easy to design, but difficult to implement unless the right tools are used.

We believe that the only way in which we will be able to take advantage of multiprocessor systems is to combine the methods with which programs for single processors are currently generated with suitable parallel processing systems. The alternative approach in which completely new technology is invented to deal with the multiprocessor system is unlikely to become popular in any other than a research environment, since most software development takes place by evolution of existing codes rather than the generation of new ones.

While there clearly remains a lot of work to be done before parallel program generation is taken for granted, much progress has been made and tools already exist today which greatly simplify the process.

Author Biography

Adam Kolowa worked for three years as a graduate student in Caltech's very prestigious parallel processing group. After graduating, he became interested in developing systems with ultra-high performance and worked extensively on optimization strategies and optimized software for applications on high-performance computers. In 1987, he jointly founded ParaSoft Corporation, the leading parallel computing company, of which he is now the chairman.

ParaSoft's main product is Express, which is software that adheres to the tenets outlined in this paper.

Kolowa's interest is in applying Express software in a manner that scales through all levels of parallel computation from networks of conventional workstations up through the machines in the Federal Government's High Performance Computing Initiative. He is also involved in the "Gigabit" project, which is building homogenous, physically distributed "meta-computers" based, in part, on the Express system.

Kolowa obtained his Ph.D in Physics from the California Institute of Technology.

Jon Flower, who received his Ph.D in Physics, was also a member of the prestigious parallel processing group at Caltech. Flower was initially interested in the field of High Energy Physics but soon became more interested in the ways that the parallel computer could be used by people with less computer background leading to an emphasis on the tools which would make the system useful.

With Kolowa, Flower founded ParaSoft in 1987, and became president in 1989. He was a prime architect of the Express system. Express is a parallel processing system designed to meet the needs of application developers through stages of the development life cycle from early understanding and visualization of a sequential application through code development, debugging, optimization and maintenance on a high-performance parallel computer.

26

Quality Management
The Secret to High Productivity

by H. Glen Weekley and Marcel Markus

Introduction

Quality management is the key to high productivity in software engineering. Raising the quality of both software engineering processes and deliverables will have an immediate effect on productivity throughout the life cycle of a system.

The application of strategies such as Information Engineering (IE) supports this by providing a platform for increasing the quality of the software engineering process, and therefore the quality of the delivered system.

In this chapter we define productivity and quality as they relate to software engineering. We then discuss the goals of quality management and describe the elements of a system we have developed to reach these goals within an IE environment.

Steps toward Productivity

There are two ways to boost productivity in software development. Developers can either do things faster or do fewer things.

Doing things faster is the conventional approach. Examples include more efficient techniques, graphical models that speed communication, and CASE tools. These provide some gains, but success is limited to small portions of the life cycle. Application generators, for example, can boost productivity in construction, yet this makes up only 5% percent of the life cycle.

More dramatic results come from doing fewer things. A software development strategy rooted in elimination of needless or redundant efforts will show productivity gains in orders of magnitude. At the risk of oversimplifying the issue, we see doing fewer things having two parts as well: doing things right, and doing the right things.

Doing things right is primarily a quality management issue. It is based on avoiding rework of inferior work products and confusion from defective work products. Doing the right things is both a business and an engineering issue. It puts the focus on what is important, so as not to waste valuable resources in areas of lesser value to the organization than those supporting corporate strategy and market advantage.

This chapter describes a Quality Management System (QMS) designed to ensure that all software development activities are done right, and an integrated IE approach that ensures the right things are being done. Implementation of both will result in the highest productivity pay-off.

Doing Things Right: The Management of Quality

Quality has been defined in many ways for practical application to the business environment. Philip Crosby speaks of "conformance to requirements," J. Juran proposes "fitness for use," Edwards Deming cites "predictability, uniformity, and cost suited to the market," and IBM defines quality as "delighted customers."

From a software engineering point of view, quality can best be described as "satisfying business objectives while minimizing life cycle costs."

Each definition is the basis for a formal methodology of quality management that leads to continual improvement of measured quality of a company's products and services. It is now widely recognized that quality does not just happen: it must be incorporated in every business process as an integral set of objectives and procedures. Quality must be managed on an ongoing basis to achieve predefined quality objectives.

Conceptually, quality management in the software engineering environment is not different from quality management in any other manufacturing environment. It requires a definition of quality criteria for all products or deliverables produced (whether intermediate or final), a formalized, repeatable production process, and a quality assurance process.

Quality management ensures that quality objectives and activities are embedded in the software development life cycle (SDLC) as components that are as essential as the SDLC methodology itself.

However, an SDLC methodology is only one component of a software engineering QMS. It contributes to, but is no guarantee for, quality improvement when implemented without the framework of a formalized QMS.

Goals of Quality Management

The ultimate goal of a software engineering QMS is increased productivity: producing a product of continually increasing quality for continually decreasing costs. This may seem to contradict the notion that quality costs.

Implementation of quality management is an investment with a substantial return. Development, implementation and maintenance of the QMS will indeed require a significant investment, but the benefits will more than compensate for these costs.

Quality management contributes to cost reduction goals by accomplishing the following objectives:

- A significant reduction of rework through the detection and correction of defects in deliverables as early as possible in the life cycle, ensuring that defects do not pollute further phases of the development process.

- Higher reliability of the delivered system, as the majority of defects have been removed during the development phases, prior to the delivery of the system to the user.

- Continuous improvement of the software engineering process itself through defect detection techniques, causal analysis and process improvement activities, addressing the root causes of defects and ensuring they are removed (see Fig. 26.1).

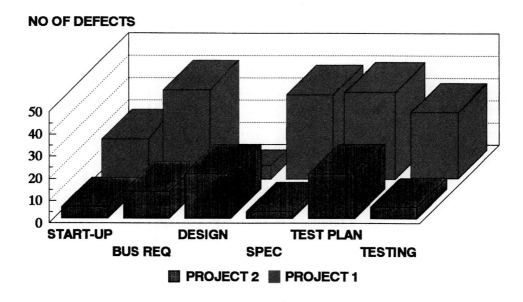

Data: collected in UK March 1990 - May 1991

Fig. 26.1 Defects found.

Building a Quality Management System

Quality management should be based on some universal principles, such as zero-defect deliverables, "do it right the first time," and consistency and measurability. In this chapter we describe a Quality Management System that integrates quality management, quality assurance, and project management.

Key components of the system are the appointment of Quality Control Managers and Inspectors and the development of a Quality Manual, a Project Control Handbook, and a Quality Metrics Database.

Successful implementation requires meeting the following conditions:

- Management of the organization must be fully committed to the implementation of a QMS.

- The QMS must be fully documented, which requires the definition of quality criteria for project management and life cycle deliverables, as well as procedures for quality assurance activities.

- The traditional project organization must be reexamined in order to accommodate the required quality assurance activities (see Fig. 26.2).

- All software engineering staff must be trained in the use of the QMS and empowered to "halt the production line" when quality is compromised.

- The organization of the IS department must include the position of Quality Manager, responsible for all quality assurance activities.

- The QMS must include causal analysis and process-improvement procedures to ensure that root causes of detected defects are addressed.

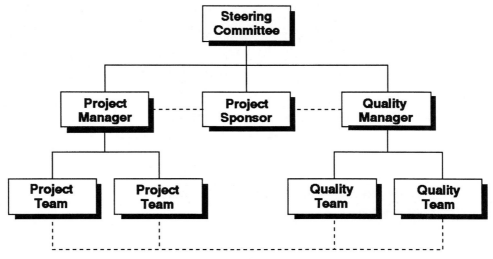

Fig. 26.2 Quality oriented project hierarchy.

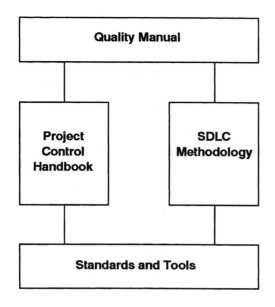

Fig. 26.3 QMS.

The QMS must be designed so that project management and quality management work hand-in-hand to achieve the desired qualitative objectives.

The structure of the QMS will determine its flexibility (see Fig. 26.3).

When designed in a modular fashion, it will allow for easy adaptation to a forever-changing IS environment, and it won't require a major overhaul when, for instance, the organization changes its SDLC methodology.

Quality Manual

The baseline quality criteria should be contained in a Quality Manual, which defines the framework of the QMS, identifies management responsibility, and provides quality criteria for generic project processes: start-up, project plan, quality plan, requirements definition, design, construction, testing, implementation, and maintenance. In addition, the Quality Manual describes the required quality assurance organization and activities such as the inspection of deliverables.

Project Control Handbook

It is not sufficient to define only the quality criteria for the software engineering process. The QMS needs to provide detailed descriptions of all processes required to meet the quality criteria. These are contained in a Project Control Handbook that, together with the Quality Manual, provides the basis for both project and quality management.

Costs of quality management

The costs of quality, provided quality objectives are set and managed within the framework of a formal software engineering QMS, are always negative. Experience has shown that the additional costs for all quality management activities, including inspections of intermediate deliverables, amount to a maximum of 15% of the overall project costs. The return on this investment, however, can be higher than 500%.

Experience of Computer Task Group in Europe has shown that the use of a QMS on several projects resulted in a return on investment of 496%, as seen in Fig. 26.4. This percentage can increase as project members and the quality management team become more experienced with QMS.

The quality inspection process

Many organizations, and indeed many quality experts such as Dr. Edwards Deming, consider inspections counter-productive in assuring quality. They argue that when "doing it right the first time"—the ultimate goal of quality management—there should be no need for inspections.

While this is true for a repetitive production process, where a single product is produced in large quantities, it is not true for software development. Even though

PROJECT PHASE	NO OF DEFECTS	EARN RATIO	VALUE	
START-UP	23	1:100	£88,166	
BUSINESS REQ.	52	1:50	£99,667	
DESIGN	20	1:30	£23,000	
SPECIFICATION	41	1:20	£31,433	
TEST PLANS	59	1:10	£22,616	
TESTING	35	1:5	£6,708	
TOTALS	230		£271,590	
COST OF QUALITY ASSURANCE:			£45,563	
RETURN ON INVESTMENT:			£226,027	496%

Fig. 26.4 Return on investment.

the QMS may define the production process in terms of basic steps and procedures, the end product, which is the system delivered to the user, is always unique.

It must conform to unique user requirements and is based on a process of requirements definition that is very dependent on the human factor. Because of this human dependency, undetected defects in the intermediate deliverables might have a devastating effect on both the quality of the system and cost of rework.

The inspection process consists of formalized steps to find and categorize as many defects as possible in a deliverable. The process as applied to the deliverables of the SDLC, was originally developed by Michael E. Fagan at IBM's Kingston Laboratory. It applies statistical process control to the inspection of documents and can be applied to any deliverable or document. It is a form of testing before the hardware platform comes into play, and is more effective than reviews, walkthroughs, or peer reviews, all of which it replaces.

Each step is managed to a strict time limit to ensure a basis for measuring the effectiveness of the QMS, and to ensure that an optimum inspection rate is maintained; that is, that the largest number of defects is found for the lowest cost in resources.

Inspections must be organized and managed by a trained quality manager or other moderator. The inspectors are invited to the inspection process on an as-required basis, and they may be recruited from anywhere in the organization, both within and outside of the IS department.

During the inspection process, the inspector checks the document under inspection against the higher-level input documents, such as the process description, standards, and quality criteria.

In addition, the inspector is issued a checklist to aid in the inspection and often specializes in one particular type of defect. A language specialist, for example, would look for language that is unclear, not concise, ambiguous, or not measurable. A standards specialist would look for violations of standards in both documentation and design. A logic specialist would trace conclusions through the process description to the higher-level documentation.

The defects detected are subjected to a causal analysis, the results of which are fed into a Quality Metrics Database for further analysis and action. The author of the inspected document, who would have participated in the inspection process, corrects the defects found and returns the corrected document to a moderator. The moderator either organizes for a reinspection or releases the document for use in the next phase (see Fig. 26.5).

The benefits of inspections are most visible during the early phases of a project. Defects found in a requirements definition document can cost 100 times as much to correct at the implementation stage. This earn ratio is proportionally reduced as the project progresses. Another benefit of the inspection process is the ability to collect quality metrics.

The number of defects found in a given deliverable is an excellent measure of

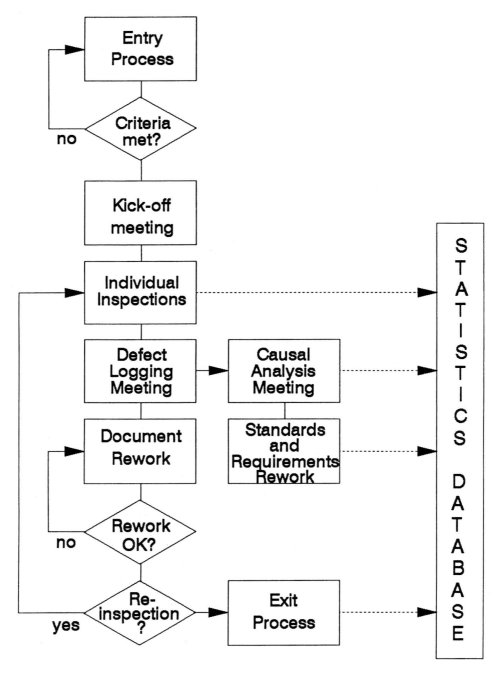

Fig. 26.5 QMS process.

quality, provided it can be related to other factors that influence the production of that deliverable.

Quality metrics

To measure the quality of our software engineering efforts, and more particularly the effect of a QMS, it is necessary to collect data on the quality aspects of processes and deliverables. This requires that both the production process (the software engineering project elements) and the quality assurance processes are structured and repeatable, and that we must be able to express their characteristics in measurable terms. Basic statistics to be collected include:

- Person-hours spent on a particular phase, preferably specified by activity and task
- Person-hours spent on project management and quality management, again specified by activity and task
- Duration of the phase, in working days
- Complexity of the work-effort, expressed in Function Points (other measuring criteria can be used, but Function Point analysis, while not perfect, provides the most comprehensive representation)
- Number of defects detected during the inspection process, specified by defect type and severity
- Person-hours spent on rework, correcting the defects found during the inspection
- Person-hours spent on quality assurance activities, including kick-off meetings, inspections, defect-logging meetings, causal analysis meetings, and all organizational and administrative activities

In addition to the above metrics, data should be collected on project properties such as project type, project environment, SDLC methodology, deliverable due dates, and similar items.

Computer Task Group has developed a Quality Metrics Database in order to capture and analyze this data. Quality metrics can now be analyzed to identify software quality and productivity trends, and consistent adherence to the QMS, including the collection of quality metrics, allows us to express quality and productivity in numerical terms.

Quality standards

To avoid having to develop software engineering quality standards from scratch, it is advisable to use the existing standards of the International Standards Organization, ISO 9001, supplemented with ISO 9004, or the *Tickit guide to software quality management* that is developed and published by the British Department of Trade and Industry. These standards provide a basis for the development and implementation of a software engineering QMS.

Ultimately, it may be advisable to apply for ISO 9001 certification, thus obtaining an internationally recognized certificate that testifies to the quality of your IS operation.

The Quality Management System described above has been audited by an independent assessment organization and was found in compliance with the standards prescribed by ISO 9001, EN 29001 and BS 5750 Part 1.

Standards and tools

Standards, tools, and aids play an important role in every QMS. The use of standards allows an organization to ensure that pre-determined quality criteria are consistently adhered to. Tools will facilitate this process. The QMS references the appropriate standards and tools wherever applicable, and provides a mechanism for ensuring that they are indeed adhered to and used.

SDLC methodology

A QMS will not work without a formal software engineering methodology, but does not prescribe the use of any one in particular. Quality management has benefits when applied with a home-grown SDM-based methodology as well as with standard methodologies implemented within the context of broad-based Information Engineering strategies.

The more rigorous the strategy for linking software development with business applications, the greater the productivity benefits gained from applying quality management.

In the following material, we discuss the integration of a QMS with an Information Engineering software development strategy.

Doing the Right Things: Information Engineering

Given scarce resources in most information systems development organizations, and the large backlog of information systems requests, it is very important to make efforts count—to do the right thing.

We view six aspects of Information Engineering as critical to the quality process:

1. Strategic foundation
2. Emphasis on user involvement
3. Commitment to engineering discipline
4. Leveraging of technology
5. Focus on stability
6. Maintenance of a comprehensive knowledge base

These fundamental IE principles provide the context for doing the right things with high quality. We discuss each in more detail in the next sections.

Strategic foundation

Information Engineering provides the structure and discipline for ensuring that software development efforts are right for the enterprise strategy. It is this aspect, more than any other, that ensures that we are doing the right things.

Its potential benefits are derived from a disciplined focus on strategic business direction. It provides management with the mechanisms to control counter-productive efforts and redirect them to accomplish the enterprise strategy. It is a structured discipline for directing effort to high-value information systems.

Information Strategy Planning activities, such as Business Driver Modeling, provide the structure for linking information components. This establishes a purpose dimension to guide downstream information technology efforts and ensure they accomplish the most important informational objectives.

Business Driver Modeling also provides rigorous, structured definitions of business requirements within a hierarchy of critical success factors (CSF). This CSF hierarchy links the strategy to logical informational requirements. A tight integration of development components, from planning to analysis to design to application generation, ensures that all software reflects the correct business purpose.

User involvement

Heavy involvement of users or business experts is essential for effective information systems development. Information Engineering requires user participation throughout the process, with an emphasis on business issues, rather than technology issues, early in the cycle.

Information Engineering emphasizes the use of techniques such as modeling Joint Application Design (JAD) and prototyping to facilitate communication among users and developers. The use of graphical representations provides the vehicle for communication of requirements facilitating user participation in the development and review of the various models. User involvement addresses both doing the right things and doing them correctly.

Engineering discipline

Engineering discipline integrates and applies the formal techniques that ensure that the desired quality result is obtained.

Furthermore, the extensive level of detail, and the sheer quantity of development facts about information technology, dictate the use of automated procedures to remember and manage them. Automation of these approaches is necessary to obtain required levels of quality and productivity. Formal approaches ensure consistency and correctness not heretofore obtainable. Significant reductions in risks of failure and overruns of schedules and budgets result from using engineering discipline.

The increasingly complex information requirements, the need for rapid change, short development cycle times, and better quality require application of engineering rigor to attain these goals at a manageable risk level.

Technology leverage

Information Engineering was created with the leveraging of technology in mind. Managing the large amounts of information about the information systems requires sophisticated technology. Elimination of time-consuming, tedious, error-prone tasks requires CASE tools. These tools with graphics-oriented work stations also provide an efficient communications medium.

Leveraging technology supports the determination of the right things to do and then assists in doing them right throughout the life cycle. While it is theoretically possible to implement Information Engineering without technology, in practice, CASE tools are necessary to support the principles and successfully attain the objectives of Information Engineering.

Stability

Because we must cope with change, Information Engineering isolates areas of stability and areas of change. It has been noted that the data required by a business change far less than the processes or functions performed by the business. A process model changes frequently as processes change. A data model changes only when the nature of the business changes, or when the enterprise enters a new line of business. Logical models change only when the business changes. A physical model changes when technology changes (see Fig. 26.6).

Information Engineering isolates the models to provide stability and the capability of quickly analyzing the impact of change based on the type of change. Technology changes do not affect the logical models, but do require systems design and construction attention. A change in a business process affects the function half of the

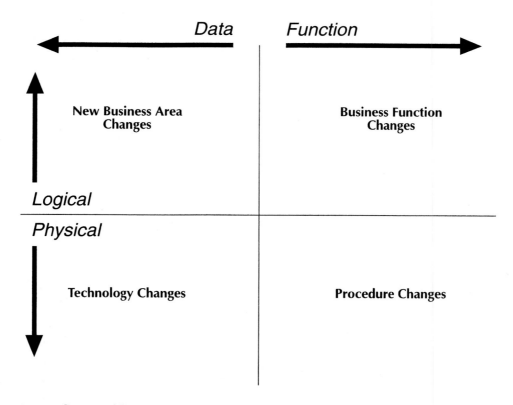

Fig. 26.6 Greater stability.

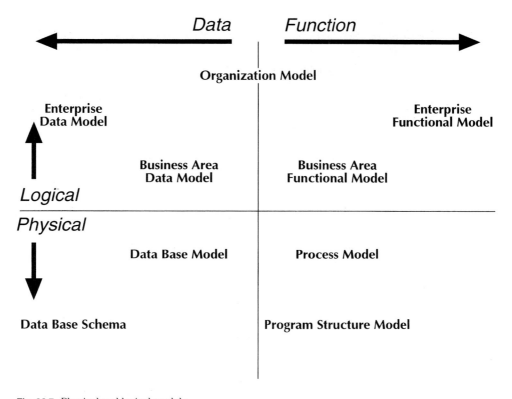

Fig. 26.7 Physical and logical models.

process. In Fig. 26.7, stability is greater in the upper left quadrant, decreasing as we move down and to the right.

The various models that Information Engineering uses as mechanisms to manage change and provide stability, are the enterprise data models, the business area models, and the physical models. These models help us to efficiently identify the right things to do in order to implement the required changes.

Comprehensive knowledge base

Information about the company and its use of information should be captured once—and only once! Prior to Information Engineering, many systems development efforts began from scratch each time, reinventing and duplicating previous efforts. The enterprise strategies and models need be created only once and form the basis for all information projects unless there is a change in the strategy or business.

Reusable information discovered by a project and placed in this knowledge base is made available to subsequent projects. The knowledge base containing all of this information also contains details of the organization structure and the functions performed.

The knowledge base is public—available to all who need the information. Private knowledge critical to the viability of the enterprise is no longer hidden in the far reaches of the organization, inaccessible to those needing it. This knowledge base contains the reusable components available to software development and maintenance teams. Reusing development components means we do not have to build them again, another case of not doing development work, thereby increasing productivity.

Life cycle implications

The benefits of operating a Quality Management System in the context of an IE environment are apparent throughout the software development life cycle. Quality management eliminates improper or inadequate application of prepared information infrastructure, project management, methodology, techniques, CASE, and development staff skills.

There is a dramatic relationship between the point in the systems development life cycle at which defects are detected and the size in duration, effort and costs of the completed system. CTG's research has been verified by metrics collected in connection with implementations of our QMS. The life cycle is as follows:

- Information infrastructure: the development environment, including methodology, CASE, organizational structure, skills, and facilities.

- Information strategy planning: the Business Driver Model, Information Architecture, Technology Architecture, Systems Development Infrastructure, Business Area Definition, Project Prioritization, and Project Plans providing purpose and direction for information efforts.

- Business Area Analysis 1 (BAA1): Business Requirements Model, Data Model, and Activity Model defining business requirements for information.

- Business Area Analysis 2 (BAA2): refinement of the BAA1 model to include additional detail to define the business systems requirements.

- Business systems design: translation of requirements into software specifications.

- Test planning & coding: test strategy and planning, and translation of software specifications to code.

- Testing: software testing to ensure it meets specifications and business requirements.

- Operational system: software has been assembled into systems and placed into operation.

The average ratios shown in Fig. 26.8 have been proven to be close to actual individual project observations. This indicates that if a defect is detected during software testing (the most common detection point in most situations), it will require $TEST \div ISP = 40 \div 2 = 20$ times the effort to correct the defect than it would have taken, if detected, to correct it during Information Strategy Planning.

This point is supported by an example reported by a CTG client. Lack of a data architecture and an Information Strategy Planning work product led to significant rework of code to implement changes required by an unexpected database implementation. We estimate that this portion of the development effort cost 20 times what it would have under optimal conditions.

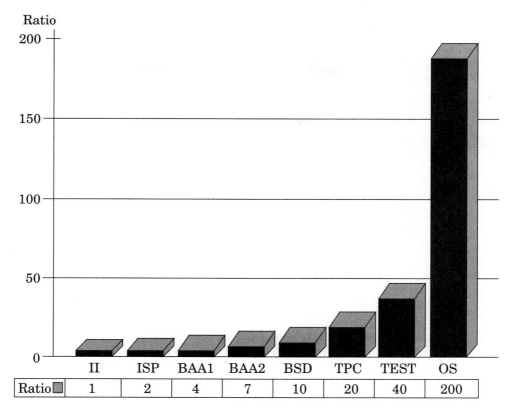

Ratio								
	II	ISP	BAA1	BAA2	BSD	TPC	TEST	OS
Ratio	1	2	4	7	10	20	40	200

Fig. 26.8 Defect cost ratio, life cycle point.

Conclusion

The design and implementation of a software engineering Quality Management System is a major task, and requires dedication and commitment on the part of all those involved, from the IS Director to the Junior Programmer. The fruits of successfully operating a QMS, however, are plentiful. It is an essential element of the drive toward higher quality and productivity in our industry.

A QMS provides the mechanism to ensure quality and enjoy the benefits of improved productivity. IE provides the system development approach to preparation of required work products. Both QMS and IE are readily available, but based on what we see in most information systems development environments today, their potential is largely untapped.

Within an Information Engineering environment, we expect methodologies and techniques, as well as CASE tools, to continue evolving. This evolution will be driven by business necessity, creating new "business drivers" for the software development business within all organizations. These high-level business drivers will be increasing the demand for better quality software, more complex systems, shorter development and maintenance cycles, and truly integrated application systems. All business drivers require a combination of quality and Information Engineering.

As the evolution in Information Engineering and quality management continues, organizations must plan for their evolution. It is essential to formally improve Information Engineering mechanisms and formally manage quality. This is the secret to high productivity.

Author Biography

H. Glen Weekley, Senior Management Consultant with the Strategic Research and Consulting organization at Computer Task Group (CTG), has specialized in Information Engineering consultation with emphasis on migration to Information Engineering and CASE, Information Strategy Planning, and Business Area Analysis since the inception of Information Engineering. He has more than 25 years experience in large scale systems development, selection and implementation, and application of Information Engineering methods to developing strategies and information technologies.

Before joining CTG, he was the national partner-in-charge of Arthur Young's systems consulting practice. Mr. Weekley was heavily involved with James Martin and other Information Engineering pioneers in the early formalization of the underlying principles of Information Engineering and the application of successful techniques to the practical use of Information Engineering.

He is a frequent speaker at international information technology seminars and is involved with industry leaders in innovative efforts in advanced strategic systems approaches.

Marcel Markus is Corporate Quality Process Manager for Computer Task Group, Inc. (CTG). Markus joined CTG in 1990, when the firm acquired Rendeck International, a European professional-services firm. He began his career in data processing in 1971 and has held various positions including those of programmer, analyst and project manager.

Mr. Markus joined Rendeck in 1981 as Project Manager and was promoted to Branch Manager of Rendeck's Southend-on-Sea, UK, business unit in 1989. As Branch Manager, Markus was responsible for sales, administration, staff management, business planning and quality control.

Mr. Markus has extensive experience in designing and implementing quality systems in accordance with international standards. As Branch Manager, Southend-on-Sea, he was instrumental in gaining the International Standards Organization (ISO) 9001 TickIT Quality Standard Certification for Software Development for the branch, This is the UK's "official seal of approval" for applying international quality standards to systems development.

In 1992, Markus was named Corporate Quality Process Manager and now supports the development and implementation of CTG's IQ Quality Management Process, a corporate-wide initiative to manage quality at every level of CTG.

References

Aguayo, Rafael and Dr. Edwards Deming. *The American who taught the Japanese about quality.* Simon & Schuster, Inc.

Feigenbaum, Armand V. *Total quality control.* McGraw-Hill.

Walton, Mary. 1991. *Deming management at work.* Putnam Publishing.

Part

2

This section is a compendium of techniques, guidelines, and philosophies that will assist the developer in understanding and then putting into place a quality/productivity program. The 42 chapters contained in this section offer the reader a wealth of information and advice in a multitude of areas, including management of resources, methods, quality, and metrics.
  Each chapter is composed of the following:

- *Abstract, which discusses the goals and principles behind the technique.*

- *Procedures/Issues/Policies, a step-by-step implementation section.*

- *Selected Bibliography, sources for further reading.*

- *Reference, where the reader can contain a detailed version of the technique described in the chapter.*

27

Kellner's Nontechnological Issues in Software Engineering

Abstract

Although much of the emphasis in current literature is on the technical issues of software engineering, a number of substantive nontechnological problems pose dangers to the effective practice of software engineering. A lack of software engineering productivity can be caused by managerial, organizational, economic, political, legal, behavioral, psychological, and social factors.

To achieve an acceptable level of software engineering productivity, as much emphasis must be placed on "people" issues as on technological issues. As Boehm (1981) puts it, "Personnel attributes and human relations activities provide by far the largest source of opportunity for improving software productivity."

Procedures/Issues/Policies

1. Recognize that the process of software engineering is "sufficiently confused and incoherent that nontechnological factors impede the effective application of technology" (Humphrey 1989).

2. There are many nontechnological issues that are intertwined with software engineering. Although any of these are potential impediments, the Kellner panel focused on these three:

   — The software engineering profession, for the most part, has not developed a block of capable/competent managers.

   — In spite of a concerted effort towards making software development an engineering discipline, it is still very much of an individual creative activity, rather than a team effort.

— Little has been done to reduce performance differences among individuals or across teams.

3. Poor management produces:

— Unrealistic project plans due to poor planning/scheduling/estimation skills
— Lack of teamwork due to inability to build and manage effective teams
— Poor project execution due to inadequate organization, delegation and monitoring
— Technical problems due to lack of management understanding of disciplines such as quality assurance, configuration management
— Inadequately trained staff due to a short-sighted rather than a long-term perspective

4. Possible solutions to poor management problem:

— Definition of dual career paths for technical and managerial staff
— Training in managerial skills and techniques
— Active mentoring and supervision by senior managers
— Increased delegation of responsibility and matching authority

5. Reasons for lack of teamwork:

— Desire for autonomy
— A culture that reinforces individual efforts more than team efforts
— Concentration of key application knowledge by a few individuals
— Desire for privacy
— The "not invented here" syndrome translated to the "not invented by me" syndrome
— Large productivity differences from one individual to another
— Political considerations between powerful individuals and managers

6. Possible solutions to teamwork problem:

— Objective assessment of team contributions with appropriate rewards
— Development of an organizational culture that condones/rewards group efforts
— Active efforts to disperse crucial application knowledge across project staff
— Improvements in communication and coordination across organizational layers
— Adoption of egoless programming techniques

7. Large performance differences between individuals negate productivity increases. Boehm (1981) estimates that productivity ranges of 3:1 to 5:1 are typical, with some studies documenting differences as high as 26:1 among experienced programmers. This variability is often due to:

— Misguided staffing practices
— Poor team development
— Inattention to the critical role of motivation
— Poor management

8. Techniques to increase effective level of productivity:
   — Enhanced training
   — Investment in productivity tools and methods
   — Standard practices
   — Professional development opportunities
   — Recognition
   — Effective staffing
   — Top talent
   — Job matching
   — Career progression
   — Team balance
   — Improved management

Selected Bibliography

Boehm, Barry W. 1981. *Software engineering economics*. Prentice-Hall.

Brooks, Fred P. 1987. No silver bullet. *Computer*. 20 (4): 10–19.

Curtis, Bill, Herb Krasner, and Neil Iscoe. 1988. A field study of the software design process for large systems. *Communications of the ACM*. 31 (11): 1268–1287.

Humphrey, Watts S. 1989. *Managing the software process*. Addison-Wesley.

Humphrey, Watts S., David H. Kitson, and Tim C. Kasse. 1989. *The state of software engineering practice: A preliminary report*. Technical report number CMU/SEI-89-TR-1, Software Engineering Institute, Carnegie Mellon University. February 1989.

Reference

Kellner, Marc I., Software Engineering Institute, with panelists Bill Curtis, Software Engineering Institute; Tom DeMarco, The Atlantic Systems Guild; Kouichi Kisida, Software Research Associates, Inc.; Maurice Schlumberger, Cap Gemeini Innovation; and Colin Tully, Independent Consultant for IEEE. 1991. pp.144–146.

Martin and Carey Survey of Success in Converting Prototypes to Operational Systems

Abstract

The use of prototyping has increased within the ranks of MIS groups during the last few years. But there has been a difference of opinion as to how a prototype should be implemented, as well as in the steps taken to make the prototype operational. One school of thought stresses that the prototype is never meant to become an operational system at all. Therefore, the languages used, as well as the platform selected, should all be experimental. On the other side of the argument are those that stress that the prototypical system should be as close to the operational system as possible. This disagreement has left MIS organizations without clear guidelines for the use of prototypes in their organizations.

Martin and Carey performed an extensive survey of a sector of MIS shops within the manufacturing industry and found that "prototype models were usually not thrown away, prototypes were usually programmed in the same language as the operational system, prototyping in third generational languages was common, and prototyping models were documented as they were developed."

The Martin and Carey findings, while contrary to much of the literature on prototyping, are important in that they open a fresh perspective on an important topic.

According to Martin and Carey, "Prototyping is the process of quickly building a model of the final software system which is used primarily as a communication tool to assess and meet the information needs of the user."

This survey found that the use of prototyping was born out of some major difficulties found in the traditional software development approach, including:

1. End users don't often possess a clear and concise understanding of what they need and what they want.

2. The methodologies and tools currently employed by MIS, data-flow diagrams, and the like, cannot demonstrate the workings of an actual system to the liking, or understanding, of a naive end-user.

3. As the development team grows, so does the complexity of communication between group members.

4. Systems developed along traditional lines are often difficult to learn and use.

5. As the technology becomes more complex, so do the systems that are created. As a result systems are often developed over longer time periods.

6. Traditional approaches have been plagued by late delivery and costly overruns.

7. It comes as no surprise to MIS staff that there exists a rather large application development backlog. According to Martin and Carey, "The users who requested them are frustrated, disillusioned, and ready to revolt."

As observed in the abstract, there are two schools of thought concerning prototypes. Each school has adopted a distinct type of prototype. The iterative type (labeled Type I by Martin and Carey) implements the final version of the prototype after a series of modifications. The Martin and Carey Type II prototype, the throwaway, is often built in a 4th-generation language and is, indeed, only a model of the final system. At prototype's end, the 4th-generation model is "thrown away" and the system is ultimately implemented in a 3rd-generation language.

Procedures/Issues/Policies

1. In general, the use of prototyping appears to more appropriate for small decision-support systems than for large transaction-processing systems. Decision-support systems may beneficially use Type I iterative systems. However, it has also been found that a transaction processing system might benefit from a Type II throwaway prototype.

2. In planning a prototype the development team should take note of the possible differences between the prototype and operational environments. These differences include:

   —Language
   —Range of transactions
   —Documentation requirements
   —Computer architecture
   —Access control
   —Procedures

3. The programming language for the ultimate operational system should be self-documenting. There are inherent differences between the 3rd-generation lan-

guages of the operational environment and the 4th-generation languages of the prototype environment. These include:

—4GLs are not as self-documenting as 3GLs.
—4GLs more than likely have features not available in 3GLs, such as rapid database inquiry.
—4GLs often use recursive paths not compatible with the structured, top-down operational language requirements.

4. Usually, 20% of a systems inputs represent 80% of the transaction volume. Therefore, it is this 20% that should be the domain of prototyping. According to Martin and Carey this is because "a prototype is designed to show users what typically will happen, rather all that can happen."

5. Turning a prototype into an operational system requires the development team to account for 100% of the systems' transactions, rather than the 20% accountable for in the prototype.

6. Prototypes are often run on a microcomputer because the PC is portable for demonstrations, it will not be disrupted by operational problems, and it will not disrupt operations systems.

7. Systems are composed of more than just software. Systems also include hardware, people, and data. The procedures used to tie all of these together in the prototype is far less complex than the procedures required in an operational system.

8. Conversion from an iterative prototype to a full operational system is complex and time-consuming. Steps required include:

—Language conversion
—Expansion to full transaction range
—Extensive documentation
—Change from micro environment to operational platform
—Establishment of access control
—Development of procedures

9. The pain of prototype-to-operational-system conversion can be eased somewhat by careful development of the prototype. Approaches that accomplish this goal include:

—The prototype should be programmed in the same language as the ultimate operational system.
—Document the prototype as it evolves.
—Develop the prototype on the ultimate platform. If the system is intended for use on a mainframe, then prototype it on a mainframe.

10. The Martin and Carey survey documented the prototyping characteristics discussed above as being the techniques used in a segment of commercial industry. The specific survey results are as follows:

—Prototype models were not usually thrown away.
—Throwaway prototypes were not actually thrown away. They were often used for other purposes, such as training.

—Prototypes were usually programmed in the same language as the operational system.

—Prototyping in 3GLs was not uncommon. According to Martin and Carey, "The power of reusable code for a 3GL such as COBOL should not be underestimated."

—Prototyping models were being documented as they were developed.

—The primary goal of the prototype process was user communications and involvement, not system development efficiency.

Selected Bibliography

Carey, J.M. 1989. Prototyping: Alternative systems development methodology. *Information software technology*. 31 (8).

Carey, J.M. and R. McLeod, Jr. 1987. Use of system development methodology and tools. *Journal of systems management*. 39 (3): 30–35.

Kingler, D.E. 1986. Rapid prototyping revisited. *Datamation*. 32: 131–132.

Martin, M.P. 1987. Designing systems for change. *Journal of systems management*. 39 (7): 14–18.

Martin, M.P. 1988. The transition between the prototype and the operational environment. *Proceedings of the Western Region of Decision Sciences Institute*. April 1988.

Reference

Martin, M.P. and J.M. Carey. 1991. Converting prototypes to operational systems: Evidence from preliminary industrial survey. *Information and software technology*. 33 (5): 351–356.

29

Putnam's Trends in Measurement, Estimation, and Control

Abstract

Although most MIS managers have read about the different techniques of measurement, estimation, and control, they are still confused about how to apply them to their own situation. In addition, a plethora of information about this topic has served to only confuse these practitioners, rather than enlighten them.

Putnam estimates that, in the development of complex systems, from 50% to 70% of these projects come in either late, over budget, or in error. Most academicians, as well as notables in the field, Putnam included, conclude that one of the major problems is that MIS departments have not developed the facilities to gauge where they are or where they should be.

The old standby, lines of code (LOC), is, according to Putnam, "the worst metric." Twelve years of Putnam's research has shown that "both the numerator (number of lines) and the denominator (number of man-months) vary with a host of factors related to the environment and management practices in complex, ill-understood, non-linear ways that cause it to behave unintuitively." The result is that the lines of code metric is wrong approximately 90% of the time.

In the late 1980s and now in the '90s, there has been a renewed emphasis on measurement. MIS shops are now attempting to evaluate the reliability of software.

In this chapter, a series of issues is raised in this area that the professional intent on installing a measurement program will want to review carefully.

Procedures/Issues/Policies

1. Putnam defines a *set of workable metrics* as that which is simple, single-valued, and a set which the boss understands. The following is the set that he recommends:

   —Quantity of function (such as source lines of code and Function Points)
   —Schedule (the elapsed calendar time)
   —People (the monthly head count)
   —Effort (the sum of the people applied over time)
   —Defects (the number of valid problem trouble reports over some time interval. This can easily be converted to mean time to defect)

2. Making Total Quality realistic in a software engineering environment:

   —Take quality seriously
   —Take productivity improvement seriously
   —Measure progress with the right metrics
   —Set realistic goals
   —Focus MIS investment and education on the weaker spots
   —Aim for a small gain every day

3. Use statistical process control on projects. This technique couples statistical techniques with the metrics previously outlined. The basics of software control include:

   —Milestone accomplishments (schedule)
   —Effort expenditure (in man-months)
   —Code production
   —Defect identification (trouble reports)

4. These statistics should be captured each month and compared with the plan.

5. Unfavorable variations indicate slippage and overrun.

6. Statistical software packages should be used because a simple extrapolation to predict the future is not useful. Statistical curve-fitting techniques, readily available in this sort of software, are a desirable tool for control.

7. Putnam's outlook for the 1990s: Control offices will be established to measure, plan, and control projects. This will be call the software-data repository, and will be responsible for measuring process-productivity improvement, as well as for generating realistic and consistent work plans for the individual project teams.

8. Executive managers will begin to take a more active interest in development because of the realization that it is of strategic importance to the organization.

Reference

Putnam, L.H. 1991. Trends in measurement, estimation, and control. *IEEE software*. March 1991. 105–107.

Sprague's Technique for Software Configuration Management in a Measurement-based Software Engineering Program

Abstract

The role of Software Configuration Management (SCM) has significantly increased over the last few years. Sprague enumerates several reasons for SCM's expanded role:

- The size of software projects has grown, meaning that there are more components to manage.
- The introduction of CASE tools has increased the number and types of machine-readable objects that must be maintained.
- The advent of new computing topologies and application structures.

These reasons, coupled with an increasing awareness of the competitive and strategic organizational issues vis-a-vis technology, has placed an emphasis on being able to control the technology environment.

Sprague's definition of SCM expands on the traditional meaning, which is control over the source code. Sprague emphasizes that SCM should consider all of the work products associated with a project, including:

- Contracts
- Memorandums
- Letters

- Project plans
- Schedules
- System and software requirements
- Design documentation
- Source, object, and executable code
- Data
- Build and installation files
- Test descriptions, results and reports
- Systems and network options
- Metrics
- Technical reports
- Education and training documents
- Presentation slides
- Videos
- Business models and plans

SCM is a formal engineering discipline, as described in the 1983 IEEE Standard 828-1983, *Standard for software configuration management plans*, is the means through which the integrity of the software product is recorded, communicated, and controlled. Derived from hardware-oriented Configuration Management (CM), SCM's objective is the cost-effective management of a software system's life cycle and the resultant configuration. As Sprague suggests, "It is the process of ensuring the software and associated products are visible, traceable, and formally controlled throughout their evolution."

Perhaps the most important concept behind SCM is baseline management. A *baseline* is a specification or product that has been formally reviewed and agreed upon, and thereafter serves as the basis for further development, and one that can be changed only through formal change control procedures.

Four functions are employed to manage the baseline and its products: configuration identification, configuration control, configuration status accounting, and configuration auditing.

This chapter presents an overview of SCM as well as a process for implementing it.

Procedures/Issues/Policies

1. *Configuration identification* is the process of designating the configuration items in a system and recording their characteristics. This process entails the determination of the constituent parts of the software, the determination of the relationship of those parts, the assignment of a label and a name to each part, and the graphical depiction of the identified software.

2. *Configuration control* provides the administrative mechanism for precipitating, preparing, evaluating, approving/disapproving, and implementing every change

to all the products in a baseline. The purpose of configuration control is to assure:

—Comprehensive system impact analysis
—Cost and schedule impact analysis
—Optimum and coordinated implementation
—Accurate configuration records
—Supportability

3. *Configuration status accounting* is the process of collecting, recording and reporting on configuration control information. The following information is typically maintained as well as archived:

—The time at which each baseline was established.
—The time at which each item and change was included in the baseline.
—A description of each software configuration item.
—The status of each software-related engineering change.
—The description of each software change.
—The documentation status for each baseline.
—The changes planned for each identified future baseline.

4. *Configuration auditing* is the process of verifying that all required configuration items have been produced, that the current version agrees with the specified requirements, that the technical documentation describes the configuration items, and that all change requests have been resolved.

Procedures for developing an SCM process

1. Develop an SCMP: the first step is to develop a plan tailored to the needs of the project/organization. The plan address the four components of SCM previously described. The SCMP should address the following:

—The characteristics of the work products controlled
—The work products to be controlled
—The different interfaces to be managed
—The expected duration of the project
—The available resources
—The organizational responsibilities of project members
—The identification procedures that will be used on each project
—The procedures for checking items into and out of the software libraries
—The procedures for managing the change process
—The authority, membership, and decision-making process of the group charged with this information's control
—The procedures to create and approve the promotion of a baseline
—The membership data that will be collected, stored and reported
—The procedures to collect, store, and report the measurement data
—The mechanism to transfer objects between repositories
—The procedures for releasing versions
—The automated tools that will be used to support the SCM process
—The procedure for recovering work products in the event of a disaster

2. Implement the SCMP: this step requires that those charged with the SCM take actions to ensure that the SCM is implemented. This implies that the SCMP be periodically reviewed—and revised, if necessary.

3. Identify and control the work products: this task is accomplished by identifying each object checked into the repository, securing an electronic or paper copy of the object and placing the object in a location where it cannot be modified, and, finally, making a log entry describing the events that took place during the transaction.

4. Collect, store, and report preliminary measurements: this should be done at each phase of the development project. The benefits derived from collecting and analyzing the measurements at each stage provides the manager with insight into how the project is doing in terms of cost, schedule, and size.

5. Transfer the work products to work group responsible for SCM who will secure and control it.

6. Deliver the work products to the customer.

7. Collect, store, and report the final measurements to project members, users and senior management.

Selected Bibliography

Bryan, W.L. and S. Siegel. 1988. *Software product assurance: Techniques for reducing software risk*. New York, N.Y.; Elsevier Science Publishing.

Forte, Gene. 1990. Configuration management survey. *CASE outlook*. 90 (2): 24–51.

Humphrey, W.S. 1989. *Managing the software process*. New York, N.Y.: Addison-Wesley Publishing Co.

Tichy, Walter F. 1989. Tools for software configuration management. Presented at the 11th International Conference on Software Engineering, May 15–18, 1989.

Reference

Sprague, Kristopher G. 1991. The role of software configuration management in a measurement-based software engineering program. *ACM SIGSOFT software engineering notes*. 16 (2): 1–10.

Corbin's Methodology for Establishing a Software Development Environment

Abstract

The SDE (Software Development Environment) is actually the integration of a number of processes, tools, standards, methodologies, and related elements whose purpose is to provide a framework for building quality software. This chapter discusses the elements of an SDE and shows how one can be developed.

Procedures/Issues/Policies

1. The elements of SDE include:
   —Project management
   —Business plan
   —Architecture
   —Methodologies
   —Techniques
   —Tools
   —Metrics
   —Policies and procedures
   —Technology platform
   —Support
   —Standards
   —Education and training

2. The benefits of SDE include:

—Improved problem definition
—Selection of the "right" problem according to the customer
—Joint customer/IS responsibility and accountability
—Acknowledgment of customer ownership of system
—Reduced costs of systems development and maintenance
—Reusability of software, models and data definitions
—Acceptance of the disciplined approach to software engineering using a consistent methodology
—Productivity improvements through team efforts and tools such as CASE

3. Sample goals of SDE are:

—Reduce systems development costs
—Reduce maintenance costs
—Reduce MIS turnover rate

These goals should be quantifiable wherever possible. For example, the first goal could be stated as "reduce systems development costs by 50% over the next five years."

4. Architecture: many organizations do not have a formal, documented architecture. There are three types:

—Business Architecture is a model of the business and identifies such things as processes and entities in the form of models.
—Computing Architecture, at a minimum, identifies hardware, software, and data communications. This breaks out into components such as operating systems, data resource management, network protocols, and user interface.
—Enterprise Architecture is a combination of the Business and Computing Architectures.

5. Business plan:

—Create a Steering Committee that provides direction to the MIS function.
—Translate the organization's business plan into an actionable MIS plan that supports the business' goals and objectives.
—The Steering Committee should be responsible for funding projects, setting priorities, resolving business issues and reviewing MIS policies and procedures.

6. Education and training: make sure that analysts, programmers and users are all trained and ready to start the development project. Training might include the following:

—Software engineering concepts
—Prototyping
—System development life cycle
—Joint application development
—Software quality assurance and testing
—Project management
—Data and process modeling
—CASE

7. Methodologies: whether the methodology chosen by the MIS department is a standard one, from a vendor or developed internally, the MIS group must follow one to ensure consistency from project to project. This will enable staff to be able to move from project to project without retraining while, at the same time, ensuring consistent deliverables. Questions to ask when selecting a methodology are:

—Does your methodology support the entire systems development life cycle?
—Does it include maintenance?
—Is it clearly documented?
—Does it focus on deliverables instead of activities?
—Is it CASE tool independent?
—Can you use your metrics and techniques with it?

8. Project management: questions to ask include:

—Do you have a formal project management discipline in place?
—Do you have a training program to support this?
—Is a software tool used?
—Do you have program planning and control to help manage the project?
—Do you get routine reports showing the project work breakdown structure, status reports, resource loading and cost projections?
—Is there a formal reporting mechanism done on a timely basis to resolve problems?

9. Standards: some of the areas in which standards are required are:

—Systems analysis and design
—Data administration
—Database administration
—Systems testing
—Prototyping
—Documentation
—Data entry
—Systems production
—Change/configuration management

Questions to ask include:

—Have you identified all of the standards that are required to support your SDE?
—Do you have someone responsible for developing and maintaining standards?

10. Support options include:

—External consulting
—A sharing arrangement where you can provide services in exchange for those needed
—User groups
—Special interest groups

11. Automated tool questions include:

—Have you identified the tools you need in the SDE?
—Have they been approved, acquired, and installed?
—Do they support the methodologies?

—Do they support the technology platform?
—Do they support the standards?
—Is technical support available to support the tools?
—Do you have templates for use in systems development?
—Do you have a data dictionary, or repository for your data?
—Do you have tools to support each phase of the life cycle?

Reference

Corbin, D.S. 1991. Establishing the software development environment. *Journal of systems management*. September 1991. 28–31.

Couger's Bottom-up Approach to Creativity Improvement in IS Development

Abstract

The majority of IS organizations use a top-down approach to generating productivity improvements. In this chapter, a process for generating via a series of bottom-up creativity techniques is addressed.

The authors are all staff members of the United Technologies Microelectronic Center who, upon a six-month review of all available IS literature, found that very little research had been published in the area of creativity generation techniques in IS organizations.

The four authors decided to cull creativity generating techniques that had been proven successful in other disciplines. As a result, a two-pronged approach was selected for the UTMC creativity program:

- Improvement of the environment for creativity and innovation
- Training in specific techniques for creativity generation and evaluation

The results of the institution of this approach were exciting. According to the authors the creativity program more than paid for itself in the efficiency improvements alone, both in savings of computer processing time and computer programming time. In addition, the UTMC group saw great improvements in the effectiveness of their systems.

Procedures/Issues/Policies

1. Survey participants to obtain perceptions on the environment for creativity and innovation. This same instrument should be used to obtain new perceptions as a measurement of the results.

2. Participants should be asked to keep a "creativity log" in which they keep track of their creativity improvements.

3. Training workshop instituted to teach a variety of creativity generation and evaluation techniques.

4. One-third of the workshop was spent in discussing how to improve the climate for creativity in the IS organization. The methodology used for this assessment was to ask the employees to identify positive and negative contributors to the creativity environment.

5. Creativity generation/evaluation techniques used:

   —Analogy/metaphor: an *analogy* is a statement about how objects, people, situations or actions are similar in process or relationship. *Metaphors*, on the other hand, are merely figures of speech. Both of these techniques can be used to create fictional situations for gaining new perspectives on problem definition and resolution.

   —Brainstorming: this technique is perhaps the most familiar of all the techniques discussed here. It is used to generate a large quantity of ideas in a short period of time.

   —Blue slip: ideas are individually generated and recorded on a 3"× 5" slip of blue paper. Done anonymously to make people feel more at ease, people readily share ideas. Since each idea is on a separate piece of blue paper, the sorting and grouping of like ideas is facilitated.

   —Extrapolation: a technique or approach, already used by the organization, is stretched to apply to a new problem.

   —Progressive abstraction technique: by moving through progressively higher levels of abstraction, it is possible to generate alternative problem definitions from an original problem. When a problem is enlarged in a systematic way, it is possible to generate many new definitions that can then be evaluated for their usefulness and feasibility. Once an appropriate level of abstraction is reached, possible solutions are more easily identified.

   —5Ws and H technique: this is the traditional, and journalistic, approach of who-what-where-when-why-how. Using this technique serves to expand a person's view of the problem and to assist in making sure that all related aspects of the problem have been addressed and considered.

   —Force field analysis technique: the name of this technique comes from its ability to identify forces contributing to or hindering a solution to a problem. This technique stimulates creative thinking in three ways: it defines direction; it identifies strengths that can be maximized; and it identifies weaknesses that can be minimized.

—Peaceful setting: this is not so much of a technique as an environment. Taking people away from their hectic surroundings enables "a less cluttered open mental process."

—Problem reversal: reversing a problem statement often provides a different framework for analysis. For example, in attempting to come up with ways to improve productivity, try considering the opposite, how to decrease productivity.

—Associations/image technique: most of us have played the game, at one time or another, where a person names a person, place or thing and asks for the first thing that pops into the second person's mind. The linking or combining process is another way of expanding the solution space.

—Wishful thinking: this technique enables people to loosen analytical parameters to consider a larger set of alternatives than they might ordinarily consider. By permitting a degree of fantasy into the process, the result just might be a new and unique approach.

6. Follow-up sessions are scheduled for reinforcement. At these meetings, which are primarily staff meetings, employees were invited to identify results of creative activity.

Reference

Couger, J.D., S.C. McIntyre, L.F. Higgins, and T.A. Snow. 1991. Using a bottom-up approach to creativity improvement in IS development. *Journal of systems management*. September 1991: 23–36.

Shetty's Seven Principles of Quality Leaders

Abstract

Shetty, a professor of management at Utah State University's College of Business, and the co-editor of *The quest for competitiveness*, suggests that even though most corporate executives believe that quality and productivity are the most critical issues facing American business, many do not know how to achieve it. Shetty lists organizations that have vigorously attacked this challenge: Hewlett-Packard, IBM, Procter and Gamble, Johnson & Johnson, Maytag, Dana Corporation, Intel, Texas Instruments, 3M, Caterpillar, Delta, Marriott, McDonald's, Dow Chemical, Xerox, and General Electric.

Shetty's chapter discusses the common principles shared by this elite group.

Procedures/Issues/Policies

Principle 1: Quality improvement requires the firm commitment of top management.

- All top management, including the CEO, must be personally committed to quality. The keyword here is *personally*. Many CEOs pay only lip service to this particular edict. Therefore, top management must be consistent and reflect its commitment through the company's philosophy, goals, policies, priorities, and executive behavior. Steps management can take to accomplish this end include establishing and communicating a clear vision of corporate philosophy, principles, and objectives relevant to product and service quality.

- Channel resources toward these objectives and define roles and responsibilities in this endeavor.

- Invest time to learn about quality issues and monitor the progress of any initiatives.
- Encourage communication between management and employees, among departments, and among various units of the firm and customers.
- Be a good role model in communication and action.

Principle 2: Quality is a strategic issue.

- It must be a party of a company's goals and strategies.
- Must be consistent with and reinforce a company's other strategic objectives.
- Must be integrated into budgets and plans—the way the company does business.
- It must be a corporate mission with planned goals and strategies.
- Quality should be at the heart of every action.

Principle 3: employees are the key to consistent quality.

- The organization must have a people-oriented philosophy.
- Poorly managed people convey their disdain for quality and service when they work.
- Pay special attention to employee recruitment, selection and socialization.
- Reinforce socialization and quality process with continuous training and education. This, to include training in:
  —Awareness of quality,
  —Each employee's role in the process,
  —Statistical process control, and
  —Problem-solving techniques.
- Incorporate quality into performance appraisal and reward systems.
- Encourage employee participation and involvement.
- Effective communication throughout the department, between departments, and throughout the organization is required to reinforce the deep commitment of management and creates an awareness and understanding of the role of quality and customer service.

Principle 4: Quality standards and measurements must be customer-driven and can be measured by:

- Formal customer surveys
- Focus groups
- Customer complaints
- Quality audits
- Testing panels
- Statistical quality controls
- Interaction with customers

Principle 5: Many programs and techniques can be used to improve quality. Techniques and programs used to improve quality include:

- Statistical quality control
- Quality circles
- Suggestion systems
- Quality-of-work-life projects
- Competitive benchmarking

Principle 6: All company activities have potential for improving product quality; therefore teamwork is vital.

- Quality improvement requires close cooperation between managers and employees and among departments.
- Total quality management involves preventing errors at the point where work is performed.
- Every employee and department is responsible for quality.

Principle 7: Quality is a never-ending process.

- Quality must be planned.
- Quality must be organized.
- Quality must be monitored.
- Quality must be continuously revitalized.

References

Shetty, Y.K. 1991. A point of view: Seven principles of quality leaders. *National productivity review*. Winter 1991–1992: 3–7.

Shetty, Y.K. 1991. *The quest for competitiveness*. Quorum Books.

Simmons' Statistics Concerning the Effect that Communications Has on Group Productivity

Abstract

In this chapter, the author details the many factors that dominate software group productivity. He defines *dominator* as a single factor that causes productivity to decline ten-fold. The two dominators that are discussed are communications and design partition.

What follows is a set of rules and statistics that the reader can use as a comparison in his or her own efforts to increase productivity.

Procedures/Issues/Policies

1. Factors that developers must cope with in developing large systems include:

   —Personnel turnover
   —Hardware/software turnover
   —Major ideas incorporated late in the game
   —Latent bugs

2. A Delphi survey performed by Scott and Simmons to uncover factors that affect productivity found that the main factors are:

   —External documentation
   —Programming language
   —Programming tools
   —Programmer experience
   —Communications

—Independent modules for task assignment (design partition)

—Well-defined programming practices

3. Improvement statistics:

—Any step towards the use of structured techniques, interactive development, inspections etc., can improve productivity by up to 25%.

—Use of these techniques in combination could yield improvements of between 25% and 50%.

—Change in programming language can, by itself, yield a productivity improvement of more than 50%.

—Gains of between 50 and 75% can be achieved by single high achievers or teams of high achievers.

—Gains of 100% can be achieved by database user languages, application generators and software reuse.

4. Dominators are factors that can suppress the effects of other factors and can reduce software group productivity by an order of magnitude.

5. Poor design partition can dominate group productivity. To obtain high productivity in the development of large software systems, the designer must break down the system in chunks that can be developed in parallel. The difference between great and average designers is an order of magnitude.

6. Communications can dominate productivity. Most project problems arise as the result of poor communications between workers. If there are n workers on the team, then there are $n(n-1) \div 2$ interfaces across which there may be communications problems.

7. Productivity of individual programmers varies as much as 26:1.

8. An individual working alone has no interruptions from fellow group members. Therefore, the productivity can be quite high for a motivated individual. It is estimated that one programmer working 60 hours a week can complete a project in the same calendar time as two others working normal hours, but at ¾ the cost.

9. Small groups of experienced and productive software developers can create large systems. An example is given of a company, Pyburn Systems. They scour the country for the best analytical thinkers. Its senior programmers typically earn $125,000 a year and can be paid bonuses of two to three times that amount. They work in small teams, never more than five, to produce large, complex systems. In comparison, most MIS departments produce large systems using normal development teams with developers of average ability.

10. In general, the difference between the cost to produce an individual program to be run by the program author, and the cost to produce a programming system product developed by a software group, is at least nine times more expensive.

11. There is a point where coordination overheads outweigh any benefits that can be obtained by the addition of further staff. Statistics that support this were pioneered during the 19th century in work on military organization. It was noted that as the number of workers who had to communicate increased arithmetically

from two to three to four to five, the number of communication channels among them increased geometrically from one to three to six to ten. From this study, it was concluded eight people is the upper limit of effective staff size for cooperative projects.

12. In studies, it has been shown that when the number of staff increased to 12 or more, the efficiency of the group decreased to less than 30%.

13. The productive time of a typical software developer during a working day can vary from 51% to 79%. It was found that the average duration of work interruption was five minutes for a typical programmer. The average time to regain a train of thought after an interruption was two minutes. Thus, the average total time spent on an interruption was seven minutes.

    If we assume five productive hours each day, then each interruption takes 2.33% of the working day, ten interruptions would take up 23.3% of the day, and 20 interruptions would take almost 50% of the working day.

14. The optimum group size for a software development team is between five to eight members. The overall design should be partitioned into successively smaller chunks until the development group has a chunk of software to develop that minimizes intra-group and inter-group communications.

Selected Bibliography

Factor, R.M. and W.B. Smith. 1988. A discipline for improving software productivity. *AT&T tech journal*. July/August 1988: 2–9.

Grady, R.B. and D.L Caswell. 1987. *Software metrics: Establishing a company-wide program*. Englewood Cliffs, N.J.: Prentice Hall.

Jones, C. 1977. *Program quality and programmer productivity*. IBM Technical Report TR 02.764. January 1977: 42–78.

Scott, R.F. and D.B. Simmons. 1974. Programmer productivity and the Delphi technique. *Datamation*. May 1974: 72–73.

Simmons, D.B. 1972. The art of writing large programs. *Computer*. March/April 1972: 43–49.

Software Productivity Metrics Working Group. 1989. Standard for software productivity metrics. IEEE, Standard P1045/32.0. 20th November 1989.

Reference

Simmons, D.B. 1991. Communications: A software group productivity dominator. *Software engineering journal*. November 1991. 454–462.

Gould's Points on Usability

Abstract

Few in the industry have added usability design to their rostrum of design issues. However, the authors note that this process leads to usable, useful, likable computer systems and applications. The authors present strong evidence that the readers can use to support their own efforts in this, perhaps, new terrain. This chapter also details a process that can be used to design effective and usable systems.

In effect, this chapter proposes:

- Greater reliance on existing methodologies for establishing testable usability and productivity-enhancing goals.

- A new method for identifying and focusing attention on long-term trends about the effects that computer applications have on end-user productivity.

- A new approach to application development, particularly the development of user interfaces.

The authors conclude that a three-way split among style of the user interface, content of the user interface, and the functional code, allows changes to be made in the user interface that still preserves the integrity of the functional code. Iterative design, a necessity when looking toward usability, proceeds rapidly.

On the style side, a particular style can be prototyped and iteratively engineered. From the set of styles developed over time, a subset of workable, usable styles will emerge that have attained the favor of organizations or end users.

Ultimately, the best work of both the style side and the functional side of development will be better leveraged.

Procedures/Issues/Policies

1. The usability process consists of four activities:

   —Early focus on users via interviews, surveys, observations, and participatory design with an aim toward understanding users' cognitive, behavioral, and attitudinal characteristics.

   —All facets of usability, for example user interface, help system, training plan, and documentation, should evolve in parallel instead of sequentially, and should be under one management.

   —There should be early, and continual, user testing. This should include observation and measurement of user behavior and careful evaluation of feedback. Ultimately there should exist a strong motivation to make design changes.

   —Iterative design must be used. Since the system under design must be continually modified due to results of behavioral tests of function, the system must have the ability to be continually changed.

2. This type of development effort has been used with great success as follows:

   —Xerox's Star system
   —Apple's Lisa system
   —IBM Audio Distribution Systems (ADS)
   —IBM's Rexx
   —Tektronix's Graphic Input Workstation
   —Boeing's banking terminal
   —Digital Equipment Corporation's VAX text processing utility
   —IBM's QMF
   —Lotus Development Corporation's Lotus 1-2-3

3. Six interacting, organizational reasons why usability design is not being used:

   —Usability is seldom a goal in development.

   —There is a belief that usability cannot be measured, even though there is much evidence to the contrary.

   —There is an apparent conflict between meeting deadlines and achieving usability. Project managers often have a lack of confidence in managing something that does not have clear goals nor the tools to efficiently address problems as they arise.

   —Designers report that software development is not organized to carry out the process of usability. Iterative design is thought to be too risky, time-consuming, and difficult.

   —Designers need better tools to do iterative design.

   —Nearly every new application creates its own user interface that creates an enormous amount of work. Also, these interfaces are not usually developed by people skilled in user-interface design.

4. Usability metrics can be created. They must be clearly stated, easily communicated, and verifiable. The results must be made public. Experience has shown that these results are then taken seriously by management. This has always been the case in logging system performance data. This operation-room metric is, in

and of itself, a viable usability metric. Measures here include percent system available, downtime per day, and average user satisfaction rating. Digital Equipment Corporation has developed a Usability Engineering approach that is analogous, as shown in Fig. 35.1.

5. Goals creation is a group process. The group must decide what the relevant usability attributes are, how to measure them, and what the target goals should be. The goals are clearly stated and communicated, just as they are for other system components.

6. End-user activity involves four operations: filling in forms, selecting among prescribed choices, manipulating lists, and reading information.

7. The four end-user operations can be tied to four corresponding building blocks that are sufficient to conceptually describe user interfaces. The operations are: form blocks, choice blocks, list blocks, and info blocks.

8. It is possible to separate the design of these blocks, that is, the user interface from the functional code. In the process described here, experts structure their applications in terms of these form, choice, list, and info blocks. Style designers write rules about how these blocks will be rendered on an end-user's screen under various circumstances. The benefits of this approach are: groups can work independently and in parallel, promotes code reuse and iterative design.

9. Content or application experts know the jobs of the end users. They can structure this knowledge into a computer-executable form. Application experts create the user-interface content specifications.

10. Application (content) programmers write the programs.

11. Style designers have skills in human factors and graphic design. Their role is mainly of advocate; they identify problems and describe solutions. They specify style rules.

12. Style programmers write programs necessary for making an interaction work.

Attribute	Measuring Concept	Measuring Method	Worst Case	Planned Level	Best Case	Now Level
Installability	Install Task	Time to install	1 day with media	1 hour without media	10 minutes with media	many cannot install
.						
.						
Learning Rate						
Fear of Seeming Foolish						

source: Digital Equipment Corporation.

Fig. 35.1 DEC's usability goals.

13. Content (application) specifications are created by the application expert and include the messages to end-users, flow of control, connections to function, and guidance to style.

14. Content (application) actions are created by application programmers. These are atomic programs with general utility. For example, a module might transfer the contents of one list to another.

15. Style specifications are created by the style designers. These are the rules regulating the set of human-computer interaction techniques used to render content, including interaction methods (e.g., entry versus selection), appearance of the end-user's screen, and the interaction devices.

16. The team works with a series of tools. Over time, they build up a library of well-tested approaches to human interface which can then be mapped onto an application's content blocks.

Selected Bibliography

Attewell, Paul. 1990. The productivity paradox. Unpublished manuscript.

Good, M., T.M. Spine, J. Whiteside, and P. George. 1986. User-derived impact analysis as a tool for usability engineering. *Human factors in computing systems CHI'86 proceedings*. pp 241–246. New York, N.Y.: ACM.

Gould, J.D. 1988. How to design usable systems. *Handbook of human-computer interaction*. ed. M. Helander. pp. 757–789. Elsevier Science. North-Holland Publishers.

Hartson, R. 1989. User interface management control and communication. *IEEE software*. January 1989: 62–70.

Wiecha, C.W., W. Bennett, S. Boies, and J. Gould. 1989. Generating highly interactive user interfaces. *Proceedings of CHI'88*. pp. 277–282. April 30 – May 4, 1989. Austin, Texas. New York, N.Y.: ACM.

Reference

Gould J.D., S.J. Boies, and C. Lewis. 1991. Making usable, useful, productivity-enhancing computer applications. *Communications of the ACM*. 34 (1)

Prescott's Guidelines for Using Structured Methodology

Abstract

The science of software engineering is composed of many methodologies, and each of these methodologies has its own variations. In this chapter, Prescott offers an itemized set of guidelines for those interested in using structured methodology to ensure their project's success.

Structured methodology is an approach to defining a particular task and defining a solution to that task. It provides a methodology for partitioning a complex task into a manageable series of "black boxes."

The underlying organization of this network of black boxes progresses from abstraction at the top level to details at the lower levels. Not only are the specifics of each black box charted out, but the interfaces between each of these black boxes is specified as well. One of the main reasons for using structured methodology is the sheer complexity and cost of a problem. The discipline associated with this technique is reflected in the need to document each particular phase of development to ensure compliance with demanding requirements for quality, performance, and reliability.

Procedures/Issues/Policies

1. Structured methodology will be successful only if:

   —The company's management is willing to make a firm commitment to the substantial time investment required to build a quality project.

   —A Software Development Plan for the development of software is used. It provides management with the means to coordinate schedules, control resources, initiate actions, and monitor progress of the development effort. It also provides detailed knowledge of the schedule, organization, and resource allocation planned by the contractor. In addition, it contains definitions/discussions of software quality and configuration management, as well as design and programming standards and conventions.

—Walkthroughs of at least five people for up to 1.75 hours at the most are held in the requirements, design, coding, and testing phases.

2. A software requirement must be expressed in very clear English.

3. Decompose each function into related subfunctions. For example Initialization can decompose into Initialize Local Variables and Initialize Global Variables subfunctions.

4. For each function or task and subfunction write a narrative that clearly describes the function in terms of what the function does. The source of the required data and its destination as output from the function must also be defined and documented. The narrative should include the following:

—Module name
—Module called by
—Module purpose
—Inputs
—Outputs
—Unit description

5. Define a local database that will house the data items pertinent to the data requirements.

6. For each function, a detailed design document must be created that will, ultimately, be used to create the code. This document contains the following information:

—Function's name
—Function's purpose
—Description
—Calling sequence, if this sub-module is called by another module or calls another module
—Calling parameters, if called or calling, then what are the parameters passed?
—The files it updates
—The variables that it uses
—Algorithm: pseudo-coded processing logic such as: clear error flag; if code entered is equal to code in table; update table

7. Module is then coded using programming standards that enforce readability and understanding.

8. A test plan is created that takes into consideration schedule, environment, and available resources.

9. Test procedures for each requirement must be documented. This translates into a series of test cases or scenarios. The test, the input, and the expected output are documented in a Requirements Traceability Matrix, which establishes the

correspondence between a software product specification and the successful testing of each such specification.

10. Systems integration and maintenance must be considered.

11. Tools and techniques that assist in the process of structured methodology:
    —Use of formal walkthroughs
    —A structured approach to software design, coding and testing
    —Use of structured programming
    —The use of standardized coding conventions
    —The use of graphics devices such as a functional block diagram for module specification

Reference

Prescott, Jon R. 1991. Using structured methodology for software project success. *Journal of systems management*. July 1991: 28–31.

Kemayel's Controllable Factors in Programmer Productivity

Abstract

This chapter, based on extensive research performed in Tunisia by the authors, seeks to identify the characteristics of the programmer's work potential. The impact of certain controllable factors in the productivity of programmers is investigated.

These factors are divided into three categories: factors pertaining to personnel, factors pertaining to the process, and factors pertaining to the user community.

Procedures/Issues/Policies

1. Programmer productivity paradoxes:

   —There is an enormous variance in the productivity of programmers. This variance can be as wide as a factor of 1:10 (other researchers report an even wider variance). There is a large opportunity to improve programmer productivity within this wide range.

   —Productivity invariance with respect to experience: according to statistical measures by Boehm, when the experience of a programmer increases from one month to three years (a 36-fold increase), productivity is improved by only 34%. This appears to show that experience seems to have no effect on software project costs.

   —Productivity invariance with respect to tools: according to Boehm, the difference in productivity between a programmer who uses no tools at all and one who uses the most up-to-date, powerful tools available, on the most powerful machines, is no larger than 50%.

—Suitability of motivation factors: studies have shown that programmers have a motivation pattern that is different from that of their managers and from workers in other industries. This difference might well explain why some well-intentioned software managers fail to motivate their programmers.

2. Thirty-three productivity factors that are proposed can be divided into three categories: factors related to personnel, factors related to the software process, factors related to the user community.

3. Personnel factors: motivation factors and experience factors are two sets of controllable factors likely to affect the productivity of data processing personnel.

4. Personnel motivation consists of many factors. Sixteen of them, derived from research follow:

    —Recognition: the reaction of the organization to the programmer's performance. Indifference leads to a drop in motivation, which leads to a decline in productivity.

    —Achievement: the satisfaction that the programmer gets from doing a challenging task. This implies that the organization must keep supplying the programmer with challenging tasks to maintain motivation.

    —The work: the nature of the tasks that must be executed is a powerful motivational tool for a programmer.

    —Responsibility: this is derived from basic management theory; that is, if you want something to happen, make someone specifically responsible for it.

    —Advancement: a programmer who feels that he or she has the possibility of career advancement in the organization is more motivated than one who does not.

    —Salary: a programmer who feels that he or she is being paid adequately, and who anticipates that salary increases will continue on par with performance, will be more motivated than one who does not.

    —Possibility for growth: this factor measures the possibilities for professional growth within a programmer's company.

    —Interpersonal relations with subordinates.

    —Status: this measures the importance of the worker in his or her company. Items considered include participation at meetings, participation in decision making, ceremonial functions, usage of restricted services, and privileges of the corporation.

    —Interpersonal relations with superiors: this is controllable to the extent that the manager has latitude in assigning group leaders.

    —Interpersonal relations with peers: since teamwork is a key ingredient for the success of any group effort, the manager should take care in dividing staff into working groups.

    —Technical supervision: this measures the willingness of the programmer's supervisor to help the programmer solve technical problems, orient efforts and make choices.

—Company policy and administration: this factor measures how clearly the command structure of the company is defined, how rational it is, and how easy it is to determine who each worker reports to.

—Working conditions: this factor represents working conditions in the traditional sense, such as office space and light.

—Factors in personal life: given that the programmer's personal life influences motivation and job performance, the manager can assign key positions or tasks to those programmers that have the best circumstances.

—Job security is a very important factor.

5. Personnel experience is equally as important. Four factors are discussed:

—Applications domain experience.

—Virtual machine experience: the aggregate of hardware, operating system, utilities, and software packages.

—Programming language experience.

—Experience with the user community: measures to what extent the programmer is familiar with the user community as a working partner.

6. Project management and programming environments are two classes of controllable factors identified by the authors as pertaining to the software process.

7. Project management consists of four controllable factors:

—Use of a goal structure: measures to what extent the programming team uses a goal structure, and to what extent the team depends on the goal structure for their day-to-day decision making.

—Adherence to a software life cycle: to what extent does a team use, and depend, on a software life cycle.

—Adherence to an activity distribution: measures to what extent the programming team uses a precise definition of life cycle activities and to what extent they depend on it for decision making.

—Use of cost estimation procedures: to what extent does the programming team use a software cost-estimation model and to what extent do they depend on it for decision making.

8. Programming environment is composed of four controllable factors:

—Programming tools: this measures to what extent the programmer uses software tools (such as debuggers and editors), and how powerful these tools are.

—Modern programming practices: to what extent does the programmer use modern programming practices (such as modular programming, program libraries, and reuse) and how powerful they are.

—Programming standards: to what extent are standards used, how stringent are they, and how strictly are they adhered to. Examples include test standards, verification standards, validation standards and unit size standards.

—Power of equipment used: Barry Boehm introduced two factors pertaining to the power of equipment used: a factor that measures memory space limitations and a factor that measures time limitations.

9. The participation of users has been found to have an important impact on programmer productivity. Well-prepared users reduce the cost of software maintenance.

   —Previous education in computing: this factor measures the duration level of the users' previous education in computing.
   —Experience in computing: what is the user's previous computing experience? Previous experience gives users a better sense of what computers can do for them and enables them to express their desires more effectively.
   —Experience with the type of application: experience in building computer systems in the same application domain is valuable. The major incentive for rapid prototyping is to have a high rating for this factor.
   —Experience with the group of programmers/analysts.

10. Survey results on Tunisian subjects include the following:

   —Of the 16 motivation factors, five were statistically significant and account for 18.89% of programmer productivity: technical supervision, working conditions, achievement, responsibilities, and recognition.
   —Of the four personnel experience factors, only two were found to be statistically significant and account for 7.49% of programmer productivity: experience with the virtual machine, and the user community.
   —Of the factors used to access project management, two proved significant and explain 5.57% of programmer productivity: the definition and use of a software life cycle, and software cost estimation.
   —In the programming environment area, two factors explained 9.62% of programmer productivity: the use of modern programming practices, and the power of equipment used for development.
   —Two user factors were found to be significant and explained a 5.33% of programmer productivity: experience of the user community with computers, and the experience of the user community with the group of programmers and analysts.

Selected Bibliography

Basili, V.R. and D.M. Weiss. 1984. A methodology for collecting valid software engineering data. *IEEE transactions on software engineering*. SE-10: 728–737.

Boehm, B.W. 1981. *Software engineering economics*. Englewood Cliffs, N.J.: Prentice Hall.

Mills, H.D. 1983. *Programmer productivity*. Boston, Ma.: Little, Brown and Co.

Reference

Kemayel, L., A. Mili, and I. Ouederni. 1991. Controllable factors for programmer productivity: A statistical study. *Journal of systems software*. 16: 151–163.

AT&T's "Estimeeting" Process for Developing Estimates

Abstract

This chapter presents a method for estimating a software development effort in the early phases of a large software-intensive project. For each feature of the project to be estimated, a "feature team" generates a detailed feature definition that is used in what the authors term an "estimeeting."

Using this process, it is possible to build-in software quality, by design, in the early stages of development and not add in quality later in a series of fixes to problems uncovered in testing. Building in quality requires "front loading" the development process, yielding better designs. Errors are both fewer and more easily and cleanly isolated and repaired.

More complete work in the early stages can lead to earlier identification of tools or special tests needed. If the estimates for a project are too low, then project staffing will also be too low. As needs become apparent, staff are "back-end loaded," which is the reverse of that desirable for a high-quality product.

The estimeeting process described in this chapter describes a process that can be used to accurately estimate a software project. The benefits of this process, as identified by the authors are as follows:

- Better estimates: the ability to more accurately predict resources.

- Earlier and closer subsystem involvement: subsystem owners attend meetings earlier, see what new features may be down the pike, and as a result, make allowances for those features.

- Early direct relationships: the meetings foster teamwork.

- Early expert high-level designs: byproducts of these meetings are ideas that are useful for the next level of design.

- Problem detection: there is a better understanding of potential problems of resources and performance.

- General acceptance of estimates: results are readily acceptable as official.

- Clearly defined milestones: the process has clearly defined outputs and events.

- Better transitions to development: smoother transitions between stages.

- Better quality: a multi-expertise team leads to better definition, requirements, and design.

- Features interactions and synergy: a better understanding of how all features interact.

- Project knowledge base: improve the expertise and knowledge base for estimators, helping to produce more system experts.

- Confidence: increased confidence in the estimates by the Product Management organization.

Procedures/Issues/Policies

1. "An estimeeting is a standardized working meeting with regularly attending estimators. The meeting capitalizes on the synergy of having the key people together. The preparation for and agenda of these meetings are described. Success requires good feature requirements and a high-level design proposal in advance and attendance by a specific group of experienced people."

2. The Front-End Process constitutes the selection process through which feature candidates are picked for development. It begins with a list of feature candidates and ends when a subset has been approved for development. This process attempts to balance the conflicting needs of business. One of these needs is to respond quickly to changes in market conditions. A conflicting need is to reduce "throw-away" efforts by deciding early what will be developed. Another need is to reduce risks. These conflicting needs can be resolved by reviewing the list of features three times, during which the set of potential features in a release is refined and distilled.

   Each of the three iterations generates a list of features for which further work will proceed, but work is stopped on features that don't make the cuts. These eliminated features might be reconsidered for a later release. The needs of the market are considered as well as the technical feasibility. Estimates of development cost will play a critical role.

3. Project-planning: estimates are used for project management once the project begins. In addition to project planning, long-range planning is also based on development estimates. Multi-release planning tries to account for: experienced staff, test facilities, and interactions with other products such as billing.

4. Software is grouped into subsystems. The subsystems are organized functionally for the various tasks to be performed by the ultimate product. Each subsystem is the responsibility of people knowledgeable in the details of existing hardware and software and standard industry practice for the subsystem function.

5. The large size of a project has implications. Project planning and management have large economic impacts: estimating errors can have serious consequences.

6. Estimating can be broken down into two major parts. The first is job size, which is the size and complexity of the code, and the second part is the effort required once the size is known. This effort depends on the productivity of the development organization.

7. In this model, people compare the job they are estimating with their own experience. Estimates are made on a system with many components. This breaking down of the problem into components is a key element of this methodology, which has these advantages:

—The components will match the past jobs done by the estimators better.
—Statistical errors in estimating the components often cancel, giving a higher probability that the result is correct.
—Potentially overlooked parts of the job have a better chance of being identified.

8. The estimeeting methodology evolved from three principles:

—Estimates are important numbers since they help determine product content. Underestimating can cause failure to meet commitments, with dire consequences for business. Estimates affect quality because they control the distribution of effort over the development cycle.
—Experienced people give the best estimates. Estimators compare the job to be estimated with one from their own experience. Therefore the more extensive the experience, the more accurate the estimate will be.
—Cooperative meetings give excellent results. It has been proven that team consensus improves on the best individual solution.

9. The concept behind the estimeeting is to gather people highly experienced in all the major aspects of feature and subsystem development with others having the authority to represent the technical viewpoint of their organizations. In this meeting, they come to a common understanding of a new feature, agree on an informal, non-binding, high-level design proposal, and estimate the development effort in their own areas of expertise.

10. With a preliminary recommendations feature list, a schedule is determined, and for each feature on the list, a feature team is formed. Over a chosen time period, each team produces two outputs—the external feature requirements (FSP) and the internal feature design (FAP).

11. These documents are distributed to estimators—the engineers with in-depth knowledge of the subsystems. The estimators are not on feature teams: they represent the development interests of their subsystems and receive these requirements and design documents for every feature that affects their subsystems.

12. Team members are drawn from the concerned organizations (systems engineering, development, etc.). Some individuals join more than one feature team. Each feature team is responsible for estimeeting preparation, presentation, and follow-up for its feature. Although composition of the team might evolve, it is initially composed of:

—The systems engineer, who owns and insures the completeness and timely delivery of the FSP with the feature's mandatory and optional requirements. The engineer presents the requirements at the estimeeting.

—The feature engineer, who owns the technical aspects of the feature's operation. Even when the feature is in production, the feature engineer will serve as a point-of-contact with a vested interest in design and resolution of issues. Along with the system architect, the feature engineer owns and generates the high-level design proposal (FAP) and identifies subsystems that are affected. This person gives the high-level design and subsystem impact portions of the estimeeting presentation.

—The system architect works with the feature engineer on the FAP and insures its completeness and timely delivery. The system architect describes the FAP's architectural impact during the estimeeting. In non-estimeeting work, the system architect develops broad architectural guidelines.

—The planner is a technical person who participates in the Front-End Process early in the release cycle. The planner is knowledgeable about proposed features when feature teams are formed. The planner is the coordinator of the feature teams and may co-author the FAP. After the estimeeting the responsibility for the feature moves from the planner to the feature engineer. Planners share their expertise about the features.

—The product manager is responsible for ensuring that the scope and design of the feature remains consistent with the strategic intent and cost goals throughout the estimeeting process.

13. The FAP can be thought of as an existence proof for the feature. It is an informal document that does not require sign-off signatures. The intent is to quickly produce this document with a minimum cost. The FAP contains:

—A description of new internal architectures, where applicable.

—A high-level functional description of how each feature works from the hardware and software design viewpoints.

—An itemization of all affected areas internal and external to each feature.

—The expected feature performance.

—Dependencies or interactions with other new or existing features.

—Open issues of design and architecture and proposed solutions.

14. The FSP consists of:

—Feature operation (typical user scenarios)
—Feature interaction with other features
—Feature impact

—Constraints

—Restrictions

15. Contents of the subsystem estimating form include:

—Feature name and number

—Date of estimate

—Estimator's name

—Area (subsystem) represented

—Estimator's experience (in years) in this area

—Estimator's preparation time

—Consultation time (in hours) with FAP authors

—Estimator's quality assessment (1 to 5 scale) of FSP and FAP

—Estimate for mandatory part of feature

—Estimate for optional part of feature

—Assumptions made to arrive at estimate

—Concerns and uncertainties that could affect the estimate

—Itemized work areas that make up estimate

16. Prior to the first estimeeting the following package is assembled:

—Cover sheet with meeting specifics and feature-team membership

—People expected to attend

—FSP (external requirements)

—FAP (design and system-impact checklist)

—Subsystem estimating form

17. The estimeeting takes about two hours for a single feature. A moderator begins by introducing the feature-team members and briefly discusses the agenda and ground rules.

18. The system engineer presents feature description and requirements, delineating what is optional and what is mandatory.

19. The system architect and feature engineer jointly present the feature design. The architect gives the architectural impact perspective and the feature engineer covers the effect on subsystems.

20. A secretary, often the planner, takes notes and records assumptions and issues. A question-and-answer period typically follows the presentations.

21. Estimators are asked to complete their individual subsystem estimating forms in an "estimate collection" interval. Estimators and engineers consult with each other over finer points.

22. Following the estimeeting, the feature engineer is responsible for resolving any open issues resulting from the estimeeting and for collecting any outstanding subsystem estimates. The feature engineer then completes a Feature Estimate Summary form, audits the estimeeting outputs for completeness, and reports the estimeeting results. The estimate, FSP, and FAP now become the formal output of the Front-End Process and form the project baseline.

Selected Bibliography

Lehder, Jr., W.D, D.P. Smith, and W.D. Yu. 1988. Software estimation technology. *AT&T technology journal.* 67 (July/Aug): 10–18.

Londeix, B. 1987. *Cost estimation for software development.* Reading, Ma: Addison-Wesley.

Myers. W. 1989. Allow plenty of time for large-scale software. *IEEE software.* 6 (7): 92.

Reference

Taff, L.M., J.W. Borchering, and W.R. Hudgins, Jr. 1991. Estimeetings: Development estimates and a Front-End Process for a large project. *IEEE transactions on software engineering.* 17 (8): 839–849.

39

Burns' Framework for Building Dependable Systems

Abstract

The role and importance of nonfunctional requirements in the development of complex critical applications have, up until now, been inadequately appreciated. Experience has shown that this approach fails to produce dependable systems.

Nonfunctional requirements include dependability (e.g., reliability, availability, safety, and security), timeliness (e.g., responsiveness, orderliness, freshness, temporal predictability, and temporal controllability), and dynamic change management (i.e., incorporating evolutionary changes into a non-stop system).

The purpose of the framework described in this chapter is to:

- Impose a design discipline that ensures that appropriate abstractions are used at each level of the design.

- Allow assertions to be developed that the nonfunctional requirements can be met by the design if implemented in a particular environment.

- Allow interactions between these nonfunctional requirements to be analyzed so that dependencies can be identified.

- Allow the nonfunctional and functional requirements to be traded off against each other.

Procedures/Issues/Policies

1. A constructive way of describing the process of system design is a progression of increasingly specific commitments that define properties of the system design, which designers operating at a more detailed level are not at liberty to change. For example, early in the design there might be commitments already made to the structure of a system in terms of module definitions and relationships.

2. Those aspects of a design to which no commitment is made at some particular level in the design hierarchy are the subject of obligations that lower levels of design must address. For example, the behavior of the defined "committed to" modules is the subject of obligations that must be met during further design and implementation.

3. The process of refining a design—transforming obligations into commitments—is often subject to constraints that are imposed primarily by the execution environment.

4. The execution environment is the set of hardware and software components on top of which a system is built. It may impose both resource constraints (e.g., processor speed) and constraints of mechanism (e.g., data locking).

5. The framework controls the introduction of necessary implementation details into the design process by distinguishing two phases in the construction of an architectural design of any application:

   —Logical architecture embodies commitments that can be made independently of the constraints imposed by the execution environment and is aimed at satisfying the functional requirements.
   —Physical architecture takes constraints into account and embraces the nonfunctional requirements.

6. The nonfunctional requirements of an application can be considered as projections onto the physical architecture—distinct projects apply to timeliness, safety and so on. The physical architecture makes it explicit where projections interact and enable criteria to be developed that cater to these interactions.

7. The framework is grounded in the object-oriented approach to system design. The object-oriented approach is widely regarded as offering a conceptual framework for mastering the complexities of the design process, shown as follows:

   —Objects are an adequate modeling tool for the functional requirements of the system.
   —They can be used to provide traceability through all stages of the design process.
   —They are an adequate basis for expressing nonfunctional requirements.
   —They provide an appropriate granularity for replication, checkpointing, dynamic change management, configuration, and dynamic reconfiguration.
   —They assist error containment through encapsulation.
   —They can support dynamic security through access-right mechanisms on operations.

—They can represent entities to be scheduled.

—Commonly encountered standard architectures can be implemented by means of redefined classes and methods.

8. The logical architecture is concerned with defining a set of object classes, their interfaces, and relationships, which together meet all the functional requirements. In the logical architecture, communication between the classes is represented by invocation of methods.

9. The physical architecture is concerned with objects; that is, instances of the classes defined in the logical architecture. It refines the logical architecture in two ways:

—It instantiates objects from the classes defined in the logical architecture and maps them onto the target execution environment.

—It annotates the objects and their methods with attributes (such as deadlines) derived from the nonfunctional requirements.

Selected Bibliography

Burns, A. and A.M. Lister. 1990. An architectural framework for timely and reliable distributed information systems (TARDIS): description and case study. YCS. 140. Department of Computer Science, University of York.

Burns, A. and A.J. Wellings. 1989. *Real-time systems and their programming languages*. Addison Wesley.

Meyer, B. 1987. Reusability: the case study for object-oriented design. *IEEE software*. 4 (2), 50–64.

Meyer, B. 1988. *Object-oriented software construction*. Englewood Cliffs, N.J.: Prentice-Hall.

Reference

Burns, A. and A.M. Lister. 1991. A framework for building dependable systems. *The computer journal*. 34 (2): 173–181.

Avison's Multiview Meta-Methodology

Abstract

There is a proliferation of systems-development methodologies with much resultant confusion. In fact, it has been estimated that hundreds of more-or-less similar methodologies exist. In practice, most organizations have developed their own methodology.

There have been many attempts to compare methodologies. Research by one of the authors has managed to categorize these methodologies into six broad themes.

This chapter describes a contingency framework, called "Multiview," which includes descriptions of relevant techniques and tools. Analysts and users select those aspects of the approach that are appropriate to the application; in effect, creating a unique methodology for each application.

Procedures/Issues/Policies

1. Some problems with using existing methodologies include:

    —Failure to meet management needs
    —Unambitious systems design
    —Inflexibility due to the output-driven design
    —User dissatisfaction
    —Inadequate documentation
    —Maintenance workload
    —Application backlog

2. Category 1: systems approach highlights the importance of the relationship between an organization and its environment, and the importance for multi-disciplinary teams to understand organizations.

Category 2: planning approaches involve strategic management in information systems work so that their needs are analyzed and that information systems that do more than computerize the operations level applications are implemented. This approach attempts to identify the needs of management and plans ways to meet those needs.

Category 3: in a participative approach, all users are expected to contribute to, and gain from, any information system; this should increase the potential for success.

Category 4: prototyping enables users to comment on the proposed information system, its inputs, processing, and outputs—before the system design is completed.

Category 5: structured approaches aid the understanding of a complex problem through functional decomposition and associated documentation techniques. This approach tends to emphasize decision trees, decision tables, data-flow diagrams, and similar items.

Category 6: data analysis is a useful modeling tool in which the data model produced is likely to be relevant for a longer period than models of processes that might be unstable.

3. It has been suggested that one approach cannot be the answer:

—The tools and techniques appropriate for one set of circumstances may not be appropriate for others.
—The "fuzziness" of some applications requires an attack on a number of fronts.
—As an information system develops it takes on very different perspectives. Any adopted methodology should be able to incorporate these views.

4. It has been argued that the contingency approach to information systems development, an approach where the methodology chosen will depend on the particular circumstances in which it will be applied, might be the solution. The methodology selected will be contingent on the particular situation according to its level of uncertainty.

5. The choice of tools and techniques used in an application following a contingency framework will depend on:

—The comprehensiveness and depth of the information systems design process required.
—Whether the designers choose a goal-oriented strategy or an alternative-oriented strategy. The goal-oriented strategy negotiates on what is to be achieved, and then finds ways to accomplish the tasks. The alternative-oriented strategy does not assume that consensus can be reached on the goals, but rather that negotiation must occur on how things should be done.
—The choice of an appropriate adaptation strategy reflecting on the perception of future events. One choice is to ignore future requirements, the second is to presume they are predictable, and the third is to presume that they are unpredictable and can be dealt with.
—The choice of an appropriate implementation strategy.

6. Multiview is a contingency approach that provides a flexible framework as an alternative to choosing between methodologies or standardizing on one methodology.

Multiview is a blended methodology that draws on each of the six methodology categories. It is an explorative structure that can be called a meta-methodology.

7. The Multiview meta-methodology:

—Step 1: analysis of human activity. This stage concerns the search for a view of the organization—a subjective and objective perception of the problem situation using diagrams and pictures. Through debate within the organization, relevant systems that might relieve problem themes are identified. The root definition describes the system on which to focus attention. The root definition is analyzed to make sure that all necessary elements have been identified, including the system owner, the client, the transformation that takes place, and the environment in which it takes place.

—Step 2: analysis of information. At this stage, the entities and functions of the system described are analyzed. By using functional decomposition, it is possible to break down the main function (clear in a well-formed root definition) into subfunctions. Using data-flow diagrams, it is possible to analyze the sequence of events. In developing an entity model, the problem solver extracts and names entities, relationships between entities, and the attributes that describe the entities.

—Step 3: analysis and design of socio-technical aspects. At this stage, the problem solver produces a design from: an analysis of people and their needs; the working environment; and consideration for the organizational structure, computers, and the necessary work tasks. The social and technical objectives are set. Alternatives are specified and compared so that the best solution can be selected. Then computer tasks, role tasks, and people tasks can be defined. The emphasis at this stage is not on development, but on a statement of alternatives, according to important social and technical considerations.

—Step 4: design of the human computer interface. Decisions are made such as batch versus on-line versus command, and similar items. Specific conversations and interactions are then designed. The users are expected to be the major contributors to this stage. Technical requirements to fulfill these human-computer interfaces can then be designed.

—Step 5: design of technical aspects. Using the entity model created in Step 2 and the technical requirements from Step 4, a more technical view is taken by the analyst because human considerations are already integrated with the forthcoming technical considerations. The technical design will include the application subsystems and the non-application subsystems—the information retrieval subsystem, database, database maintenance subsystem, the control subsystem, etc.

8. These five stages incorporate five views that are appropriate to the progressive development of an analysis and design project. Because it is a multi-view approach, it covers computer-related questions and matters relating to people and business functions. Each step addresses one of the following five questions:

—How is the information system supposed to further the aims of the organization that will use the system?

—How will it fit into the working lives of the people in the organization who will use the system?

—How can concerned individuals best relate to the computer in terms of operating it and using its output?

—What information-processing function is the system to perform?

—What is the technical specification of a system that will come close enough to doing the things specified in the above four questions?

Selected Bibliography

Avison, D.E. and G. Fitzgerald. 1988. *Information systems development: Methodologies, techniques and tools*. Oxford: Blackwell Scientific Publications.

Avison, D.E. and A.T. Wood-Harper. 1986. Multiview: An exploration in informal system development. *Australian computer journal*. 18 (4).

Avison, D.E. and A.T. Wood-Harper. 1990. *Multiview: An exploration information systems development*. Oxford: Blackwell Scientific Publications.

Davies, L.J. and A.T. Wood-Harper. 1989. Information systems development: Theoretical frameworks. *Journal of applied systems analysis*. 16.

Hirschheim, R. and H.R. Klein. 1989. Four paradigms for information systems development. *Communications of the ACM*. 32 (10).

Iivari, J. 1989. A methodology for IS Development as an organizational change: A pragmatic contingency approach. In Klein & Kumar.

Reference

Avison, D.E. and A.T. Wood-Harper. 1991. Information systems development research: An exploration of ideas in practice. *The computer journal*. 34 (2).

Byrne's Reverse Engineering Technique

Abstract

The problem of reusing an existing system in a different programming language is a problem that can be solved in three ways: manually rewrite the existing system, use an automatic language translator, or redesign and re-implement the system.

There are problems with each of these approaches. Manually translated source code often retains the style and flavor of the original implementation. This approach is labor-intensive and error-prone.

Automatic translation, a better technique, has problems as well. The source language might not yield itself to simple translation into the target language. Most automated translator tools perform the easier parts of the translation process, leaving the more complex details for a human being. Perhaps the biggest problem with this technique is, as the author suggests, its tendency to replicate the same problems plaguing the original version—in other words, "garbage in, garbage out."

Of the three approaches, redesign and re-implementation has the best chances of producing a successful system. But this technique also has disadvantages. This approach has the highest cost since it is the equivalent of building a new system. Perhaps the most serious disadvantage is that for many systems, it may not be possible to redesign from the system requirements, since the requirements might not exist.

Reverse engineering provides a new approach. Reverse engineering can produce a reconstructed design that captures the functionality of the system. This chapter describes a reverse engineering technique that successfully translated a FORTRAN program into the Ada language.

Procedures/Issues/Policies

1. Collect information. The reverse engineering process begins by extracting detailed design information, and from that information extracting a high-level design abstraction. Detailed design information is extracted from the source code and existing design documents. This information includes structure charts as well as data descriptions to describe processing details. In this step, all possible information about the program is collected. Information sources include source code, design documents, and documentation for system calls and external routines. Personnel experienced with the software should also be identified. This last requirement is not to be underestimated. The lack of "domain knowledge" can make design recovery extremely difficult, if not impossible.

2. Examine information. In this step, the information collected in step 1 is examined to allow the person(s) doing the recovery work to become familiar with the system and its parts. Staff responsible for reverse engineering formulate a plan for dissection and recording the recovered information. It should be noted that becoming familiar with the language implementation of the module can bias the reverse engineering effort by influencing the perspective of what should be recovered and how it should be expressed.

3. Extract the structure. The information is reviewed in an attempt to identify the program structure. This review is used to create a set of structure charts where each node in the chart corresponds to a routine called in the program. Therefore, the charts record the calling hierarchy of the program. For each edge in the chart, the data passed to a node and returned by that node must be recorded. It should be noted that there is a general availability of software tools to assist in the structure-chart development. Associating structure chart nodes with source code routines raises the issue of traceability. In reverse engineering, it is desirable to record the links between the recovered design and the original source code or documentation. In this case, it would be desirable to give a node a meaningful name and to record the name of the implemented function to which it corresponds. As the structure chart is recorded, the data items passed between nodes should also be recorded.

4. Record functionality. Record the processing done by each node. At this step, the program routines' functionality, as well as the functionality of system and library routines, are described either in English or in a more formal notation. If debugging statements are used within the program, then they should also be recorded. Conditional compilation code—the procedural code that directs the software to a particular hardware platform—needs to be reviewed carefully.

5. Record data-flow. The recovered program structure and processing logic can be analyzed to identify the data transformations in the software that show the actual data processing performed in the program. This information can be used to develop a set of hierarchical data-flow diagrams that model the software.

6. Record control-flow. At this stage, the high-level control of the program is identified. This refers to the level of control that affects the overall software operation. A problem in this step might be in distinguishing between low-level control struc-

tures that involved the implementation of a routine, and high-level control structures that served to control the software operation. The former should be included as part of the processing described in the detailed design: the latter needs to be recorded in a control-flow diagram and its control specification. The author found that there is a temptation to recover too much of the control structure.

7. Review the recovered design. The recovered design is reviewed for consistency. At this stage, missing items are identified and an attempt is made to locate them. The design is checked to see if it accurately represents the program.

8. Generate documentation. The purpose of this step is to generate design documentation. Information explaining the purpose of the program, program overview, history, etc., will be recorded.

Selected Bibliography

Biggerstaff, T.J. 1989. Design recovery for maintenance and reuse. *Computer*. 22 (7): 36–49.

Chikofsky, E.J. and J.H. Cross, II. 1990. Reverse engineering and design recovery: A taxonomy. *IEEE software*. 7 (1): 13–17.

Choi, S.C. and W. Scacchi. 1990. Extracting and restructuring the design of large systems. *IEEE software*. 7 (1): 66–71.

Ricketts, J.A., J.C. DelMonaco, and M.W. Weeks. Data reengineering for application systems. Paper presented at Conference on Software Maintenance. pp 174–179. 16–19 October, 1989. Miami Florida.

Reference

Byrne, E.J. 1991. Software reverse engineering: A case study. *Software—practice and experience*. 21 (12): 1349–1364.

Prieto-Diaz's Reusability Model

Abstract

Software *reuse* is still far from being a standard practice in the software engineering community, even though it was conceived over 20 years ago. The problem, according to Prieto-Diaz, is not one of technology but of an unwillingness to address the most important issues that influence software reuse.

A model for implementing software reuse programs is discussed in this chapter. This model is based on an incremental strategy, and addresses many issues, that were thought to be external to the software process. These issues include managerial, economic, performance, cultural, and technology transfer. The approach addressed here is practical, effective, and has potential to make reuse a regular practice in the software development process.

Procedures/Issues/Policies

1. Factors that influence reuse include the following:

   —Managerial factors: organizational, motivational and financial
   —Economic factors: integrating reuse in cost-benefit analysis, system costing and estimating, pricing criteria, contracting strategies, and support costs
   —Legal factors: software copyright, liability, proprietary issues, and contractual requirements

2. Justifications for an incremental approach include:

   —Provides an immediate return on investment
   —Builds confidence within the organization
   —Easier to manage
   —Allows for tuning and refining the reuse process
   —Facilitates monitoring and evaluating reuse

3. A key ingredient is *management support*, which is a common factor in all successful reuse programs (such as those reused by Raytheon, Toshiba, and Hartford). This commitment is necessary because reuse programs demand changes in the manner of software development.

4. Inputs to the reuse program include software from existing systems and requirements for future systems.

5. The products of a reuse program include a series of software catalogs, an automated library system, generic architectures, and a collection of reusable components.

6. The assessment reports include feasibility analysis, domain stability assessment, cost-benefit analysis, and an implementation plan.

7. Questions for a feasibility analysis include:

   —Does the organization have enough financial and human resources to implement a reuse program?
   —Can the organization afford it?
   —Is reuse necessary in the organization?
   —Does the organization want to do it?
   —Is management committed to implementing a reuse program?
   —How many systems of the same kind will be produced?
   —Are variations from implementation to implementation large or small?
   —Is existing software already available for reuse?
   —What is the estimated cost for each alternative?
   —Does a critical mass of software engineers exist?
   —Is software production large enough to justify a reuse program?

8. Questions for an analysis of domain suitability follow:

   —Is the domain, or line of business, broad or narrow?
   —Is the domain mature and well understood or is it new and not well understood?
   —Is the domain complex or simple?
   —Is the domain stable or rapidly changing?
   —Is the domain very technology dependent?
   —Is the domain in a state of developing concepts or does it rely on well established principles, methods and formalisms?

9. Questions for cost benefit analysis:

   —How much does it cost?
   —Is a reuse program economically feasible?
   —What alternatives exist for implementing a reuse program?
   —What is the scope?
   —How big a program is contemplated?
   —What are the expectations?
   —What is the desired level of reuse (partial, opportunistic, formal, or total)?

10. The following organizational structure is recommended to establish a successful reuse program:

    —Asset management group provides initiatives, funding and policies for reuse.
    —Identification and qualification group identifies potential reusability areas and collects and certifies new additions to the collection.
    —Maintenance group maintains and updates reusable software components.
    —Development group creates new reusable components.
    —Reuser support group assists and trains users and runs tests and evaluations of reusable components.
    —Librarian updates and distributes catalogs, classifies new assets, maintains library system, and manages asset orders. Several roles may be assigned to one person. However, a staff size for a large corporate endeavor might exceed 10 people.

11. A reuse program can be implemented in four basic stages: Initiation, Expansion, Contraction, and Steady State.

12. Stage 1: Initiation. Existing software is analyzed to select potentially reusable components. Descriptors of these components are extracted manually or automatically, and a preliminary index is produced. A stage 1 catalog is produced. This catalog informs software engineers in the organization about potentially reusable software.

13. Stage 2: Expansion. The size of the catalogs increases as more of the existing software is identified for reuse. At this point, a classification scheme is necessary. An initial faceted-classification scheme is produced and included with the stage 2 catalog. Based on the feasibility study, a case can be made to support an automated library system.

    The faceted-classification scheme requires the resources of a librarian and a domain expert. A faceted scheme provides basic domain models in the form of taxonomies and standard descriptions or lexicons, which in turn support bootstrapping the domain analysis process.

14. Stage 3: Contraction. In this stage, domain analysis is the key activity. Early domain models from stage 2, coupled with more detailed information from existing systems and from requirements for future systems are used for domain analysis. Standard architectures and functional models are derived, and common components are grouped to support basic generic functions.

    Redundant and ineffective components are identified and retired from the collection. This results in contraction in the size of the collection. The collection and classification are updated and a stage 3 catalog is made available. In this stage, a domain analyst, one or more domain experts, a software engineer, and a librarian are required.

15. Stage 4: Steady State. Now that the essential components have been identified for a specific domain, these components are progressively replaced by components supporting domain specific functions. These components are reusable since they are designed to plug directly into the architecture.

Selected Bibliography

Barnes, B.H. and T.B. Bollinger. 1991. Making reuse cost-effective. *IEEE software*. 8 (1): 13–24.

Basili, V.R. and H.D. Rombach. 1988. *Towards a comprehensive framework for reuse: A reuse-enabling software evolution environment*. Tech. Report CS-TR-2158. College Park, Md.: Dept of Computer Science. University of Maryland.

Frakes, W.B. 1991. A survey of software reuse. Position paper for the First International Workshop on Software Reuse. July, 1991. Dortmund, Germany.

Freeman, P. 1983. Reusable software engineering: Concepts and research directions. In *Workshop on reusability in programming*. ed. Alan Perlis. pp 3–26. Newport, R.I.: ITT Programming.

Prieto-Diaz, R. Implementing faceted classification for software reuse. *Communications of the ACM*. 34 (5): 88–97.

Reference

Prieto-Diaz, R. 1991. Making software reuse work: An implementation model. *ACM SIGSOFT, software engineering notes*. 16 (3): 61–68.

Farbey's Considerations on Software Quality Metrics during the Requirements Phase

Abstract

In this chapter Farbey expands on the general view of quality as the difference between what is expected and what is experienced:

$$\text{Quality} = \text{Expectations} - \text{Experience}$$

Four questions are addressed:

1. Effectiveness: does the specification, considered as a solution, solve the right problem?

2. Serviceability: does the specification, considered as a starting point, provide a firm basis on which to proceed?

3. Prediction: does the requirement specification (together with the system test specification) provide useful measures for predicting the final quality outcome?

4. Process: does the process by which the specification is produced encourage effectiveness, serviceability, and quality prediction?

Procedures/Issues/Policies

1. Effectiveness: the first question concerns the quality of the specification as a so-lution—how well does the specification capture the problem? The ultimate effec-tiveness of a system depends not on the quality of software or the specification, but on the degree to which the problem is correctly perceived. Focus on the spec-ification as a product by asking questions such as:

   —Is the process by which it has been produced conducive to bringing out and clarifying objectives?
   —Is it complete in that it exhausts the objectives and needs that are known?
   —Is the specification maintainable?
   —Is the specification readable?

   Quality attributes covered here include:

   —Functionality: does the specification capture all of the required functions?
   —Performance: does the specification meet the users' demands?
   —Usability: ease of use, learning and relearning.

2. Serviceability: the second question concerns the quality of the specification's content and the implications for later system development. The following is a list of questions of efficiency, in this context meaning "doing things right":

   —Are the requirements consistent?
   —Are the requirements clearly understood?
   —Are the requirements compatible with the methods of later development stages?
   —Are the requirements readable?
   —Are the requirements modifiable?
   —Are the requirements traceable?
   —Are the requirements usable after implementation?
   —Are the requirements maintainable?
   —Are the requirements in compliance with documentation standards?

3. Prediction: the third question concerns the value of measures of quality that will act as predictor measurements for the eventual quality of the finished software. A predictor metric is used to predict the value of a property of a system that will only become directly observable during a later stage of system development.

4. Process: three processes of development are worth considering:

   —Life-cycle process such as Structured Systems Analysis and Design (SSADM), which is based on a waterfall model. In this model, requirements specification occurs at an early stage and is then fixed as would be any associated metrics.
   —Prototyping approach offers an early normalization, but also offers a more flex-ible model of system development that recognizes the problem of changing re-quirements.
   —Approaches that recognize specifically the social setting in which requirements specifications takes place.

Control of quality during any process will probably consist of instituting checklists together with a program for completing them and acting on the results. Questions to ask at this point include:

—Is the system easy to learn?
—Is the system easy to relearn?
—Is there stability and maturity in the system?

Selected Bibliography

Schafer. G. 1988. *Functional analysis of office requirements - A multi-perspective approach*. Chichester, U.K.: John Wiley.

Stamper, R. Information: Mystical fluid or a subject for scientific inquiry. Paper presented at Computer Journal Symposium. November 1984.

Watts, R. 1988. *Measuring software quality*. Manchester, U.K.: NCC.

Reference

Farbey, B. 1990. Software quality metrics: Considerations about requirements and requirement specifications. *Information and software technology*. 32 (1): 60–64.

Redmill's Quality Considerations in the Management of Software-based Development Projects

Abstract

It comes as no surprise that the majority of software development projects are late, over budget, and out of specification. Project managers point to a number of technical problems, most of which are related to specific technical tasks in software development. This chapter shows that inadequate management and a lack of attention to quality are the main causes of the problem.

Procedures/Issues/Policies

1. The most common reasons given by project managers for failure to meet budget, time scale and specification are as follows:

   —Incomplete and ambiguous requirements
   —Incomplete and imprecise specifications
   —Difficulties in modeling systems
   —Uncertainties in cost and resource estimates
   —General lack of visibility
   —Difficulties with progress monitoring
   —Complicated error and change control
   —Lack of agreed metrics
   —Difficulties in controlling maintenance
   —Lack of common terminology
   —Uncertainties in software/hardware apportionment

—Rapid changes in technology
—Determining suitability of languages
—Measuring and predicting reliability
—Problems with interfacing
—Problems with integration

2. Audits of systems development efforts reveal shortcomings in projects such as:

—Lack of standards
—Failure to comply with existing standards
—Non-adherence to model in use
—No sign-off at end of stages
—Lack of project plans
—No project control statistics recorded or stored
—No Quality Assurance (QA) procedures
—No change-control procedures
—No configuration control procedures
—Records of test data and results not kept

3. The three causes for the lack of control of projects are:

—Attitude toward quality
—Attitude toward management
—Attitude toward project

4. In finding solutions, the principal reasons for project management shortcomings should be reviewed. The reasons might include that the project manager:

—Has no experience working where a quality culture predominates
—Has not been trained in Total Quality Management (TQM)
—Has not received adequate management training
—Has not been managed in accordance with TQM principles by supervisors
—Has not overcome an inclination towards technical matters and finds that they offer a more friendly environment than the less familiar affairs of management

5. Solutions include the following:

—Training: project manager and team must be trained in TQM.
—Management commitment must always be seen to be 100%.
—Standards: a comprehensive set of standards for all aspects of work should be instituted and used. The project life cycle must be covered, as well as other pertinent issues.
—Guidelines, procedures, and checklists should be available to assist workers to meet the standards and QA agents to check the products.
—QA should be carried out at all stages of the life cycle and for all end products.
—The QA team should be independent of the development team.
—Audits should be carried out during the project to ensure that management and QA procedures are being adhered to. The project manager should always initiate a review of the auditors' recommendations and of all resulting correction action.

—Planning: the project manager should be fastidious in drawing up plans and ensuring their use for control. Plans should include the project plan, stage plans, and a quality plan that details the quality requirements of the project.

—Reporting: a reporting system should be instituted to ensure that problems are quickly escalated to the management level appropriate to the action needed.

—Feedback: statistics that assist in project control and the improvement of quality should be collected, analyzed, and used.

—Continuous review: the whole quality system (components, mode of operation, and quality of results) should be reviewed and improved continuously.

—The project manager must not be too technically involved. Technical duties should be delegated to a development team manager who reports to project manager.

—A non-technical support team should be appointed to assist in non-developmental matters, including coordination and interpretation of resource and time statistics, recording all expenditures and tracking against the budget, and tracking milestones. This team should report to project manager.

Selected Bibliography

Rathbone, M. 1988. Software quality system. *Computer techniques*. February 1988.

Redmill, F.J. 1987. Difficulties of specifying users' requirements for computer systems and methods of mitigating them. *British telecommunication engineering*. 6 (1).

Wingrove, A. 1987. Software failures are management failures. In *Software reliability: achievement and assessment*. ed. B. Littlewood. Oxford, U.K.: Blackwell.

Reference

Redmill, F.J. 1990. Considering quality in the management of software-based development projects. *Information and software technology*. 32 (1): 18–22.

Contel's Software Metrics in the Process Maturity Framework

Abstract

The Contel Technology Center's Software Engineering laboratory has as one of its prime goals the improvement of software engineering productivity. As a result of work in this area, the authors have suggested a set of metrics for which data are to be collected and analyzed. This set of metrics is based on a process maturity framework developed at the Software Engineering Institute at Carnegie Mellon University. The SEI framework divides organizations into five levels based on how mature (organized, professional, aligned to software tenets, etc.) the organization is. The five levels range from initial, or ad hoc, to an optimizing environment.

Contel recommends that metrics be divided into five levels as well. Each level is based on the amount of information made available to the development process. As the development process matures and improves, additional metrics can be collected and analyzed.

Procedures/Issues/Policies

1. Level 1: Initial Process. This level is characterized by an ad hoc approach to software development. Inputs to the process are not well defined, but the outputs are as expected. Preliminary baseline project metrics should be gathered at this level to form a basis for comparison as improvements are made and maturity increases, This can be accomplished by comparing new project measurements with baseline measurements.

2. Level 2: Repeatable Process. At this level the process is repeatable in much the same way that a subroutine is repeatable. The requirements act as input, the code as output, and constraints are such things as budget and schedule. Even

though proper inputs produce proper outputs, there is no means to discern easily how the outputs are actually produced. Only project-related metrics make sense at this level since the activities within the actual transitions from input to output are not available to be measured. Measures are this level can include:

—Amount of effort needed to develop the system
—Overall project cost
—Software size: non-commented lines of code, Function Points, and object and method count
—Personnel effort: actual person-months of effort, report person-months of effort
—Requirements volatility: requirements changes

3. Level 3: Defined Process. At this level the activities of the process are clearly defined. This additional structure means that the input to and output from each well-defined functional activity can be examined, which permits a measurement of the intermediate products. Measures include:

—Requirements complexity: number of distinct objects and actions addressed in requirements
—Design complexity: number of design modules, Cyclomatic complexity, McCabe design complexity
—Code complexity: number of code modules, Cyclomatic complexity
—Test complexity: number of paths to test, of object-oriented development, then number of object interfaces to test
—Quality metrics: defects discovered, defects discovered per unit size (defect density), requirements faults discovered, design faults discovered, and fault density for each product
—Pages of documentation

4. Level 4: Managed Process. At this level, feedback from early project activities are used to set priorities for later project activities. Activities are readily compared and contrasted, and the effects of changes in one activity can be tracked in the others. Measurements can be made across activities and are used to control and stabilize the process so that productivity and quality can match expectation. Metrics, although derived from the following data, are tailored to the individual organization. The following types of data are recommended to be collected:

—Process type: what process model is used and how it correlates to positive or negative consequences.
—Amount of producer reuse: how much of the system is designed for reuse. This includes reuse of requirements, design modules, test plans, and code.
—Amount of consumer reuse: how much does the project reuse components from other projects. This includes reuse of requirements, design modules, test plans, and code. (By reusing tested, proven components, effort can be minimized and quality can be improved.)
—Defect identification: how and when are defects discovered? Knowing this will indicate whether those process activities are effective.
—Use of defect density model for testing: to what extent does the number of defects determine when testing is complete? This controls and focuses testing as

well as increases the quality of the final product.

—Use of configuration management: is a configuration management scheme imposed on the development process? This permits traceability, which can be used to assess the impact of alterations.

—Module completion over time: at what rates are modules being completed? This reflects the degree to which the process and development environment facilitate implementation and testing.

5. Level 5: Optimizing Process. At this level, measures from activities are used to change and improve the process. This process change might affect the organization and the project as well. Studies by SEI report that 85% of organizations are at level 1, 14% at level 2, and 1% at level 3. None of the firms surveyed had reached levels 4 or 5. Therefore, the authors have not recommended a set of metrics for level 5.

6. Steps to take in using metrics include:

—Assess the process: determine the level of process maturity.
—Determine the appropriate metrics to collect.
—Recommend metrics, tools and techniques.
—Estimate project cost and schedule.
—Collect appropriate level of metrics.
—Construct project database of metrics data that can be used for analysis and to track value of metrics over time.
—Cost and schedule evaluation: when the project is complete, evaluate the initial estimates of cost and schedule for accuracy. Determine which of the factors may account for discrepancies between the predicted and actual values.
—Form a basis for future estimates.

Selected Bibliography

Boehm, B.W. 1988. A spiral model of software development and enhancement. *IEEE computer*. May 1988.

Conte, S.D., H.E. Dunsmore, and V.Y. Shen. 1986. *Software engineering metrics and models*. Menlo Park, Ca.: Benjamin-Cummings.

Humphrey, W. 1989. *Managing the software process*. Reading, Ma.: Addison-Wesley.

Pfleeger, S.L. 1989. Recommendations for an initial set of metrics. Technical report CTC-TR-89-017. Chantilly, Va.: Contel Technology Center.

Reference

Pfleeger, S.L. and C. McGowan. 1990. Software metrics in the process maturity framework. *Journal of systems software*. 12: 255–261.

Kydd's Technique to Induce Productivity through Shared Information Technology

Abstract

Organizations have made large investments in shared information technology (SIT) over the years under the guise of electronic mail systems, distributed databases, and group decision-support systems. The authors of this chapter contend that SIT may not be appropriate for every organization. In order for SIT to be successful, the corporate culture must be one that supports sharing of information across boundaries. In this chapter, we find general guidelines that can be used concerning conditions under which high-return SIT can be implemented.

Procedures/Issues/Policies

1. There are two organizational prerequisites for successful investment in SIT:

   —The organizational culture must be "right"; that is, appropriate for and supportive of information sharing.
   —Successful execution of a significant number of jobs must require timely access to shared information.

2. In "excellent" companies there is a great deal of communication among people in different functional areas. There might also be cross-functional management of cost, quality, and scheduling. This implies that communication occurs across traditional organizational boundaries and that information is shared.

3. In traditional American businesses, organization is through a hierarchical structure in which corporate norms have dictated that communications paths follow the hierarchy—allowing certain managers to monopolize information. SIT, in contrast, allows workers to work in a cooperative manner across traditional organizational boundaries.

4. Rich communications media foster productivity in group meetings, one-on-one meetings, and telephone contacts.

5. Guidelines for implementing high return SIT:

—Assess the environment within the organization to determine whether shared information will further the strategic objectives of the organization. In addition, determine whether or not the culture of the organization fosters information sharing.

—If SIT is not strategically important, defer SIT until it is.

—If SIT is strategically important, but the culture does not encourage information sharing, then plan and implement an improvement program that focuses on a single, measurable objective of strategic importance (such as a quality improvement program) and requires involvement by everyone in the organization. The objective is to develop a culture in which everyone is concerned with continuous improvement, measurable results, and shared information. Ensure that management behavior is consistent with the objectives of the program and that the organization's reward system encourages information sharing.

—If the improvement program is successful, develop a plan for implementing SIT. This plan should include steps for developing an information infrastructure with standardized definitions of key data elements, an information technology infrastructure that provides access to both corporate and external databases, and a uniform set of user-friendly tools. This set should include tools that establish communication protocols between individuals and reinforce the new collaborative norms.

Selected Bibliography

Draft, R.L. and R.H. Lengel. 1986. Organizational information requirements, media richness, and structural design. *Management science*. 5: 554–571.

Reference

Kydd, C.T. and L.H. Jones. 1989. Corporate productivity and shared information technology. *Information & management*. 17 (5): 277–281.

Bellcore's Software Quality Metrics

Abstract

The Bellcore Quality Assurance Engineering Software group (QAES) for Bellcore Client Companies (BCCs) has developed and implemented a comprehensive quality assurance program that focuses on resolving the underlying problems associated with developing quality software.

The objective of Bellcore's QAES's surveillance program is to develop "cooperative" relationships that cause vendors to focus on: implementing methods and techniques to improve software-development control; improving the effectiveness of the underlying process used to develop and support software, thus improving quality; and understanding the needs and requirements of the BCCs. This chapter discusses this approach and explores the measurements utilized whose objective are:

- Assure adequate vendor quality control
- Minimize defects
- Optimize buyer satisfaction

Procedures/Issues/Policies

1. Assure adequate vendor quality control: measures have been implemented in the surveillance program to track the accomplishment of milestone criteria. These include:

   - Requirements, design, coding, and unit test-phase measurements such as:
     —Phase deliverable completion
     —Number of open correction action requests
     —Review coverage

- Test-phase measurements

  —Test coverage as measured by structure, functions, or paths
  —Number of test cases executed and passed
  —Number of trouble reports
  —Number of open trouble reports by severity
  —Trouble report initiation rates
  —Product-specific quality, reliability, and stability

2. Minimize defects and improve the effectiveness of the software development process:

   - Review of software development artifacts (e.g., requirements specifications and code) and testing results provide measurable evidence about the effectiveness of the implemented software processes; that is, specific information about the type and quantity of defects produced.

   - Specific measurements used in "real time" to minimize defects include:

     —Average number of defects detected in modules and subsystems by type
     —Historical system, subsystem, and module fault densities
     —Number of defects detected during reviews

3. A long-term approach is the collection of comprehensive defect data. Information about defect type, its origin, the mechanism used for detection, and defect severity, are required to isolate ineffective processes and detection mechanisms. Defects found during reviews and testing are classified according to the phase detected (x-axis) and originated (y-axis).

   After defect data are accumulated, simple calculations will determine the percentage of total defects attributable to certain phases of the life cycle and the effectiveness of phase-defect detection methods. For example, the percentage of total defects attributable to "requirements" is calculated as the total number of requirements defects divided by the number of defects multiplied by 100.

4. Quality and reliability measures include:

   —Number and duration of system outages due to software failure
   —Number of customer trouble reports
   —Customer trouble report cause analysis
   —Patch statistics, where a *patch* is defined as an interim fix

5. Buyer support measures include:

   —Customer service response time
   —Number of open trouble reports
   —Site distribution of open fault reports
   —Aging of open customer trouble reports by severity
   —Time-to-correct customer trouble reports

Selected Bibliography

Grady, R.B. 1987. Measuring and managing software maintenance. *IEEE software.* September 1987: 35–45.

Jones, T.C. 1986. *Programmer productivity.* New York, N.Y.; McGraw-Hill.

Reference

Hon, S.E. 1990. Assuring software quality through measurements: A buyer's perspective. *Journal of systems software.* 13: 117–130.

Keyes' Value of Information

Abstract

If it's perceived that there will be difficulty in making the point that the corporate information resource is a worthy vehicle to protect with a dictionary workbench, then calculating the Value of Information (VOI) will a useful exercise. The calculation will assist the organization in determining the true worth of its investment in information.

The ultimate goal of this exercise is to assign a dollar value to each unit of information. In this way, an organization, used to assessing relative worth based on bottom-line statistics, can instantly recognize the value of information in understandable terms.

Procedures/Issues/Policies

The steps that should be taken for this assessment follow:

1. Assign each system (i.e., payroll) a weighting factor relative to its importance to the organization. Permissible weighting factors for this exercise are: 1 for a low relative value, 2 for a middle relative value, and 3 for a high relative value.

2. For each data element within a system, assign a weighting factor that shows that data element's importance relative to that system. Again use the weighting factors 1–3.

3. Multiply these two numbers together to get the total weighting factor of a data element relative to all data in the organization.

4. For each data element, note the number of systems in which this data element is cross-referenced. For example, it is possible that "customer name" is used in the

sales system, the inventory system, and a marketing system. This would give us a total of three systems.

For each data element, multiply the number of systems in which it appears by the total weighting factor from step 3 above.

5. Convert this number to a percentage by comparing it to the total number of systems in the organization.

6. Using the last audited net income amount for the organization (this could be a quarter or an entire year), calculate the VOI by multiplying the percentage calculated in instruction five by the net income amount.

Reference

Keyes, Jessica. 1992. *INFOTRENDS: The competitive use of information.* New York, N.Y.: McGraw-Hill.

Pfleeger's Method for CASE Tool Selection Based on Process Maturity

Abstract

A wide variety of CASE tools are available in the software market for various applications in the software-development process. It is not a trivial issue for an organization to make the appropriate selections and incorporate CASE tools at the right stages for its own environment. The five process maturity levels defined by the Software Engineering Institute can be used as guidelines for an organization to determine the proper CASE tools to use based on its own process maturity.

It is obvious that the CASE tools chosen for a particular project have direct effects on the success of a project in terms of productivity, schedule, quality, etc. Without any clearly defined procedures or guidelines, it is rather difficult for an organization to make intelligent decisions for selecting proper CASE tools for a particular process and project. The method presented here clearly defines the most suitable types of tools to use based on the software-development process maturity of an organization. It is valuable for either organizations that have already introduced CASE tools with emphasis on continuous process improvement, or organizations planning on migrating from no previous CASE tools involvement to a process with fully integrated CASE tools support.

Procedures/Issues/Policies

The following table describes the characteristics for each process maturity level defined by the Software Engineering Institute.

Level	Characteristics
5. Optimizing	Improvement fed back to process
4. Managed	Measured process (quantitative)
3. Defined	Process defined, institutionalized
2. Repeatable	Process dependent on individuals
1. Initial	Ad hoc

Level 1: Initial process

For level 1 of process maturity, the inputs are not well defined; however, the outputs are usually defined. The software process neither defines nor controls the transition from inputs to outputs. The CASE tools selection for this level should focus on adding structure and definition to the process inputs and outputs. A tool that structures and controls the requirements is useful at this level of maturity.

Level 2: Repeatable process

For level 2 of process maturity, the process inputs, outputs, and constraints are identified. This process is repeatable. Proper inputs will always produce proper outputs, even though there is no mechanism to keep track of how the outputs are produced. The process at level 2 is completely dependent on the individuals working on the project. The CASE tools selection for this level should focus on documenting and retaining the information produced in the software-development process, and making it available to other members of the project team. Tools for requirements modeling, specification, and analysis are useful, and a project management tool will help track the project constraints.

Level 3: Defined process

For level 3 of process maturity, the process is refined into activities according to various phases in the development cycle. The entry and exit criteria for all activities in the process are clearly defined. The inputs for any particular activity should be ready and evaluated before the actual activity occurs. The inputs and outputs associated with each activity are considered intermediate products. The CASE tools selection for this level should focus on measuring the characteristics of the intermediate products to ensure that goals are met and to monitor the process deviations. CASE tools should be selected to produce, analyze, and organize those intermediate products.

Level 4: Managed process

At level 4 of process maturity, the software development process tends to be dynamic in the sense that feedback and experience from early project activities can be used to determine and modify later project activity priorities. The effectiveness of process factors such as reuse, testing, and reviews can be evaluated. The causal analysis can be done throughout the development process to prevent future mistakes and to analyze defects injected in the early activities. The software-development process is now carefully controlled rather than just monitored. The CASE tools selection for this level should focus on collecting and analyzing process-wide metrics for confidence measurement and course correction to allow management and control of the development process.

Level 5: Optimizing process

Level 5 is the ultimate level of process maturity. Projects at this level are fully dynamic in terms of real-time intra- and inter-process improvements and modifications. The software process evolves and corrects itself. The CASE tools selection for this level should focus on dynamic evaluation, configuration, and reconfiguration of an environment based on the current process status to ensure that the product confidence level is met. Process programming and process simulation tools should be considered.

Selected Bibliography

Boehm, B.W. A spiral model of software development and enhancement. *Computer*. May 1988.

Humphrey, W. 1989. *Managing the software process*. Reading, Ma.: Addison-Wesley.

National Bureau of Standards. 1983. Guidelines: A framework for the evaluation and comparison of software development tools. FIPS Publication 99. Gaithersburg, Md.

Pfleeger, S.L. and C.L. McGowan. 1990. Software metrics in a process maturity framework. *Journal of system software*. July 1990.

Reference

Pfleeger, S.L. and J.C. Fitzgerald, Jr. 1991. Software metrics tool kit: Support for selection, collection and analysis. *Information and software technology*. 33 (7).

50

McCabe's Complexity Metric

Abstract

McCabe's metric to asses the complexity of software is perhaps one of the most well-known and well-used metrics. It is presented here in a simplified format.

Procedures/Issues/Policies

McCabe's proposal for a cyclomatic complexity number was the first to attempt to objectively quantify the "flow of control" complexity of software.

The metric is computed by decomposing the program into a directed graph that represents its flow of control. The cyclomatic complexity number is than calculated using the formula

$$V(g) = Edges - Nodes + 2$$

In its shortened form, the cyclomatic complexity number is a count of decision points within a program with a single entry and a single exit plus one.

Reference

McCabe, T. 1976. A complexity measure. *IEEE transactions on software engineering*. December 1976: 308–320.

Halstead's Effort Measure

Abstract

In the 1970s, Maurice Halstead developed a theory on software behavior. Some of his findings evolved into software metrics: one of these is referred to as "Effort," or just "E," and is a well-known complexity metric.

Procedures/Issues/Policies

The Effort measure is calculated as:

$$E = \text{Volume} \div \text{Level}$$

where Volume is the size of a piece of code and Level is a measure of how "abstract" the program is. The abstract level varies from almost 0 for programs with a low abstract level to almost 1 for programs that are highly abstract.

Reference

Halstead, M. 1977. *Elements of software science*. New York, N.Y.: Elsevier.

DEC's Overview of Software Metrics

Abstract

Nowhere is productivity and quality more important than at a hardware/software vendor. DEC's view of productivity and quality is presented in this chapter, and provides a fine overview of the principles of this book.

Procedures/Issues/Policies

1. Software productivity: why do we care?

   —Expectations of customers and users
   —Increasing complexity
   —Effective use of technology
   —Missed opportunities
   —Shortage of skilled software developers
   —Increasing need for higher quality software

2. Productivity: what do we really want?

   —Better products
   —Better focus
   —Better resource utilization
   —Better control

3. Productivity: why measure?

   —Quantify the project's progress
   —Quantify attributes of the software system

4. Why use metrics?

   —Understand and manage the process
   —Measure the impact of change on the process: new methods and training
   —Know when you've met a goal: usability, performance, and test coverage

5. Software system metrics:

   - Characterization of the system parts

     —Requirements
     —Specifications
     —Code
     —Documentation
     —Tests
     —Training

   - Attributes include

     —Usability
     —Maintainability
     —Extendibility
     —Size
     —Defect level
     —Performance
     —Completeness

6. Software development process metrics:

   - Characterizations of the system-developing process

   - Attributes include

     —Development cost
     —Schedule predictability
     —Defect discovery rate
     —Repair

7. Metrics characteristics

   —Collectable
   —Reproducible
   —Pertinent
   —System independent

8. Questions to ask:

   —How time is spent on a project?
   —Has the defect rate decreased?
   —What tools are being used?
   —What are the reasons for rework?
   —Are problem reports under control?
   —Is this a reasonable schedule?

9. Caveats

- Behavior modifies toward what is being measured
- Measure the important attributes
- Measure multiple attributes

    —Size versus quality
    —Source code versus source + comments
    —Executable lines of code versus data declarations

10. Product metrics

    —Size: lines of code, pages of documentation, number and size of test, token count, and function count
    —Complexity: decision count, variable count, number of modules, size/volume, and depth of nesting
    —Reliability: count of changes required by phase, count of discovered defects, defect density (= number of defects ÷ size), and count of changed lines of code

11. Process metrics

    —Complexity: time to design, code, and test; defect discovery rate by phase; cost to develop; number of external interfaces; and defect fix rate
    —Methods and tool use: number of tools used and why, project-infrastructure tools, and tools not used and why not
    —Resource metrics: years experience with team, years experience with language, years experience with type of software, MIPS per person, support personnel to engineering personnel ratio, and non-project time to project time ratio
    —Productivity: percent of time to redesign, percent of time to redo, schedule variance, and effort variance

12. What is productivity?

    —How is it defined?
    —In what context is it defined?
    —What about quality and predictability?
    —Productivity itself isn't the goal

13. Classes of productivity

    —Product: quality, reliability, bug rate, maintainability, and complexity level
    —People: how much is done in a unit of time, what are the effects of training, type of problem, morale, and creativity versus discipline
    —Process: what can be automated and at what cost, predictability of what is delivered and when, solving system problems, and installing control

14. Operational definitions

    —Identify the attributes
    —Determine the metric and measuring technique

—Measure to understand where you are
—Establish the worst and the best planned cases
—Modify process
—Re-measure to see what's changed
—Reiterate
—Work with available data
—Determine additional data needed and collection method

15. Software quality dimensions

—Software capabilities
—Publications
—Packaging
—Ease of installation
—Ease of use
—Performance
—Reliability
—Maintainability
—Compatibility
—Evolvability
—Cost
—Timeliness

16. The relative cost of fixing problems can be shown as follows:

—Just before code   1.0
—During code   1.5
—Just before test   10.0
—During test   60.0
—In the field   100.0

Reference

Digital Equipment Corporation. 1990. Software metrics: An overview - Tools for managing software development. Company presentation.

Hewlett-Packard's Total Quality Control (TQC) Guidelines for Software Engineering Productivity

Abstract

Engineering productivity is extremely important to HP because they rely on new product development to maintain their competitive strength. HP introduces an average one new product every business day. A total of 70% of HP's engineers are involved in software development, and half of all R&D projects are exclusively devoted to software development.

It was this significant investment in software development that prompted HP's president to issue a challenge to achieve a ten-fold improvement in software quality within five years. He also asked that new product development time be reduced by 50%.

This chapter points out the techniques HP utilized to meet this vast quality and productivity challenge.

Procedures/Issues/Policies

1. HP's productivity equation is

   Productivity = (function of doing the right things) × (function of doing things right)

2. Cultural and organizational issues addressed in order to motivate and support positive changes:

   - Productivity managers are used in each division to

     —Understand productivity and quality issues
     —Evaluate, select, and install CASE tools

—Communicate best software engineering practices
—Train staff

Establish productivity and quality metrics

- A group productivity council is created to share the best R&D practices across divisions for

    —Metrics definition
    —Metrics tracking
    —Productivity councils
    —Software quality and productivity assessment
    —Communication of best practices

3. Software metrics council is created, composed of both R&D and QA managers and engineers, whose objective is to identify key software metrics and promote their use.

4. Project/Product quality metrics

    —Break-even time measures return on investment. It is defined as the time until development costs are offset by profits. The three numbers plotted are: R&D investment in dollars, operating profit in dollars and time, and sales revenue in dollars and time.
    —Time-to-market measures responsiveness and competitiveness. It is defined as the time from project go-ahead until market release.
    —Kiviat diagram measures variables that affect software quality and productivity. It is a bulls-eye chart that graphs results of quality and productivity assessment.

5. Process quality metrics

    —Progress rate measures schedule accuracy. It is defined as the ratio of planned to actual development time.
    —"Open critical and serious KPRs" measures effectiveness of support processes. It is defined as the number of service requests classified as known problems (of severity levels "critical" or "serious") that are not signed off.
    —Post-release defect density measures effectiveness of design and test processes. It is defined as the total number of defects reported during the first 12 months after product shipment.

6. People quality metrics: the turnover rate measures morale, which is the percentage of engineers leaving company; and training measures the investment in career development, and is defined as the number of training hours per engineer per year.

7. Basic software quality metrics

    —Code size: *KNCSS*, which is thousands of lines of non-comment source statements
    —Number of pre-release defects requiring repair
    —Pre-release defect density (defects ÷ KNCSS)
    —Calendar months for pre-release QA
    —Total pre-release QA test hours
    —Number of post-release defects reported after one year

—Post-release defect density (defects ÷ KNCSS)
—Calendar months from investigation checkpoint to release

8. Strategy for code reuse

—Share code (use exactly as-is) whenever possible
—If sharing is not possible, try to leverage (minimal modifications)
—If neither sharing nor leveraging is possible, look for similar algorithms (design reuse)
—As a last resort, invent something new

9. The Systems Software Certifications program is established to ensure measurable, consistent, high-quality software. The four metrics chosen are:

—Breadth: measures the testing coverage of user accessible and product internal functionality
—Depth: measures the proportion of instructions or blocks of instructions executed during testing
—Reliability: measures how stable and robust a product is and its ability to recover gracefully from error conditions
—Defect density: measures the quantity and severity of reported defects found and a product's readiness for use.

Reference

Hewlett-Packard. 1989. Software engineering productivity.

54

Motorola's Six Sigma Defect Reduction Effort

Abstract

In 1987, Motorola set in motion a five-year quality improvement program. The term Six Sigma is one used by statisticians and engineers to describe a state of zero defects. The result of this program produced productivity gains of 40% as well as Motorola winning the Malcolm Baldridge National Quality award in 1988.
Benefits include:

- Increased productivity by 40%
- Reduced backlog from years to months
- Increased customer service levels
- Shifted IS time from correcting mistakes to value-added work
- Better staff motivation
- Reduced costs by $1.5 billion

Procedures/Issues/Policies

1. Identify your product. Determine what is the service or product you are producing. IS must align what they do with customer desires.

2. Identify customer requirements. IS must determine what the customer perceives as a defect-free product or service. The unit of work that the user deals with must be considered. For example, in a general ledger system, the user worries about defects per journal voucher, not defects per thousand lines of code.

3. Diagnose the frequency and source of errors. Four categories of metrics were established to target defect reduction:

—New software development
—Service delivery
—Cycle time
—Customer satisfaction, which is composed of a detailed service with the intent of validating the first three metrics

4. Define a process for doing the task. Motorola refers to this process as "mapping," but closely aligned to the re-engineering process. The process involves using personal computer-based tools to determine flow-through of processes and answering the following questions:

—Which processes can be eliminated?
—Which processes can be simplified?

5. Mistake-proof the process. By streamlining a process and eliminating any unnecessary steps, it is possible to make the process mistake-proof. By using metrics, a process control mechanism is put into place so that problems can be addressed before they affect output.

6. Put permanent control measures in place. Once Six Sigma is reached, this level must be maintained. At this step, the Six Sigma metrics are set-up to be used to continuously monitor the process. Monthly quality review meetings are held where each person discusses their metric, its trend, diagnosis of source cause of errors, and the action plan to correct the errors.

Reference

Rifkin, G. 1991. No more defects. *Computerworld*. 15 July 1991: 59–62.

Lederer's Management Guidelines for Better Cost Estimating

Abstract

Estimating software project costs inaccurately wastes limited resources, causes expected contributions to be missed, and ultimately destroys the credibility of estimators and developers. This chapter results from a study of the cost estimating practices reported by 115 computing managers and professionals.

Procedures/Issues/Policies

1. Causes of inaccurate estimates include (listed in order of descending value):

   —Frequent requests for changes
   —Overlooked tasks
   —Users' lack of understanding of their own requirements
   —Insufficient communication between user and analyst
   —Poor or imprecise problem definition
   —Insufficient analysis when performing estimate
   —Lack of coordination between systems development, technical services, operations, and other areas
   —Lack of an adequate methodology or guidelines for estimating
   —Personnel changes in information systems department
   —Insufficient test time
   —Lack of historical data regarding past estimates and actual costs
   —Lack of setting and reviewing standard durations used in estimating

—Pressure from managers, users, or others to increase or decrease estimate

—Inability to anticipate skills of project team members

—Red tape

—Lack of project control when comparing estimates and actual costs

—Users' lack of understanding of data processing

—Inability to identify failures in previous estimates

—Reduction of project scope or quality in order to stay within the estimate, resulting in extra work later

—Lack of careful management examination of estimate

—Lack of participation in estimating by systems analysts and programmers

—Performance reviews do not consider estimate accuracy

—Lack of diligence by systems analysts and programmers

—Management removing "padding" from the estimate

2. Influences on the estimate include (listed in order of descending value):

—Complexity of proposed system

—Required integration with other systems

—Complexity of programs in system

—Size of the system in number of functions

—Capabilities of the project team members

—Size of the system in number of programs

—Project team's experience with the application

—Anticipated frequency or extent of potential changes in user requirements

—Project team's experience with the programming language

—Data management system

—Size of project team

—Extent of programming or documentation standards

—Availability of software productivity tools

—Development mode (batch or on-line)

—Programming language used

—Project team's experience with the hardware

—Availability of testing aids

—Availability of test time on the hardware

—Computer memory and secondary storage constraints

—Size of the system in number of lines of code

3. The uses of cost estimates (listed in order of descending value):

—To staff projects

—To control or monitor project implementation

—To select proposed projects for implementation

—To schedule projects

—To quote the charges to users for projects

—To audit project success

—To evaluate project developers

—To evaluate project estimators

4. Software packages in use (listed in order of descending value):

—Estimacs
—Spectrum/Estimator
—In-house package
—Project Workbench
—Nolan/Prompt
—AGS PAC III
—DEC/VAX Software Project Manager
—Microsoft Project

5. Guideline one: assign the initial estimating task to the final developers. There are two schools of thought concerning estimating. One is that a separate group of people should be given the responsibility for estimating all software projects, much in the same way as a professional estimator performs all construction project estimates. This study found that this was not valid—the best estimates come from the ultimate developers of the product.

6. Guideline two: delay accepting the initial estimate until the end of a thorough study. If the estimators do not develop an accurate initial estimate, then they should not present it until it is as accurate as possible. Project overruns are a direct result of improvising an estimate. Coming up with an estimate under pressure serves no purpose, since the researchers found that revising an estimate might not correct it.

7. Guideline three: anticipate and control user changes. Estimators should thoroughly understand (before they estimate the costs)the user requirements that motivated the proposed system. By doing so, they might reduce, and therefore control, frequent change requests.

8. Guideline four: monitor the progress of the proposed project. The study found that the percentage of large projects that overrun their estimates, and the percentage of those for which formal monitoring of project progress is done (by comparing it to its project plan) was negative. Thus, formal monitoring is important.

9. Guideline five: evaluate proposed project progress by using independent auditors. Project monitoring is usually done by those involved with it. The survey shows, however, that more accurate estimates occur when independent auditors are present. Apparently, an independent evaluation is an advance warning to estimators and developers that computing management is concerned with creating and meeting an accurate estimate. It also reduces cheating.

   Twenty-five percent of systems analysts and programmers refrain from accurately reporting their hours in order to meet estimates, 36% of computing departments postpone the delivery of part of a project, and then claim on-time delivery for the rest of the project, and 68% of the projects in this study had programmers work a disproportionate amount of time in the final days of the project to meet the targeted completion date.

10. Guideline six: use the estimate to evaluate project personnel. More accurate estimates are produced when this evaluation is made. The authors recommend in-

forming personnel in advance of the intended use of the estimate, and giving favorable recognition to those personnel whose projects meet estimates.

11. Guideline seven: Computing management should carefully study and approve the cost estimate. For 58% of an organization's large projects, a cost/benefit analysis is used to justify systems development. Computing management approval, rather than user management approval, increases estimating accuracy.

12. Guideline eight: Rely on documented facts, standards, and simple arithmetic formulas rather than guessing, using intuition or personal memory, and complex formulas.

13. Guideline nine: Don't rely on cost estimating software for an accurate estimate. The study found that the use of software-estimating packages had no significant effect on reducing overruns.

Selected Bibliography

Albrecht, A.J. 1979. Measuring application development productivity. *GUIDE/SHARE application development symposium proceedings*. October 1979: 83–92.

Conte, S.D., H.E. Dunsmore, and V.Y. Shen. 1986. *Software engineering metrics and models*. Menlo Park, Ca.: Benjamin/Cummings Publishing Company, Inc.

Lederer, A.L., R. Mirani, B.S. Neo, C. Pollard, J. Prasad, and K. Ramamurthy. 1990. Information system cost estimating: A management perspective. *MIS quarterly*. 14 (2): 159–178.

Reference

Lederer, A.L. and J. Prasad. 1992. Nine management guidelines for better cost estimating. *Communications of the ACM*. 35 (2): 51–59.

56

Kanter's Methodology for Justifying Investment in Information Technology

Abstract

A survey of over 100 corporate CEOs found that 64% felt that their organizations were not getting the most return from their information systems investments. This short chapter focuses on how to justify the IS function.

Procedures/Issues/Policies

1. Decide if you need to justify past expenditures or if you want to work on new expenditures only. A strong argument can be made for comprehensive budgeting of past activities as a base point for future planning.

2. After the scope is decided, sort budgets by many categories such as specific department and activity, or by qualitative breakouts such as architecture, skills mix, and systems development.

3 Many IS executives measure information technology expenditures against industry averages. To assure balance, analyze by major application areas such as marketing, manufacturing, or finance. Use third-party yardsticks, such as those following, to measure strategic or competitive advantage applications:

- Computerworld Premier 100, based on a six-part formula that includes (where % = weight value):

   —Annual IS budget as a percentage of revenue (30%)
   —Market value of equipment as a percentage of revenue (15%)

—Company profitability over five years (15%)
—Percentage of IS budget for people (10%)
—Percentage of IS budget on education (15%)
—Number of PCs or Terminals as a percentage of total headcount (15%)

- CIO Magazine Top 100, where experts evaluate MIS operations on four factors that foster competitive edge:

  —Demonstrated importance of customer service
  —Not "who you know," but how you connect to them
  —Value of information, equal to money as an asset
  —Illuminate shifts in IS usage

- Nolan, Norton. Starts with IT expenditure by industry compared to total revenue, then adds:

  —Application portfolio by function
  —Compared to business strategy
  —Broken out by spending for institutional systems, professional support, physical automation, and external support

- SoCal Gas Company. Based on a University of St. Louis method, the company evolved a four-point plan:

  —Economic impact (65 points)
  —Strategic alignment (22 points)
  —MIS support (13 points)
  —Definition uncertainty (add or subtract points)

- Rivard & Kaiser places a value on intangible and probability returns, including:

  —Incremental analysis
  —Value analysis
  —Expected value
  —Worst case, most likely case, and best case analysis

- Index Group PRISM, which makes broad use of questionnaires to measure user satisfaction and performance within corporate culture and strategy guidelines.

4. Do a qualitative survey, application by application, of all major systems. Have two groups respond. IS staff should rate the cost/value in terms of maintainability, adequacy of hardware/software, staffing requirements, etc., of each application. Each user department should rate effectiveness of each application in terms of mission, fulfillment, timeliness, adequacy, method of reporting, productivity benefit, etc.

   This survey permits you to gain alignment and reach a consensus for action, make cuts, and clearly identify high return-on-investment applications.

5. The next step is to assess future costs. The best approach builds on basic value analysis as represented by the return-on-investment measurement. In this instance, it is important to place a value on intangible benefits and the strategic uses of information technology.

As an example, placing terminals in customers' offices has an intangible value unless you ask how much more will that customer buy? Or how many customers do we normally lose in a year, and how many will we keep now? The answers can be found by extrapolation, projection, or survey.

The expected-value method can be used to assess the probabilities of certain outcomes. This allows you to draw and adjust quantified value conclusions of the type that senior management will respect.

For example, assume that the average annual downtime for a paper mill is two weeks, with each week costing $2 million. A new information system has a goal of reducing downtime by improving maintenance decisions. If the assumption is made that a 50% chance downtime can be reduced by 10%, then these are tangible figures that can be brought to management.

References

Kanter, J. 1990. It's time to justify your organization's investment in information technology. *Cambex storage*. 1 (1).

From a paper prepared for MIS sponsors of Babson College's Center for Information Management.

57

The "Make-Buy" Decision

Abstract

Many projects can make use of package software to satisfy all or part of a functional requirement. In making this decision, as part of the planning step, the purchase cost of the package must be weighed against the development costs estimated. As part of this process the questions in this chapter should be answered.

Procedures/Issues/Policies

1. Does the vendor-supplied software meet all functional requirements defined in the scope of the plan? If not, what percentage of the function will have to be enhanced or added locally? What costs are associated with these enhancements?

2. Has the vendor-supplied software been developed using software engineering methods? Is it maintainable? Does a good documentation base exist? What documentation is supplied with the package?

3. Does the vendor-supplied software meet human interface requirements for the system to be developed?

4. Does the vendor-supplied software already have a user base? How many users are working in an identical environment (hardware, operating system, database)? Are current users happy with the package? Are they happy with the vendor's support of the package? Is there a user group?

5. What is the vendor's policy on software maintenance, error correction, and reporting? What are the vendor's rates for future adaptation or software enhancements? Does a maintenance contract exist? Is the vendor the original developer of the package?

6. Will the vendor supply the source code, or will the source code be placed in escrow?

7. Have adequate benchmark and validation tests been conducted on the vendor's software?

8. Is there more than one candidate vendor package? Have all the candidates been evaluated? Have benchmark tests been conducted?

9. How are new releases of the package handled? How long are the older releases supported? What is the frequency (based on past performance) of new releases?

10. Is special training required to use the package? To operate the package? Is training conducted at the local site? Is there any cost associated with training?

Reference

General Electric Company. 1986. *Software engineering handbook*. New York, N.Y.; McGraw-Hill.

58

Software Selection from Multiple Packages

Abstract

Many projects can make use of package software to satisfy part or all of a functional requirement. In making this decision during planning, the purchase cost of the package must be weighed against estimated development costs. The decision is further complicated when more than one software package is evaluated. This chapter provides a recommended evaluation procedure.

Procedures/Issues/Policies

1. Cost is the real cost of vendor-supplied software (purchase price + cost to modify + cost to add + maintenance fee).
2. Service and support: based on other users with identical environments.
3. Documentation: for users and local maintenance.
4. Expandability/flexibility: needed to address future applications or changes in environment.
5. Reputation of the vendor and the vendor-supplied software.
6. Stability, based on the age of the package and the number of releases over the past two years.
7. Machine or operating system dependency based on programming languages used and special features tied to special hardware.
8. Completeness of function and performance, based on software scope.

A Software Evaluation Matrix should be developed to evaluate software packages. First, establish a weight factor, based on importance, for each characteristic. Grade each candidate package on a scale of 1 to 10 for each characteristic listed above. The final grade for each package is:

$$\Sigma \left[(\text{characteristic})_k \times (\text{weight factor})_k \right]$$

where k = 1 to 8.

Reference

General Electric Company. 1986. *Software engineering handbook*. New York, N.Y.: McGraw-Hill.

59

COCOMO Model

ABSTRACT:

The COnstructive COst MOdel (COCOMO) describes factors that affect the ultimate cost of computer software. The factors fall into four broad categories: product, computer, personnel, and project. Each of these factors are assigned quantitative values.

The software development effort is modeled as a nonlinear function of the number of estimated lines of code to be developed. COCOMO equations take the form of:

$$m = c_1 \times KLOC^a \times PROD(f_i)$$

where

m	=	number of person-months for development effort
c_1	=	model coefficient
a	=	model exponent
f_i	=	cost factor (i = 1 to 16)

Each model cost factor is assigned values based on the degree of its importance and impact.

Procedures/Issues/Policies

Cost Factors

1. Product cost factors

   —Required software reliability: degree to which effort will be expended to assure software reliability (number of reviews and quality assurance effort)

   —Data base size: size and complexity of the database to be developed or integrated (number of information elements and access methods)

   —Software product complexity: logical and structural complexity of the software to be developed

2. Computer cost factors

—Execution time constraints: degree to which program execution time is tied to successful accomplishment of software requirements
—Memory constraint: memory limitations
—Environmental volatility: frequency and extent to which the environment external to the software (i.e., operating system, hardware, etc.) will change during development
—Computer turnaround time: responsiveness of the programming environment

3. Personnel cost factors

—Analyst capability: experience and expertise
—Application experience: experience of development personnel with user application domain
—Programmer capability: experience and expertise
—Environment expertise: experience and expertise with software environment
—Language experience: experience and expertise in programming language

4. Project cost factors

—Programming practices: use of modern programming practices during project
—Software tools: availability of software tools for each of the software engineering steps
—Schedule constraints: the degree to which scheduling constraints will affect the application of software engineering techniques

5. Other cost considerations

—Language: cost per source instruction in assembly language is about twice the cost per source instruction in a higher-level language.
—Real-time applications: cost/instruction is about five times that of conventional applications.
—Point on learning curve: an experienced programming group requires 50% to 100% more effort to develop an unfamiliar program than some variant of a familiar program.
—Amount of documentation: documentation costs run about 10% of the total software development cost.
—Amount of previous software used: the cost of adapting existing software into a new project may be determined by estimating the modification and interface costs for the new application.
—Representations of development environment: the added cost required to adapt software to actual operational conditions can be quite significant—up to 95%—but can only be estimated subjectively.

References

Boehm, B. 1981. *Software engineering economics*. Englewood Cliffs, N.J.: Prentice-Hall.

Boehm, B. 1975. The high cost of software. In *Practical strategies for developing large software systems*, ed. E. Horowitz, pp 4–14. Reading, Ma.: Addison-Wesley.

IEEE Standard Dictionary of Measures to Produce Reliable Software

Abstract

The IEEE standards were written with the objective of providing the software community with defined measures currently used as indicators of reliability. By emphasizing early reliability assessment, this standard supports methods through measurement to improve product reliability.

This chapter presents a subset of the IEEE standard, easily adaptable by the general IS community.

Procedures/Issues/Policies

1. Fault density. This measure can be used to predict remaining faults (by comparison with expected fault density), determine if sufficient testing has been completed, and establish standard fault densities for comparison and prediction.

$$F_d = \frac{F}{KSLOC}$$

where

F = total number of unique faults found in a given interval resulting in failures of a specified severity level

$KSLOC$ = number of source lines of executable code and non-executable data declarations in thousands

2. Defect density. This measure can be used after design and code inspections of a new development or large block modifications. If the defect density is outside the norm after several inspections, it is an indication of a problem.

$$DD = \frac{\displaystyle\sum_{i=1}^{I} D_i}{KSLOD}$$

where

D_i = total number of unique defects detected during the "i"th design or code inspection process
I = total number of inspections
$KSLOD$ = number of source lines of executable code and non-executable data declarations in thousands (in design phase)

3. Cumulative failure profile. This is a graphical method used to: predict reliability, estimate additional testing time to reach an acceptable reliable system, and identify modules and subsystems that require additional testing. A plot is drawn of cumulative failures versus a suitable time base.

4. Fault-days number. This measure is the number of days that faults are in the system, from their creation to their removal. For each fault detected and removed, during any phase, the number of days from its creation to its removal is determined in "fault-days." The fault-days are then totaled, for all faults detected and removed, to get the fault-days number at the system level, including all faults detected and removed up to the delivery date. In those cases where the creation date of the fault is not known, the fault is assumed to have been created at the middle of the phase in which it was introduced.

5. Functional or modular test coverage. This measure is used to quantify a software test coverage index for a software delivery. From the system's functional requirements, a cross-reference listing of associated modules must first be created.

Functional (modular) test coverage index = $FE \div FT$

where

FE = number of the software functional (modular) requirements for which all test cases have been satisfactorily completed
FT = total number of software functional (modular) requirements

6. Requirements traceability. This measure aids in identifying requirements that are either missing from, or in addition to, the original requirements.

$$TM = (R1 \div R2) \times 100$$

where

$R1$ = number of requirements met by the architecture
$R2$ = number of original requirements

7. Software maturity index. This measure is used to quantify the readiness of a software product. Changes from previous baselines to the current baselines are an indication of the current product stability.

$$SMI = \frac{(M_T - F_a + F_c + F_{del})}{M_T}$$

where

SMI = maturity index
M_T = number of software functions (modules) in the current delivery
F_a = number of software functions (modules) in the current delivery that are additions to the previous delivery
F_c = number of software functions (modules) in the current delivery that include internal changes from a previous delivery
F_{del} = number of software functions (modules) in the previous delivery that are deleted in the current delivery

The Software Maturity Index may be estimated as:

$$SMI = \frac{M_T - F_c}{M_T}$$

8. Number of conflicting requirements. This measure is used to determine the reliability of a software system resulting from the software architecture under consideration, as represented by a specification based on the entity-relationship-attributed model. What is required is a list of the systems inputs, its outputs, and a list of the functions performed by each program.

The mappings from the software architecture to the requirements are identified. Mappings from the same specification item to more than one different requirements are examined for requirements inconsistency. Additionally, mappings from more than one specification item to a single requirement are examined for specification inconsistency.

9. Cyclomatic complexity. This measure is used to determine the structured complexity of a coded module. The use of this measure is designed to limit the complexity of the module, thereby promoting understandability of the module.

$$C = E - N + 1$$

where

C = complexity
N = number of nodes (sequential groups of program statements)
E = number of edges (program flows between nodes)

10. Design structure. This measure is used to determine the simplicity of the detailed design of a software program. The values determined can be used to identify problem areas within the software design.

$$DSM = \sum_{i=1}^{6} W_i D_i$$

where

DSM = design structure measure
P1 = total number of modules in program
P2 = number of modules dependent on input or output
P3 = number of modules dependent on prior processing (state)
P4 = number of database elements
P5 = number of non-unique database elements
P6 = number of database segments
P7 = number of modules not single entrance/single exit

The design structure is the weighted sum of six derivatives determined by using the primitives given above.

D_1 = designed organized top down
D_2 = module dependence (P2/P1)
D_3 = module dependent on prior processing (P3/P1)
D_4 = database size (P5/P4)
D_5 = database compartmentalization (P6/P4)
D_6 = module single entrance/exit (P7/P1)

The weights (W_i) are assigned by the user based on the priority of each associated derivative. Each W_i has a value between 0 and 1.

11. Test coverage. This is a measure of completeness of the testing process from both the developer and user perspective. The measure relates directly to the development, integration, and operational test stages of product development.

$$TC(\%) = \frac{\text{(implemented capabilities)}}{\text{(required capabilities)}}$$

$$\times \frac{\text{(program primitives tested)}}{\text{(total program primitives)}} \times 100$$

where

—Program functional primitives are modules, segments, statements, branches, or paths
—Data functional primitives are classes of data
—Requirement primitives are test cases or functional capabilities

12. Data or information flow complexity. This is a structural complexity or procedural complexity measure that can be used to evaluate the information-flow

structure of large scale systems, the procedure and module information-flow structure, the complexity of the interconnections between modules, the degree of simplicity of relationships between subsystems, and to correlate total observed failures and software reliability with data complexity.

$$\text{weighted IFC} = \text{length} \times (\text{fanin} \times \text{fanout})^2$$

where

IFC = information flow complexity

fanin = local flows into a procedure + number of data structures form which the procedure retrieves data

fanout = local flows from a procedure + number of data structures that the procedure updates

length = number of source statements in a procedure (excluding comments)

The flow of information between modules and/or subsystems needs to be determined either through the use of automated techniques or charting mechanisms. A local flow from module A to B exists if one of the following occurs:

1. A calls B
2. B calls A and A returns a value to B that is passed by B
3. Both A and B are called by another module that passes a value from A to B.

13. Mean time to failure. This measure is the basic parameter required by most software reliability models. Detailed record keeping of failure occurrences that accurately track the time (calendar or execution) at which the faults manifest themselves, is essential.

14. Software documentation and source listings. The objective of this measure is to collect information that identify the parts of the software maintenance products that may be inadequate for use in a software maintenance environment, Questionnaires are used to examine the format and content of the documentation and source-code attributes from a maintainability perspective.

The questionnaires examine the following product characteristics:

1. modularity
2. Descriptiveness
3. Consistency
4. Simplicity
5. Expandability
6. Testability

Two questionnaires, the Software Documentation Questionnaire and the Software Source Listing Questionnaire, are used to evaluate the software products in a desk audit.

For the software documentation evaluation, the resource documents should include those that contain the program design specifications, program testing information and procedures, program maintenance information, and guidelines used in preparation of the documentation. Typical areas covered by the questionnaire include:

1. The documentation indicates that data storage locations are not used for more than one type of data structure.
2. Parameter inputs and outputs for each module are explained in the documentation.
3. Programming conventions for I/O processing have been established and followed.
4. The documentation indicates the resource (storage, timing, tape drives, disks, etc.) allocation is fixed throughout program execution.
5. The documentation indicates that there is a reasonable time margin for each major time-critical program function.
6. The documentation indicates that the program has been designed to accommodate software test probes to aid in identifying processing performance.

The software source listings evaluation reviews either high-order language or assembler source code. Multiple evaluations using the questionnaire are conducted for the unit level of the program (module). The modules selected should represent a sample size of at least 10% of the total source code. Typical areas include:

1. Each function of this module is an easily recognizable block of code.
2. The quantity of comments does not detract from the legibility of the source listings.
3. Mathematical models as described/derived in the documentation correspond to the mathematical equations used in the source listing.
4. Esoteric (clever) programming is avoided in this module.
5. The size of any data structure that affects the processing logic of this module is parameterized.
6. Intermediate results within this module can be selectively collected for display without code modification.

Note: The information contained herein is copyrighted information of the IEEE, extracted from IEEE Std. 982.1-1988, IEEE Standard Dictionary of Measures to Produce Reliable Software. This information was written within the context of IEEE Std 982.1- 1988 and the IEEE takes no responsibility for or liability for damages resulting from the reader's misinterpretation of said information resulting from the placement and context of this publication. Information is reproduced with the permission of the IEEE.

Reference

IEEE Standards Department. 1988. Standard of measures to produce reliable software. Standard 982.1-1988. Piscataway, N.J.: IEEE.

IEEE Framework for Measures

Abstract

Software reliability measurements take place in an environment that includes user needs and requirements, a process for developing products meeting those needs, and user environment within which the delivered software satisfies those needs. This measurement environment establishes a framework for determining and interpreting software reliability indicators.

This chapter provides IEEE's recommended process for measurement, which formalizes the data collection practices in both development and support. It provides for product evaluation at major milestones in the life cycle. It also relates measures from one life cycle phase to another. It is the basis for product reliability measurement.

Procedures/Issues/Policies

The process can be described in nine stages. These stages might overlap or occur in different sequences depending on organization needs. Each of these stages in the measurement process influences the production of a delivered product with the potential for high reliability.

Other factors influencing the measurement process include the following: a firm management commitment to continually assess product and process maturity or stability, or both, during the project; use of trained personnel in applying measures to the project in a useful way; software support tools; and a clear understanding of the distinctions among errors, faults, and failures.

1. Product Measures

   —Errors, faults, and failures is the count of defects with respect to human cause, program bugs, and observed system malfunctions.
   —Mean time to failure and failure rate are derivative measures of defect occurrence and time.

—Reliability growth and projection is the assessment of change in the failure-free state of the product under testing or operation.

—Remaining product faults is the assessment of how fault-free is the product in development, test, or maintenance.

—Completeness and consistency is the assessment of the presence and agreement of all necessary software system parts

—Complexity is the assessment of complicating factors in a system

2. Process Measures

—Management control measures address the quantity and distribution of error and faults and the trend of the costs required for defect removal.

—Coverage measures allow one to monitor the ability of developers and managers to guarantee the required completeness in all the activities of the lifecycle and to support the definition of corrective actions.

—Risk, benefit, and cost evaluation measures support delivery decisions based both on technical and cost criteria. Risk can be assessed based on residual faults present in the product at delivery and the cost associated with the resulting support activity.

3. Errors, faults and failures

—Error: a human action that results in software containing a fault.

—Fault: an accidental condition that causes a functional unit to fail in performing its required function. It is also a manifestation of an error in software that, if encountered, might cause a failure.

—Failure: the termination of the ability of a function unit to perform its required function. It is also an event in which a system or system component does not perform a required function within specified limits. A failure might be produced when a fault is encountered.

4. Stage 1: plan organizational strategy. Initiate a planning process. Form a planning group and review reliability constraints and objectives, giving consideration to user needs and requirements. Identify the reliability characteristics of a software product necessary to achieve these objectives. Establish a strategy for measuring and managing software reliability. Document practices for conducting measurements.

5. Stage 2: determine software reliability goals. Define the reliability goals for the software being developed in order to optimize reliability in light of realistic assessments of project constraints, including size scope, cost, and schedule.

Review the requirements for the specific development effort in order to determine the desired characteristics of the delivered software. For each characteristic, identify specific reliability goals that can be demonstrated by the software, or measured against a particular value or condition. Establish an acceptable range of values. Consideration should be given to user needs and requirements.

Establish intermediate reliability goals at various points in the development effort.

6. Stage 3: implement measurement process. Establish a software reliability measurement process that best fits an organization's needs. Review the rest of the

process and select those stages that best lead to optimum reliability. Add to or enhance these stages as needed. Consider the following suggestions:

—Select appropriate data collection and measurement practices designed to optimize software reliability.

—Document the measures required, the intermediate and final milestones (when measurements are taken), the data collection requirements, and the acceptable values for each measure.

—Assign responsibilities for performing and monitoring measurements, and provide necessary support for these activities from across the internal organization.

—Initiate a measure selection and evaluation process.

—Prepare educational materials for training personnel in concepts, principles, and practices of software reliability and reliability measures.

7. Stage 4: select potential measurements. Identify potential measurements to be made that would be helpful in achieving the reliability goals established in stage 2.

8. Stage 5: prepare data collection and measurement plan. Prepare a data collection and measurement plan for the development and support effort. For each potential measurement, determine the primitives needed to perform the measurement. Data should be organized so that information related to events during the development effort can be properly recorded in a database and retained for historical purposes.

   For each intermediate reliability goal identified in stage 2, identify the measurements needed to achieve the goal. Identify the points during development when the measurements are to be taken. Establish acceptable values, or a range of values, to assess whether the intermediate reliability goals are achieved.

   Include in the plan an approach for monitoring the measurement effort. The responsibility for collecting and reporting data, verifying its accuracy, computing the measurements, and interpreting the results should be described.

9. Stage 6: monitor the measurements. Once the data collection and reporting begins, monitor the measurements and the progress made during development, so as to manage the reliability and thereby achieve the goals for the delivered product. The measurements assist in determining whether the intermediate reliability goals are achieved and whether the final goal is achievable. Analyze the measurement and determine if the results are sufficient to satisfy the reliability goals. Decide whether a measurement assists in affirming the reliability of the product or process being measured. Take corrective action.

10. Stage 7: assess reliability. Analyze the measurements to ensure that reliability of the delivered software satisfies the reliability objectives and that the reliability as measured, is acceptable.

    Identify the assessment steps that are consistent with the reliability objectives documented in the data collection and measurement plan. Check the consistency of the acceptance criteria and the sufficiency of tests to satisfactorily demonstrate that the reliability objectives have been achieved. Identify the organization responsible for determining final acceptance of the software reliability. Document the steps in assessing the software reliability.

11. Stage 8: use software. Assess the effectiveness of the measurement effort and perform necessary correction action. Conduct a follow-up analysis of the measurement effort to evaluate reliability assessment and development practices, record lessons learned and evaluate user satisfaction with the software's reliability.

12. Stage 9: retain software measurement data. Retain measurement data on the software throughout the development and operation phases for use on future projects. These data provide a baseline for reliability improvement and an opportunity to compare the same measures across completed projects. This information can assist in developing future guidelines and standards.

Reference

IEEE Standards Department. 1989. IEEE guide for the use of IEEE standard dictionary of measures to produce reliable software. Standard 982.2-1988. June 12, 1989. Piscataway, N.J.: IEEE.

Gillies' Method for Humanization of the Software Factory

Abstract

In order to introduce the CASE technology successfully to an organization, the human issues such as goals, objectives, fears, and job impacts, must be taken into consideration first. A method is presented here to address those human issues and, at the same time, to develop a quality definition that is accepted by the entire software development community of an organization. The method takes the following approach:

- To educate people about quality
- To resolve different viewpoints of quality
- To reach a realistic consensus view of quality that is achievable by all parties

CASE technology has been widely used in the computer software industry for many years. While more CASE tools become available and CASE technology becomes mature, it is more noticeable that CASE education is more than just the technology. The human issues must also be focused so that when those issues are addressed, the CASE users (such as software development staff) will be more likely to perceive that the new technology will serve as an aid to the staff instead of being a threat to their jobs. The method described here should be considered as part of CASE education when introducing any new CASE technology to an organization. This will ensure that the cooperation of staff will help in realizing the new technology's potential.

Procedures/Issues/Policies

1. Educate people about quality. The following definitions of quality can serve as a starting point for education on quality,

   Quality is the degree of excellence (The Oxford English Dictionary).

   Quality is the totality of features and characteristics of a product or services that bear on its ability to satisfy specified or implied needs (The International Organization for Standardization 1986).

   —The transcendent view: relates quality to innate excellence.
   —The product-based view: the economist's view—the higher the quality, the higher the cost.
   —The user-based view can be summarized as fitness for purpose.
   —The manufacturing view: quality measured in terms of conformance to requirements.
   —The value-based view: the ability to provide what the user wants at an affordable cost (Garvin 1984).

   Quality means the degree of user satisfaction. Previously, good quality meant that a national or an in-house standard was satisfied. This is necessary, but it is not sufficient alone for producing high-quality products. Quality depends upon user satisfaction:

   —Software match to specification
   —Specification match to user needs (Yasuda 1989)

   It is important to realize that the purpose of having a starting point for a discussion of quality is to appreciate that the definition of quality varies dramatically depending on the viewpoint. Any one of the previous quality definitions is not sufficient by itself, but is necessary to be considered for reaching a corporate consensus on quality.

2. Resolve different viewpoints of quality: establish relationship characteristics. This is accomplished through a two-part exercise involving an enabler and a mix of personnel from developers and users. The first part of the exercise focuses on reaching a consensus on quality that reflects the beliefs of all parties. The second part of the exercise focuses on understanding the interrelationship and conflicts that exist between different quality criteria. Relationships between characteristics are classified in terms of trade-offs (if A is enhanced, B is degraded), affinity (if A is enhanced, B is affected), and resonance (if A is enhanced, B is enhanced).

   The purpose of establishing the relationship between quality characteristics is for people to have realistic expectations. All quality criteria are desirable, but perfection is almost impossible to achieve with all aspects of quality characteristics included. Previous experiences indicate that the success of quality improvement is based on a those critical criteria, not the entire set. The relationships help people to clearly appreciate the consequences of emphasizing only those characteristics.

3. Reach a realistic consensus view of quality. The purpose of this step is to ensure a higher probability for the acceptance of the quality definition and improvement. Note that if all parties involved feel that the quality consensus takes their special needs into consideration and understand the needs of others, it is more

likely that the quality consensus will be accepted. In an environment where quality consensus is reached and clearly defined, CASE technology can then be introduced as the means to achieve the specific goals identified in the quality consensus model. This, obviously, increases the likelihood of CASE being viewed as an aid rather than a hindrance to the software developer.

Selected Bibliography

Gavin, D. 1984. What does product quality mean? *Sloane management review*. 4.

Gilb, T. 1988. *Principles of software engineering management*. Reading, Ma.: Addison-Wesley.

International Organization for Standardization. 1986.

Yasuda, K. 1989. Software quality assurance activities in Japan. In *Japanese perspectives in software engineering*. Reading, Ma.: Addison-Wesley.

Reference

Gillies, A.C. 1991. Humanization of the software factory. *Information and software technology*. 33 (9): 641–646.

Pfleeger's Approach to Software Metrics Tool Evaluation

Abstract

As technology advance, the process and environment for software development are constantly changing. Different projects usually employ different quantified data for use in terms of project management, control, and forecast. For an organization that employs software metrics tools in its software development environment, it is not uncommon to have a wide range of software metrics tools available to use for various projects.

Often, time-product managers make the selection of tools based on sources such as previous experience, vendor specifications, and inputs from other groups. As more software metrics tools are acquired, it becomes more important to identify the characteristics common to each tool, and have the information stored in a repository. The repository is desirable because the comparison can be easily made among various tools to select the best set of tools to use at any time.

Software metrics are widely used in understanding, managing, and controlling the software development process. Attempts have been made to apply metrics to the characteristics of various aspects of software development. Software metrics tools are often used to collect and analyze data specific to project process maturity, development environment, and management needs and preferences. The approach suggested here describes a comprehensive way to collect essential information for each software metrics tool, and describes a project metrics database that supports monitoring, decision making, trend analysis, predictions, and setting up standards for future projects.

Procedures/Issues/Policies

A two-staged approach to evaluation is described below.

1. First stage: paper evaluation. This stage includes activities such as reviewing the product literature and documentation from various sources, such as vendors and third-party evaluations. The first level of information is a set of basic tool data collected according to the following sample categories:

   —Tool name
   —Vendor name
   —Vendor address
   —Contact
   —Evaluation date

   The tool information is further refined by following a scheme known as "faceted classification," which defines orthogonal facets as independent indices used to group similar objects. Each facet describes an attribute of an object that cannot be described by any other facets. The repository storing the evaluation result will be organized according to the facets employed. The following set of facets are suggested:

   —Purpose of the tool
   —Software development activity
   —Process maturity level
   —Methodology
   —Language
   —Operating system
   —Platform
   —Target application

2. Second stage: extended evaluation. This stage involves the use of a tool in a real-life setting with hands-on evaluation. The results of the evaluation are recorded as the third level of information according to the following sample categories:

   —Version number
   —Platform evaluated
   —Operation system used
   —Cost
   —Tool strength

   The fourth level of information is collected by performing subjective evaluations of the tool's strengths and weakness. The sample categories are listed below:

   —Performance and speed
   —Data import and export
   —User interface
   —Documentation
   —Tool accuracy
   —Vendor support
   —Cost

For each category, a raw score is obtained based on the evaluation results. A weight, based on project needs and goals, is assigned. The final score for each category is computed by multiplying the raw score by the assigned weight. The overall rating of the tool is calculated by adding the final score for each category.

The repository will hold all four levels of information for each evaluated tool. Project managers can then retrieve the level of information desired, and build the software metrics tools kit based on interests and needs.

Selected Bibliography

Humphrey, W. 1989. *Managing the software process.* Reading, Ma.: Addison-Wesley.

Pfleeger, S.L. 1989. Recommendations for an initial set of software metrics. Technical report CTC-TR-89-017. Contel Technology Center.

Pfleeger, S.L. and C.L. and McGowan. 1990. Software metrics in a process maturity framework. *Journal of system software.* July 1990.

Prieto-Diaz, R. and P. Freeman. 1987. Classifying software for reusability. *IEEE software.*

Reference

Pfleeger, S.L. and J.C. Fitzgerald, Jr. 1991. Software metrics tool kit: Support for selection, collection and analysis. *Information and software technology.* 33 (7): 477–482.

Maiden's Method for Reuse of Analogous Specifications through Human Involvement in Reuse Process

Abstract

The concept of software reuse has been applied in various software deliverables, such as design, coding, and test cases, and has been realized with the advance of CASE tools revolution. An alternative paradigm is proposed for the reuse of specifications during requirement analysis, through the analogy concept. The analogy-recognition process is knowledge-intensive, and requires the software analyst's involvement in a pragmatic approach to perform problem classification, reusable-specification candidate selection, and customizing the selected reusable specification for the new problem domain.

Specification reuse is a concept that should be implemented at some level higher than the reusable code or reusable design level. Reusable code or reusable design addresses only isolated, piece-wise solutions that usually are identified at the design or coding phase of the software life cycle. However, reusable specification must be identified during the requirement analysis, thus providing a better picture of software productivity and quality during those early stages of software life cycle, and avoiding costly faults and omissions that could happen in later stages.

Procedures/Issues/Policies

A good definition of *analogy* is made by Carbonell (1985): "Analogical problem solving consists of transferring knowledge from past problem solving episodes to new problems that share significant aspects with corresponding past experience—and using transferred knowledge to construct solutions to new problems."

Analogy is not a process that performs matches for syntactic similarities. Analogy, basically, is a process that transfers, in its entirety, a network of domain and method knowledge representing solution. Analogy is concerned with finding the affinities between the problem domains rather than just the reusable specifications. The domain and method knowledge are best presented by a set of interconnected causal relations constrained by abstraction.

Normally, domain and method knowledge are stored separately in the existing systems, but expert software engineers usually memorize abstract and concrete specifications in a form integrated with domain and method knowledge. Method and problem domain knowledge are usually required by intelligent CASE tools to assist the analytic problem-solving process. This indicates that specification reuse must be a human-supported task, and the important role of the software analyst must be emphasized to achieve a successful analogy process.

The analogy process for specification reuse can never be achieved solely by software tools, and involves the following steps in which extensive analyst participation is essential:

1. Retrieve the correct specification from a repository. Considerable knowledge is obviously needed to understand different problem domains and the analogy between them. An analyst is required to bring knowledge of the target domain to the process, which requires that key features of the new problem be defined and applied as inputs to the reusable specifications-retrieval mechanism. The key features are used to match critical features of those candidate software-engineering problems in the repository. This is normally an iterative process of retrieval and understanding.

2. Selection of candidate specifications under the same problem category. The requirement analyst must use his knowledge of the target and the reusable domains to understand each candidate and compare it to the functional and nonfunctional requirements of the target problem. Supports, such as diagnostics and explanation tools, are needed for the analyst to identify those possible misconceptions about the analogy and to guide the analyst during specification reuse so that the most appropriate specification will be selected.

3. Customization of the selected specification to the new domain. This also requires an analyst with extensive knowledge of the target and reusable domains to make successful modifications to a reusable specification. Functional requirements of the new problem should be tested against the analogous specifications. Prototyping is appropriate to provide confidence that the reused specification will most likely meet the target problem requirements.

Selected Bibliography

Carbonell, J.G. 1985. Derivational analogy: A theory of reconstructive problem solving and expertise acquisition. Technical report CMU-CS-85-115. Pittsburgh, Pa.: Computer Science Department, Carnegie-Mellon University.

Maiden, N.A.M. 1991. Analogy as a paradigm for specification reuse. *Software engineering journal.* 6 (1): 3–15.

Maiden, N.A.M. and A.G. Sutcliffe. 1991. Analogical matching for specification reuse. In *Proceedings of the 6th knowledge-based software engineering conference.* Piscataway, N.J.: IEEE Computer Society Press.

Reference

Maiden, N.A.M. 1991. Saving reuse from the noose: Reuse of analogous specification through human involvement in reuse process. *Information and software technology.* 33 (10): 780–790.

Tate's Approaches to Measuring the Size of Application Products with CASE Tools

Abstract

CASE tools have been widely used in the software development environment. CASE tools have evolved equipped with the capability to generate end products in various forms, including programming language source codes, graphical user interface, and data dictionary entries. This implies that lines of code (LOC) count, in many cases, is no longer adequate for measuring productivity and process performance. Methods such as dictionary token counts, vector metrics, and function metrics are considered alternative approaches for productivity measurements.

The purpose of measuring the size of CASE application product is basically an attempt to measure the technology productivity or the development productivity or both. Technology productivity indicates the performance of a specific type of CASE technology or CASE tool. Development productivity focuses on the performance of an individual developer or a development group.

Software deliverables come in various forms. It is necessary to include all objects of the end products in order to make comprehensive measurements. These measurements can then be used to produce tangible productivity numbers such as development cost, development effort, or time per unit size of the job done, and others.

Procedures/Issues/Policies

The overall size of any software product basically should consist of representations from all object types delivered for the end product, and can be determined by one of the following ways:

1. Find a common measure, for example, lines of code counts, for all objects.
2. Construct a composite measure that is a function of different weighted objects. This is commonly known as Function Points or Function Weight.

Three different methods are listed as possible approaches for the measurement of CASE application products (CAPs).

1. Dictionary token counts: CASE tools are concerned with a wide array of object types, such as source codes, entities, relationships, data types, data flows, graphical interfaces, and forms. All objects should be entered in a dictionary as tokens or fields. Those tokens can then be weighted and added together to form a single measurement. The following advantages are noted: tokens are simple and easy to count; tokens provide a useful measure across many CASE tools; a token can be considered as an atomic decision instance that the developer makes, thus better representing the software development effort as a whole.

   Note that tokens are most suitable for general purposes and for objective target sizes.

2. Size metric vectors: this approach implies that a concept, such as size, has more than one dimension and should not be represented in a single value. Objects such as data-flow diagram, data model, and user interface, can be sized separately. The size metric vectors should be tailored based on the end-product objects.

   Note that size metric vectors should not replace common or composite size metrics. They are simply complementary to one another.

3. Function metric vectors (composite units-of-size measure): one common composite measure is Function Points. The composite measures provides early size measures based on a partial system model. The success of composite measures is based on the purpose for which they are constructed and their suitability for that purpose. Some possible purposes include the forecast of: downstream effort/cost for particular stages and CAP parts, or for a completed CAP; downstream development time for similar categories; downstream size in tokens and/or lines of source or machine code.

   Composite metrics are most suitable for particular purposes since they assign weights to different component types, and object counts can be tailored for special needs.

Selected Bibliography

Basili, V.R. and H.D. Rombach. 1988. The TAME project: Towards improvements oriented software environments. *IEEE transactions on software engineering.* 14 (6): 758–773.

Verner, J. 1989. A generic model for software size estimation based on component partitioning. PhD Thesis. New Zealand: Massey University.

Verner, J., G. Tate, B. Jackson, and R. Hayward. 1989. Technology dependence in function point analysis: A case study and critical review. In *Proceedings of the 11th international conference on software engineering*. May 1989, Pittsburgh, Pa.

Reference

Tate, G. and J.M. Verner. 1991. Approaches to measuring size of application products with CASE tools. *Information and software technology*. 33 (9): 622–628.

Linkman's Method for Controlling Programs through Measurement

Abstract

A controlled development and maintenance program is essential for bringing down the cost associated with the software development life cycle. The control mechanism can be implemented by first setting up specific goals and then selecting the right set of metrics for measuring against those goals.

Goals have to be tangible and balanced, or they will be too remote to be considered achievable. Intermediate targets are needed for monitoring the project progress and making sure that the project is on the right track. Project data collection and analysis should also be part of the control mechanism.

A four-step procedure is outlined for establishing targets and the means for assessment. The procedure is not focused on any particular set of metrics; rather it is based on the belief that metrics should be selected on the basis of goals. This procedure is suitable for setting up goals for either the entire project deliverables, or for any partial product created in the software life cycle.

Procedures/Issues/Policies

1. Define measurable goals: establishing project goals is similar to the development process for project deliverables. Software projects usually start with abstract problem concepts: the final project deliverables are obtained by continuously partitioning and refining the problem into tangible and manageable pieces. Final, quantified goals can be transformed from initial, intangible goals by following the same divide and conquer method for software deliverables. Three sources of information are helpful to establishing the targets: historical data, under the as-

sumptions that data are available, the development environment is stable, and projects are similar in terms of type, size, and complexity; synthetic data, such as modeling results, are useful if models used are calibrated to specific development environments; expert opinions.

2. Maintain balanced goals: the measurable goals are usually established on the basis of the following four factors: cost, schedule, effort, and quality. It is feasible to achieve just a single goal, but it is always a challenge to deliver a project with the minimum staff and resource, on time, and within budget. It needs to be kept in mind that trade-offs are always involved and all issues should be addressed to reach a set of balanced goals.

3. Set up intermediate goals: a project should never be measured only at its end point. Checkpoints should be set up to provide confidence that the project is running on course. The common practice involves: setting up quantifiable targets for each phase, measuring the actual values against the targets, and establishing a plan to make corrections for any deviations. The four factors in step 2 should be broken down into phase or activity for setting up intermediate targets. Measurements for cost and effort can be divided into machine and human resources according to the software life cycle phase, so that expenditures can be monitored to ensure the project is running within budget.

   Schedule should always be defined in terms of milestones or check points to ensure that intermediate products can be evaluated and the final product will be delivered on time. Quality of intermediate products should always be measured to guarantee the final deliverable will meet its target goal.

4. Establish means of assessment: two aspects are involved in this activity: The first is data collection. Based on the project characteristics such as size, complexity, and level of control, a decision should be made in terms of whether a manual data-collection process or an automated data-collection process should be used. If a manual method is applied, then the availability of the collection medium at the right time should be emphasized. The second is data analysis. The following two types of analyses should be considered:

   —Project analysis: this type of analysis consists of checkpoint analysis and continuous analysis (trend analysis), and is concerned with verifying that the intermediate targets are met to ensure that the project is on the right track.
   —Component analysis: this type of analysis concentrates on the finer level of details of the end product, and is concerned with identifying those components in the product that might require special attention and action. The complete process includes deciding on the set of measures to be analyzed, identifying the components detected as anomalous using measured data, finding out the root cause of the anomalies, and taking actions to make correction.

Selected Bibliography

Kitchenham, B.A., L.M. Packard, and S.G. Linkman. An evaluation of some design metrics. *Software engineering journal.* 5 (1): 50–58.

Linkman, S.G. 1990. Quantitative monitoring of software development by time-based and inter-checkpoint monitoring. *Software engineering journal.* 5 (1): 43–49.

Walker, J.G. and B.A. Kitchenham. 1989. Quality requirements specification and evaluation. In *Measurement for software control and assurance,* ed. B.A. Kitchenham and B. Littlewood. Elsevier Applied Science.

Reference

Linkman, S.G. and J.G. Walker. 1991. Controlling programs through measurement. *Information and software technology.* 33 (1): 93–102.

67

Zachman's Framework

Abstract

In his seminal work, Zachman makes the observation that, just as a builder needs a detailed set of plans for a building, a systems developer needs a detailed set of plans for a complex system. He continues this observation by saying that different types of plans are prepared by different parties for different purposes, and represent what are really very different views of the same building. Zachman created an architectural framework, which is basically a "set of representations" of differing orientations and focuses. This chapter gives a brief overview of Zachman's framework.

Procedures/Issues/Policies

1. The framework is a two-dimensional classification of the various components of an information systems architecture. One dimension consists of scope description, business model, information system model, technology model, and detailed description. The second dimension consists of data description, process description, and network description.

2. Zachman's framework:

Description	Data Description	Process Description	Network
Scope Description			
Business Model			
Information Systems Model			
Technology Model			
Detailed Description			

3 At the Scope Description Level

—Data description: a list of entities relevant to the business or project.
—Process description: a list of business processes.
—Network description: a list of locations at which the business operates, or at which the processes of interest are performed.

4. At the Business Model level

—Data description: an entity-relationship diagram.
—Process description: might be a functional flow diagram
—Network description: some form of logistic definition of the enterprise.

5. At the Information System Model level

—Data description: a detailed logical data model with all the necessary data element definitions.
—Process description: might be a detailed data flow diagram with supporting documentation.
—Network Description: plan for system distribution.

6. At the Technology Model level

—Data description: detailed definition of the external schemas.
—Process description: detailed structure chart with complete module specifications.
—Network description: system architecture of processors, nodes and communication lines.

7. At the Detailed Description level
    —Data description: describes actual files, records, fields, and so on, as under-
    stood by the data management software.
    —Process description: consists of the programs.
    —Network description: is in the form used by the communications software.

Reference

Zachman, J.A. 1987. A framework for information systems architecture. *IBM systems journal*. 26 (3).

68

Malcolm Baldridge Quality Award

Abstract

The Malcolm Baldridge Quality Award is an annual award that recognizes American companies that excel in quality achievement and quality management.
The Award promotes:

- Awareness of quality as an increasingly important element in competitiveness.
- Understanding the requirements for quality excellence.
- Sharing of information on successful quality strategies and benefits derived from implementation of these strategies.

Although only one part of the examination is related to technology, all the Baldridge award tenets of quality apply to the IT process. In this chapter, a synopsis of the requirements are highlighted.

Procedures/Issues/Policies

1. The award is built upon a number of key concepts, as follows:

   —Quality is defined by the customer.
   —The senior leadership of business needs to create clear quality values and build the values into company operations.
   —Quality excellence derives form well-designed and well-executed systems and processes.
   —Continuous improvement must be part of the management of all systems and processes.
   —Companies need to develop goals as well as strategic and operational plans to achieve quality leadership.

—Shortening the response time of all operations and processes of the company needs to be part of the quality improvement effort.

—Operations and decisions of the company needs to be based upon facts and data.

—All employees must be suitably trained, developed, and involved in quality activities.

—Design quality and defect and error prevention should be major elements of the quality system.

—Companies need to communicate quality requirements to suppliers, and work to elevate supplier quality performance.

2. Examination Categories/Items

	Maximum Points
1.0 Leadership	100
1.1 Senior Executive Leadership	40
1.2 Quality Values	15
1.3 Management for Quality	25
1.4 Public Responsibility	20
2.0 Information and Analysis	70
2.1 Scope and Management of Quality Data and Information	20
2.2 Competitive Comparisons and Benchmarks	30
2.3 Analysis of Quality Data and Information	20
3.0 Strategic Quality Planning	60
3.1 Strategic Quality Planning Process	35
3.2 Quality Goals and Plans	25
4.0 Human Resource Utilization	150
4.1 Human Resource Management	20
4.2 Employee Involvement	40
4.3 Quality Education and Training	40
4.4 Employee Recognition and Performance Measurement	25
4.5 Employee Well-Being and Morale	25
5.0 Quality Assurance of Product and Services	140
5.1 Design and Introduction of Quality Products and Services	35
5.2 Process Quality Control	20
5.3 Continuous Improvement of Processes	20
5.4 Quality Assessment	15
5.5 Documentation	10

Reference

United States Department of Commerce, National Institute of Standards and Technology, Gaithersburg, Maryland 20899

69

Bharadwaj and Mattson's Programming Environments for Parallel Distributed Computing

Abstract

Computer programmers take for granted the existence of a common programming model. This model, as embodied in high-level programming languages such as C or Fortran, shields programmers from machine-specific details and lets them focus on algorithms rather than hardware.

Parallel computing on machines composed of merchant microelectronic components can provide orders of magnitude more CPU cycles at costs that are orders of magnitude lower than traditional high-performance computers. However, the difficulty, and therefore, the cost of producing and maintaining software for these multiprocessors is at least an order of magnitude greater than it is to produce similar software for conventional computers. Hence, the user needs to devote the utmost attention to software tools for developing, debugging, and maintaining parallel software. Indeed, the total cost of a parallel computational approach to a problem is much more sensitive to software costs than to hardware costs.

Parallel computing (which includes distributed computing on local or wide area networks) at this time lacks a commonly accepted programming model. Until broad consensus forms around a particular programming model, each parallel programmer must choose a model and a programming environment that expresses that model. Failing to do so sacrifices productivity by exposing low-level, hardware issues to the programmer and forcing a reprogramming of the software for every new parallel platform.

While there are many programming models for parallel computing as implemented in hundreds of programming environments, we have restricted our discussion to MIMD computers. MIMD systems are multiprocessor computers where each processor has its own instruction and data streams. There are four main classes of parallel computing models:

1. Communication libraries.

2. Data Parallel Languages.

3. Coordination languages.

4. Inherently parallel languages.

In this chapter, we will introduce each of these classes and identify issues to consider when making a selection. These issues are:

Portability
Expressiveness
Code Reuse
The Learning Curve
Debugging
Performance
Support

We will introduce each issue and discuss how well each programming model handles it.

Classifications of Parallel Programming Environments

In this section we describe each of the four main parallel programming models.

Communication libraries are libraries of modules for process management and communication. Since they are implemented as libraries, they cannot utilize the compiler for optimization or syntactic support. The library-based implementation, however, has the advantage of interfacing easily with a variety of sequential languages. Examples of communication libraries are TCGMSG (Harrison, 1992), PVM (Geist, 1992), and P4 (Lusk, 1992).

Data Parallel languages usually are based on sequential languages such as Fortran. They consist of the base language plus syntax to express data distribution and parallel operations. Examples are Fortran-D and the new proposed High-Performance Fortran language.

Coordination languages are compact languages or language extensions whose primary function is to coordinate the execution of a number of processes where coordination refers to communication, process management, and synchronization. These environments are implemented as languages rather than libraries. This makes it possible to provide compiler support for a more flexible syntax as well as various optimizations. The major example of a coordination language that is in widespread use is Linda® (Carriero and Gelernter, 1990).[1] In Linda, all process coordination occurs in terms of operations on a virtual shared memory.

The final class contains inherently parallel languages. While the other three classes are all based on existing sequential languages, the class of inherently parallel languages consists of languages that are designed specifically for parallel computing. These languages can be explicitly parallel (the user must directly specify which components execute in parallel); or they can be implicitly parallel (parallelism is automatically extracted from the program).

A discussion of programming environments for MIMD computing would not be complete without a mention of tools that automatically parallelize sequential programs. In our opinion, these tools will never be effective for general parallel computing. Sequential programs are inherently limited in their ability to express parallelism that may be hidden in a code. Automatic parallelism may be effective for a limited portion of the program, but the programmer would still need to explicitly code the rest of the program. Therefore, these tools will only be useful in providing a "first pass" mapping onto environments from one of our four classes and cannot qualify as a stand-alone parallel programming environment.

Issues in Selecting a Parallel Programming Environment

Portability

Portable programs can be moved from one computer to another by simply recompiling the code. Portability is axiomatic among programmers of sequential computers. Parallel programmers, however, often ignore portability and use native (low-level) tools particular to a given parallel computer.

The use of nonportable code inflates the risks associated with parallel computing. Every year, a number of parallel computer manufacturers fail, while a few more arrive to take their place. Software developers who write nonportable code for a parallel computer expose themselves to this volatility.

Each of the programming environment classes supports portability. In fact, portability has been one of the key motivations for the creation of these environments.

Expressiveness

Expressiveness refers to the ability of a programming environment to support a diversity of algorithms. With an expressive programming environment, a program's structure follows from the needs of the algorithm—not the needs of the programming environment. While subjective, this issue is of vital importance to achieving high levels of productivity.

Expressive parallel programming environments naturally should support the views of program development that carry over from sequential computing to parallel computing. A well-known maxim used to highlight the most important aspects of sequential programming is:

```
data structures + algorithms = program
```

This has been extended by N. Carriero to read:

```
distributed data structures + algorithms = parallel program
```

Hence, we expect that an expressive programming environment must support distributed data structures as well as direct process interaction.

Coordination languages and inherently parallel languages are more expressive than other approaches. These environments provide distributed data structures as well as more direct communication constructs. Therefore, they let programmers express the full range of parallel algorithms easily and naturally.

The other classes do well on a subset of parallel algorithms, but not on general algorithms. Data parallel languages are very good for data parallel algorithms, but are unable to express control or functional parallelism. Communication libraries are quite effective for algorithms designed around data decomposition strategies, but do not provide general support for distributed data structures.

Code reuse

Code reuse has become one of the key buzzwords of modern software engineering. The high cost of software throughout its life cycle requires that code be written to permit reuse in later programs.

Parallel programmers face a magnified version of this problem: reuse and conversion of the existing base of sequential software that runs into the hundreds of millions, if not billions of lines. Parallel computers require unique software constructs to support the multiple threads of execution. Complete reengineering of existing sequential codes is both undesirable and costly. Moreover, in many cases, programs have outlived the availability of programmers who understand the algorithms well enough to recode them.

Parallel programming environments based on standard languages will do well with code reuse, at least in the sense that they permit reuse of sequential code. Communication libraries, coordination languages, and data parallel languages all provide excellent support in this area. However, users should keep in mind that simple code reuse is not the whole story, since most sequential programs require reorganization in order to achieve effective parallel performance.

Inherently parallel languages support code reuse, but require additional programmer effort in the form of language interface modules that must be explicitly written for each case.

The learning curve

Software engineers are expensive, so they must become productive with any given programming environment as quickly as possible. Often, effective software engineers place their major focus on the programming task at hand and view time spent coping with a new programming environment as expensive overhead. Therefore, the learning curve for the parallel programming environment must be short.

A short learning curve results from making the parallel environment similar to sequential ones and minimizing the number of new constructs that must be learned. This favors communication libraries and coordination languages. The most extreme example of a short learning curve is given by the shared memory coordination language, Linda, for which only 6 operations must be mastered.

Data parallel languages are also based on familiar languages. However, they require the use of data parallel algorithmic approaches and subtle data distribution directives that have no sequential analogues and may be difficult to learn.

Finally, inherently parallel languages are entirely new languages. They incur a steep learning curve penalty because of the need to master both new programming concepts and new language syntax.

Program debugging

Programmers are faced with daunting tasks when they must debug parallel programs. Parallel programs contain both sequential and parallel components, so all of the problems of debugging sequential programs remain, along with a host of new problems unique to parallel programming.

We believe that the best way to debug parallel programs is to use a two-phase approach. First, the environment should interface to standard (and therefore familiar) debuggers for the sequential components of the program. Second, the programming model itself should be designed so that the unique parallel logic can be easily debugged. The best way to support debugging of parallel logic is to make the logic visually apparent. In other words, the programming environment should support visualization of the detailed progress of the parallel algorithm. This will let software engineers verify their parallel algorithms and see where problems emerge.

All of the programming environment classes naturally interface to existing sequential debuggers, with the exception of the inherently parallel languages. They, by definition, require unique debuggers to go along with the unique parallel language syntax and semantics.

Debugging the parallel portion of a program is more difficult. Of the various environments, only shared memory coordination languages like Linda provide a visualizable model of the parallel computation. In such languages, all parallelism is expressed in terms of operations on persistent objects rather than transient events. These objects can be represented visually with simple icons, while processes can be represented by numbered icons whose shapes reflect their most recently executed parallel operations. This results in a dynamic picture of the operation of a parallel program which is remarkably easy to grasp and provides a great aid to debugging the parallel program.

Performance

The only reason to use parallel computers is to get high performance. This means that any useful programming environment must let processes interact (communicate) effectively. We have observed that virtually all successful environments do a good job of providing high communication performance subject to the physical constraints imposed by the underlying hardware. As a general rule, however, we would note that the actual communication overhead is relatively unimportant to achieving excellent parallel performance. This is because a good candidate algorithm for parallelization will have a relatively small amount of required communication. For such algorithms, high overall performance can be achieved even with relatively slow communication.

In general, we have found that all classes of parallel programming environments are capable of achieving reasonable communication performance across the full range of supported architectures. As a result, this matter does not usually serve as a differentiating factor among them.

Support

Most programming environments for parallel computers were developed at universities or national laboratories and are in the public domain. However, it would be a mistake to think of the use of these environments as being free of charge. If a public domain programming environment is used, then the user must be prepared to support that environment.

The costs associated with supporting a parallel programming environment can be formidable. Parallel and distributed computers are at the cutting edge of technology and can be unstable and difficult to program. Finding staff with the required knowledge of communication and networking technology might also prove difficult.

Therefore, we believe that it is more cost-effective to buy a commercially supported environment. Commercially supported programming environments exist for each class, with end-user prices that are well under the costs of building an in-house support infrastructure. When all considerations are weighed, commercially supported software is the most cost-effective way to go!

Conclusion

In this chapter, we have discussed the importance of using a consistent programming environment for parallel and distributed computing. We defined four classes of programming environments and focused on the task of selecting among them.

Selecting a programming environment is one of the most important decisions made in a parallel computing project. One might hope that one class of programming environments would be clearly the best, but, unfortunately, too much depends on the particular application and matters of personal preference. However, shared memory coordination languages rank consistently high in our analysis, and they seem a good choice in a wide variety of situations.

Selecting the best parallel programming environment is important. But even more important is selecting a parallel computing environment in the first place. Most programmer time is spent maintaining and supporting software, so any portable programming environment providing a consistent model of parallel, multiprocessor systems is far better than native, low-level tools.

Selected Bibliography

Carriero, N. and D. Gelernter. *How to write parallel programs: A first course*. Cambridge: MIT Press, 1990.

Feo, John. *SISAL users manual*. Lawrance Livermore National Laboratory, 1992.

Foster, Ian and Steven Tuecke. *Parallel programming with PCN*. Argonne National Laboratory, 1993.

Geist, Al, et al. *PVM users manual*. Oakridge National Laboratory, 1992.

Harrison, Robert J. *TCGMSG users manual*. Pacific Northwest National Laboratory, 1993.

The HPFF working group. *High performance fortran standard, Draft 1.0*. Rice University, 1993.

Lusk, Rusty and Ralph Butler. *P4 users manual*. Argonne National Laboratory, 1992.

Scientific Computing Associates, Inc. *C-Linda user guide and reference manual*, 1992.

Reference

Carriero, N. and D. Gelernter, "Coordination languages and their significance," Comm. ACM, Feb. 1992.

Mattson, TG "Is there a crisis in parallel computing software?", *Supercomputing review*, 4:2, Feb. 1991, pp. 38–40.

Contributors

Sudy Bharadwaj is currently Director of Sales at Scientific Computing Associates, Inc., a firm specializing in state-of-the-art tools for numerical computation and parallel processing. Mr. Bharadwaj has held executive-level sales and marketing positions for parallel and vector processing software vendors. Mr. Bharadwaj began his career in software development in graphics, graphical user interface development, and parallel and vector precompiler development. Mr. Bharadwaj holds a degree in Computer Science from the State University of New York in Buffalo.

Timothy G. Mattson holds a Ph.D. in chemistry for his work on computational methods in quantum scattering theory. His work in parallel computing began during a post-doctoral position at Caltech as a member of the concurrent computation project. His industrial experience includes signal processing, applied mathematics, computational physics, and software tools for writing portable software for parallel computers.

Dr. Mattson is the director of product engineering at Scientific Computing Associates, Inc., where he works with the company's Linda products. In addition, Dr. Mattson is a research scientist in the Computer Science Department at Yale University, conducting research in global optimization theory and applications of parallel computing to computational chemistry.

Index

ABOUT JESSICA KEYES

Jessica Keyes is president of Techinsider/New Art Inc., a technology consultancy/market research firm specializing in productivity and high-technology applications to business requirements. She is publisher of TECHINSIDER reports, as well as Computer Market Letter. Organizer and leader of TECHINSIDER seminars, Keyes has given seminars for such prestigious universities as Boston University, University of Illinois, James Madison University, and San Francisco State University. Prior to founding Techinsider, Keyes was Managing Director of R&D for the New York Stock Exchange and has been an officer with Swiss Bank Co. and Banker's Trust, both in New York City. She has over 15 years of technical experience in such diverse areas as AI, CASE, and reengineering. She also holds an M.B.A. from New York University.

A noted columnist and correspondent with over 150 articles published in such journals as *Software Magazine*, *Computerworld*, *Corporate Computing*, and *AI Expert*, Jessica is also the author of four books, including *Infotrends: The Competitive Use of Information*, published by McGraw-Hill. She is currently working on *The McGraw-Hill Handbook of Multimedia*.

DISK WARRANTY

This software is protected by both United States copyright law and international copyright treaty provision. You must treat this software just like a book, except that you may copy it into a computer to be used and you may make archival copies of the software for the sole purpose of backing up your software and protecting your investment from loss.

By saying, "just like a book," McGraw-Hill means, for example, that this software may be used by any number of people and may be freely moved from one computer location to another, so long as there is no possibility of its being used at one location or on one computer while it is being used at another. Just as a book cannot be read by two different people in two different places at the same time, neither can the software be used by two different people in two different places at the same time (unless, of course, McGraw-Hill's copyright is being violated).

LIMITED WARRANTY

McGraw-Hill warrants the physical diskette(s) enclosed herein to be free of defects in materials and workmanship for a period of sixty days from the purchase date. If McGraw-Hill receives written notification within the warranty period of defects in materials or workmanship, and such notification is determined by McGraw-Hill to be correct, McGraw-Hill will replace the defective diskette(s). Send requests to:

Customer Service
TAB/McGraw-Hill
13311 Monterey Ave.
Blue Ridge Summit, PA 17294-0850

The entire and exclusive liability and remedy for breach of this Limited Warranty shall be limited to replacement of defective diskette(s) and shall not include or extend to any claim for or right to cover any other damages, including but not limited to, loss of profit, data, or use of the software, or special, incidental, or consequential damages or other similar claims, even if McGraw-Hill has been specifically advised of the possibility of such damages. In no event will McGraw-Hill's liability for any damages to you or any other person ever exceed the lower of suggested list price or actual price paid for the license to use the software, regardless of any form of the claim.

McGRAW-HILL, INC. SPECIFICALLY DISCLAIMS ALL OTHER WARRANTIES, EXPRESS OR IMPLIED, INCLUDING BUT NOT LIMITED TO, ANY IMPLIED WARRANTY OF MERCHANTABILITY OR FITNESS FOR A PARTICULAR PURPOSE. Specifically, McGraw-Hill makes no representation or warranty that the software is fit for any particular purpose and any implied warranty of merchantability is limited to the sixty-day duration of the Limited Warranty covering the physical diskette(s) only (and not the software) and is otherwise expressly and specifically disclaimed.

This limited warranty gives you specific legal rights, you may have others which may vary from state to state. Some states do not allow the exclusion of incidental or consequential damages, or the limitation on how long an implied warranty lasts, so some of the above may not apply to you.